PAGE 30

ON THE ROAD

YOUR COMPLETE DESTINATION GUIDE
In-depth reviews, detailed listings and insider tips

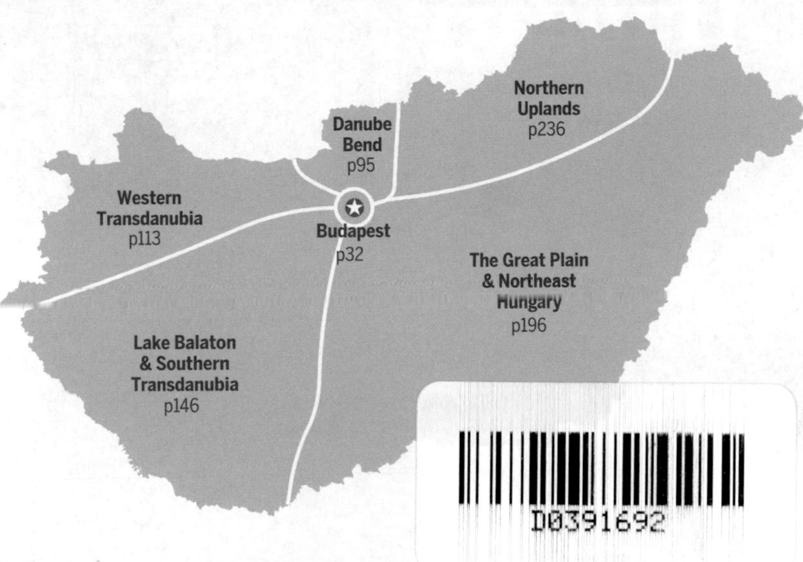

PAGE 301

SURVIVAL GUIDE

VITAL PRACTICAL INFORMATION TO HELP YOU HAVE A SMOOTH TRIP

THIS EDITION WRITTEN AND RESEARCHED BY

Steve Fallon,
Anna Kaminski, Caroline Sieg

welcome to Hungary

Super Structures

Hungary's scenery is more gentle than striking, more pretty than stunning. But you can't say the same thing about the built environment across the land. Architecturally Hungary is a treasure trove, with everything from Roman ruins and medieval town houses to baroque churches, neoclassical public buildings and Art Nouveau bathhouses and schools. And we're not just talking about Budapest here; walk through Szeged or Kecskemét, Debrecen or Sopron and you'll discover an architectural gem at virtually every turn. Some people (ourselves included) go out of their way for another glimpse of their 'hidden' favourites, like the Reök Palace in Szeged, the buildings of Kőszeg's Jurisics tér or the Mosque Church in Pécs. It's almost as if they're afraid these delightful structures will crumble and disappear unless they are regularly drenched in admiring glances.

In Hot Water

Hungarians have been 'taking the waters' supplied by an estimated 300 thermal springs since togas were all the rage and Aquincum was the big Smoke. They still do – for therapeutic, medicinal and recreational purposes – but the venues have changed somewhat. Today they range from authentic bathhouses dating from the Turkish occupation and Art Nouveau palaces to clinical sanatoriums straight

Hungary has always marched to a different drummer – speaking a language, preparing dishes and drinking wines like no others. It's Europe at its most exotic.

(left) Gellért Baths (p55), Budapest
(below) Wine tasting at Tokaj's Rákóczi Cellar (p262)

out of a Thomas Mann novel. This is where the older generation like to rejuvenate and catch up on the local gossip. More and more though, you'll see clear, chlorinated waters in organically shaped pools that bubble, squirt and spurt at different rhythms and temperatures alongside the requisite wellness centre offering a myriad of treatments. Good for the kids, good for the grown-ups, good for the whole family.

Eat, Drink & Be Magyar

There is a lot more to Hungarian food than goulash – it remains one of the most sophisticated styles of cooking in Europe. Magyars even go so far as to say there are three essential world cuisines: French, Chinese and their own. That may be a bit of an exaggeration but Hungary's reputation as a food centre dates largely from the late 19th century and the first half of the 20th and, despite a fallow period during the chilly days of communism, is once again commanding attention. So too are the nation's world-renowned wines – from the big-bodied reds of Villány and white Olazrizling from Badacsony to honey-gold Tokaj.

Hungary

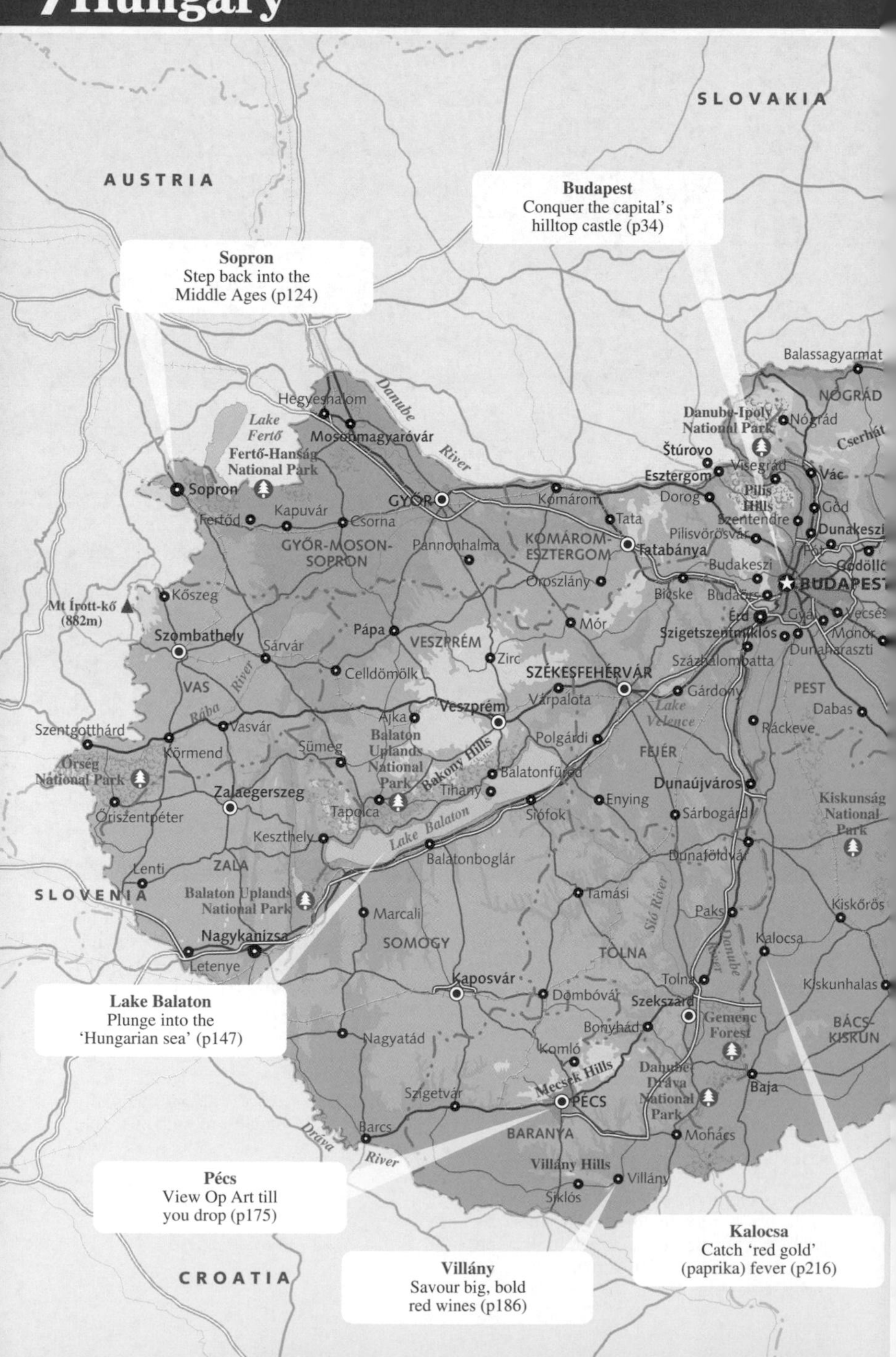

Budapest
Conquer the capital's hilltop castle (p34)
Sopron
Step back into the Middle Ages (p124)
Lake Balaton
Plunge into the 'Hungarian sea' (p147)
Pécs
View Op Art till you drop (p175)
Villány
Savour big, bold red wines (p186)
Kalocsa
Catch 'red gold' (paprika) fever (p216)
SLOVAKIA
AUSTRIA
SLOVENIA
CROATIA
Danube River
Lake Fertő
Fertő-Hanság National Park
Sopron
Hegyeshalom
Mosonmagyaróvár
Győr
Fertőd
Kapuvár
Csorna
GYŐR-MOSON-SOPRON
Pannonhalma
Mt Írott-kő (882m)
Kőszeg
Szombathely
Sárvár
VAS
Rába River
Pápa
VESZPRÉM
Celldömölk
Zirc
Szentgotthárd
Vasvár
Körmend
Őrség National Park
Őriszentpéter
Zalaegerszeg
Sümeg
Ajka
Veszprém
Balaton Uplands National Park
Bakony Hills
Tapolca
Tihany
Balatonfüred
Keszthely
Lake Balaton
Siófok
Balatonboglár
Lenti
ZALA
Nagykanizsa
Letenye
Marcali
SOMOGY
Kaposvár
Nagyatád
Szigetvár
Barcs
Dráva River
Pécs
Mecsek Hills
Komló
BARANYA
Villány Hills
Villány
Siklós
Mohács
Danube-Dráva National Park
Bonyhád
Dombóvár
Szekszárd
Gemenc Forest
Baja
Tolna
TOLNA
Tamási
Sió River
Paks
Kalocsa
Dunaföldvár
Sárbogárd
Enying
Dunaújváros
FEJÉR
Polgárdi
Várpalota
Székesfehérvár
Lake Velence
Gárdony
Mór
Oroszlány
Komárom
Tata
Tatabánya
KOMÁROM-ESZTERGOM
Esztergom
Štúrovo
Dorog
Visegrád
Pilis Hills
Szentendre
Pilisvörösvár
Budakeszi
Bicske
Budaörs
Érd
Szigetszentmiklós
Százhalombatta
Budapest
Gyál
Vecsés
Monor
Dunaharaszti
PEST
Dabas
Ráckeve
Danube-Ipoly National Park
Nógrád
NÓGRÁD
Balassagyarmat
Cserhát
Vác
Göd
Dunakeszi
Gödöllő
Kiskunság National Park
Kiskőrös
Kiskunhalas
BÁCS-KISKUN

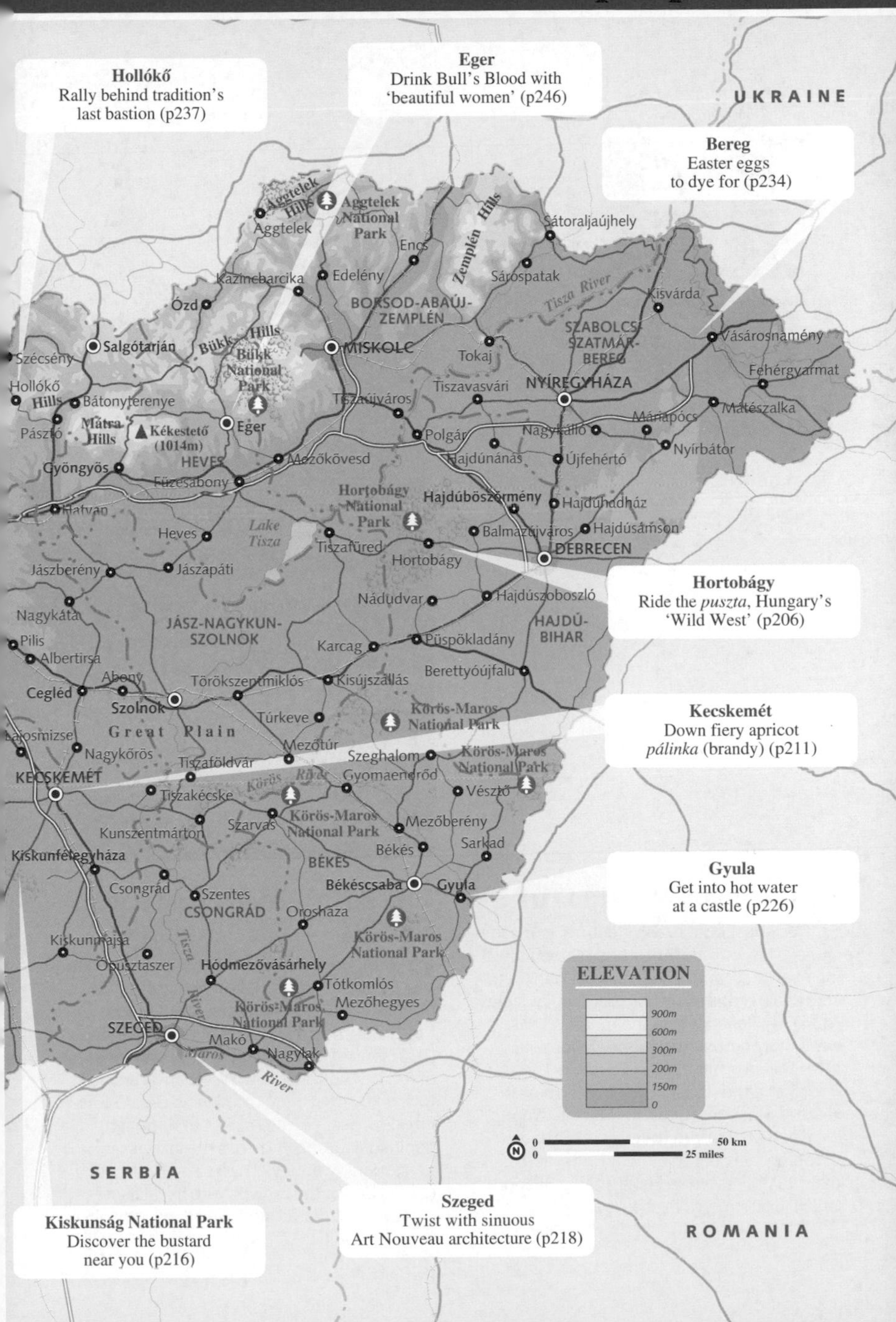
Hollókő
Rally behind tradition's last bastion (p237)
Eger
Drink Bull's Blood with 'beautiful women' (p246)
Bereg
Easter eggs to dye for (p234)
Hortobágy
Ride the puszta, Hungary's 'Wild West' (p206)
Kecskemét
Down fiery apricot pálinka (brandy) (p211)
Gyula
Get into hot water at a castle (p226)
Szeged
Twist with sinuous Art Nouveau architecture (p218)
Kiskunság National Park
Discover the bustard near you (p216)
UKRAINE
SERBIA
ROMANIA
ELEVATION
900m
600m
300m
200m
150m
0
0
50 km
0
25 miles
Aggtelek Hills
Aggtelek National Park
Aggtelek
Zemplén Hills
Sátoraljaújhely
Encs
Sárospatak
Edelény
Kazincbarcika
Ózd
BORSOD-ABAÚJ-ZEMPLÉN
Tisza River
Kisvárda
SZABOLCS-SZATMÁR-BEREG
Vásárosnamény
Salgótarján
Bükk Hills
Bükk National Park
MISKOLC
Tokaj
Szécsény
Hollókő
Fehérgyarmat
NYÍREGYHÁZA
Tiszavasvári
Hills
Bátonyterenye
Tiszaújváros
Máriapócs
Mátészalka
Mátra Hills
Kékestető (1014m)
Eger
Polgár
Nagykálló
Pásztó
Nyírbátor
HEVES
Mezőkövesd
Hajdúnánás
Újfehértó
Gyöngyös
Füzesabony
Hortobágy National Park
Hajdúböszörmény
Hajdúhadház
Hatvan
Heves
Lake Tisza
Balmazújváros
Hajdúsámson
Tiszafüred
DEBRECEN
Hortobágy
Jászberény
Jászapáti
Nádudvar
Hajdúszoboszló
Nagykáta
JÁSZ-NAGYKUN-SZOLNOK
HAJDÚ-BIHAR
Pilis
Karcag
Püspökladány
Albertirsa
Abony
Törökszentmiklós
Kisújszállás
Berettyóújfalu
Cegléd
Szolnok
Körös-Maros National Park
Túrkeve
Great Plain
Lajosmizse
Nagykőrös
Mezőtúr
Szeghalom
Tiszaföldvár
KECSKEMÉT
Körös River
Gyomaendrőd
Vésztő
Tiszakécske
Szarvas
Mezőberény
Kunszentmárton
Békés
Sarkad
Kiskunfélegyháza
BÉKÉS
Békéscsaba
Gyula
Csongrád
Szentes
CSONGRÁD
Orosháza
Tisza River
Kiskunmajsa
Ópusztaszer
Hódmezővásárhely
Tótkomlós
Mezőhegyes
SZEGED
Makó
Nagylak
Maros River

14 TOP EXPERIENCES

Budapest's Castle Hill

1 Budapest boasts architectural gems in spades, but the limestone plateau towering over the Danube River's west bank is the Hungarian capital's most spectacular sight (p34). Enclosed within the medieval castle walls, numerous attractions vie for your attention, from the splendid Great Throne Room and the treasures of the Budapest History Museum (p35), to the claustrophobic Castle Labyrinth (p40) and the show-stopping view of Parliament (p46) across the river in Pest from Fishermen's Bastion (p35). Fishermen's Bastion, top

Lake Balaton's Northern Shore

2 Hungary's 'sea' (and Continental Europe's largest lake) is where the populace comes to sun and swim in summertime. The quieter side of Lake Balaton (p147) mixes sizzling beaches and oodles of fun on the water with historic waterside towns like Keszthely (p150) and Balatonfüred (p164). Tihany (p159), a 30m-high peninsula jutting 4km into the lake, is home to a stunning abbey church, and Badacsony (p156) draws the crowds with its lakeside location, cultivated slopes and robust white wines. Reflection of Tihany's Abbey Church (p161), right

1

JON ARNOLD / GETTY IMAGES ©

2

ILONA NAGY / GETTY IMAGES ©

Thermal Baths

3 With more than 300 thermal hot springs (p297) in public use across Hungary, it's not hard to find a place to take the waters. Some of the thermal baths, like the Rudas (p55) and Király (p55) in Budapest and part of the Turkish Bath (p249) in Eger, date back to the 16th century. Increasingly popular are waterparks catering to a larger audience. Among the most unusual spa experiences in Hungary are floating on a thermal lake at Hévíz (p155) and getting into hot water at a castle at Gyula (p226). Széchenyi Baths (p54), Budapest, top

Wine & Pálinka

4 Hungarian wines (p292), made here for millennia, are celebrated the world over. Honey-gold sweet Tokaj (p261) and crimson-red Bull's Blood from Eger (p246) are the best known. Don't overlook the big-bodied reds of Villány (p187) or Somló's flinty whites. Beyond the fruit of the vine is *pálinka*, a fruit-flavoured brandy (think apricots, plums, even raspberries) that kicks like a mule. And then there's the increasingly popular aperitif Unicum, chocolate-brown in colour and as bitter as a loser's tears.

MARTIN MOOS / GETTY IMAGES ©

DAVID BORLAND / GETTY IMAGES ©

Szeged

5 The cultural capital of the Great Plain and Hungary's third-largest city, Szeged (p218) is filled with eye-popping Art Nouveau masterpieces, students, open-air cafes and green spaces, straddling the ever-present Tisza River. Theatre, opera and all types of classical and popular music performances abound, culminating in the Szeged Open-Air Festival (p221) in summer. Szeged is also justly famed for its edibles, including the distinctive fish soup made with local paprika and Pick (p220), Hungary's finest salami. Cupola of Szeged's New Synagogue (p219), top

Pécs

6 This gem of a city (p175) is blessed with rarities of Turkish architecture and early Christian and Roman tombs. Its Mosque Church (p177) is the largest Ottoman structure still standing in Hungary, while the Hassan Jakovali Mosque (p180) has survived the centuries in excellent condition. Pécs is exceptionally rich in art and museums. What's more, the climate is mild – almost Mediterranean-like – and you can't help noticing all the almond trees in bloom or in fruit here. Basilica of St Peter (p179), bottom

Hollókő

7 It may consist of a mere two streets, but Hollókő (p237) is the most beautiful of Hungary's villages. Its 65 whitewashed houses, little changed since their construction in the 17th and 18th centuries, are pure examples of traditional folk architecture and have been on Unesco's World Heritage list for 25 years. Most importantly, it is a bastion of traditional Hungarian culture, holding fast to the folk art of the ethnic Palóc people (p241) and some of their ancient customs. Local women from Hollókő, top left

Paprika

8 Paprika, the sine qua non of Hungarian cuisine (p217), may not be exactly what you expect. All in all, it's pretty mild stuff and a taco with salsa or a chicken vindaloo from the corner takeaway tastes more fiery. But the fact remains that many Hungarian dishes such as *pörkölt* (stew of beef, pork or most commonly veal) and *halászlé* (fish soup) wouldn't be, well, Hungarian dishes without the addition of the 'red gold' spice grown around Szeged and Kalocsa (p216). It comes in varying degrees of piquancy and is a culinary and culturally Magyar essential.

Sopron

9 Sopron (p124) has the most intact medieval centre in Hungary, its cobbled streets lined with one Gothic or colourful early baroque facade after another. A wander though the back streets here is like stepping back in time. The icing on the cake is the town's Roman ruins. But architecture aside, the little town that brought down the Iron Curtain beckons with its many vineyards and cellars where you can sample the local wine. Trinity Column (p124), top right

9

FUNKYSTOCK / GETTY IMAGES ©

Bird-watching

10 With 250 resident species, several of them endangered and many rare, birds are plentiful in Hungary and you don't have to go out of your way to observe our feathered friends. Head to the Hortobágy (p207) on the Great Plain to see autumn migrations, or to one of the many lakes, such as Tisza (p200), to see aquatic birdlife. Bustards proliferate in Kiskunság National Park (p216) near Kecskemét, while white storks nesting atop chimneys in eastern Hungary are quite a sight from May to October.

A great bustard, right

10

MORALES / GETTY IMAGES ©

Art Nouveau

11 Art Nouveau architecture and its Viennese variant, Secessionism, abound in Hungary. Superb examples, built largely during the country's 'Golden Age' in the late 19th and early 20th centuries, can be seen in cities like Budapest, Szeged and Kecskemét. The style's sinuous curves and flowing, asymmetrical forms, colourful tiles and other decorative elements stand out like beacons in a sea of refined and elegant baroque and mannered, geometric neoclassical buildings – it will have you gasping with delight. Art Nouveau architecture on Szervita tér, Budapest

Eger

12 Everyone loves Eger (p246), and it's immediately apparent why. Beautifully preserved baroque architecture gives the town a relaxed, almost Mediterranean feel; it is flanked by two of the Northern Uplands' most beautiful ranges of hills – Bükk (p246) and Mátra (p241)– and it is the home of some of Hungary's best wines, including the celebrated Bull's Blood, which can be sampled at cellars in the evocatively named Valley of the Beautiful Women, within walking distance of the city. Minorite Church of St Anthony of Padua (p248), right

JOHN ELK / GETTY IMAGES ©

LASZLO BELICZAY / CORBIS ©

LONELY PLANET / GETTY IMAGES ©

The Puszta

13 Hungarians tend to view the *puszta* (p197) – the Great Plain – romantically, as a region full of hardy shepherds fighting the wind and snow in winter and trying not to go stir-crazy in summer as the notorious *délibabok* (mirages) rise off the baking soil. It's a romantic notion, but the endless plains can be explored in Kiskunság National Park (p216) and Hortobágy (p207). Mount a mighty steed yourself or watch as Hungarian cowboys ride with five horses in hand in a spectacular show of skill and horsemanship. Wild horses in Hortobágy National Park, top right

Folkloric Northeast

14 Preserved through generations, Hungary's folk art traditions (p285) bring everyday objects to life. Differences in colours and styles easily identify the art's originating region. You'll find exquisite detailed embroidery, pottery, hand-painted or carved wood, dyed Easter eggs and graphic woven cloth right across the country, but the epicentre is in Bereg (p234). The culture of the tiny villages of this region in the far northeast of Hungary has much to do with their neighbours to the east, including the brightly dyed Easter eggs. Decorated Easter eggs, above

need to know

Currency
» Hungarian forint (Ft; international currency code: HUF)

Language
» Hungarian

When to Go

High Season (Jul–Aug)
» Summer is warm, sunny and unusually long.

» Resorts at Lake Balaton and Mátra Hills book out; expect long queues at attractions and high prices everywhere.

» Many cities grind to a halt in August.

Shoulder (Apr–Jun, Sept–Oct)
» Holidaymakers have gone home and prices drop.

» Spring is glorious, though it can be wet in May and early June.

» Autumn is particularly special in the hills; festivals mark the *szüret* (grape harvest).

Low Season (Nov–Mar)
» November is rainy, and winter is cold and often bleak.

» Many sights reduce their hours sharply or close altogether.

» Prices are rock-bottom.

Your Daily Budget

Budget up to 10,000Ft
» Dorm bed: 2500–5000Ft

» Meal at self-service restaurant: 1200Ft

» Free or discounted entry to some national museums for EU citizens

Midrange 20,000Ft
» Single/double private room: from 6000/8000Ft

» Two-course meal with drink: 3500–6000Ft

» Cocktail: from 1200Ft

Top end over 30,000Ft
» Double room in superior hotel: from 16,500Ft

» Dinner for two with wine at a good restaurant: from 10,000Ft

» All-inclusive ticket at a spa/waterpark: adult/child 3000/1800Ft

Money

» ATMs are everywhere in Hungary, even in small villages. Credit cards, especially Visa, MasterCard and American Express, are widely accepted.

Visas

» Citizens of all European countries and of Australia, Canada, Israel, Japan, New Zealand and the USA do not require visas for visits of up to 90 days.

Mobile Phones

» Most North American phones won't work here. Consider buying a rechargeable SIM chip at mobile-phone shops and newsagents, which cuts the cost of making local calls.

Driving/ Transport

» Drive on the right; the steering wheel is on the left side of the car. Trains are punctual but slow, and buses are often a necessary alternative.

Websites

» **Hungarian National Tourist Office** (www.gotohungary.com) The single best website on Hungary; make it your first portal of call.

» **Caboodle** (www.caboodle.hu) English-language portal, with daily news, features and events.

» **Tourinform** (www.tourinform.hu) Good for visitor-centre locations.

» **Lonely Planet** (www.lonelyplanet.com) Destination information, hotel bookings, travellers' forum, plus more.

» **Hungary Museums** (www.museum.hu) A list of every museum in the land currently open to the public.

Exchange Rates

Australia	A$1	232Ft
Canada	C$1	223Ft
Europe	€1	284Ft
Japan	¥100	282Ft
New Zealand	NZ$1	182Ft
UK	UK£1	356Ft
USA	US$1	224Ft

For current exchange rates, see www.xe.com.

Important Numbers

Hungary Country Code	36
Ambulance	104
Europe-wide Emergency Number	112
Fire	105
Police	107
24-hour Car Assistance	188

Arriving in Hungary

» **Ferenc Liszt International Airport** (p310)

Minibuses, buses and trains to central Budapest, 4am to midnight, 400Ft to 3200Ft; taxi from 5500Ft.

» **Keleti, Nyugati & Déli train stations**

All three stations are on metro lines of that name; trams and/or night buses call when the metro is closed.

» **Népliget & Stadionok bus stations**

Both are on the M3 metro line and served by trams 1 and 1A.

Leaving a Tip

The way you tip in a restaurant or cafe in Hungary is unusual. You never leave the money on the table (it's considered rude), but instead tell the waiter how much you're paying in total. For example, if the bill is 3600Ft, you're paying with a 5000Ft note and you think the waiter deserves a gratuity of about 10%, first ask if service is included – some places now add it to the bill automatically – but if it's not, tell the waiter you're paying 4000Ft, or that you want 1000Ft back.

Everyone needs a helping hand when they visit a country for the first time. There are phrases to learn, customs to get used to and etiquette to understand. The following section will help demystify Hungary so your first trip goes just as smoothly as your fifth.

Language

Hungarians like to boast that their language ranks with Japanese and Arabic as among the world's most difficult to master. All languages are challenging for non-native speakers, but it is true: Hungarian is difficult to learn well. However, this should not put you off attempting a few words and phrases. Without some German language skills, it's the only way you'll make yourself understood in the more remote parts of the country. For more on what to say and how to speak *Magyarul* (in Hungarian; literally 'Hungarian-ly'), see p317.

Booking Ahead

Reserving a room, even if only for the first night of your stay, is the best way to ensure a smooth start to your trip. These phrases should see you through a call if English isn't spoken.

Hello.	Szervusztok.	*ser*·vus·tawk
I would like to book a single/double room.	Szeretnék egy egyágyas/ duplaágyas szobátfoglalni.	*se*·ret·nayk ej *ej*·aa·dyosh/ *dup*·lo·aa·dyosh *saw*·baat *fawg*·lol·ni
My name is...	A nevem...	o *ne*·vem...
from (2 July) to (6 July)	(Július kettõ)tõl (Július hat)ig	(*yū*·li·ush *ket*·tēū)·tēūl (*yū*·li·ush *hot*)·ig
How much is it per night/person?	Mennyibe kerül egy éjszakára/fõre?	*men'*·nyi·be *ke*·rewl ej *ay*·so·kaa·ro/*fēū*·re
Thank you very much.	Nagyon köszönöm.	*no*·dyawn *keu*·seu·neum

What to Wear

In general, Hungarian dress is very casual; many people attend classical-music concerts and even the opera in jeans. There are no particular items to remember, apart from an umbrella for late spring and autumn, and a warm hat (everyone wears them) for winter, unless you plan to do some serious hiking or other sport. A swimsuit for the mixed-sex thermal spas and pools is a good idea, as are plastic sandals or thongs (flip-flops). The summer fashions and beachwear are daringly brief, even by Western standards. Hungarians let their hair – and most of their clothes – down in the warmer months at lake and riverside resorts; going topless is almost the norm for women here.

What to Pack

- Passport
- Credit card
- Driver's licence
- Phrasebook
- Money belt
- Medical kit
- Mobile phone charger
- Adapter plug
- Small kettle or coil immersion heater for hot drinks
- Earplugs
- Hat/cap for sun
- Swimsuit
- Swimming towel
- Thongs/flip-flops
- Waterproof clothing
- Umbrella
- Padlock
- Torch (flashlight)
- Pocketknife
- Camera
- Clothes pins/pegs

Checklist

» Check the validity of your passport.

» Take a look at some of the 'what's on' and English-language media websites.

» Make any necessary bookings (for sights, accommodation and/or travel).

» Check your airline's baggage restrictions.

» Inform your credit/debit card company you're going abroad.

» Organise travel insurance (see p306).

» Check to see if you can use your mobile (see p308).

Etiquette

Hungarians are almost always extremely polite in their social interactions, and the language can be very courtly – even when doing business with the butcher or having your haircut.

» Greetings
An older man will often kiss a woman's hand, and young people's standard greeting to their elders is *Csókolom* ('I kiss it' – 'it' being the hand, of course). People of all ages, even close friends, shake hands profusely when meeting up.

» Asking for Help
Say *legyen szíves* ('be so kind as') to attract attention; say *bocsánat* ('sorry') to apologise.

» Religion
Dress modestly and be quiet and respectful when visiting any religious building.

» Eating & Drinking
If you're invited to someone's home, bring a bunch of flowers (available in profusion all year) or a bottle of good local wine.

» Name Days
As much as their birthdays, Hungarians celebrate their name day, which is usually the Catholic feast day of their patron saint (all Hungarian calendars list them). Flowers, sweets or a bottle of wine are the usual gifts. Tradition allows you to present them up to eight days after the event.

Tipping

» When to Tip
Hungarians are very tip-conscious and nearly everyone routinely hands gratuities to waiters, hairdressers and taxi drivers; doctors and dentists accept 'gratitude money', and even petrol-station attendants and thermal-spa attendants expect a coin or two.

» Taxis
Most people just round up the fare.

» Restaurants
Always ask if service is included, as this is becoming increasingly common. If it is not, tip between 10% and 15% and follow the usual Hungarian procedure (see p15).

» Bars
If you go to the bar to get drinks, there's no need to tip; if drinks are brought to your table, tip as in restaurants.

Money

Credit and debit cards can be used almost everywhere and there is usually no minimum-purchase requirement. Visa and MasterCard are the most popular options; American Express is less frequently accepted. Chip-and-pin is the norm for card transactions, though business establishments now accept signatures as an alternative if the card has no chip. ATMs are everywhere, but be warned that those at branches of OTP, the national savings bank, dispense 20,000Ft notes, which can be hard to break. Hungary's value-added (or sales) tax of between 5% and 27% on goods and services is Europe's highest. Visitors are not exempt, but non-EU residents can claim refunds (see p306).

if you like...

Cuisine

Hungary can boast Eastern Europe's finest cuisine. It's very meaty, it's true, but it's big on flavour. Try one of the staples, like paprika-laced *pörkölt* (a stew not unlike what we call goulash) or *gulyá* (or *gulyásleves*), a thick beef soup. And don't overlook specialities such as *libamaj* (goose liver prepared in an infinite number of ways) and *halászlé*, a rich fish soup.

Budapest Choose between Hungarian staples, trendy cellar eateries, Michelin-starred restaurants and everything in between (p70).

Fish Locally caught Lake Balaton fish is a must. The most popular varieties are pikeperch, catfish and carp (p147).

Sopron Sample locally produced red Kékfrankos and white Traminer in the many cellars of a town known for its wine since Roman times (p129).

Bereg The deep-purple *szilva* (plums) of this region in the northeast yield the finest *lekvár* (jam) and *pálinka* (brandy) (p234).

Patisseries Every town offers several *cukrászdák* (cake shops or patisseries) selling sweet creations, but the granddaddy is Budapest's Gerbeaud (p78).

Architecture

Hungary's architectural waltz through history begins with the Romans at Szombathely and Aquincum in Budapest, moves to the early Christian sites in Pécs, climbs up to the castles of the Northern Uplands, and into the many splendid baroque churches across the land. Neoclassicism steps in with fine public buildings in Debrecen and Nyíregyháza. But taking centre stage is the Art Nouveau/ Secessionism found in abundance in Budapest, Szeged and Kecskemét.

Budapest Wander through Budapest's historical heart and see how many different architectural styles you can spot (p34).

Kőszeg Visit Jurisics tér for a visual feast of Renaissance, baroque, Gothic and neoclassical features (p140).

Pécs Home to the most significant architectural relics of Turkish rule, an early Christian World Heritage Site and a clutch of baroque structures (p177).

Boldogkőváralja Everyone's idea of the perfect castle is the 13th-century hilltop fortress northwest of Tokaj (p264).

Synagogues There are some fine example of Jewish houses of worship through Hungary, but especially in Szeged, Eger, Esztergom and Vác.

Scenery

Hungary cannot claim any point higher than 1000m, and it's nowhere near the sea. Yet the country has an amazingly varied topography. There's the low-lying salty grasslands of the Great Plain, a half-dozen ranges of hills to the north and northeast, and two major (and very scenic) rivers: the Danube and the Tisza. Hungary also has well over 1000 lakes, of which the largest and most famous is Balaton.

Őrség Drive past peaceful meadows and through the hills of Őrség National Park for a glimpse of traditional village life (p145).

Pannonhalma Head for the hilltop abbey for all-encompassing views of the surrounding Kisalföld countryside (p116).

Tihany This 30m-high pensinsula is home to wild and vineyard-filled swathes of green and the most dramatic views across Lake Balaton (p159).

Hortobágy The real Hortobágy on the Great Plain and the one in paintings, poems and active imaginations gets mixed, but it remains stunningly beautiful (p206).

Visegrád The view from the mighty fortress completed in 1259 will convince you that the Danube really does 'bend' (p105).

» Cherry *rétes* (strudel; p27)

Folk Art

Hungary has one of the richest folk traditions in Europe, and this is where the country often comes to the fore in art. Folk art and fine art are inextricably linked; the music of Béla Bartók and the ceramic sculptures of Szentendre's Margit Kovács, for example, are deeply rooted in traditional culture.

Budapest Check out the work of artisans from all over Hungary at Budapest's **Festival of Folk Arts** in August, held in and around Buda Castle (p57).

Sopron Folk art and crafts are on display at the handicraft fair during Sopron Festival Weeks in July (p127).

Sárköz Head for the heart of folk-weaving country for ornate embroidered fabrics and carved wooden housewares (p193).

Mezőkövesd Intricate embroidered roses and hand-painted flowers on dark-wood furniture are the hallmarks of the Matyó people based here (p252).

Nádudvar The sombre black-on-black pottery of this town on the Great Plain is striking from the first sighting (p210).

Kalocsa Technicolour wall-painting, embroidery and painted pottery from this paprika town is celebrated nationwide (p216).

Thermal Spas

Since the time of the Romans in the 2nd century AD, citizens have enjoyed Hungary's abundant thermal waters. The choice of venues is enormous and much varied, but the trend today is for extra-large spas with a wellness centre offering services from A to Z for the adults and a huge water park for the kids.

Hévíz Gyógy-tó, Europe's largest thermal lake, is therapeutic, medicinal and filled with lotuses (p155).

Budapest From Turkish hammams and palace-like baths to outdoor whirlpools, you are completely spoiled for choice in the capital (p54).

Sárvár Flit between outdoor and indoor thermal pools, saunas and state-of-the-art spa offerings, with every type of pampering imaginable (p139).

Harkány From mud cures to relaxing in the medicinal waters, this bath near Pécs can cure a range of maladies (p188).

Hajdúszoboszló This Texas-sized thermal bathing centre and water park is the country's largest and equipped with every spa feature on earth (p209).

Gyula This is where you can find out what it's like to take the waters in the shadow of a medieval castle (p226).

Festivals

Hungary paints the town red year-round nowadays; the days when nothing got scheduled in August are well and truly over. Choose from among themed festivals that celebrate things like Jewish culture and folklore, classical music or jazz, and new crops of grapes (or cherries or apples).

Sopron Celebrate Sopron's grape harvest by sampling its many fine reds and whites, accompanied by music and folk dancing (p127).

Mohács The Busójárás carnival in February/March brings out masked creatures, lively processions, folk music and plenty of dancing in the streets (p194).

Budapest Immerse yourself in Budapest's distinguished Jewish heritage during a 10-day extravaganza in late August/early September (p61).

Szeged The Szeged Open-Air Festival in July is the most important in the country and showcases every branch of the performing arts (p221).

Hollókő Easter in this folkloric village in the Cserhát Hills sees women in colourful traditional costumes parading through the streets (p240).

Debrecen The Debrecen Flower Carnival in August is arguably Hungary's most colourful festival (p203).

month by month

Top Events

1. **Budapest Spring Festival**, March & April
2. **Sziget Music Festival**, August
3. **Busójárás**, February
4. **Szeged Open-Air Festival**, July & August
5. **Hollókő Easter Festival**, April

January

Hungary is still festive after the Christmas holidays. It's cold but the skies are bright blue. There may be a light dusting of snow on church spires and possibly ice floes in the Danube and Tisza.

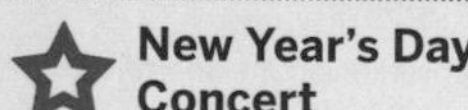

New Year's Day Concert

This annual event, usually held in Budapest's Duna Palota on 1 January, ushers in the new year and is the favourite of the capital's glitterati. (www.hungaria koncert.hu)

February

By February winter has hung on a bit too long and the days are cold, short and bleak. Many attractions will remained closed (or keep shortened hours) until March.

Busójárás

Pre-Lenten carnival involving anthropomorphic costumes, held in Mohács on the weekend before Ash Wednesday. (www.mohacs.hu)

March

This is an excellent month to visit Hungary. Women have put their furs back in the closet, and it's the start of the concert and theatre season in many cities.

Budapest Spring Fesitval

Hungary's largest cultural festival, with some 200 events staged at 60 venues throughout the capital. (www.festivalcity.hu)

April

It looks and feels and smells like an old-fashioned spring in April, like the times before the season turned into a 15-minute interval between winter and summer.

Hollókő Easter Festival

Traditional costumes and folk traditions welcome in spring in this World Heritage-listed village. (www.holloko.hu)

May

The selection of fresh vegetables and fruit is not great in winter, but in spring a cycle of bounty begins, starting with asparagus.

Gyöngyös Wine Days

The first of a pair of wine festivals in this pretty town in the Mátra Hills (the other one is in September) takes place in late May and celebrates the region's Hárslevelű (Linden Leaf), a green-tinted white wine that is both spicy and slightly sweet. (www.matrainfo.hu)

June

Late spring is wonderful but the month of June can be pretty wet, especially early in the month. Beware the start of the holiday crowds.

Hungarian Dance Festival

The prestigious Hungarian Dance Festival is held biannually in Győr in late June. (www.hungariandance festival.hu)

Museum Night

Hundreds of museums across the country mark the summer solstice in mid-June by re-opening their doors at 6pm on a Saturday and not closing them till the wee hours, sometimes as late as 2am. Great fun.

Danube International Multicultural Festival

Authentic folk music and dance, with performers from around Hungary and Europe, held in mid-June in towns and cities on or near the Danube, including Kalocsa and Szekszárd. (www.cioff.org)

Sopron Festival Weeks

Theatre, world and folk music, folk dancing and a handicraft fair, held in Sopron. (www.prokultura.hu)

July

School's out for the summer, so now you're competing not only with foreign visitors but local ones too. Book early for Balaton and the Mátra Hills.

Szeged Open-Air Festival

The most celebrated open-air festival in Hungary, with opera, ballet, classical music and folk dancing, held in Szeged. (www.szegediszabadteri.hu)

Winged Dragon International Street Theatre Festival

Some 50 music and puppet performances are held in and around historical buildings in Nyírbátor in the Northeast. (www.szarnyas-sarkany.hu)

Balaton Sound Festival

A lakeside adjunct of the hugely popular Sziget Festival in Budapest, held at Zamárdi, near Balatonfüred, over four days in July, boasts almost as impressive a line-up of bands. (www.sziget.hu/balatonsound)

Veszprém Festival

Veszprém Fest, one of the premier festivals in the Balaton region and held over four days in mid-July, attracts headline performers in jazz and classical music.

August

Hungary used to come to a grinding halt in what was called the 'cucumber-growing month', but that's all changed now and August is festival month.

Debrecen Flower Carnival

Week-long spectacular in Debrecen kicked off by a parade of flower floats on St Stephen's Day (20 August). (www.iranydebrecen.hu/info/flower-carnival)

Formula 1 Hungarian Grand Prix

Hungary's prime sporting event, held in early August in Magyoród, 24km northeast of the capital. (www.hungaroring.hu)

Haydn at Eszterháza Festival

A week of classical music performance at the Esterházy Palace in Fertőd.

Hortobágy Bridge Fair

This 100-year-old fair in Hortobágy has dance, street theatre, folklore performances and the occasional horse and pony.

Sziget Music Festival

Now one of the biggest and most popular music festivals in Europe, held on Budapest's Hajógyár Island. (www.sziget.hu)

Jewish Summer Festival

Some 10 days of folk music and dancing, including the celebrated Csángo Festival, held in Jászberény. (www.jaszbereny.hu)

Zemplén Festival

Classical music festival launched by the Ferenc Liszt Chamber Orchestra and held in venues around Zemplén, especially Sárospatak. (www.zemplenfestival.hu)

September

September brings summer to a close. It's a good time to visit as there's still a lot going on, wine is starting to flow and peak-season prices are over.

Grape Harvest Festivals

Festivals in honour of the the grape harvest are held in late September in all wine-producing areas of Hungary, including Tokaj, Balatonfürd, Szekszárd and Gyöngyös. The Budapest International Wine Festival (p61), held in the Castle

District, is when Hungary's foremost vintners introduce their vintages to the public.

October

Though the days are getting shorter and everyone is back into their routines, autumn is beautiful, particularly in the Northern Uplands and Buda Hills.

Budapest International Marathon

Eastern Europe's most celebrated race goes along the Danube and across its bridges in early October. (www.budapestmarathon.com)

November

The month kicks off immediately with a public holiday – All Saints' Day on 1 November. After that the winter season begins with many museums and other tourist attractions around the country sharply curtailing their hours or closing altogether.

Balaton International Egg Festival

It takes place in an odd venue – Siófok on Lake Balaton, a place not well known for its folk art – and at the wrong time of year (isn't it Advent, heralding Christmas?), but this unusual festival celebrates the painted Easter egg in all of its guises. (www.tojasfesztival.hu)

December

The build-up to Christmas intensifies as the month wears on, and the arrival of decorations, trees and coloured lights is a welcome sight.

New Year's Gala & Ball

The annual calendar's most coveted ticket is this gala concert and ball held at the Hungarian State Opera House (p82) in Budapest on 31 December.

itineraries

Whether you've got six days or 60, these itineraries provide a starting point for the trip of a lifetime. Want more inspiration? Head online to lonelyplanet.com/thorntree to chat with other travellers.

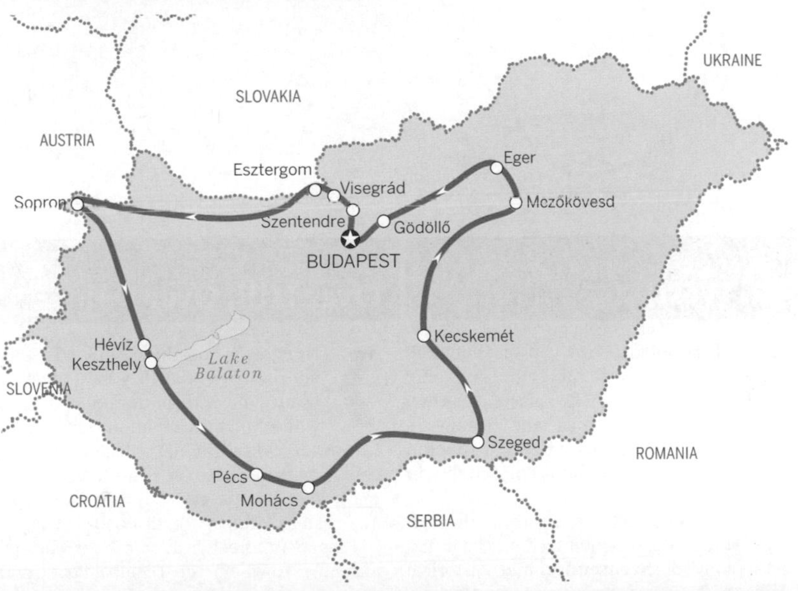

Ten Days
Essential Hungary

This itinerary offers you the best of Hungary and will give you a taste of the country's historical wealth and natural beauty.

From **Budapest**, make your way north to the towns of the Danube Bend – picture-postcard **Szentendre**, royal **Visegrád** and holy **Esztergom**. The road continues west along the Danube to **Sopron**, Hungary's finest medieval city. Travel south to Lake Balaton and recharge your batteries at lovely **Keszthely** and nearby **Hévíz**, which boasts its own thermal lake. **Pécs**, Hungary's 'Mediterranean' town, is south; from there carry on east to **Mohács**, the site of Hungary's famous defeat at the hands of the Ottomans in 1526. A car ferry will take you to the right bank of the Danube and the road eastward to **Szeged**, the university town that is forever young. **Kecskemét**, city of apricots and Art Nouveau, is to the north. Enough of the flatlands of the Great Plain? Head to the hills and delightful **Eger** but make a detour to **Mezőkövesd**, celebrated for its folk art. Head west for Budapest, stopping at **Gödöllő**, the summer retreat of Emperor Franz Joseph and his beloved consort Elisabeth.

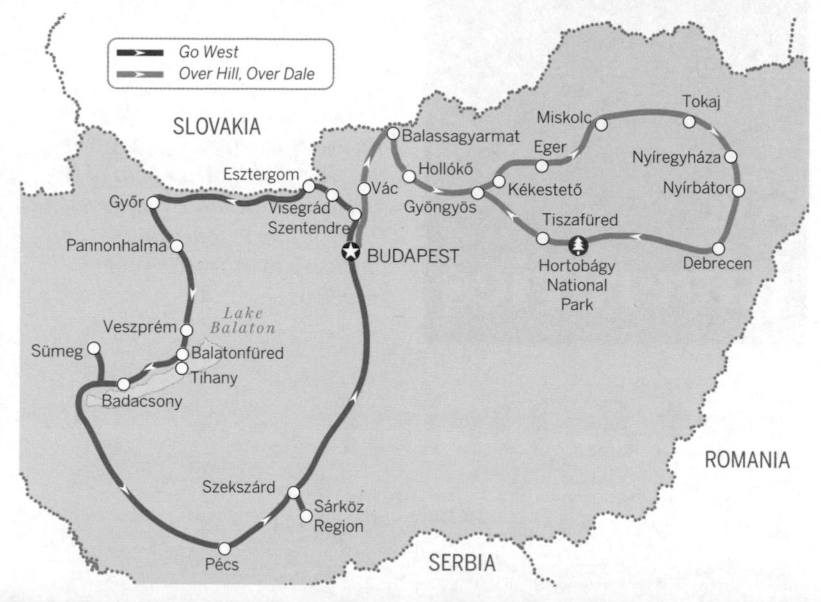

One week
Go West!

This 690km road trip of Hungary's west has something for everyone: castles, churches, palaces, thermal spas, rolling hills and Hungary's biggest lake. It's mostly an easy drive, and you should be able to do it comfortably in a week.

From **Budapest** head north through the Danube Bend region to the former artist colony of **Szentendre** and historical **Visegrád**, before arriving at **Esztergom**, Hungary's most sacred city. The road continues west along the Danube to **Győr**, an industrial city with a medieval core that's surprisingly rich in historical buildings and monuments. From here, head south to **Pannonhalma**, where the awesome abbey is on Unesco's World Heritage List, and on to **Veszprém**, the 'city of queens'. The scenic northern coast road of Lake Balaton is your next port of call, with its towns of **Balatonfüred**, **Tihany** and **Badacsony**. Make a quick detour to **Sümeg** and its dramatic castle before turning south again to **Pécs**, the jewel of the south. Return to the capital, but take time to sample the sublime red wines of **Szekszárd** and the folkloric **Sárköz** region along the way.

One week
Over Hill, Over Dale

Hungary's 'northern uplands' are not dramatic. But they have a gentle beauty all of their own, and nestled within the hills are important historical towns and traditional villages. We've included part of the Great Plain too, so you'll really get the 'ups' and 'downs' of northern and eastern Hungary on this 650km trip.

From **Budapest** head north to **Vác**, an attractive town on the Danube Bend, and then on to **Balassagyarmat**, capital of the traditional Palóc region. Continue east and then south through the rolling Cserhát Hills to **Hollókő**, a 'museum town' of folk art. The road winds through the eastern Cserhát and the foothills of the Mátra Hills to **Gyöngyös**, where you'll start a challenging drive through the hills and past **Kékestető**, Hungary's highest point. Lovely **Eger** awaits you at the end of the road. It's then on to sprawling **Miskolc** and the traditionally sweet wines of **Tokaj** before a quick stop at **Nyíregyháza**. Head southwest for **Nyírbátor**, where connections with Dracula are too close for comfort, and then **Debrecen**, nicknamed the 'Calvinist Rome' and Hungary's second-largest city. For a taste of Hungary's Great Plain head west through **Hortobágy National Park** to **Tiszafüred** and back to Budapest.

Eat & Drink Like a Local

When to Go

Food festivals take place year-round, celebrating everything from asparagus and honey to the lowly pumpkin (vegetable marrow, if the truth be known) and, of course, the grape.

Spring (Mar–May)

A late winter menu of preserved foods is consigned to the trash heap as the springtime cycle begins, starting with lettuces, *spárga* (asparagus) and then all the soft fruits. Ham figures largely at events like the **Hollókő Easter Festival** (www.holloko.hu).

Summer (Jun–Aug)

The bounty continues with strawberries, raspberries and cherries giving way to plums. Count on lots of grills and *gulyás* cooked in a *bogrács* (cauldron) at the **Hortobágy Bridge Fair** (www.hnp.hu).

Autumn (Sep–Nov)

Dozens of wine festivals occur during the harvest. The most important one is the **Budapest International Wine Festival** (www.winefestival.hu).

Winter (Dec–Feb)

The selection of fresh vegetables and fruit is not great but the hunting season is on, the mushrooms and nuts have been collected and Christmas treats await.

It's not difficult to live like a local while travelling in Hungary. The natives are friendly, the food is excellent (and never *too* strange) and the wine even better. And there are lots of things here that everyone everywhere likes: fresh produce, sweet cakes and fruit-flavoured brandy that kicks like a mule.

Food Experiences

There is so much fresh produce in Hungary and so many interesting and unusual specialties you might need some guidance.

Meals of a Lifetime

» Ikon (p205), **Debrecen** Arguably the most inventive restaurant in provincial Hungary; unforgettable *fois gras* on *pain d'épices* (spice bread).

» Padlizsán (p111), **Esztergom** Dramatic setting below a cliff, soft music at night and modern, very imaginative Hungarian dishes.

» Imola Udvarház Borétterem (p251), **Eger** Award-winning and very stylish eatery at the foot of Eger Castle with a top-notch menu and wine list.

» Kisbuda Gyöngye (p73), **Budapest** Traditional but elegant *fin-de-siècle* restaurant in Óbuda specialising in goose liver.

» Matróz (p123), **Győr** Market-side restaurant with some of the best fish soup west of the Danube River.

» Mandula (p187), **Villány** This is *the* place to book for an extravagant, belt-challenging wining and dining experience.

Cheap Eats

Many *hentesáru boltok* (butcher shops) have a *büfé* (snack bar) selling boiled or fried *kolbász* (sausage), *virsli* (frankfurters), *hurka* (blood sausage/black pudding), roast chicken and pickled vegetables. Point to what you want; the staff will weigh it and hand you a slip of paper with the price. You usually pay at the *pénztár* (cashier) and hand the stamped receipt back to the staff for your food.

Food stalls sell the same sorts of things, as well as fish when located near lakes or rivers. One of the more popular snacks in Hungary is *lángos*, deep-fried dough with various toppings (usually cheese and sour cream), available at food stalls throughout Hungary. *Pogácsa*, a kind of dry, savoury scone introduced by the Turks, is the preferred snack among beer drinkers.

Dare to Try

Hungarians will happily consume *libamáj* (goose liver) and, to a lesser extent, *kacsamáj* (duck liver) whenever the opportunity presents itself, be it cold *zsírjában* (in its own fat), *roston sült* (pan-fried) with apples, or as *pástétom* (pâté), but they generally eschew other forms of offal. The most unusual Hungarian dishes are meatless and quite inviting. Cold fruit soups such as *meggyleves* (sour cherry soup) or *fahéjas-almaleves* (cinnamon apple soup) are a positive delight on a warm summer's evening. Dishes such as *makós metélt* (vermicelli topped with poppy seeds) may look bizarre and fall neither in the savoury nor sweet category, but you won't soon forget the taste.

Hungarian Specialties

Bread, Dumplings & Noodles

There's a saying that Hungarians 'eat bread with bread'. Since the reign of King Matthias Corvinus in the 15th century, leftover *kenyér* (bread) has been used to thicken soups and stews; *kifli* (crescent-shaped rolls) gained popularity during the Turkish occupation. Uniquely Magyar are the flour-based *galuska* (dumplings) and *tarhonya* (barley-shaped egg pasta) served with *pörkölt* and *paprikás* dishes.

Soups

A Hungarian meal always starts with *leves* (soup). This is usually something relatively light like *gombaleves* (mushroom soup) or *húsgombócleves* (tiny liver dumplings in bouillon). More substantial soups are *gulyás* (or *gulyásleves*), a thick beef soup, and *bableves*, a hearty bean soup usually made with meat. Another big favourite is *halászlé* (fisherman's soup), a rich soup of fish stock, poached carp or catfish, tomatoes, green peppers and paprika.

Meat & Stews

Hungarians eat an astonishing amount of meat. Pork, beef, veal and poultry are the meats most commonly consumed, and they can be breaded and fried, baked, simmered in *lecsó* (savoury mix of peppers, tomatoes and onions) and turned into some paprika-flavoured creation.

The most popular dish prepared with paprika, the sine qua non of Hungarian cuisine, is the thick beef soup *gulyás* (or *gulyásleves*), usually eaten as main course. *Pörkölt* ('stew') is closer to what foreigners call 'goulash'; the addition of sour cream, a reduction in paprika and the use of white meat such as chicken makes the dish *paprikás*.

Goose legs and livers and turkey breasts – though not much else of either bird – make an appearance on most menus. But lamb, mutton and rabbit are rarely seen.

Fish

Freshwater fish, such as *fogas* (great pike-perch) and the younger, smaller and more prized *süllő* (both indigenous to Lake Balaton), and *ponty* (carp) from the nation's rivers and streams, are plentiful but often overcooked by Western standards.

Vegetables

Fresh salad is often called *vitamin saláta* here and is generally available when lettuce is in season; almost everything else is *savanyúság* (literally 'sourness'), which can be anything from mildly sour-sweet cucumbers and pickled peppers to very acidic sauerkraut. Such things go surprisingly very well with heavy meat dishes.

The traditional way of preparing *zöldség* (vegetables) is in *főzelék*, Hungary's unique 'twice-cooked' vegetable dishes. Here peas, green beans, lentils, vegetable marrow or cabbage are fried or boiled and then mixed into a roux with milk. This dish is sometimes topped with a few slices of meat and eaten at lunch.

In restaurants, vegetarians can usually order any number of types of *főzelék*, as well as *gombafejek rántva* (fried mushroom caps) and pasta and noodle dishes with cheese, such as *túróscsusza* and *sztrapacska*. Other meatless dishes include *gombaleves* (mushroom soup), *gyümölcsleves* (fruit soup) in season, *rántott sajt* (fried cheese) and *sajtoskenyér* (sliced bread with soft cheese). *Bableves* (bean soup) usually – but not always – contains meat. *Palacsinta* (pancakes) may be savoury and made with *sajt* (cheese) or *gomba* (mushrooms), or sweet and prepared with *dió* (nuts) or *mák* (poppy seeds).

Sweets & Desserts

Hungarians love sweets. Desserts eaten at the end of a meal include *Somlói galuska*, sponge cake with chocolate and whipped cream, and *Gundel palacsinta* (flambéed pancake with chocolate and nuts). More complicated pastries, such as *Dobos torta*, a layered chocolate and cream cake with a caramelised brown-sugar top, and the wonderful *rétes* (strudel), filled with poppy seeds, cherry preserves or *túró* (curd or cottage cheese), are usually consumed mid-afternoon in a *cukrászda* (pâtisserie or cake shop).

How to Eat & Drink Like a Local

When to Eat

For the most part Hungarians are not big eaters of *reggeli* (breakfast), preferring a cup of tea or coffee with a plain bread roll at the kitchen table or on the way to work. *Ebéd* (lunch), eaten at around 1pm, is traditionally the main meal in the countryside and can consist of two or three courses, but this is no longer the case for working people in the cities and towns. *Vacsora* (dinner or supper) is less substantial when eaten at home, often just sliced meats, cheese and some pickled vegetables.

Choosing Your Restaurant

An *étterem* is a restaurant with a large selection of dishes, sometimes including international options. A *vendéglő* (or *kisvendéglő*) is smaller and is supposed to serve inexpensive regional dishes or 'home cooking', but the name is now 'cute' enough for a lot of large places to use it. An *étkezde* or *kifőzde* is something like a diner, smaller and cheaper than a *kisvendéglő* and often with seating at a counter. The overused term *csárda* originally signified a country inn with rustic atmosphere, Gypsy music and hearty local dishes; now any place that strings dried peppers and a couple of painted plates on the wall is one. A *bisztró* is a much cheaper sit-down place that is often *önkiszolgáló* (self-service). A *büfé* is cheaper still and with a very limited menu. Food stalls, known as *Lacikonyha* (literally 'Larry's kitchen') or *pecsenyesütő* (roast ovens), can be found near markets, parks or train stations. A *kávéház*, 'coffee house' or cafe, is the best place to get something hot or nonalcoholic and cold. An *eszpresszó*, along with being a type of coffee, is essentially a coffee house too, but it usually also sells alcoholic drinks and light snacks.

Other useful words include *élelmiszer* (grocery store), *csemege* (delicatessen) and *piac* (market).

Menu Advice

Restaurant menus are often translated into German, English and sometimes French with mixed degrees of success; a certain freshwater fish called 'crap' regularly appears on many. Two very important words on a menu to note include *készételek* ('ready-made', including dishes like *gulyásleves* and *pörkölt*) and *frissensültek* (dishes 'made to order').

Drinking à la Magyar

Hungarians love their wine and take it seriously (see p292). In summer, spritzers (or wine coolers) of red or white wine and mineral water are consumed in large quantities; knowing the hierarchy and the art of mixing a spritzer to taste is important and will definitely win you the badge of 'honorary local'. A *kisfröccs* (small spritzer) is 10cL wine and the same amount of mineral water; a *nagyfröccs* (big spritzer) doubles the quantity of wine. A *hosszúlépés* (long step) is 10cL of wine and 20cL of water while a *házmester* (janitor) trebles the amount of wine. Any bar in town will serve you these but don't expect one at a *borozó*, a traditional 'wine bar' – usually a dive – serving rotgut. Stronger libations include the fruit-flavoured brandy *pálinka* and Unicum, a bitter aperitif nicknamed the 'Hungarian national accelerator'.

regions at a glance

Budapest

Spas ✓✓✓
Jewish Heritage ✓✓✓
Food & Drink ✓✓✓

Taking the Waters
The 'city of healing waters' has enough thermal baths to satisfy the most wanton of appetites for wet fun. Some date back to the Turkish occupation, others are likened to swimming in a cathedral.

Under the Stars
Beside being home to Europe's largest and most splendid synagogue, Budapest has seen a resurgence of Jewish culture, music and cuisine. On the sombre end of the spectrum, the ordeal of the Jewish community in WWII is well documented in the superb Holocaust Memorial.

On the Town
The eating scene in Budapest is as distinguished as in any capital worth its salt. Here you'll find hearty *pörkölt* (a stew not unlike goulash) and poppy-seed strudel alongside Michelin-starred food-as-art. Nightlife venues range from swanky cocktail bars to the local phenomenon of pub-in-a-ruin.

p32

Danube Bend

Hiking ✓✓✓
Churches ✓✓
The Danube ✓✓✓

Going Walkabout
Deceivingly close to built-up Budapest, the Danube Bend offers excellent chances for hiking for a day or even longer. The verdant Börzsöny and Pilis Hills are both criss-crossed by well-marked paths and trails and accessible by public transport.

Prayer Time
If ecclesiastical architecture is your thing, head north. As the seat of the Roman Catholic Church in Hungary, Esztergom boasts its largest church, and Szentendre is filled with Serbian Orthodox churches.

River Cruising
The Bend is where you get to look the Danube right in the face, and what better way to do that than by getting on it? You can reach Szentendre, Visegrád and even Esztergom by ferry and/or hydrofoil.

p95

Western Transdanubia

Architecture ✓✓✓
Roman Sites ✓✓
Wine ✓✓

Sacred & Profane
From the 1000-year old abbey in Pannonhalma to the imposing castle in Sárvár – former home of Hungary's own Countess Dracula – Western Transdanubia is an architectural treasure box.

Roamin' Romans
Sopron's location on the ancient Amber Route and the vast imperial cemeteries uncovered near Szombathely offer a wealth of Roman treasures – from the sarcophagi in Sopron's Fabricius House to freshly excavated graves full of funereal offerings now in Szombathely's Iseum site.

The Red & White
Western Transdanubia's climate is ideal for making wine and this age-old art is still widely practised here, particularly around Sopron.

p113

Lake Balaton & Southern Transdanubia

Architecture ✓✓✓
Activities ✓✓
Wine ✓

Architecture on Show

A diverse wealth of structures resides here – from Sümeg's imposing hilltop castle to Hungary's most celebrated mosque church in Pécs to delightful rural villages with open-air museums of folk architecture.

In Hot Water

Whether you play and unwind in medicinal thermal lakes and Hungary's 600-sq-km 'sea' or opt to hike and ride a horse around the rolling Mecsek Hills, Balaton Uplands National Park and the wild Tihany peninsula beckon.

Vine Results

The Badascony region produces the exquisite Olazrizling, one of the country's memorable dry white wines, while further south you'll find the tannin-rich reds of Villány and varietals like Cabernet Francs and Merlots.

p146

The Great Plain & Northeast Hungary

Folk Art ✓✓✓
Activities ✓✓
Architecture ✓✓✓

Stitch in Time

The Great Plain can claim a number of places synonymous with folk art, including Nádudvar, Hódmezővásárhely and Kalocsa, but no place compares with the Bereg region of Northeast Hungary.

Ride 'em Cowboy

The Hortobágy is where to watch the most ambitious riding show on earth, with cowboys riding five-in-hand. And if you can't beat 'em, join 'em and saddle up yourself.

Sinuous Curves

Get a look up close at Hungary's most extravagant and colourful architecture – Art Nouveau/ Secessionism – in Szeged and Kecskemét, both of which have superb examples from the late 19th and early 20th centuries.

p196

Northern Uplands

Wine ✓✓✓
Castles ✓✓✓
Activities ✓✓

Overflowing Glass

This region can claim honey-sweet Tokaj wine. Need we say more? Well, we will. There's also Eger's famed red Bull's Blood and sharp white Hárslevelű from Gyöngyös.

Castle Capers

A half-dozen of Hungary's most picturesque and historic castles and fortresses can be found in the hilly region to the north, including Boldogkő, Diósgyőr, Eger, Hollókő and Sárospatak.

Choo-Choo Trains

The little boy or girl in you will love the region's narrow-gauge trains that run through the forest at Lillafüred, the Mátra Hills and Szilvásvárad.

p236

Every listing is recommended by our authors, and their favourite places are listed first

Look out for these icons:

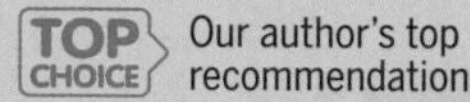
Our author's top recommendation

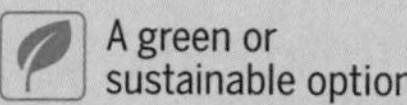
A green or sustainable option

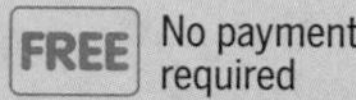
No payment required

See the Index for a full list of destinations covered in this book.

On the Road

Budapest

AREA CODE ☎1 / POP 1.74 MILLION

Includes »

Best Places to Eat

- » Onyx (p73)
- » Klassz (p74)
- » Mák Bistro (p74)
- » Gepárd És Űrhajó (p73)
- » Bistro 181 (p73)

Best Places to Stay

- » Four Seasons Gresham Palace Budapest (p66)
- » Brody House (p65)
- » Lánchíd 19 (p65)
- » Zara Boutique Hotel Budapest (p65)
- » Blue Danube Hostel (p65)

Why Go?

There's no other city in Hungary like Budapest – everything of importance starts or ends here. It is the beauty of Budapest that sets it apart. Straddling a gentle curve in the Danube, it is flanked by the Buda Hills on the west bank and the start of the Great Plain to the east. Architecturally it is a gem, with enough examples of baroque, neoclassical, Eclectic and Art Nouveau (Secessionist) to satisfy anyone.

Besides the heady mix of museums and shopping streets, outdoor entertainment areas called *kertek* (literally 'gardens') and 'ruin pubs' heave with party-makers in the warmer months, and there are numerous thermal baths in which to pamper yourself.

Like any capital city, Budapest does have a gritty side. But come spring (or summer, or a brisk autumn day, or dusk), when the city is at its loveliest, cross the Danube on foot and you will see why this passionate and vibrant city remains unmissable.

When To Go

Budapest

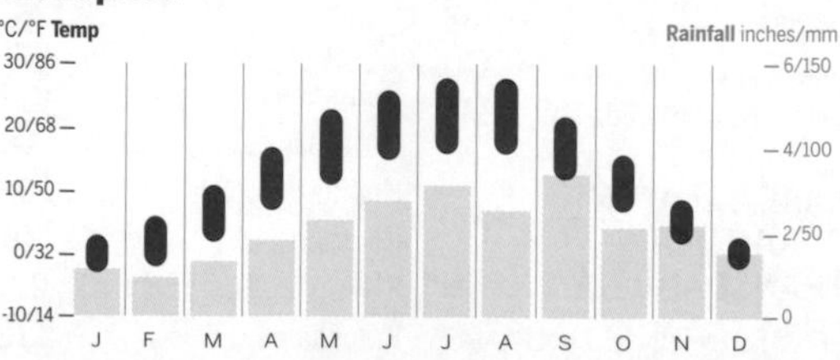

March Catch the Budapest Spring Festival (p57), the city's most important cultural fest

August Budapest welcomes racing fans at the Formula 1 Hungarian Grand Prix (p57)

December Wrap up the year in style at the New Year's Gala & Ball (p61)

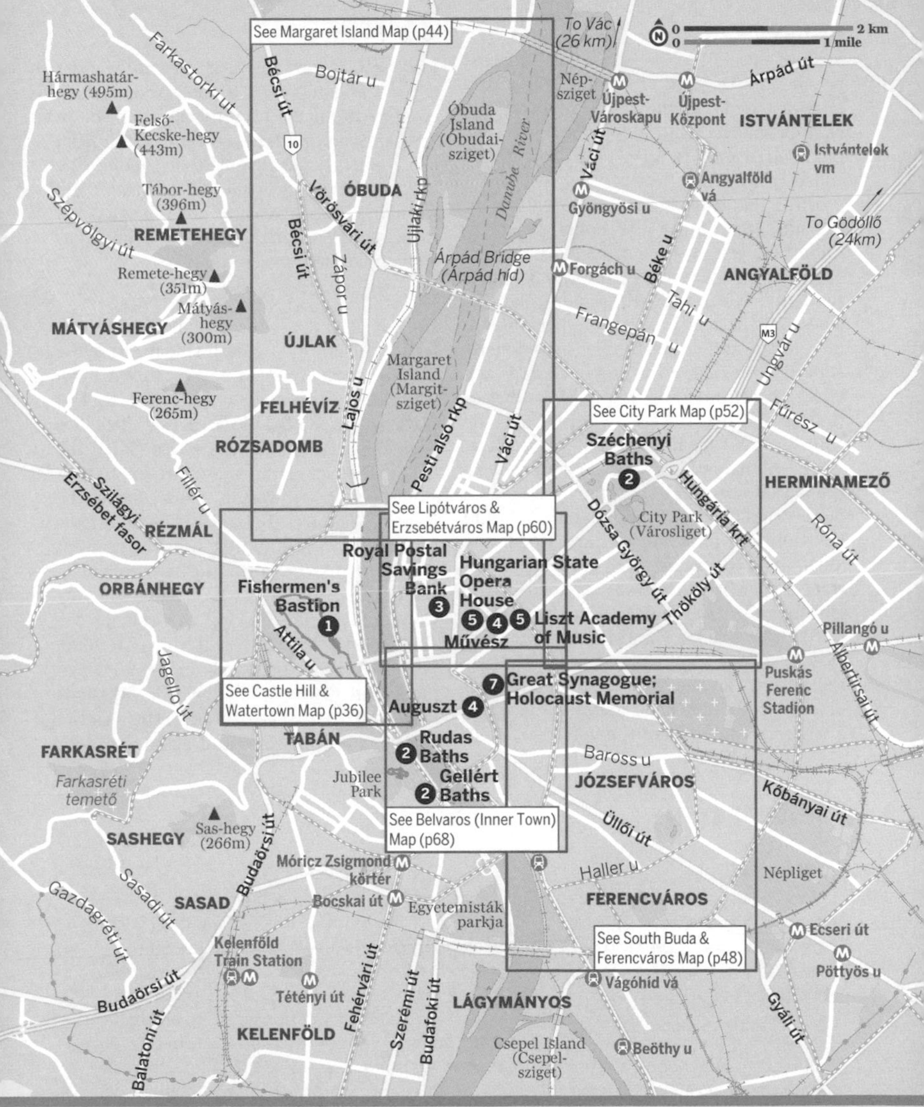

Budapest Highlights

❶ Taking in the views of the Danube and the rest of the city from **Fishermen's Bastion** (p35) on Castle Hill

❷ Soaking the afternoon away Turkish-style in a thermal **bath** (p55), either in **Gellért Baths'** (p55) Art Nouveau 'cathedral' or in the **park** (p54)

❸ Ogling the sinuous curves and asymmetrical forms of the city's incomparable Art Nouveau architecture, such as that of the **Royal Postal Savings Bank** (p52)

❹ Enjoying a slice of something sweet at a traditional cafe like **Művész** (p78) or **Auguszt** (p78) in Pest

❺ Taking in an evening of music at the **Hungarian State Opera House** (p82) or the **Liszt Academy of Music** (p54)

❻ Sizing up the monumental socialist mistakes on display at **Memento Park** (p92), a well-manicured trash heap of history

❼ Exploring Budapest's Jewish culture, from a visit to the **Great Synagogue** (p49) to the sombre **Holocaust Memorial** (p49)

History

Strictly speaking, the story of Budapest began only in 1873, when hilly Buda and historic Óbuda, on the western bank of the Danube, merged with industrial Pest on the flat eastern side, to form what was at first called Pest-Buda.

Until the Huns forced them to flee in the mid-5th century, the Romans had an important colony here named Aquincum. The Magyars arrived five centuries later, but Buda and Pest remained no more than villages until the 12th century, when foreign merchants and tradespeople settled here. King Béla IV built a fortress in Buda in the late 13th century, but it was King Charles Robert (Károly Róbert) who moved the court from Visegrád to Buda 50 years later.

The Mongols burned Buda and Pest to the ground in 1241, beginning a pattern of destruction and rebuilding that would last until the mid-20th century. Under the Turks, both towns lost most of their populations, and when they were defeated by the Habsburgs in the late 17th century, Buda Castle was in ruins. The 1848–49 revolution, WWII and the 1956 Uprising all took their toll, but in the late 20th century Budapest emerged from under the communist yoke as a vibrant, cosmopolitan capital.

Sights

Budapest is an excellent city to wander around and there are sights around every corner – from the brightly tiled gem of an Art Nouveau building to women fresh from the countryside hawking their homemade *barack lekvár* (apricot jam). Castle Hill in Buda offers a treasure box of sights, but most is in Pest. Think of Margaret Island as a green buffer between the two.

BUDA

Hilly, leafy Buda is more than just a pretty face. The majestic western side fronting the Danube was home to a prosperous town when Pest was merely a village. **Castle Hill** (Várhegy; Map p36; 16, 16/a, 116, M M2 Batthyány tér, Széll Kálmán tér, 19, 41) – also called the Castle District – the kilometre-long limestone plateau towering 170m above the Danube, features Budapest's most important medieval monuments and museums, and is a Unesco World Heritage Site. The site of the medieval town of Buda, the area went into decline during the rule of the Turks (1541–1686). Left in ruins in 1686, 1849 and rather decisively in 1945 – when the Nazis held out against the Russians here for seven weeks – the Castle District has been rebuilt time and again. Now it's

BUDAPEST IN...

Two Days

If you have just a couple of days in Budapest (what were you thinking?) spend most of the first day on **Castle Hill**, taking in the views, visiting a museum or two and perhaps having lunch at **Cafe Miró** or **21 Magyar Vendéglő**. In the afternoon, ride the **Sikló** down to Clark Ádám tér and, depending on what day it is, make your way to the **Rudas Baths** or **Gellért Baths**. In the evening, head to Liszt Ferenc tér for drinks and then to **Klassz** for dinner, finishing the evening off in a 'ruin pub' or 'rubble bar' (in an abandoned or disused building) such as **Instant**. Next day, concentrate on the two icons of Hungarian nationhood and the places that house them: the Crown of St Stephen in the **Parliament** building and the saint-king's mortal remains in **St Stephen's Basilica**. Take a late-afternoon cake break at **Gerbeaud** and catch a performance at the **Liszt Academy of Music** or **Hungarian State Opera House**.

Four Days

With another couple of days to look around the city, take a morning **walking tour** up Andrássy út, stopping off and visiting whatever interests you along the way – don't miss the **Terror House**. The cafe and cake shop **Lukács** is en route, and you could also take the waters at the **Széchenyi Baths**. Then delve into the city's Jewish heritage by visiting the **Great Synagogue** and **Holocaust Memorial**, and follow up with dinner at **Rosenstein**. The following day, why not take in destinations further afield, such as **Memento Park**, or ride into the Buda Hills on the **Cog Railway**? Be back in time for a farewell pub crawl or, if it's the right season, a well-watered tour of the city's best 'gardens', such as **Ötkert**.

a mostly pedestrianised maze of cobbled streets and museums, consisting of two distinct parts: the Old Town where commoners once lived, and the Royal Palace.

Óbuda is the oldest part of Buda (in Hungarian, 'ó' means 'ancient'), stretching to the north and west of Castle Hill. It is home to the most complete Roman ruins in Hungary – the Roman settlement of Aquincum.

Further northwest lie the **Buda Hills** – the city's green playground, complete with cable car, cog railway, great hiking trails and spectacular views.

Gellért Hill, a 200-million-year old, 235m-high slab of granite southeast of Castle Hill, is crowned with a fortress and the Liberty Monument. Its pinnacle was allegedly a favourite gathering spot for a bit of 'double, double toil and trouble', according to the 17th-century witch trial transcripts. And who can blame them? The view from here of the Royal Palace and Danube is particularly fabulous in the evenings with the bridges lit up.

Royal Palace PALACE

(Királyi Palota; Map p36; I Szent György tér) A succession of palaces has stood on this spot for the past seven centuries – razed and rebuilt at least a half-dozen times. Béla IV established a royal residence here in the mid-13th century, and subsequent kings added to the original Gothic and Renaissance structure. The palace was levelled in the battle to rout the Turks in 1686, and the Habsburgs rebuilt it as a much smaller baroque edifice but spent little time here. Over time the palace was extended, but it was destroyed in 1945 after serving as the last stronghold of the Nazis. The decision was then made to rebuild it as the 18th-century version, but on a larger scale and with a brand-new baroque facade. The result is what you see today, home to two important museums as well as the **National Széchenyi Library** (Országos Széchenyi Könyvtár; ☎224 3700; www.oszk.hu; I Szent György tér, Royal Palace, Wing F; ⌚10am-9pm Tue-Sat; 🚌19, 41).

There are two entrances to the Royal Palace. The first is via the splendid **Habsburg Steps** (Map p36), southeast of Szent György tér and through an ornamental gateway dating from 1903. The second is via **Corvinus Gate** (Map p36), with its big, black raven symbolising King Matthias Corvinus, southwest of the square.

Fishermen's Bastion MONUMENT

(Halászbástya; Map p36; I Szentháromság tér; adult/concession 540/220Ft; ⌚9am-11pm mid-Mar–mid-Oct) Just east of Matthias Church, Fishermen's Bastion is a neo-Gothic folly that looks simply too new and well-scrubbed to be medieval. Built as a viewing platform in 1905 by Frigyes Schulek, its name was taken from the medieval guild of fishermen responsible for defending this stretch of wall. The seven white turrets represent the Magyar tribes that entered the Carpathian Basin in the late 9th century. From here, the views of Pest and the Danube are superb.

Budapest History Museum MUSEUM

(Budapesti Történeti Múzeum; Map p36; www.btm.hu; I Szent György tér 2; adult/concession 1500/750Ft; ⌚10am-6pm Tue-Sun Mar-Oct, reduced hours Nov-Feb; 🚌16, 16/a, 116, 🚌19, 41) This wonderful museum puts the 2000 years of the city's history into perspective over the course of four floors, rather than bombarding you with an array of objects. From the basement, you can enter restored palace rooms dating from the 15th century. There are three vaulted halls, one with a magnificent Renaissance door frame in red marble bearing the seal of Queen Beatrice and tiles with a raven and a ring (the seal of her husband, King Matthias Corvinus), leading to the Gothic Hall, the Royal Cellar and the 14th-century Tower Chapel.

Exhibits on the ground floor showcase Budapest during the Middle Ages, with important Gothic statues of courtiers, squires and saints discovered during excavations in 1974. There are also artefacts recently recovered from a well dating from Turkish times, most notably a 14th-century tapestry of the Hungarian coat of arms with the fleur-de-lis of the House of Anjou. The 1st-floor exhibit 'Budapest in Modern Times' traces the history of the city from the expulsion of the Turks in 1686 through the horrors of 20th-century war, to Hungary's entry into the EU. On the floor above, the exhibits show Budapest from prehistoric times to the arrival of the Avars in the late 6th century.

Hungarian National Gallery GALLERY

(Nemzeti Galéria; Map p36; www.mng.hu; I Szent György tér 6; adult/concession 1200/600Ft; ⌚10am-6pm Tue-Sun; 🚌16, 16/a, 116, 🚌19, 41) The Hungarian National Gallery is an overwhelming collection, spread across four floors, which traces Hungarian art from the 11th century to the present. The largest collections include

Castle Hill & Watertown

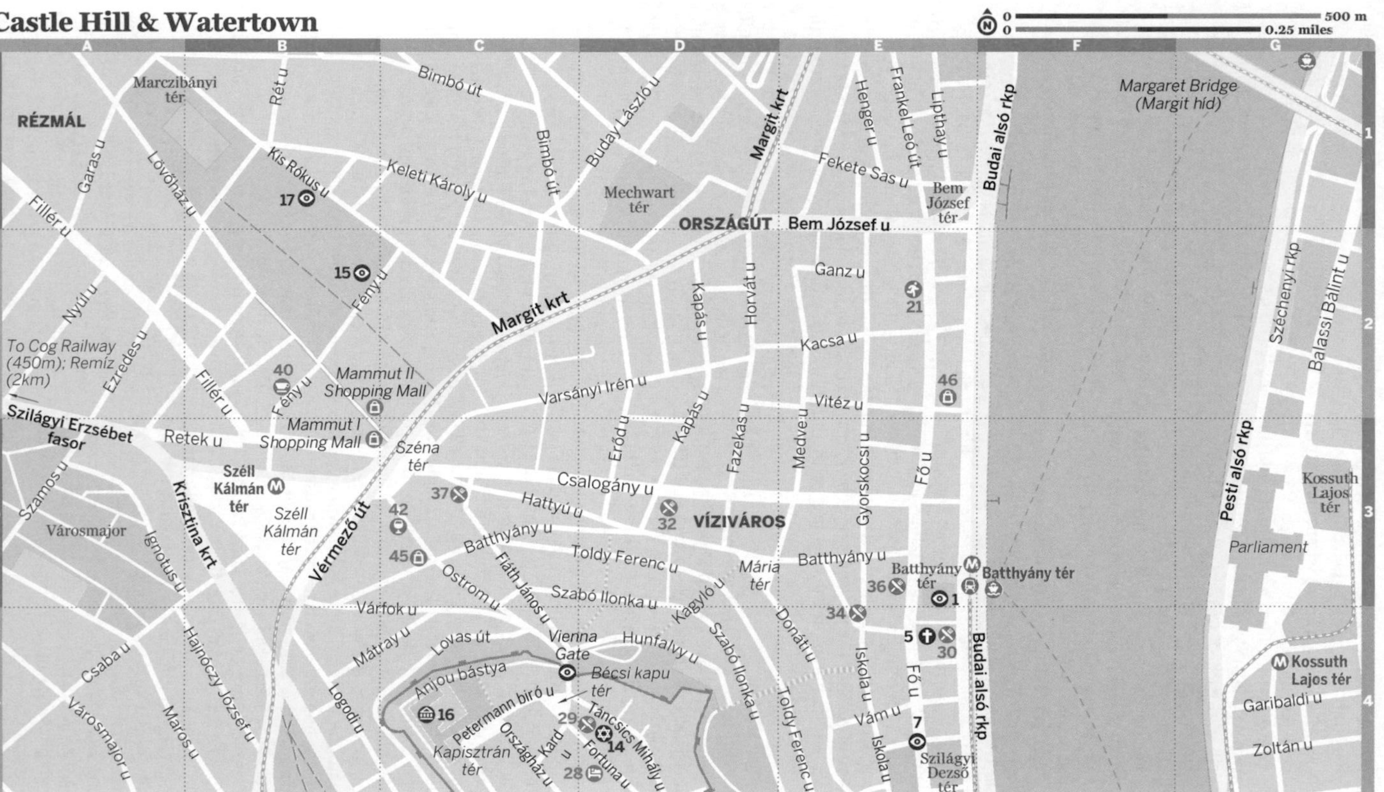

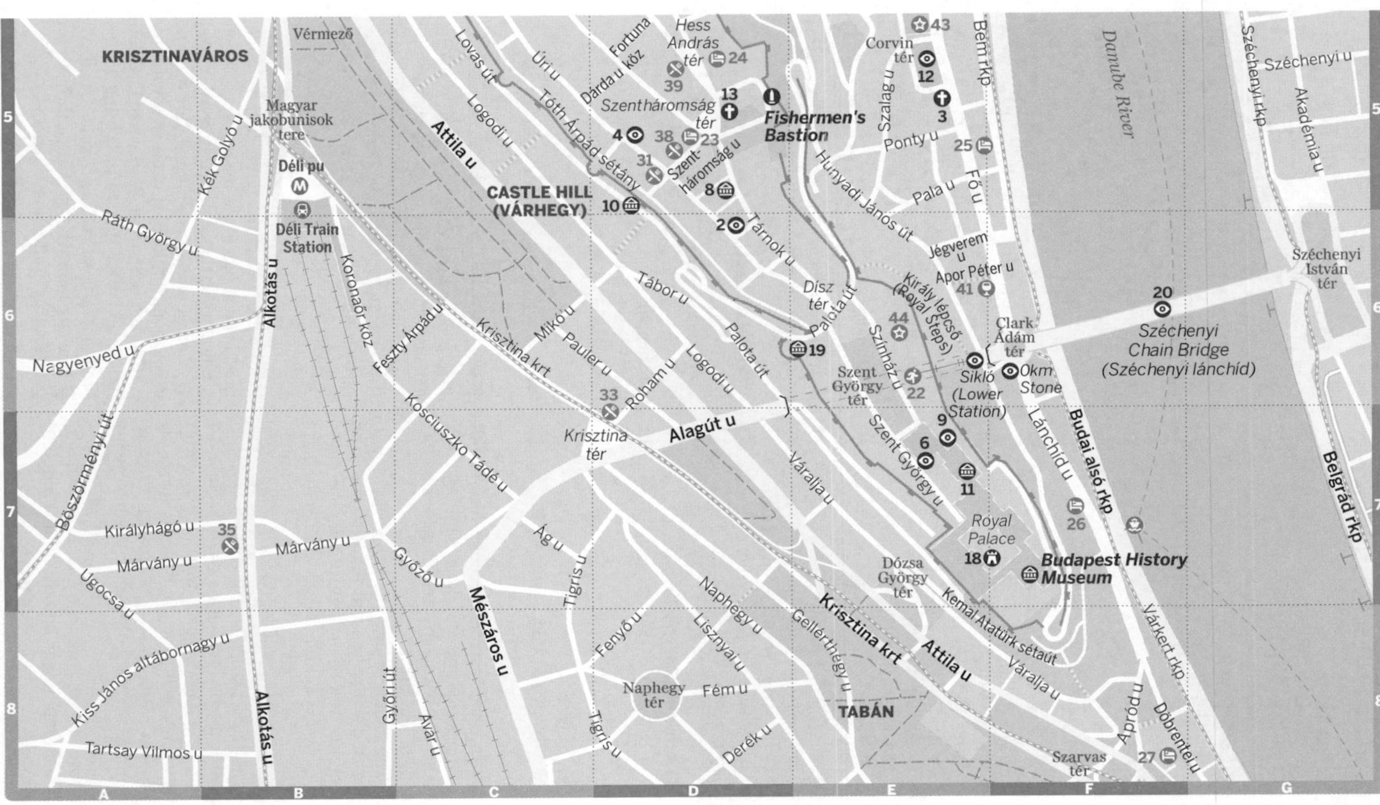
KRISZTINAVÁROS
Vérmező
Magyar jakobunisok tere
Déli pu
Déli Train Station
Kék Golyó u
Ráth György u
Alkotás u
Nagyenyed u
Böszörményi út
Királyhágó u
Márvány u
35
Ugocsa u
Kiss János altábornagy u
Tartsay Vilmos u
Lovas út
Úri u
Fortuna
Dárda u köz
Hess András tér
24
39
13
Szentháromság tér
Fishermen's Bastion
4
38
23
31
Szent-háromság u
8
Tóth Árpád sétány
Logodi u
Attila u
CASTLE HILL (VÁRHEGY)
10
2
Tárnok u
Hunyadi János út
Szalag u
Corvin tér
43
12
3
Ponty u
25
Pala u
Fő u
Bem rkp
Danube River
Jégverem u
Apor Péter u
41
Király lépcső (Royal Steps)
Dísz tér
Palota út
19
44
Színház u
Tábor u
Koronaőr köz
Feszty Árpád u
Krisztina krt
Mikó u
Pauler u
Roham u
Logodi u
Palota út
33
Krisztina tér
Alagút u
Kosciuszko Tádé u
Szent György tér
22
Clark Ádám tér
Sikló (Lower Station)
0km Stone
20
Széchenyi Chain Bridge (Széchenyi lánchíd)
Széchenyi István tér
Széchenyi rkp
Széchenyi u
Akadémia u
9
6
11
Szent György u
Váralja u
Lánchíd u
Budai alsó rkp
26
Royal Palace
18
Budapest History Museum
Belgrád rkp
Várkert rkp
Dózsa György tér
Kemal Atatürk sétaút
Váralja u
Attila u
Krisztina krt
Gellérthegy u
Naphegy u
Lisznyai u
Fenyő u
Naphegy tér
Fém u
Tigris u
Ág u
Mészáros u
Győző u
Győri út
Avar u
Derék u
TABÁN
Szarvas tér
27
Apród u
Döbrentei u

Castle Hill & Watertown

Top Sights

Budapest History Museum ... F7
Fishermen's Bastion ... D5

Sights

1 Batthyány tér ... E3
2 Buda Castle Labyrinth ... D6
3 Capuchin Church ... E5
4 Castle Hill ... D5
5 Church of St Anne ... E4
6 Corvinus Gate ... E7
7 Fő Utca ... E4
8 Golden Eagle Pharmacy Museum ... D5
9 Habsburg Steps ... E7
10 Hospital In The Rock ... D5
11 Hungarian National Gallery ... E7
12 Lajos Fountain ... E5
13 Matthias Church ... D5
14 Medieval Jewish Prayer House ... D4
15 Millennium Park ... B2
16 Museum of Military History ... C4
17 Palace of Wonders ... B1
18 Royal Palace ... F7
19 Royal Wine House & Wine Cellar Museum ... E6
20 Széchenyi Chain Bridge ... F6

Activities, Courses & Tours

21 Király ... E2
22 Sikló ... E6

Sleeping

23 Burg Hotel ... D5
24 Hilton Budapest ... D5
25 Hotel Victoria ... E5
26 Lánchíd 19 ... F7
27 Orion Hotel ... F8
28 St George Residence ... D4

Eating

29 21 Magyar Vendéglő ... D4
30 Angelika Kávéház ... E4
31 Cafe Miró ... D5
32 Csalogány 26 ... D3
33 Déryné Bisztró ... D7
34 Éden ... E4
35 Mongolian Barbecue ... B7
36 Nagyi Palacsintázója ... E3
37 Nagyi Palacsintázója ... C3
38 Ruszwurm Cukrászda ... D5
39 Vár a Speiz ... D5

Drinking

40 Auguszt Cukrászda ... B2
41 Lánchíd Söröző ... E6
42 Oscar American Bar ... C3

Entertainment

43 Buda Concert Hall ... E5
44 National Dance Theatre ... E6

Shopping

45 Bortársaság ... C3
46 Herend Village Pottery ... E2

medieval and Renaissance stonework, Gothic wooden sculptures and panel paintings, late-Gothic winged altars, and late Renaissance and baroque art.

The names behind the Hungarian paintings and sculpture from the 19th and 20th centuries may be unfamiliar, but collectively these works communicate what some have described as a 'patriotic sorrow' – the muted grief of generations for their country. The sombreness permeates some of the works of realist Mihály Munkácsy, such as *The Last Day of a Condemned Man*. Other works that may catch your eye include the overly wrought Romantic Nationalist 'heroic' paintings by Gyula Benczúr, the harrowing depictions of war and the dispossessed by László Mednyánszky, the unique portraits by József Rippl-Rónai, and the almost religious canvases by Tivadar Csontváry.

FREE Citadella FORT

(Map p68; www.citadella.hu; 24hr) The Citadella is a fortress that never saw battle. Built by the Habsburgs using forced labour after the 1848–49 War of Independence to deter further insurrection from Pest, the Citadella was obsolete by the time it was ready (1851) and became municipal property in 1894, serving variously as a prison camp, homeless shelter and anti-aircraft battery. Today the Citadella has some big guns and open-air displays in the central courtyard, as well as offering budget accommodation with access to some of the best views in town.

To reach here from Pest, cross Elizabeth Bridge and take the stairs leading up behind the statue of St Gellért, or cross Liberty Bridge and follow Verejték utca through the park starting at the Cave Chapel.

Aquincum Museum ARCHAEOLOGICAL SITE

(Aquincumi Múzeum; Map p44; www.aquincum.hu; III Szentendre út 139; adult/student & senior 1500/600Ft; archaeological park only 1000/300Ft; park 9am-6pm Tue-Sun May-Sep, reduced hours Apr & Oct, museum 10am-6pm Tue-Sun May-Sep, reduced hours Apr & Oct) The most complete Roman civilian town in Hungary, Aquincum had paved streets and fairly sumptuous single-storey houses with courtyards, fountains and mosaic floors, as well as sophisticated drainage (flushing toilets!) and heating systems. As you walk among the ruins, you can see the outlines of the big public baths, a market, an early Christian church and a temple dedicated to the god Mithras.

The museum on the western edge of Aquincum puts the ruins in perspective, with a vast collection of coins, artefacts and wall paintings. Look out for the replica of a 3rd-century portable organ called a hydra (and the mosaic illustrating how it was played) and the mock-up of a Roman bath. Most of the big sculptures and stone sarcophagi are outside, to the left of the old museum building or behind it in the lapidarium.

Matthias Church CHURCH

(Mátyás Templom; Map p36; www.matyas-temlom.hu; I Szentháromság tér 2; adult/concession 1000/700Ft; 9am-5pm Mon-Fri, 9am-1pm Sat, 1-5pm Sun) The pointed spire and colourful tiled roof of this neo-Gothic church rise above the streets of Castle Hill. Budapest residents are divided over its exterior: some deplore it as too flashy, while others consider it an architectural masterpiece. Parts of Matthias Church (named for King Matthias Corvinus, who was wed here twice) date back some 500 years – most notably the carvings above the southern entrance. The rest was designed by the architect Frigyes Schulek in 1896. Highlights of the interior are the remarkable stained glass windows, and the tomb of King Béla III in one of the chapels along the north wall. This is the only medieval royal tomb to have survived.

Liberty Monument MONUMENT

(Szabadság szobor; Map p68) A 14m-tall, dramatically striding woman with great muscle definition, the Liberty Monument lies to the east of the Citadella. Originally commissioned by Admiral Horthy as a memorial to his son, who perished in a wartime plane crash, the sculpture was adapted in 1947 to serve as tribute to Soviet soldiers who died liberating Budapest in 1945 – the woman's propeller was replaced with a generic palm frond proclaiming freedom. However, the victims' names in Cyrillic letters on the plinth and statue of the Soviet soldier that flanked her were removed in 1992 and banished to Memento Park (see boxed text, p92). Ms Liberty herself remained, as an unofficial symbol of the city. Today the monument is dedicated to 'Those who gave up their lives for Hungary's independence, freedom and prosperity'.

Golden Eagle Pharmacy Museum MUSEUM

(Arany Sas Patika; Map p36; www.semmelweis.museum.hu; I Tárnok utca 18; adult/concession 500/250Ft; 10.30am-6pm Tue-Sun mid-Mar–Oct, reduced hours Nov–mid-Mar; 16, 16/a, 116) Just north of Dísz tér on the site of Budapest's first apothecary (1681), this museum contains unusual displays of medieval medicine, including a mock-up of an alchemist's laboratory complete with dried bats and pickled octopus in jars, and a small 'spice rack' used by 17th-century travellers to store their daily fixes of curative herbs. (But what's with the stuffed crocodile hanging from the ceiling?)

Hospital In The Rock MUSEUM

(Sziklakórház; Map p36; 70 701 0101; www.hospitalintherock.com; I Lovas út 4/c; adult/6-25yr & 62-70yr/under 6yr & over 70 3600/1800Ft/free; 10am-7pm Tue-Sun; 16, 16/a,116) Part of the Castle Hill caves network, this hospital was used extensively during the siege of Budapest in WWII and the 1956 Uprising. As well as original medical equipment, it contains 100 wax figures. The hour-long guided tour includes a walk through a Cold War nuclear bunker and is much more than a quick tramp through dank corridors: you learn about how the natural cave system was adapted to work as a hospital, and about the inhuman conditions staff had to work in while tending people wounded in the Uprising. Gritty stuff.

Vasarely Museum GALLERY

(Map p44; 388 7551; www.vasarely.hu; III Szentlélek tér 6; adult/6-26yr & 62-70yr/under 6yr & over 70yr 800/400Ft/free; 10am-5.30pm Tue-Sun; 86, HÉV Árpád híd) Housed in the crumbling Zichy Mansion, this museum contains the works of Victor Vasarely, the late 'father of Op Art', famous for his 3D optical illusion works. The collection ranges from his early sketches to playful, mesmerising pieces using geometric shapes to great effect, such as *Tlinko-F* and *Ibadan-Pos-*, which are fun to watch as they 'swell' and 'move' around the canvas.

WORTH A TRIP

THE (BUDA) HILLS ARE ALIVE...

...with the sound of hikers' footsteps, the chug-chug-chug of the tiny railway and the clamour of picnickers who climb the 500m-high **Buda Hills** to escape hot, dusty Pest in summer. Keen hikers may wish to equip themselves with Cartographia's 1:25,000 *A Budai-hegység* map (No 6) and if you wish to partake in hobbit-esque activity, there are a couple of beautiful caves to explore – Pálvölgy Cave (p56) and Szemlőhegy Cave (p56) (with a guided tour, mind). And if you want some culture on top of your nature, **Béla Bartók Memorial House** (Bartók Béla Emlékház; ☎394 2100; www.bartokmuseum.hu; II Csalán út 29; adult/senior & student 1200/600Ft; ⏰10am-5pm Tue-Sun; 🚌5, 29), the house where the great composer resided from 1932 until 1940, allows a peek into the man's life.

Getting to the hills is part of the fun. On the Buda side, take either tram 59 or 61 from Széll Kálmán tér to the circular Hotel Budapest (II Szilágyi Erzsébet fasor 47). Directly opposite is the terminus of the **Cog Railway** (Fogaskerekű vasút; www.bkv.hu; Szilágyi Erzsébet fasor 14-16; admission 320Ft; ⏰5am-11pm), just in case you didn't come here to 'climb ev'ry mountain'. Built in 1874, the cog climbs 3.7km in 14 minutes, three or four times an hour, to **Széchenyi-hegy** (427m), one of the prettiest residential areas in Buda.

At Széchenyi-hegy, train enthusiasts (and children) are likely to be drawn to the narrow-gauge **Children's Railway** (Gyermekvasút; www.gyermekvasut.hu; adult/child 1 section 500/300Ft, entire line 700/350Ft; ⏰closed Mon Sep-Apr), two minutes to the south on Hegyhát út. The railway has eight stops and was built in 1951 by Pioneers (socialist Scouts); it is now staffed entirely by schoolchildren aged 10 to 14 (the engineer excepted). The little train chugs along for 12km, terminating at Hűvösvölgy.

There are walks fanning out from any of the stops along the Children's Railway line, or you can return to Széll Kálmán tér on tram 61 from Hűvösvölgy. A more interesting way down, however, is to get off at **János-hegy**, the fourth stop on the Children's Railway and the highest point (527m) in the hills. Take the 101 steps up the 23.5m-tall **Elizabeth Lookout** (Erzsébet kilátó), and on clear days you'll be rewarded with views of Slovakia's Tatra Mountains. About 700m to the east is the **chairlift** (Libegő; www.bkv.hu; adult/child 800/500Ft; ⏰9am-7pm Jul & Aug, 9.30am-5pm May, Jun & Sep, 10am-4pm Oct-Apr, closed 2nd & 4th Mon of every month), which will take you 1040m down to Zugligeti út. From here, bus 291 returns to Szilágyi Erzsébet fasor.

Imre Varga Exhibition House GALLERY
(Varga Imre Kiállítóháza; Map p44; www.budapestgaleria.hu; III Laktanya utca 7; adult/child 800/400Ft; ⏰10am-6pm Tue-Sun; 🚌86) Part of the Budapest Gallery, this exhibition space includes sculptures, statues, medals and drawings by Imre Varga, one of Hungary's foremost sculptors. Specialising in works made of moulded sheet metal, Varga chose a varied array of subjects – from Greek legendary figures (Prometheus) to prominent communist figures (Lenin, Béla Kun), as well as commemorating the Holocaust and honouring the Swedish humanitarian Raoul Wallenberg – but his work is always fresh and never derivative.

Buda Castle Labyrinth LABYRINTH
(Budavári Labirintus; Map p36; www.labirintus.com; I Úri utca 9; adult/senior & student/under 12yr 2000/1500/600Ft; ⏰10am-7pm; 🚌16, 16/a, 116) The 1200m-long cave system under Castle Hill offers relief from the heat on a hot summer's day – it's always 20°C down here. The Labyrinth recently played host to a real-life drama that's at least as interesting as the contents of the cavern and tunnel network (examples of stone carvery, mist, ominous music á la *Phantom of the Opera*, and a photo exhibition of caves around the world). On 29 July 2011, police stormed the Labyrinth, chasing out the visitors and panicking foreign tourists, who believed some kind of terror attack had occurred. Apparently, after running the place successfully for 27 years, the owner didn't have a license. Since then, it has been run in a fairly humdrum fashion by whoever took over. But after a court ruled in late 2012 that the police actions against the original owner were unjust, hope was revived that the Labyrinth experience might be restored to its former glory. Watch this space.

Roman Military Amphitheatre ARCHAEOLOGICAL SITE
(Római Katonai Amfiteátrum; Map p44; III Pacsirtamező utca; ⌚24hr; 🚌86) Built in the 2nd century for the Roman garrisons, this amphitheatre about 800m south of Flórián tér and across the road from Aquincum could accommodate up to 15,000 spectators and was larger than Rome's Colosseum. The remainder of the military camp extended north to Flórián tér. Take bus 86 to Flórián tér and descend at III Nagyszombat utca.

Royal Wine House & Wine Cellar Museum MUSEUM
(Borház és Pincemúzeum; Map p36; ☎267 1100; www.kiralyiborok.com; I Szent György tér Nyugati sétány; admission adult/student & senior 990/750Ft; ⌚noon-8pm daily May-Sep, noon-8pm Tue-Sun Oct-Apr) Housed in what once were the royal cellars below Szent György tér dating back to the 13th century, this attraction offers a crash course in Hungarian viticulture in the heart of the Castle District. Tastings cost 1990/2490/3790Ft for three/four/six wines (try not to swallow!). You can also try various types of Hungarian sparkling wine and *pálinka* (fruit brandy), which you can swallow.

Elizabeth Bridge BRIDGE
(Erzsébet híd; Map p68; 🚌15, 115, 🚋19, 41, 2) Elizabeth Bridge, a gleaming white suspension bridge, enjoys a special place in the hearts of many Budapesters both as the first newly designed bridge to reopen after WWII (in 1964) and because its design is a copy of a bridge the Germans destroyed in 1945. Having since become one of the unofficial symbols of the city, it boasts a higher arch than the other bridges and offers dramatic views of both Castle and Gellért Hills and the more attractive bridges to the north and south.

Széchenyi Chain Bridge BRIDGE
(Széchenyi lánchíd; Map p36) A twin-towered structure to the south, this is the city's oldest and arguably most beautiful bridge. Named in honour of its initiator, Count István Széchenyi, it was actually built by Scotsman Adam Clark. When it opened in 1849, Chain Bridge was unique for two reasons: it was the first permanent dry link between Buda and Pest; and the aristocracy – previously exempt from all taxation – had to pay a toll to use it, like everybody else.

Gül Baba's Tomb ISLAMIC
(Gül Baba türbéje; Map p44; ☎326 0062; II Türbe tér 1; adult/child/student 600/300/450Ft; ⌚10am-6pm Tue-Sun; 🚋4, 6 or 17) This octagonal tomb contains the remains of Gül Baba, an Ottoman Dervish poet who took part in the capture of Buda in 1541 and died suddenly afterwards, his funeral attended by none other than Sultan Suleiman the Magnificent. Gül Baba is known in Hungary as the 'Father of Roses', possibly for the flowers left at his tomb. This is a pilgrimage place for Muslims; remove your shoes before entering. To reach the tomb from Török utca, running parallel to Frankel Leó út, walk west along steep, cobbled Gül Baba utca to the set of steps just past house No 16.

Batthyány tér SQUARE
(Map p36; Ⓜ M2 Batthyány tér, 🚋19, 41) Batthyány tér is the centre of Víziváros and the best place to snap the photogenic Parliament building across the river. On the southern side is the 18th-century baroque **Church of St Anne** (Szent Ana templom; Map p36; I Batthyány tér 7; Ⓜ M2 Batthyány tér, 🚋19, 41), with one of the most eye-catching interiors of any church in Budapest.

A TRIO OF GALLERIES

You've seen Budapest's grand art museums, but there's so much more to the city's creative scene. Here are three great little galleries that you may have missed:

» **2B Galéria** (Map p68; www.2b-org.hu; IX Ráday utca 47; ⌚2-6pm Mon-Fri, 10am-2pm Sat; Ⓜ M3 Corvin negyed, 🚋4, 6) The exhibitions at this gallery range from merely eclectic to deeply thought provoking – such as an exhibition focusing on the extension of perception, with blind and partially sighted volunteers helping prepare the audiovisual installations.

» **A38 Exhibition Space** Works by up-and-coming artists at A38 (p81), Budapest's only floating gallery/bar/concert venue.

» **Vintage Galéria** (Map p68; www.vintage.hu; V Magyar utca 26; ⌚2-6pm Tue-Fri; Ⓜ M2 Astoria, 🚋47, 49) A private gallery featuring striking contemporary photography.

Millennium Park OUTDOORS

(Millenáris Park; Map p36; ☎336 4000; www.millenaris.hu; II Kis Rókus utca 16-20; ⏲6am-1am; Ⓜ M2 Széll Kálmán tér, 🚊4 or 6) Millennium Park is an attractive landscaped complex, comprising fountains, ponds, little bridges, a theatre, gallery and, for kids, the wonderful **Palace of Wonders** (Csodák Palotája; Map p36; www.csodapalota.hu; II Kis Rókus utca 16-20, Bldg D; adult/student & child 1500/1250Ft; ⏲10am-8pm; Ⓜ M2 Széll Kálmán tér). It's an interactive playhouse for children of all ages, with 'smart' toys and puzzles, most with a scientific bent. You can also enter the park from Fény utca 20–22 and Lövőház utca 37.

Kiscelli Museum MUSEUM

(Kiscelli Múzeum; Map p44; ☎1-388 8560; www.budapestgaleria.hu; III Kiscelli utca 108; adult/6-26yr & 62-70yr 1000/500Ft; ⏲10am-6pm Tue-Sun Apr-Oct, to 4pm Nov-Mar; 🚌160, 165, 🚊17) Housed in an 18th-century monastery southwest of Flórián tér, the Kiscelli Museum contains two excellent sections. The **Contemporary City History Collection** (Újkori Várostörténeti Gyűjtemény) has a complete 19th-century apothecary, moved here from Kálvin tér and comprising a wonderful assembly of ancient signboards advertising shops and other trades, and rooms (both public and private) furnished with Empire, Biedermeier and Art Nouveau furniture and bric-a-brac. Upstairs, the **Municipal Picture Gallery** (Fővárosi Képtár) has an impressive collection of artworks by József Rippl-Rónai, Lajos Tihanyi, István Csók and Béla Czóbel, among others.

Museum of Military History MUSEUM

(Hadtörténeti Múzeum; Map p36; ☎325 1600; www.militaria.hu; I Tóth Árpád sétány 40; adult/senior/student 1100/350/550Ft; ⏲10am-6pm Tue-Sun Apr-Sep, reduced hours Oct-Mar; 🚌16, 16/a, 116) Loaded with weaponry dating from before the Turkish conquest, the Museum of Military History also does a good job with uniforms, medals, flags and battle-themed fine art. Exhibits focus particularly on the 1848–49 War of Independence and the Hungarian Royal Army under the command of Admiral Miklós Horthy (1918–43), but there are plenty of tools of modern warfare both in and outside – cannons, mines, an array of guns... Outside is a mock-up of the electrified fence that once separated Hungary from Austria, and 'Thirteen Days', the exhibition dedicated to the 1956 Uprising, is said to be particularly worthwhile.

Cave Chapel RELIGIOUS

(Sziklakápolna; Map p68; XI Szent Gellért rakpart 1/a; ⏲10am-7pm; 🚌47, 49, 19, 41) Located on a small hill directly north of the landmark Art Nouveau **Danubius Gellért Hotel** (1918), the chapel was built into a cave in 1926. It was the seat of the Pauline order until 1951, when the communists arrested and imprisoned the priests and sealed the cave off. It was reopened and reconsecrated in 1992, with its stone cross (destroyed in the 1940s) re-erected above the entrance. Behind the chapel is a monastery, with neo-Gothic turrets that are visible from Liberty Bridge.

Fő Utca HISTORIC

(Map p36; 🚌86) Fő utca is the arrow-straight 'Main Street' running from Clark Ádám tér through Víziváros. It was originally laid down by the Romans, who were fond of straight lines. At the former **Capuchin Church** (Map p36; I Fő utca 30-32; 🚊19, 41), used as a mosque during the Turkish occupation, you can see the remains of an Islamic-style ogee-arched door and window on the southern side. Around the corner there's the seal of King Matthias Corvinus – a raven with a ring in its beak – and a little square called Corvin tér with the delightful 1904 **Lajos Fountain** (Lajos kútja; Map p36). The Eclectic building on the north side at No 8 is the Buda Concert Hall (p84). To the north is the **Iron Stump** – an odd-looking tree trunk into which itinerant artisans and merchants drove nails to mark their visit.

Medieval Jewish Prayer House JEWISH

(Középkori Zsidó Imaház; Map p36; I Táncsics Mihály utca 26; adult/child 600/300Ft; ⏲10am-5pm Tue-Sun May-Oct; 🚌16, 16/a, 116) With parts dating from the late 14th century, this tiny ancient house of worship has documents and items linked to the Jewish community of Buda, as well as Gothic stone carvings and tombstones. Jews originally settled in Buda in the 13th century, at the invitation of King Béla IV, and remained throughout the Ottoman occupation, but when the Austrians liberated the town, the prosperous Jewish community was accused of collaborating with the Turks and destroyed.

MARGARET ISLAND & NORTHERN PEST

A part of neither Buda nor Pest, Margaret Island (Margit-sziget), which stretches for 2.5km in the middle of the Danube, was the domain of one religious order or another until the Turks came and turned what was then

RAOUL WALLENBERG: RIGHTEOUS GENTILE

At Yad Vashem, a museum in Jerusalem dedicated to the Holocaust, there is a row of trees called the 'Avenue of the Righteous among Nations'. They represent some of the approximately 21,300 gentiles (non-Jews) who either saved Jews during the Holocaust or came to their defence by putting their own lives at risk. Among them was Raoul Wallenberg, the Swedish diplomat and businessman who rescued as many as 35,000 Hungarian Jews during WWII.

Wallenberg began working in 1936 for a trading firm whose owner was a Hungarian Jew. In July 1944 the Swedish Foreign Ministry, at the request of Jewish and refugee organisations in the USA, sent the 32-year-old Wallenberg on a rescue mission to Budapest as an attaché to its embassy. By that time almost half a million Jews in Hungary had been sent to Nazi death camps in Germany and Poland.

Immediately, Wallenberg began issuing Swedish 'protective passports' and set up 'safe houses', flying the flags of Sweden and other neutral countries, where Jews could seek asylum. He even followed German 'death marches' and deportation trains, distributing food, clothing and passports, and actually freeing some 500 people along the way.

When the Soviet army entered Budapest in January 1945, Wallenberg was summoned to report to Soviet Marchal Rodion Malinovsky and subsequently arrested for espionage (his privileged background and Sweden's theoretically neutral but actually pro-Nazi Germany stance during the war compromised him) and sent to Moscow's notorious Lubyanka prison. In 1957, responding to reports that Wallenberg had been seen alive in a labour camp, the Soviet Union announced that he had died of a heart attack in 1947. Several witnesses claimed sightings of Wallenberg into the late 1980s, but none was ever confirmed and most historians believe he was executed in the Lubyanka in 1947. For Wallenberg's family, however, the case remains open.

Wallenberg has been made an honorary citizen of the USA, Canada, Israel and, most recently (in 2003), the city of Budapest.

called the Island of Rabbits into – appropriately enough – a harem. It's been a public park open to everyone since the mid-19th century, named after King Béla IV's daughter Margaret (Margit).

While not teeming with unmissable sights, its gardens and shaded walkways are lovely places to stroll. As the island is mostly off limits to cars, cyclists also feel welcome here.

The easiest way to get to Margaret Island from Buda or Pest is via tram 4 or 6, while bus 26 covers the length of the island. You can hire a bicycle from one of several stands, including **Bringóhintó** (Map p44; www.bringohinto.hu; mountain bike per half-hr/hr/day 690/990/2800Ft, pedal coach for 4 people per half-hr/hr 1980/2980Ft; 8am-dusk) beside the refreshment stand near the Japanese Garden in the northern part of the island.

Franciscan Church and Monastery RUIN
(Ferences templom és kolostor; Map p44; 26) The ruins – no more than a tower and a wall dating from the late 13th century – are in the centre of the island. The Habsburg Archduke Joseph built a summer residence here when he inherited the island in 1867 and it was later converted into a hotel, which operated until 1949.

Dominican Convent RUIN
(Domonkos kolostor; Map p44; 26) The remains of the 13th century Dominican convent lie northeast of the Franciscan Church and Monastery. The convent's most famous resident was St Margaret (1242–71), the daughter of King Béla IV, after whom the island takes its name. Kings were wont to do as they please with their daughters and, as the story goes, Béla IV vowed that Margaret would commit herself to a life of devotion in a nunnery if the Mongols were driven from Hungary. They were and she did – at nine years of age. Still, if we're to believe the description in *Lives of the Saints*, she seemed to enjoy her gilded cage, especially the mortification-of-the-flesh parts. St Margaret, canonised only in 1943, commands something of a cult following in Hungary. A red marble sepulchre cover surrounded by a wrought-iron grille marks her original resting place, and there's a much-visited brick shrine with votive offerings located a short distance to the southeast.

Margaret Island

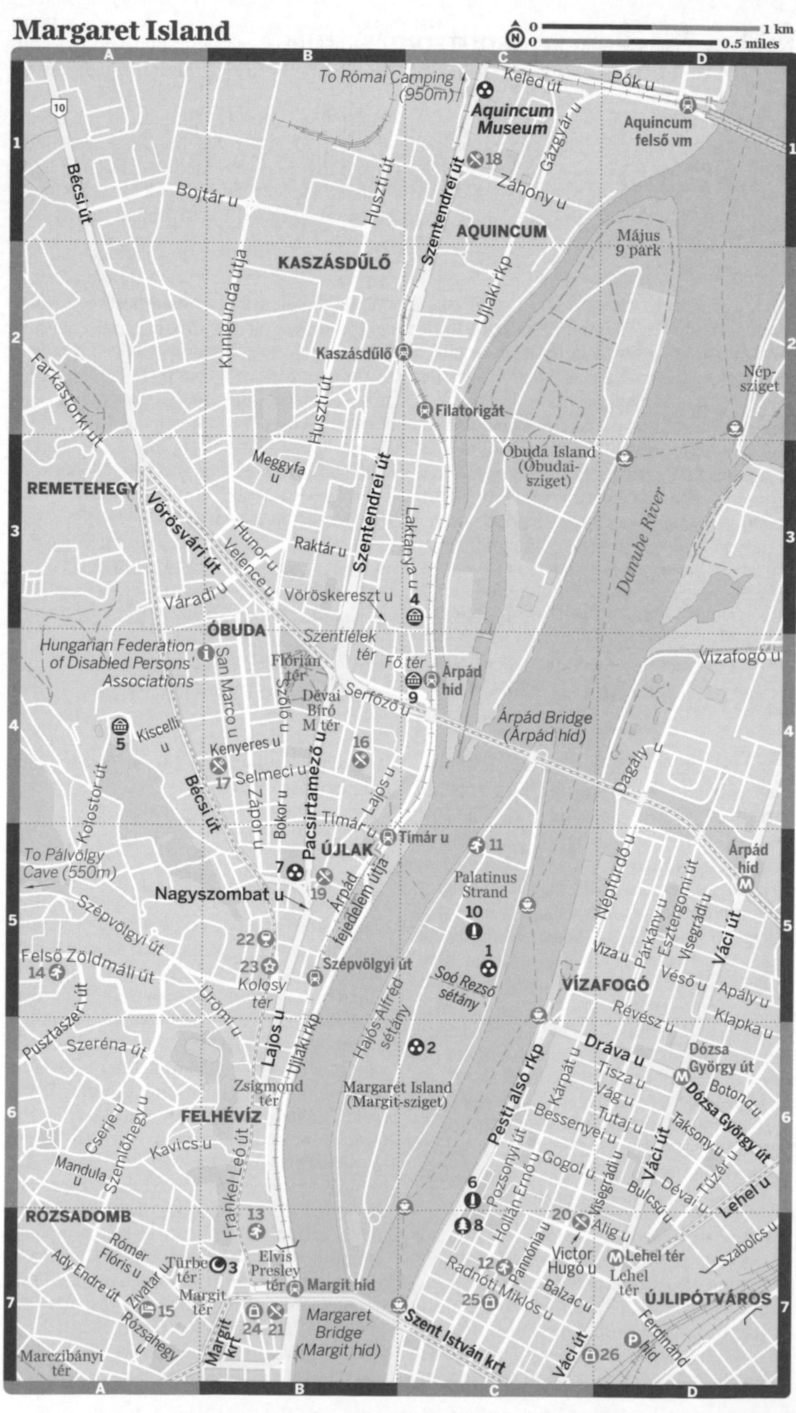

Szent István Park PARK
(Szent István körút; Map p44; 15, 115) Northeast of the Palatinus Houses (the oldest houses in the Újlipótváros neighbourhood) is 'St Stephen's Park', where a statue shows **Raoul Wallenberg** (Map p44; XIII Szent István Park) doing battle with a snake that personified evil. *Kígyóölo* (Serpent Slayer) was erected in 1999 to replace another that had been mysteriously removed the night before its unveiling in 1948.

St Gellért Monument MONUMENT
(Map p68) Looking down on Elizabeth Bridge from Gellért Hill is the St Gellért Monument. Gellért was an Italian missionary whom King Stephen invited to Hungary to convert the natives. The monument marks the spot where the bishop was hurled to his death in 1046, allegedly in a spiked barrel (though some say it was a wheelbarrow), by pagan Hungarians resisting the new faith.

Water Tower TOWER
(Víztorony; Map p44; 26) The octagonal water tower, erected in 1911 in the north-central part of the island, rises 66m above an open-air theatre used for free performances during summer. A quick huff and puff up the 153 steps to the tower's **Lookout Gallery** (Kilátó Galéria; Map p44; Margitsziget, víztorony; adult/child 400/250Ft; 11am-7pm May-Oct; 26) will earn you a stunning 360-degree view from the cupola terrace of the island, Buda and Pest.

Queen Elizabeth Statue MONUMENT
(Map p68; I Döbrentei tér; 19, 41) To the north of Elizabeth Bridge and through an underpass is a statue of Queen Elizabeth. As Habsburg empress, Hungarian queen and consort to Franz Joseph, 'Sissi' was much loved by Magyars because, among other things, she learned to speak Hungarian. She was assassinated by an Italian anarchist in Geneva in 1898.

PEST

While Buda might sometimes seem like a garden, Pest is an urban jungle, with an abundance of architecture, museums, historic buildings and broad boulevards that are unmatched on the other side of the Danube.

Belváros (also known as Inner Town) is the heart of Pest. The area north of Ferenciek tere is full of flashy boutiques and well-touristed bars and restaurants, while the neighbourhood to the south is mostly pedestrianised and trendy. Just north of Belváros is quieter **Lipótváros** (Leopold Town), named in honour of Archduke Leopold, the grandson of Empress Maria-Theresa – a scattering of government ministries, 19th-century apartment blocks and grand squares. **Újlipótváros** ('New Leopold Town'), north of Lipótváros and to the east of Margaret Island, is a predominantly upper middle class and Jewish area before WWII, where many of the 'safe houses' were located during the war. **Erzsébetváros** ('Elizabeth

Margaret Island

Top Sights
Aquincum Museum ... C1

Sights
1 Dominican Convent ... C5
2 Franciscan Church and Monastery ... C6
3 Gül Baba's Tomb ... B7
4 Imre Varga Exhibition House ... C3
5 Kiscelli Museum ... A4
Lookout Gallery ... (see 10)
6 Raoul Wallenberg Memorial ... C6
7 Roman Military Amphitheatre ... B5
8 Szent István Park ... C7
9 Vasarely Museum ... C4
10 Water Tower ... C5

Activities, Courses & Tours
11 Bringóhintó ... C5
12 Happy Bike ... C7
13 Lukács ... B7
14 Szemlőhegy Cave ... A5

Sleeping
15 Hotel Papillon ... A7

Eating
16 Kéhli ... B4
17 Kisbuda Gyöngye ... B4
18 Nagyi Palacsintázója ... C1
19 Pastrami ... B5
20 Trófea Grill ... C7
21 Trófea Grill ... B7

Drinking
22 Puskás Pancho ... B5

Entertainment
23 Cinema Hall ... B5

Shopping
24 BÁV (Buda branch) ... B7
25 Matyó Design ... C7
26 West End City Centre ... C7

BUDAPEST FOR CHILDREN

Budapest abounds in places that will delight children, and there is always a special child's entry rate (and often a family one) to paying attractions. Group visits to many areas of the city can be designed around a rest stop or picnic at, say, City Park, on Margaret Island or along the Danube.

Kids love transport and the city's many unusual forms of conveyance – from the **Cog Railway** and **Children's Railway** (p40) in the Buda Hills (where there are also some gentle hiking trails suitable for young 'uns) and the **Sikló** (Map p36; I Szent György tér; one way/return adult 900/1800Ft, child 550/1000Ft; ⏲7.30am-10pm, closed 1st & 3rd Mon of month; 🚌16, 🚎19, 41) funicular climbing up to Castle Hill to the trams, trolleybuses and M1 metro – will fascinate and entertain, as will the model railways at the **Transport Museum** (p51) in City Park. Children will also be mesmerised by the acrobatics and contortions at the **Municipal Great Circus** (p84), the veritable Noah's Ark of wild things at **Budapest Zoo** (p53) and puppet antics at the **Budapest Puppet Theatre** (p84).

More 'educational' (well, hands-on) destinations include the just-for-kids **Palace of Wonders** in **Buda's Millennium Park** (p42).

Budding archaeologists will get a lot out of a visit to **Aquincum** (p39), and older children may also appreciate a boat ride along the Danube, a Segway tour, or a venture into the damp darkness of the **Pálvölgy** and **Szemlőhegy** caves (p56). The outdoor **Széchenyi Baths** (p54) are also suitable for older water babies.

Lonely Planet's *Travel with Children* includes all sorts of useful information and advice for people travelling with little ones.

Town') – Budapest's liveliest nightlife district, sits between two busy squares, Oktogon and Blaha Lujza tér. Bisected by the Big Ring road, it is bordered by the attractive Andrassy út boulevard to the north, which ends at City Park. The western side of Elizabeth Town is still predominantly Jewish, with a kosher bakery and half a dozen synagogues; this was also the ghetto where Jews were forced to live behind wooden fences when the Nazis occupied Hungary in 1944.

South of Erzsébetváros lies **Józsefváros** – a mix of lovely 19th-century town houses and villas around the Little Ring road and lively student digs. The neighbourhood south of Belváros is **Ferencváros**, home to some controversial contemporary architecture and the lively, pedestrianised Rádayutca, packed with cafes and restaurants.

City Park – Pest's green lung, and a former royal hunting ground, is bordered to the west by Heroes' Square (Hősök tere), and is home to Budapest's largest baths.

Parliament HISTORIC BUILDING

(Országház; Map p60; ☎441 4904; www.parlament.hu; V Kossuth Lajos tér 1-3; adult/concession/EU citizen 3500/1750Ft/free; ⏲8am-4pm Mon-Sat, to 2pm Sun) Parliament's spiky neo-Gothic form dominates the Pest side of the river. It was designed by Imre Steindl, who died just before it was completed in 1902. The melange of architectural styles – neo-Gothic, neo-Romanesque, neobaroque – is surprisingly harmonious.

You'll only get to see three of the 690 sumptuously decorated rooms on a guided tour of the North Wing: the main staircase and landing, the Loge Hall and the Congress Hall, where the House of Lords of the one-time bicameral assembly sat until 1944. The Crown of St Stephen, the nation's most important national treasure, is on display on the landing. From the Middle Ages onwards, it was lost, stolen and found on many occasions and finally returned to Hungary by President Carter in 1978. Tours are conducted in eight languages; the English-language ones are at 10am, noon and 2pm. Book ahead, either in person or by email.

St Stephen's Basilica CHURCH

(Szent István Bazilika; Map p60; www.basilica.hu; V Szent István tér; adult/concession 500/300Ft; ⏲9am-5pm Apr-Sep, 10am-4pm Oct-Mar) The main attraction inside the splendid red-marble and gold Basilica is the Holy Right – the mummified right hand of St Stephen (raising the question: what happened to the rest of the man?) in the Holy Right Chapel behind the main altar. The most venerated object of the Hungarian Catholic church, the hand was returned to Hungary by Habsburg Empress Maria Theresa in 1771, after it was discovered in a monastery in Bosnia. Like the Crown of St Stephen, it was snatched by the bad guys after WWII but was soon handed over to the, er, rightful (ugh!) owners.

Budapest's neoclassical cathedral took more than 50 years to build and was completed in 1906. Much of the interruption had to do with a fiasco in 1868 when the dome collapsed during a storm. The structure had to be demolished and rebuilt from the ground up. After a complete facelift in 2003, the interior is no longer gloomy and its dome, reached by lift and 146 steps, offers a superb 360-degree view of the city.

Terror House MUSEUM

(Terror Háza; Map p60; www.terrorhaza.hu; VI Andrássy út 60; adult/concession 2000/1000Ft; ⏲10am-6pm Tue-Sun) This building, dominated in dark succession first by the dreaded Arrow Cross, then the Nazis and then the Political Police under the Soviets, is instantly recognisable by the word 'terror' spelled out in sunlight on its facade. An ultra-modern, highly interactive museum, Terror Háza di-

BUDAPEST'S JEWS

Jews have lived in Hungary since the 9th century AD; Budapest's large Jewish community in particular steadily contributed to Hungary's scholarly, artistic and commercial progress. After WWI, from which Hungary emerged the loser, Jews were blamed for the economic depression that followed and the territories lost. In 1920 the notorious Numerus Clausus legislation came into play, limiting to 6% the number of Jewish students admitted to universities. Jews fared better in Hungary in the lead-up to WWII than in other eastern European countries, despite Hungary being Germany's ally, but pressure was put on the Hungarian government to adopt Jewish laws (based on the Nazi Nuremburg laws) in 1938, 1940 and 1941, which progressively stripped Jews of property rights, the right to belong to various professions and even to have sexual intercourse with non-Jews.

Following Hungary's occupation by German forces in March 1944, Jews were forced to wear the yellow Star of David and their movement within the city was severely restricted. In July 1944 about 200,000 Jews were moved into 2000 homes within Erzsébetváros, which became the main ghetto. Though more than 15,000 Budapest Jews had already died before the German occupation – worked to death in labour camps or as service personnel accompanying Hungarian troops – they had managed to avoid mass deportation to death camps. Then, just 10 months before the end of the war, about half of Budapest's Jewish population was sent to Auschwitz and other death camps. At the same time, agents of neutral states were working to save Jews by moving them into protected houses within Budapest. Nevertheless, the gangs of the fascist Arrow Cross Party, in power from mid-October 1944, roamed the city in search of Jews, killing them indiscriminately.

Soviet troops liberated the two ghettos on 16 January 1945. When other Jews returned from labour camps and came out of hiding, it transpired that the pre-war Jewish population of Hungary (about 246,000) had been reduced by about half. Still, Budapest Jews fared better than their brethren in the provinces, who were almost all deported to death camps.

There has been a renaissance of Jewish culture and music in Budapest since the fall of the Iron Curtain, in festivals, cuisine and synagogue attendance. The Jewish Summer Festival, held in late July, is a week of music, exhibitions, cuisine and more, with a number of events held at the Great Synagogue (p49). Other important Jewish sites include the Holocaust Memorial Centre (p49) and the traditional Jewish businesses that survive in Erzsébetváros ('Elizabeth Town'), where you can also find a number of kosher restaurants.

But while there has been a renaissance of Jewish culture and music, there has also been a resurgence of openly expressed anti-Semitism. In November 2012, Marton Gyongyosi, an MP for the far right Jobbik party, called for the government to compile a national list of Hungarian Jews, especially Jewish government members, whom he described as a 'national security risk' for alleged solidarity with Israel. The outrage caused by this remark led the leaders of the right, centre and left-wing parties to address a demonstration against anti-Semitism in front of the Parliament building, pledging support to the Jewish community. Viktor Orban, the prime minister, stated that the remark was 'unworthy of Hungary'. Still, being a Jew in Budapest (and Hungary) now, as before, is a mixed blessing.

South Buda & Ferencváros

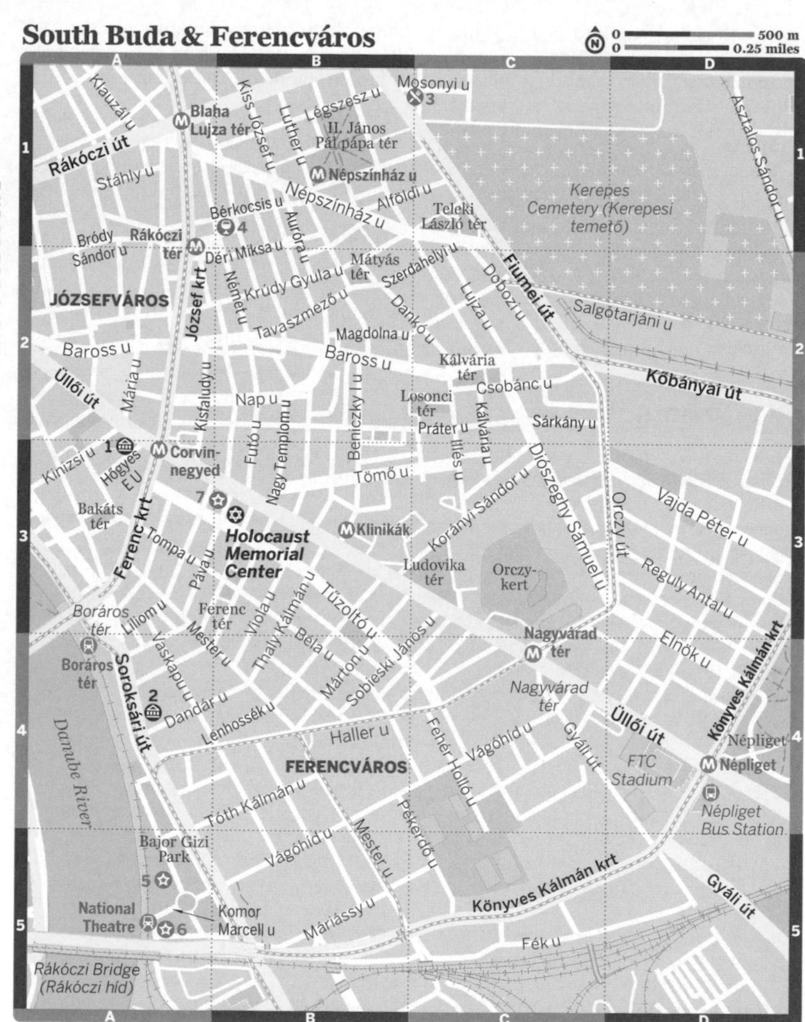

vides opinion among Budapest residents: some see it as a fitting tribute to the victims of two terror regimes, while others see it as a Disney-like trivialisation of the horror Hungarians experienced under the Nazis and their local collaborators, and then under the Soviets, with more emphasis on gimmicks (such as the maze made from bricks of lard) than solid historical evidence.

Either way, it packs a visual punch, starting from the jarring introduction of a tank in the central courtyard and the giant wall of victims' photos. The impact is continued through the interactive map of Europe as it falls to the Nazis, a collection of dramatic black-and-white photos and videos of Nazi victory and a carpet map of deportation centres, accompanied throughout by urgent music. There are personal effects (letters, crosses, a tiny pin with a Star of David) of those who were deported and victims of every political persuasion who were taken for interrogation and torture right here in the basement.

Elsewhere, exhibits are dedicated to the 1956 Uprising, the persecution of various religions and implements of torture, and the known victimisers who are named and

South Buda & Ferencváros

shamed in a collection of photographs. The lift deliberately travels at snail's pace to allow you to watch a video of an execution, but perhaps the most harrowing displays are the reconstructed prison cells (collectively called the 'gym', with reinforced walls to mask the screams) and the final Hall of Tears gallery.

TOP CHOICE Great Synagogue JEWISH
(Nagy zsinagóga; Map p68; ☎343 6756; www.dohanystreetsynagogue.hu; VII Dohány utca 2-8; adult/student & child 2750/2050Ft; ⊙10am-5.30pm Sun-Thu, to 4pm Fri Apr-Oct, reduced hours Nov-Mar) The Great Synagogue is the largest Jewish house of worship in the world outside New York City and can seat 3000 people. Built in 1859, the synagogue blends Romantic style with Moorish architectural elements. The Hebrew above the entrance translates as: 'Make me a sanctuary and I will dwell among them' (Exodus 25:8). In an annexe of the synagogue is the Hungarian Jewish Museum, with a wealth of Torahs, a silver Kiddush cup, *besamim* (spice boxes) and other objects pertaining to religious and everyday life, and an 18th-century handwritten book of the local Burial Society. The Holocaust Memorial Room relates the events of 1944–45 through graphic photographs that include the infamous mass murder of doctors and patients at a hospital on XII Maros utca.

On the synagogue's north side, behind the small and tranquil cemetery, a **Holocaust Memorial** (Map p68; opposite VII Wesselényi utca 6; MM2 Astoria, 47, 49) stands over the mass graves of people murdered by the Nazis in 1944–45. On the leaves of the metal 'tree of life' are the family names of some of the hundreds of thousands of victims.

TOP CHOICE Holocaust Memorial Center JEWISH
(Holokauszt Emlékközpont; Map p48; ☎455 3322; www.hdke.hu; IX Páva utca 39; adult/student & child 1000Ft/free; ⊙10am-6pm Tue-Sun; MM3 Ferenc körút) Part interactive museum, part educational foundation and housed in a striking, fortress-like building, the superb Holocaust Memorial Center opened in 2004 on the 60th anniversary of the start of the Holocaust in Hungary. The thematic permanent exhibition traces the rise of anti-Semitism in Hungary and follows the path to genocide of Hungary's Jewish and Roma communities, from the initial deprivation of rights through the increasing removal of freedom, dignity and, finally, mass deportations to German death camps in 1944–45.

The exhibits consist of a series of maps, graphic videos, photographs, personal effects and interactive displays. The music is festive to begin with, but the final exhibits are accompanied by the pounding heartbeat of the doomed communities. The videos of the death camps, taken by the liberators, are particularly harrowing, featuring piles of corpses and emaciated survivors. A sublimely restored, irregularly shaped synagogue in the central courtyard, designed by Leopold Baumhorn and completed in 1924, hosts temporary exhibitions, while an 8m wall outside features the names of Hungarian victims of the Holocaust. An absolute must-see.

Hungarian State Opera House CULTURAL BUILDING
(Magyar Állami Operaház; Map p60; ☎332 8197; www.operavisit.hu; VI Andrássy út 22; tours adult/concession 3000/2000Ft; ⊙tours 3pm & 4pm) The neo-Renaissance Hungarian State Opera House was designed by Miklós Ybl in 1884 and is among the city's most beautiful buildings. Its facade is decorated with statues of muses and opera greats such as Puccini and Mozart, while its interior dazzles with marble columns, gilded vaulted ceilings and chandeliers, and superb acoustics (considered the third best in Europe). If you cannot attend a performance, at least join one of the English-language guided tours. Tickets are available from the souvenir shop inside to the left.

Museum of Fine Arts MUSEUM

(Szépmüvészeti Múzeum; Map p52; www.mfab.hu; XIV Dózsa György út 41; adult/concession 1800/900Ft, temporary exhibitions 3800/2000Ft; ⌚10am-6pm Tue-Sun) On the northern side of Heroes' Square, the Museum of Fine Arts houses the city's outstanding collection of foreign artworks. Besides the Egyptian and Graeco-Roman artefacts, such as the Orpheus floor mosaic, intricate gold Roman earrings and medieval Spanish altarpieces, there's a superb Old Masters collection. The thousands of works from the Dutch and Flemish, Spanish, Italian, German, French and British schools between the 13th and 18th centuries include *The Garden of Earthly Delights* by Hieronymus Bosch, with its oversized strawberries, and the humorous *Centaur at the Village Blacksmith's Shop* by Arnold Böcklin. Among the eccelsiastically themed works, see how many you can spot with anatomically incorrect crucifixions (through the palm rather than the wrist). There are also 19th- and 20th-century paintings, watercolours, graphics and sculpture, including some important impressionist works, and usually a couple of excellent temporary exhibitions. Free English-language tours of key galleries depart at 11am Tuesday to Saturday, 2pm Tuesday and Friday, and 1pm Wednesday and Thursday.

Ludwig Museum of Contemporary Art MUSEUM

(Ludwig Kortárs Művészeti Múzeum; Map p48; ☎555 3444; www.ludwigmuseum.hu; IX Komor Marcell utca 1; adult/student & child 1300/650Ft; ⌚10am-8pm Tue-Sun; 📶; 🚋2) Housed in the architecturally controversial Palace of Arts, with its faux-wood panelling and themed halls (Glass Hall, Blue Hall), the Ludwig Museum is Hungary's most important collector and exhibitor of international contemporary art. Works by American, Russian, German and French artists span the past 50 years, while Hungarian, Czech, Slovakian, Romanian, Polish and Slovenian works date from the 1990s. The museum frequently holds cutting-edge temporary exhibitions that include photography, installations and much more. To get here, take HEV train 7 to the Közvágóhíd stop.

Hungarian National Museum MUSEUM

(Magyar Nemzeti Múzeum; Map p68; www.mnm.hu; VIII Múzeum körút 14-16; adult/concession 1100/550Ft; ⌚10am-6pm Tue-Sun) The National Museum, housed in a large neoclassical building, was founded in 1802 when Count Ferenc Széchényi donated his collection of art, maps and manuscripts to the state. Today it contains the nation's most important collection of historical relics, presented as a range of rather old-fashioned but still awe-inspiring exhibits. The 1st floor traces the history of the Carpathian Basin from earliest times to the end of the Avar period in the early 9th century, while upstairs you follow the Magyar people from the conquest of the Carpathian Basin to the end of communism. In the basement, a lapidarium has finds from Roman, medieval and early modern times. Look out for the enormous 3rd-century Roman mosaic from Balácapuszta, near Veszprém; the crimson silk royal coronation robe (or mantle) stitched by nuns in 1031; the reconstructed 3rd-century Roman villa from Pannonia; the treasury room with preconquest gold jewellery; the stunning baroque library; Beethoven's Broadwood piano; and communist propaganda posters.

Váci Utca STREET

(Map p68; 🚌7, Ⓜ M1 Vörösmarty tér, M3 Ferenciek tere, 🚋2) The best way to see the posher side of the Inner Town is to walk up pedestrianised Váci utca, the capital's premier – and most expensive – shopping strip, with designer clothes, expensive jewellery shops, the odd pub and some bookshops for browsing. Many of the buildings are worth closer inspection, but it's a narrow space and you'll need to crane your neck. **Thonet House** (Map p68; V Váci utca 11/a; 🚋2) is a masterpiece built by Ödön Lechner in 1890, and a florist-cum-gift shop called **Philanthia** (Map p68; V Váci utca 9; 🚋2) has an original – and very rare – Art Nouveau interior.

Museum of Applied Arts MUSEUM

(Iparművészeti Múzeum; Map p68; www.imm.hu; IX Üllői út 33-37; adult/student 1100/550Ft; ⌚10am-6pm Tue-Sun; Ⓜ M3 Corvin-negyed, 🚋4, 6) The Museum of Applied Arts owns a king's ransom of 18th- and 19th-century Hungarian furniture, Art Nouveau and Secessionist artefacts, and objects related to the history of trades and crafts (glass-making, bookbinding, goldsmithing, leatherwork). A small part of the collection forms the 400-piece 'Collectors and Treasures' and 'Ottoman Carpets' exhibits on the 1st floor, and almost everything else is in the four or five temporary exhibitions on display at any given time. A combined ticket (2700/1400Ft per adult/child) will get you into everything. The building, designed by Art Nouveau master Ödön Lechner and decorated with Zsolnay ceramic tiles, was completed for the Millenary Exhibition in 1896.

Transport Museum MUSEUM

(Közlekedési Múzeum; Map p52; www.km.iif.hu; XIV Városligeti körút 11; adult/child 1400/700Ft; ⏲10am-5pm Tue-Fri, to 6pm Sat & Sun May-Sep, reduced hours Oct-Apr) One of the most enjoyable museums in Budapest, this is not just for children and trainspotters (though both would be delighted by the scale models of ancient trains, some of which run). Trains aside, there are classic late-19th-century automobiles and sailing boats, lots of those old wooden bicycles called 'bone-shakers', a few hands-on exhibits and lots of show-and-tell from the attendants. Outside are pieces retrieved from the original Danube bridges after the bombings of WWII, and a cafe in an old MÁV coach.

Franz Liszt Memorial Museum MUSEUM

(Liszt Ferenc Emlékmúzeum; Map p60; ☎322 9804; www.lisztmuseum.hu; VI Vörösmarty utca 35; adult/child 1000/500Ft; ⏲10am-6pm Mon-Fri, 9am-5pm Sat; Ⓜ M1 Vörösmarty utca) The great composer declared himself Hungarian despite not speaking the language, and this small but perfectly formed museum is housed in the Old Music Academy, where he lived in a 1st-floor apartment for five years until his death in 1886. Among his personal effects and musical instruments, keep an eye out for a tiny glass piano and his travelling keyboard. Concerts (included in the entry fee) are usually held here on Saturday at 11am.

Egyetem Tér SQUARE

(University Square; 🚌15, 115, M3 V Ferenciek tere) At the centre of the Inner Town lies 'University Square', its name referring to a branch of the prestigious **Loránd Eötvös Science University** (ELTE; Map p68; V Egyetem tér 1-3) located here. Beside the main university building stands the **University Church** (Egyetemi templom; Map p68; ☎318 0555; V Papnövelde utca 5-7; ⏲7am-7pm; Ⓜ M3 Kálvin tér), a lovely baroque structure constructed by Hungary's only indigenous monastic order, the Paulines, and consecrated in 1742. Over the altar inside is a copy of Poland's much-revered Black Madonna of Częstochowa.

Ferenc Hopp Museum of East Asian Art MUSEUM

(Hopp Ferenc Kelet-Ázsiai Művészeti Múzeum; Map p52; www.hoppmuzeum.hu; VI Andrássy út 103; adult/child 1000/500Ft; ⏲10am-6pm Tue-Sun; Ⓜ M1 Bajza utca) Housed in the former villa of its benefactor and namesake, the museum showcases an absorbing collection of Chinese and Japanese ceramics, porcelain, textiles and sculpture, Indonesian *wayang* puppets and Indian statuary, as well as Lamaist sculpture and scroll paintings from Tibet.

Palace of Art MUSEUM

(Műczarnok; Map p52; www.mucsarnok.hu; XIV Hősök tere; adult/concession 1500/800Ft; ⏲10am-6pm Tue, Wed & Fri-Sun, noon-8pm Thu; Ⓜ M1 Hősök tere) This splendid building, one of the city's largest exhibition spaces, focuses on visual art. About five or six major exhibitions are staged annually. One explored the theme 'What is a Hungarian?' through painting, photography, installations and video.

Széchenyi István Tér PLAZA

(Map p68; 🚌16, 105, 🚋2) Named in 1947 after the long-serving (1933–45) American president, Roosevelt tér was renamed in May 2011 after the developer of the Chain Bridge it faces; it offers one of Pest's best views of Castle Hill. On the southern end of the square is a **statue of Ferenc Deák** (Map p68), the Hungarian minister largely responsible for the Compromise of 1867, which brought about the dual monarchy of Austria and Hungary. The Art Nouveau building with gold tiles to the east is the **Gresham Palace**, built by an English insurance company in 1907 (and wonderfully photogenic from the Buda side of the bridge). It now houses the sumptuous **Four Seasons Gresham Palace Hotel**. The **Hungarian Academy of Sciences** (Magyar Tudományos Akadémia; Map p60; V Roosevelt tér 9), founded by Count István Széchenyi (see p133) is at the northern end of the square.

Ethnography Museum MUSEUM

(Néprajzi Múzeum; Map p60; www.neprajz.hu; V Kossuth Lajos tér 12; adult/concession 1000/500Ft; combined ticket for all exhibitions 1400Ft; ⏲10am-6pm Tue-Sun) The Ethnography Museum, opposite the Parliament building, once housed the Supreme Court, which explains the fresco of Justitia, goddess of justice, on the entrance hall ceiling. Besides providing an easy introduction to traditional Hungarian life, with decent mock-ups of peasant houses from the Őrség and Sárköz regions of Western

City Park

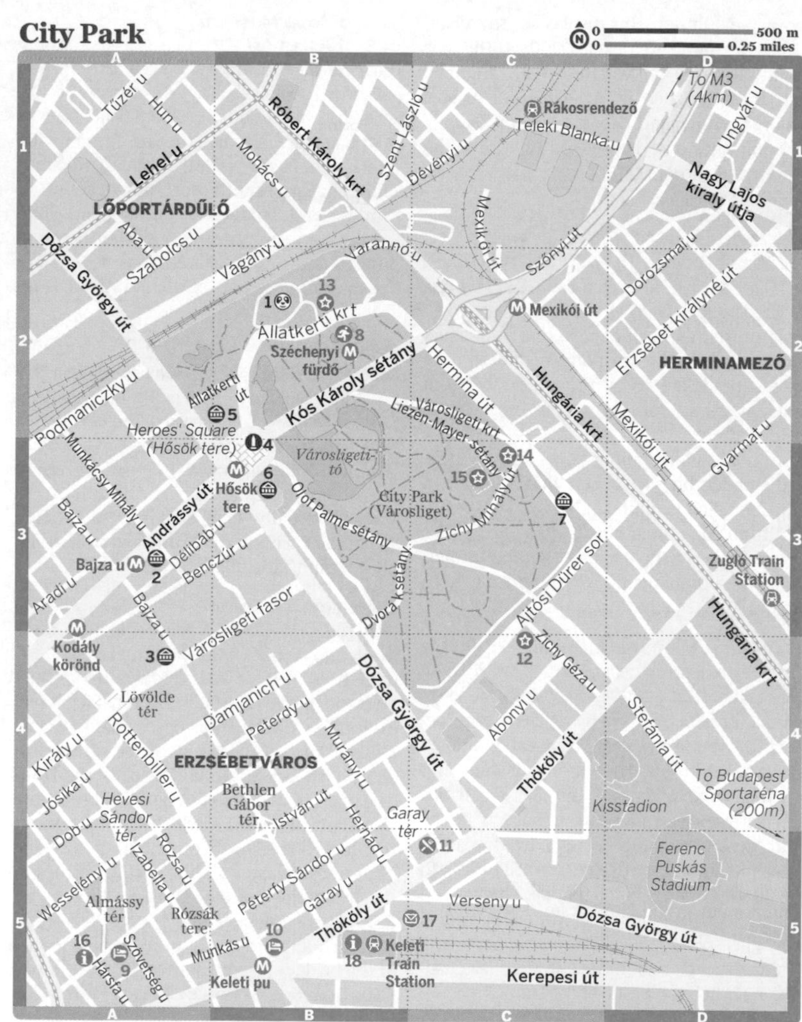

and Southern Transdanubia, folk dress and crafts, there are some priceless objects collected from Transylvania. On the 2nd floor, well-presented temporary exhibitions deal with cultures from further afield: Africa, Asia, Oceania and the Americas.

Szabadság tér SQUARE

(Liberty Square; 🚌15) 'Liberty Square', one of the largest in the city, is a few minutes' walk northeast of Széchenyi István tér. At its centre is a **Soviet army memorial** (Map p60) captioned 'Glory to the Soviet liberators of the city', the last of its kind still standing in Budapest. It's fenced off to prevent vandalism by those who don't agree with its sentiment. Other notable buildings include the pile of Secessionist splendour that is the former **Royal Postal Savings Bank** (Map p60; V Hold utca 4; 🚌15, 115) and the **National Bank of Hungary** (Magyar Nemzeti Bank; Map p60; V Szabadság tér 9; 🚌15, 115) next door, featuring one of the most exceptional entrance halls in the city.

Kossuth Lajos tér SQUARE

(Map p60; Ⓜ M2 Kossuth Lajos tér) West of Szabadság tér is Kossuth Lajos tér, the site

City Park

Sights
1 Budapest Zoo ... B2
2 Ferenc Hopp Museum of East Asian Art ... A3
3 György Ráth Museum ... A4
4 Millenary Monument ... B3
5 Museum of Fine Arts ... B2
6 Palace of Art ... B3
7 Transport Museum ... C3

Activities, Courses & Tours
8 Széchenyi Baths ... B2

Sleeping
9 Centre of Rural Tourism ... A5
10 Hotel Baross ... B5

Eating
11 Olimpia ... C5

Entertainment
12 Dürer Kert ... C4
13 Municipal Great Circus ... B2
14 Pántlika ... C3
15 Pecsa Music Hall ... C3

Information
16 Centre of Rural Tourism ... A5
17 Keleti Train Station Branch ... C5
18 Wasteels ... B5

of Budapest's Parliament – the city's most photographed building. Southeast of the square in Vértanúk tere is a statue of Imre Nagy, the reformist communist prime minister who was executed in 1958 for his role in the Uprising two years earlier. Just around the corner is **Bedő House** (Bedő-ház; Map p60; ☎269 4622; www.magyarszecessziohaza.hu; V Honvéd utca 3; adult/student & child 1500/1000Ft; ⊙10am-5pm Tue-Sat; Ⓜ M2 Kossuth Lajos tér), a stunning Art Nouveau apartment block (1903) designed by Emil Vidor, its three floors crammed with furniture, porcelain, ironwork, paintings and objets d'art. A block west of the square, on the riverbank, is **Shoes on the Danube**, (Cipők a Duparton; Map p60; V Pesti alsó rakpart; 🚊2, 2A) a monument to the Hungarian Jews shot and thrown into the Danube by members of the fascist Arrow Cross Party in 1944, by sculptor Gyula Pauer and film director Can Togay. It's a simple affair – 60 pairs of old-style boots and shoes in cast iron, tossed higgledy-piggledy on the bank of the river – but it is one of the most poignant monuments yet unveiled in this city of so many tears.

Rumbach Sebestyén Utca Synagogue — JEWISH

(Rumbach Sebestyén utcai zsinagóga; Map p68; VII Rumbach Sebestyén utca 11; admission 600Ft; ⊙10am-5.30pm Sun-Thu, to 3pm Fri; Ⓜ M2 Astoria, 🚊4, 6) This Moorish synagogue, built in 1872 by Austrian Secessionist architect Otto Wagner for the conservatives, has had a facelift and is stunning inside. Check out the original stained-glass windows, which miraculously survived WWII.

György Ráth Museum — MUSEUM

(Ráth György Múzeum; Map p52; ☎342 3916; www.hoppmuzeum.hu; VI Városligeti fasor 12; adult/child 400/250Ft; ⊙10am-6pm Tue-Sun) The Ferenc Hopp Museum's temporary exhibits are shown at the György Ráth Museum, located in an Art Nouveau residence a few minutes' walk southwards down Bajza utca.

Millenary Monument — MONUMENT

(Ezeréves emlékmű; Map p52; XIV Heroes' Sq; Ⓜ M1 Hősök tere) In the centre of Heroes' Square is a 36m-high pillar backed by colonnades. Atop the pillar is the Angel Gabriel, holding the Hungarian crown and a cross. At the base are Árpád and the six other Magyar chieftains who occupied the Carpathian Basin in the late 9th century. The 14 statues in the colonnades represent rulers and statesmen, from King Stephen on the left to Lajos Kossuth on the right. The four allegorical figures at the top are, from left to right, Work and Prosperity, War, Peace, and Knowledge and Glory.

Budapest Zoo — ZOO

(Budapesti Állatkert; Map p52; www.zoobudapest.com; XIV Állatkerti körút 6-12; adult/child/family 2200/1600/6400Ft; ⊙9am-6.30pm Mon-Thu, to 7pm Fri-Sun May-Aug, reduced hours Sep-Apr; Ⓜ M1 Széchenyi fürdő, 72) This large zoo, which opened with 500 animals in 1866, has a good collection, including big cats, hippopotamuses, polar bear and giraffe, and its themed houses (wetlands, Madagascar, nocturnal Australia) are world-class. Away from the beasties, have a look at the Secessionist animal houses built in the early 20th

GET THE BEST SEAT IN THE HOUSE

In the large concert hall of the Liszt Academy of Music, try to nab the first seat from the left in the 8th row, which will give you the best view of the stage.

century, such as the Elephant House, with pachyderm heads in beetle-green Zsolnay ceramic, and the Palm House with an aquarium erected by the Eiffel Company of Paris.

Liszt Academy of Music NOTABLE BUILDING
(Liszt Zeneakadémia; Map p60; ☎462 4600; www.zeneakademia.hu; VI Liszt Ferenc tér 8; MM1 Oktogon) The academy, a block southeast of Oktogon, was built in 1907 and has a bronze statue of the composer above the entrance. It attracts students from all over the world and is one of Budapest's top concert venues. The interior, with large and small concert halls richly embellished with Zsolnay porcelain and frescoes, is worth a look even if you're not attending a performance.

Orthodox Synagogue JEWISH
(Ortodox zsinagóga; Map p68; ☎342 1072; VII Kazinczy utca 29-31; admission 1000Ft; ⏲10am-3.30pm Sun-Thu, to 12.30pm Fri; MM2 Astoria, 🚋47, 49) There were once a half-dozen synagogues and prayer houses in the Jewish Quarter, reserved for different sects and ethnic groups (conservatives, Orthodox, Poles, Sephardics etc). The Orthodox Synagogue, which can also be accessed from Dob utca 35, was built in 1913 but hasn't been used since WWII.

Zwack Unicum Museum MUSEUM
(Zwack Unicum Múzeum; Map p48; www.zwackunicum.hu; IX Soroksári út 26; adult/student & senior 2000/1000Ft; ⏲10am-6pm Mon-Fri; 🚋2, 24) Unicum, the thick, brown, bitter-tasting aperitif made from 40 herbs – and clocking in at 42% alcohol – was supposedly named by Franz Joseph himself. If you really can't get enough of the stuff, visit this very commercial museum, which traces the history of the product since it was first made in 1790 and invites visitors to buy big at its sample store. Enter from Dandár utca.

Activities

Budapest is chock-a-block with things to keep you occupied outdoors. From taking the waters and cycling to caving and canoeing, it's all in or within easy access of the capital.

Thermal Baths

Budapest lies on the geological fault separating the Buda Hills from the Great Plain and more than 30,000 cu metres of warm to scalding (21°C to 76°C) mineral water gushes forth each day from some 123 thermal springs. As a result, 'taking the waters' at one of the many *gyógyfürdő* (thermal baths) is a real Budapest experience

Depending on the time of day, some baths are for men or women only. There are usually mixed days as well, and some baths are always mixed. On single-sex days or in same-sex sections, men usually are handed drawstring loincloths and women apronlike garments. You must wear a bathing suit on mixed-sex days; if by chance you've forgotten yours, you can hire one.

Most of the baths offer a full range of serious medical treatments, plus pampering services such as massages and pedicures. Specify what you want when buying your ticket. Admission costs start from 2300Ft.

Some of the baths look a little rough around the edges, but the water is cleaned regularly. Still, a pair of flip-flops is good for walking around in. It's possible to rent a towel at most but not all baths; bring your own if possible. Many pools in the baths require you to wear a bathing cap; bring your own or wear the disposable one provided or sold for a nominal fee.

Most baths come with lockers operated by electronic bracelets; specify that you want a locker when paying your entry fee. In others, find an unoccupied locker or cabin, get changed and then find an attendant to lock it for you and give you a numbered tag to tie to yourself. (The number does not match the locker number, so you need to remember it.)

Some baths date from Turkish times, some are Art Nouveau marvels, some allow you to play chess while you bathe and others look as though they could be film sets for Thomas Mann's *Magic Mountain*. If you need help choosing, **Budapest Spas and Hot Springs** (www.spasbudapest.com) is an excellent source of information.

Széchenyi Baths BATHHOUSE
(Széchenyi Fürdő; Map p52; ☎363 3210; www.spasbudapest.com; XIV Állatkerti út 1; ticket with locker/cabin weekdays 3400/3800Ft, weekends 3550/3950Ft; ⏲6am-10pm; MM1 Széchenyi fürdő) At the northern end of City Park, the Széchenyi Baths is unusual for three reasons: its immense size (a dozen thermal baths and five outdoor swimming pools);

its bright, clean atmosphere; and its water temperatures (up to 38°C), which really are what the wall plaques say they are. It's mixed at all times, there's a spiral whirlpool in one of the outdoor pools and you often see local men playing chess while bathing.

TOP CHOICE Gellért Baths BATHHOUSE

(Gellért Fürdő; Map p68; ☎466 6166; www.spasbudapest.com; XI Kelenhegyi út, Danubius Hotel Gellért; with/without private changing room 3200/4300Ft; ⏰6am-8pm) Soaking in the Art Nouveau Gellért Baths, open to both men and women in separate sections (Monday to Saturday; mixed on Sunday), has been likened to taking a bath in a cathedral. The eight thermal pools range in temperature from 26°C to 38°C, and the water is good for pains in the joints, arthritis and blood circulation. The outdoor pools are always mixed and one of the pools has recently been extended. There is also a wave machine in use in warmer months.

Rudas Baths BATHHOUSE

(Rudas Gyógyfürdő; Map p68; ☎356 1322; www.spasbudapest.com; I Döbrentei tér 9; day ticket with/without cabin use weekdays 2300/2000Ft, weekends 3300/3000Ft; ⏰men 6am-8pm Mon & Wed-Fri, women 6am-8pm Tue, mixed 10pm-4am Fri, 6am-8pm & 10pm-4am Sat, 8am-6pm Sun; 🚌5, 7, 8, 86, 🚋18, 19) Built in 1566, the stunningly renovated Rudas Baths is the most Turkish of all the baths in Budapest, with an octagonal pool, domed cupola with coloured glass and massive columns. Things can get very sociable during mixed-gender bathing on weekend nights. A bathing costume is compulsory. Water massage, aroma relax massage and other treatments are available. Check times in advance as opening hours differ for mixed and single-sex bathing.

Király BATHHOUSE

(Király Gyógyfürdő; Map p36; ☎202 3688; www.spasbudapest.com; II Fő utca 84; daily ticket with cabin 2300Ft; ⏰9am-9pm; 🚌86) The four pools here, with water temperatures between 26°C and 40°C, are genuine Turkish baths erected in 1570, and have a wonderful skylit central dome (though the place is begging for renovation). Bathing is mixed every day of the week, so pack a swimsuit. A range of massages and pedicures are on offer.

Lukács BATHHOUSE

(Lukács Gyógyfürdő; Map p44; ☎326 1695; www.spasbudapest.com; II Frankel Leó út 25-29; all-day ticket with locker/cabin weekdays 2800/2900Ft, weekends 3200/3300Ft; ⏰6am-8pm; 🚌86, 🚋17) Housed in a sprawling 19th-century complex, these baths are popular with spa aficionados. The thermal baths (temperatures 22°C to 40°C) are mixed and there are three swimming pools. Besides five types of massage (underwater jet massage, aroma massage...), there are also on offer mud treatment, sauna, steam room and salt chamber treatment for asthmatics.

Cycling

More and more cyclists are taking advantage of Budapest's growing network of dedicated cycle routes. Parts of Budapest, including City and Népliget Parks, Margaret Island and the Buda Hills, are excellent places for cycling. You can rent bicycles from Yellow Zebra Bikes (p57) and other outlets.

Dynamo Bike & Bake CYCLING

(Map p68; ☎06 30 868 1107; www.dynamobike.com; V Képíró utca 6; bike rental per 24/48/72 hours 3300/6000/9000Ft; ⏰Mon, Wed-Fri 8am-7pm, Sat & Sun 9am-3pm; Ⓜ M3 Kálvin tér, 🚋47, 49) A fantastic little cake shop–cum–bike rental, Dynamo is run by a keen cycling guide who appreciates the value of good equipment. The hybrid urban bikes and mountain bikes are brand new and meticulously maintained.

LOCAL KNOWLEDGE

A DIFFERENT VIEW

You've been to Fishermen's Bastion, the Citadella, Buda Hills. You've seen all the great views, right? Wrong. Here are three unlikely places from which to catch an unexpectedly good view of the city:

» The roof garden of the **West End City Centre** (Map p44; www.westend.hu; VI Váci út 1-3; ⏰8am-11pm; Ⓜ M3 Nyugati pályaudvar) is particularly good at dusk, when the streets below are illuminated.

» **Institut Français** (I Fő utca 17; 🚌19, 41) offers a fantastic view of Parliament, the Chain Bridge and their surrounds from its 4th floor Mediatheque.

» **Sky Bar** (www.expohotelbudapest.com/sky_bar; X Expo tér 2, Expo Hotel Budapest; ⏰5pm-2am; 🚆Kőbánya felső Vasútállomás), 12 floors up at the Expo Hotel Budapest, at the height of 50m, offers stunning views of Pest.

Rental includes safety gear as well as maps and advice. Cycling tours can be arranged at reasonably short notice.

Budapest Bike CYCLING
(Map p68; ☎06 30 944 5533; www.budapestbike.hu; VII Wesselényi utca 13; 6/24/48hr hire 2000/3000/5000Ft; ⏲9am-6pm mid-Mar–mid-Oct, other months by appointment; Ⓜ M2 Astoria, 🚊4, 6) Bikes are available year-round, and bike tours, tours of the baths and pub crawls are also on the menu.

Caving

Budapest has three caves open for walk-through guided tours (usually in Hungarian). The best two are listed here.

Pálvölgy Cave CAVING
(Pálvölgyi-barlang; ☎325 9505; www.palvolgyi.atw.hu; II Szépvölgyi út 162/a; adult/child 1200/960Ft; ⏲10am-4pm Tue-Sun; 🚌65) The second-largest in Hungary, this 19km-long cave was discovered in 1904 and is noted for its stalactites and bats. The 500m route involves climbing some 120 steps and a ladder, and may not be suitable for the elderly or children under five. The temperature is a constant 8°C, so wear a jacket or jumper. Tours lasting either one hour or 25 minutes depart from 10.15am to 3.15pm. Take bus 65 from Kolosy tér in Óbuda.

Szemlőhegy Cave CAVING
(Szemlőhegyi-barlang; Map p44; ☎325 6001; www.szemlohegyi.atw.hu; II Pusztaszeri út 35; adult/child 1000/800Ft; ⏲10am-4pm Wed-Mon; 🚌29) A beautiful cave, with stalactites, stalagmites and weird grapelike formations, Szemlőhegy has a temperature of 12°C. Tours last between 35 and 49 minutes and start on the hour, every hour. Take bus 29 from Kolosy tér in Óbuda.

Language Courses

The most prestigious Hungarian-language school in the land, the Debrecen Summer University has a **Budapest branch** (Map p60; ☎320 5751; www.nyariegyetem.hu/bp; V Váci utca 63, 2nd fl; M2 Kossuth Lajos tér) offering intensive courses lasting three weeks (60 hours) for 78,000Ft and regular evening classes of 60/84 hours for 58,000/79,000Ft. The city also has other options for getting to grips with Magyar.

Fungarian LANGUAGE COURSE
(Map p68; ☎06 20 357 2503; www.fungarian.com; VII Dohány utca 1/a, Katapult Kávézó; €15/person; ⏲2-3pm daily; 🚌8, 112, 239, Ⓜ M2 Astoria, 🚊47, 49) While you may not learn one of Europe's most complex languages in an hour, as the brochure promises, you will leave this enjoyable cafe session with a few useful phrases under your belt. The price of the lesson includes a drink, and further lessons can be arranged on request.

Hungarian Language School LANGUAGE COURSE
(Map p68; ☎266 2617; www.magyar-iskola.hu; VIII Bródy Sándor utca 4, 1st fl; Ⓜ M3 Kálvin tér, M2 Astoria, 🚊47, 49) Evening, morning and individual classes available. About €6 per lesson or 48,500Ft for a block of 32 lessons.

Tours

Boat

River Ride BUS TOUR, BOAT TOUR
(Map p60; ☎332 2555; www.riverride.com; V Széchenyi István tér 7-8; adult/child 7500/5000Ft; 🚊2) A strange and hugely entertaining two-hour tour on this bright yellow amphibious bus takes you overland and into the river. Three to four departures daily year round, from Széchenyi István tér; check website for timetable.

Legenda BOAT TOUR
(Map p68; ☎266 4190; www.legenda.hu; V Vigadó tér, pier 7; daytime adult/student/child 4300/3300/2150Ft; night adult/student/child 5300/4100/2650Ft; 🚊2) Day and night cruises on the Danube, with taped commentary in up to 30 languages. Night cruises are more attractive, with Buda Castle, Parliament, Gellért Hill and the Citadella all lit up. Dining cruises are also available. Check website for timetable.

Mahart PassNave BOAT TOUR
(Map p68; ☎484 4013; www.mahartpassnave.hu; V Belgrád Rakpart, Landing Stage pier 3; ⏲10am-10pm May-Sep, 11am-8pm Oct-Dec & Apr) Hour-long cruises between Margaret and Rákóczi bridges, departing hourly in high season and at 1pm and 5pm in low season.

Bus

Program Centrum BUS TOUR, BOAT TOUR
(Map p68; ☎1-317 7767; www.programcentrum.hu; V Erzsébet tér 9-11; adult/12-18yr/child €22/16/10; Ⓜ M1/M2/M3 Deák Ferenc tér, 🚊47, 49) Ticket valid for two bus routes (one with taped commentary in 23 languages, one with live commentary in English and German), two hour-long river cruises (daytime and evening), two walking tours, a beer and a bowl of goulash.

Cycling

Yellow Zebra Bikes CYCLING

(Map p60; ☎269 3843; www.yellowzebrabikes.com; VI Lázár utca 16 ; 1hr/half-day/full-day hire from 500/2000/2500Ft; ⏲10am-6pm Nov-Mar, 8.30am-8pm Apr-Oct; Ⓜ M1 Opera) Long-established and very reliable, Yellow Zebra Bikes rents out bicycles year-round from the Discover Budapest office near the Opera House, as well as from a meeting point just behind the Budapest Info office. It also runs cycling tours of the city (adult/student 6000/5500Ft) that take in Heroes' Square, City Park, inner Pest and Castle Hill in about 3½ hours. Tours, including the bike, depart from the Budapest Info office at 11am from March to November, and 11am and 5pm in July and August. There is also an internet access spot here.

Specialist

City Segway Tours GUIDED TOUR

(Map p60; ☎269 3843; www.citysegwaytours.com/budapest; VI Lázár utca 16; €48-75; ⏲10am & 2.30pm; Ⓜ M1 Opera, M3 Arany János utca) One of the most entertaining ways of seeing the city. Tours vary from about 1½ hours to four hours, giving you plenty of time to practise your Segway skills. These wheeled excursions take in such sights as St Stephen's Basilica, the Opera House, Chain Bridge and other sights of inner Pest. Superior Segway and Grand Segway tours depart at 10am daily, and the Mini Segway Tour leaves at 2.30pm.

Walking

Free Budapest Tours WALKING TOUR

(Map p68; ☎06 20 534 5819; www.freebudapesttours.eu; Deák Ferenc tér; ⏲10.30am & 2.30pm) Entertaining and knowledgeable guides offer two highly professional tours of the city: Essential Pest, an afternoon tour taking in the highlights of the Inner Town (1½ hours); and From Pest to Buda, a morning tour of Inner Town's highlights, plus the banks of the Danube and Castle District (2½ hours). The tours are free; the guides work for tips only (be generous!). Meeting point is near the Deák Ferenc tér metro at the Budapest Sightseeing Bus stop (Andrássy út 2). Evening thematic tours – Literary Walk and Behind The Night pub crawls – cost €10 per person.

Absolute Walking Tours GUIDED TOUR

(Map p60; ☎269 3843; www.absolutetours.com; VI Lázár utca 16; ⏲10am daily; Ⓜ M1 Opera) This very reliable outfit has, among other tours, a 3½-hour guided promenade through City Park, central Pest and Castle Hill. Cracker specialist tours include the Hammer & Sickle, Alternative Budapest and Hungaro Gastro Food & Wine Experience. There are also speciality tours: Behind the Iron Curtain (with a visit to Memento Park), Jewish Budapest Heritage, and caving and Segway tours. Tours depart from the Discover Budapest office.

Festivals & Events

Budapest has a crowded calendar of festivals, with something happening pretty much every month. Look out for the tourist board's annual *Events Calendar* for a complete listing.

January

New Year's Day Concert MUSIC

(www.hungariakoncert.hu) This is an annual event, usually held in the Duna Palota on January 1 to herald the new year.

March

Budapest Spring Festival PERFORMING ARTS

(www.festivalcity.hu) The capital's largest and most important cultural fixture, with 200 events, takes place for two weeks in late March/early April, at five dozen venues across the city.

Budapest Fringe Festival PERFORMING ARTS

(www.budapestfringe.com) A three-day festival of non-mainstream theatre, music and dance, held in Millennium Park and other venues around town, as a kind of sideshow to the Budapest Spring Festival.

April

National Dance House Festival PERFORMING ARTS

(www.tanchaztalalkozo.hu/eng) Hungary's biggest *táncház*, with performances by folk artists and dance bands and traditional crafts, held over two days in early April at the Buda Concert Hall and other venues.

June

Danube Carnival PERFORMING ARTS

(www.cioff.org) A 10-day pan-Hungarian international carnival of folk, world and modern music and dance, held from mid-June in Vörösmarty tér and on Margaret Island.

August

Formula 1 Hungarian Grand Prix RACING

(☎info 28 444 444; www.hungaroring.hu; Hungaroring; weekend seating Super Gold €400, Gold

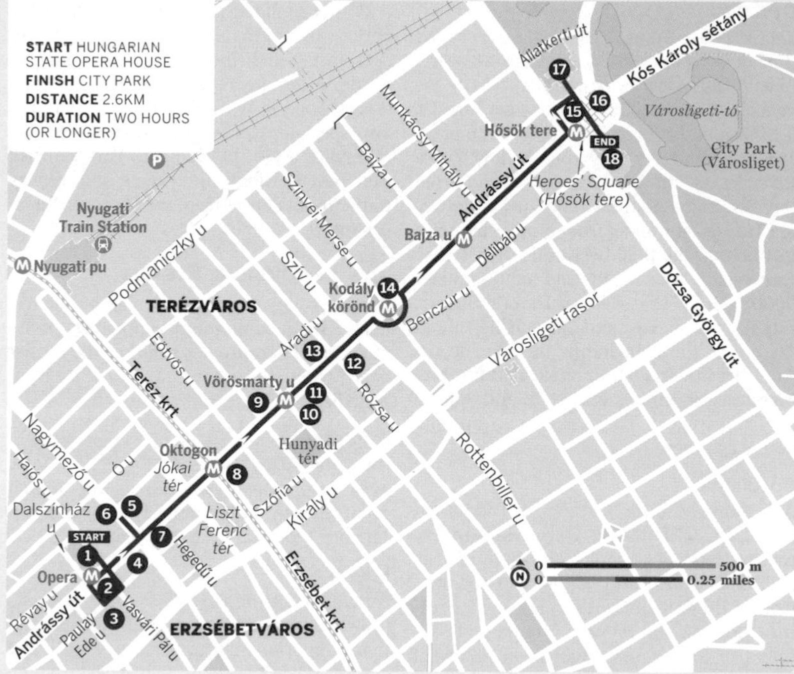

Walking Tour

Budapest

This is an easy walk, which starts a little north of Deák Ferenc tér and follows attractive Andrássy út to Heroes' Sq (Hősök tere).

Andrássy út splits away from Bajcsy-Zsilinszky út about 200m north of Deák Ferenc tér. On the right you will see the **1 Hungarian State Opera House**. In the niche at the left of the carriage entrance is a statue of Ferenc Erkel, the father of Hungarian opera, and a statue of composer Ferenc Liszt stands in the one at right. At 1st-floor level are statues of the muses of opera, while those of the great composers Tchaikovsky, Verdi and Mozart are at 2nd-floor level.

Opposite the Opera House, **2 Dreschler Palace** was designed by Art Nouveau master builder Ödön Lechner in 1882. It once housed the Hungarian State Ballet Institute, but has stood eerily empty since the late 1990s. For something even more magical, walk down Dalszínház utca to the **3 New Theatre**, a Secessionist gem (1909) embellished with monkey faces, globes and geometric designs that look like an early version of Art Deco.

The old-world cafe **4 Művész** is one block up. The next cross street is Nagymező utca, 'the Broadway of Budapest', with a number of theatres, such as the **5 Budapest Operetta** at No 17 and the restored **6 Thália**.

Next, you will pass the **7 statue of Géza Hofi** (1936–2002), the stand-up comedian who was transformed over the course of his career from working-class underdog to star of the stage.

Two blocks up, Andrássy út meets the Big Ring road at Oktogon, a busy intersection. Look out for the building at **8 Teréz körút 13**, an exact replica of Florence's Palazzo Strozzi. Two blocks beyond, the word 'terror' is written in sunlight on the former secret-police building, now home to the **9 Terror House**. It was here that many activists before and after WWII were taken for interrogation and torture. A plaque on the outside reads in part: 'We cannot forget the horror of terror, and the victims will always be remembered.'

Along the next two blocks you'll pass some very grand buildings: the ⑩ **Old Kunsthalle – Academy of Fine Arts**, somewhat resembling Palazzo Bevilacqua in Verona, with the **Budapest Puppet Theatre** in the basement at No 69; the ⑪ **Hungarian University of Fine Arts**, founded in 1871; and the headquarters of ⑫ **MÁV**, the national railway. The posh cafe and cake shop ⑬ **Lukács** is opposite.

The next square is ⑭ **Kodály körönd**, one of the most beautiful in the city, with the facades of some of the four neo-Renaissance town houses given a facelift.

The last stretch of Andrássy út and the surrounding neighbourhoods are packed with stunning old mansions that are among the most desirable addresses in the city.

Andrássy út ends at ⑮ **Heroes' Square** (Hősök tere), just west of City Park. The square is defined by the ⑯ **Millenary Monument** (Ezeréves emlékmű). Beneath the tall column and under a stone slab is an empty coffin representing the unknown insurgents of the 1956 Uprising. Archangel Gabriel stands on top of the column; according to legend, he came to King Stephen in a dream and offered him the crown. To the north of the monument is the ⑰ **Museum of Fine Arts** and its rich collection of Old Masters. The building was commissioned by Parliament for the 1896 Millenary Celebration of the Hungarian tribes arriving in present-day Hungary. To the south is the ornate ⑱ **Palace of Art** (Műcsarnok), which also opened in 1896.

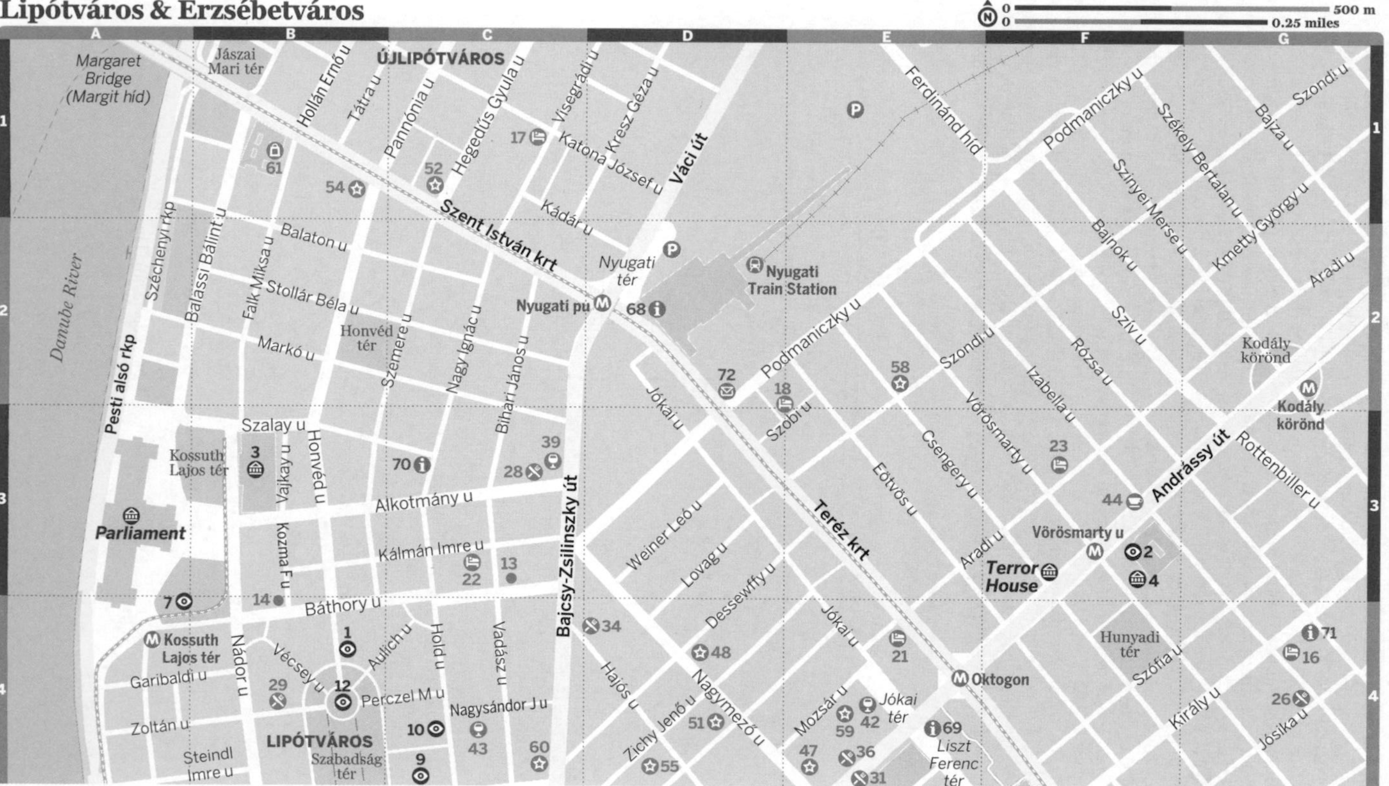
Lipótváros & Erzsébetváros
0.25 miles
500 m
Danube River
Margaret Bridge (Margit híd)
Jászai Mari tér
ÚJLIPÓTVÁROS
Hollán Ernő u
Tátra u
Pannónia u
Hegedűs Gyula u
Visegrádi u
Kresz Géza u
Katona József u
Váci út
Ferdinánd híd
Podmaniczky u
Székely Bertalan u
Szinyei Merse u
Bajza u
Szondi u
Kmetty György u
Bajnok u
Aradi u
Szív u
Kodály körönd
Kodály körönd
Kádár u
Szent István krt
Nyugati tér
Nyugati Train Station
Nyugati pu
Széchenyi rkp
Balassi Bálint u
Falk Miksa u
Balaton u
Stollár Béla u
Honvéd tér
Markó u
Szemere u
Nagy Ignác u
Bihari János u
Pesti alsó rkp
Podmaniczky u
Szondi u
Rózsa u
Izabella u
Vörösmarty u
Csengery u
Eötvös u
Jókai u
Szobi u
Szalay u
Kossuth Lajos tér
Vajkay u
Honvéd u
Alkotmány u
Kozma F u
Kálmán Imre u
Parliament
Bajcsy-Zsilinszky út
Andrássy út
Rottenbiller u
Vörösmarty u
Terror House
Weiner Leó u
Lovag u
Teréz krt
Aradi u
Báthory u
Dessewffy u
Jókai u
Hunyadi tér
Kossuth Lajos tér
Garibaldi u
Nádor u
Vécsey u
Aulich u
Hold u
Vadász u
Hajós u
Nagymező u
Szófia u
Oktogon
Perczel M u
Nagysándor J u
Zichy Jenő u
Mozsár u
Jókai tér
Liszt Ferenc tér
Király u
Jósika u
Zoltán u
Steindl Imre u
LIPÓTVÁROS
Szabadság tér

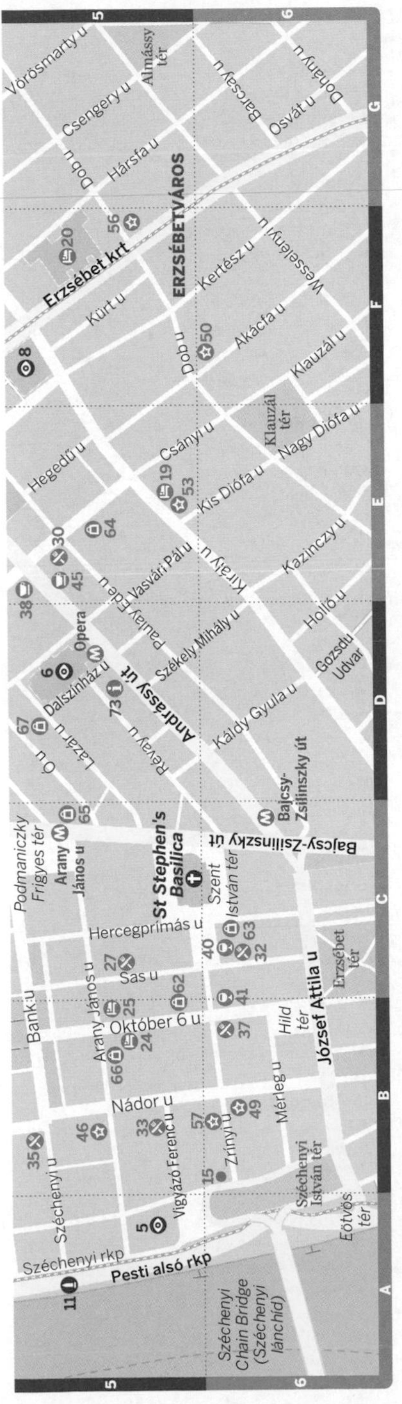

€300-320, Silver €225-250; standing room weekend/Sunday €110/€100) Reintroduced in 1986 after a hiatus of half a century, the Formula 1 Hungarian Grand Prix is part of the World Championship Series and takes place at the Hungaroring at Mogyoród, northeast of Budapest, in August.

Sziget Music Festival MUSIC

(www.sziget.hu) One of the biggest and most popular music festivals in Europe, held in mid-August on Budapest's Hajógyár (Óbuda) Island.

Budapest Festival of Folk Arts FOLK ART

(Budapest Craft Days) Check out the work of artisans from all over Hungary at Budapest's Craft Days festival, held in and around Buda Castle for three days in mid-August.

Jewish Summer Festival JEWISH

(www.jewishfestival.hu) A 10-day festival starting at the end of August, showcasing the best of Jewish culture, from gastronomy to music, theatre and film. Many events take place at Pest's Great Synagogue (p49).

September

Budapest International Wine Festival WINE

(www.winefestival.hu) Hungary's foremost winemakers introduce their wines at this ultra-popular event, held in the Castle District in mid-September.

October

Budapest International Marathon RUNNING

(www.budapestmarathon.com) Eastern Europe's most celebrated race steps out along the Danube and across its bridges in early October.

CAFE Budapest PERFORMING ARTS

(Contemporary Art Festival; www.cafebudapest.hu) Contemporary art takes many forms during this week-long festival: poetry slams, modern theatre, jazz marathon and a 'Night of the Contemporary Galleries', to name a few.

December

New Year's Gala & Ball MUSIC

(www.opera.hu) The annual calendar's most-coveted ticket is to this gala concert and ball, held at the Hungarian State Opera House on 31 December. Book well in advance at 3-15 Hajós utca, or via phone (☎332 4816).

Lipótváros & Erzsébetváros

Top Sights

Parliament A3
St Stephen's Basilica C5
Terror House F3

Sights

1 Bedő House B4
2 Budapest Puppet Theatre F3
3 Ethnography Museum B3
4 Franz Liszt Memorial Museum F3
5 Hungarian Academy of Sciences A5
6 Hungarian State Opera House D5
7 Kossuth Lajos tér A4
8 Liszt Academy of Music F5
9 National Bank of Hungary C4
10 Royal Postal Savings Bank C4
11 Shoes on the Danube A5
12 Soviet Army Memorial B4

Activities, Courses & Tours

Absolute Walking Tours .... (see 67)
City Segway Tours .... (see 67)
13 Cityrama C3
14 Debrecen Summer University Branch B4
15 River Ride B6
Yellow Zebra Bikes .... (see 67)

Sleeping

16 Association of Hungarian Rural & Agrotourism G4
17 Aventura Hostel C1
18 Carpe Noctem D2
19 Connection Guest House E5
20 Corinthia Grand Hotel Royal F5
21 Home-Made Hostel E4
22 Hotel Parlament C3
23 Kapital Inn F3
24 To-Ma B5
25 Trendy Budapest B&B Hostel B5

Eating

26 Bistro 181 .... G4
Bock Bisztró .... (see 20)
27 Café Kör C5
Első Pesti Rétesház .... (see 24)
28 Hummus Bar C3
29 Iguana B4
30 Két Szerecsen E5
31 Klassz E4
32 LaciPecsenye C6
33 Mák Bistro B5
34 Marquis de Salade D4
35 Momotaro Ramen B5
36 Ring Cafe E4
37 Tom-George B6

Drinking

38 Alexandra Book Cafe E5
39 Becketts Irish Bar C3
40 DiVino Borbár C6
41 Innio C6
42 Kiadó Kocsma E4
43 Le Cafe-Mystery C4
44 Lukács Cukrászda F3
45 Művész Kávéház E5

Entertainment

46 Aranytíz Cultural Centre B5
47 Budapest Operetta E4
Budapest Puppet Theatre .... (see 2)
48 Club AlterEgo D4
49 Duna Palota B6
50 Fogasház F6
Hungarian State Opera House .... (see 6)
51 Instant D4
52 Kino C1
53 Kuplung E5
54 Morrison's 2 .... B1
55 Most! D4
56 Örökmozgó F5
57 Ötkert B6
58 Pótkulcs E2
59 Rocktogon Pub & Roll E4
60 Szikra Cool Tour House C4

Shopping

61 Báv B1
62 Bestsellers B5
63 Bortársaság (Basilica branch) C6
64 Cancan E5
65 Haas & Czjzek C5
66 Originart B5
67 Treehugger Dan's Bookstore D5

Information

68 Budapest Info D2
69 Budapest Info (Oktogon Branch) E4
70 District V Police Station C3
71 National Federation of Rural & Agrotourism G4
72 Nyugati Train Station Branch D2
73 Ticket Express D5

LOCAL KNOWLEDGE

SIMPLICISSIMUS' SECRETS

András Török, aka Simplicissimus, is the author of the cult *Budapest: A Critical Guide*, still going strong after seven editions. As this mix of anecdotes, city walks, advice and history testifies, the author/lecturer/translator/graphic designer/business consultant and columnist for the monthly magazine *Budapest* knows the city inside out. We ask him to share some of his vast knowledge of the city.

When did you write the first edition and why? Twenty-six years ago. Hungarian travel books at the time infuriated me – very dry. So I wrote the way people talked.

Where do you go to get away from the hustle and bustle of the city? Small, lesser-known museums such as the György Ráth Museum (p53), and Café Művész (p78) at 9am, when it has just opened and there's no one else there.

What's a real treat for you when you dine out? The seafood at Philippe Le Belge – it's very expensive, but worth it. I also love Olimpia (p74), a tiny place, only for 20 people or so, always packed, and the chef is always coming up with something creative.

If you wanted to admire Budapest at night, where's a good vantage point? The roof garden of the West End City Centre (p55), believe it or not. Also, the cafe (p79) on the top floor of Alexandra Bookshop – just look out the window.

When's the best time to visit the flea markets? Early in the morning, 7am-ish. That's when all the local characters come bargain-hunting.

The 'pub in a ruin' trend kicked off a decade ago – what's the latest trend? Ruin Pub version two. The whole scene's fragile, since the buildings are rented for a few months at a time, but now we have 'trendy cosmo bistro in a ruin' rather than just something that's rough around the edges.

Sleeping

Budapest has more than a hundred youth hostels, with all the facilities that backpackers have come to expect: free wi-fi, lockers, tours, kitchen, TV lounge and laundry facilities. Hostelling International (HI) cards or their equivalents are not required at any hostels in Budapest, but they might bag you a discount of up to 10%. You're looking at around 2800Ft to 4700FT for a dorm bed, about 9000Ft for a double.

Private rooms generally cost 6000Ft to 7500Ft for a single, 7000Ft to 8500Ft for a double and 9000Ft to 13,000Ft for a small apartment, but have become less popular with the advent of affordable, centrally located guesthouses. Tourinform in Budapest does not arrange private accommodation, but will direct you to a travel agency, such as **To-Ma** (Map p60; 353 0819; www.tomatour.hu; V Október 6 utca 22; 9am-noon & 1-8pm Mon-Fri, 9am-5pm Sat & Sun; M1/2/3 Deák Ferenc tér), that does.

The city has scores of *panzió* (pensions) and guesthouses, but many are on the outskirts of Pest or in the Buda Hills and not very convenient unless you have your own transport. The number of mid-range options for quality guesthouses and hotels in central Budapest is growing, costing between 15,000Ft and 33,500Ft for a double at any time of year.

Luxury accommodation is not difficult to find, either. Double-room rates at top-end hotels start at around 33,500Ft. From there, the sky's the limit.

BUDA

TOP CHOICE **Lánchíd 19** BOUTIQUE HOTEL €€€
(Map p36; 419 1900; www.lanchid19hotel.hu; I Lánchíd utca 19; r €108-325; 19, 41) This new, boutique hotel facing the Danube has wow factor in spades. It's not just us who think so – it won the European Hotel Design Award for Best Architecture in 2008, among other awards, and watching its facade form pictures as special sensors reflect the movement of the Danube, we can't help but agree. Each of the 45 rooms and three 'panoramic' suites is decorated in individual, minimalist style, with distinctive artwork and a unique chair ('can you *sit* on that?') designed by art college students. And you can't lose with the views: at the front it's the Danube, and at the back Buda Castle.

St George Residence BOUTIQUE HOTEL €€€
(Map p36; ☎393 5700; www.stgeorgehotel.hu; I Fortuna utca 4; ste from €174-404; P 🛜 🐾; 🚌16, 16/a, 161) Housed in a venerable 700-year-old building in the heart of Castle District, this boutique hotel is all period grandeur. Its four classes of suites feature such touches as green marble, imported Italian furniture and Jacuzzis (a welcome anachronism). If you wish to stay here during Formula I season, be prepared to book a year in advance.

TOP CHOICE **Hotel Papillon** HOTEL €€
(Map p44; ☎212 4750; www.hotelpapillon.hu; II Rózsahegy utca 3/b; s/d/tr €60/75/95, apt €100-120; P ❄ @ 🛜 🏊) Though it's no relation to the famous French prisoner, this small hotel in Rózsadomb has a family guesthouse feel and a friendly owner. The rooms, while not instantly memorable, are spotless and modern, and some have balconies. There's a delightfully leafy back garden with a small swimming pool, and one of the apartments has a lovely roof terrace.

Back Pack Guesthouse HOSTEL €
(☎385 8946; www.backpackbudapest.hu; XI Takács Menyhért utca 33; beds in yurt 3000Ft, dm large/small 3800/4500Ft, d 11,000Ft; P @ 🛜) Catering to budget travellers since 1992, this laid-back hostel – Budapest's first! – sits in a colourfully painted suburban 'villa' in south Buda, and while not central, it's perpetually full. The Back Pack is relatively small, but the fun (and, in season, sleeping bodies) spills out into a lovely landscaped garden, with hammocks, a yurt and a Thai-style lounging platform. It's the perfect place for an Ayurvedic massage or arranging a caving/cycling trip. The upbeat attitude of the friendly, much-travelled owner/manager seems to permeate the place, and the welcome is always warm.

Beatrix Panzió GUESTHOUSE €€
(275 0550; www.beatrixhotel.hu; II Széher út 3; s/d/tr from €50/60/70, apt from €80-210; P @ 🛜 🐾; 🚌29, 🚋18, 61) Run by a small, devoted team, this is an attractive award-winning pension in a quiet residential neighbourhood on the way to the Buda Hills. Surrounding the property is a lovely garden with fishpond, sun terraces and a grill for BBQs. There's a really friendly vibe and guests often end up socialising together. Take tram 61 to Kelemen László utca stop, walk two blocks southwest along Bognár utca and turn right into Széher út.

Grand Hostel Budapest HOSTEL €
(www.grandhostel.hu; XII Hüvösvölgyi utca 69; dm €3600-4500, s/d from €8400/13,500Ft; P @ 🛜; 🚋61) 'Grand' may be tooting their own horn a bit, but this colourful hostel does come pretty close, with its cavern-like cocktail bar, tiled rooms, communal cook-offs and DJ nights. There's a sociable feel and the staff are happy to help arrange all manner of excursions. To get here, take tram 61 to the Kelemen Laszlo utca stop.

Danubius Gellért Hotel LUXURY HOTEL €€€
(Map p68; ☎889 5500; www.danubiusgroup.com/gellert; XI Szent Gellért tér 1; d/ste from €170/268; P ❄ @ 🛜 🏊) Budapest's grande dame is a post-WWI Art Nouveau pile with loads of character. The main draw here are the splendid thermal baths, with recently enlarged outdoor pool, Zsolnay ceramic fountains and arched glass entrance hall – free for guests. Prices depend on which way your room faces (the river views are good, but light sleepers should be mindful of the trams).

Hilton Budapest HOTEL €€€
(Map p36; ☎889 6600; www.budapest.hilton.com; I Hess András tér 1-3; r/ste from €160/360; P ❄ 🛜 🐾; 🚌16, 16/a, 116) Perched above the Danube on Castle Hill, the Hilton is a harmonious blend of old and new, incorporating the wall of a former Jesuit cloister and enclosing the remains of a 14th-century Dominican church and baroque college. The rooms are rather sombre, but the location is hard to beat and the views of the river are fantastic. Cheekily, they charge extra for wi-fi.

Burg Hotel HOTEL €€
(Map p36; ☎212 0269; www.burghotelbudapest.com; I Szentháromság tér 7-8; s/d/ste from €105/115/134; P ❄ 🛜) You won't be writing home about the rooms at this small hotel – forgettable pastels and chintzy bedspreads – but you *will* be able to see Matthias Church, as it's right in front of the hotel. The spic-and-span rooms come equipped with all mod cons, and this is one of the very, very few midrange options on Castle Hill.

Hotel Victoria HOTEL €€
(Map p36; ☎457 8080; www.victoria.hu; I Bem rakpart 11; s/d from €109/115; P ❄ @ 🛜) Contemporary decor, friendly service, great breakfast, easy access to public transport... this elegant little hotel ticks all those boxes and more. Its 27 comfortable and spacious rooms come with larger-than-life views of Parliament and the Danube, and the 19th-

century Jenő Hubay Music Hall attached to the hotel serves as a small theatre and concert venue.

Orion Hotel HOTEL €€
(Map p36; ☎356 8583; www.bestwestern-ce.com/orion; I Döbrentei utca 13; s/d/ste from €70/90/120; ; 18, 19, 41) Part of the Best Western chain, this cosy place hidden away in the Tabán district is within easy walking distance of the Castle District and comes with super-helpful staff and a relaxed atmosphere. The 30 rooms are bright and of a good size, and there's a small sauna for guest use.

Római Camping CAMPGROUND €
(☎388 7167; www.romaicamping.hu; III Szentendrei út 189; campsite for 1/2/van/caravan 4720/6000/5665/7220Ft, bungalow for 2/4 6000/12,000Ft; year-round; P) Located in a leafy park north of the city, opposite the popular Rómaifürdő swimming pool complex, the city's largest camping ground attracts mostly caravans, but the camping spots get access to hot showers *and* wi-fi.

Hotel Citadella HOTEL €
(Map p68; ☎466 5794; www.citadella.hu; XI Citadella sétány; dm/r/tr 3200/12,850/15,000Ft; 27, 19, 41) We're choosing this one because of the location atop Gellért Hill rather than the facilities – though the dozen guest rooms are extra large, retain some of their original features and have their own shower (toilets are on the circular corridor). The single dorm packs in 14 people, but you do get dibs on the incredible nighttime view of the Danube.

PEST

TOP CHOICE Brody House BOUTIQUE HOTEL €€
(Map p68; ☎266 1211; www.brodyhouse.com; VIII Bródy Sándor utca 10; r €70-105; ; M3 Kálvin tér, 47, 49) 'Brody' must be the new term for cutting-edge cool, because the eight individually decorated rooms are just that. From the wrought-iron features of Ludo and the stand-alone bathtub of Tinei to the creamy class of Claret and bright colours of Yusuke, each space has a strong personality, enhanced by artwork of the artist it's named after. And you don't even have to leave the building to get a superb meal.

TOP CHOICE Zara Boutique Hotel Budapest BOUTIQUE HOTEL €€
(Map p68; ☎357 6170; www.boutiquehotelbudapest.com; V Só utca 6; s/d €159/169; P; 47, 49) While we would argue that a hotel with 74 rooms is rather large to describe itself as 'boutique', there's no arguing with the stylish interiors – all parquet floors and designer wallpaper, with modern creature comforts such as satellite TV. The hotel is cobbled together from two buildings, linked by an open-air corridor. Make sure you ask for a room facing Só utca, as half of them look onto a less-than-pretty *udvar* (courtyard).

TOP CHOICE Blue Danube Hostel HOSTEL €
(Map p68; ☎06 30 532 6146; huqwerty@yahoo.com; VII Kazinczy utca 5; s 7330-8800Ft, d 10,265-11,730Ft; ; 8, 112, 239, M2 Astoria, 47, 49) This place gets top marks for the sheer effort that super-knowledgeable host Sándor puts into making his guests feel welcome, equipping them with maps and advice and even picking them up at ungodly hours. The hostel consists of several rooms in a self-contained apartment in the city's most happening nightlife area. The owner has another 'spillover' property where guests can stay if this place fills up.

TOP CHOICE KM Saga Guest Residence GUESTHOUSE €
(Map p68; ☎215 6883, 217 1934; www.km-saga.hu; IX Lónyay utca 17, 3rd fl; s €25-63, d €28-80;) This unique place has five themed rooms, an eclectic mix of 19th-century furnishings and a hospitable, multilingual Hungarian-American owner, Shandor. It's essentially a gay B&B, but everyone is welcome. Two rooms share a bathroom.

Gerlóczy Rooms Delux BOUTIQUE HOTEL €€
(Map p68; ☎501 400; www.gerloczy.hu; V Gerlóczy utca 1; r €90;) The 15 individually decorated rooms in this revamped 1890s building are decked out in sombre shades, but details such as the stained glass, Art Nouveau touches and original wrought-iron staircase give the place character. Try to nab one of the two rooms with balconies. Great cafe and restaurant downstairs, too.

Hotel Art HOTEL €€
(Map p68; ☎266 2166; www.hotelart.hu; V Király Pál utca 12; s €79-151, d €99-159; P) The 'art' in question refers to the Art Deco (including a pink facade) in the public areas, fitness centre and sauna, but the 32 guest rooms at this Best Western branch are quite ordinary (though comfortable and well located), except for the few with separate sitting and sleeping areas. Rooms on the 5th floor have mansard roofs.

Maverick Hostel HOSTEL €

(Map p68; ☎267 3166; www.maverickhostel.com; V Ferenciek tere 2, 2nd floor, apt 16; dm/d/tr/q €18-20/52-60/81/100; @ 🛜 🐾; M M3 Ferenciek tere) The splendid hallway with glass roof suggests something out of the ordinary, and this hostel certainly lives up to its name. With plush beds (rather than bunks) in dorms, nice touches such as stained-glass windows and chandeliers, a wonderfully comfortable common area and fully equipped kitchen, this place is fantastic value, especially given its location in the heart of the city.

Zara Continental Hotel HOTEL €€

(Map p68; ☎1-815 1000; www.continentalhotelbudapest.com; VII Dohány utca 42-44; r/ste from €75/158 ; P ❄ @ 🛜 🏊 🐾; 🚌73, M M2 Blaha Lujza tér, 🚋4, 6) No expense has been spared in transforming the former Hungária Fúrdő (Hungária Bath) into this stunning hotel, with a huge atrium lobby retaining some of the original 19th-century building's features and some 272 spacious and stylish rooms decked out largely in shades of brown (Zara's signature colour). Standout features include the panoramic rooftop garden with swimming pool.

Kapital Inn BOUTIQUE €€€

(Map p60; ☎06 30 915 2029; www.kapitalinn.com; VI Aradi utca 30, 4th fl; r €79-125; @; 🚋4, 6) This gay-owned and -operated B&B offers quite luxurious accommodation in four rooms up under the stars. The 56-sq-metre terrace has to be seen to be believed. Guests get to use a little office with its own laptop, the breakfast room and bar has a fridge stocked with goodies that can be raided at will, and the 1893 entrance to the building is a stucco masterpiece. Alas, there's no lift and the cheaper pair of rooms shares a bathroom.

Hotel Palazzo Zichy HISTORIC HOTEL €€€

(Map p68; ☎235 4000; www.hotel-palazzo-zichy.hu; VII Lőrinc pap tér 2; r/ste from €139/169; P ❄ @ 🛜 🐾; M M3 Corvin negyed, Kálvin tér, 🚋4, 6) The 'palace', once a sumptuous 19th-century residence belonging to the aristocratic Zichy family, has been transformed into a lovely hotel, with its original features, such as wrought-iron bannisters, blending seamlessly with the ultra-modern decor. The rooms, all charcoals and creams, are enlivened by red glasstopped desks, the showers are terrific, and there's a sauna and fitness room in the basement for guest use.

TOP CHOICE **Four Seasons Gresham Palace Budapest** LUXURY HOTEL €€€

(Map p68; ☎2686000; www.fourseasons.com/budapest; V Széchenyi István tér 5-6; r/ste from €325/1125; P ❄ @ 🛜 🏊) This magnificent 179-room hotel was created out of the long-derelict Art Nouveau Gresham Palace (1907), and no expense was spared to piece back together its famous wrought-iron Peacock Gates, Zsolnay tiles and splendid mosaics. The hotel truly lives up to the 'palace' part of its name, and the opulence is complimented by impeccable service and sumptuous modern features, such as the infinity pool and state-of-the-art spa with Hungarian mud therapy. You got the dosh? This is simply the best hotel in town.

Budapest Rooms B&B €€

(Map p68; ☎630 4743; www.budapestrooms.eu; VII Szentkirályi utca 15; s/d/tr/q €48/62/78/84; 🛜; 🚌8, 112, 239, 🚋47, 49, Astoria) A small B&B consisting of just four tranquil rooms, individually decorated in soothing colours, with great showers, and presided over by one of the nicest, most helpful hosts in town. The fully equipped kitchen is a boon for self-caterers, and if you don't feel like cooking Budapest's most happening district is only a couple of blocks away.

Corinthia Grand Hotel Royal LUXURY HOTEL €€€

(Map p60; ☎479 4000; www.corinthia.hu; VII Erzsébet körút 43-49; r/ste from €140/347; P ❄ @ 🛜 🏊) Decades in the remaking, the one-time Royal Hotel is now a very grand, 414-room, five-star hotel. Its lobby – a double atrium with a massive marble staircase – is among the most impressive in the capital, and the Royal Spa, dating back to 1886 but now as modern as tomorrow, awaits you with an impressive range of treatments and massages.

Kempinski Hotel Corvinus LUXURY HOTEL €€€

(Map p68; ☎429 3777; www.kempinski-budapest.com; V Erzsébet tér 7-8; r/ste from €229/349; P ❄ @ 🛜 🏊; M M1/2/3 Deák Ferenc tér) Essentially for business travellers on hefty expense accounts, the Kempinski has European service, American efficiency, Hungarian charm and fusion Japanese cuisine. The 366 guest rooms and suites remain among the classiest in town and fitness and pampering facilities abound; an extra nice touch is a mini-art gallery showcasing up-and-coming talent.

Hotel Baross HOTEL €€
(Map p52; ☎461 3010; www.barosshotel.hu; VII Baross tér 15, 4th-6th fl; d/tr/q €250/350/400; ❄@🛜🐾; Ⓜ M2 Keleti pályaudvar) The main advantage of the Baross is its convenient location, directly opposite Keleti train station, though the rooms – spacious and decorated in neutral shades – don't let down the side either. The very blue inner courtyard is a delight and the buffet breakfast ample; our only complaint is that the wi-fi works only in the lobby.

Bohem Art Hotel BOUTIQUE HOTEL €€€
(Map p68; ☎327 9020; www.bohemarthotel.hu; V Molnár utca 35; r/ste from €249/349; ❄@🛜; 🚌15, 115, Ⓜ M3 Kálvin tér, 🚊47, 49) Though the rooms at this delightful, small hotel are a little on the compact side, each is individually decorated, with giant prints and bold touches of colour amid monochrome decor and ultra-modern furnishings. The stylish bar attracts a young, sophisticated crowd and the champagne buffet breakfast is one of the best in the city, with a great choice of dishes and, of course, bubbly.

Trendy Budapest B&B Hostel HOSTEL €
(Map p60; ☎30 611 9541; www.trendybudapesthostel.com; V Oktober 6 utca 19; d/q from €29/44; @🛜; 🚌15, 115, Ⓜ M2 Kossuth tér, M3 Arany János utca) Bright, stylish and spacious, the rooms at this apartment B&B live up to the name. Each room is individually decorated, with designer wallpaper and pinks, reds and creams predominating. Its ideal location in the centre of Pest is paired with the owner's excellent knowledge of the city's hotspots. Two of the rooms share facilities.

Carpe Noctem HOSTEL €
(Map p60; ☎20 365 8749; www.carpenoctemhostel.com; VI Szobi utca 5, 3/8a; dm 8000Ft; @🛜; Ⓜ M3 Nyugati pálaudvar, 🚊4, 6) As the name suggests, this sociable joint, run by an English/Aussie team, is all about making the most of the night, so expect bar crawls and nocturnal outings. A great place to meet fellow travellers for a bit of crush-your-beer-can-against-your-forehead action – you can sleep your happy hangover off later on the comfy orthopaedic mattresses.

Loft Hostel HOSTEL €
(Map p68; ☎328 0916; www.lofthostel.hu; V Veres Pálné utca 19; dm 4200-5000Ft, d 13,000Ft; @🛜) This hostel may well succeed in its loft-y aspirations to be the strongest backpacker magnet in town. Travellers end up lingering longer than expected, seduced by the owner's Hungarian cooking and the wonderfully friendly atmosphere. The showers are among the best in town and it feels just like staying at a friend's house. Bike rental and tours available.

Soho Hotel BOUTIQUE HOTEL €€€
(Map p68; ☎872 8216; www.sohohotel.hu; VII Dohány utca 64; s/d/ste €189/199/249; P❄@🛜) Those with a taste for the macabre will adore the dark baroque elegance of the two vampire-themed suites at this delightfully stylish boutique hotel. We also love the lobby bar in eye-popping reds, blues and lime greens, the nonallergenic rooms with bamboo matting on the walls and parquet floors, and the music/film theme throughout (check out the portraits of Bono, George Michael and Marilyn).

11th Hour Hostel HOSTEL €
(Map p68; ☎266 2153; www.11thhourcinemahostel.com; V Magyar utca 11; dm 2385-3845Ft d 13,000-14,000Ft; @🛜; 🚌8, 112, 239, Ⓜ M2 Astoria, 🚊47, 49) Highlights at this lively hostel include the courtyard bar and low-lit common room with a huge projection screen for watching films, as well as a sociable vibe, table football and regular bar crawls on the menu – it's not the place to catch up on your sleep. The bathrooms could be a tad cleaner.

Connection Guest House GUESTHOUSE €€
(Map p60; ☎267 7104; www.connectionguesthouse.com; VII Király utca 41; s/d from €45/60; @🛜) Spotless, stylish and (great) service are the three key words at this very central gay pension located above a leafy courtyard. It attracts a young crowd due to its proximity to the hottest nightlife district in town. Three of the seven rooms share facilities on the corridor. Light sleepers should ask for rooms other than 6 and 7, as Király utca can be noisy at night.

Home-Made Hostel HOSTEL €
(Map p60; ☎302 2103; www.homemadehostel.com; VI Teréz körút 22; dm/d from 5500/15,000Ft; @🛜) This extremely welcoming and homey hostel has recycled tables hanging upside-down from the ceiling and old valises under the beds serving as lockers. The warm atmosphere will make you want to stay forever, and the friendly staff organise bar tours, teach you to cook Hungarian dishes and hold surprise events weekly.

Belváros (Inner Town)

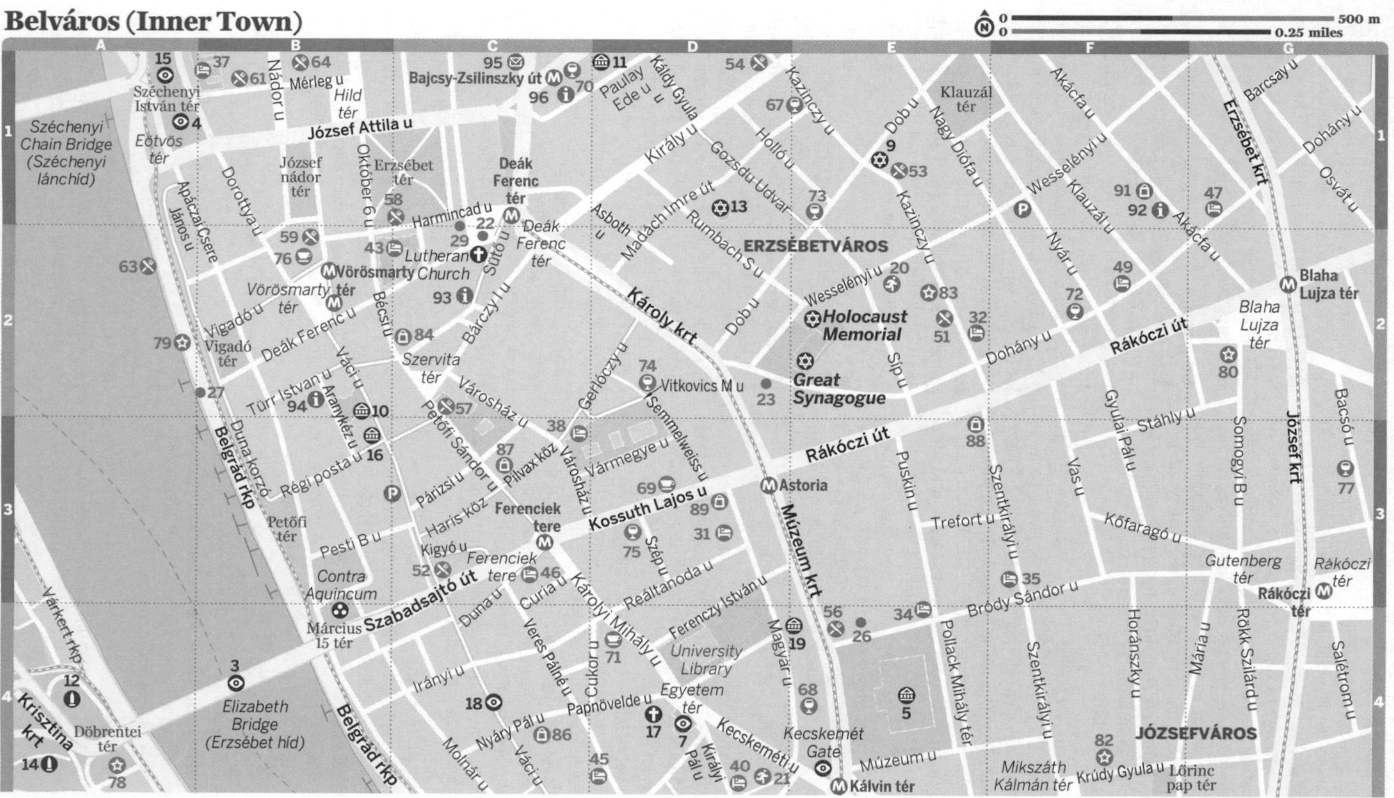

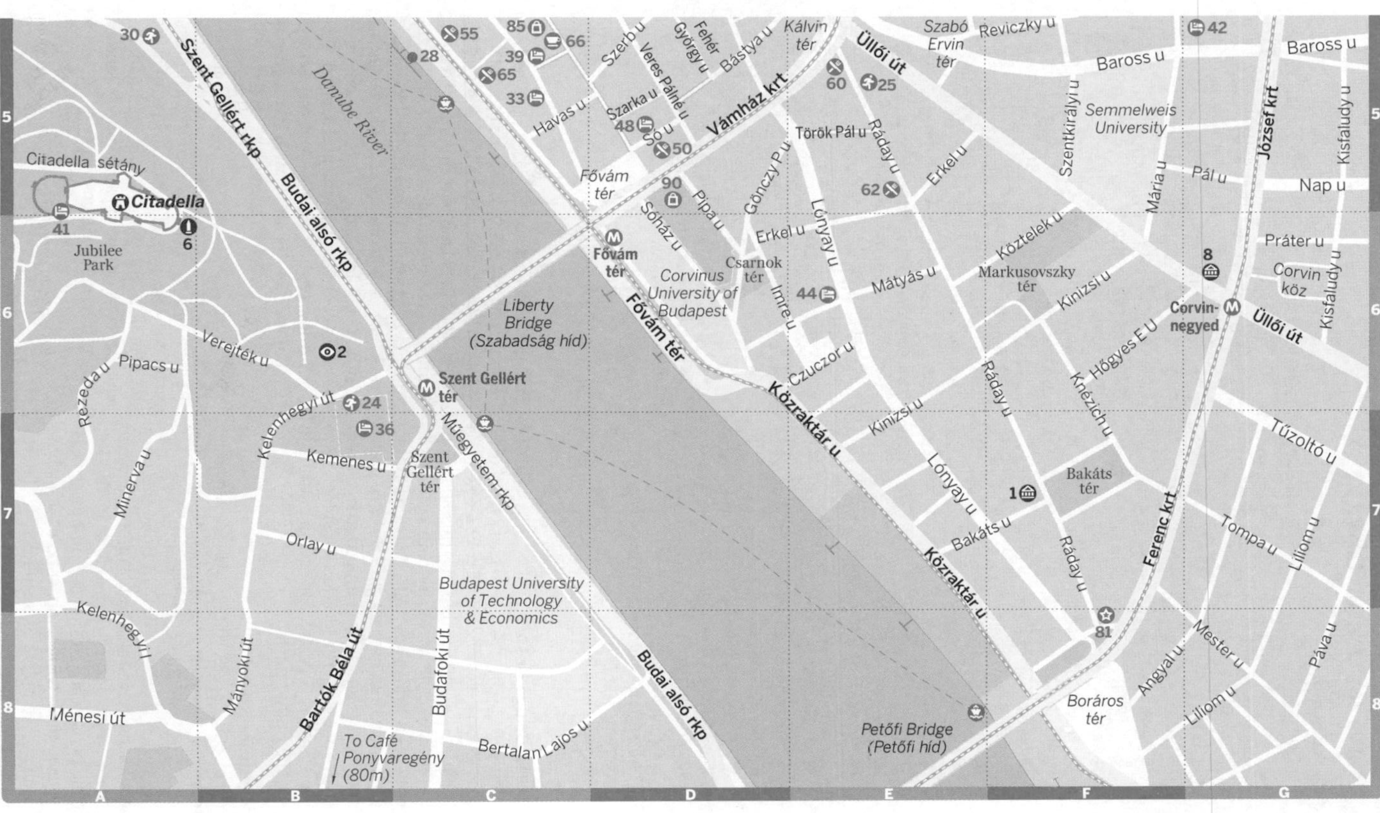

Szent Gellért rkp
Budai alsó rkp
Danube River
Citadella sétány
Citadella
Jubilee Park
Pipacs u
Rezeda u
Minerva u
Verejték u
Kelenhegyi út
Kelenhegyi u
Kemenes u
Orlay u
Ménesi út
Mányoki út
Bartók Béla út
Szent Gellért tér
Szent Gellért tér
Műegyetem rkp
Budafoki út
Budapest University of Technology & Economics
Bertalan Lajos u
To Café Ponyvaregény (80m)
Liberty Bridge (Szabadság híd)
Fővám tér
Fővám tér
Fővám tér
Corvinus University of Budapest
Sóház u
Pipa u
Csarnok tér
Imre u
Erkel u
Gönczy P u
Vámház krt
Havas u
Szarka u
Só u
Szerb u
Veres Pálné u
Fehér György u
Bástya u
Kálvin tér
Török Pál u
Lónyay u
Ráday u
Erkel u
Üllői út
Szabó Ervin tér
Reviczky u
Mátyás u
Czuczor u
Közraktár u
Kinizsi u
Markusovszky tér
Köztelek u
Szentkirályi u
Semmelweis University
Baross u
Mária u
Pál u
Nap u
Kisfaludy u
Práter u
Corvin köz
József krt
Corvin-negyed
Högyes E U
Knézich u
Bakáts tér
Bakáts u
Petőfi Bridge (Petőfi híd)
Boráros tér
Ferenc krt
Angyal u
Mester u
Liliom u
Tompa u
Tűzoltó u
Páva u

Belváros (Inner Town)

Top Sights

Citadella A5
Great Synagogue E2
Holocaust Memorial E2

Sights

1 2B Galería F7
2 Cave Chapel B6
3 Elizabeth Bridge B4
4 Ferenc Deák Statue A1
5 Hungarian National Museum E4
6 Liberty Monument A6
7 Loránd Eötvös Science University D4
8 Museum of Applied Arts G6
9 Orthodox Synagogue E1
10 Philanthia B2
11 Postal Museum D1
12 Queen Elizabeth Statue A4
13 Rumbach Sebestyén Utca Synagogue D1
14 St Gellért Monument A4
15 Széchenyi István Tér A1
16 Thonet House B3
17 University Church D4
18 Váci Utca C4
19 Vintage Galería E4

Activities, Courses & Tours

20 Budapest Bike E2
21 Dynamo Bike & Bake D4
22 Free Budapest Tours C2
23 Fungarian D2
24 Gellért Baths B6
25 Hungarian Equestrian Tourism Association E5
26 Hungarian Language School E4
27 Legenda B2
28 Mahart PassNave C5
29 Program Centrum C1
30 Rudas Baths A5

Sleeping

31 11th Hour Hostel D3
32 Blue Danube Hostel E2
33 Bohem Art Hotel C5
34 Brody House E4
35 Budapest Rooms F3
36 Danubius Gellért Hotel B7
37 Four Seasons Gresham Palace Budapest B1
38 Gerlóczy Rooms Delux C3
39 Green Bridge Hostel C5
40 Hotel Art D4
41 Hotel Citadella A5
42 Hotel Palazzo Zichy G5
43 Kempinski Hotel Corvinus C2
44 KM Saga Guest Residence E6
45 Loft Hostel D4
46 Maverick Hostel C3
47 Soho Hotel G1
48 Zara Boutique Hotel Budapest D5

Green Bridge Hostel HOSTEL €

(Map p68; ☎266 6922; www.greenbridgehostel.com; V Molnár utca 22-24; dm €15-19, d €50; Ⓜ M3 Kálvin tér, 🚊47, 49) Few hostels truly stand out in terms of comfort, location and reception, but Green Bridge has it all, in spades. Bunks are nowhere to be seen, and the free coffee and lockers and fully equipped guest kitchen are bonuses. The location, one block from the Danube, is perfect for evening strolls to see the lit-up bridges.

Aventura Hostel HOSTEL €€

(Map p60; ☎239 0789; www.aventurahostel.com; XIII Visegrádi utca 12, 1st fl; dm/d/apt 4300/15,000/18,800Ft; @ 📶) Run by two affable ladies, Aventura has got to be the most chilled hostel in Budapest, with four themed rooms, beds rather than bunks in the loft (tall people need to duck!), in-house massage and even retro apartments for those wanting complete self-sufficiency. There's no real common area, though.

Hotel Parlament HOTEL €€

(Map p60; ☎374 6000; www.parlament-hotel.hu; V Kálmán Imre utca 19; r €118-170; P ❄ @ 📶; 🚌15, 115, Ⓜ M2 Kossuth Lajos tér) This Best Western branch is all minimalist decor, with bright touches of colour livening up the blacks and greys. The pine floors are anti-allergenic, the staff super-helpful, and there's an adorable wellness centre with sauna and Jacuzzi. Test your knowledge of famous Magyars on the 'design wall' in the lobby, with photographs and names etched in the glass.

Eating

As a rough guide, a two-course sit-down meal for one person with a glass of wine or beer for less than 3500Ft in Budapest can be considered 'cheap', while a moderately priced meal will cost you up to 7500Ft. There's a big jump to an 'expensive' meal (7500Ft to 11,000Ft), and 'very expensive' is anything above that.

49 Zara Continental Hotel F2

Eating

50 Bangkok D5
51 Bors Gasztro Bár E2
52 Buddha Bar C3
53 Carmel Pince E1
54 Fausto D1
55 Gepárd És Űrhajó C5
56 Múzeum E4
57 Nagyi Palacsintázója C2
58 Nobu C1
59 Onyx B2
60 Pata Negra E5
61 Salaam Bombay B1
62 Soul Café E5
63 Spoon A2
64 Tigris B1
65 Trattoria Toscana C5

Drinking

66 1000 Tea C5
67 400 Bar E1
68 Action Bár E4
69 Auguszt Cukrászda D3
70 Boutiq' Bar C1
71 Centrál Kávéház D4
72 Coxx Men's Bar F2
73 Dobló E1
74 Eklektika Restolounge D2
75 Funny Carrot D3
76 Gerbeaud B2
77 Hintaló G3

Entertainment

78 Cinetrip A4
79 Columbus A2
80 Corvintető G2
81 Jedermann F8
82 Nothin' But The Blues F4
83 Szimpla Kert E2

Shopping

84 BÁV (Belváros branch) C2
85 Intuita C5
86 Kamchatka Design C4
87 Magma C3
88 Magyar Pálinka Háza E3
89 Mono Fashion D3
90 Nagycsarnok D5
91 Romani Design F1

Information

92 BKV Lost & Found Office F1
93 Budapest Info (Main Office) C2
94 Ibusz B2
95 Main Post Office C1
96 Vista C1

Transport

Mahart PassNave .... (see 28)

Historically, Budapest's cafe culture was once as famous as Vienna's, but by the time communism collapsed in 1989 there were scarcely a dozen cafes or cake shops left. Luckily, the trend has reversed, with trendy cafes popping up all over the city and a few grand insitutions left over from the 19th-century heyday. Leafy VI Liszt Ferenc tér is surrounded by hip cafes, and there are a few on IX Ráday utca and V Szent István tér behind St Stephen's Basilica.

International fast-food places are a dime a dozen, but old-style self-service restaurants are disappearing fast from Budapest. Little restaurants called *étkezdék*, canteens not unlike British 'cafs' that serve simple but very tasty Hungarian dishes, are sprinkled throughout Pest.

The city has become very cosmopolitan and you can find pretty much any cuisine that tickles your fancy: Indian, Middle Eastern, Japanese, Chinese, Italian, French and Thai. Good places to eat out include the streets by St Stephen's Basilica in Belváros, Ráday utca in southern Pest and the streets off Andrassy út. Besides international cuisine, there are a number of fine dining establishments, including two Michelin-starred restaurants.

The lion's share of the city's approximately 20 large food markets are in Pest, and self-caterers shouldn't have trouble finding 24-hour supermarkets in either half of the city.

BUDA

TOP CHOICE **Vár a Speiz** HUNGARIAN, INTERNATIONAL €€€
(Map p36; ☎488 7416; www.varaspeiz.hu; I Hess András tér 6; mains 3800-11,400Ft; 16, 16/a, 116) Beautifully presented, imaginative takes on Hungarian dishes rule the roost here (goulash, veal ragout), with the occasional international influence (Argentinian steak with duck fois gras), and it's all superb. In deference to Western tastes, the Hungarian

classic *mohn nudle* (noodles with sugar and crushed poppyseeds) is presented as a dessert rather than a main.

Csalogány 26 HUNGARIAN €€€
(Map p36; ☎201 7892; www.csalogany26.hu; I Csalogány utca 26; 4-/8-course menus 8000/12,000Ft; ⏲noon-3pm & 7-10pm Tue-Sat) While the name and decor are underwhelming, the modern, imaginative take on Hungarian cuisine certainly does not fail to dazzle. Choose four or eight dishes from either of two concise menus. The choice between roast suckling pig and duck liver with spelt is a tough one. The poppyseed tart with pumpkin ice cream is truly inspired, and always has us leaning towards Menu II.

21 Magyar Vendéglő HUNGARIAN €€
(Map p36; ☎202 2113; www.21restaurant.hu; I Fortuna utca 21; mains 3460-5360Ft; 🚌16, 16/a, 116) This unimaginatively named joint sits right in the heart of Castle District. Think exposed brick chic and innovative takes on Hungarian classics, but minus half the fat and accompanied by some great wines, some of which are bottled right here. Try the Hortobágy pancake stuffed with goose liver.

Fuji Japán JAPANESE €€€
(☎325 7111; www.fujirestaurant.hu; II Csatárka út 54; sashimi 3800-12,500Ft, mains 2200-7200Ft; ⏲noon-11pm; 🚌29) Above Rózsadomb in district II and on the corner of Zöld lomb utca and Zöldkert út, Fuji is a long way to schlep for sushi, sashimi and other Japanese dishes like sukiyaki and teppanyaki. But this is the most authentic Japanese game in town, judging from the repeat clientele who nip in regularly for noodles and more.

Cafe Miró INTERNATIONAL €€
(Map p36; ☎201 2375; www.cafemiro.hu; I Úri utca 30; mains 2490-4490Ft; 📶✍; 🚌16, 16/a, 116) Its interior inspired by Joan Miró's art, this welcome addition to the Castle District eating scene is great for enormous fruit smoothies in summer, the selection of teas and soups for colder days and imaginative dishes such as grilled goat's cheese, honey and pear salad, and pearl barley risotto with pork. Efficient service, too.

Remíz HUNGARIAN €€
(☎275 1396; www.remiz.hu; II Budakeszi út 5; mains 3280-5250Ft; 🚋61) Next to a *remíz* (tram depot) in the Buda Hills, this virtual institution remains popular for its reliable food (try the grilled dishes, especially the ribs, or the wonderfully juicy duck), competitive prices and verdant garden terrace. Portions match the biggest of appetites, and service is flawless.

Nagyi Palacsintázója HUNGARIAN €
(Granny's Palacsinta Place; Map p36; www.nagyipali.hu; I Hattyú utca 16; pancakes 160-680Ft; ⏲24hr; ✍) Sometimes all you're hankering after is a pancake, and Granny's Palacsinta Place has a bewildering array – stuffed with cottage cheese and dill, Mexican meat, peanut butter and banana, poppyseed and apple...you get the picture. The place is open round the clock and always packed. There are other 24-hour branches in **Buda** (Map p36; I Batthyány tér 5; Ⓜ M2 Batthyány tér), **Óbuda** (Map p44; III Szentendrei út 131; 🚆HEV train to Aquincum felső station) and **Pest** (Map p68; V Petőfi Sándor utca 17–19; Ⓜ M3 Ferenciek tere).

Náncsi Néni HUNGARIAN €
(Auntie Nancy; ☎397 2742; II Ördögárok út 80; soups & starters 750-1500Ft, mains 2350-3200Ft; ⏲noon-midnight) 'Auntie Náncsi' (the nickname for any loopy old lady in Hungarian) is a perennial favourite with Hungarians and expats alike. Housed in a wood-panelled cabin in Hűvösvölgy, it specialises in game in autumn and winter. In summer the lighter fare and garden seating are the attraction. Take bus 157 to Hűvösvölgy stop; the restaurant is across the street.

Pastrami INTERNATIONAL €€
(Map p44; ☎430 1731; www.pastrami.hu; III Lajos utca 93-99; mains 1800-5900Ft; ⏲8am-11pm; 🚌86, 🚋17, 🚆HÉV Tímár utca) The attempt to re-create New York's celebrated pastrami and Reuben sandwiches here is laudable (the meat is custom-cured locally), and there's so much more, from soups, salads, risottos and pastas to Hungarian goose leg with cabbage. To top it off, these guys make their own ice cream and the breakfasts are ample.

Kéhli HUNGARIAN €€
(Map p44; ☎368 0613; www.kehli.hu; III Mókus utca 22; mains 1990-6980Ft; ⏲noon-11.30pm; 🚌86) A self-consciously rustic but stylish place in Óbuda, Kéhli has some of the best traditional Hungarian food in town. In fact, one of Hungary's best-loved writers, the novelist Gyula Krúdy (1878–1933), who lived in nearby Dugovits Titusz tér, enjoyed Kéhli's bone marrow on toast (990Ft as a starter) so much that he included it in one of his novels.

Ruszwurm Cukrászda CAFE €
(Map p36; www.ruszwurm.hu; I Szentháromság utca 7; cakes 380-580Ft; ⏲10am-7pm) This thimble-sized cafe dating back to 1827 is the perfect place for coffee and cakes in the Castle District, though it can get pretty crowded and it's almost always impossible to get a seat.

Éden VEGETARIAN, VEGAN €
(Map p36; ☎20 337 7575; www.edenivegan.hu; I Iskola utca 31; mains 830-1050Ft; ⏲8am-9pm Mon-Thu, to 6pm Fri, 11am-9pm Sun; ✎; 🚌86) In a new location in an old town house (dating from 1811) just below Castle Hill, this self-service place offers solid, healthy vegetarian platters and ragouts, washed down with fresh juices; it's the only place in town catering to vegans. Seating is in the main dining room on the ground floor or, in warmer months, in an atrium courtyard.

Angelika Kávéház CAFE €
(Map p36; ☎225 1653; www.angelikacafe.hu; I Batthyány tér 7; desserts 790Ft; sandwiches 1850-2450Ft; ⏲9am-midnight Apr-Oct, 9am-11pm Nov-Mar; Ⓜ M2 Batthyány tér) Angelika is a charming cafe attached to an 18th-century church, with a raised terrace. The more substantial dishes – salads, sandwiches, pastas and meat and fish – are not likely to win any culinary prizes, but you should come here for the desserts and views across the square to the Danube.

Kisbuda Gyöngye HUNGARIAN €€
(Map p44; ☎368 6402; www.remiz.hu; III Kenyeres utca 34; mains 2680-5220Ft; ⏲closed Sun) This is a traditional and very elegant Hungarian restaurant run by a friendly family in Óbuda; the antiques-cluttered dining room and attentive service create a *fin-de-siècle* atmosphere. Try the excellent goose liver speciality with a glass of Tokaj, or a more pedestrian dish such as *tanyasi csirke paprikás* (farmhouse chicken paprika).

Déryné Bisztró BISTRO €€
(Map p36; ☎225 1407; www.cafederyne.hu; I Krisztina tér 3; mains 1850-4950Ft; ⏲7.30am-midnight Sun-Wed, to 1am Thu-Sat; 🚌16, 105, 178, 🚋18) An adorable bistro near the entrance to the tunnel running under Castle Hill, with a young, lively clientele flocking to its horseshoe-shaped bar in the evening. In warm weather, the terrace is a great spot for a full English breakfast or to polish off one of the Mediterranean or Hungarian dishes on offer. Great daily specials, too.

Mongolian Barbecue ASIAN €€
(Map p36; www.mongolianbbq.hu; XII Márvány utca 19/a; buffet before/after 5pm & weekends 3490/4990Ft; ⏲noon-5pm & 6pm-11pm; 🚌105, 🚋61) One of those all-you-can-eat Asian places where you choose the raw ingredients and legions of cooks stir-fry it for you. The difference here is that as much beer, wine and sangria you can quaff is included in the price. During summer there's also seating in an attractive, tree-filled courtyard.

PEST

TOP CHOICE **Gepárd És Űrhajó** HUNGARIAN €€
(Cheetah & Rocket; Map p68; ☎06 70 329 7815; www.gepardesurhajo.com; V Belgrád Rakpart 18; mains 2490-3490Ft; ⏲noon-midnight; Ⓜ M3 Ferenciek tere, 🚋2) It's difficult not to love the 'Cheetah and Rocket' for three reasons: the name, the excellent wine (they stock more than 100 vintages), and the food – inspired takes on Hungarian dishes such as wild meat stew with porcini mushrooms and lamb trotters with sheep-cheese polenta. The meats are cooked to perfection and the weekly specials are based on seasonal ingredients. Beam us up, Spotty!

TOP CHOICE **Bistro 181** FRENCH €
(Map p60; ☎06 30 651 0880; www.bistro181.hu; VII Izabella utca 38; mains 1600-2900Ft; ⏲noon-3pm & 6-11pm Tue-Sat; Ⓜ M1 Vörösmarty utca, 🚋4, 6) The Provence-inspired menu at this warmly lit cellar bistro is succinct and accompanied by a menu of 10 carefully selected French wines. Each dish, from the French onion soup and warm chicken liver salad to Provençal beef stew, is cooked to perfection by the chef who's transplanted from Avignon. You decide whether the lemon cake is indeed 'the world's best'!

TOP CHOICE **Onyx** EUROPEAN €€€
(Map p68; ☎30 508 0622; www.onyxrestaurant.hu; V Vörösmarty tér 7-8; tasting menus 22,900-25,900Ft, mains 6900-10,900Ft; ⏲noon-2pm Tue-Fri, 6.30-11pm Tue-Sat; ✎; Ⓜ M1 Vörösmarty tér) Picture the scene: music tinkling gently from a grand piano in the corner and a white-gloved gentleman bringing you dish after dish that is as pleasing to the eye as to the palate. It's difficult to fault this place, with the exemplary service, wine expertly paired with two superb multicourse tasting menus, and standout mains such as saddle of lamb with sweetbread-stuffed ravioli and Danube salmon with crispy veal. There's a

separate menu for vegetarians as well. If you've spent your life looking for the perfect tiramisu you may have just found it. Superb.

TOP CHOICE Mák Bistro INTERNATIONAL €€

(Map p60; ☎06 30 723 9383; www.makbistro.hu; V Vigyázó Ferenc utca 4; mains 3200-5600Ft; ⊙noon-3pm & 6pm-midnight Tue-Sat) With a new chef at the helm, Mák Bistro has gone from strength to strength. Kata Talás is responsible for such ambitious pairings of flavours as scallops with grapefruit and sardine with mango, and she doesn't shy away from using offal, either. You may be seduced by more traditional mains – Mangalica spare ribs, sirloin with polenta – and the chocolate millefeuille really is to die for. It's only a matter of time before Mák joins Budapest's Michelin-starred elite.

Fausto ITALIAN €€€

(Map p68; ☎277 6210; www.fausto.hu; VI Székely Mihály utca 2; mains 4500-12,000Ft; ⊙noon-3pm & 6-11pm Mon-Fri, 6-11pm Sat; ✎; Ⓜ M1 Opera) The most upmarket (and expensive) Italian restaurant in town, Fausto offers inspired pasta dishes such as black ravioli with salmon and beetroot, and mains such as deer loin with white polenta. Daily specials and vegetarian choices abound, and the Italian wine selection is huge. With its exemplary service, it remains one of the most pleasant dining experiences in Budapest.

Tom-George ITALIAN €€€

(Map p60; ☎266 3525; www.tomgeorge.hu; V Október 6 utca 8; starters 1850-3600Ft, mains 2250-9000Ft; ⊙noon-midnight; 📶; 🚌15, 115, Ⓜ M1/M2/M3 Deák tér) Uber-trendy – it could be in London or New York – the service here is great, the decor *très contemporain* and the Italian dishes – from homemade pasta to veal chops – are excellent. Even if you don't approve of murdering ecclesiastical figures, try the priest-strangler pasta, or if you're not too hungry, nurse one from a long list of cocktails at the bar. Reservations recommended.

Bock Bisztró BISTRO €€

(Map p60; ☎321 0340; www.bockbisztro.hu; VII Erzsébet körút 43-49; mains 3700-7100; Ⓜ M1 Oktogon, 🚋4, 6) The city's business clientele pack the large dining room of this wine restaurant at lunchtimes, drawn by the likes of 'ox cheek, retro style', fois gras bruleé and duck with sour cherry. The chef must be some kind of mad genius – some of the pairings of ingredients don't sound as if they'd work, but they come together beautifully. Everything is impeccably executed, the service is spot on and we dare you to finish your meal with the 'bizarre' ice cream selection.

Olimpia HUNGARIAN €€€

(Map p52; ☎321 2805; www.alparutca.hu; VII Alpár utca 5; 2/3-course lunches 1950/2350Ft; 4/5/6/7-course dinners 5900/7000/7900/8500Ft; ⊙noon-3pm & 7-10pm Mon-Fri, 7-10pm Sat; 🚌79, Ⓜ M2 Keleti pályaudvar) Each night, these kitchen wizards conjure up an incredible seven-course menu of dishes using traditional Hungarian recipes with clever modern twists and seasonal ingredients. Tuesdays are fresh-fish days, so expect the likes of scallops with pear and honey. And relax: you're in for a leisurely evening. Reservations essential for dinner and recommended for lunch.

TOP CHOICE Klassz INTERNATIONAL €€

(Map p60; www.klasszetterem.hu; VI Andrássy út 41; mains 1890-4390Ft; ⊙11.30am-11pm Mon-Sat, 11.30am-6pm Sun) Unusually for a wine restaurant, the food here is of a very high standard and the cooking uniformly excellent – from the foie gras to the native Mangalitsa pork, both permanent fixtures on the menu. More unusual dishes include mint-mustard lamb trotters and venison ribs with duck liver ragout. We love the big, bright dining room on two levels and the homey floral wallpaper. We don't love having to wait for a table – reservations are not accepted – but we will, again and again.

Rosenstein HUNGARIAN €€

(Map p48; ☎333 3492; www.rosenstein.hu; VIII Mosonyi utca 3; mains 3300-6200Ft; ⊙noon-11pm Mon-Sat; 🚌5, 7, 173, 178, Ⓜ M2 Keleti pályaudvar, 🚋24) A top-notch Hungarian restaurant in an unlikely location, with Jewish tastes and aromas and super service. Family-run, it's been here for years, so expect everyone to know each other. Standout dishes include smoked tenderloin with Tokaj sauce. Daily lunch specials such as roast duck with braised cabbage and lamb stew go for as little as 2200Ft.

Salaam Bombay INDIAN €€

(Map p68; ☎411 1252; www.salaambombay.hu; V Mérleg utca 6; mains 1490-3900Ft; ⊙noon-3pm & 6-11pm; ✎) If you hanker after a fix of authentic curry or tandoori in a bright, upbeat environment, look no further than this attractive eatery just east of Széchenyi tér. Don't believe us? Even staffers at the Indian embassy are said to come here regularly. There's a large choice of vegetarian dishes – the aubergine (eggplant) ones stand out. Lunch specials from 980Ft.

Momotaro Ramen ASIAN €€
(Map p60; ☎269 3802; www.momotaroramen.com; V Széchenyi utca 16; dumplings 600-1400Ft; noodles 1150-1800Ft; mains 1800-4750Ft; ⏰11am-10.30pm Tue-Sun; ⓥ) Besides the oodles of noodles with and without soup (hot-and-sour ramen, vegie ramen) this Chinese/Japanese hybrid also does possibly the best dumplings in town: the steamed vegetable and pork versions particularly stand out. More substantial dishes are also on the menu.

Tigris HUNGARIAN €€
(Map p68; ☎317 3715; www.tigrisrestaurant.hu; V Mérleg utca 10; mains 3800-5700Ft; ⏰noon-midnight Mon-Sat; 🚌15, Ⓜ M1/M2/M3 Deák tér, 🚌2) This is upscale Hungarian food at its best, with the lIkes of goose-liver crème brûlée, saddle of wild rabbit with roasted mushrooms and Mangalica tenderloin, served within classy old-school surroundings and using Zsolnay tableware. The restaurant's owner is also a vintner and there's a wide range of Gere vintages to be paired expertly with your dishes.

Két Szerecsen BISTRO €
(Map p60; ☎434 1984; www.ketszerecsen.hu; VI Nagymező utca 14; mains about 2500Ft; ⏰8am-midnight Mon-Fri, 9am-midnight Sat & Sun; ⓥ; 🚌70, 78, 105, Ⓜ M1 Opera) This vaulted cellar-like bistro is watched over by a James Bond-esque angel, and its menu is that of an ambitious coffee house that has turned its hand to imaginative international cuisine. You can find everything from fried camembert to tapas to Thai curry, accompanied by an extensive list of Hungarian wines and *pálinkas*. Two-course weekly lunch specials are 990Ft.

Ring Cafe BURGERS €
(Map p60; ☎331 5790; www.ringcafe.hu; VI Andrássy utca 38; burgers 1490-3290Ft; ⏰9am-late Mon-Fri, 10am-1am Sat, 10am-10pm Sun; 📶) When we tell you that this place does the best burgers in town, we're not messing about. From the smoky jalapeno burger and imaginative lamb burger with rosemary pesto to the burger topped with fois gras and the Angus steak burger, these are guaranteed to satisfy your late-night carnivorous cravings. With imaginative sandwiches and salads and egg-and-bacon power breakfasts to boot, it's little wonder this place is perpetually packed.

> **SPEND LIKE A PAUPER, EAT LIKE A PRINCE**
>
> If you wish to partake of Budapest's gastronomic feasts offered by Onyx (p73), Fausto (p74), Mák Bistro (p74), Tigris and others without drifting into insolvency, visit at lunchtime, when three-course menus go for as little as 2200Ft. Reservations are even more essential than at dinnertime, though.

Pata Negra SPANISH €
(Map p68; ☎215 5616; www.patanegra.hu; IX Kálvin tér 8; tapas 520-1850Ft, plates 950-2200Ft; ⓥ; Ⓜ M3 Kálvin tér, 🚌47, 49) The 'Black Foot', named after a breed of pig used to make Spain's most prized cured ham, is a lovely Spanish tapas bar featuring classic dishes such as *calamares a la romana* (battered squid rings), *albondigas* (meatballs) and *gambas al ajillo* (garlic prawns), with Hungarian touches like duck liver with apple. Don't miss the ham and cheese plates.

Marquis de Salade EUROPEAN €
(Map p60; ☎302 4086; www.marquisdesalade.hu; VI Hajós utca 43; mains 2600-4000Ft; ⏰noon-1am; ⓥ; 🚌109, Ⓜ M3 Arany János utca) This basement restaurant is a strange hybrid, with dishes from Russia and Azerbaijan as well as from Hungary. It's difficult to go wrong with the likes of *pelmeni* (boiled dumplings stuffed with meat) or the lamb with aubergine cooked in a clay pot. Of the excellent vegetarian dishes, we particularly like the stuffed aubergine (eggplant) with walnut sauce.

Bors Gasztro Bár SANDWICHES €
(Map p68; www.facebook.com/BorsGasztroBar; VII Kazinczy utca 10; mains from 790Ft; ⏰11.30am-9pm; ⓥ) We love this thimble-sized place, and not just for its hearty, imaginative soups (how about sweet potato with coconut?) – the grilled baguettes are equally good: try 'French Lady' (red onion jam, chicken, cranberry) or 'Brain Dead' (with pig's brains as the main ingredient). It's not really a sit-down kind of place; most people loiter by the doorway.

Soul Café INTERNATIONAL €

(Map p68; ☎217 6986; www.soulcafe.hu; IX Ráday utca 11-13; mains 1800-3700Ft) One of the better choices along a street with about a million seemingly identical cafes with outdoor terraces, this one shines with its Italian-inspired menu (try the excellent pappardelle with porcini mushrooms), efficient service and great apple cake with mascarpone mousse.

Carmel Pince JEWISH €€

(Map p68; ☎322 1834; www.carmel.hu; VII Kazinczy utca 31; starters 1500-2800Ft, mains 3800-6000Ft; ⏰noon-11pm Sun-Fri, noon-2pm & 6-11pm Sat; 📶🅥; 🚌8, 112, 239, Ⓜ M2 Astoria, 🚋47, 49, 74) This bona fide glatt-kosher eatery, housed within a cavernous whitewashed interior that puts you in mind of a synagogue, serves hearty portions of authentic Ashkenazi specialities, such as gefilte fish, matzo ball soup, chopped chicken liver and *cholent* (hearty brisket and kugel dumpling casserole) that's almost as good as the one Aunt Goldie used to make!

Első Pesti Rétesház HUNGARIAN €

(Map p60; www.reteshaz.com; V Október 6 utca 22; strudel 360Ft; ⏰9am-11pm; 🚌15, 115, Ⓜ M3 Arany János utca) There are Hungarian mains on the menu as well, but the main reason to come to Strudel House is, of course, for the strudel – all 13 varieties of it. The fillings, wrapped in razor-thin filo pastry right in front of you, range from the classic poppy seed and cottage cheese with sour cherry to savoury cabbage.

Múzeum HUNGARIAN €€

(Map p68; ☎267 0375; www.muzeumkavehaz.hu; VIII Múzeum körút 12; mains 2800-6700Ft; ⏰6pm-midnight Mon-Sat) This is the place to come if you like to dine in old-world style, with a piano tinkling softly in the background. It's a venerable cafe-restaurant that is still going strong after over 125 years at the same location, near the Hungarian National Museum. The goose-liver dishes are to die for, and there's a good selection of Hungarian wines.

LaciPecsenye HUNGARIAN €€

(Map p60; ☎333 1717; www.lacipecsenye.eu; V Sas utca 11; mains 2800-4700Ft; ⏰noon-midnight) Inside this minimalist-chic bistro, the changing daily mains written on black slate are brought to you by unsmiling young staff in 'Who the **** is Laci?' T-shirts. Dishes are mostly for the carnivorously inclined and some are truly inspired, such as calamari stuffed with meat and anything with duck liver. Don't skip out on the pumpkin cake, either.

Spoon INTERNATIONAL €€€

(Map p68; ☎411 0933; www.spooncafe.hu; off V Vigadó tér 3; starters 2900-9900Ft, mains 2850-9850Ft; ⏰noon-midnight; 🅥; 🚋2) If you like the idea of dining on the high waters while tethered to the bank, Spoon's for you. Though the name suggests a liquid lunch (soup), international fusion dishes are served, such as veal cheeks with rosehip sauce and scallops with ginger-mango salsa, and some great vegetarian choices. You can't beat the views of the castle and Chain Bridge.

Buddha Bar ASIAN €€

(Map p68; ☎799 7300; www.buddhabarhotel.hu; V Váci utca 34; mains 3200-5400Ft; ⏰7pm-11pm Sun-Wed, to midnight Thu-Sat; Ⓜ M3 Ferenciek tere) It's difficult to say whether this is an Asian restaurant or a temple. The focal point in the dimmed lighting is a giant golden Buddha, the furnishings create the illusion of colonial opulence, the music is ambient lounge, and the menu stampedes from gyoza to sushi to tempura and Thai curry. The food's overpriced, but we love the ambience.

Nobu JAPANESE €€€

(Map p68; ☎429 4242; www.noburestaurants.com/budapest; V Erzsébet tér 7-8, Kempinski Hotel Corvinus; sashimi per piece 700-1400Ft; mains 4800-10,900Ft; ⏰noon-3pm & 6-11.45pm; Ⓜ M1 Vörösmarty tér) Unpretentious service, chilled beats and excellent sushi and sashimi define Budapest's Nobu branch. Unless you go for the Alaskan black cod (10,900Ft), all the bento boxes allow you to appreciate the chefs' skills without going bankrupt.

Iguana MEXICAN €€

(Map p60; ☎331 4352; www.iguana.hu; V Zoltán utca 16; mains 1790-4690Ft; ⏰11.30am-1am; 🅥; 🚌15, Ⓜ M2 Kossuth Lajos tér) Bustling Iguana serves decent-enough Tex-Mex food, so you'll find the usual suspects: nachos with guacamole, chilli con carne and tacos *al pastor* (with specially marinated pork). It's hard to say whether the pull is the enchilada and burrito combination *platos* (plates), the fajitas or the frenetic and boozy 'we-party-every-night' atmosphere provided by its colourful decor and canned music.

Café Kör INTERNATIONAL €

(Map p60; ☎311 0053; www.cafekor.com; V Sas utca 17; mains 1180-4290Ft; ⏰10am-10pm Mon-Sat; 🚌15 or 115, Ⓜ M3 Arany János) Just behind the Basilica of St Stephen, the 'Circle Café' is a long-standing favourite for lunch or dinner, but also a great place for a light meal at any time, including breakfast (150Ft to 790Ft), which is served till noon. Salads, desserts and daily specials are usually very good.

Trattoria Toscana ITALIAN €€
(Map p68; ☎327 0045; www.toscana.hu; V Belgrád rakpart 13; starters 1490-4590Ft, mains 2890-4990Ft; ⏲noon-midnight; 🖉; 🚌15, 115, 🚊2) Located beside the Danube, this trattoria serves rustic and very authentic Italian and Tuscan food, including *crema di fagioli* (a hearty soup of beans and fresh pasta) and a wonderful Tuscan farmer's platter of prepared meats. The pizza and pasta dishes are excellent too (try the spaghetti with garlic and Venus clams), as are the perfectly cooked risottos.

Bangkok THAI €€
(Map p68; ☎266 0584; www.thaietterem.hu; V Só utca 3; soups & starters 950-2190Ft, mains 1990-5390Ft; ⏲noon-11pm; 🖉; 🚊47, 49) Bangkok is done up in Asian-style kitsch that recalls takeaway places around the world. The Thai- and Laotian-inspired dishes are reasonably authentic though, and service is all but seamless. If you want your *tom yum* (hot-and-sour soup) properly spicy, speak up when ordering, and don't miss out on the caramel duck with bamboo.

Trófea Grill BUFFET €€
(Map p44; ☎270 0366; www.trofeagrill.hu; XIII Visegrádi utca 50/a; lunch weekdays/weekends 3899/5499Ft, dinner 5499Ft; ⏲noon-midnight Mon-Fri, 11.30am-midnight Sat, 11.30am-9pm Sun) This is the place to head when you really could eat a horse, as this all-you-can-eat has an enormous buffet of more than 100 cold and hot dishes, including plenty of meaty options. The price includes all-you-can-quaff draft beer, wine and soft drinks as well. There's also a Buda **branch** (Map p44; ☎438 9090; I Margit körút 2; lunch Mon-Fri 3399Ft, Sat & Sun 4999Ft, dinner Mon-Thu 4499Ft, Fri-Sun 4999Ft; 🚊4, 6), where the opening times are the same but the prices lower.

Hummus Bar MIDDLE EASTERN €
(Map p60; ☎302 1385; www.hummusbar.hu; V Alkotmány utca 20; dishes 900-1500Ft; ⏲11am-10pm Mon-Sat, noon-10pm Sun; 🖉; Ⓜ M2 Kossuth Lajos tér, M3 Nyugati pályaudvar) Branches of this popular Middle Eastern eatery are popping up all over town, and we are happy to recommend the vegie platters here in particular. Enjoy the hummus au naturel on pita or in a dish with accompaniments, and sample the mini-salads. If you're extra hungry, the *shakshuka* (aubergine with vegetable sauce and eggs) should do the trick.

🍷 Drinking

Budapest – and particularly Pest – is loaded with pubs and bars, and there are enough to satisfy all tastes. In summer the preferred drinking venues are the outdoor *kertek* ('garden' bars). The liveliest part of town is district VII, Erzsébetváros.

BUDA

Oscar American Bar BAR
(Map p36; ☎06 20 214 2525; www.oscarbar.hu; I Ostrom utca 14; ⏲5pm-2am Mon-Thu, to 4am Fri & Sat; Ⓜ M2 Széll Kálmán tér) The decor here is cinema-inspired – film memorabilia on the wood-panelled walls, the eponymous Oscar statue, leather directors' chairs – and the beautiful crowd often acts as though it's on camera. Not to worry, the potent cocktails, from daiquiris and cosmopolitans to mojitos, go down a treat. There's music most nights.

Café Ponyvaregény CAFE
(☎209 9580; www.cafeponyvaregeny.hu; XI Bercsényi utca 5; coffee 660-770Ft; ⏲10am-midnight Mon-Sat, 2-10pm Sun; 🚊18, 19, 47, 49) The 'Pulp Fiction' has become a bit of a cult hit with locals (not unlike the namesake film), thanks to its eclectic decor, great coffee and nice touches such as old books and fringed lampshades. In fact, it's become so popular they've had to open a second branch (www.cafeponyvaregeny.hu; XI Kopaszi gát).

Lánchíd Söröző BAR
(Map p36; ☎214 3144; www.lanchidsorozo.hu; I Fő utca 4; 🚌16, 86, 🚊19, 41) The 'Chain Bridge Pub', at the southern end of Fő utca, has a wonderful retro Magyar feel to it, with old movie posters and advertisements on the walls, red-checked cloths on the tables and plenty of *pálinka* on the drinks menu. Friendly service as well.

Tranzit Art Café CAFE
(www.tranzitcafe.com; XI Kosztolányi Dezső tér 7; lunch 1200Ft; ⏲9am-11pm Mon-Fri, 10am-10pm Sat & Sun) An abandoned bus station has been turned into a friendly cafe with artwork on walls, hammocks in the green courtyard to lie in while you sip your shake, plus good breakfasts (eggs, ciabatta) and two-course lunches. Occasional events include art exhibitions and live music.

Puskás Pancho BAR
(Map p44; 333 5656; www.symbolbudapest.hu; III Bécsi út 56; 11.30am-midnight; 86, 17) One of Buda's most popular sports pubs, themed after the Hungarian footballer nicknamed 'Pancho' in Spain, is part of the enormous Symbol complex in Óbuda. Football on the big screen and a mix of Spanish and Hungarian dishes complement each other nicely.

PEST

400 Bar CAFE, BAR
(Map p68; www.400bar.hu; VII Kazinczy utca 52; 11am-3am Mon-Wed & Sun, to 5am Thu-Sat) A large, popular cafe-bar with an attractive terrace, located in a pedestrian zone in the heart of the nightlife district. Great for coffee, cocktails, shooters and generally meeting new people.

Lukács Cukrászda CAFE
(Map p60; www.lukacscukraszda.com; VI Andrássy út 70; 9am-7.30pm) This cafe is dressed up in the finest of decadence, all mirrors and marble and gold, with soft piano music in the background. The selection of cakes (590Ft to 1320Ft) is excellent and all the tempting goodies are made from organic ingredients – a bonus!

Auguszt Cukrászda CAFE
(Map p68; www.augusztcukraszda.hu; V Kossuth Lajos utca 14-16; 10am-6pm Tue-Fri, from 9am Sat; 8, 112, 239, M2 Astoria, M3 Ferenciek tere) Not the original branch of the splendid 1870 institution, but the most central and convenient one. Take a seat within the opulent interior and choose one (or more!) of the delectable cakes on display (520Ft to 790Ft), washed down by a selection of loose-leaf or fresh herbal teas. Other branches are in Buda, west (XI Sasadi út 190; 59) and north (Map p36; II Fény utca 8; M2 Széll Kálmán tér) of Castle Hill, respectively.

Művész Kávéház CAFE
(Artist Coffeehouse; Map p60; 343 3544; www.muveszkavehaz.hu; VI Andrássy út 29; cakes 590-790Ft; 9am-10pm Mon-Sat, 10am-10pm Sun; M1 Opera) Almost opposite the State Opera House, this venerable coffee house (here since 1898) is an interesting place to people-watch – especially from the terrace – over a cup or two of cappucino art and a slice of decent cake.

1000 Tea TEAHOUSE
(Map p68; 337 8217; www.1000tea.hu; V Váci utca 65; noon-9pm Mon-Thu, noon-10pm Fri & Sat; 15, 115) In a small courtyard off lower Váci utca, this is the place if you want to sip a soothing blend made by tea-serious staff and lounge on pillows in a Japanese-style tearoom. We haven't tried counting (just to make sure there *are* 1000 teas), but the selection of loose-leaf black, green, yellow and white teas is vast.

Gerbeaud CAFE
(Map p68; 429 9000; www.gerbeaud.hu; V Vörösmarty tér 7; cakes from 750Ft; 9am-9pm; M1 Vörösmarty tér) Founded in 1858, Gerbeaud has been the most fashionable meeting place for the city's elite since 1870. Along with exquisitely prepared cakes and pastries, it serves Continental breakfast, sandwiches and some of the best ice-cream sundaes in town.

Centrál Kávéház COFFEE HOUSE
(Map p68; www.centralkavehaz.hu; V Károlyi Mihály utca 9; breakfast 1790-2190Ft; cakes 390-550Ft; 8am-11pm; 8, 112, 239, M2 Blaha Lujza tér, 4, 6) This grande dame, dating back to 1897, is still jostling to reclaim her title as *the* place to sit and look intellectual in Pest after reopening a few years ago following extensive renovations. It serves meals as well as lighter fare, such as sandwiches, and chef's specials such as 'Jewish egg'.

Innio WINE BAR
(Map p60; V Október 6 utca 9; 8am-midnight Sun-Thu, to 2am Fri & Sat; 15, 115, M1/M2/M3 Deák Tér) On weekends, you have to jostle Budapest's bold and beautiful just to get some elbow room inside this trendy bar. Perch on a stool and imbibe some Hungarian wine to a pounding electronica soundtrack, try some *pálinka* or else drop by on a weekday for a quiet lunch – this place does some imaginative salads and fusion mains.

Becketts Irish Bar BAR
(Map p60; 311 1035; www.becketts.hu; V Alkotmány utca 20; noon-1am Sun-Thu, to 2am Fri & Sat; M3 Nyugati pályaudvar, 4, 6) Of the capital's ubiquitous 'Irish' pubs, this is arguably the best (and definitely the largest) of the lot, with all-day Irish breakfasts (think English breakfast but with white pudding), a lively young crowd and football matches on the big screen.

DiVino Borbár WINE BAR
(Map p60; 06 70 935 3980; www.divinoborbar.hu; V Szent István tér 3; 4pm-midnight Sun-Wed, to 2am Thu-Sat) Central, free-flowing and always

heaving, DiVino is Budapest's most popular winebar and the crowds spilling out into the square in front of the basilica will tell you that immediately. The choice of wines (supposedly only from vintners aged under 35) at this self-service place is enormous; choose from scores at the bar but be careful: those 0.1L glasses (800Ft to 2000Ft) go down quickly.

Dobló WINE BAR
(Map p68; ☎06 20 398 8863; www.budapestwine.com; VII Dob utca 20; ⏰5pm-midnight Sun & Tue, to 3am Wed-Sat; 74) Brick-lined and candlelit, Dobló on Dob is where you go to taste Hungarian wines, with scores available by the 12.5cL glass for 900Ft to 1500Ft. Or do an organised tasting of five wines for 5850Ft (10,500Ft for nine sweet wines). There's useful blotter too – salads, sandwiches and mixed platters of meat or cheese (2500ft).

Boutiq' Bar COCKTAIL BAR
(Map p68; ☎06 30 229 1821; www.boutiqbar.hu; V Paulay Ede utca 5; ⏰6pm-2am Tue-Sat; Ⓜ M1 Bajcsy-Zsilinszky utca) Some may call this self-styled 'neo-speakeasy' pretentious (servers in penguin suits; reservations required), but the cocktail range is vast and uses quality alcohol and real fruit juice. Some, invented inhouse, are positively inspired: try the Scotland Yard (1650Ft), made with Ballantine's, honey, peach brandy and Angostura bitters.

Alexandra Book Cafe CAFE
(Map p60; VI Andrassy út 39; ⏰10am-10pm; Ⓜ M1 Oktogon, Opera, 🚊4, 6) Inside one of Budapest's best bookshops, this glitzy cafe in the revamped Ceremonial Hall shows off Károly Lutz frescoes and other touches of opulence. Great spot for a light lunch or coffee pre- or post-browse.

Hintaló BAR
(Map p68; www.hintaloiszoda.hu; VIII Bacsó Béla utca 15; ⏰3pm-1am Mon-Fri, 5pm-1am Sat; Ⓜ M2 Blaha Lujza tér, 🚊4, 6) The 'Rocking Horse' (with approporiate decor) is a two-story affair with Czech beers on tap, friendly bar staff whose eye you can actually catch and DJs some nights.

Kiadó Kocsma PUB
(Map p60; VI Jókai tér 3; ⏰10am-1am Mon-Fri, 11am-1am Sat & Sun) If you're wondering why the decor at this two-level pub – a student and boho refuge – is faux-Moorish upstairs and English-pub–esque downstairs, it's because two venues were originally combined. A great place for a swift pint, and while it's a stone's throw from the soulless watering holes around Liszt Ferenc tér, it's light-years ahead in attitude and presentation.

Macska BAR
(Map p48; VIII Bércoscis utca 23; ⏰4pm-1am Sun-Thu, to 2am Fri & Sat; Ⓜ M2 Blaha Lujza tér, 🚊4, 6) 'Cat' is a peculiar little cafe-bar, with vegie and vegan dishes on the menu, and, as befitting its name, felines in various guises as part of its eclectic decor. Chilled atmosphere and occasional DJ appearances.

☆ Entertainment

For a city of its size, Budapest has a huge choice of things to do and places to go after dark – from opera and (participatory) folk dancing to live jazz and pulsating clubs with some of the best DJs in central Europe.

Your best source of information in English about what's on in the city is the freebie **Budapest Funzine** (www.budapestfunzine.hu), available at hotels, bars, cinemas and wherever tourists congregate. The monthly freebie **Koncert Kalendárium** (www.koncertkalendarium.com) has more serious offerings, of classical concerts, opera, dance and the like.

Authentic *táncház*, literally 'dance house' but really folk-music workshops, are held at various locations throughout the week, but less frequently in summer. Very useful listings can be found on the **Dance House Guild** (www.tanchaz.hu) and **Folkrádió** (www.folkradio.hu) websites. The former also lists bands playing other types of traditional music, such as klezmer (Jewish folk music).

Nightclubs

Not all clubs and music bars in Budapest levy a cover charge, but those that do will ask for between 1500Ft and 3000Ft at the door. The trendier (and trashier) places usually let women in for free.

BOOKING AGENCIES

You can book almost anything online at www.jegymester.hu and www.kulturinfo.hu. Another useful booking agency is **Ticket Express** (Map p60; ☎030 303 0999; www.tex.hu; VI Andrássy út 18; ⏰10am-6.30pm Mon-Fri, to 3pm Sat), the largest ticket office network in the city.

THE RISE OF THE RUIN

A visit to the capital just isn't complete without a visit to a *romkocsma* ('pub in a ruin'), part of the exclusively Budapest phenomenon that kicked off around the year 2000. The idea was simple: find a ruin or abandoned building in downtown Pest, rent the cellar or ground floor, have some artist friends come round and paint murals – but don't fix it up too much, since the rough-around-the-edges atmosphere is part of the draw – get a band playing and the booze flowing, *et voilá*!

Since 2007, a related summer trend has taken off: the roof pub. It's a similar concept, only you rent out a rooftop rather than a cellar and turn it into a watering hole.

Another Budapest institution, especially during the long and hot summers, is the so-called *kertek*, literally 'gardens' – but in Budapest that can be any outdoor spot that has been converted into an entertainment zone, including courtyards and any available stretch along the river.

All three have a transient feel, as the venues (and their locations) can change from year to year and a definitive list is usually not available until spring. The best single source of information is **Caboodle** (www.caboodle.hu). While they may not last the distance from one year to the next, some of the more popular ones in recent years have been:

Corvintető (Map p68; 06 20 772 2984; www.corvinteto.com; VIII Blaha Lujza tér 1-2; 6pm-5am; M2 Blaha Lujza tér) An 'underground garden above the city', the first of the roof pubs, offering excellent concerts, a cocktail lounge and DJ nights on the rooftop of the former Corvin department store off Somogyi Béla utca.

Dürer Kert (Map p52; 06 1 789 4444; www.durerkert.com; XIV Ajtósi Dürer sor 19-21; 4pm-5am; 1, 74, 75) A very relaxed open space on the southwestern edge of City Park, boasting some of the best DJs on the 'garden' circuit. The garden is just lovely in summer.

Ötkert (Map p60; http://otkert.blogspot.com; V Zrínyi utca 4 ; noon-late Mon-Sat; 15, 115, 2) Edgy urban design? Check. Courtyard full of revellers? Check. Not your typical 'pub in a ruin', this is the trend's latest incarnation, a trendy nightspot made to look a bit rough, but with more upmarket clientele.

Kuplung (Map p60; www.kuplung.net; VI Király utca 46; 5pm-4am Mon-Sat, 6pm-4am Sun; M1 Opera) Grease monkeys, ahoy! A former garage, gritty and grimy on the outside, the 'Klutch' established itself as one of the most happening places in town, with DJs, live acts and, for the more dextrous in the audience, table tennis and table football.

Fogasház (Map p60; www.fogashaz.hu; VII Akácfa utca 51; 10am-4am; 923, M1 Opera, Oktogon, 4, 6) The atmospheric courtyard here heaves with revellers in search of a drink, a DJ set or just a sit-around with 10 of their closest friends.

Szimpla Kert (Map p68; 352 4198; www.szimpla.hu; VII Kazinczy 14; noon-3am; 74) The oldest of the ruin pubs, Szimpla has 'winterised' (sort of) and opens year-round. Think brick walls, industrial decor, and a lively drinking scene.

Instant The wackiest of them all, with psychedelic decor and a non-stop party on several floors. Words don't do it justice!

TOP CHOICE **Cinetrip** CLUB

(Map p68; www.cinetrip.hu; Rudas Baths; admission from 8000Ft; 10pm-3.30am Sat; 7, 86, 18, 19) This is an only-in-Budapest kind of experience that combines dancing, a sound-and-light show, acrobatics and bathing, and certainly gives a new meaning to 'wet 'n' wild'! The current location is Rudas Baths, and if there's an event happening there while you're in town it's not to be missed. Check website for schedules.

Instant CLUB

(Map p60; 06 30 830 8747; www.instant.co.hu; VI Nagymező utca 38; 1pm-3am; M1 Opera, 70, 78) We love, love, love this 'rubble bar' on Pest's most vibrant nightlife strip. Also known as the Enchanted Forest, its decor is something like Alice in Wonderland on some serious 'shrooms, and you really have to go there to see what it's like for yourself. It has six bars, three dance floors and two garden spaces for bopping, relaxing and chilling. If you want a taste of things to come and can't wait till lunchtime, head for the ground-floor coffee shop (open 8am to 10pm).

Cinema Hall CLUB

(Map p44; www.cinemahall.hu; III Bécsi út 38-44; 9pm-6am Fri & Sat; 17, HÉV Szépvölgyi út) Despite the name, don't expect any movie screenings here. This enormous nightspot is divided into four distinct areas, hosting big-name DJs and other live acts. It's in Óbuda, but well worth getting out to if you want to party until dawn; the enormous dance floor really gets jumping in the wee hours. Take the HEV train to the Szépvölgyi út stop, then walk three blocks west to Kolosy tér. It's on the west side of the square.

Morrison's 2 CLUB

(Map p60; 374 3329; www.morrisons.hu; V Szent István körút 11; 5pm-4am Mon-Sat) One of Budapest's biggest party venues, this cavernous cellar club attracts a student crowd every night of the week except Sunday, with its four dance floors, half-dozen bars (including one in a covered courtyard) and nice little enticements such as free beer and free entry for blondes (on certain nights). Expect DJs, karaoke, funk, house and retro hits, fuelled with plenty of cheap booze.

Gay & Lesbian Venues

There are no specific girl bars in Budapest, though Eklektika Restolounge might fit the bill.

Club AlterEgo GAY

(Map p60; www.alteregoclub.hu; VI Dessewffy utca 33; 10pm-6am Fri & Sat) Budapest's premier gay club, with the most chic (think attitude) crowd and best dance music.

Action Bar BAR

(Map p68; 266 9148; www.action.gay.hu; V Magyar utca 42; admission 1000Ft; 9pm-4am; 909, 914, 979, M3 Kálvin tér) Action is the bustling cellar bar to head to if you want just that. With a strip show on Friday nights, 'oral academy' on Saturdays, events such as 'bear club', and toilets with see-through walls, you know what to expect.

Coxx Men's Bar BAR

(Map p68; 344 4884; www.coxx.hu; VII Dohány utca 38; 9pm-4am Sun-Thu, to 5am Fri & Sat; 7, M2 Astoria, 47, 49) Probably the cruisiest game in town, this boldly named meet/meat rack has a long, brick-lined cellar bar and some significant play areas in the back featuring slings, wet rooms and more. You might soon find yourself 'behind bars' in more ways than one.

Chicken Exit MUSIC

(www.facebook.com/chickenexit) Themed indie, indie rock, synthpop, thrash and other music parties for a young lesbian, bisexual, bicurious and gay crowd at different locations around the city. Friendly vibe.

Funny Carrot BAR

(Map p68; www.funnycarrot.hu; V Szép utca 1/b; 7pm-6am; 7, 8, 78, 908, 921, M2 Astoria, M3 Ferenciek tere, 47, 49) Cavernous decor and comfy lounge seats at this laidback gay bar are perfect for a quiet tête-a-tête. Try not to snigger at the name.

Le Cafe-Mystery BAR

(Map p60; 06 30 350 0253; www.mysterybar.hu; V Nagysándor József utca 3; 4pm-2am; ; M3 Arany János utca) The original neighbourhood gay bar in the city has changed its name (and decor) a couple of times, but it's still a friendly little place where you can nurse your cocktail and hook your laptop up to the projector if you so desire.

Eklektika Restolounge LESBIAN

(Map p68; www.eklektika.hu; VI Nagymező utca 30; noon-midnight) There are no specifically lesbian bars in town that we know about, but this chilled-out eatery/bakery and lounge is probably the closest you're gonna get. It has a completely new look but the same ol' friendly vibe and gay-friendly crowd.

Live Music

TOP CHOICE **A38** LIVE MUSIC

(A38 Ship; 464 3940; www.a38.hu; XI Pázmány Péter sétány 3-11; 11am-4pm, terraces 4pm-4am Tue-Sat; 906, 4, 6) Moored on the Buda side just south of Petőfi Bridge, the A38 is a decommissioned Ukrainian stone hauler ship from 1968 that has been recycled as a major live-music venue. The combination of great live bands, its bar and the location have seen it named 'best bar in the world', according to Lonely Planet's 2012 poll. Who are we to argue?

TOP CHOICE **Pótkulcs** LIVE MUSIC

(Map p60; 269 1050; www.potkulcs.hu; VI Csengery utca 65/b; 5pm-1.30am Sun-Wed, 5pm-2.30am Thu-Sat; M3 Nyugati pályaudvar) You can't really pigeonhole the 'Spare Key' – this terrific little venue's menu of music spans from klezmer (Jewish folk music), Afro rock and reggae to 'well-hung folk music'. Live performances Tuesday to Saturday; other nights, you can cosy up on the sofas or trawl through the bar's vast selection of beers and spirits.

Szikra Cool Tour House LIVE MUSIC
(Map p60; www.szikra.eu; IV Bajcsy-Zsilinszky utca 31; ⏲9am-2am Mon-Thu, to 6am Fri, 10am-6am Sat, to 2am Sun; MM3 Arany János utca) Having relocated to new premises, the 'Spark' (*szikra* in Hungarian) culture centre continues to draw a diverse young crowd with equally diverse offerings, from DJ nights and other live acts to salsa nights and film screenings.

Jedermann LIVE MUSIC
(Map p68; www.jedermannkavezo.blogspot.com; XI Ráday utca 58; ⏲8am-1am) This very mellow spot attached to the Goethe Institute and decorated with jazz posters fills up with students and intellectuals, who come for the great lunches and brunches or just to read a book or chat to the friendly Dutch owner. Jazz gigs most nights, and in summer the courtyard terrace out back is a pleasant refuge.

Rocktogon Pub & Roll LIVE MUSIC
(Map p60; www.rocktogon.hu; VI Moszár utca 9; MM1 Oktogon) With a name like this, it's little surprise that the Rocktogon hosts AC/DC and Motörhead tribute bands alongside the odd DJ performance. The crowd tends to be young, energetic and with a preference for heavy make-up, piercings and dark colours. A lively bar.

Budapest Sportaréna LIVE MUSIC
(☎422 2682; www.budapestarena.hu; XIV Stefánia út 2; ⏲box office 9am-6pm Mon-Fri; MM2 Stadionok) This purpose-built 12,500-seat arena, named after local pugilist László Papp, is where big local and international acts (Muse, Beyoncé etc) perform.

Pecsa Music Hall LIVE MUSIC
(Map p52; ☎848 0206; www.petoficsarnok.hu; XIV Zichy Mihály út 14; MM1 Széchenyi fürdő, 72, 74) In the southeast corner of City Park, Pecsa Music Hall plays host to local and international rock, blues and metal gigs, with the venue intimate enough for you to be sprinkled with the guitarists' sweat in the mosh pit on rowdier nights. Intense!

Columbus LIVE MUSIC
(Map p68; ☎266 9013; www.columbuspub.hu; V Vigadó tér, Pier no. 4; ⏲noon-midnight; 2) This boat-cum-jazz-club, moored in the Danube just off the northern end of V Vigadó tér, hosts live big-name local and international acts nightly and salsa nights most Fridays, with the gentle movement of the boat adding a bit of spice to the dancing. Music starts at 8pm.

Nothin' But The Blues BLUES, JAZZ
(Map p68; ☎06 20 322 8602; www.bluespub.hu; VIII Krúdy Gyula utca 6; ⏲11am-midnight Mon-Wed, to 4am Thu-Sat; 47, 49) The oldest blues venue in town, NBB has been wailing for around two decades. The name may be accurate Thursday to Saturday from about 7.30pm, when there's usually a live guitarist, but acts vary the rest of the week.

Aranytíz Cultural Centre TRADITIONAL MUSIC
(Aranytíz Művelődési Központ; Map p60; ☎354 3400; www.aranytiz.hu; V Arany János utca 10; ⏲bookings 2-9pm Mon & Wed, 9am-3pm Sat) At this cultural centre in the north of the Inner Town, you'll find performances by various folk groups as well as the occasional salsa night.

Pántlika BAR, CLUB
(Map p52; www.pantlika.hu; XIV Városligeti körút; ⏲noon-midnight; 1, 1/a, 72, 74) A communist-era kiosk crammed with retro memorabilia and with an incredible selection of *pálinka*. The hearty Hungarian food coming from the kitchen fuels the action on the outdoor terrace. Eclectic DJ sets some nights.

Most! LIVE MUSIC
(Map p60; www.mostjelen.blogspot.com; VI Zichy Jenő utca 17; ⏲11am-2am Mon & Tue, to 4am Wed-Fri, 4pm-4am Sat, 4pm-2am Sun) This eclectic bar-cafe-performance space with roof terrace wears many hats. *Most!* means 'Now!' and it's at its best when local pop and rock acts take to the stage, or when decent local DJs are spinning a set.

Duna Palota CLASSICAL MUSIC
(Danube Palace; Map p60; ☎235 5500; www.dunapalota.hu; V Zrínyi utca 5; tickets 3000-10,500Ft; 15, 115) The elaborate 'Danube Palace' hosts cultural perfomances, including light classical music concerts and folk music, throughout the week from May to October.

Hungarian State Opera House OPERA
(Magyar Állami Operaház; Map p60; ☎bookings 814 7225; www.opera.hu; VI Andrássy út 22) The opera house is home both to the state opera company and the Hungarian National Ballet, and is said to have the third-best acoustics

in Europe after Milan's La Scala and the Opéra Garnier in Paris. Worth visiting at least once, to admire the incredibly richly decorated interior as much as to view a performance. Black tie not necessary – dress code for a night at the opera here is relaxed.

Budapest Operetta OPERA
(Budapesti Operettszínház; Map p60; ☎bookings 312 4866; www.operettszinhaz.hu; VI Nagymező utca 17; tickets 1000-15,000Ft; ⊙bookings 10am-7pm Mon-Fri, 1-7pm Sat & Sun; MM1 Opera) This theatre presents operettas, which are always a riot – especially campy ones such as *The Gypsy Princess* by Imre Kálmán – with their over-the-top staging and costumes. There's an interesting bronze statue of the composer outside the main entrance.

Palace of Arts MUSIC, DANCE
(Művészetek Palotája; Map p48; ☎bookings 555 3300, info 555 3001; www.mupa.hu; IX Komor Marcell utca 1; tickets 1000-5000Ft; ⊙bookings 10am-6pm; 2) The main concert halls at this palatial arts centre alongside the Danube and just opposite the National Theatre are the 1700-seat Béla Bartók National Concert Hall and the smaller Festival Theatre accommodating up to 450 people. Both are purported to have the best acoustics in Budapest and are great places to see anything from *Madame Butterfly* to *ABBA – The Show*.

Dance

There are several excellent options for modern dance fans, including **Mu Színház** (☎209 4014; www.mu.hu; XI Kőrösy József utca 17; tickets about 2000Ft; 4) in south Buda, where virtually everyone involved in Hungarian dance got their start.

National Dance Theatre DANCE
(Nemzeti Táncszínház; Map p36; ☎201 4407, bookings 1-375 8649; www.nemzetitancszinhaz.hu; I Színház utca 1-3; tickets 2200-5000Ft; ⊙bookings 10am-6pm Mon-Thu, to 5pm Fri; 16, 16/a, 116) The only 18th century building in town to still function as a theatre hosts ballet, international acts, modern dance, folk dance and more, including the **Hungarian National Ballet** (www.opera.hu) and **Budapest Dance Theatre** (www.budapestdancetheatre.hu), one of the most exciting contemporary troupes in the city.

Trafó House of Contemporary Arts DANCE
(Trafó Kortárs Művészetek Háza; Map p48; ☎bookings 215 1600; www.trafo.hu; IX Liliom utca 41; tickets 1000-3500Ft; ⊙bookings 4-8pm; MM3 Ferenc körút) This stage in Ferencváros presents the cream of the crop of dance, acrobatics and

ROMA'S BUDAPEST BREAKTHROUGHS

The Roma people have lived in Hungary since the 14th century; now, as then, they are the poorest, most marginalised part of Hungarian society, facing widespread discrimination and occasional attacks from neo-fascist groups such as Véderő.

Nevertheless, some positives are emerging. As part of the Decade of Roma Inclusion 2005–2015 – a political commitment made by the governments of 12 European countries with large Roma populations (including Romania, Hungary, Croatia and Spain) to improve the socio-economic status and social inclusion of Roma – several projects have been set up. One has been the **Chachipe Map** (www.chachipe.org) international photo contest, displayed at the time of writing in Budapest's Szabadsag tér, featuring Roma and non-Roma living side by side. Alternately touching (a boy dressed as Michael Jackson dancing in a ruined building) and harrowing (a wary little girl in the town of Gyöngyöspata, where a neo-fascist group set up camp to intimidate the locals), these images are helping to raise awareness in the capital about the Roma people and their contribution to Hungarian society.

Budapest's Citibank Citi Service Centre headquarters are also displaying paintings by talented Roma artists, including the internationally renowned Tibor Balogh, an orphan and the first Roma to be admitted to the Hungarian Academy of Fine Arts, whose bold, sometimes provocative work has appeared in Venice and beyond.

The Romani Design (p85) cooperative, established in 2009, is making inroads into Budapest's fashion scene, using traditional designs and contemporary methods to produce vibrant, colourful clothing, jewellery and accessories. Workshops are periodically held to pass skills on to young Roma fashion designers.

music such as hip hop and blues, including international acts.

Buda Concert Hall — DANCE

(Budai Vigadó; Map p36; ☎225 6049; www.hagyomanyokhaza.hu; I Corvin tér 8; 86, M2 Batthyány tér, 19, 41) The 30 artistes of the Hungarian State Folk Ensemble (Magyar Állami Népi Együttes) perform at Buda Concert Hall on Tuesday and Thursday from May to early October, with occasional performances the rest of the year.

Theatre

International Buda Stage — THEATRE

(IBS; ☎391 2525; www.ibsszinpad.hu; II Tárogató út 2-4; tickets free-3200Ft; bookings 10am-6pm Mon-Fri; 29, 61) Found on the way to the Buda Hills, the theatre at the International Business School has occasional performances – often comedies – in English, as well as folk theatre and dance.

National Theatre — THEATRE

(Nemzeti Színház; Map p48; ☎bookings 476 6868; www.nemzetiszinhaz.hu; IX Bajor Gizi park 1; tickets 1200-4000Ft; bookings 10am-6pm Mon-Fri, 2-6pm Sat ; 2) This rather eclectic venue is the place to go if you want to brave a play in Hungarian (including Shakespeare's works) or just go to check out the bizarre and very controversial venue, built in 2002 according to the designs of Mária Siklós.

Budapest Puppet Theatre — THEATRE

(Budapest Bábszínház; Map p60; ☎bookings 342 2702; www.budapest-babszinhaz.hu; VI Andrássy út 69; tickets 800-1800Ft; M1 Vörösmarty utca) The puppet theatre usually doesn't require fluency in Hungarian for its shows, designed for children (such as *Puss in Boots*) and performed in daytime hours. Consult the website for program schedules.

Cinema

A couple of dozen cinemas screen English-language films with Hungarian subtitles. Check out the film listings in the *Budapest Funzine* (p79). Watch out for 'm.f.', meaning the film is dubbed into Hungarian. Tickets cost between 850Ft and 1970Ft.

Kino — CINEMA

(Map p60; ☎950 6846; www.akino.hu; XIII Szent István körút 16; 4, 6) Formerly the Szindbád cinema, named after the seminal (and eponymous) 1971 film by director Zoltán Huszárik and based on the novel by Gyula Krúdy, this revamped movie house shows good Hungarian and foreign films with subtitles. Internationally themed film festivals are also held.

Cinema City MOM Park — CINEMA

(☎999 6161; www.cinemacity.hu; XII Alkotás út 53; 61) The only multiplex cinema in the city to show blockbusters both in their original language and with subtitles.

Örökmozgó — CINEMA

(Map p60; ☎342 2167; www.filmarchive.hu; VII Erzsébet körút 39; 4, 6) Part of the Hungarian Film Institute, this cinema (whose name vaguely translates as 'moving picture') screens an excellent assortment of foreign classic films in their original languages.

Circus

Municipal Great Circus — CIRCUS

(Fővárosi Nagycirkusz; Map p52; ☎343 9630; www.circus.hu; XIV Állatkerti körút 7; adult 1900-3900Ft, senior 1700-2900Ft, child 1500-2700Ft; performances 3pm daily plus 11am & 7pm Sat, 11am Sun; M1 Széchenyi fürdő) Europe's only permanent big top has everything one would expect from a circus, including acrobats, daredevils on horseback, performing parrots and ice shows in season.

Shopping

Budapest is a great place to satisfy the urge to buy. Some people consider the city's flea markets the highlight – not just as places to indulge their vice, but as the consummate Budapest experience. Shops are generally open from 9am or 10am to 6pm during the week and till 1pm on Saturday.

TOP CHOICE Ecseri Piac — MARKET

(XIX Nagykőrösi út 156; 6am-4pm Mon-Fri, to 3pm Sat, 8am-1pm Sun) One of the biggest flea markets in Central Europe, selling everything from antique jewellery and Soviet army watches to Fred Astaire–style top hats. Saturday is said to be the best day to go; dealers get here early for diamonds amid the rust. Take bus 54 from Boráros tér in Pest or, for a quicker journey, the red-numbered express bus 84E, 89E or 94E from the Határ utca stop on the M3 metro line and get off at the Fiume utca stop. Then follow the crowds over the pedestrian bridge.

Matyó Design — FASHION

(Map p44; ☎06 20 453 1137, 06 20 327 6875; www.matyodesign.hu; XIII Radnóti Miklós utca 25, 2nd fl; 75, 76) This is one of those companies that makes you wonder why someone didn't think of it before... Two sisters who grew up in a small village near Mezőkövesd in northern Hungary have taken the Matyó needlework famous in that area and put a new spin on it. Goodbye, voluminous skirts and heavy vests embellished with embroidery; hello, jeans, T-shirts and other contemporary apparel, as well as baby clothes. Stunning stuff.

Magma HOMEWARES
(Map p68; ☎235 0277; www.magma.hu; V Petőfi Sándor utca 11; ⏰10am-7pm Mon-Fri, to 3pm Sat; Ⓜ M3 Ferenciek tere) This excellent showroom in the heart of the Inner Town focuses exclusively on Hungarian design and talented designers, with everything from glassware and porcelain to textiles and furniture, offering unique gift ideas.

Báv ANTIQUES
(Bizományi Kereskedőház és Záloghitel; Map p60; www.bav.hu; XIII Szent István körút 3; ⏰10am-6pm Mon-Fri, to 2pm Sat; 🚋4, 6) This chain of pawn and secondhand shops, with a number of branches around town, is always a fun place to comb for trinkets and treasures, especially if you don't have time to get to the flea markets. Check out this branch for chinaware, textiles and furniture. Other stores include the **Belváros branch** (Map p68; ☎429 3020; V Bécsi utca 1-3; M1/2/3 Deák Ferenc tér) for knickknacks, porcelain, glassware and artwork, and the **Buda branch** (Map p44; ☎315 0417; II Frankel Leó utca 13 & II Margit körút 4; 🚋4, 6) for jewellery, lamps and fine porcelain.

Intuita HANDICRAFTS
(Map p68; www.intuitashop.com; V Váci utca 67; ⏰10am-6pm Mon-Fri, to 4pm Sat; 🚋2, 2/a) You're not about to find painted eggs and *pálinka* here, but rather one-of-a-kind, modern Hungarian crafted items such as hand-blown glass, jewellery, ceramics and bound books. Great gift ideas. There's a second branch a couple of doors down at Váci utca 61.

Romani Design FASHION, CLOTHING
(Map p68; www.romani.hu; VII Akácfa utca 20; ⏰10am-6pm Mon-Fri; Ⓜ M2 Blaha Lujza tér, 🚋4, 6) Roma-designed clothing (mostly for women), jewellery and accessories – brightly coloured and theatrical, as one would expect. Designer Erica Varga's jewellery (mostly silver) and clothing incorporate good-luck motifs such as the four-leaf clover, horseshoe and lentils. That's right, lentils!

Haas & Czjzek PORCELAIN, GLASS
(Map p60; ☎302 2820; www.porcelan.hu; VI Bajcsy-Zsilinszky út 23; ⏰10am-7pm Mon-Fri, to 3pm Sat; Ⓜ M3 Arany János utca) Just up from Deák Ferenc tér, this chinaware and crystal shop, here since 1879, sells Herend and Zsolnay porcelain as well as more affordable, Hungarian-made Hollóháza and Alföldi pieces.

Herend Village Pottery PORCELAIN, HOMEWARES
(Map p36; ☎356 7899; www.herendimajolika.hu; II Bem rakpart 37; ⏰9am-5pm Tue-Fri, to noon Sat; Ⓜ M2 Batthyány tér, 🚋19, 41) An alternative to what some might consider overwrought Herend porcelain is the hardwearing Herend pottery and dishes decorated with bold fruit patterns sold here. You can also enter from II Fő utca 61.

THREE FOR THE CATWALK...KIND OF

Budapest – and Hungary in general – is brimming with creative fashion talent. Here are three places to pick some local designer creations:

Mono Fashion (Map p68; www.monofashion.hu; V Kossuth Lajos utca 20; ⏰11am-8pm Mon-Fri, 10am-6pm Sat; Ⓜ M2 Astoria, 🚋47, 49) The best creations by young designers such as Nanushka, USE, Je Suis Belle and Tank Theory, ranging from casual streetwear to elegant attire. Stocks its own NUBU clothing line for men and women, and works by contemporary artists.

Kamchatka Design (Map p68; www.kamchatkedesign.com; V Nyári Pál utca 7; ⏰noon-6pm Mon-Fri, 10am-2pm Sat; Ⓜ M3 Ferenciek tere, 🚋2, 2/a) Stylish, casual women's wear, locally designed and made by Márta Schulteisz. Some lovely accessories, too.

Cancan (Map p60; www.cancan.hu; VI Nagymező utca 6; ⏰10am-7pm Mon-Fri, to 4pm Sat; Ⓜ M1 Opera) Designer bikinis, tankinis and men's swimwear (by non-Hungarian names), as well as fabulous women's underwear and accessories by **Suck Right!** (www.suckright.co.hu) designer Viktória Csepleő, which is rather like Alice in Wonderland meets Morticia Addams.

Originart HANDICRAFTS
(Map p60; www.originart.hu; V Arany János utca 18; ⌚10am-6pm Mon-Sat; 🚌15, 115, Ⓜ M3 Arany János utca) Hungarian handicrafts guaranteed to put a smile on your face, from brightly painted ceramic figures and ceramics in general to jewellery boxes, mugs and acrylic paintings. All very playful and with kiddie appeal.

Bestsellers BOOKS
(Map p60; www.bestsellers.hu; V Október 6 utca 11; ⌚9am-6.30pm Mon-Fri, 10am-5pm Sat, 10am-4pm Sun) Probably the best English-language bookshop in town, with fiction, travel guides and lots of Hungarica, as well as a large selection of newspapers and magazines, Hungarian literature translated into English, plus helpful staff.

Nagycsarnok MARKET
(Great Market; Map p68; IX Vámház körút 1-3; ⌚9am-6pm Mon-Sat) This is Budapest's biggest market, though it has become a tourist magnet since its renovation for the Millecentenary celebrations in 1996. Still, plenty of locals head here for fruit, vegetables, deli items, fish and meat, and it's a fantastic place to pick up local salamis, cheeses, paprika, foie gras and garlands of dried peppers and garlic to give your kitchen that Hungarian touch.

Bortársaság WINE
(Map p36; ☎212 2569; www.bortarsasag.hu; I Batthyány utca 59; ⌚10am-7pm Mon-Fri, to 6pm Sat) Once known as the Budapest Wine Society, this place has a half-dozen retail outlets with an exceptional selection of Hungarian wines. No one, but no one, knows Hungarian wines like these people do. Central for Pest is the **Basilica branch** (Map p60; ☎328 0341; V Szent István tér 3; ⌚noon-8pm Mon-Fri, 10am-4pm Sat; M3 Arany János utca).

Magyar Pálinka Háza DRINK
(Hungarian Pálinka House; Map p68; ☎06 30 421 5463; www.magyarpalinkahaza.hu; VIII Rákóczi út 17; ⌚9am-7pm Mon-Sat) If you've discovered that *pálinka,* a kind of eau-de-vie flavoured with fruits and berries, is your poison, this large shop a short distance from Astoria stocks hundreds of varieties to take home with you.

Treehugger Dan's Bookstore BOOKS
(Map p60; www.treehuggerdans.com; VI Lázár utca 16; ⌚10am-6pm Mon-Fri, to 4pm Sat) A hugely popular second-hand business with thousands of English-language books in large new premises, Treehugger Dan's accepts trade-ins and serves organic fair-trade coffee.

Information

Dangers & Annoyances

No parts of Budapest are 'off limits' to visitors, although some locals now avoid Margaret Island after dark during the low season, and both residents and visitors give the dodgier parts of the VIII and IX districts (areas of prostitution) a wide berth.

Pickpocketing is most common in markets, the Castle District, Váci utca and Hősök tere, near major hotels and on certain popular buses (such as 7) and trams (2, 4, 6, 47 and 49), though opportunistic pickpocketing can occur on any form of public transport, particularly during rush hour.

Taking a taxi in Budapest can be an expensive and even unpleasant experience.

If you've left something on any form of public transport in Budapest, contact the **BKV Lost**

SCAMS

There are a number of scams common to Budapest, and we're told they've been on the rise.

» Scams involving attractive young women, gullible guys, expensive drinks in nightclubs and then a frog-marching to the nearest ATM by gorillas-in-residence have been all the rage in Budapest for well over a decade. Guys, please, do yourself a favour – if it seems too good to be true, it is.

» Taxi drivers are known for overcharging and taking advantage of passengers unfamiliar with local currency by switching large-denomination notes for smaller ones and demanding extra payment. Only ever take taxis from reputable companies and make sure you know exactly how much cash you're handing over.

» Some travellers in Budapest have complained of men in fake policemen's uniforms demanding to see tourists' passports and money, ostensibly to check for fraudulent notes. They then either run away with the money or switch large-denomination notes for small ones.

& Found Office (Map p68; ☎461 6688; VII Akácfa utca 18; ⏰8am-5pm Mon-Fri; Ⓜ M2 Blaha Lujza tér).

Discount Cards

Budapest Card (www.budapestinfo.hu; 24/48/72hr card 3900/9900/7900Ft) This card, valid for one, two or three days, offers discounted admission to 60 museums and other sights, unlimited travel on all forms of public transport, and discounts for organised tours, car rental, thermal baths and at selected shops and restaurants. The 48-hour card is more expensive than the 72-hour because it offers free rides on the Giragge Hop-On/Hop-Off bus and a river cruise. Unless you're planning on seeing most of the sights in the booklet you get with the cards, the value they represent isn't that great, since most of the discounts on attractions are 10% to 30%. Available at Tourinform offices, travel agencies, hotels, the airport and main metro stations, and online.

Emergency

If you need to report a crime, or a lost or stolen passport or credit card, first call the **central emergency number** (☎112), the **police** (☎107) or the **English-language crime hotline** (☎438 8080; ⏰8am-8pm). Any crime must then be reported at the police station of the district you're in. In central Pest that's the **Belváros-Lipótváros Police Station** (Map p60; ☎373 1000; V Szalay utca 11-13; Ⓜ M2 Kossuth Lajos tér).

Internet Access

More and more cafes, restaurants and bars are offering free wi-fi to paying customers, as a result of which internet cafes are rapidly becoming obsolete. All the accommodation options reviewed in this chapter also offer internet access and/or wi-fi, which is free in most cases (though not in some upmarket lodgings). Tourinform offers internet access for 150Ft per 15 minutes, and there are a number of internet cafes in town, but some tend to open and close at a rapid rate.

Fougou (VII Wesselenyi utca 57; 200Ft/hour; ⏰7am-2am; Ⓜ M2 Blaha Lujza tér, 🚋4, 6) Large internet cafe with a call centre attached.

Internet Buda (II Margit körút 15-17; 200Ft/hour; ⏰8am-midnight; 🚋4, 6) Large internet cafe with photocopying and other services available.

Internet Resources

Budapest Tourism Office (www.budapestinfo.hu) Budapest's best overall website.

Caboodle (www.caboodle.hu) Hungary's best English-language portal, with daily news, features and events, plus links to, among other sites, Politics.hu and the incomparable Pestiside.hu (subtitled 'The Daily Dish of Cosmopolitan Budapest').

Xpat Loop (www.xpatloop.com) Website aimed at Budapest's expat community, with opinion pieces and plenty of dining and entertainment listings.

Budapest Sun Online (www.budapestsun.com) Popular English weekly, with local news, interviews and listings.

Left Luggage

Budapest's three major train stations and two bus stations all have left-luggage offices and/or lockers.

Medical Services

Consultation and treatment in private clinics doesn't come cheap in Budapest, so make sure your travel insurance covers you. Dental treatment, on the other hand, is both good and inexpensive by European standards.

CLINICS

FirstMed Centers (☎24hr emergency hotline 224 9090; www.firstmedcenters.com; I Hattyú utca 14, 5th fl; ⏰8am-8pm Mon-Fri, to 2pm Sat) This private medical and dental clinic has round-the-clock emergency treatment that is as expensive as you'll find in Europe (a basic consultation for 10 to 20 minutes costs from 19,200Ft to 38,200Ft.

SOS Dent (☎269 6010; www.smilistic.com; VI Király utca 14; ⏰24hr) Consultations at this dental surgery are free (8am to 8pm), with extractions costing from €31 to €38, fillings from €46 and crowns from €120.

PHARMACIES

Each of Budapest's 23 districts has a rostered all-night pharmacy; a sign on the door of any pharmacy will help you locate the nearest 24-hour one. There are conveniently located pharmacies in the city centre.

Déli Gyógyszertár (☎355 4691; XII Alkotás utca 1/b; ⏰7am-8pm Mon-Fri, to 2pm Sat; Ⓜ M2 Déli pályaudvar)

WANT MORE?

For in-depth information, reviews and recommendations at your fingertips, head to the Apple App Store to purchase Lonely Planet's *Budapest City Guide* iPhone app.

Alternatively, head to **Lonely Planet** (www.lonelyplanet.com/hungary/budapest) for planning advice, author recommendations, traveller reviews and insider tips.

Teréz Gyógyszertár (☎311 4439; VI Teréz körút 4; ⌚8am-8pm Mon-Fri, to 2pm Sat)

Money

There are ATMs everywhere in Budapest, including in the train and bus stations and at airport terminals. ATMs at branches of OTP (the national savings bank) dish out difficult-to-break 20,000Ft notes. Money changers (particularly those along V Váci utca) don't tend to give good rates, so go to a bank instead if possible.

K&H Bank (V Deák Ferenc utca 1; ⌚8am-5pm Mon, to 4pm Tue-Thu, to 3pm Fri; ⓂM1 Vörösmarty tér) Conveniently located on the main shopping drag.

OTP Bank (V Deák Ferenc utca 7-9; ⌚8am-6pm Mon, to 5pm Tue-Thu, to 4pm Fri; ⓂM1 Vörösmarty tér) The National Savings Bank offers among the best exchange rates for cash and travellers cheques.

Post

Main Post Office (Map p68; V Bajcsy-Zsilinsky út 16, Belváros main post office; ⌚8am-8pm Mon-Fri, to 2pm Sat; ⓂM1 Bajcsy-Zsilinsky utca)

Nyugati Train Station Branch (Map p60; VI Teréz körút 51-53, Nyugati train station; ⌚7am-8pm Mon-Fri, 8am-6pm Sat; ⓂM3 Nyugati pályaudvar)

Keleti Train Station Branch (Map p52; VIII Kerepesi út 2-6, Keleti train station; ⌚7am-9pm Mon-Fri, 8am-2pm Sat; ⓂM2 Keleti pályaudvar)

Telephone

If you're going to spend more than just a few days in Budapest and expect to use your phone quite a bit, consider buying a rechargeable SIM chip, which may reduce the cost of making local calls (but for a European mobile, check with your service provider as you may get an even better deal with them).

Telenor (www.telenor.hu; II Lövőház utca 2-6, Mammut I, 2nd floor; ⌚9am-8pm Mon-Sat, to 6pm Sun; ⓂM2 Széll Kálmán tér, 🚊4, 6)

T-Mobile (www.t-mobile.hu; V Petőfi Sándor utca 12; ⌚9am-7pm Mon-Fri, 10am-1pm Sat; ⓂM3 Ferenciek tere)

Vodafone (www.vodaphone.hu; VI Váci út1-3, West End City Centre, 1st fl; ⌚10am-9pm Mon-Sat, to 6pm Sun; ⓂNyugati pályaudvar)

Tourist Information

Budapest Info (Map p60; ☎438 8080; www.budapestinfo.hu) has info desks in the arrivals sections of all three Ferenc Lizst International Airport terminals, as well as two main branches in the city.

Budapest Info – Main Office (Map p68; ☎438 8080; V Sütő utca 2; ⌚8am-8pm) The best single source of information about Budapest.

Budapest Info – Oktogon Branch (Map p60; VI Liszt Ferenc tér 11; ⌚10am-6pm Mon-Fri; ⓂM1 Oktogon, 🚊4, 6)

Travel Agencies

Ibusz (Map p68; ☎501 4910; www.ibusz.hu; V Aranykéz utca 4-6; ⌚9am-6pm Mon-Fri, to 1pm Sat; ⓂM1/2/3 Deák Ferenc tér) Ibusz is arguably the best agency for private accommodation, and its main office also changes money, books all types of accommodation and sells transport tickets.

Vista (Map p68; ☎429 9999; www.vista.hu; VI Andrássy utca 1; ⌚9.30am-6pm Mon-Fri, 10am-4.30pm Sat; ⓂM1 Bajcsy-Zsilinski út) Vista is an excellent destination for all travel needs, both outbound (air tickets, package tours etc) and incoming (room bookings, organised tours, study etc).

Wasteels (Map p52; ☎210 2802; www.wasteels.hu; VIII Kerepesi út 2-6; ⌚8am-8pm Mon-Fri, to 6pm Sat; ⓂM2 Keleti pályaudvar) This agency next to platform No 9 at Keleti train station sells BIJ-26 discounted train tickets for those aged 26 years and under, but you must have a student or youth card to get the discounted fares.

ℹ Getting There & Away

Air

Budapest's Ferenc Liszt International Airport (p310), 24km southeast of the city centre, has two modern terminals, and an older one (Terminal 1) about 5km to the west that is no longer in use but still connected to the other two terminals by bus 200E. Airlines to/from countries with the Schengen border fly from Terminal 2A, while other international flights and budget airlines use Terminal 2B next door. Both Terminal 2A and 2B have ATMs and Interchange currency exchange desks, while Terminal 2A also has car rental desks and a left-luggage office. Budapest can be reached from destinations worldwide, but is most widely served from continental Europe by budget airlines such as EasyJet (p310), **Germanwings** (4U; www.germanwings.com) and **Wizz Air** (W6; www.wizzair.com).

Boat

Mahart PassNave (Map p68; ☎484 4000; www.mahartpassnave.hu; V Belgrád rakpart; ⌚8am-6pm Mon-Fri) runs hydrofoils to Bratislava and Vienna from late April to late September, arriving at and departing from the **International Ferry Pier** (Nemzetközi hajóállomás; ☎318 1223; V Belgrád rakpart). Hydrofoils depart Budapest on Mondays and Wednesdays at 9am, returning from Vienna on Tuesdays and Thursdays. Adult one-way and return fares to Vienna are €99 and €125 respectively. Transporting a bicycle costs €25 each way.

Bus

All international buses and domestic buses to and from western Hungary arrive at and depart from **Népliget bus station** (☎219 8030; IX Üllői út 131) in Pest. The **international ticket office** (☎219 8020; ⏰6am-6pm Mon-Fri, to 4pm Sat & Sun) is upstairs. Eurolines (p311) is represented here, as is its Hungarian associate Volánbusz (p311). There's a **left-luggage office** (⏰6am-9pm) downstairs, which charges 340Ft per piece per day.

Stadion bus station (☎220 6227; XIV Hungária körút 48-52) generally serves cities and towns in eastern Hungary. The **ticket office** (⏰6am-6pm Mon-Fri, to 5pm Sat & Sun) and the **left-luggage office** (per piece 340Ft; ⏰6am-7pm) are on the ground floor.

Car & Motorcycle

Assistance and/or advice for motorists is available from the **Hungarian Automobile Club** (Magyar Autóklub; ☎188; www.autoclub.hu; Berda József utca 15; 🚊4 , 6).

For information about traffic and public road conditions in the capital, ring Főinform (p314).

Train

Budapest has three main train stations:

Keleti pályaudvar (Keleti Pályaudvar; VIII Kerepesi út 2-6; Ⓜ M3 Keleti pályaudvar) handles most international trains, as well as domestic traffic from the north and northeast.

Nyugati pályaudvar (Western train station; VI Teréz körút 55-57; Ⓜ M3 Nyugati pályaudvar) deals with some international trains (eg Romania), as well as domestic trains for the Danube Bend and the Great Plain.

Déli pályaudvar (Southern train station; I Krisztina körút 37; Ⓜ M2 Déli pályaudvar) handles trains to some destinations in the south (eg Osijek in Croatia and Sarajevo in Bosnia).

All train have amenities, including left-luggage lockers that cost between 400Ft and 600Ft a day. You'll also find post offices and grocery stores that are open late. All three stations are on metro lines, and night buses serve them when the metro is closed. To save queuing at the train stations, buy your tickets at the **MÁV-Start passenger service centre.** (☎512 7921; www.mav-start.hu; V József Attila utca 16; ⏰9am-6pm Mon-Fri)

ℹ Getting Around

Budapest is easy to navigate, as the Danube separates east and west (Pest and Buda). There is a safe, efficient and inexpensive public transport system that is rapidly being upgraded and will never have you waiting more than five or 10 minutes for any conveyance. Five types of transport are in general use: metro trains on three (and, in 2014, four) city lines, green HÉV trains on four suburban lines, blue buses, yellow trams and red trolleybuses. You can also get around by bicycle, car and motorbike.

Daytime public transport in Budapest runs from about 4.15am to between 9pm and 11.30pm, depending on the line. From 11.30pm to just after 4am, a network of about 35 night buses kicks in, generally running every half-hour to hour.

To/From The Airport

Fő Taxi (☎222 2222; www.fotaxi.hu) now has the monopoly on picking up taxi passengers at the airport. Fares to most locations in Pest are 5300Ft, and in Buda 5500Ft to 6000Ft. Of course, you can take any taxi to the airport and several companies have a flat-rate discounted fare to and from Ferihegy. **City Taxi** (☎211 1111; www.citytaxi.hu) charges 5000Ft between the airport and Pest, and 5500Ft between Ferenc Liszt and Buda.

The **Airport Shuttle Minibusz** (☎296 8555; www.airportshuttle.hu; one way/return 3200/5500Ft) ferries passengers in nine-seat vans from the airport's terminals directly to their hotel, hostel or residence (one-way and return cost 3200Ft and 5500Ft). Tickets are available at a clearly marked desk in the arrivals hall, though you may have to wait while the van fills up. You need to book your journey *to* the airport 12 hours in advance, but remember that, with up to eight pick-ups en route, this can be a nerve-wracking way to go if you're running late.

The cheapest (and slowest) way to get into the city centre from Terminals 2A and 2B is to take city bus 200E (320Ft; look for the stop on the footpath between Terminals 2A and 2B), which terminates at the Kőbánya-Kispest metro station. From there, take the M3 metro into the city centre.

Bicycle

More and more cyclists are seen on the streets and avenues of Budapest these days, taking advantage of the city's growing network of bike paths. The main roads in the city might be a bit too busy to allow enjoyable cycling, but the side streets are fine and there are some areas (eg City Park, Margaret Island) where cycling is positively ideal. Bike rental is available from Dynamo Bike & Bake (p55) and Budapest Bike (p56), among others.

Boat

BKV (Budapest Transport Company; ☎258 4636; www.bkv.hu) passenger ferries run a scheduled, 11-stop passenger ferry from Millenniumi Városközpont in southern Pest either to Újpest or Rómaifürdő in the very north of the city every half an hour between 8.30am and 7.30pm and less frequently on weekends (tickets 400ft; bike transport 400Ft). It's an 11.5km scenic commuting route that takes just under two hours. Though BKV also does leisure cruises, these passenger ferries give you the same views and are cheaper. The most convenient place to embark in Pest is IX Boráros tér, just north of Petőfi Bridge, while the ferry stop closest to the Castle District is I Batthyány tér.

From early April to late October Mahart PassNave (p88) also runs excursion boats on the Danube from Budapest to Szentendre, and between early May and late September hydrofoils from Budapest to Vác, Visegrád, Nagymoros and Esztergom. Boats usually leave from the Vigadó tér Pier, off V Vigadó tér on the Pest side, and sometimes pick up and discharge passengers from the ferry stop at I Batthyány tér on the Buda side, which is on the M2 metro line.

Bus

Budapest is covered by an extensive system of 240 or so day and night bus routes. On certain lines, a bus may have an 'E' after its number, indicating it's an express and makes limited stops. Buses run from about 4.15am to between 9 and 11.30pm, depending on the route. From 11.30pm to 4am, a network of 35 or so night buses takes over (the numbers are three-digit and begin with '9'), running every 15 to 60 minutes, depending on the route.

Useful bus routes (marked with blue lines on most Budapest maps) include:

» **7** Cuts across a large swathe of central Pest from XIV Bosnyák tér and down VII Rákóczi út, before crossing Elizabeth Bridge to Kelenföldi train station in southern Buda. 7E covers the same route, but with fewer stops.

» **15** Covers much of Inner Town from IX Boráros tér to XIII Lehel tér north of Nyugati train station.

» **86** Runs the length of Buda from XI Kosztolányi Dezső tér to Óbuda.

» **105** Goes from V Deák Ferenc tér to XII Apor Vilmos tér in central Buda.

Car & Motorcycle

Driving around Budapest is not for the faint-hearted. Dangerous manoeuvres, extensive roadworks and serious accidents abound, and finding a place to park is next to impossible in some neighbourhoods. Use the public transport system instead. If you must drive, Főinform (p314) has information about current road conditions.

» **Hire** All major international rental firms, including Avis (p314), Budget (p314) and Europcar (p314), have offices in Budapest and at the airport. The best independent rental company is **Fox Autorent** (☎382 9000; www.foxautorent.com; VII Hársfa utca 53-55, Building I, ground floor;

FARES & TRAVEL PASSES

To ride the metro, trams, trolleybuses, buses and the HÉV (as far as the city limits), you must have a valid ticket, which you can buy at kiosks, newsstands, metro entrances, machines and, in some cases, on the bus for an extra charge. Children under the age of six and EU seniors over 65 travel for free. Bicycles can only be transported on the HÉV.

» The basic fare for all forms of transport is 350Ft (3000Ft for a block of 10), allowing you to travel as far as you like on the same metro, bus, trolleybus or tram line *without* changing/transferring. A ticket allowing unlimited stations with one change within 1½ hours costs 530Ft.

» On the metro exclusively, the base fare drops to 300Ft if you are going just three stops within 30 minutes. Tickets bought on the spot rather than in advance cost 450Ft.

» You must always travel in one continuous direction on any ticket; return trips are not allowed. Tickets have to be validated in machines at metro entrances and aboard other vehicles – inspectors will fine you for not validating your ticket.

» Travel passes are valid on all trams, buses, trolleybuses, HÉV (within the city limits) and metro lines, and you don't have to worry about validating your ticket each time you get on. The most central places to buy them are ticket offices at the Deák Ferenc tér metro station, the Nyugati pályaudvar metro station and the Déli pályaudvar metro station, all open from 6am to 8pm daily.

» One-day/three-day/seven-day travel cards cost 1650/4150/4950Ft. You'll need a photo for the fortnightly/monthly passes (7000/10,500Ft).

» Travelling 'black' (ie without a valid ticket or pass) is risky; there's an excellent chance you'll get caught. The on-the-spot fine (payable within two days) is 8000Ft, which doubles if you pay it at the **BKV office** (☎461 6800; VII Akácfa utca 22; ⏰6am-8pm Mon-Fri, 8am-1.45pm Sat) up to 30 days later, and goes up to 32,500Ft after that.

⏲8am-6pm), who also have an office at the airport, with excellent service and very competitive rates (compacts from €35/170 per day/week). A Suzuki Swift from Avis costs €55 per day and €349 per week, with unlimited kilometres, collision damage waiver (CDW) and theft protection (TP) insurance.

» **Parking** Parking costs between 200Ft and 440Ft (more on Castle Hill), generally between 8am and 6pm Monday to Friday and 8am and noon on Saturday. Illegally parked cars are clamped or towed.

Metro & HÉV

Budapest has three underground metro lines that converge (only) at Deák Ferenc tér. The little yellow (Millennium) M1 line runs from Vörösmarty tér to Mexikoi út in Pest; the red M2 line from Déli train station in Buda runs to Örs vezér tere in Pest; and the blue M3 line goes from Újpest-Központ to Kőbánya-Kispest in Pest. All three lines run from about 4am to about 11.15pm.

The city's long-awaited M4 metro line will run from Kelenföldi train station in southern Buda to XIV Bosnyák tér in northeastern Pest. The first section, between Kelenföldi and Keleti train stations, covering 7.5km and 10 stations, is due to open in 2014.

The HÉV suburban train network, which runs on four lines (north from Batthyány tér in Buda via Óbuda and Aquincum to Szentendre, south to both Csepel and Ráckeve, and east to Gödöllő), plus one side line to Csömör, is almost like an additional above ground metro line.

Taxi

Taxis in Budapest remain very cheap by European standards, but you must use caution when using their services.

Avoid at all costs taxis with no name on the door and only a removable taxi light box on the roof.

Never get into a taxi that does not have a yellow licence plate and an identification badge displayed on the dashboard (as required by law), the logo of one of the reputable taxi firms on the side doors, and a table of fares clearly visible on the right-side back door.

Make sure you know exactly how much cash you're handing over, as travellers have complained of drivers switching large-denomination notes for small ones and demanding more payment.

Not all taxi meters are set at the same rates and some are much more expensive than others, but there are price ceilings under which taxi companies are free to manoeuvre. From 6am to 10pm the highest legal flagfall is 300Ft, the per-kilometre charge 240Ft and the waiting fee 60Ft. After 10pm the per-kilometre charge rises to 300Ft.

Budapest residents rarely flag down taxis in the street. They almost always ring for one from a reputable taxi company, and fares are actually cheaper if you book over the phone.

City Taxi (☎211 1111; www.citytaxi.hu)
Fő Taxi (☎222 2222; www.fotaxi.hu)
Rádió Taxi (☎377 7777; www.radiotaxi.hu)
Taxi 4 (☎444 4444; www.taxi4.hu)

Tram

There are currently just over 30 tram lines run by BKV. They are faster and a more enjoyable way of sightseeing than buses. Most trams run from 4.30am to about 10.45pm. Important tram lines (indicated with a red line on most Budapest maps) include:

» **2 & 2A** A scenic tram that travels along the Pest side of the Danube from V Jászai Mari tér to IX Boráros tér and beyond.

» **4 & 6** Extremely useful trams that start at XI Fehérvári út and XI Móricz Zsigmond körtér in south Buda, respectively, and follow the entire length of the Big Ring road in Pest before terminating at II Moszkva tér in Buda. Tram 6 runs every 15 minutes around the clock.

» **18** Runs from southern Buda along XI Bartók Béla út, through the Tabán to Széll Kálmán tér, before carrying on into the Buda Hills.

» **19** Covers part of the same route as No 18, but then runs along the Buda side of the Danube to I Batthyány tér.

» **47 & 49** Links V Deák Ferenc tér in Pest with points in southern Buda via the Little Ring road.

» **61** Connects XI Móricz Zsigmond körtér with Déli train station and Széll Kálmán tér in Buda.

Trolleybus

Trolleybuses (indicated on maps by a broken red line) go along cross streets in central Pest and are of limited use to most visitors, with the sole exception of the ones to and from and around the City Park (70, 72 and 74).

AROUND BUDAPEST

Hungary is not huge and a good deal of the rest of the country is 'around Budapest'. Many of the towns and cities on the Danube Bend and in Transdanubia, the Northern Uplands and even the Great Plain are relatively easy day- or even half-day-trips from the capital.

Ráckeve

☎24 / POP 9728

The attractions of this town on the southeastern end of Csepel, the long island in the Danube south of Budapest, are its pretty riverside park and strand, a colourful Gothic Serbian Orthodox church (*rác* is the old

DON'T MISS

RED ALERT!

A truly mind-blowing excursion is a visit to the compact **Memento Park** (www.mementopark.hu; XXII Balatoni út 16; adult/student 1500/1000Ft; ⊙10am-dusk), 10km southwest of the city centre. Since 1993 it's been home to almost four dozen statues, busts and plaques of Lenin, Béla Kun and the other 'heroic' workers that have ended up on rubbish heaps in other former socialist countries. See if you can spot Marx and Engels (the latter appropriately in the former's shadow), and a pair of boots that used to belong to Stalin. The boots were all that remained after a crowd pulled the enormous statue down from its plinth on XIV Dózsa György út during the 1956 Uprising and took bits home with them as souvenirs. Once upon a time, these socialist-realism relics would have graced the main squares of Hungarian cities (in fact, at least four of the 42 statues were erected as recently as the late 1980s), but these are now all that's left. The Party is well and truly over.

Statues aside, there is also an exhibition centre in an old barracks, with displays about the events of 1956 and the changes since 1989, and a documentary film with rare footage of secret agents collecting information on 'subversives'. You can sate your appetite for Lenin postcards, posters, T-shirts and Soviet medals at the ticket booth.

To reach this Communist Disneyland, take tram 19 from I Batthyány tér in Buda, tram 47 or 49 from V Deák Ferenc tér in Pest or bus 7 from V Ferenciek tere in Pest, all of which go to XI Kosztolány Dezsö tér in southern Buda. Then board city bus 150 (25 minutes, every 20 to 30 minutes) for the park.

An easier, though more expensive, way is to take the direct bus (with park admission adult/child return 4900/3500Ft), departing from in front of the Le Meridien Budapest hotel on Deák Ferenc tér at 11am year-round, with an extra departure at 3pm in July and August.

Hungarian word for 'Serb') and the former Savoya Mansion, now a lovely hotel.

Sights

Savoya Mansion NOTABLE BUILDING
(Savoyai-kastély; ☎485 253; www.savoyai.hu; Kossuth Lajos utca 95) About 600m south of the HÉV station is the Savoya Mansion, the oldest baroque palace in Hungary, finished in 1722 by an Austrian architect who would later go on to design Schönbrunn Palace in Vienna. Originally the home of Prince Eugene of Savoya, who drove out the last of the Turkish occupiers from Hungary at the Battle of Zenta in 1697, the mansion was completely renovated and turned into a top-notch hotel in 1982.

Serbian Orthodox Church CHURCH
(Görög-keleti szerb templom; Viola utca 1; adult/child 400/200Ft; ⊙10am-noon & 2-5pm Tue-Sat, 2-5pm Sun) From Hősök tere in the centre of town, you can't miss the blue clock tower of the Serbian Orthodox Church to the southeast. The late-Gothic church, the oldest of its kind in Hungary, was originally built in 1487 by Serbs who fled their town of Keve ahead of the invading Turks. It was enlarged with two Renaissance side chapels in the following century, while the incongruous freestanding clock tower was added in 1758.

The walls and ceiling of the church interior are covered with colourful frescoes painted between 1765 and 1771 by an ethnic Serbian master from Albania (though they are thought to be tracings of the 15th-century originals). The scenes from the Old and New Testaments were meant to teach the Bible to illiterate parishioners.

Eating

Savoyai Kastély HUNGARIAN
(☎424 189; www.savoyai.hu; Kossuth Lajos utca 95; mains 2100-5200Ft; ⊙noon-10pm) The Savoya Mansion's atmospheric cellar restaurant is the best place in Ráckeve for kick-ass catfish goulash and other stellar examples of Hungarian cuisine: goose liver with fried apples, tenderloin stroganoff, and pancake with poppy seeds to finish. A good way to have a good look at the mansion's interior without actually staying here, too.

Getting There & Away

The easiest way to reach Ráckeve is on the HÉV suburban train (760Ft, 1¼hr, 40km, half-hourly), departing from the Vágóhíd HÉV terminus in district IX on the Pest side. The last HÉV train back to Budapest leaves Ráckeve just after 10pm.

Gödöllő

☎28 / POP 34,396

The main draw of Gödöllő (pronounced, roughly, as 'good-duh-ler') is the Gödöllő Royal Palace, which rivalled Esterházy Palace at Fertőd in Western Transdanubia in splendour and size when it was completed in the 1760s and is the largest baroque manor house in Hungary. But the town itself, full of lovely baroque buildings and monuments and host to a couple of important annual music festivals, is worth the trip.

Sights

Gödöllő Royal Palace PALACE

(Gödöllői Királyi Kastély; www.kiralyikastely.hu; Szabadság tér 1; adult/child 1800/900Ft, Baroque Theatre adult/student 1200/600Ft; ⌚10am-6pm Apr-Oct, to 5pm Tue-Sun Nov-Mar) This palace was designed in 1741 by Antal Mayerhoffer for Count Antal Grassalkovich (1694–1771), confidante of the prima donna Empress Maria Theresa, who insisted on going sledging here one summer, requiring servants to pull her along specially laid-out mounds of salt to simulate snow. After the formation of the Dual Monarchy, the palace was enlarged as a summer retreat for Emperor Franz Joseph, and soon became the favoured residence of his consort, the much-beloved Habsburg empress and Hungarian queen Elisabeth (1837–98), known as Sissi. Between WWI and WWII the regent, Admiral Miklós Horthy, also used it as a summer residence, but after the communists took over part of the mansion was used as a barracks for Soviet and Hungarian troops and as an old people's home.

Partial renovation of the mansion began in the 1990s, and the rooms have been restored to the period when the imperial couple were in residence. On the 1st floor are Franz Joseph's suites, done up in 'manly' greys and maroons, and Sissi's impressive, violet-coloured private apartments complete with portraits of her on horseback. On the 1st floor, check out in particular the **Ceremonial Hall**, all gold tracery, stucco and chandeliers, where chamber-music concerts are held throughout the year. There's also the **Queen's Reception Room**, with a Romantic-style oil painting of Sissi patriotically repairing the coronation robe of King Stephen with needle and thread; and a room dedicated to the queen's assassination by Italian anarchist Luigi Lucheni, who stabbed her to death with a

WORTH A TRIP

SZÁZHALOMBATTA ARCHAEOLOGICAL PARK

Despite being located in the unpretty settlement of Százhalombatta, the **Archaeological Park** (Régészeti Park; www.matricamuzeum.hu; Poroszlai Ildikó utca 1; adult/student 1200/660Ft; ⌚10am-6pm Tue-Sun Apr-Oct) makes a great outing for those with an interest in archaeology (or a taste for the macabre), as it's the only open-air prehistoric museum in Hungary and the country's most important Hallstatt (early Iron Age culture between 800 and 600 BC) site. The 6-hectare park sits in the middle of some of the area's more than 120 Iron Age burial mounds – Százhalombatta means '100 Mounds' – and is still undergoing excavation. There are about 10 reconstructed Bronze and Iron Age settlements, including replicas of pottery, cooking utensils, musical instruments and clothing. The highlight of the park is the 2700-year-old oak burial mound No 115, which is 7m high and houses an incredibly detailed 5.5-sq-metre burial chamber rebuilt from archaeological finds and floor plans.

The **Matrica Museum** (www.matricamuzeum.hu; Gesztenyés út 1-3; adult/student 1200/660Ft; ⌚10am-5pm Tue-Sun), part of the Archaeological Park, traces the history of the settlement from prehistoric times till today.

Some 300m northeast of the museum en route to the park, the **Harcsa Csárda** (☎06 23 354 926; www.harcsacsarda.hu; Dunafüredi út 1; mains 1450-3900Ft; ⌚11.30am-11pm Mon-Thu, to midnight Fri & Sat, noon-8pm Sun) is an old-style inn, its menu a stampede through the A–Z of Hungary's best, from catfish stew with cottage-cheese noodles to Grandma's liver dumpling soup and stuffed cabbage with pork knuckle. Bring your appetite.

To get here, take a Pécs-bound train from Déli train station (560Ft, 40 minutes, 28km, every 20 minutes).

sharpened needle file, and her subsequent immortalisation.

Unfortunately, you cannot see the secret tunnels, wide enough to accommodate a coach and horses, discovered in recent years and attributed to the Habsburgs. It is highly recommended, however, to overdose on architectural splendour by visiting the **Baroque Theatre** in the southern wing (access by guided tour only; tours cost 5300Ft for a group of up to 9, 6500Ft for 10 people or more.).

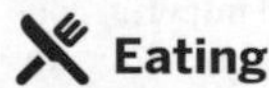

Eating

Szélkakas HUNGARIAN

(☎20-953 7375; www.godolloiszelkakas.hu; Bajcsy-Zsilinszky utca 27; mains 1700-2700Ft; ⏰11.30am-11pm Sun-Thu, to midnight Fri & Sat) The 'Weathervane' is a charming eatery with a covered garden, about 500m north of the Szabadság tér HÉV stop. The menu leans towards hearty meat and fish offerings, such as duck leg with braised red cabbage and catfish stew with garlic noodles.

ℹ Getting There & Away

Train HÉV trains from Örs vezér tere, at the terminus of the M2 metro in Pest, leave for Gödöllő (560Ft, 26km, 45 minutes) every 20 minutes to an hour throughout the day. Get off at the Szabadság tér stop (the third from last). The last train leaves this stop for Budapest at 10.45pm.

Bus Buses from Puskás Ferenc Stadion bus station in Pest serve Gödöllő (560Ft, 45 minutes, 28km, hourly). The last return bus is at about 5.30pm on weekdays and about 7.30pm on Saturday and Sunday.

Danube Bend

Includes »

Best Places to Eat & Drink

» Padlizsán (p111)
» Csülök Csárda (p111)
» Kovács-kert (p106)
» Promenade (p100)
» Kaleidoszkóp Ház (p111)

Best Places to Stay

» Mathias Rex (p100)
» Hotel Visegrád (p106)
» Tabán Panzió (p103)

Why Go?

The Danube Bend is a region of peaks and picturesque river towns to the north of Budapest. The name is quite literal: this is where hills on both banks force the river to turn sharply and flow southward. It is the most beautiful stretch of the Danube along its entire course and should not be missed.

Four historical towns vie for visitors' attention. Szentendre has its roots in Serbian culture and became an important centre for art early in the 20th century. Today it's a tourist hotspot with cobbled streets and a profusion of church spires. Round the bend is tiny Visegrád, Hungary's 'Camelot' in the 15th century and today home to Renaissance-era palace ruins and a forbidding hilltop fortress. Esztergom, once the pope's 'eyes and ears' in Hungary, is now a sleepy town with the nation's biggest cathedral, while Vác is a lovely spot with a laid-back attitude and a macabre crypt of mummies.

When to Go

Vác

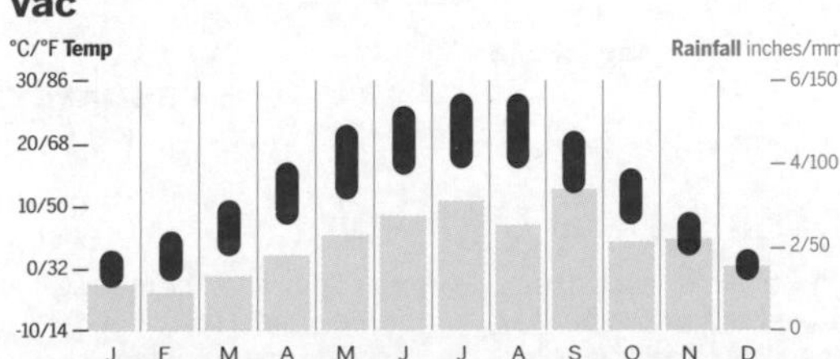

Mar–Apr Easter is the most important time of year in Orthodox Szentendre and Catholic Esztergom.

May & Sep Avoid the tourist hoards by visiting Szentendre and Visegrád in early spring or autumn.

Dec Winter is cold but atmospheric and you may even spot some ice floes in the Danube.

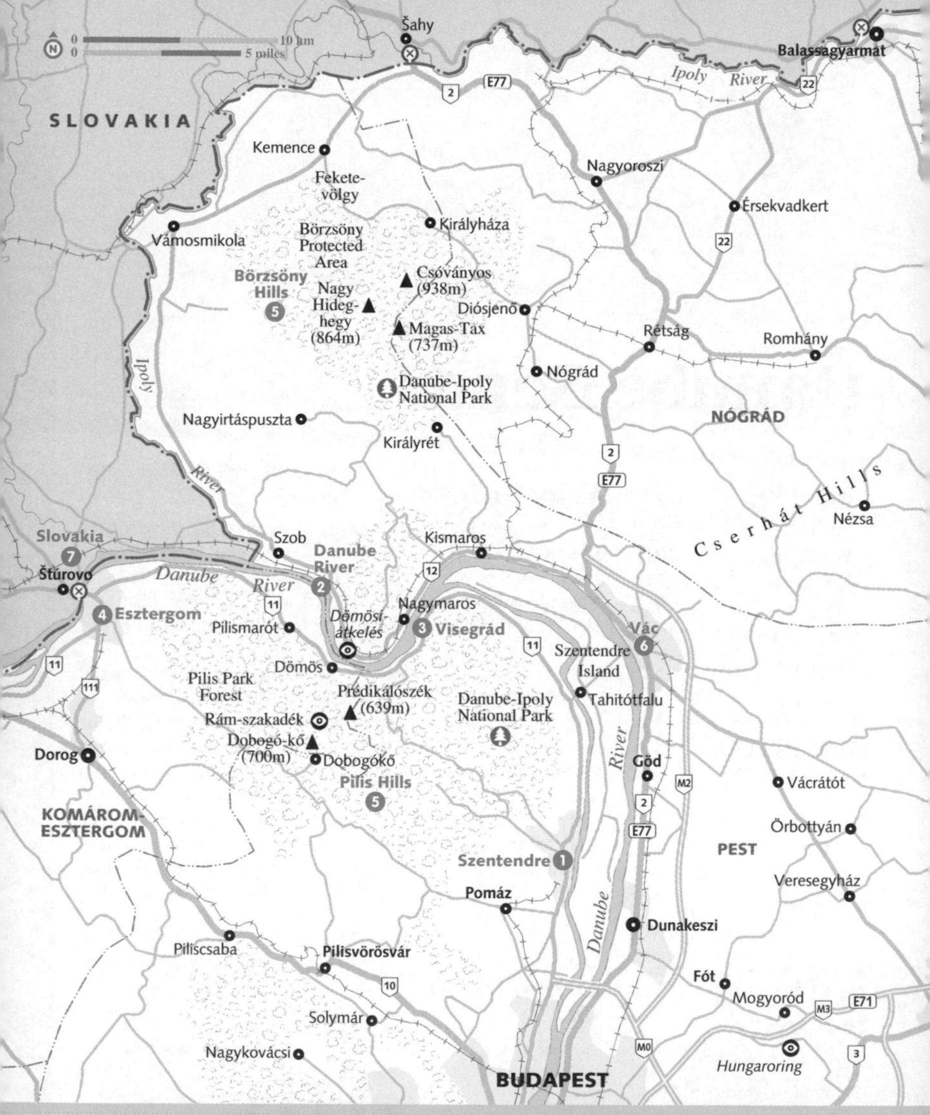

Danube Bend Highlights

1 Stroll the cobbled back streets of **Szentendre** (p97), where life remains largely untouched by the town's tourist tumult

2 Make a day of it on the **Danube**, cruising to Szentendre, Visegrád or even Esztergom by ferry or hydrofoil

3 Climb up to the medieval hilltop **citadel** (p105) at Visegrád and enjoy the wonderful views of the Danube

4 Marvel at the splendid Gothic altarpieces and paintings at the **Christian Museum** (p108) in Esztergom

5 Pick a path for a pleasurable hike through the verdant **Börzsöny** (p104) or **Pilis Hills** (p106)

6 Scare yourself half to death at the **Memento Mori** (p102) display in Vác

7 Visit Slovakia via a short stroll over the **Mária Valéria Bridge** (p109) in Esztergom

Getting There & Around

Regular buses serve towns on the west bank of the Danube, but trains only go as far as Szentendre, with a separate line running to Esztergom; the east bank, including Vác, has excellent transport links.

The river itself is a perfect highway, and regular boats ferry tourists to and from Budapest over the summer months. From May to September, a **Mahart ferry** departs Budapest's Vigadó tér at 10am Tuesday to Sunday bound for Szentendre (one way/return 1590/2390Ft, 1½ hours), returning at 5pm; the service runs on Saturday only in April.

Between May and late August there's a ferry from Vigadó tér in Budapest at 9am, calling in at Vác (11am, one-way/return 1490/2240Ft) and Visegrád (noon, 1790/2690Ft) before carrying on to Esztergom (1.45pm, 1990/2990Ft). It returns from Esztergom/Visegrád/Vác at 4.45/5.50/6.30pm, reaching Budapest at 8pm. The service is reduced to Saturday only in April and September.

Hydrofoils travel from Budapest to Visegrád (one way/return 2690/3990Ft, one hour) and Esztergom (one way/return 3990/5990Ft, 1½ hours) on Friday, Saturday and Sunday from early May to September; boats leave at 9.30am and return at 5pm from Esztergom and 5.30pm from Visegrád.

Szentendre

☎26 / POP 26,000

Szentendre ('St Andrew') is the southern gateway to the Danube Bend but has none of the imperial history or drama of Visegrád or Esztergom. As an art colony turned lucrative tourist centre and easily accessible from Budapest just 19km south, Szentendre strikes many travellers as a little too 'cute', and is crowded and relatively expensive most of the year. Still, it's an easy train trip from the capital, and the town's dozens of art museums, galleries and churches are well worth the trip. Just try to avoid it at weekends in summer.

History

Szentendre was home first to the Celts and then the Romans, who built an important border fortress here. The Magyars colonised the region in the 9th century; by the 14th century Szentendre was a prosperous estate under the supervision of Visegrád.

Serbian Orthodox Christians came here from the south in advance of the Turks in the 15th century, but the Turkish occupation of Hungary over the next two centuries brought the town's peaceful co-existence to an end, and by the end of the 17th century the town was deserted. Though Hungary was soon liberated from the Ottomans, fighting continued in the Balkans and a second wave of Serbs fled to Szentendre. Believing they would return home, but enjoying complete religious freedom under the Habsburgs, Orthodox clans built their own churches and gave the town its unique Balkan feel.

Szentendre's delightful location began to attract day trippers and painters from Budapest early last century; an artists colony

THE DUSTLESS HIGHWAY

No other river in Europe is as evocative, or important, as the Danube. It has been immortalised in legends, tales, songs, paintings and films through the ages, and has played an essential role in the cultural and economic life of millions of people since the earliest human populations settled along its banks.

Originating in Germany's Black Forest, the river cuts an unstoppable swathe through – or along the border of – 10 countries and, after more than 2800km, empties into the Black Sea in Romania. It is second only in length to the Volga in Europe (although at 6400km, the Amazon dwarfs both) and, contrary to popular belief, is green-brown rather than blue (or 'blond', as the Hungarians say). Around 2400km of its length is navigable, making it a major transport route across the continent.

Even though only 12% of the river's length is located in the country, Hungary is vastly affected by the Danube. The entire country lies within the Danube river basin which, being so flat is highly prone to flooding. As early as the 16th century, large dyke systems were built for flood protection, but it's hard to stop water running where it wants to. The capital was devastated by flooding in 1775 and 1838; in 2006 the river burst its banks, threatening to fill Budapest's metro system and putting the homes of tens of thousands of people in danger. It came close to doing so again in 2009.

Despite the potential danger, the river is beloved – so much so that it's been designated its own day. On 29 June every year cities along the river host festivals, family events and conferences on **Danube Day** (www.danubeday.org) in honour of the mighty river.

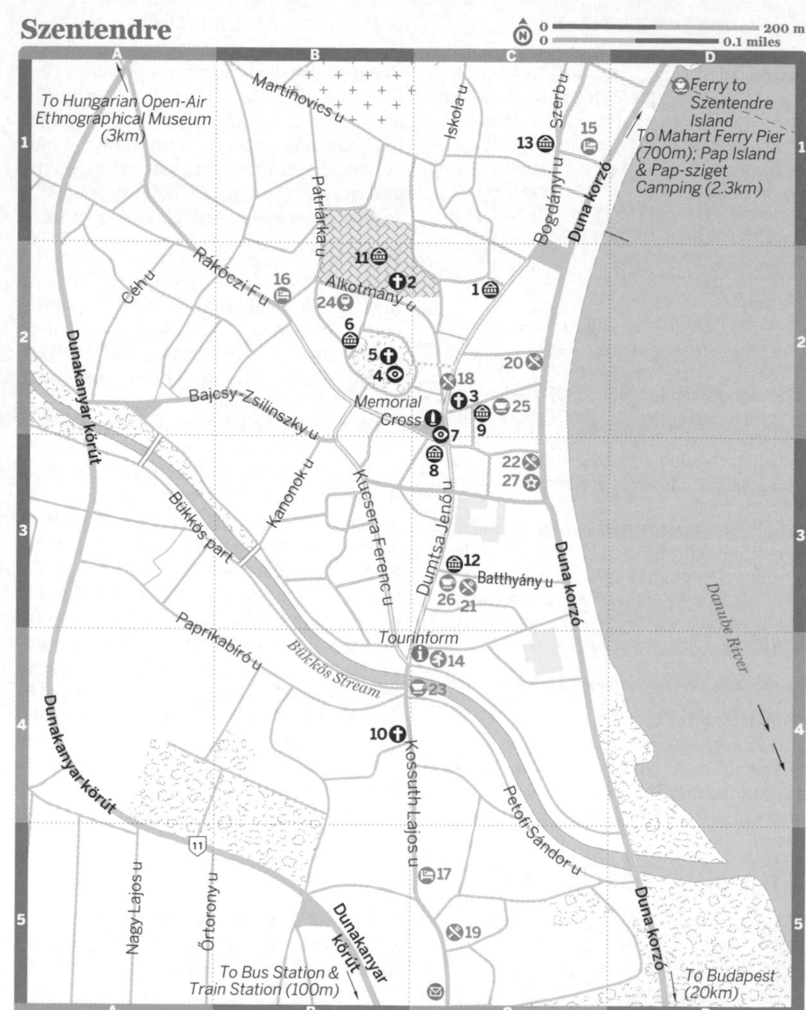

was established here in the 1920s and is still known for its art and artists.

Sights

Fő tér SQUARE

(Main Square) The colourful heart of Szentendre is surrounded by 18th- and 19th-century burghers' houses, with the **Memorial Cross** (1763), an iron cross decorated with faded icons on a marble base, in the centre. The **Kmetty Museum** (☎310 244; www.museum.hu/szentendre/kmetty; Fő tér 21; adult/child 600/300Ft; ⌚2-6pm Wed-Sun) on the southwestern side of the square, one of the town's many museums and galleries, displays the work of the cubist János Kmetty (1889–1975).

Blagoveštenska Church CHURCH

(Blagoveštenska templom; ☎310 554; Fő tér; admission 300Ft; ⌚10am-5pm Tue-Sun) The highlight of Fő tér is the Blagoveštenska Church, built in 1754. The church, with fine baroque and rococo elements, hardly looks 'eastern' from the outside, but once you are inside, the ornate iconostasis, elaborate 18th-century furnishings and canned Slavonic church music give the game away.

Szentendre

Sights
1 Anna-Ámos Collection ... C2
2 Belgrade Cathedral ... B2
3 Blagoveštenska Church ... C2
4 Castle Hill ... B2
5 Church of St John the Baptist ... B2
6 Czóbel Museum ... B2
7 Fő tér ... C2
8 Kmetty Museum ... C3
9 Margit Kovács Ceramic Collection ... C2
National Wine Museum ... (see 1)
10 Požarevačka Church ... B4
11 Serbian Ecclesiastical Art Collection ... B2
12 Szabó-Samos Marzipan Museum ... C3
13 Szentendre Art Mill ... C1

Activities, Courses & Tours
14 Rent-a-Bike ... C4

Sleeping
15 Centrum ... C1
16 Ilona ... B2
17 Mathias Rex ... C5

Eating
18 Aranysárkány ... C2
19 Erm's ... C5
20 Görög Kancsó ... C2
21 Palapa ... C3
22 Promenade ... C3

Drinking
23 Adria ... C4
24 Avakumica ... B2
25 Jovialis ... C2
26 Szabó-Samos Marzipan Museum Cafe ... C3

Entertainment
27 Danube Cultural Centre ... C3

Margit Kovács Ceramic Collection MUSEUM
(Kovács Margit Kerámiagyüjtemény; ☎310 244; www.pmmi.hu/hu/museum/6/intro; Vastagh György utca 1; adult/concession 1000/500Ft; ⏰10am-6pm) If you descend Görög utca from the main square and turn right onto Vastagh György utca you'll reach this museum (in an 18th-century salt house) dedicated to the work of Szentendre's most famous artist. Margit Kovács (1902–77) was a ceramicist who combined Hungarian folk, religious and modern themes to create Gothic-like figures. Some of her works are overly sentimental, but many others are very powerful, especially the later ones in which mortality is a central theme.

Castle Hill VIEWPOINT
(Vár-domb) Castle Hill, reached via Váralja lépcső, the narrow steps between Fõ tér 8 and 9, was the site of a fortress in the Middle Ages. All that's left of it today is the walled early-Gothic **Church of St John the Baptist** (Keresztelő Szent János Templom; Templom tér, Vár-domb; admission free), from where you get splendid views of the town. Note the frescoes painted by members of the artists' colony in the 1930s. Nearby is the **Czóbel Museum** (☎310 244; www.pmmi.hu/hu/museum/4/intro; Templom tér 1; adult/child 600/300Ft; ⏰10am-6pm Wed-Sun), which contains the works of the impressionist Béla Czóbel (1883–1976), a friend of Pablo Picasso and student of Henri Matisse.

Belgrade Cathedral CHURCH
(Belgrád Székesegyház; ☎312 399; Pátriárka utca 5; admission incl art collection 600Ft; ⏰10am-4pm Fri-Sun Jan & Feb, to 6pm Tue-Sun May-Oct, to 4pm Tue-Sun Nov-Dec) Just north of Castle Hill you'll notice the red tower of Belgrade Cathedral, completed in 1764 and seat of the Serbian Orthodox bishop in Hungary.

Serbian Ecclesiastical Art Collection MUSEUM
(Szerb Egyházművészeti Gyüjtemény; ☎312 399; Pátriárka utca 5; adult/child 600/300Ft; ⏰10am-4pm Fri-Sun Jan & Feb, to 6pm Tue-Sun Mar-Oct, to 4pm Tue-Sun Nov-Dec) The Serbian Ecclesiastical Art Collection is a treasure trove of icons, vestments and other sacred objects in precious metals. A 14th-century glass painting of the crucifixion is the oldest item on display; a 'cotton icon' of the life of Christ from the 18th century is unusual. Take a look at the defaced portrait of Christ on the wall upstairs – the story goes that a drunken *kuruc* (anti-Habsburg) mercenary slashed it and, when told the next morning what he had done, drowned himself in the Danube.

Požarevačka Church CHURCH
(☎310 554; Kossuth Lajos utca 1; admission 300Ft; ⏰by appointment) Dedicated in 1763, this late-Baroque Serbian Orthodox church has a lovely iconostasis dating from 1742. The church is on the way into town from the bus and train stations and a good introduction to Szentendre's predominant architecture.

Anna-Ámos Collection MUSEUM

(☎310 790; http://www.pmmi.hu/hu/museum/3/intro; Bogdányi utca 10-12; adult/child 600/300Ft; ⏲10am-6pm Thu-Sun Apr-Oct) Bogdányi utca, Szentendre's busy pedestrian street, leads north from Fő tér, where you'll find the excellent Anna-Ámos Collection, displaying the surrealist and expressionist paintings of husband-and-wife team Margit Anna and Imre Ámos.

Szentendre Art Mill GALLERY

(Szentendrei Művészet Malom; ☎301 701; www.szentendreprogram.hu; Bogdányi utca 32; adult/child 1000/500Ft; ⏲10am-6pm) This enormous gallery, spread over three floors of an old mill, exhibits both local and national artists and underscores Szentendre's renewed commitment to become once again a centre for serious art. Its extensive exhibition space is used for paintings, sculpture, graphics and applied arts, and its grounds are possibly the quietest spot in the touristy centre.

National Wine Museum MUSEUM

(Nemzeti Bormúzeum; ☎317 054; www.bor-kor.hu; Bogdányi utca 10; admission 200Ft, 5/9 tastings 1700/2600Ft; ⏲10am-10pm) The National Wine Museum in the Labirintus restaurant traces the development of wine-making in Hungary and offers wine tastings of between five and nine vintages.

Hungarian Open-Air Ethnographical Museum MUSEUM

(Magyar Szabadtéri Néprajzi Múzeum; ☎502 500; www.skanzen.hu; Sztaravodai út; adult/student 1500/750Ft, on festival days 1600/800Ft; ⏲9am-5pm Tue-Sun Apr-Oct, 10am-4pm Sat & Sun Nov–early Dec & Feb-Mar) Just 5km northwest of Szentendre and accessible by bus 230 from bay No 7 at the bus station, is Hungary's most ambitious *skanzen*, or open-air folk museum, with farmhouses, churches, bell towers, mills and so on set up in eight regional divisions, as well as the walls of a Roman villa excavated in the area. Craftspeople and artisans do their thing on random days (generally at the weekend) from Easter to early December (generally on Sundays and holidays), and the museum hosts festivals throughout the season.

Activities

Pap Island (Pap-sziget), 2km north of the centre, is Szentendre's playground and has a grassy *strand* (beach) for sunbathing, a **swimming pool** (☎310 697; adult/child 900/450Ft; ⏲8am-7pm May-Sep), and tennis courts and rowing boats for hire.

Rent-a-Bike BICYCLE RENTAL

(☎06 20 406 3030; Dumtsa Jenő utca 22; 1 hr/day 800/3000Ft; ⏲10am-6.30pm Mon-Fri, 9am-2pm Sat) Bicycles can be rented from the Rent-a-Bike stand next to Tourinform. Take the hourly ferry across to Szentendre Island to enjoy kilometres of uncrowded cycling paths.

Sleeping

Mathias Rex GUESTHOUSE €€

(Mathias Rex Panzió; ☎505 570; www.mathiasrexhotel.hu; Kossuth Lajos utca 16; s/d 10,000/15,000Ft, studio from 30,000Ft; ❄@) This very central *panzió* (pension or guesthouse) has a dozen rooms so clean they border on sterile but are of a good size. The décor is modern and minimalist, there's a pretty courtyard and an inexpensive cellar-restaurant occupies the basement.

Ilona GUESTHOUSE €

(Ilona Panzió; ☎313 599; www.ilonapanzio.hu; Rákóczi Ferenc utca 11; s/d 5800/8000Ft) A spiffy little guesthouse with six rooms, Ilona has plenty going for it: superb central location, secure parking, inner courtyard for breakfast and rooms in very good nick (although on the small side). This place almost feels country.

Centrum HOTEL €€

(Centrum Panzió; ☎302 500; www.hotelcentrum.hu; Bogdányi utca 15; s/d from €40/50; ❄@) Standards at the Canadian-run Centrum may have dropped a notch or two but it remains what its name implies. A stone's throw from the Danube, the hotel is in a renovated townhouse with seven bright, large rooms filled with interesting old furniture.

Pap-sziget Camping CAMPGROUND €

(Pap-sziget Kemping; ☎310 697; www.pap-sziget.hu; small/large campsite for two 4000/4400Ft, bungalows from 8600Ft; ⏲May–mid-Oct; @≋) This big, leafy camping site takes up most of Pap Island, some 2km north of Szentendre. Motel (6400Ft per double) and hostel (4800Ft per double) rooms are very basic, though the 'comfort bungalows' are slightly more, well, comfortable. Facilities include a small supermarket, a snack bar and a restaurant.

Eating

TOP CHOICE **Promenade** INTERNATIONAL €€

(☎312 626; www.promenade-szentendre.hu; Futó utca 4; mains 1850-4450Ft; ⏲11am-11pm Tue-Sun) Vaulted ceilings, whitewashed walls, a huge cellar for tasting wine and a wonderful terrace overlooking the Danube are all highlights at the Promenade, one of Szentendre's best restaurants serving, 'enlightened' Hungarian and international dishes.

Erm's HUNGARIAN €€

(☎303 388; www.erms.hu; Kossuth Lajos utca 22; mains 1590-3700Ft) Subtitled 'Csülök & Jazz', retro-style Erm's, with its walls festooned with early 20th-century memorabilia and simple wooden tables, is where to go for Hungarian-style pork knuckle in all its guises, and live music at the weekend.

Palapa MEXICAN €€

(☎302 418; www.palapa.hu; Dumtsa Jenő utca 14/a; mains 1860-4380Ft; ⏲5pm-midnight Mon-Fri, noon-midnight Sat & Sun) The Mexican food – from tacos to fajitas – at this colourful restaurant (with live music at the weekend) makes it the perfect place for a change from Hungarian fare. In warm weather the garden quickly fills up with revellers.

Aranysárkány INTERNATIONAL €€€

(Golden Dragon; ☎301 479; www.aranysarkany.hu; Alkotmány utca 1/a; mains 2400-3600Ft) The fashionable 'Golden Dragon' may sound Chinese but instead serves up mains like Angus steak and salmon fillets. It was Hungary's first private restaurant (established in 1977) and is still considered ground-breaking in the local food scene.

Görög Kancsó GREEK €€

(Greek Jug; ☎303 178; www.gorogkancsoetterem.hu; Duna korzó 9; mains 1990-3690Ft) Should you crave a fix of taramasalata and moussaka, the 'Greek Jug' can accommodate and boasts the prettiest (and leafiest) terrace in town.

Drinking

Adria CAFE

(☎06 20 448 8993; Kossuth Lajos utca 4; coffee 200-500Ft) This funky little spot by the canal has a cosy interior bedecked in bright colours and a tree-shaded terrace. Expect soulful music served alongside your choice of coffee or tea and cake. They do Balkan grilled dishes (650Ft to 1100Ft) too.

Jovialis CAFE

(☎06 30 939 4779; www.jovialis.hu; Görög utca 2; coffee 250-500Ft; ⏲10am-6pm) Our favourite new cafe in Szentendre is an ultramodern but very comfortable affair attached to the Margit Kovács Ceramic Collection (p99). The staff are founts of information.

Szabó-Samos Marzipan Museum Cafe CAFE

(☎311 931; www.szamosmarcipan.hu; Dumtsa Jenő utca 14; cakes 380-520Ft; ⏲9am-7pm) This cafe is a good place to stop for cake and ice cream, and kids will love the marzipan creations inside the **Szabó-Samos Marzipan Museum** (admission 450Ft) just opposite.

Avakumica BAR

(☎500 145; Alkotmány utca 14; ⏲8am-10pm Mon-Thu, to midnight Fri, 10am-midnight Sat, to 10pm Sun) Dive into this place, a cellar bar near Castle Hill, to escape the tourist hordes and rehydrate.

Entertainment

Danube Cultural Centre PERFORMING ARTS

(Dunaparti Művelődési Ház; ☎312 657; www.szentendreprogram.hu; Duna korzó 11/a) This centre stages theatrical performances, concerts and folk dance gatherings, and can also tell you what's on elsewhere in Szentendre.

Information

Tourinform (☎317 966; www.iranyszentendre.hu; Dumtsa Jenő utca 22; ⏲9.30am-4.30pm Mon-Fri, 10am-2pm Sat & Sun) Lots of information about Szentendre and the Danube Bend.

New Cultural Centre of Szentendre (www.szentendreprogram.hu) Solid source for online information.

OTP Bank (Dumtsa Jenő utca 6) Equipped with an ATM.

Main Post Office (Kossuth Lajos utca 23-25)

Getting There & Away

Bus

Buses from Budapest's Újpest-Városkapu train station, which is on the M3 blue metro line, run to Szentendre at least once an hour (310Ft, 25 minutes, 15km). Onward service to Visegrád (465Ft, 45 minutes, 25km, hourly) and Esztergom (930Ft, 1½ hours, 50km, hourly) is frequent.

Train

The easiest way to reach Szentendre from Budapest is to catch the HÉV suburban train from Batthyány tér in Buda (630Ft, 40 minutes, every 10 to 20 minutes). Remember that a yellow city-bus/metro ticket is good only as far as the Békásmegyer stop; you'll have to pay 320Ft extra to get to Szentendre. Also, many HÉV trains run only as far as Békásmegyer, where you must cross the platform to board the train for Szentendre. The last train leaves Szentendre for Budapest just after 11pm.

Getting Around

Buses heading north on Rte 11 to Visegrád and Esztergom will stop near Pap-sziget Camping (p100); ring the bell after you pass the Hotel

Danubius (Ady Endre utca 28) on the left. Bus 230 leaves from bay 7 at the main bus station throughout the day for the Hungarian Open-Air Ethnographical Museum (p100).

Ferries run hourly to Szentendre Island (from 5.05am to 7.35pm daily from March to October) and cost 250/100/250Ft one-way for an adult/child/bicycle.

Vác

☎27 / POP 34,500

Lying on the east side of the river, Vác is the odd one out in the Danube Bend, but its locals don't seem to mind. And it's no surprise, for this unpretentious town with a resonant history has plenty to keep people enthralled, from its collection of baroque town houses to its vault of 18th-century mummies. And it has one distinct advantage over its west-bank counterparts – glorious sunsets over the Börzsöny Hills, reflected in the Danube, which is more of a prominent feature here than in the other towns on the Bend.

History

Vác can prove its ancient origins without putting a spade into the ground. Uvcenum – the town's Latin name – is mentioned in Ptolemy's 2nd-century *Geographia* as a river crossing on an important road. King Stephen established an episcopate here in the 11th century, and within 300 years Vác was rich and powerful enough for its silver mark to become the realm's legal tender. The town's medieval centre and Gothic cathedral were destroyed during the Turkish occupation; reconstruction in the 18th century gave Vác its baroque appearance. In 1846 Vác became the first Hungarian town to be linked with Pest by rail.

Sights

Március 15 tér SQUARE

Vác's renovated main square has the town's most colourful buildings, including the **Town Hall** (1764), considered a baroque masterpiece. Note the statue of Justice and the seals held by the two figures on the gable – they represent Hungary and Bishop Kristóf Migazzi, the driving force behind Vác's reconstruction more than two centuries ago. In the square's centre, you'll see the entrance to a **crypt** (adult/concession 600/350Ft; 2-6pm Wed-Fri, 10am-6pm Sat & Sun May-Oct), the only remnant of the medieval Church of St Michael. Tourinform (p104) holds the key.

Dominican Church CHURCH

(Fehérek temploma; ☎305 988; Március 15 tér 24; admission free) Dominating the southeast side of Március 15 tér is the 18th-century Dominican (or White Friars') Church. Its interior is richly decorated in the baroque and rococo styles, but the doors are normally locked outside service times.

Memento Mori MUSEUM

(☎500 750; Március 15 tér 19; adult/concession 1000/500Ft; 10am-6pm Tue-Sun) This bizarre exhibit contains three mummies and assorted artefacts recovered from the crypt of the Dominican Church. It's not for the faint-hearted. The crypt functioned as a place of burial in the 18th century, but was later bricked up and forgotten. A cool temperature year-round and minimal ventilation kept the bodies and clothes of the deceased in good condition for centuries. When renovation work on the church began in 1994, the crypt was rediscovered and a total of 262 bodies were exhumed. It was a gold mine for historians and helped to shed light on the burial practices and way of life in the 18th century. Most of the mummies are now in the vaults of the Hungarian National Museum in Budapest but three – a man, woman and baby – are on display here. Memento Mori also showcases a number of colourfully painted coffins, clothes and jewellery of the deceased, a registry of those buried and a history of the church and its crypt.

Vác Diocesan Museum MUSEUM

(☎319 494; Március 15 tér 4; adult/concession 600/300Ft; 2-6pm Wed-Fri, 10am-6pm Sat & Sun May-Oct) Housed in what was once the Palace of the Great Provost, this museum displays just a small portion of the wealth the Catholic Church amassed in Vác over the centuries.

Vác Cathedral CHURCH

(Váci székesegyház; Konstantin tér; admission free; 10am-noon & 1.30-5pm Mon-Sat, 7.30am-7pm Sun) Tree-lined Konstantin tér, to the southeast of Március 15 tér, is dominated by the town's colossal cathedral, which dates from 1775 and was one of the first examples of neoclassical architecture in Hungary. The frescoes on the vaulted dome and the altarpiece are by the celebrated artist Franz Anton Maulbertsch and well worth a look.

Triumphal Arch MONUMENT
(Diadalív-kapu; Dózsa György út) North of the main square is the only Triumphal Arch found in Hungary. It was built by Bishop Migazzi in honour of a state visit by Empress Maria Theresa and her husband Francis of Lorraine in 1764.

Vác Synagogue JEWISH
(Eötvös utca 5) Near the bus stop is the town's renovated 19th-century synagogue. The interior is yet to be finished, but when complete it will be used as an exhibition hall.

Wine Museum MUSEUM
(☎307 238; Március 15 tér 20; admission 600Ft; ⏰noon-8pm Mon-Sat) Vác's Wine Museum has an exceptional collection of more than 2500 Hungarian wines, including Tokaji Aszú from 1880. Wine tastings can be arranged.

Activities

Vác Strandfürdő SWIMMING
(www.vacisport.hu; Ady Endre sétány; 1100/630Ft) The Vác Strandfürdő has **outdoor pools** (⏰6am-8pm Jun-Sep) and an **indoor pool** (⏰6am-8pm Mon-Fri, 7am-8pm Sat & Sun May-Sep, 6am-8pm Mon-Fri, 6am-7pm Sat, 7am-5pm Sun Oct-Apr) on the southern edge of the 'beach', accessible from Ady Endre sétány.

MÁV Nostalgia TRAIN TOUR
(☎1-269 5242; www.mavnosztalgia.hu; one-way adult/child 1900/1290Ft) Once a month in May, June and July MÁV Nostalgia runs a *nosztalgiavonat* (vintage steam train) from Nyugati station in Budapest (departs at 9.50am) to Szob (arrives 11.30am) via Vác (10.40am) and Nagymaros-Visegrád; the train returns to Vác at 4pm. One-way tickets are adult/child 2900/1490Ft and return 3900/2290Ft. Be sure to double-check this service and schedule before making plans.

Sleeping

TOP CHOICE **Tabán Panzió** GUESTHOUSE €€
(Alt Vendégház; ☎06 30 910 3428, 316 860; altvendeghaz@invitel.hu; Tabán utca 25; s/d 5000/12,000Ft; ❄📶) Staying at this small guesthouse above the Danube is like staying with nice relatives. The owners are more than happy to while away the hours chatting, and the breakfast will keep you going all day. The four rooms (No 3 has a balcony) are kitschy but cosy, and there's a fully equipped kitchen with a river view and a small garden for guests' use.

Fónagy & Walter GUESTHOUSE €€
(☎310 682; www.fonagy.hu; Budapesti főút 36; r 12,500Ft; @📶) Fónagy & Walter is a homey little guesthouse 850m southeast of the main square. Its five rooms – suites almost, accommodating up to four people – are overly decorated but comfortable, the well-stocked wine cellar is outstanding and the owners occasionally fire up the grill in the courtyard.

Vörössipka HOTEL €€
(Red Cap; ☎501 055; okktart@netelek.hu; Honvéd utca 14; s/d 9000/14,000Ft; ❄@📶) It's a titch away from the action east of the centre, but the 'Red Cap' has 15 generous-sized (if somewhat austere) rooms, a sun-filled breakfast room and a friendly owner.

Eating

Váci Remete Pince HUNGARIAN €€
(☎06 30 944 3538, 302 199; Fürdő lépcső 3; mains 1850-3290Ft) This wonderful eatery with a covered terrace and awesome views of the Danube impresses with its top-notch wine selection, fine spread of Hungarian specialities and excellent service.

Momo SEAFOOD €€€
(☎300 833; Tímár utca 9; mains 2150-3950Ft) Pricey but worth it, Momo offers excellent fish and grilled dishes and has a lovely terrace overlooking parkland and the river.

Barlang Bar INTERNATIONAL €€
(Cave Bar; ☎501 760; Március 15 tér 12; pizzas 650-2350Ft, mains 1200-3100Ft) With its fluorescent lighting and red booths, this cellar restaurant/bar below the main square looks as though it would be more at home in Budapest than Vác. Its international menu is appealing and, thankfully, there is outdoor seating on the square in summer.

Drinking

Duna Presszó CAFE €
(☎305 839; Március 15 tér 13; cakes 450Ft; ⏰9am-9pm Sun-Thu, to 10pm Fri & Sat) Duna is the quintessential cafe: darkwood furniture, chandeliers, excellent cake and ice cream and a loyal following throughout the day. It's very central and useful for something warm or cold at any time of the day.

Eszterházy Kávézó CAFE
(Eszterházy utca; ice cream 110Ft, cakes 180-340Ft; ⏰5.30am-7pm) This pleasant little cafe with outside seating is the perfect spot for refreshments while on a stroll along the Danube.

☆ Entertainment

Imre Madách Cultural Centre PERFORMING ARTS
(☎316 411; Dr Csányi László körút 63) This circular centre can help you with what's on in Vác – theatre, concerts and kid's shows. Concerts are occasionally held in the cathedral, the Dominican Church and the former Bishop's Palace.

ℹ Information

Tourinform (☎316 160; www.tourinformvac.hu; Március 15 tér 17; ⌚8am-5pm Mon-Fri, to 2pm Sat mid-Jun–Aug, 9am-5pm Mon-Fri, 10am-noon Sat Sep–mid-Jun) Overlooking the main square.

Vác Website (www.vac.hu) Useful and multilingual.

OTP Bank (Széchenyi utca) In the Dunakanyar shopping centre.

Main Post Office (Posta Park 2) Some 300m east of the main square.

ℹ Getting There & Away

Boat

Car ferries (1500/430/430Ft per car/bicycle/person, hourly 6am to 8pm) cross over to Szentendre Island from the ferry pier on Ady Endre sétány; a bridge connects the island's west bank with the mainland at Tahitótfalu. From there, hourly buses run to Szentendre.

Bus

Catch buses from the station 400m northeast of Március 15 tér.

DESTINATION	PRICE	TIME	KM	FREQUENCY
Balassagyarmat	930Ft	1¼hr	45	7 daily
Budapest	560Ft	45-55min	30	half-hourly
Diósjenő	465Ft	50min	25	up to 9 Mon-Sat
Nógrád	350Ft	30min	20	up to 9 Mon-Sat
Salgótarján	1860Ft	2½hr	95	7 daily
Vácrátót	310Ft	30min	14	hourly

Train

The train station is 600m northeast of Március 15 tér.

DESTINATION	PRICE	TIME	KM	FREQUENCY
Balassagyarmat	1300Ft	2hr	70	7 daily
Budapest	650Ft	45min	34	half-hourly
Vácrátót	250Ft	12min	10	hourly

Around Vác

BÖRZSÖNY HILLS

These hills begin the series of ranges that make up Hungary's Northern Uplands, and – along with the Pilis Hills on the opposite side of the Danube – form Hungary's 600-sq-km **Danube-Ipoly National Park** (Duna-Ipoly Nemzeti Park; www.dinpi.hu). There's very good hiking, but make sure you get hold of Cartographia's 1:40,000 map *Börzsöny* (No 5; 1215Ft), which is available at Tourinform in Vác.

Nógrád, with the ruins of a hilltop castle dating from the 12th century, could be considered the gateway to the Börzsöny. **Diósjenő**, 6km north, is a good base for exploring the hills and has a few accommodation options, including **Diósjenő Camping** (☎35-364 134; www.patakpart.hu; Petőfi Sándor utca 61; campsite per person/tent 800/1000Ft, 2-person bungalows 6000Ft; ⌚May-Sep) which features bungalows with cookers and bathrooms. From here you can strike out west along marked trails to **Nady Hideg-hegy** (864m) or **Magas-Tax** (737m). The Börzsöny's highest peak, **Csóványos** (938m), lies to the west of Diósjenő and is a much more difficult climb.

If you're under your own steam, take the beautiful restricted road from Diósjenő to Kemence via Királyháza; it follows the cool and shady Kemence Stream. Just before Kemence, there is a turn-off south to the beautiful **Fekete-völgy** (Black Valley), and the **Feketevölgy Pension** (☎06 30 520 0277, 27-587 110; www.feketevolgy.hu; s/d from 9000/12,900Ft; 🍽), a peaceful oasis set well back in the forest. Kemence itself is a nondescript town with a few guesthouses and restaurants, internet access and an ATM.

Hourly trains travelling north out of Vác pass through Nógrád (465Ft, 40 minutes, 24km) and Diósjenő (560Ft, 49 minutes, 29km); both can also be reached by bus from Vác.

Visegrád

☎26 / POP 1860

Visegrád (from the Slavic words for 'high castle') has the most history of the four main towns on the Danube Bend. While much of it has crumbled to dust over the centuries, reminders of its grand past can still be seen in its Renaissance palace and 13th-century citadel, which offers spectacular views from high above a curve in the river.

History

The Romans built a border fortress just north of the present castle in the 4th century, and it was still being used by Slovak settlers 600 years later. After the Mongol invasion in 1241, King Béla IV began work on a lower castle by the river and then on the hilltop citadel. Less than a century later, embattled King Charles Robert of Anjou moved the royal household to Visegrád.

For almost 200 years, Visegrád was Hungary's 'other' (often summer) capital and an important diplomatic centre. But Visegrád's real golden age came during the reign of King Matthias Corvinus (r 1458–90) and Queen Beatrix, who had Italian Renaissance craftsmen rebuild the Gothic palace. The sheer size of the residence, and its stonework, fountains and gardens, were the talk of 15th-century Europe.

The destruction of Visegrád came first with the Turks and later in 1702, when the Habsburgs blew up the citadel to prevent Hungarian independence fighters from using it as a base. All trace of the palace was lost until the 1930s, when archaeologists uncovered the ruins.

Sights

Royal Palace PALACE

(Királyi Palota; ☎597 010; www.visegradmuzeum.hu; Fő utca 29; adult/concession 1100/550Ft; ⊙9am-5pm Tue-Sun) The main attraction in town is the Royal Palace, just inland from the river. Once boasting 350 rooms, the palace today is a mere shadow of its former self and has been only partly reconstructed. The dozen or so rooms that can be visited are mostly the royal suites centred on the Court of Honour and its Hercules Fountain, a replica of the original Renaissance piece. Moving from room to room, you'll discover more reconstructions and replicas: a cold and clammy royal bedchamber from the 1400s, a warmer kitchen and, in the courtyard to the east, the Lion Fountain in red marble. Also of note is the petite St George's Chapel (1366), but once again, it's not original. The history of the palace and its reconstruction, along with architectural finds, including richly carved stones dating from the 14th century, is told in the archaeological exhibition and lapidarium.

Solomon's Tower TOWER

(Salamon Torony; ☎398 026; adult/concession 700/350Ft; ⊙9am-5pm Tue-Sun May-Sep) North of the main town and just a short walk up Görgey lépcső from the Mahart ferry port, 13th-century Solomon's Tower was once part of a lower castle used to control river traffic. These days, what's left the of stocky, hexagonal keep, with walls up to 8m thick, houses one of the palace's original Gothic fountains, along with exhibits related to town history.

Visegrád Citadel FORTRESS

(Visegrádi Fellegvár; ☎598 080; adult/child & student 1400/700Ft; ⊙9am-5pm mid-Mar–Apr & Oct, to 6pm May-Sep, to 4pm Nov-Mar) Just north of Solomon's Tower, a trail marked 'Fellegvár' (Fortress) leads to Visegrád Citadel (1259), sitting atop a 350m hill and surrounded by moats hewn from solid rock. Completed in 1259, the citadel was the repository for the Hungarian crown jewels until 1440, when Elizabeth of Luxembourg, the daughter of King Sigismund, stole them with the help of her lady-in-waiting and hurried off to Székesfehérvár to have her infant son László crowned king. (The crown was returned to the citadel in 1464 and held here – under a stronger lock, no doubt – until the Turkish invasion.)

There's a small pictorial exhibit in the residential rooms on the west side of the citadel and two smaller displays near the east gate: one on hunting and falconry, the other on traditional occupations in the region (stone-cutting, charcoal burning, beekeeping and fishing). However, the real highlight is just walking along the ramparts of this eyrie and admiring the views of the Börzsöny Hills and the Danube, which are arguably the best in the region.

An alternative, less steep path leads to the citadel from the town centre area. Find the trail (Kálvária sétány) starting behind the Catholic church on Fő tér. You can also reach it by City-Bus (p106) minibus.

Activities

Walks & Hikes WALKING

There are some easy walks and hikes in the immediate vicinity of Visegrád Citadel – to the 377m-high **Nagy-Villám Lookout Tower** (Nagy-Villám Kilátó; adult/child 800/400Ft; ⊙10am-6pm), for example. Across from Jurta Camping is the sod-and-wood Forest Cultural House designed by Imre Makovecz; it caters to visiting school groups only but is worth a glimpse.

Bobsled Track ADVENTURE SPORTS
(bob-pálya; ☎397 397; adult/child 400/300Ft; ⏲9am-6pm Mon-Fri, to 7pm Sat & Sun Apr-Sep, 11am-4pm Oct-Mar) A 700m bobsled track, on which you wend your way down a metal chute while sitting on a felt-bottomed cart, is on the hillside below the lookout. In winter it becomes a toboggan track.

Sleeping

Hotel Visegrád HOTEL €€€
(☎397 034; www.hotelvisegrad.hu; Rév utca 15; s/d from €62/74; ❄@🛜🏊) This very flash new four-star spa hotel opposite the Nagymaros ferry pier has 71 finely tuned rooms with all the trimmings as well as several pools (inside and out), sauna, steam room and treatments available.

Hotel Honti HOTEL €€
(☎398 120; www.hotelhonti.hu; Fő utca 66; hotel s/d €45/65, guesthouse s/d €40/55, campsites per person/tent/caravan 1100/600/1200Ft; ❄@🛜) This friendly, please-everyone establishment has seven homey rooms in its guesthouse on quiet Fő utca and 23 in its hotel facing Rte 11. The hotel's large garden and table-tennis table are for guest use, and bicycles are also available for rent (2000Ft per day). There's now a camping ground next to the guesthouse, catering largely to motorists.

Vár HOTEL €€
(☎397 522; www.varhotel.hu; Fő utca 9; s 9000-10,500Ft, d 15,500-17,500Ft) A massive facelift and a nip and a tuck have turned the 20 old-style rooms in a lovely old landmark building into retro delights. Lovely courtyard, and the century-old cellar is a treat.

Jurta Camping CAMPGROUND €
(Jurta Kemping; ☎398 217; www.mogyorohegy-erdeiiskola.hu/jurta-kemping; Mogyoróhegy; campsites per adult/child/tent or car/caravan 1100/900/1100/1300Ft; ⏲May-Sep) About 2km northeast of the citadel is this nicely situated campsite near meadows and woods. It is, however, far from the centre, and the shuttle service is infrequent.

Eating

Kovács-kert HUNGARIAN €€
(☎398 123; www.kovacs-kertetterem.hu; Rév utca 4; mains 1590-2490Ft) This adorable restaurant just up from the Nagymaros ferry has a large photo menu covering a fine array of Hungarian standards. Its leafy terrace seating is a welcome relief in the warmer summer months.

Sirály INTERNATIONAL €€
(☎398 376; www.siralyvisegrad.hu; Rév utca 15; mains 2100-3600Ft) Next door to the Hotel Visegrád but very much retaining its own identity, the 'Seagull' is a classy, up-to-the-moment eatery serving international and Hungarian favourites. Unusually, the selection of 'real' vegetarian dishes is generous.

Don Vito Pizzeria PIZZERIA €
(☎397 230; www.donvitovisegrad.hu; Fő utca 83; pizza 990-1950Ft, pasta 1590-1890Ft; 🥗) Don Vito is quite a joint for such a small town. Its collection of gangster memorabilia is impressive as is its selection of top-shelf liquor. The list of pizzas is long, and lo and behold, there are even vegetarian main courses to choose from.

Information

Visegrád Tours (☎398 160; www.visegradtours.hu; Rév utca 15; ⏲8am-5pm) Inside the Hotel Visegrád; the only place with information on the town.

Visegrád Website (www.visegrad.hu) General information on Visegrád in English.

Dunakanyar Takarékszövetkezet (Rév utca 9) Bank with ATM next to the Hotel Visegrád.

Post Office (Fő utca 77; ⏲8am-4pm Mon-Fri)

Getting There & Away

Boat

Hourly ferries cross the Danube to Nagymaros (per person/bicycle/car 420/420/1400Ft) from around 6am to just before 9pm.

Bus

No train line reaches Visegrád but buses are very frequent (745Ft, 1¼ hours, 39km) to/from Budapest's Újpest-Városkapu train station, Szentendre (465Ft, 45 minutes, 25km) and Esztergom (560Ft, 45 minutes, 26km).

Getting Around

City-Bus (☎397 372; www.city-bus.hu; up to 6 people 2500Ft; ⏲9am-6pm Apr-Sep) City-Bus operates a taxi van service between the Mahart ferry pier (opposite the Vár hotel), and the citadel via the Nagymaros ferry pier.

Around Visegrád

Pilis Hills

Directly to the south and southwest of Visegrád are the Pilis Hills, an area of rolling ranges blanketed in oak and beech woods. Once the private hunting grounds of Matthias Corvinus, the hills are now

Budapest's outdoor playground, criss-crossed by a lot more hiking trails than roads. The entire region, which covers 250 sq km, falls within the scope of the **Danube-Ipoly National Park** (Duna-Ipoly Nemzeti Park; www.dinpi.hu); the Börzsöny Hills, north of the Danube, make up the rest it.

A good starting point for exploring the hills is **Dobogó-kő** (700m), the region's largest settlement. From here, marked trails head off to various vantage points in the park, including **Prédikálószék** (Pulpit Seat), a 639m crag for experienced hikers and climbers only, and **Rám-szakadék** (Rám Precipice), from where you can descend to Dömös, 6km southwest of Visegrád, in around three hours. Some of the best bird-watching in western Hungary is in these hills but make sure you arm yourself with *Pilis Visegrádi-hegység*, the 1:40,000 Pilis and Visegrád Hills map (No 16; 1215Ft)

Transport to Dobogókő is limited; up to four buses daily travel to/from Esztergom (370Ft, 40 minutes, 19km), and up to nine on weekdays to/from the HÉV station in Pomáz (465Ft, 30 minutes, 21km), two stops before Szentendre.

GERARD GORMAN: BIRDER

Gerard Gorman, author of the *Birds of Hungary*, *Birding in Eastern Europe* and dozens of other books and articles on the subject, owns and operates **Probirder** (www.probirder.com), an informational website and guide service based in Budapest.

Hungary: the centre of the known universe for birds and birding. Discuss. Well, Hungary is just one of the ornithological crossroads in Europe. Poland can be great and parts of Romania are fantastic. Hungary does have an excellent reputation in part due to all the books and articles published about it.

That's a lot of feathers in your cap. So have the numbers of birders in Hungary grown exponentially? There's a lot of activity around Lake Tisza, for example. Domestically there's been an increase among young people but it's nothing like in the UK or America or Scandinavia. Tisza-tó? They're not really birders, just people looking for a day out. There are lots of good birds there but very few real guides, especially ones who speak foreign languages.

Fly me to... The Pilis deserve a mention, but I don't take people there – too developed. For highlands I'd go to the Bükk or the Zemplén. Hortobágy has always been a magnet but it's 2½ hours from Budapest and much less birder-friendly these days, with its complicated system of restricted areas and passes. Increasingly I frequent the northern area of Kiskunság National Park around Apaj. It's an hour from here and they have the great bustard there.

Um, the great what? *Otis tadra*, the national bird of Hungary. It's a goose-like bird weighing in at 10kg to 16kg, with a wing span of up to 1.5m. – the heaviest European land bird capable of flying. It's endangered and very localised and Hungary's population of 1300 birds is the largest one in Central and Eastern Europe. Everyone wants to see one, but for such a big bird, individual sightings can be elusive. You have to know exactly which fields they frequent, and these change. But that is where a guide comes in. I find them 99.99% of the time.

Do birders tweet? Social media like Facebook and Twitter? In a word, yes.

OK, you saw that coming. What's the Holy Grail of birding in Hungary then? There are two: the saker falcon and the eastern imperial eagle. These are Asiatic birds that reach Europe uniquely via the Carpathian Basin. You don't get them in Western Europe and Hungary is the best place to see them in the world. The great bustard may be the national bird but Spain and Portugal are full of them, too.

Bustard schmustard, isn't that the saker falcon on the 'tail' of the 50Ft coin? Yes, and its reputation goes even further. A friend with the national parks wanted to gain more protection for birds of prey here. He circulated the idea that the *turul*, the sacred bird of the ancient Hungarians, was in fact the saker falcon. Now every school kids knows this. 'That's our ancient bird,' they say with pride. Like the *turul*, the saker falcon has become totemic.

Esztergom

☎33 / POP 30,850

Esztergom's massive basilica, sitting high above the town and Danube River, is an incredible sight, rising out of what seems like nowhere in a rural stretch of country. But Esztergom's attraction goes deeper than the domed structure: the country's first king, St Stephen, was born here in 975; it was a royal seat from the late 10th to the mid-13th centuries; and it has been the seat of Roman Catholicism in Hungary for more than a thousand years.

History

Castle Hill (Vár-hegy), towering over the city centre, was the site of the Roman settlement of Solva Mansio in the 1st century AD, and it is thought that Marcus Aurelius finished his *Meditations* in a camp nearby during the second half of the 2nd century.

Prince Géza chose Esztergom as his capital, and his son Vajk (later Stephen) was crowned king here in 1000. Stephen founded one of the country's two archbishoprics at Esztergom and built a basilica, bits of which can be seen in the Castle Museum.

Esztergom lost its political significance when King Béla IV moved the capital to Buda after the Mongol invasion in 1241. It remained the ecclesiastical seat, but Esztergom's capture by the Turks in 1543 interrupted the church's activities, and the city's archbishop fled to Nagyszombat (now Trnava in Slovakia). The church did not re-establish its base in this 'Hungarian Rome' until the early 19th century.

Sights

Esztergom Basilica CHURCH

(Esztergomi Bazilika; ☎402 354; www.bazilika-esztergom.hu; Szent István tér 1; admission free; ⏲8am-6pm Apr-Sep, to 4pm Oct-Mar) The basilica, the largest church in Hungary, is on Castle Hill, and its 72m-high central dome can be seen for many kilometres around. The building of the present neoclassical church was begun in 1822 on the site of its 12th-century counterpart destroyed by the Turks. József Hild, who designed the cathedral at Eger, was involved in the final stages, and the basilica was consecrated in 1856 with a sung Mass composed by Franz Liszt.

The grey church is colossal, measuring 117m long and 47m wide. Its highlight is the red-and-white marble Bakócz Chapel on the south side, which is a splendid example of Italian Renaissance stone-carving and sculpture. The chapel escaped most – though not all – of the Turks' axes; notice the smashed-in faces of Gabriel and missing heads of other angels above the altar. The copy of Titian's *Assumption* over the church's main altar is said to be the world's largest painting on a single canvas.

On the northwest side of the church is the entrance to the basilica's **treasury** (kincstár; adult/child 800/400Ft; ⏲9am-5pm Mar-Oct, 11am-4pm Tue-Sun Nov & Dec), an Aladdin's cave of vestments and church plate in gold and silver and studded with jewels. It is the richest ecclesiastical collection in Hungary.

The door to the right as you enter the basilica leads to the **crypt** (altemplom; admission 200Ft; ⏲9am-5pm Mar-Oct, 11am-2.45pm Nov-Feb), a series of eerie vaults down 50 steps with tombs guarded by monoliths representing Mourning and Eternity. Among those at rest here is Cardinal József Mindszenty. It's worth making the tortuous climb up to the **cupola** (600Ft; ⏲9.30am-5.30pm Apr-Oct) for the outstanding views over the city; the 400 steps leading up to it are to the left of the crypt entrance.

Castle Museum MUSEUM

(Vármúzeum; ☎415 986; www.mnmvarmuzeuma.hu; Szent István tér 1; adult/concession 1800/900Ft, courtyard only 500/250Ft; ⏲10am-6pm Tue-Sun Apr-Sep, to 4pm Tue-Sun Oct-Mar) At the southern end of Castle Hill, the Castle Museum is housed in the former Royal Palace, which was built mostly by French architects in the 12th century, during Esztergom's golden age. The palace was largely destroyed by the Turks; today the structure is a combination of modern brickwork and medieval stone masonry.

The museum concentrates on archaeological finds from the town and its surrounding area, the majority of which is pottery dating from the 11th century onwards. Other points of interest include some of the basilica's original ornate capitals and a fantastic view across the Danube to Slovakia.

Christian Museum MUSEUM

(Keresztény Múzeum; ☎413 880; www.christianmuseum.hu; Berényi Zsigmond utca 2; adult/concession 900/450Ft; ⏲10am-5pm Wed-Sun Mar-Nov) Below Castle Hill in the picturesque riverbank Watertown (Víziváros) district is the former Bishop's Palace, today housing the Christian Museum with the finest collection of medieval religious art in Hungary.

It contains Hungarian Gothic triptychs and altarpieces; later works by German, Dutch and Italian masters; tapestries and what is arguably the most beautiful object in the nation: the sublime Holy Sepulchre of Garamszentbenedek (1480), a wheeled cart in the shape of a cathedral, with richly carved figures of the 12 Apostles and Roman soldiers guarding Christ's tomb. The sepulchre was used during Easter Week processions and was painstakingly restored in the 1970s.

Be sure to see Tamás Kolozsvári's Calvary altar panel (1427), which was influenced by Italian art; the late-Gothic *Christ's Passion* (1506) by 'Master M S'; the gruesome *Martyrdom of the Three Apostles* (1490) by the so-called Master of the Martyr Apostles; and the *Temptation of St Anthony* (1530) by Jan Wellens de Cock, with its druglike visions of devils and temptresses. Audio guides are available for 500Ft, and guided tours in English and German for 3000Ft.

The fastest way to reach the museum from Castle Hill is to walk down steep Macskaút, which can be accessed from just behind the basilica.

Mária Valéria Bridge BRIDGE

Cross the bridge from Watertown over to Primate Island (Prímás-sziget) and to the southwest is the Mária Valéria Bridge, connecting Esztergom with the Slovakian city of Štúrovo. Destroyed during WWII, the bridge only reopened in 2002. The bridge's original Customs House (Vámház) is on the left as you cross.

Danube Museum MUSEUM

(Duna Múzeum; ☎500 250; www.dunamuzeum.hu; Kölcsey utca 2; adult/child 600/300Ft; ⌚9am-5pm Wed-Mon May-Oct, 10am-4pm Wed-Mon Nov-Apr) This surprisingly interesting (and quite high-tech) museum has exhibits on all aspects of the history and use of Hungary's mightiest river. With all the hands-on exhibits, it's a great place for kids.

Activities

Aquasziget SPA

(☎511 100; www.aquasziget.hu; Táncsics Mihály utca 5; adult/child day pass 2950/1600Ft; ⌚10am-8pm Mon-Fri, from 9am Sat & Sun) At the northern end of Primate Island is Esztergom's Aquasziget, an enormous spa and water park with a plethora of indoor and outdoor pools, curly waterslides and a full wellness centre.

Szent István Strandfürdő SWIMMING POOL

(www.palatinus-to.hu/szent_istvan_strandfurdo; Kis-Duna sétány 1; adult/concession 1100/800Ft; ⌚6am-7pm) Just east of the Little Danube are outdoor thermal pools and stretches of grass 'beach', as well as indoor pools open year-round.

Sleeping

Alabárdos Panzió GUESTHOUSE €€

(☎312 640; www.alabardospanzio.hu; Bajcsy-Zsilinszky utca 49; s/d 8500/11,500Ft, apt from 20,100Ft; ❄📶) This mustard-yellow landmark up a small hill isn't flashy but does provide neat, tidy and sizeable accommodation in 23 rooms and apartments. The laundry room and big breakfast are pluses.

CARDINAL MINDSZENTY

Born József Pehm in 1892 in the village of Csehimindszent near Szombathely, Mindszenty was politically active from the time of his ordination in 1915. Imprisoned under the short-lived regime of communist Béla Kun in 1919 and again when the fascist Arrow Cross came to power in 1944, Mindszenty was made Archbishop of Esztergom – and thus Primate of Hungary – in 1945, and cardinal the following year.

In 1948, when he refused to secularise Hungary's Roman Catholic schools under the new communist regime, Mindszenty was arrested, tortured and sentenced to life imprisonment for treason. Released during the 1956 Uprising, he took refuge in the US Embassy on Szabadság tér in Budapest when the communists returned to power. He would remain there until September 1971.

As relations between the Kádár regime and the Holy See began to improve in the late 1960s, the Vatican made several requests for the cardinal to leave Hungary, which he refused to do. Following the intervention of US President Richard Nixon, Mindszenty left for Vienna, where he continued to criticise the Vatican's relations with the regime in Hungary. He retired in 1974 and died the following year. But as he had vowed not to return to his homeland until the last Soviet soldier had left Hungarian soil, Mindszenty's remains were not returned until 1991.

Esztergom

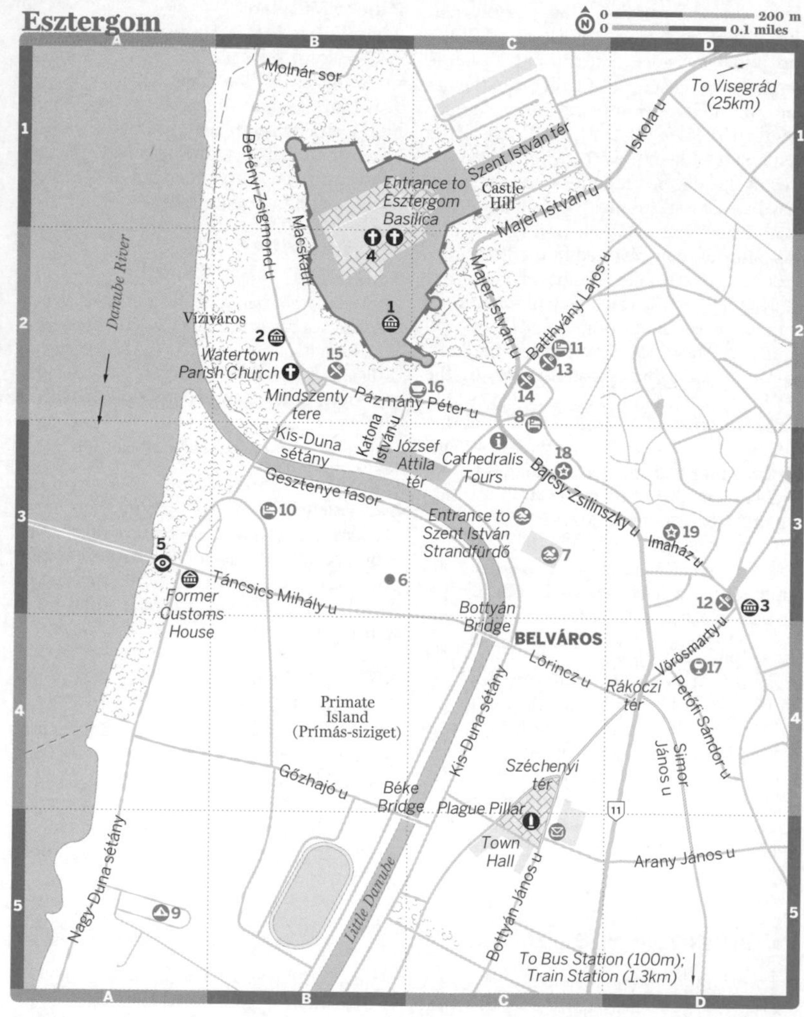

Ria Panzió GUESTHOUSE €€
(☎06 20 938 3091, 313 115; www.riapanzio.com; Batthyány Lajos utca 11; s/d 9000/12,000Ft; ❄@📶) This 11-room guesthouse in a converted town house just down from the basilica has quiet, cosy rooms; a tiny fitness centre in a one-time wine cellar; and bicycles to rent (100Ft per day).

Hotel Esztergom HOTEL €€
(☎412 555; www.hotel-esztergom.hu; Helischer J utca, Prímás-sziget; s/d 14,000/16,000Ft; ❄@📶🏊) Hotel Esztergom claims a leafy and quite tranquil spot on Primate Island and has 36 up-to-date guestrooms, a restaurant and a roof terrace. There's a sports centre with a tennis court, and guests can use a nearby swimming pool.

Gran Camping CAMPGROUND €
(☎06 30 948 9563, 402 513; www.grancamping-fortanex.hu; Nagy-Duna sétány 3; campsites per adult/child/tent/tent & car 1400/800/1100/1400Ft, bungalows from 16,000Ft, dm/d/tr 3000/12,000/14,000Ft; ⏲May-Sep; @🏊) Small but centrally located on Primate Island, Gran Camping has space for 500 souls in various forms of accommodation (including a hostel

Esztergom

Sights

1 Castle Museum ... B2
2 Christian Museum ... B2
3 Danube Museum ... D3
4 Esztergom Basilica ... B2
5 Mária Valéria Bridge ... A3

Activities, Courses & Tours

6 Aquasziget ... B3
7 Szent István Strandfürdő ... C3

Sleeping

8 Alabárdos Panzió ... C2
9 Gran Camping ... A5
10 Hotel Esztergom ... B3
11 Ria Panzió ... C2

Eating

12 Café Trafó ... D3
13 Csülök Csárda ... C2
14 Múzeumkert ... C2
15 Padlizsán ... B2

Drinking

16 Kaleidoszkóp Ház ... C2
17 Maláta Bar ... D4

Entertainment

18 All-In Music Cafe ... C3
19 Esztergom City Theatre & Cultural House ... D3

with dormitory accommodation) as well as a good-sized swimming pool.

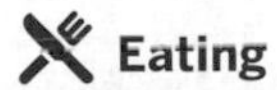

Eating

TOP CHOICE Padlizsán HUNGARIAN €€
(☎311 212; Pázmány Péter utca 21; mains 1550-3000Ft) With a sheer rock face topped by a castle bastion as the backdrop to its courtyard, Padlizsán has the most dramatic setting of any restaurant in Esztergom. And its menu doesn't let the show down either, featuring modern Hungarian dishes (the perch with almonds is excellent) and imaginative salads. The dining room feels like an intimate parlour and there's soft live music most nights.

Csülök Csárda HUNGARIAN €€€
(☎412 420; Batthyány Lajos utca 9; mains 1980-3890Ft) The 'Pork Knuckle Inn' – guess the speciality here – is a charming eatery that is popular with visitors and locals alike. It serves up good home-style cooking (try the bean soup, 1790Ft) and the portions are huge.There are some antique kitchen items on display here, too.

Múzeumkert HUNGARIAN €€
(☎404 440; www.muzeumkertetterem.hu; Batthyány Lajos utca 1; mains 1290-2790Ft) This jack-of-all-trades near the basilica – it's a restaurant, pizzeria and sophisticated cocktail bar – has a delightful inner courtyard and wonderful, upbeat modern decor. Lovely place to spend an evening.

Drinking

Kaleidoszkóp Ház CAFE
(www.kaleidoszkophaz.hu; Pázmány Péter utca 7; coffee 250Ft; ⏲noon-9pm Tue-Sat, 4-9pm Sun) This cafe-cum-cultural centre in Watertown with mix-and-match furnishings, a steady stream of events and a shop selling a rare mix of must-have unnecessaries is the coolest spot in Esztergom.

Maláta Bar BAR
(Vörösmarty utca 3; ⏲4pm-2am) If you want to kick your heels up, head for this popular pub-bar with a retro Hungarian look (curios and 'antiqued' stuff) and canned music. It's the liveliest – and latest – venue in town.

Café Trafó CAFE-BAR
(☎403 980; www.trafocafe.hu; Vörösmarty utca 15; coffee 270-640Ft, beer 390Ft; ⏲7am-2am Mon-Sat, 8am-midnight Sun) This cosy cafe-bar housed in a litle glass house opposite the Danube Museum has plenty of tree shade and a large terrace for hot summer days. It's a wonderful place to take a breather, sit back and relax at any time.

Entertainment

For up-to-date information about what's on, check the listings in the biweekly freebie *Komárom-Esztergomi Est.*

Esztergom City Theatre & Cultural House PERFORMING ARTS
(Esztergomi Várszínház és Művelődési Ház; ☎313 888; www.esztergomkultura.hu; Imaház utca 2/b) What was once the synagogue for Esztergom's Jewish community, the oldest in

Hungary, and built in the Moorish Romantic style by Lipót Baumhorn in 1888, now contains the town's theatre and cultural centre. Ask here about organ concerts at the basilica in summer, ancient Hungarian music performances at the Castle Museum and plays and other theatrical performances staged here.

All-In Music Cafe LIVE MUSIC
(http://hovamenjek.hu/esztergom/all-in-music-cafe; Bajcsy-Zsilinszky utca 35; beer 450Ft; ⊙5-10pm Sun-Thur 5pm-1am Fri & Sat) Boasting the largest selection of wines and *pálinka* (fruit brandy) as well as some pretty hot live rock and blues, this is our favourite new evening hang-out, located just down from the basilica.

Information

Cathedralis Tours (☎520 260; Bajcsy-Zsilinszky utca 26; ⊙9am-6pm Mon-Fri, 9am-noon Sat (in summer) With the closing of Gran Tours, this private travel agency is the only place in town for information.

Esztergom Website (www.esztergom.hu) Hungarian only, but with English-language links.

OTP Bank (Rákóczi tér 2-4) Has a 24hr ATM.

Post Office (Arany János utca 2) Enter from Széchenyi tér.

Getting There & Away

Bus

Esztergom has excellent bus connections, including those to the following destinations:

DESTINATION	PRICE	TIME	KM	FREQUENCY
Budapest	930Ft	70min	46	half-hourly
Dobogókő	370Ft	40min	20	2 to 3 daily
Komárom	1120Ft	1½hr	60	up to 7 daily
Szentendre	930Ft	1½hr	50	hourly
Tata	1120Ft	1hr 40min	54	hourly
Veszprém	2830Ft	3½hr	145	2 daily
Visegrád	560Ft	45min	26	hourly

Train

To get to Western Transdanubia and points beyond, take a train to Komárom.

DESTINATION	PRICE	TIME	KM	FREQUENCY
Budapest	1120Ft	1½hr	53	hourly
Komárom	1120Ft	1½hr	53	2 daily

Western Transdanubia

Includes »

Best Places to Eat

- Taverna Flórián (p143)
- La Maréda (p123)
- Pityer (p136)
- Kalóz Fregatt (p117)
- Vadkörte (p145)

Best Places to Stay

- Hilltop (p116)
- Kastély (p132)
- Portré Hotel (p142)
- Spirit Hotel (p140)
- Wieden Panzió (p128)

Why Go?

A visit to Western Transdanubia is a must for anyone wishing to see remnants of Hungary's Roman legacy, medieval heritage and baroque splendour.

This swathe of land bordering Austria, Slovenia and Slovakia largely avoided the Ottoman destruction wrought on the country in the 16th and 17th centuries. Its seminal towns – Sopron, Kőszeg and Győr – all managed to save their medieval centres from total devastation, and exploring their cobbled streets and hidden courtyards is a magical experience. Equally rewarding are reminders of Roman settlement in Szombathely, with its rich collection of ruins and a wealth of funereal treasures. Even the Romanesque period has its say in these parts – the Benedictine Abbey Church of Ják is among the finest examples of 13th-century architecture in the country.

Wine connoisseurs will also enjoy the trip, as the region is known for its fine tipple – particularly its reds.

When to Go

Sopron

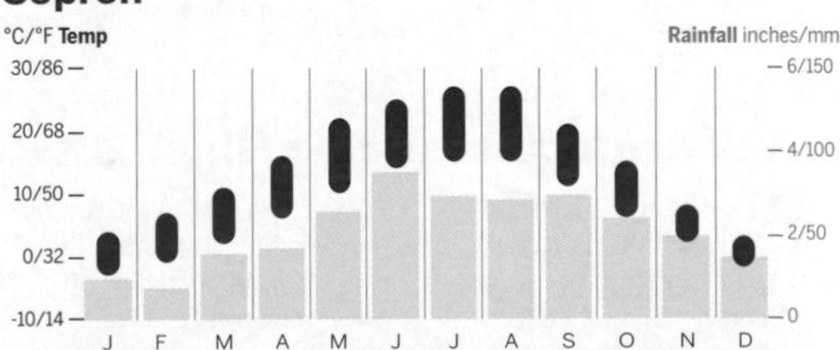

May A great time to visit Őrség National Park, with warm weather but few crowds.

July Rock out to a host of local and international musicians at the VOLT festival in Sopron.

October Get your fill of Hungary's best wines in Sopron and Győr after the grape harvest.

History

The Danube River was the limit of Roman expansion in what is now Hungary, and most of today's Western Transdanubia formed the province of Pannonia Superior. The Romans had a big hand in the area's development, building some of their most important towns here, including Arrabona (Győr), Scarbantia (Sopron) and Savaria (Szombathely). Because of their positions on the Amber trade route from northern Europe to the Adriatic Sea and Byzantium, and the influx of such ethnic groups as Germans and Slovaks, these towns prospered in the Middle Ages. Episcopates were established, castles were built and many of the towns were granted special royal privileges.

A large part of Western Transdanubia remained in the hands of the Habsburgs during the Turkish occupation, and it was thus spared the ruination suffered in the south and on the Great Plain. As a result, some of the best examples of Romanesque and Gothic architecture in the country can be found here, as well as Hungary's first baroque churches.

Tata

✆34 / POP 25,026

There is no escaping water in Tata, a small historical town with a massive lake as its centrepiece, surrounded by the remains of a proud castle and a smattering of neoclassical mansions. This is the legacy of the Esterházy family, who paid for the town's facelift in the 18th century, employing the skills of architect Jakab Fellner. In medieval times, Tata was the favourite retreat of kings, though it fell into disrepair after being ravaged by the Turks in 1683. Tata's many watermills, left over from its heyday, are now in various

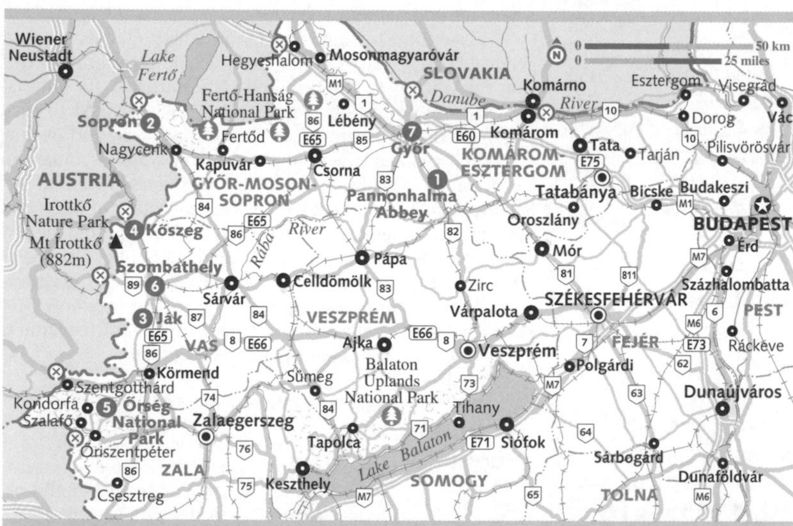

Western Transdanubia Highlights

1. Exploring 1000-year old **Pannonhalma Abbey** (p116) – the architecturally splendid spiritual heart of Hungary in a lofty hilltop location
2. Wandering the cobbled streets and peeking into picturesque hidden courtyards of **Sopron's** medieval Inner Town (p124)
3. Calling in at Ják to admire the beautiful, intricately carved stone portal of the **abbey church** (p137)
4. Lingering in Kőszeg's **Jurisics tér** (p141), arguably Hungary's finest medieval centre
5. Exploring **Őrség National Park** (p145), a region of unspoilt rural beauty where three countries meet
6. Pondering the wealth of Roman remains at **Iseum** (p133), Szombathely's superb archaeological museum
7. Visiting the tomb of Bishop Vilmos Apor and marvelling at Imre Patkó's collection of exotic objects in **Győr**

WORTH A TRIP

PÁPA – A TOWN TO DYE FOR

If you've ever worn a blue garment of some description, you have a link to Pápa, a medieval market town with a Calvinist bent. The link is indigo dye. Used in traditional textiles, be it blouses or tablecloths, blue dyeing has a long-standing tradition in Hungary and in Pápa in particular, where you will find the imaginatively titled and popular **Blue Dyeing Museum** (Kékfestő Múzeum; Március 15 tér 12; adult/child 800/600Ft; ⌚9am-5pm Tue-Sun Apr-Oct, to 4pm Tue-Sat Nov-Mar). The traditional cold indigo vat-dyeing method of textile printing has been around in Hungary since 1786, when an immigrant from Saxony by the name of Carl Friedrich Kluge established a factory for that very purpose. While this factory-cum-museum ceased operations in 1956, the machines remain in perfect working order, and if you're lucky, you can sometimes catch a demonstration; if not, the beautiful finished products, such as the elaborate wall hangings, are worth a visit in themselves.

Pápa is easily reached by train from Győr (930Ft; one hour; 48km; hourly).

states of disrepair, but this genteel decay is tempered by the beauty of the town's natural surroundings.

Sights & Activities

Old Lake LAKE

(Öreg-tó) Tata's focal point and its most striking feature is the vast lake, around which you'll find a smattering of other attractions. This 'Wetland of International Importance', protected by the Ramsar Convention, attracts a considerable number and variety of waterfowl, such as migrating geese, best spotted between September and November. In the summer, the lake is served by boats, which depart from the piers just southwest of the castle, on the eastern shore of the lake and also halfway along the eastern side of the lake.

Old Castle CASTLE

(Öregvár; adult/student 800/400Ft; ⌚10am-6pm Tue-Sun) The sturdy remains of the medieval castle – one of four original towers and a palace wing – were rebuilt in neo-Gothic style at the end of the 19th century to mark a visit by Emperor Franz Joseph. Once a royal retreat for kings Sigismund and Matthias, today they house the **Domokos Kuny Museum** (☎381 251; adult/senior & student 600/300Ft; ⌚10am-6pm Tue-Sun mid-Apr–mid-Oct, to 2pm Wed-Fri, to 4pm Sat-Sun mid-Oct–mid-Apr). On the ground floor are a mishmash of archaeological finds from nearby Roman settlements, bits of the 12th-century Benedictine monastery near Oroszlány and contemporary drawings of the castle in its heyday. The 'Life in the Old Castle' exhibit on the 1st floor is interesting; don't miss the cathedral-like green-tiled Gothic stove that takes pride of place in the Knights' Hall. Material on the 2nd floor comprises the black-and-white sketches of János Schadl and the work of a dozen 18th-century artisans, including Kuny, a master ceramicist. Tata porcelain was well known for centuries (the crayfish, once abundant in the lake, was a common motif) and the craft indirectly led to the foundation of the porcelain factory at Herend, near Veszprém.

Museum of Graeco-Roman Statue Replicas MUSEUM

(Görög-Római Szobormásolatok Múzeuma; Hősök tere 7; adult/student 200/100Ft; ⌚10am-6pm Tue-Sun Apr-Oct) Displayed in this renovated Romantic-style former synagogue are plaster copies of stone sculptures that lined the walkways of Cseke-tó in the 19th century, including Venus de Milo.

Holy Cross Church CHURCH

(Szent Kereszt templom) Dominating the square is this 18th-century church, also known as the Great Church, one of architect Jakab Fellner's works. Inside you'll find modern ceiling frescoes and simple walls (simple for the baroque period, that is), as well as Fellner's body in the crypt and his statue outside the church.

Small Lake LAKE

(Cseke-tó) Small Lake (different to Öreg-tó, the vast Old Lake) is surrounded by the protected 200-hectare **English Park** (Angolpark) – a relaxing place for a walk or a day of fishing. The park itself, which was established in 1783 by the Esterházy family, contains an open-air theatre and 18th-century folly ruins built using Roman stones.

PANNONHALMA ABBEY

Not even the power of Stalin could shut down this splendid **abbey** (Pannonhalmi főapátság; ☎570 191; www.bences.hu; Vár utca 1; foreign-language tours adult/student/family 2500/1500/6300Ft; ⏰9am-4pm Tue-Sun Apr & Oct–mid-Nov, 9am-5pm daily Jun-Sep, 10am-3pm Tue-Sun mid-Nov–Mar, Transports Tue-Sun mid-Nov–Mar) that crowns the top of a hill in the small village of Pannonhalma. In a country filled with religious sites, nothing comes close to Pannonhalma Abbey in terms of architectural splendour and historical significance. It was here that the legendary Árpád expressed his pleasure with the beauty of his new territory after its conquest by the Magyar.

Still a functioning monastery today, it was originally founded in 996 by monks from Venice and Prague, who came on the invitation of Prince Géza. Its creation marked the beginning of Christianity in Hungary; Géza's son, King Stephen, converted the pagan Magyars with the Benedictines' help. The monastery is an eclectic mix of architectural styles with its buildings razed, rebuilt and restored over the centuries. It served as a mosque during the Turkish occupation and as a refuge for Jews in autumn 1944 under the protection of the International Red Cross. Today it runs one of the best secondary schools in the country and, since the early 1990s, the brethren have revived the monastery's age-old tradition of winemaking at the award-winning **Archabbey Winery** (www.apatsagipinceszet.hu; tours by appointment 700Ft, with 3/5 wine tastings 1800/2700Ft).

Access is by tour only. The centrepiece of the central courtyard is the statue of the first abbot, Asztrik, who brought the crown of King Stephen to Hungary from Rome, and a relief of King Stephen himself presenting his son Imre to the tutor Bishop Gellért. From here there are dramatic views of the Kisalföld range and the rolling countryside, while looming behind you is the neoclassical clock tower built in the early 19th century.

The main entrance to **St Martin's Basilica** (Szent Márton-bazilika), built in the early 12th century, is through the Porta Speciosa. This red-limestone doorway comprising a series of arches was recarved in the mid-19th century by the Stornos, a controversial family of

Cifra Mill HISTORIC SITE
(Cifra-malom; Váralja utca 3) East of the old castle is the 16th-century Cifra Mill – the most intact of what is left of Tata's 14 watermills – interesting for its red-marble window frames and five rapidly deteriorating water wheels lying against the eastern outside wall.

German Minority Museum MUSEUM
(Német Nemzetiségi Múzeum; ☎381 251; Alkotmány utca 1; adult/student 400/200Ft; ⏰9am-6.30pm Wed-Thu Apr–mid-Oct, other times by appointment) Tata was predominantly German-speaking for centuries, and the 'Living Together for 1100 Years' exhibition inside the Nepomucenus Mill explores all aspects of the German experience in Hungary, from traditional attire to photos of pro-Hitler marches before WWII. You must be able to read German or Hungarian to fully appreciate this museum.

Esterházy Mansion MUSEUM
(Esterházy Kastély; Kastel tér; adult/student 400/200Ft; ⏰10am-6pm Wed-Sun May-Sep) Designed by Jakab Fellner in 1764 and used as a hospital for many years, this mansion has now been restored and hosts temporary exhibitions.

Clock Tower HISTORIC BUILDING
(óratorony; Országgyűlés tér) The octagonal wooden clock tower is a lot older than it looks. Made by József Éder in 1763, it once housed what may well have been Europe's tiniest prison.

Fényes Fürdő THERMAL BATHS, SPA
(www.fenyesfurdo.hu; Fényes fasor; adult/child 1100/650Ft; ⏰9am-7pm May–mid-Sep) This spa complex and campground north of the city centre has thermal spas and several huge pools – both indoor and outdoor – including a paddling pool for your little ones and a water slide for big 'uns.

Sleeping

TOP CHOICE **Hilltop** HOTEL €€€
(☎550 440; www.hilltop.eu; Neszmély; s/d/tr 12,500/14,300/16,000Ft; 📶🏊) Not only does Hilltop have expansive views of Slovakia and a 30km stretch of the Danube River, but it's located in the middle of the vineyards

restorers who imposed 19th-century Romantic notions of Romanesque and Gothic architecture on ancient buildings. The fresco above the doorway depicts the church's patron, St Martin of Tours. To the right below the columns is probably the oldest graffiti in Hungary: 'Benedict Padary was here in 1578', in Latin.

Inside the pleasantly austere stone church, well-worn steps lead down into the 13th-century crypt. The red-marble niche allegedly covers the wooden throne of St Stephen and a marble slab inscribed with 'Ottó 1912–2011' marks the burial spot of the heart of Otto von Habsburg – the last Crown Prince of Austria-Hungary and one of the leaders of Austrian anti-Nazi resistance (the rest of him is buried in Vienna).

In the cloister arcade, you'll notice the little faces carved in stone on the wall. They represent human emotions and vices, such as wrath, greed and conceit, and are meant to remind monks of the baseness and transitory nature of human existence. In the cloister garden a Gothic sundial offers a sobering thought: 'Una Vestrum Ultima Mea' (One of you will be my last).

The most beautiful part of the abbey is the neoclassical library built in 1836 by János Packh, who was involved in designing the Esztergom Basilica. It contains some 400,000 volumes – many of them priceless historical records – making it the largest private library in Hungary. On display is a copy of the priceless Deed of Foundation of the Abbey Church of Tihany, dating from 1055 and written in Latin; it also contains about 50 Hungarian place names, making it the earliest surviving example of written Hungarian. The library's interior may look like marble, but it is actually wood made to look like the more expensive stone. An ingenious system of mirrors within the skylights reflects and redirects natural light throughout the room.

In the heart of the village, **Borbirodalom** (www.borbirodalom.hu; Szabadság tér 27; ⌚noon-10pm) has an extensive selection of wines from the nearby Pannonhalma-Sokoróalja region in its cellar, and a gourmet menu that includes venison and goose liver.

Frequent buses serve Győr (465Ft; 30 minutes; 21km; half-hourly).

from which it makes its very own wine. Rooms are accordingly tasteful and modern and the restaurant on-site serves regional and seasonal specialities along with local reds and whites. Wine courses and wine tasting sessions are available. Hilltop is best reached with your own transport; find it 15km northeast of Tata just past the tiny village of Dunaszentmiklós.

Parti Panzio B&B €€€
(☎481 577; www.partipanzio.hu; Boróka utca 6-8; s/d 12,000/16,800Ft;) A lovely 12-room guesthouse near the eastern side of the lake. Rooms are decked out in soothing creams; extras include a spa and sauna alongside the indoor pool, and the breakfast is hearty.

Öreg-tó Camping CAMPGROUND €
(☎383 496; www.tatacamping.hu; Fáklya utca 2; campsite per adult/child/tent 900/500/600Ft, d 8000Ft; P) Large, well-kept campground with a youthful vibe, a stone's throw from the eastern shore of the lake. There are tent plots as well as several fully equipped bungalows. Also, with food stalls nearby, you won't have to wander far to get a meal.

Kristály Hotel HOTEL €€€
(☎383 577; www.hktata.hu; Ady Endre utca 22; s/d from 22,000/29,500Ft; P) This beautifully appointed hotel on the main drag has been lovingly renovated – it now wins first prize in Tata's 'best in show' competition. Rooms are tastefully designed and come with little surprises, such as fresh fruit and flowers. The restaurant comes well recommended. Wi-fi in lobby only.

Eating

Büfés (snack bars) line Fáklya utca near Öreg-tó Camping and along Deák Ferenc utca, near the pier where you can rent boats.

TOP CHOICE **Kalóz Fregatt** INTERNATIONAL €€
(www.kalozfregatt.hu; Almási utca 2; mains 1990-3200Ft;) The most imaginative eatery in town, this corsair-themed joint offers everything from 'paunch warmers' such as goulash and soup with liver dumplings to 'Old Pirate's Favourite' (pork chops with all the trimmings) and 'Surprise on Board' (we won't spoil it!). If you're not famished, half-portions are available.

Halászcsárda Tata HUNGARIAN €€
(www.halaszcsardatata.hu; Tópart utca; mains 1500-2800Ft;) With cute covered picnic benches by the lakefront, jolly orange tablecloths and plenty of flowers, this tavern is a sure bet for a plethora of fish dishes (though there are a few meat and veggie offerings to placate non-pescatarians, too).

Zöld Lovag MEDIEVAL €
(Adu Endre utca 17; mains around 1800Ft) Medieval-themed restaurants in Hungary are a dime a dozen, but this is one of the better ones when it comes to the food: portions big enough to satisfy a famished jouster, served on wooden platters.

Information

OTP Bank (Ady Endre utca 1-3) Has an exchange machine and ATM.

Tourinform (586 045; tata@tourinform.hu; Ady Endre utca 9; 8am-5pm Mon-Fri, 10am-7pm Sat-Sun mid-Jun–Aug, 8am-4pm Mon-Fri Sep-Jun) Central, with very helpful staff.

Getting There & Away

Bus

Main centres, such as Győr (1490Ft, 1½ hours, 72km, three daily except Sunday), Budapest (1490Ft, 1½ hours, 77km, once daily) and Esztergom (1120Ft, 1½ hours, 54km, hourly), are connected to Tata.

Train

Tata has excellent links with Budapest (1490Ft, one hour, 74km, hourly) and Győr (1120Ft, one hour, 57km, hourly). There are trains to Sopron (2800Ft, two to 2½ hours, 142km, four daily) via Győr, and Szombathely (3200Ft, 2½ to three hours, 174km, six daily). To get to Slovakia, take the train to Komárom (370Ft, 20 minutes, 20km, hourly) and walk across the border.

Getting Around

Bus 1 links the main train station with the bus station and Kossuth tér. Bus 3 will take you to Fényes Fürdő.

Győr

96 / POP 131,267

This large city with the funny name (pronounced 'jyeur') is a surprisingly splendid place. Hidden behind an industrial facade, its medieval heart is dense with religious and historical attractions.

Győr is situated in the heart of Kisalföld (Little Plain) at the meeting point of the Mosoni-Danube and Rába Rivers. It was settled by Celts, Romans and Avars – the latter building a circular fort (a *gyűrű*, from which the town took its name) – before King Stephen established a bishopric at Győr in the 11th century. Győr has come under attack several times, with the Ottomans capturing the town for four years in the late 16th century; in 1809, Napoleon's forces destroyed the formidable castle, and during WWII the Allies targeted the town's factories and railway, though this busy hub has bounced back since.

Sights

Basilica CHURCH
(Bazilika; 8am-noon & 2-6pm) Chapter Hill (Káptalan-domb), the oldest part of the city, is criss-crossed with quiet cobbled streets and tight alleyways and dominated by the Basilica, with foundations dating back to the 11th century. Over the ensuing centuries the religious centre of Győr gained an amalgam of styles: Romanesque apses, a neoclassical facade and a Gothic chapel riding piggyback on the south side. The baroque, dark interior, with red-marble accents – including stunning frescoes by Franz Anton Maulbertsch; the main altar; the bishop's throne and the pews hewn from Dalmatian oak – dates from the 17th and 18th centuries.

The real highlight here is the Herm of László, an incredible and priceless goldwork dating from the early 15th century. Housed in the Gothic Héderváry Chapel, the herm is a bust reliquary of one of Hungary's earliest king-saints László (r 1077–95). Once a year on 27 June it is taken from its resting place and paraded around the city.

If you're looking for miracles, move to the north aisle and the Weeping Icon of Mary, an altarpiece brought from Galway by the Irish Bishop of Clonfert in 1649, who had been sent packing by Oliver Cromwell. Some 40 years later – on St Patrick's Day no less – it began to cry tears of blood and is still a pilgrimage site today.

The Basilica also features the tomb of Bishop Vilmos Apor, shot by the Soviet 'liberators' in 1945 for trying to protect local women and girls from rape, and beatified by the Pope in 1997.

Imre Patkó Collection MUSEUM
(Széchenyi tér 5; adult/senior & student 600/300Ft; 10am-6pm Tue-Sun Apr-Sep, to 4pm rest of year) Journalist and art historian Imre Patkó was a traveller and an art collector, and this is a

fascinating trawl through his life's trappings. In the 20th-century art collection, the dark *Bone Music*, the sombre *Burned People* and the mesmerising *Ice World* stand out. On the 3rd floor, among the objects collected during Patkó's time in India, Tibet, Vietnam and West Africa, you may spot a ceremonial broom from Burma, wooden carvings from the Congo and Cameroon, a 19th-century opium pipe and an Australian boomerang. The museum is located in the 17th-century **Iron Stump House** (Vastuskós Ház), a former caravanserai entered from Stelczer Lajos utca. It still sports the log into which itinerant artisans would drive a nail to mark their visit.

Margit Kovács Ceramic Collection MUSEUM
(Kovács Margit kerámiagyűjtemény; Apáca utca 1; adult/senior & student 600/300Ft; ⏲10am-6pm Tue-Sun) This branch of the City Art Museum is devoted to the celebrated, Győr-born ceramicist Margit Kovács (1902–77). Many of her works deal with rural and family life and have touches of folk art and religious imagery, while her later pieces are more abstract. Although her best work is located in Szentendre, the 100 or so pieces on show here are a pleasure to view, including a sorrowful terracotta Virgin, nativity scene and some dapper soldiers.

FREE **Szécheny Pharmacy Museum** MUSEUM
(Szécheny Patikamúzeum; Széchenyi tér 9; ⏲7.40am-4pm Mon-Fri) Odds are you've never purchased aspirin in such splendid surroundings. This working apothecary features a vaulted rococo ceiling, fabulous frescoes with religious and herbal themes, displays of mysterious ampoules, and a couple of politically incorrect statues of black savages holding up ye olde porcelain jars.

János Xánthus Museum MUSEUM
(www.gymsmuzeum.hu; Széchenyi tér 5; adult/senior & student 700/350Ft; ⏲10am-6pm Tue-Sun Apr-Sep, to 4pm Oct-Mar) Győr's main museum is named after a local 19th-century traveller and naturalist. The exterior of this peach-coloured museum building with its all-seeing eye is as interesting as the collection, parts of which are a philatelist's wet dream. You have to trawl through the fairly ho-hum archaeological remains and the like to spot the gems, such as the miniscule boots created by a shoemaker in a bid to show off his skills and be accepted by the appropriate guild.

Péter Váczy Museum MUSEUM
(Nefelejcs köz 3; adult/student & child 800/400Ft; ⏲10am-6pm Tue-Sun Mar-Oct, to 5pm rest of year) This is the private collection of an anticommunist history professor with a clear passion for antiques. Housed inside the late-Renaissance **Hungarian Ispita** (Magyar Ispita; Nefelejcs köz 3), which was once a charity hospital, this eclectic assortment runs the gamut from Greek and Roman relics to Chinese terracotta figures and Baroque and Renaissance furniture.

FREE **Zichy Palace** MUSEUM
(Zichy palota; Liszt Ferenc utca 20; ⏲8am-3.30pm Mon-Thu, to noon Fri, noon-6pm Sat) In the stunning baroque Zichy Palace, sometimes used for concerts and plays, you'll find the engaging **Doll Exhibition**, consisting of 72 mostly 19th-century dolls and furniture. Look for the 1960s 'rocker' dolls and the thoroughly contemporary Harry Potter addition.

Synagogue JEWISH
(Kossuth Lajos utca 5; adult/student & child 500/250Ft; ⏲10am-6pm Wed-Sun) Across the Rába River, the richly decorated octagonal cupola, galleries and tabernacle of the city's erstwhile synagogue, built in 1870, poke above the treeline. The former Jewish house of worship now plays host to János Vasilescu's private collection of contemporary Hungarian art, but the true star here is the beautifully restored interior. In the former Jewish school next door is the city's music academy.

Diocesan Treasury and Library MUSEUM
(Egyházmegyei kincstár és könyvtár; Káptalandomb 26; adult/senior & student 800/400Ft; ⏲10am-4pm Tue-Sun Mar-Oct) One of the richest collections of sacred relics in Hungary, this treasury features Gothic chalices, a Renaissance mitre embroidered with pearls, a 14th-century gold monstrance from Budapest's Clarissa Convent and a bloodied part of Bishop Vilmos's shirt. The showstopper here is the priceless library, containing almost 70,000 volumes printed before 1850, including an 11th-century codex.

Napoleon House HISTORIC BUILDING
(Király utca 4; adult/senior & student 800/400Ft; ⏲10am-6pm Mon-Fri, 9am-1pm Sat) The trivia that accompanies this building is of greater interest than its present-day contents – a small art gallery. A certain diminutive French conqueror spent the night here on

Győr

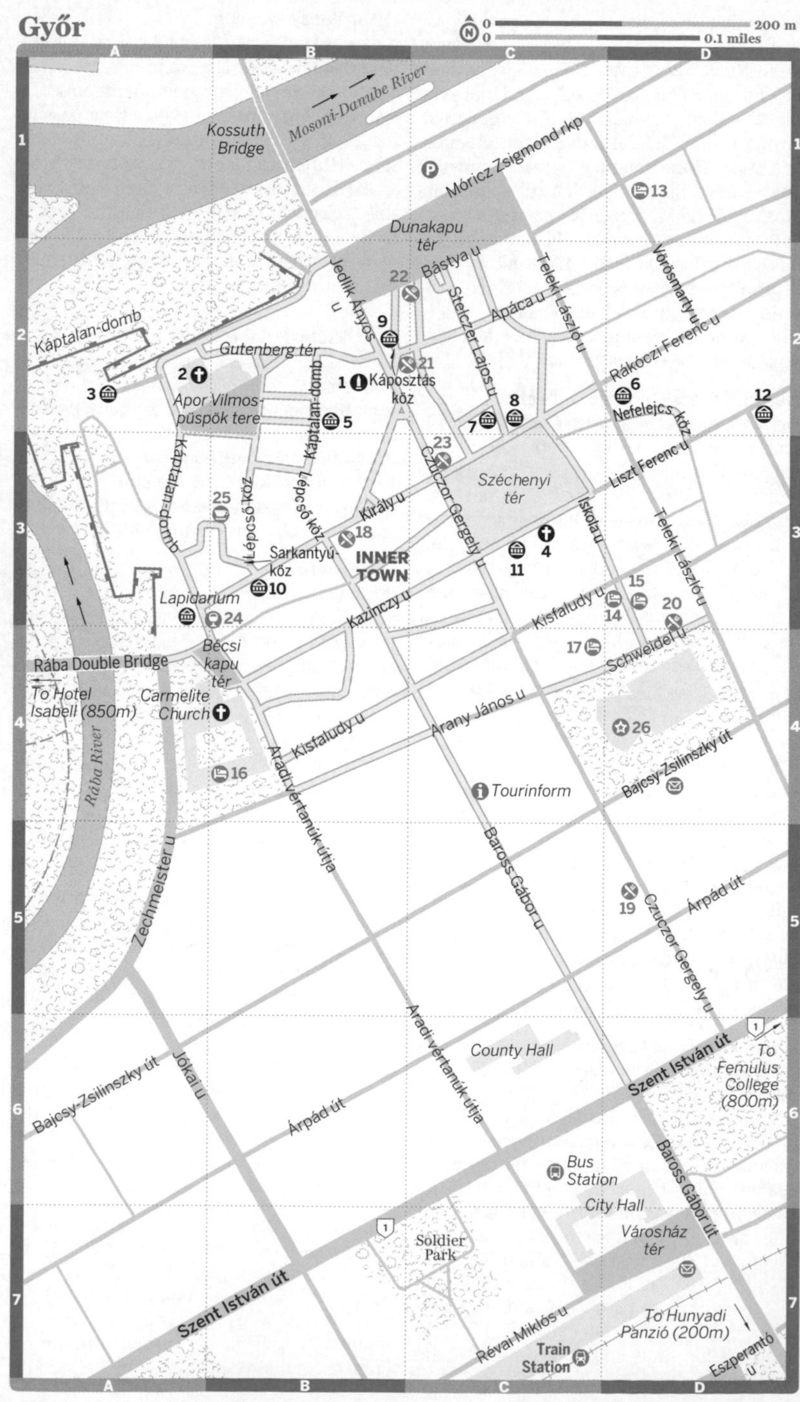

0 200 m
0 0.1 miles
A
B
C
D
1
2
3
4
5
6
7
Mosoni-Danube River
Kossuth Bridge
Móricz Zsigmond rkp
Dunakapu tér
Bástya u
Jedlik Ányos u
Stelczer Lajos u
Apáca u
Teleki László u
Vörösmarty u
Rákóczi Ferenc u
Káptalan-domb
Gutenberg tér
Káposztás köz
Apor Vilmos püspök tere
Nefelejcs köz
Liszt Ferenc u
Széchenyi tér
Czuczor Gergely u
Király u
Lépcső köz
Sarkantyú-köz
INNER TOWN
Iskola u
Kisfaludy u
Schweidel u
Kazinczy u
Lapidarium
Rába Double Bridge
To Hotel Isabell (850m)
Bécsi kapu tér
Carmelite Church
Arany János u
Kisfaludy u
Aradi vértanúk útja
Rába River
Tourinform
Bajcsy-Zsilinszky út
Zechmeister u
Baross Gábor u
Árpád út
County Hall
Jókai u
Szent István út
To Femulus College (800m)
Bus Station
City Hall
Baross Gábor út
Városház tér
Soldier Park
Révai Miklós u
To Hunyadi Panzió (200m)
Train Station
Eszperantó u

Győr

Sights

- 1 Ark of the Covenant B2
- 2 Basilica A2
- 3 Bishop's Castle A2
- 4 Church of St Ignatius C3
- City Museum .... (see 10)
- 5 Diocesan Treasury and Library B2
- Doll Exhibition .... (see 12)
- 6 Hungarian Ispita D2
- Imre Patkó Collection .... (see 7)
- 7 Iron Stump House C2
- 8 János Xánthus Museum C2
- 9 Margit Kovács Ceramic Collection B2
- 10 Napoleon House B3
- Péter Váczy Museum .... (see 6)
- 11 Szécheny Pharmacy Museum C3
- 12 Zichy Palace D2

Sleeping

- 13 Duna D1
- 14 Hotel Fonte D3
- 15 Kertész Pension D3
- 16 Klastrom Hotel B4
- 17 Teátrum C4

Eating

- 18 Bergman Cukrászda B3
- 19 Komédiás D5
- 20 La Dolce Vita D3
- 21 La Maréda B2
- 22 Matróz C2
- 23 Pálffy Étterem C3

Drinking

- 24 John Bull Pub B3
- 25 Mandala B3

Entertainment

- 26 Győr National Theatre D4

31 August 1809 after his troops took the castle and wrecked it. Why did Monsieur Bonaparte choose Győr to make his grand entrée into Hungary? Apparently the city was near a battle site; an inscription on the Arc de Triomphe in Paris recalls '*la bataille de Raab*'.

Bishop's Castle HISTORIC BUILDING
(Püspökvár; Káptalandomb 1; adult/senior & student 1000/500Ft; ⌚10am-4pm Tue-Sun) This fortress-like structure with an attractive 14th-century tower (rebuilt in the 18th century) is partially closed to the public. You can, however, visit the exhibition inside the tower (ticket office is behind the Basilica).

Ark of the Covenant MONUMENT
(Frigyszekrény szobor; Jedlik Ányos utca) Local tradition has it that in 1731, King Charles (Károly) III erected the ark, the city's finest baroque monument, to appease the angry people of Győr after one of his soldiers accidentally knocked a monstrance containing the Blessed Sacrament out of the bishop's hands during a religious procession.

Church of St Ignatius CHURCH
Dating from 1641, this Jesuit and later Benedictine church sits on the south side of the enormous Széchenyi tér – the town's marketplace in the Middle Ages. The 17th-century white-stucco side chapels and the ceiling frescoes painted by the Viennese baroque artist Paul Troger in 1744 are worth a look.

Activities

Raba Quelle SPA
(☎514 900; www.gyortermal.hu; Fürdő tér 1; adult/child 2450/1900Ft; ⌚thermal baths 9am-8.30pm Sun-Thu, to 9pm Fri-Sat, pool 6am-8pm Mon-Sat, open-air pool 8am-8pm May-Aug) Győr's complex of thermal baths, pools, water slides and fitness and wellness centres, offering every treatment imaginable. Travellers have complained, though, that some facilities were shut when they visited, but no reduction in entry price offered.

Festivals & Events

Hungarian Dance Festival DANCE
(www.magyartancfesztival.hu) Held biannually in late June.

Sleeping

Hotel Isabell HOTEL €€€
(☎528 020; www.isabellhotel.hu; Lakatos utca 15; s/d €66/80, ste €95; P@) This pastel, flower-adorned little hotel is possibly Győr's nicest, not least thanks to the efforts of its brisk, cheerful staff. The attic rooms are compact and bright, with nice little touches such as fresh flowers. There's a sauna for guest use, too.

LOCAL KNOWLEDGE

CSABA GRÓZER: BOWMAKER

The Magyar, who settled in Hungary in the 10th century, excelled at archery – a skill they'd inherited from their Skythian and Hun ancestors, as well as their weapon of choice, the recurve composite bow. Those reinforced bows were used by Magyar cavalry in battle for centuries until they were eventually phased out with the advent of guns. Examples of medieval Magyar bows can be seen at Budapest's National Museum. Traditional horseback archery has been revived in Europe in recent years by Lajos Kassai from Kaposmero in southern Hungary (www.horsebackarcherybg.com), who also perfected the speed-shooting technique.

His northern Hungarian counterpart, Csaba Grózer (www.grozerbows.com), began pursuing his dream of making traditional bows – from recurve Hungarian to Mongol, Scythian, Persian and Assyrian – more than 20 years ago, when traditional archery was out of fashion. Now he is a renowned bowyer, has popularised the sport of traditional archery both in his native Hungary and worldwide and has recently provided bows for UK's BBC1 *Robin Hood* series. To visit his workshop, make arrangements in advance and take a train from Győr to Mosonmagyaróvár (745Ft, 20 to 25 minutes; hourly), then take a taxi from the station to Templom utca 14 in the village of Feketeerdő (1500Ft, 15 minutes).

How popular is archery as a sport in Hungary? You can say that archery is in our blood; it goes back many centuries. But when I started making traditional bows, everyone was shooting sports bows. I was lucky to have met British archery enthusiast, Roy Simpson, who promoted my work. Today, traditional bows have well overtaken sports bows in popularity.

What is the process of making a bow? If you take a composite bow – a combination of wood, leather and horn – first you shape the wood, then prepare the horn material – mountain goat or grey cattle horn is good – and flatten it. Then take apart small pieces of sinew or fibreglass and bind the two together, mould the horn to the approximate shape of the bow, bit by bit; glue the two together, leave it for a couple of months, then add another layer. Depending on the type of finish, a bow can take between three months to a year to complete.

What else do you do? In summer particularly we have a lot of groups coming to the workshop for archery demos. I also arrange horseback archery demonstrations and lessons on my property nearby.

Teátrum GUESTHOUSE €€
(☎310 640; www.teatrum.hu; Schweidel utca 7; s/d/tr 9500/12,500/15,000Ft; 📶) Arguably the best B&B in town, with warm, cosy guestrooms featuring plenty of natural wood and compact, spotless bathrooms. A very central location, friendly staff and a perpetually busy restaurant on the ground floor seal the deal.

Klastrom Hotel HOTEL €€€
(☎516 910; www.klastrom.hu; Zechmeister utca 1; s/d from €50/70; 📶) Though the bright, charming rooms at this converted 300-year-old Carmelite convent are former monks' cells, you will hardly be expected to take up an austere, monastic lifestyle. A plethora of perks include a sauna, solarium, pub with a vaulted ceiling, oxygen bar and a restaurant with seating in a leafy and peaceful inner garden. The best rooms face the courtyard.

Hotel Fonte HOTEL €€€
(☎513 810; www.hotelfonte.hu; Kisfaludy utca 38; s/d from 16,300/19,300Ft; P ❄ @ 📶) The cream exterior of this centrally located business hotel hides bright, carpeted rooms with all mod cons. An extensive buffet breakfast is included, and the on-site restaurant is one of the best in town. There are also bikes for rent for those who want to get out and about.

Hunyadi Panzió GUESTHOUSE €€
(☎329 162; www.hunyadi-gyor.hu; Hunyadi utca 10; s/d 8900/11,900Ft; P ❄ @ 📶) While this B&B may not be super-central, it is located right near the bus and train stations. The canary-yellow rooms are spic-and-span and guests can enjoy the garden terrace in warmer months.

Duna GUESTHOUSE €€€
(☎329 084; www.dunapanzio.hu; Vörösmarty utca 5; s/d 7500/11,500Ft; P 📶) The powder-blue Duna guesthouse distinguishes itself with its attentive service and thoughtful details, such as a small play area for children. The rooms are a little worn, but clean and comfortable. Best not to visit in the depths of winter, as some guests have complained of inadequate heating.

Kertész Pension GUESTHOUSE €€
(☎317 461; www.kerteszpanzio.com; Iskola utca 11; s/d 8000/12,000Ft; @) The 'Gardener' has very simple rooms, but it's well located in central Győr, staff couldn't be more friendly and there's an attractive, wood-panelled bar.

Eating

TOP CHOICE **La Maréda** INTERNATIONAL €€€
(☎510 982; www.lamareda.hu; Apáca utca 4; mains 2680-4850Ft) The most creative restaurant in town, La Maréda specialises in true fusion cuisine. Everything on the seasonal menu – from venison saddle with goat's cheese and spicy pumpkin cream to roast duck (pink and juicy in the middle!) with quince jelly – is expertly seasoned and presented beautifully enough to deserve the accolade 'food as art'. Yet the service is wonderfully unpretentious and attentive.

Matróz SEAFOOD €€
(http://matroz-vendeglo.internettudakozo.hu; Dunakapu tér 3; mains 1200-2180Ft) The fishing nets hanging from the ceiling of this vaulted brick cellar, the life belt and the nautically themed stained-glass windows give the game away: this busy cellar-like place specialises in fish, and plenty of it. Though few can resist catfish prepared in the 'Good Woman's Style' or the carp soup, there are also pork medallions, liver and turkey dishes.

Pálffy Étterem HUNGARIAN €€
(www.palffyetterem.hu; Jedlik Ányos utca 19; mains 1490-7000Ft) The cellar part of this exceedingly popular restaurant, accessorised with wrought-iron chandeliers and halberds, feels like a medieval banqueting hall – an impression aided by the vast quantities of hearty, mainly carnivorous dishes, such as goulash, ribs and 'frizzled trotters with beer'. Bring a king's ransom in diamonds if you wish to order the goose liver.

Komédiás HUNGARIAN €€
(Czuczor Gergely utca 30; mains 1700-3000Ft; ⏲closed Sun) An upscale cellar eatery decorated in postmodern greys and blacks, the 'Comedian' caters to a firm local following with a thoroughly Hungarian menu. It has courtyard seating, which is a delight in the warmer months, and there are good-value set-lunch menus on weekdays (1000Ft).

Bergman Cukrászda PASTICCERIA €
(Király utca 17; cakes 650Ft) Old-world patisserie specialising in excellent cakes. Either the Art Nouveau interior or the small outdoor seating area is a good place to while away the day over a cup of coffee.

La Dolce Vita PIZZA €
(www.pizzza.hu; Schweidel utca 23; mains 850-1350Ft; ⏲closed Sun; 🖉) Okay, so the menu ticks all the predictable boxes: an array of pizzas, risottos, prosciutto and melon for starters, tiramisu and panna cotta for dessert. But it's all decent quality and very central to boot.

Drinking & Entertainment

A good source of information for what's on in Győr is the free fortnightly magazine *Győri Est*.

John Bull Pub PUB
(☎618 320; www.johnbullpub.hu; Aradi vertanuk utca 3) Made to look like a classic English pub – all dark leather and wood panelling – this is the hottest spot in town. Besides the beers and ales, there's an extensive selection of local wines and creative, hearty dishes (try the brains). If you want to dine here, don't even think about coming without a reservation.

Mandala TEAHOUSE
(Sarkantyú köz 7; ⏲10am-10pm Mon-Thu, to 11pm Fri-Sat, 2-8pm Sun) This small teahouse festooned with Tibetan prayer flags and rattling with wind chimes has more tea varieties on offer than some Hungarian towns. Choose your poison and relax in a super-chilled environment.

Győr National Theatre THEATRE
(Győri Nemzeti Színház; ☎box office 520 611; www.gyoriszinhaz.hu; Czuczor Gergely utca 7; ⏲10am-1pm Mon-Fri, 2-6pm Tue-Fri) This modern, technically advanced structure is home to the celebrated **Győr Ballet** (www.gyoribalett.hu), as well as the city's opera company and the philharmonic orchestra.

Information

OTP Bank (Baross Gábor utca 16)

Main Post Office (Bajcsy-Zsilinszky út 46; 8am-6pm Mon-Fri) The main post office is opposite the Győr National Theatre. Another branch is available at the train station (Révai Miklós utca 8), south of the colossal city hall.

Tourinform (311 771; www.gyortourism.hu; Baross Gábor utca 21-23; 9am-6pm Mon-Fri, to 7pm Sat-Sun Jun-Aug, to 5pm Mon-Fri, to 1pm Sat Sep-May) Large new office with helpful staff and plenty of informative brochures.

Getting There & Away

Bus Destinations from Győr include the following:

DESTINATION	PRICE	TIME	KM	FREQUENCY
Balatonfüred	2200Ft	2½hr	100km	5 daily
Budapest	2520Ft	2hr	28km	1 daily
Esztergom	2200Ft	2¼hr	102km	1-2 daily
Keszthely	2520Ft	3hr	136km	5 daily
Pannonhalma	650Ft	33min	21km	hourly
Pápa	930Ft	1hr	48km	8 daily
Pécs	4200Ft	4½-5hr	254km	2 daily
Sopron	1680Ft	2-2½hr	87km	hourly
Szombathely	2200Ft	2½hr	110km	3-4 daily
Tapolca	2200Ft	2½hr	106km	3 daily
Tata	1120Ft	1¼hr	58km	1 daily
Veszprém	1680Ft	1¾hr	86km	5 daily

Train Győr is a train hub with convenient connections to Budapest (2520Ft, 1½ to two hours, 131km, half-hourly) and Vienna (3350Ft, 1½ hours, 119km, 13 daily). Other destinations include Szombathely (2200Ft, 1½ to two hours, 103km, hourly) and Veszprém (1490Ft, two hours, 79km, five daily), via Pannonhalma.

Sopron

99 / POP 60,755

Hungary's 'most faithful city' (a reference to the 1921 referendum, when Sopron opted to stay part of Hungary rather than be absorbed into Austria) has been around for a while. First settled by the Celts, then the Romans (as a trading spot along the Amber Route from the Baltic Sea to the Adriatic and Byzantium), then a succession of Germans, Avars, Slavs and Magyars. In recent years, this little town also indirectly brought about the most dramatic event of the late 20th century – the fall of the Iron Curtain (p131). Today it is the most beautiful town in western Hungary, its medieval Inner Town (Belváros) intact and its cobbled streets a pleasure to wander. If that weren't enough, it's also famous for its wine, surrounded as it is by flourishing vineyards.

Sights

THE INNER TOWN

Firewatch Tower TOWER

(Tűztorony; Fő tér) The 60m-high tower – from which trumpeters would warn of fire, mark the hour, and watch for salespeople trying to smuggle in non-Sopron wine – is a true architectural hybrid. The 2m-thick square base, built on a Roman gate, dates from the 12th century and the cylindrical middle and arcaded balcony from the 16th century, while the baroque spire was added in 1681. A narrow spiral staircase snakes its way up to the summit where you get an all-encompassing view of the Lővér Hills to the southwest, the Austrian Alps to the west and the entire Inner Town before you. The tower was under renovation at the time of writing but due to reopen in late 2012, as is the brand-new visitors' centre at its base. **Fidelity Gate** (Fő tér, below Firewatch Tower) shows 'Hungaria' receiving the *civitas fidelissima* (Latin for 'the most loyal citizenry') of Sopron. It was erected the year after the 1921 referendum in which the citizens of Sopron voted to remain part of Hungary.

Goat Church CHURCH

(Kecsketemplom; Templom utca 1; 7am-9pm May-Sep, 8am-6pm Mon-Sat Oct-Apr) Dominating the southern side of the main square, this mostly Gothic church gets its unusual name from the legend that the church was built thanks to the treasure unearthed by a goat (hence the stone goat being cuddled by an angel on a pillar). Originally built in the late 13th century, the church has a mostly baroque interior with a splendid red-marble pulpit in the centre of the south aisle, which dates from the 15th century. Better yet is the church's **Chapter Hall** (Középkori Káptalan Terem; info 338 843; Templom utca 1; admission free; 10am-noon & 2-5pm mid-May–Sep), located off the main nave. Part of a 14th-century Benedictine monastery, it has fading frescoes and grotesque stone carvings – mainly animals with human heads – representing the deadly sins of humankind.

Directly in front of the chutch is the tall, corkscrew-like 1701 **Trinity Column**

(Szentháromság oszlop; Fő tér) – among the finest examples of a 'plague pillar' in Hungary – paid for by two Sopron residents to celebrate the end of the plague at the end of the 17th century.

Storno House MUSEUM
(Storno Ház és Gyűjtemény; www.soprontourist.info/en/sopron//museums; adult/senior & student 1300/750Ft; ⏲10am-6pm Tue-Sun Apr-Sep, 2-6pm Oct-Mar) Storno House, built in 1417, has an illustrious history, not least because King Matthias stayed here in 1482–3 and Franz Liszt played a number of concerts here in the mid-19th century. After that, it was taken over by the Swiss-Italian family of Ferenc Storno, chimney sweep turned art restorer, whose recarving of Romanesque and Gothic monuments throughout Transdanubia divides opinions to this day. To their credit, the much-maligned Stornos did rescue many altarpieces and church furnishings from oblivion, and their house is a Gothic treasure trove. The 2nd floor of Storno House has the wonderful **Storno Collection** (Storno Gyűjtemény; ☎311 327; adult/senior & student 1000/500Ft); its highlights include the beautiful enclosed balcony with leaded windows and frescoes, an extensive collection of medieval weaponry, leather chairs with designs depicting Mephisto with his dragons, and door frames made from pews taken from 15th-century **St George's Church** on Szent György utca.

Fabricius House MUSEUM
(www.soprontourist.info/en/sopron//museums; Fő tér 6; adult/senior & student 1000/500Ft; ⏲10am-6pm Tue-Sun Apr-Sep, to 2pm Oct-Mar) The baroque Fabricius House was built on Roman foundations and is divided into three distinct sections. The main **archaeological exhibition** (adult/senior & student 700/350Ft; ⏲10am-6pm Tue-Sun Apr-Sep, to 2pm Oct-Mar) covers Celtic, Roman and Hungarian periods of history on its lower floors, the standout artefact being the 1200-year-old Cunpald Goblet – don't miss the 'whispering gallery' either. The basement, which used to be a Roman bathhouse, now fittingly features some of the most impressive Roman remains in Sopron: sarcophagi and Scarbantia-era statues reconstructed from fragments (including enormous statues of Juno, Jupiter and Minerva). Finally, upstairs are the **urban flats** (polgári lakások; ☎311 327; adult/senior & student 700/350Ft; ⏲10am-6pm Tue-Sun Apr-Sep, 2-6pm Oct-Mar), with rooms tracing the changes in interior furnishings between the 17th and 18th centuries – of interest to those with a passion for antique furniture.

Old Synagogue MUSEUM
(Ó Zsinagóga; Új utca 22; adult/student 700/350Ft; ⏲10am-6pm Tue-Sun May-Oct) Új utca was known as Zsidó utca (Jewish St) until the Jews were evicted from Sopron in 1526 after being accused of plotting with Turks. It features a remnant of the medieval community's existence – the Old Synagogue, built in the 14th century and containing two rooms, one for each sex (note the women's windows along the west wall). The main room contains a medieval 'holy of holies', with geometric designs and trees carved in stone, and some incongruous-looking stained-glass windows. The inscriptions on the walls date from 1490. There's a reconstructed *mikvah* (ritual bath) in the courtyard as well as a plaque commemorating the devastation of Sopron's Jewish community under the Nazis in 1944.

Pharmacy Museum MUSEUM
(Patikamúzeum; Fő tér 2) Housed in a 19th-century pharmacy in a Gothic building just off the main square and under renovation at the time of writing, this collection of curios comprises an assortment of ancient pharmaceutical tools, cures and books. Look for oddities such as the amulet to ward off the evil eye and the hat against epilepsy.

Scarbantia Forum RUIN
(☎321 804; Új utca 1; adult/senior & student 300/150Ft; ⏲8am-4pm Mon-Fri, 10am-5pm Sat-Sun) The Scarbantia Forum is an original Roman-era marketplace recently discovered under – and accessible through – an office block.

Roman Ruins RUIN
(Szabadtéri rom) As the plaque on the ground in Fő tér reminds you, Sopron used to be an important stop along the Amber Road, and fragments of Sopron's Roman past – in the form of reconstructed Roman walls and outlines of 2nd-century buildings – can be found at the open-air ruins behind the city's town hall. At the time of writing, a footpath was being built that will shortly encircle the remnants of the city's defensive walls and other ruins of interest.

Sopron

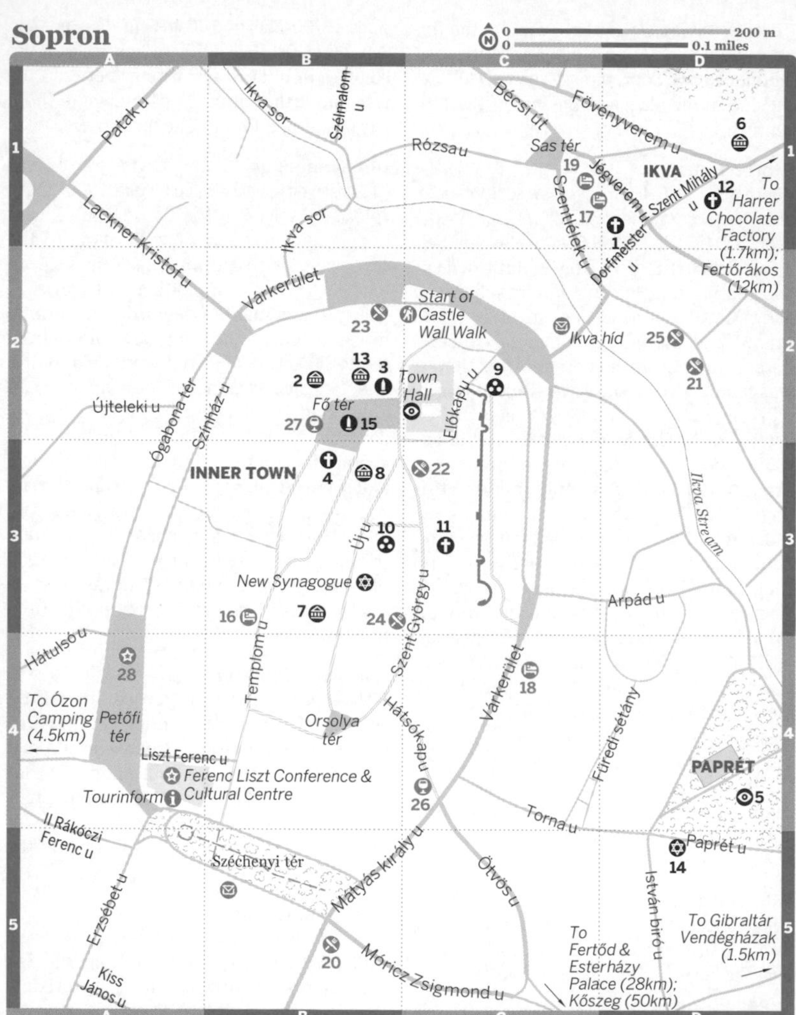

OUTSIDE THE INNER TOWN

St Michael's Church & Chapel of St James CHURCH

(Szent Mihály-templom & Szent Jakab-kápolna; Szent Mihály utca) At the top of the Lővér Hills, is St Michael's Church (Szent Mihály-templom), built between the 13th and 15th centuries and featuring some impressive gargoyles. Behind St Michael's to the south is the little Romanesque-Gothic Chapel of St James (Szent Jakab-kápolna), the oldest structure in Sopron and originally an ossuary. Not much escaped the Stornos' handiwork when they 'renovated' St Michael's – they even added the spire. Check out the lovely polychrome Stations of the Cross (1892) in the churchyard and the large number of tombstones with German family names.

Harrer Chocolate Factory CHOCOLATE FACTORY

(Harrer Csokoládéműhely és Cukrászda; ☎505 904; www.harrercafe.com; Faller Jenő utca 4; adult/child 1990/1490Ft; ⏰10am & 2pm daily by appointment) Sopron's answer to Willy Wonka's Chocolate Factory, the Austrian confectioner dynasty Harrer aims to initiate you into the mysteries of pralines, truffles, flavoured chocolate

Sopron

Sights

Archaeological Exhibition .... (see 2)
1 Church of the Holy Spirit D1
2 Fabricius House B2
Fidelity Gate................................. (see 3)
3 Firewatch Tower B2
4 Goat Church B3
5 Holocaust Memorial D4
6 House of the Two Moors..................... D1
Medieval Chapter Hall................. (see 4)
7 Old Synagogue.................................... B3
8 Pharmacy Museum B3
9 Roman Ruins C2
10 Scarbantia Forum................................ B3
11 St George's Church C3
12 St Michael's Church & Chapel of St James D1
Storno Collection .... (see 13)
13 Storno House B2
14 Synagogue... D5
15 Trinity Column..................................... B2
Urban Flats .... (see 2)

Sleeping

Erhardt Pension .... (see 21)
16 Hotel Wollner B3
17 Jégverem Fogadó C1
18 Pannonia Med Hotel C4
19 Wieden Panzió....................................... C1

Eating

20 Alcatraz B5
21 Erhardt Restaurant & Wine Cellar.. D2
22 Forum Pizzeria C3
23 Graben B2
Jégverem .... (see 17)
24 Liszt Salon.. B3
25 Stubi... D2

Drinking

26 Cezár Pince.. C4
27 Gyógygödör Borozó B2

Entertainment

28 Petőfi Theatre.. A4

and so much more. Visits to the factory (book in advance) involve a video on the production of chocolate and lots of chocolate tasting, be it dipping fruit into chocolate fountains, sampling Harrer's raw, dark, milk and flavoured chocolates, or sipping champagne alongside your truffles. You may well hate the stuff for weeks afterwards.

Synagogue JEWISH
(Paprét utca 14) Evidence of Sopron's Jewish past can be seen at the crumbling synagogue east of the Inner Town, boarded up and falling into disrepair. A plaque tells passers-by that '1640 martyrs' were taken from here to Auschwitz on 5 July 1944. A **Holocaust memorial** across the street, erected with much political chest-beating in 2004, features sculptures of jackets with the Star of David and a pile of shoes, which represent Auschwitz remains.

Church of the Holy Spirit CHURCH
(Szentlék-templom; Dorfmeister utca) The interior of this 15th-century church is rather dark, but if you time your visit for midday, you'll be able catch a glimpse of some fine wall and ceiling frescoes by Dorfmeister, as well as a stupendously ornate altar.

House of the Two Moors HISTORIC BUILDING
(Két mór ház; Szent Mihály utca 9) Fashioned from two 17th-century peasant houses, the ornate gate of this house is guarded by two large statues, previously painted an exaggerated black to represent the darker-skinned Moors, which are now painted white.

Festivals & Events

Tickets to various events are available from the ticket office in the Ferenc Liszt Conference and Cultural Centre.

Spring Days CULTURAL FESTIVAL
Music, theatre and dance in March.

Sopron Festival Weeks MUSIC
All manner of concerts, plus exhibitions in Sopron's squares from mid-June to mid-July.

VOLT MUSIC
Hugely popular music festival in early July; mostly Hungarian bands but some international acts also.

Grape Harvest WINE
Wine tasting, music and folk dancing to celebrate the grape harvest in October.

Sleeping

Ózon Camping CAMPGROUND €
(☎523 370; Erdei Malom köz 3; campsite per tent/adult/child 2000/1600/1500Ft; ⊙mid-Apr–mid-Oct;) This delightful campground with 50 sites has everything you could want, from fridges and washing machines to a restaurant, heated swimming pool and other sports facilities. It's set in a leafy valley about 4.5km west of the Inner Town (take bus 3, 10 or 10/b) in the green of the Lővér Hills.

Wieden Panzió GUESTHOUSE €€
(☎523 222; www.wieden.hu; Sas tér 13; s/d from 7000/9900Ft;) Sopron's loveliest guesthouse is located in an attractive old townhouse a stone's throw from Inner Town (well, three minutes' walk). Rooms are spacious, bright and coloured in peaceful hues; bigger apartments are also an option.

Hotel Wollner HOTEL €€€
(☎524 400; www.wollner.hu; s/d €75/90;) This refined family-run hotel offers just 14 spacious, tastefully decorated rooms in the heart of Inner Town. The menu at the fine restaurant is short, but each dish is superbly executed and the cavernous wine cellar is one of the better places to sample Sopron's famous wines.

Jégverem Fogadó GUESTHOUSE €
(☎510 113; www.jegverem.hu; Jégverem utca 1; s/d 6900/8900Ft;) It's difficult not to like a guesthouse that displays a symbol of a little man with an ice pick perched on a giant ice cube (the inn is on top of an 18th-century ice cellar). Booking in advance is essential, since there are only five suite-like rooms; the restaurant comes highly recommended whether you're staying here or not.

Pannonia Med Hotel HOTEL €€€
(☎312 180; www.pannoniahotel.com; Várkerület 75; s/d from €50/59, ste from €97;) There's still a taste of yesteryear grandeur in the antique-furnished rooms and suites at Sopron's plush, century-old hotel, coupled with a thoroughly modern wellness centre with pool, sauna and gym. If you're in Sopron to get your teeth done, you needn't even step outside: the hotel comes with its own dentist.

Erhardt Pension GUESTHOUSE €€
(☎506 711; www.erhardt-pension.com; Balfi utca 10; s/d from €35/50;) This is in a great central spot and comprises one of the best restaurants in town, accommodating staff and nine compact, homey rooms decked out in soothing creams and browns, complete with super-comfy mattresses. And if you happen to be sampling the local wines in the extensive wine cellar, your bed is just a stagger away.

Gibraltár Vendégházak GUESTHOUSE €€
(☎338 502; www.gibraltarvendeghaz.hu; M. Berc-senyi utca 35; s/d from 7500/9250Ft; ) This brand new guesthouse may be a 15-minute walk from the centre, but the trek is worth it for the view and the lovely proprietress, who goes out of her way to make you feel welcome. Spacious, well-furnished rooms and delicious home-cooked breakfast seal the deal.

Eating

TOP CHOICE **Erhardt Restaurant & Wine Cellar** INTERNATIONAL €€€
(☎506 711; www.borvendeglo.hu; Balfi út 10; mains 1400-3500Ft;) One of the best restaurants in town, with a wooden-beamed ceiling and paintings of rural scenes complementing the imaginative dishes, such as paprika catfish with parsley gnocchi. There's an extensive selection of Sopron wines to choose from (also available for purchase at their wine cellar) and the service is top-notch.

Graben INTERNATIONAL €€
(☎340 256; www.grabenetterem.hu; Várkerület 8; mains 1690-3200Ft; ⊙8am-10pm) Located in a cosy cellar near the old city walls, Graben attracts a largely Austrian clientele with the likes of 'old man's steak', schnitzel, and game dishes. Great flavours and friendly service. In summer its terrace spreads out over an inner courtyard.

Stubi HUNGARIAN €
(Balfi utca 16; meals 600-1000Ft; ⊙noon-9pm) This is very much a local place for local people, but if you speak German (or Hungarian), the goulash, hearty cabbage and potato stew, noodles with crushed poppy seeds and sugar, and other Hungarian daily specials are the best (and cheapest) in town and the portions are large.

Jégverem HUNGARIAN €€
(www.jegverem.hu; Jégverem utca 1; mains 1200-3200Ft, lunch 750Ft) The slogan of this rustic pension restaurant is 'The Restaurant for Guzzle-guts' (we think they mean 'greedy-

guts'). It is defined by its ambitious menu, portions large enough to satisfy a famished sumo wrestler and seriously inexpensive lunch specials, including the likes of venison stew and meat stew with semolina dumplings. A clear winner.

Liszt Salon CAFE €
(Szent György utca 12; coffee 600Ft; ⌚10am-10pm) This very stylish and mature cafe attracts locals and newcomers alike with a huge array of teas and coffee and two distinct areas – one with low, comfy couches and the other featuring upright chairs and tables for bad backs. Occasional classical concerts are held here, too.

Forum Pizzeria PIZZERIA €€
(Szent György utca 3; mains 850-2990Ft) Though the menu at this popular pizzeria runs the gamut from pizza and pasta to meat, fish and Hungarian takes on Mexican dishes, pizza is what they do best and they make it right in front of you. The vaulted ceiling in the dining area makes you feel as if you're eating in a church.

Alcatraz SANDWICHES €
(Mátyás Király utca 1; gyros 550-800Ft) We could make a joke about prison food here, but we won't. Suffice to say that it's an island of quick eats, such as pizza, sandwiches and gyros, in a town with very few such places, but don't expect to be wowed gastronomically.

Drinking & Entertainment

The Sopron region is noted for its red wines, especially Kékfrankos and Merlot, and the white Tramini is also worth a try. There a number of wine cellars scattered about the city where you can try the local tipple, but watch your intake if you don't want a massive *macskajaj* ('cat's wail' – Hungarian for 'hangover') the next day.

Gyógygödör Borozó WINE BAR
(Fő tér 4; ⌚9am-10pm) The incongruously cutesy wooden furniture looks out of place inside this stone cellar, but that shouldn't detract from the pleasure of sampling the extensive collection of Sopron wines alongside inexpensive Hungarian dishes. Wine spritzers (120Ft) are also popular.

Cezár Pince WINE BAR
(Hátsókapu utca 2; ⌚closed Sun) Atmospheric cellar bar where you can imbibe the local reds while sharing large platters of cured meats, pates and salami.

Petőfi Theatre THEATRE
(☎517 517; www.prokultura.hu; Petőfi tér 1) This beautiful theatre with National Romantic-style mosaics on the front facade features both contemporary plays and Hungarian and foreign drama.

Information

City Website (www.sopron.hu) Practical and background info on the town.

Main Post Office (Széchenyi tér 7-8) There's also an Inner Town branch (Várkerület 37; ⌚8am-4pm Mon-Fri).

OTP Bank (Várkerület 96/a)

Tourinform (☎517 560; sopron@tourinform.hu; Ferenc Liszt Conference & Cultural Centre, Liszt Ferenc utca 1; ⌚9am-6pm Mon-Fri, to 7pm Sat-Sun mid-Jun–Aug, shorter hours rest of year) Free internet access and a plethora of information on Sopron and the surrounding area, including local vintners.

Getting There & Away

Bus Destinations from Sopron include the following:

DESTINATION	PRICE	TIME	KM	FREQUENCY
Balatonfüred	3130Ft	4hr	178km	2 daily
Fertőd	560Ft	45min	28km	hourly
Győr	1680Ft	2-2½hr	87km	hourly
Kőszeg	1120Ft	1¼-1½hr	59km	6 daily
Nagycenk	310Ft	20min	15km	3 hourly
Sárvár	1300Ft	1¼-1¾hr	62km	3 daily
Szombathely	1490Ft	2hr	76km	7 daily
Veszprém	2830Ft	3¼-3¾	155km	3 daily

Train There are express trains to Budapest (4200Ft, three hours, 216km, eight daily) via Győr (1680Ft, 85km, 1¼ hours, hourly) and direct trains to Vienna's Miedling (4450Ft, one to 1¼ hours, up to 15 daily). Local trains run to Szombathely (1300Ft, one hour, 62km, hourly) and Wiener Neustadt in Austria (2800Ft, 40 minutes, 34km, hourly), where you change for Vienna.

Getting Around

Buses 1 and 2, from the bus and train stations, circle the Inner Town.

Around Sopron

Sights

Lővér Hills HILLS

This range of 300m- to 400m-high foothills of the Austrian Alps, some 5km south and southwest of the city centre, is Sopron's playground. It's a great place for hiking and walking, but is not without bitter memories, for it was here that partisans and Jews were executed by Nazis and the fascist Hungarian Arrow Cross during WWII. You can climb to the top of **Károly Lookout** (Károly kilátótorony; adult/senior & student 350/200Ft; 9am-8pm May-Aug, shorter hours rest of year) on the hill (394m) west of the Lővér hotel; walk to **Taródi Castle** (Csalogány köz 8; 300Ft; vary), or 'crazy man's castle', built by eccentric local Istvan Taród in the 1950s and still owned by his descendants; if someone is in, they'll usually let you have a look around.

The hills are a 15- to 20-minute walk from the city centre.

Fertő-Hanság National Park PARK

(www.ferto-hansag.hu) The flat expanse of the Fertő-Hanság National Park begins almost at Sopron's easterly border. Made up of reedy marshland and a slither of Lake Fertő (most of the lake lies in Austrian territory), the park is a paradise for birds, and therefore bird lovers. White egrets, godwits, great crested grebes and 50,000 wild geese – among many others – use the park as refuge, particularly during the migration months in spring and autumn. Due to its gently undulating landscape, Fertő-Hanság is also a favourite of (Austrian) cyclists who take advantage of the many cycle paths through the region and numerous inexpensive lodgings in the villages along the way. (Ask Sopron's Tourinform for details of cycle paths).

By public transport, the best way to reach the park is to catch a bus to Fertőrákos (310Ft, 25 minutes, 14km, hourly) or else just cycle in.

Fertőd

99 / POP 3474

The tiny town of Fertőd, 27km east of Sopron, was put on the map in the mid-18th century when the proud Count Miklós Esterházy (nicknamed 'Miklós the Ostentacious') proclaimed that 'Anything the [Habsburg] emperor can do, I can do better'! The aristocrat went about constructing one of the largest and most opulent summer palaces in central Europe, highly deserving of the hyperbolic moniker, the 'Hungarian Versailles', and meant to rival the Parisian landmark in beauty and size.

After a century and a half of neglect (it was used as stables in the 19th century and a hospital during WWII), the palace has been partially restored to its former glory and renovations are continuing.

Sights

TOP CHOICE **Esterházy Palace** PALACE

(537 640; www.esterhaza.hu; Joseph Haydn utca 2; tour adult/senior & student 2000/1000Ft; 10am-6pm Tue-Sun mid-Mar–Oct, to 4pm Fri-Sun Nov–mid-Mar) Esterházy Palace is Fertőd's only sight, but what a sight it is! When originally completed, this horseshoe-shaped baroque and rococo palace boasted 126 rooms, a separate opera house, a hermitage (complete with a real-live cranky old man in a sack cloth who wanted to be left alone), temples to Diana and Venus, a Chinese dance house, a puppet theatre and a 250-hectare garden laid out in the French manner. Today only 23 rooms are open to the public; if you're wondering whether they were gilded with real gold, the answer is: yes, around 30kg of the stuff.

As you approach the main entrance to the so-called **Courtyard of Honour** (info 537 640; Joseph Haydn utca 2; 10am-6pm Tue-Sun mid-Mar–Oct, to 4pm Fri-Sun Nov–mid-Mar), notice the ornamental wrought-iron gate, a masterpiece of the rococo. Note also the rather violent statuary: the cherubs in the fountain and the bearded men in the alcoves on either side are seemingly intent on doing harm to the vanquished beasts with their golden tridents.

The one-hour Palace Museum tour passes through several rooms decorated in the pseudo-Chinese style that was all the rage in the late 18th century; the pillared Sala Terrena, which served as the summer dining room, with its floor of Carrara marble (heated from underneath in cold weather) and Miklós Esterházy's monogram in floral frescoes on the ceiling; and the Prince's Bed Chamber, with paintings of Amor. On the 1st floor are more sumptuous baroque and rococo salons as well as the lavish Concert Hall, where many of the works of composer Franz Joseph Haydn (a 30-year resident of the palace) were first performed, including the *Farewell Symphony* in 1772.

THE PAN-EUROPEAN PICNIC

To quote Helmut Kohl, 'the soil under the Brandenburg Gate is Hungarian soil'. Yet Sopron's pivotal role in the subsequent fall of the Berlin Wall and the collapse of the Iron Curtain is little known, as the Pan-European Picnic tends to be overshadowed by the events that followed.

The year 1989 was one of transition. Even though Central Europe still lived under the yoke of Soviet power, there were bolder and bolder calls for democracy and freedom of speech. In Hungary, the benign Communist government under Miklós Németh decided to address the issue of border control between Austria and Hungary, since Hungarians were allowed to travel freely by that point. Inspired by a speech by the visiting Otto van Habsburg, members of Hungarian opposition parties came up with the idea of a picnic, with citizens of Hungary and Austria meeting, hanging out and dismantling the barbed wire fence between the two countries (a process which started in May 1989 with the symbolic cutting of the fence by the respective foreign ministers of the two countries).

The chosen spot for the picnic on August 19 was several kilometres from Sopron, on the road between Sopronkőhida and Sankt Margareten im Burgenland. A number of East Germans, allowed to holiday by Lake Balaton, heard of the picnic and on the day, several hundred of them rushed through the gate into Austria. The border guards not only did not stop them, but some helped them through. In the turbulent weeks that followed, thousands of East Germans camped outside the West German embassy in Budapest, having heard from Hungarian border guards that it would be possible to obtain West German passports there. On 11 September, Hungary opened its borders to GDR and its Eastern European neighbours, and as a result more than 70,000 people fled to the West via Hungary. The East German government collapsed within weeks and the Berlin Wall soon followed.

Today the site consists of a park with picnic tables, displays on the events of 1989, an old watchtower and a marble monument commemorating the event. The picnic's role in the unification of Germany was marked on its 20th anniversary in 2009 by Angela Merkel, Chancellor of Germany, who visited the site.

The most striking feature of the adjacent Banqueting Hall is the Mildorfer's ceiling fresco, *Glory of Apollo*, with Apollo's chariot which seems to be gunning straight for you – regardless of where you stand.

The apartment where Haydn lived, off and on, from 1761 to 1790, is in the west wing of the baroque **Music House** (Muzsikaház; Madach sétány 1), southwest of the palace, beyond which stretch the seemingly endless French gardens. When Empress Maria Theresa attended a masked ball here in 1773, Miklós, 'the Splendour Lover', threw one of the greatest parties of all time, complete with fireworks and 24,000 Chinese lanterns, and presented the Empress with a jewel-encrusted sleigh as a parting gift.

Two major musical events at the palace are the Haydn Festival of Strings in July and the more established Haydn Esterháza Festival in late August/early September. For information and tickets check with the ticket office at the palace.

The palace may be visited only as part of a tour, and though tours tend to be in Hungarian only, you are presented with a detailed fact sheet in English so that you can follow the tour.

Two very convenient restaurants for a bite to eat are both located in Grenadier House, the former living quarters of the grenadier guards opposite the palace, and tend to be open all day, every day.

Getting There & Away

The easiest way to get here is by frequent bus from Sopron (560Ft, 45 minutes, 28km, hourly), and there are also services to Győr (1120Ft, 1¾ hours, 57km, two to four daily).

Nagycenk

99 / POP 1920

Only 15km southeast of Sopron is the site of the ancestral mansion of the Széchenyi clan – a family instrumental in transforming Hungary into its present-day entity. This sombre neoclassical manor house turned superb museum aptly reflects the temperament and sense of purpose of the Széchenyis – democrats and reformers all. Ferenc, the patriarch, donated his entire collection of books and art to the state in 1802, laying the foundations for the National Library now named in his honour. But it was his son, István (1791–1860), who made the greatest impact of any Hungarian on the economic and cultural development of the nation (see the boxed text, The Greatest Hungarian').

Sights

Széchenyi Memorial Museum MUSEUM
(Széchenyi Emlékmúzeum; www.nagycenk.hu; Kiscenki utca 3; adult/senior & student 1200/600Ft; ⏲10am-6pm Tue-Sun Apr-Oct, shorter hours rest of year) Approached through attractive grounds with sculpted vegetation, this excellent museum gives you a detailed insight into the work of István Széchenyi, as well as the man himself.

The rooms on the museum's ground floor, furnished with period pieces, trace the Széchenyi family and their role as key players in the 1848–49 War of Independence, as well as István's greatest influences – from the men whose thinking shaped his own and the widow he'd married, to significant events such as his military service and involvement in the ill-fated government of Lajos Batthyány. A sweeping baroque staircase leads to the exhibits on the 1st floor – testimony to István's many accomplishments and diverse interests – from Budapest's Chain Bridge, the Danube and Tisza Rivers' engineering works, steamboat and rail transport, to photography, silk farming and horse breeding, explored through an engaging mix of models, artefacts and maps.

While there's a taped commentary in several languages (including English) in each room (just press the button), an audioguide (200Ft) will save you the Babylonian clash of languages when others compete for the button.

FREE **Steam Train Museum** MUSEUM
(Múzeum Vasút; ⏲24hr) Steam-engine fans will be thrilled with the presence of several of these vintage leviathans at the open-air Steam Train Museum – fittingly located near the mansion of the man responsible for their introduction to Hungary. On weekends, between April and early October, you can actually ride a **narrow-gauge train** (one-way adult/child 700/350Ft; 5 daily) for 4km from the Kastély train station to Fertőboz and back.

Széchenyi Mausoleum CEMETERY
(Széchenyi tér; adult/senior & student 500/300Ft; ⏲9am-5pm Tue-Sun May-Oct) The Széchenyi Mausoleum, the final resting place of István and other family members and a great place of pilgrimage for Hungarians, is in the village cemetery across the road from St Stephen's Church.

Sleeping & Eating

TOP CHOICE **Kastély** HISTORIC HOTEL €€€
(☎360 061; www.szechenyikastelyszallo.hu; Kiscenki utca 3; s/d from €52/70) In the west wing of the mansion, this beautifully appointed inn offers large rooms with a touch of old-school charm and lovely features, such as antique chandeliers. If you can afford it, opt for room 106 or 107, which are large suites with period furniture and restful views of the six-hectare garden. Rates include entrance to the museum. The splendid dining room at the Kastély is highly rated by all and sundry, and its outdoor tables in the hotel's splendid courtyard are the only place to dine in summer.

Getting There & Away

Nagycenk is accessible from Sopron (310Ft, 20 minutes, 15km, hourly) by frequent bus. The village is on the train line linking Sopron (310Ft, 14 minutes, 12km, up to 12 daily) and Szombathely (930Ft, one hour, 50km, 12 daily). The train station is near St Stephen's church. Buses stop close to the Széchenyi mansion.

Szombathely

☎94 / POP 79,590

Szombathely means 'Saturday market' – an appropriate name for this bustling city that has been a trade settlement since 43AD, when Romans built Savaria on this site along the Amber Route. Plundered by the Huns, Longobards and Avars, Szombathely bounced back again in the Middle Ages, but the Mongols, then the Turks and the Habsburgs put a stop to that. The town began to flourish again with the appointment of the first bishop in 1777, followed by its development as an important railway hub in the 19th century. Heavy bombing during WWII and subsequent rebuilding accounts for Szombathely's architectural diversity. When it comes to Roman ruins and treasures, Szombathely is second to none.

'THE GREATEST HUNGARIAN'

The man whose visage is printed on the 5000Ft note is none other than Count István Széchenyi (1791–1860), whose contributions to the modernisation of Hungary are beyond measure. Born in Vienna and inspired by his travels around England as a young man, Széchenyi returned to Hungary determined to tackle what he considered to be his country's backwardness. To do so, he had his fingers in many a pie.

In his seminal 1830 work *Hitel* (meaning 'credit' and based on *hit* or 'trust'), he advocated sweeping economic reforms and the abolition of serfdom (he himself had distributed the bulk of his property to landless peasants two years earlier); he was afterwards put in charge of transport infrastructure by the government.

The man was simply brimming with ideas:

'In Budapest, the only way to get from Buda to Pest is by boat. So why not invite the Brits to build the Chain Bridge, and charge everyone (yes, you too, noblemen) to use it – that way we can cover the cost.'

'Not enough land for cultivation? Why, let's straighten the serpentine Tisza River, which'll give Hungary an extra 25% of arable land. As a bonus, we can now travel up the Danube as far as the Iron Gates in Romania.'

'Tired of slow boats pulled along by horses? Let's introduce steam boats to the Danube and Lake Balaton instead!'

'Transport nonexistent or too slow? The Brits can help us build railways and we can start by connecting Budapest to Vác and Szolnok by steam engine!'

'Whoever said that horseracing is a frivolous pastime! The winners can help us improve the country's breeding-horse stock; I'll start up a stud farm myself to show you how it's done!'

'We can't be importing from experts from abroad all the time. Why not get some homegrown ones? I'm willing to donate a large lump sum to help fund the Hungarian Academy of Sciences in Budapest to get the ball rolling.'

A believer in gradual development and evolution, Széchenyi became part of Lajos Batthyány's independent government in 1848; however, he reacted badly to the radicalisation of events and open conflict with Vienna caused him to have a nervous breakdown. He spent more than a decade in an asylum in Vienna in self-imposed exile and though he'd recovered sufficiently to resume writing, Széchenyi nevertheless shot himself in the head in 1860 after harassment by political police.

For all his accomplishments, Széchenyi's contemporary and fellow reformer, Lajos Kossuth, called him 'the greatest Hungarian' – an accolade this dynamic but troubled visionary retains to this day.

Sights

TOP CHOICE Iseum MUSEUM

(www.iseumsavariense.hu; Rákóczi Ferenc utca 12; adult/senior & student 800/400Ft; ⏲10am-5pm Tue-Sun) Once part of a grand 2nd-century complex of two temples dedicated to the Egyptian goddess Isis by Roman legionnaires (one of only three in Europe), Iseum was completely restored in 2011. The adjacent U-shaped hall makes a grand new home for the archaeological discoveries made at the vast Roman cemeteries at Alsópáhok and Nemesbőd, in the Szombathely region, dating back to the 1st century AD. The excellent 'Travelling to the Afterlife' exhibit currently features just a fraction of the graves still to be excavated and consists of complete skeletons, alongside the items buried with them, such as jewellery, weapons, tools and pottery, the objects and the analysis of the bones used to divine the individuals' life stories – a must for anyone with an interest in Roman history.

FREE Szombathely Cathedral CHURCH

(Szombathelyi Székeshegyház; Mindszenty József tér) This attractive Neoclassical cathedral looms above the quiet square. Built in 1797, it once featured stuccowork and frescoes by Franz Anton Maulbertsch and was supported by grand marble columns. Unfortunately, allied bombing in the final days of WWII did not

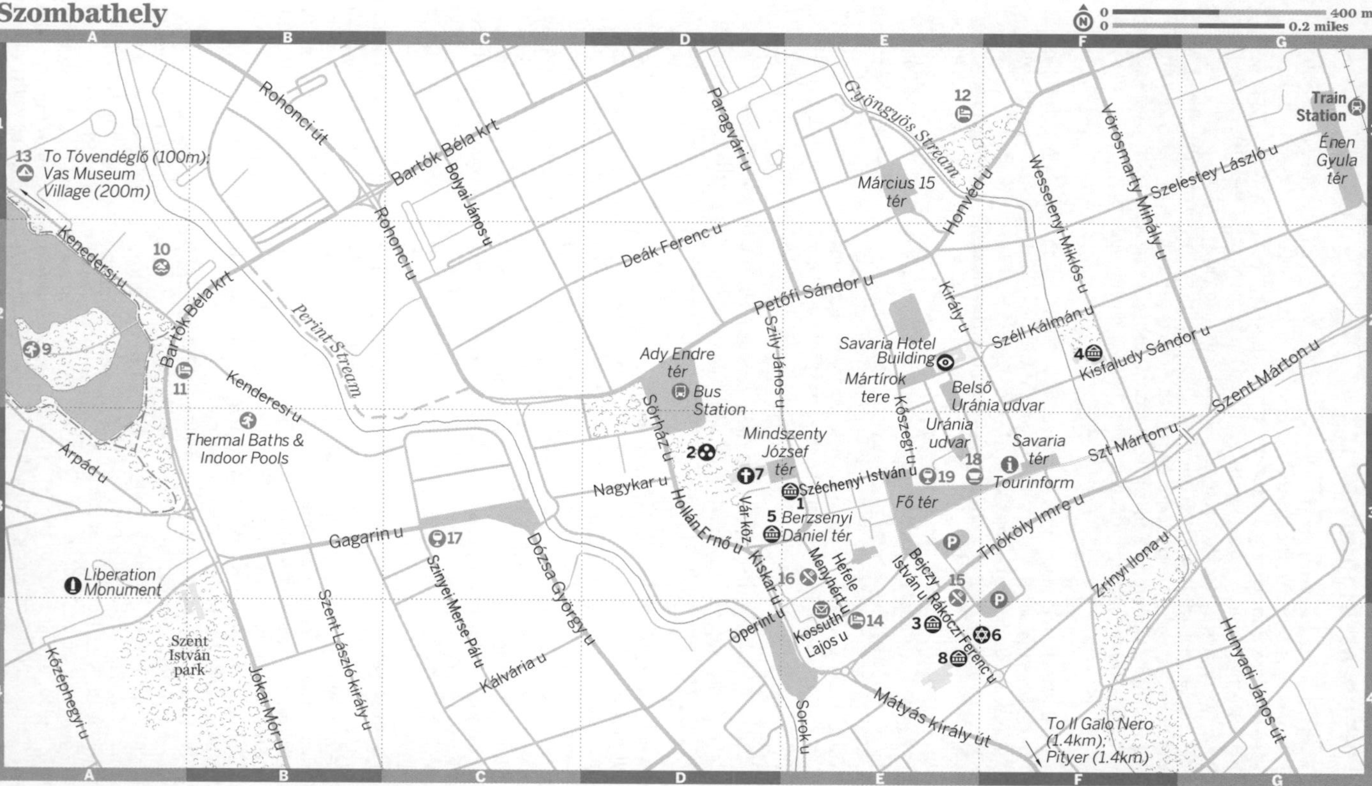
Szombathely
0 400 m
0 0.2 miles
A B C D E F G
1 2 3 4
Rohonci út
Bartók Béla krt
Bolyai János u
Rohonci u
Paragvári u
Gyöngyös Stream
12
Március 15 tér
Honvéd u
Wesselényi Miklós u
Vörösmarty Mihály u
Szelestey László u
Train Station
Énen Gyula tér
13 To Tóvendéglő (100m); Vas Museum Village (200m)
Kenedersi u
10
Deák Ferenc u
Petőfi Sándor u
Perint Stream
Király u
Széll Kálmán u
Kisfaludy Sándor u
4
Szent Márton u
9
11
Kenderesi u
Ady Endre tér
Bus Station
Szily János u
Savaria Hotel Building
Mártírok tere
Belső Uránia udvar
Uránia udvar
Kőszegi u
Thermal Baths & Indoor Pools
Sörház u
2
Mindszenty József tér
7
Széchenyi István u
1
19
18
Savaria tér
Tourinform
Szt Márton u
Árpád u
Nagykar u
Hollán Ernő u
Vár köz
5 Berzsenyi Dániel tér
Fő tér
Thököly Imre u
Gagarin u
17
Dózsa György u
Kiskar u
Hefele Menyhért u
Bejczy István u
Zrínyi Ilona u
Liberation Monument
16
15
Szinyei Merse Pál u
Szent László király u
Óperint u
Kossuth Lajos u
14
3
Rákóczi Ferenc u
6
8
Szent István park
Jókai Mór u
Kálvária u
Hunyadi János út
Középhegyi u
Sorok u
Mátyás király út
To Il Galo Nero (1.4km); Pityer (1.4km)

Szombathely

spare the cathedral, but the splendid interior has been restored with great care, featuring pink-marble pillars, a couple of Maulbertsch originals and a glorious red-and-white marble pulpit. A feature of great interest to those with a taste for the macabre is the glass coffin to the right of the entrance containing the remains of a mitre-bedecked saint.

Smidt Museum MUSEUM

(Hollán Ernő utca 2; adult/student 800/400Ft; ⊙10am-5pm Tue-Sun) A hospital superintendent by the name of Lajos Smidt was a hoarder by nature so visiting this museum gives us the opportunity to do what most of us secretly enjoy: rooting through someone's private belongings. His extraordinary collection includes antique Bibles, ornate 19th-century pistols, Iron Age swords, Roman remains, clocks, surgical equipment, Biedermeier miniatures and so much more. During your perambulations through this mansion, you may spot two legionaries' skulls, Széchenyi's wife's dancing slippers, dinosaur molars, an opium pipe, Franz Liszt's pocket watch and a tiny chess set for dolls.

Szombathely Gallery GALLERY

(www.keptar.szombathely.hu; Rákóczi Ferenc utca 12; adult/senior & student 800/400Ft; ⊙10am-5pm Tue-Sat, to 7pm Wed) This grand modern-art gallery specialises primarily in 20th-century Hungarian art, with numerous temporary exhibitions throughout the year. The permanent collection includes works by homegrown artists such as Gyula Derkovitzs, as well as a wealth of abstract and avant-garde works from the 1950s onwards and an innovative textile collection.

Bishop's Palace MUSEUM

(Püspöki palota; Mindszenty József tér 1; adult/senior & student 350/200Ft; ⊙9.30am-3.30pm Tue-Fri, to 11.30am Sat) Maulbertsch frescoes in the upstairs Reception Hall at the Baroque Bishop's Palace, built in 1783, miraculously survived the WWII air raids, but are not usually open to the public. You can, however, admire the murals of Roman ruins and gods painted in 1784 by István Dorffmeister in the Sala Terrena on the ground floor. Other rooms contain photographs of the cathedral before and just after the bombing of WWII and the Diocesan Collection and Treasury, including missals and bibles from the 14th to 18th centuries, Gothic vestments, a beautiful 15th-century monstrance from Kőszeg and even a bejewelled replica of St Stephen's Crown made in the USA.

Vas Museum Village MUSEUM

(Vasi Múzeumfalu; Árpád utca 30; adult/senior & student 800/400Ft; ⊙9am-5pm Tue-Sun Apr-Oct) On the banks of the city's fishing lake, this open-air museum contains more than 40 18th- and 19th-century farmhouses *(porták)* moved here from two dozen villages in the Őrség region. The most interesting of these are the Croatian, German and 'fenced' houses; if you're lucky, you'll catch a folk craft and dance demonstration (every other month).

Savaria Museum MUSEUM

(Kisfaludy Sándor utca 9; adult/senior & student 800/400Ft; ⊙10am-5pm Tue-Sat mid-Apr–mid-Oct, shorter hours rest of year) Those into Roman relics will love the extensive collection from the museum's namesake settlement, housed inside this large, crumbling mansion – from the impressive Roman votive altars and tomb stones to the rare milestone used to mark the distance between Rome and Savaria. Other noteworthy exhibits include the original apostle statues from the Benedictine church in Ják.

Synagogue JEWISH
(zsinagóga; Rákóczi Ferenc utca 3) This lovely, twin-towered Moorish building is the former synagogue, designed in 1881 by the Viennese architect Ludwig Schöne. Today it's a music school and the attached Béla Bartók Concert Hall (p138). All that remains of the town's formerly thriving Jewish community is a plaque that marks the spot from where '4228 of our Jewish brothers and sisters were deported to Auschwitz on 4 July 1944'.

Garden of Ruins RUIN
(Romkert; Mindszenty József tér; adult/senior & student 700/400Ft; ⌚9am-5pm Tue-Sat Apr-Nov) Here you'll find some impressive remains of the Roman Savaria, excavated here since 1938. Don't miss the beautiful mosaics of plants and geometrical designs on the floor of what was St Quirinus Basilica in the 4th century. There are also remains of Roman road markers, public baths, a customs house, shops and the medieval castle walls.

Activities

Lakes LAKE
Northwest of the city centre you'll find the Anglers' Lake and the Rowing Lake (Csónakázótó), popular with locals. **Boats** (rowing/pedal boat per hour 1000/1300Ft; ⌚1-7pm May-Sep) can be hired from the western side of the little island in the middle of the latter. Bus 27 stops near the lakes.

Tófürdő Swimming Complex SWIMMING
(☎505 689; Kenederesi utca 2; adult/child 900/700Ft; ⌚9am-8pm May-Sep) This massive water park has enormous pools as well as slides and chutes for water babies of all ages.

Sleeping

Park Hotel Pelikán HOTEL €€€
(☎513 800; www.hotelpelikan.hu; Deák Ferenc utca 5; s/d €81/105;) This highly professional hotel occupies a former orphanage and children's hospital, though you wouldn't have guessed it from the stylish decor, subtle lighting and carpets plush enough to drown in. The high ceilings make the smaller rooms seem larger, and there's a lovely indoor pool on the ground floor. Excellent international restaurant, too.

Wagner Hotel HOTEL €€€
(☎322 208; www.hotelwagner.hu; Kossuth Lajos utca 15; s/d from 11,500/18,500Ft;) A lovely hotel very close to the heart of Szombathely. It has a sunny inner courtyard, and while rooms are only big enough to swing a very small cat, they have all the mod cons. The on-site restaurant serves imaginative, well-executed international mains, such as duck with peaches.

Il Gallo Nero B&B €€
(☎509 447; www.gallonero.hu; Rumi út 21; s/d from 8400/14,500Ft) The 13 rooms at this friendly B&B have a rustic feel to them and a subtle colour scheme, though there's nothing rustic about the brand new beds. The attractive on-site restaurant with roaring fireplace serves Italian-inspired cuisine.

Tópart Camping CAMPGROUND €
(www.topartkemping.uv.hu; Kenederesi utca 6; campsite per adult/child/tent 1000/600/900Ft, bungalows for 2/4 people from 5500/11,500Ft; ⌚May-Sep;) Northwest of the city centre, near the lakes and swimming complex, this campground is spacious, friendly and family-orientated, with weekend packages that include free entry to the pool and spa. Bus 27 runs from the bus station along Bartók Béla körút, from where the camp is only a short walk.

Hotel Claudius HOTEL €€€
(☎313 760; www.claudiushotel.hu; Bartók Béla körút 39; s/d 17,400/21,400Ft;) This former Soviet monstrosity is a stunner from the inside. Public spaces have been thoroughly modernised, while rooms are sizeable, have a balcony, and are decked out in neutral shades. There's also a decent restaurant on-site with an extensive selection of local wines.

Eating

TOP CHOICE **Pityer** SEAFOOD €€
(☎508 010; Rumi útca 18; mains 1800-3400Ft) This *csárda* (Hungarian-style inn) has a lovely courtyard and its displayed fishing nets hint at the menu options: excellent fish dishes, such as catfish goulash. Portions are hearty and the large and worth the 1.5km trip from the city centre.

DON'T MISS

THE BENEDICTINE ABBEY OF JÁK

The tiny settlement of Ják (pronounced 'yuck'), 12km from Szombathely, is home to the song in stone that is the Romanesque **Benedictine Abbey Church** (Bencés apátsági templom; adult/student 300/150Ft; ⊙8am-6pm Apr-Oct, 10am-2pm Nov-Mar). The two-towered structure was founded in 1214 by Márton Nagy, a local feudal lord, though he died before its completion in 1256. Though the church miraculously escaped destruction during the Mongol invasion, it failed to escape the ravages of the Turkish occupation. The most dramatic restorations were carried out between 1896 and 1904 by Friguyes Shulek (responsible for Buda Castle's Fishermen's Bastion in Budapest), who recut or replaced most of the statues in its portal, stripped away the earlier baroque additions and added spires to the towers.

The showstopper here is undoubtedly the magnificent main portal. Carved in geometric patterns 12 layers deep and featuring carved statues of Christ and his Apostles, as well as two lions – one with a possessive paw on a decapitated human head – the portal is an exceptional piece of stonemasonry. If you think it seems to be in great condition in spite of its age, it's because renovations were completed in 1996 in time for Hungary's millennium celebrations.

Facing the portal is the tiny clover-leaf Chapel of St James (Szent Jakab-kápolna) topped with an onion dome. It was built around 1260 as a parish church, since the main church was monastic. Note the paschal lamb (symbolising Christ) over the main entrance, and the baroque altar and frescoes in the musty interior.

In stark contrast to the baroque flourishes of St James, the interior of the abbey church is rather simple and plain, though its single nave and three aisles have a much more graceful and intimate feel than most Hungarian Gothic churches. To the west and below the towers is a gallery reserved for the benefactor and his family. The rose-and-blue frescoes on the wall between the vaulting and the arches below could very well be of Márton Nagy and his progeny.

Buses from Szombathely (310Ft, 21 minutes, 14km, six to 20 daily) stop by the crossroad in the middle of the village; the abbey is just around the corner.

Tóvendéglő INTERNATIONAL €€
(☎900 700; www.to-vendeglo.hu; Rumi Rajki sétány 1; mains 1290-3490Ft) With a view overlooking the city's small lake from its terraced patio, modern Tóvendéglő has the finest location of any eatery in Szombathely. Dishes on the ambitious menu range from the robust pigs' trotters with potatoes to saffron risotto with king prawns.

Café Móló ITALIAN €€
(Rákóczi Ferenc útca 1-3; mains 1300-3000Ft) With images of Asia adorning its walls, a spacious, modern interior and huge terrace, Móló is packed in the evenings with a clientele that likes to watch sports on the big screen while fuelling themselves with a wide range of cocktails, pasta and pizza. Avoid the profiteroles like the proverbial plague, though.

Old Post Pub INTERNATIONAL €€
(Hefele Menyhért utca 2; mains 1800-2600Ft) This bright, clean eatery has more old-fashioned beer mugs than Zsa Zsa Gabor has ex-husbands, a number of beers on tap, a mixed international menu with the likes of grilled meat and chilli-based dishes, and a small summer terrace.

Drinking & Entertainment

Royal Söröző BAR
(Fő tér 16; ⊙8.30am-midnight Sun-Thu, to 1am Fri-Sat) With tables on the main square, popular Royal is a grand place for people watching. Inside, the wooden booths afford you some privacy and the dark beer is some of the best around.

M Café CAFE
(Fő tér 24, Belső Uránia udvar; coffee 470Ft; ⊙9am-10pm) Open-fronted cafe serving good coffee, cakes and something stronger for those who enjoy a liquid lunch. In summer its tables spill out onto the pavement.

Bánya Café Bar BAR
(www.banyacafe.hu; Szinyei Merse Pál utca; ⊙10am-11pm Mon-Wed, to midnight Thu, to 2am Fri, 4pm-2am Sat) This popular basement (*bánya* means 'mine') bar/club gets really packed on

weekends; expect a lively night rather than a quiet tête-à-tête with your neighbour. Good selection of cocktails and deadly *pálinka* (Hungarian fruit brandy).

Béla Bartók Concert Hall CLASSICAL MUSIC (☎313 747; www.savaria_symphony.hu; Rákóczi Ferenc utca 3) Housed in the former synagogue.

Information

City Website (www.szombathely.hu) Lots of practical and background information.

OTP Bank (Király utca 10)

Tourinform (☎514 451; szombathely@tourinform.hu; Király utca 1/a; ⏲9am-5pm Mon-Fri mid-Sep–mid-Jun, to 6pm daily mid-Jun–mid-Sep) At the eastern end of Fő tér.

Getting There & Away

Bus & Train

Bus Departures from Szombathely include:

DESTINATION	PRICE	TIME	KM	FREQUENCY
Budapest	3950Ft	4½-5½hr	240km	2 daily
Győr	2200Ft	2½hr	110km	3-4 daily
Ják	310Ft	21min	14km	4-16 daily
Kaposvár	3410Ft	3½-4½hr	188km	3 daily
Keszthely	1680Ft	2¼hr	90km	2 daily
Kőszeg	370Ft	37min	18km	hourly
Pécs	4430Ft	4½-5hr	261km	3 daily
Sárvár	650Ft	40min	35km	6-8 daily
Sopron	1490Ft	2hr	76km	4 daily
Veszprém	2200Ft	2-3hr	117km	3 daily

Train Szombathely is a major train hub, serving destinations such as:

DESTINATION	PRICE	TIME	KM	FREQUENCY
Budapest	4060Ft	3-3¾	236km	hourly
Győr	2200Ft	1¼-2hr	103km	12 daily
Körmend	620Ft	24min	26km	hourly
Kőszeg	370Ft	24min	18km	hourly
Pécs	4620Ft	4½hr	250km	3 daily
Sárvár	620Ft	20min	24km	hourly
Sopron	1300Ft	1hr	62km	hourly
Veszprém	2570Ft	2-2¾	111km	10 daily

Getting Around

Bus 27 will take you from the train station to the Vas Museum Village and the lakes.

Sárvár

☎95 / POP 15,651

The small town of Sárvár, 27km east of Szombathely on the Rába River, is famous (or notorious) for a few reasons. Its 44°C thermal waters, channelled into a state-of-the-art spa, draw visitors from all over Austria and Hungary. Sárvár's fortified castle was long home to the Nádasdy dynasty: Tamás published the first two printed books in Hungarian; Ferenc, dubbed the 'Black Captain', fought valiantly against the Turks and his grandson, Ferenc III, created one of the greatest libraries and private art collections in central Europe. To lovers of the macabre, however, it is the wife of the 'Black Captain', Erzsébet Báthory, who takes centre stage as the most prolific serial killer in history, aka the 'Blood Countess'.

Sights

Nádasdy Castle & Ferenc Nádasdy Museum MUSEUM (Várkerület 1; adult/student 800/400Ft; ⏲10am-4pm Tue-Sun) Sárvár's main sight is the pentagonal Nádasdy Castle, which dominates the town and is reachable by a low bridge across a dry moat. The palatial interior of the Ferenc Nádasdy Museum was the venue for some of the grisly murders committed in the 17th century by Erzsébet Báthory – the wife of Ferenc Nádasdy, or the 'Black Captain', though any mentions of Sárvár's most notorious resident are conspicuously omitted from the museum's displays, adding to her mystery.

Parts of the castle date from the 13th century, but most of it is 16th-century Renaissance and in good condition despite the Austrian crown confiscating much of the castle's contents as punishment for the Nádasdy family's participation in the 1670 rebellion. As a result, many of the furnishings, tapestries and objets d'art you see today were collected from other sources.

One thing the Habsburgs could not take with them was the rather dramatic ceiling fresco in the Knight's Hall, picturing Hungarians – the Black Captain included – battling the Turks, painted by Hans Rudolf Miller in the mid-17th century. The other striking feature of the hall is the ornate 16th-century cabinet of gilded dark wood and marble.

The museum also has one of the nation's best collections of weapons and armour that belonged to the Nádasdy Hussars – a regiment of fast, lightly-armed cavalry. See if you can spot the sabres in bejewelled scabbards, a rather dramatic painting of a warrior with a winged helmet on horseback, and a ceramic stove with clawed feet amidst the uniforms, paintings of the Hussars in action and other paraphernalia.

Among the exhibits about the castle and Sárvár is the printing press established here, and some of the then inflammatory Calvinist tracts it published. One work in Hungarian, entitled *The Pope Is Not the Pope – That's That* and dated 1603, was later vandalised by a Counter-Reformationist who defiantly wrote 'Lutheran scandal' across it in Latin.

Finally, there's a priceless collection of some 60 antique Hungarian maps donated by a UK-based expatriate Hungarian in 1986, the star being the 1520 map of Europe.

Activities

Sárvár Fürdő SPA

(www.sarvarfurdo.hu; Vadkert utca 1; adult/child 2800/1300Ft, adult after 4/7pm 1700/800Ft; baths 8am-10pm year-round, pools to dusk May-Oct) A huge and very modern spa and wellness complex southeast of the castle, guaranteed to leave you squeaky clean and prune-toed, Sárvár Fürdő has indoor and outdoor thermal and swimming pools, several

MURDERS MOST CRUEL: THE CASE OF THE COUNTESS DRACULA

It was the scandal of the 17th century. On the night of 29 December 1610 the Lord Palatine of Hungary, Count György Thurzó, raided the castle at Csejta (now Čachtice in western Slovakia) and caught Countess Erzsébet Báthory literally red-handed – or so he and history would later claim. Covered in blood and screaming like a demon, the widow of the celebrated Black Captain was in the process of tearing chunks out of the body of one of her servant girls with her teeth.

By the time Thurzó had finished collecting evidence from household staff and the townspeople at Čachtice and Sárvár, some 300 depositions had been given, accusing the countess of torturing, mutilating, murdering and – worst of all – disposing of the bodies of more than 600 girls and young women without so much as a Christian burial.

The case of the so-called Blood Countess or Countess Dracula has continued to grab the imagination of everyone from writers (Erzsébet is believed to have been the model for Bram Stoker's *Dracula*) to film-makers and fetishists over the centuries, and some pretty crazy theories have emerged as to why the most prolific female mass-murderer in history did it. Some say she considered the blood of young maidens to be an *elixir vitae* and bathed in it to stay young. Others point to the high incidence of lunacy in the two much-intermarried branches of the Báthory dynasty. Another possibility is that Erzsébet Báthory was the victim of a conspiracy, though she had been known to display sadistic behaviour towards her servants throughout her life.

When the Black Captain died in 1604, his widow inherited all of his estates – properties coveted by both Thurzó and Erzsébet's son-in-law Miklós Zrínyi, the poet and great-grandson of the hero of Szigetvár, who themselves were linked by marriage. Worse, the election of the countess' nephew Gábor Báthory as prince of Transylvania, a vassal state under Ottoman rule, threatened to unite the two Báthory families and strengthen the principality's position. It was in the interest of the Palatine – and the Habsburgs – to get this matriarch of the Báthory family out of the way.

Gábor was murdered in 1613 and the 'Báthory faction' in Hungary ceased to be a threat. The case against the Blood Countess never came to trial, and she remained 'between stones' (ie in a sealed chamber) at the castle until she died in 1614 at the age of 54 and was interred posthumously in the family vault in Nagyecsed.

Was Erzsébet as bloodthirsty as history has made her out to be? Did she really bite great chunks out of the girls' necks and breasts and mutilate their genitals? Much of the villagers' testimony does appear to be consistent, but to form your own conclusions read Tony Thorne's well-researched *Countess Dracula: The Life and Times of Elisabeth Bathory, the Blood Countess.*

types of sauna, a wellness and fitness centre, and a bewildering range of treatments ranging from 'lava stone massage' and 'shake-up massage' to oxygen therapy and couples' packages. You could spend weeks here.

Sleeping & Eating

Eating options are largely restricted to pensions and hotel restaurants.

TOP CHOICE **Spirit Hotel** HOTEL €€€
(☎889 500; www.spirithotel.hu; Vadkert utca 5; s/d from €117/212; P❄@☎≋) With its smooth lines and slick look, the five-star Spirit Hotel is contemporary-meets-creature-comfort, with open logwood fireplaces, mosaic-tiled floors, a silver-service restaurant and a spacey bar. Rooms are coloured in soft creams and browns and there's a full thermal spa and wellness centre offering every treatment imaginable. Spa use is available for nonguests.

Tinódi Pension GUESTHOUSE €€
(☎323 606; www.tinodifogado.hu; Hunyadi János utca 11; s/d 9000/14,000Ft; P☎) This tidy guesthouse comprises a collection of bright, wood-panelled attic rooms designed for hobbits (watch the sloping roof!) around a quiet courtyard. The cheerful restaurant won't be collecting any Michelin stars anytime soon, but there are reliable options of pizza and hot sandwiches.

Thermal Camping Sárvár CAMPGROUND €
(☎523 610; www.thermalcamping.com; Vadkert utca 1; campsite per adult/child/tent 3100/1990/1400Ft; 4-person mobile homes 28,000Ft; 2-person cabins 15,500Ft; P☎) While this completely refurbished campground mostly attracts mobile homes (with a few of its own for rent), there are also several brand-new, fully equipped cabins with terraces. Campers have use of shared facilities, including washing machines. The best bit? Unlimited free entry to the Sárvár Fürdő thermal baths next door.

Várkapu INTERNATIONAL €€
(www.varkapu.hu; Várkerület 5; mains 1500-3200Ft) This immensely popular restaurant attached to a guesthouse has an extensive international menu that changes with the seasons, large portions, restful views of the castle and the odd bit of medieval weaponry in the decor. There's a good selection of Hungarian wines and daily specials (750Ft to 1200Ft) are a bargain.

Platán Hotel HUNGARIAN €€
(www.platanhotel.hu; Hunyadi János utca 23; mains 1500-3200Ft) The walls of this *csárda* bristle with antlers, so it's only fitting that there should be game on the menu as well as hearty soups and platters for two. The rooms above the restaurant have seriously comfortable beds and guests have access to a pool, sauna and spa (at extra cost).

Information

Tourinform (☎520 178; sarvar@tourinform.hu; Várkerület 33; ⏲9am-5pm Mon-Fri, to 1pm Sat Jul & Aug, to 4pm Mon-Fri Sep-Jun) This tourist office is almost opposite the castle entrance.

Getting There & Away

Bus

Buses from Sárvár run to Budapest (3950Ft, three hours, 221km, one to two daily), Győr (1860Ft, two hours, 96km, two daily), Sopron (1300Ft, 1¼ hours, 62km, five daily), Szombathely (650Ft, one hour, 35km, 17 daily) and Vezsprém (1490Ft, 1½ hours, 77km, two daily).

Train

Sárvár is on the train line linking Szombathely (620Ft, 21 minutes, 24km, hourly) with Veszprém (1860Ft, 1½ to two hours, 100km, eight daily) and Budapest (4405Ft, 3½ hours, 224km, up to eight daily).

Kőszeg

☎94 / POP 11,783

The tranquil town of Kőszeg is sometimes called 'the nation's jewellery box', and as you pass under the pseudo-Gothic Heroes' Gate into Jurisics tér, you'll see why. What opens up before you is a treasure trove of colourful Gothic, Renaissance and baroque buildings that together make up one of the most delightful squares in Hungary. At the same time the nearby Kőszeg Hills, which include Mt Írottkő (882m), the highest point in Transdanubia, and the Írottkő Nature Park, offer numerous hiking possibilities.

Sights

Jurisics Castle CASTLE
(Rajnis József utca 9) Dominating the Old Town and originally built in the mid-13th century, the four-towered fortress has been reconstructed several times due to a major fire and is now a hotchpotch of Renaissance arcades, Gothic windows and baroque interiors. It is here that Miklós Jurisics heroically held out against the Turks and is

commemorated with a statue. Inside is a **museum** (Várműzeum; ☎info 360 240; adult/senior or child/family 460/230/900Ft; ⊙10am-5pm Tue-Sun) – at the time of writing it was closed for renovation until early 2013 – with exhibits on the history of Kőszeg from the 14th century, focusing largely on the siege of 1532 and on local wine production. Among the latter is the curious *Szőlő jővésnek könyve* (Arrival of the Grape Book), a kind of gardener's logbook of grape shoot and bud sketches begun in 1740 and updated annually on St George's Day (23 April). You can climb two of the towers for views over the town.

Jurisics tér SQUARE

The former market square, where miscreants were put in stocks during medieval times, is one of Hungary's prettiest. The facade of the red-and-yellow **Town Hall** (Városháza; Jurisics tér 8), a mixture of Gothic, Renaissance, baroque and neoclassical styles, features three coats of arms, those of Hungary, Kőszeg and Miklós Jurisics himself. The **Renaissance House** (Jurisics tér 7), built in 1668, is adorned with graffiti etched into the stucco. The 1739 **statue of the Virgin Mary**, in the middle of the square, was paid for by fining blasphemous Lutherans.

Heroes' Gate MONUMENT

(Hősök kapuja; Jurisics tér 6) This pseudo-medieval gate was erected in 1932 (when these nostalgic portals were all the rage in Hungary) to mark the 400th anniversary of Suleiman's withdrawal; memorials under the gate commemorate Hungary's fallen in WWI and WWII. Attached is the **General's House** (Tábornokház; Jurisics tér 6; adult/student 400/200Ft; ⊙10am-5pm Tue-Sun), a small museum with a missable collection of folk art and local history but with a good view of the Old Town from the top of Heroes' Gate.

Golden Unicorn Pharmacy Museum MUSEUM

(Arany Egyszarvú Patikamúzeum; Jurisics tér 11; adult/senior & student 600/300Ft; ⊙10am-5pm Tue-Sun) This ye olde apothecary has a display of medicinal plants in the attic, some exceptional 18th-century oak furniture, medicinal herbs growing in the small garden and entertaining displays on medicine through the ages, including a periodic table with the elements personified – arsenic by a serpent and mercury by the fleet-footed deity in a winged helmet.

Church of St James CHURCH

(Szent Jakab-templom) The east wall of this Gothic creation, built in 1407, contains very faded 15th-century frescoes of a giant St Christopher carrying the Christ Child, Mary Misericordia sheltering supplicants under a massive cloak, and the three magi bearing their gifts of gold, frankincense and myrrh. The altars and oaken pews are masterpieces of baroque woodcarving, and Miklós Jurisics and two of his children are buried in the crypt.

Church of the Sacred Heart CHURCH

(Jézus Szíve templom; Fő tér) The interior of this pointy neo-Gothic stunner, built in 1894, is the most beautiful for many miles around: a vivid blue that really sets off the geometric frescoes and the images of the saints on the stained glass windows – particularly striking on a sunny day.

Church of St Henry CHURCH

(Szent Imre-templom) This baroque Lutheran church with the tall steeple is dark and plain inside, as befitting its desire for austerity, but it does contain a few art treasures.

Synagogue JEWISH

(zsinagóga; Várkör 38) The circular synagogue, built in 1859, with its strange neo-Gothic towers, once served one of the oldest Jewish

FOR WHOM THE BELL TOLLS

Kőszeg has played pivotal roles in the nation's defence over the centuries. The best-known story is the storming of the town's castle by Suleiman the Magnificent's troops in August 1532, which sounds all too familiar but has a surprise ending. Miklós Jurisics' 'army' – made up of fewer than 500 soldiers and the town militia – held the fortress for 25 days against 100,000 Turks. An accord was reached when Jurisics allowed the Turks to run up their flag over the castle in a symbolic declaration of victory provided they left town immediately thereafter. The Turks kept their part of the bargain (packing their bags at 11am on 30 August), and Vienna was spared the treatment that would befall Buda nine years later. To this day the bells at the Church of the Sacred Heart peal an hour before noon to mark the withdrawal.

Kőszeg

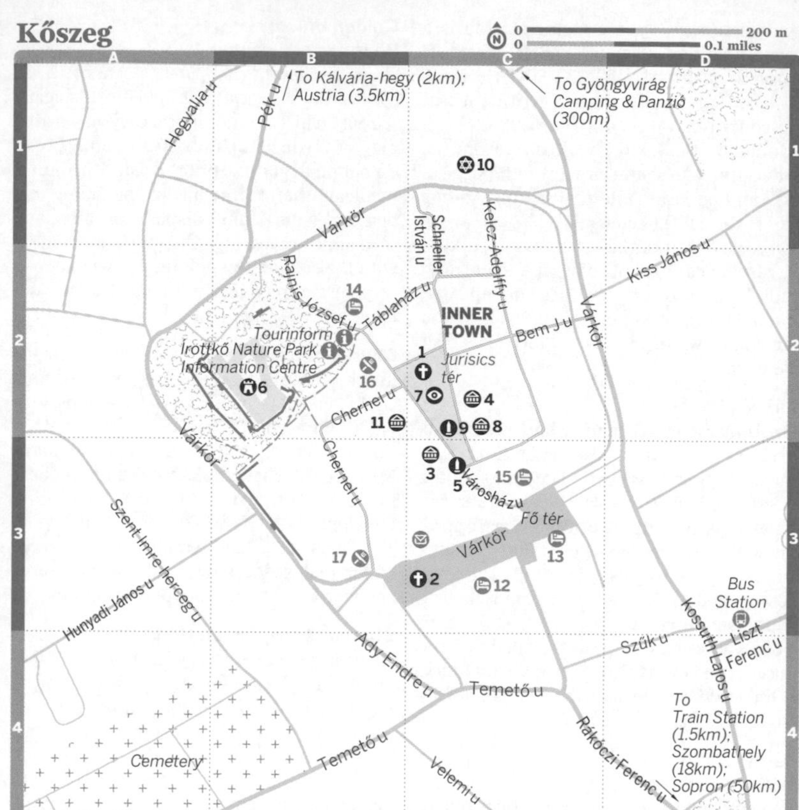

communities in Hungary, but now sits abandoned and in decay.

Activities

Hiking HIKING

The nearby Kőszeg Hills offer a number of good hiking trails, including one up to the Írottkő Peak (884m) and the lookout tower on Óház peak. Additionally, **Írottkő Nature Park** (☎563 121; www.naturpark.hu; Rajnis József út 7; ⌚8am-6pm Mon-Fri, 9am-1pm Sat mid-Apr–Oct, 8am-5pm Mon-Fri mid-Oct–mid-Apr) has several appealing cycling trails (pick up info at Tourinform). If planning on serious hiking, arm yourself with a copy of Cartographia's 1:40,000-scale *Kőszegi-hegység* (Kőszeg Hills; No 13) map.

Sleeping

Portré Hotel HOTEL €€

(☎363 170; www.portre.com; Fő tér 7; s/d 9000/14,000Ft; 📶) This positive stunner of a boutique hotel offers a half-dozen individually decorated, spacious rooms right on Fő tér. The cafe/restaurant downstairs is one of the most popular spots in town.

Írottkő Hotel HOTEL €€€

(☎360 373; www.hotelirottko.hu; Fő tér 4; s/d 15,000/20,000Ft; 📶) Kőszeg's arguably poshest hotel (though that's not saying much) has a wellness centre in the basement, instantly forgettable rooms aimed at business types and a stellar central location.

Arany Strucc Hotel HOTEL €€

(☎360 323; www.aranystrucc.hu; Várkör 124; s/d 7000/10,700Ft) Located on the site of a 1597 inn, the 'Golden Ostrich' is a worn, though wonderfully atmospheric, hotel in the heart of Kőszeg. Those of you with a sweet tooth may wish to note that it has its own confectionery workshop. Try to nab room 7 – it's the biggest and has balcony views over the main square, Fő tér.

Kőszeg

Sights

	Castle Museum	(see 6)
	Church of St Henry	(see 1)
1	Church of St James	C2
2	Church of the Sacred Heart	C3
3	General's House	C3
4	Golden Unicorn Pharmacy Museum	C2
5	Heroes' Gate	C3
6	Jurisics Castle	B2
7	Jurisics tér	C2
8	Renaissance House	C2
9	Statue of the Virgin Mary	C2
10	Synagogue	C1
11	Town Hall	B2

Sleeping

12	Arany Strucc Hotel	C3
13	Írottkő Hotel	C3
14	Pont Vendégház	B2
15	Portré Hotel	C3

Eating

16	Bécsikapu	B2
	Garabonciás Pizzeria	(see 8)
	Portré Etterém	(see 15)
17	Taverna Flórián	B3

Gyöngyvirág Camping & Panzió CAMPGROUND, GUESTHOUSE €
(360 454; www.gyongyviragpanzio.hu; Bajcsy-Zsilinszky utca 6; campsite per adult/tent 750/500Ft, s/d from 5000/6500Ft) The 'Lily of the Valley' is a great catch-all option for budget travellers: there's a small campground (with no tree cover) that backs onto the Gyöngyös River and a range of simple rooms, ranging from ones with shared bathroom to kitchen-equipped studios – ideal for self-caterers. It's a 10-minute walk to the town centre.

Pont Vendégház GUESTHOUSE €
(563 224; Táblaház utca 1; s/d from 5300/8000Ft; P) Opposite the entrance to the castle and dating back to the 1532 siege, this former burgher's house offers several simple, compact en-suite rooms decked out with antique furniture. A bargain.

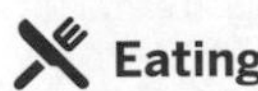

Eating

TOP CHOICE **Taverna Flórián** MEDITERRANEAN €€€
(563 072; www.tavernaflorian.hu; Várkör 59; mains 2000-4290Ft; closed Mon & Tue lunch) Beautiful cellarlike surroundings with subtle lighting, exemplary service and a succinct menu with each dish beautifully executed, make this Kőszeg's top spot. Choose from the likes of duck with pearl-barley risotto and rabbit confit – and don't skip out on dessert, either.

Bécsikapu HUNGARIAN €€
(www.becsikapu.hu; Rajnis József utca 5; mains 1300-3300Ft) Opposite the Church of St James, this is a pleasant *csárda* with a medieval-themed banqueting hall, specialising, appropriately, in large portions of meat and fish dishes; it's worth splurging on the venison steak and wild boar goulash. Wash it down with an extensive range of Hungarian wines.

Portré Etterém INTERNATIONAL €
(Fő tér 7; mains 990-1290Ft;) All things to all people, this hugely popular cafe/restaurant is a convenient stop for breakfast, an afternoon beer or a wide range of soups, salads and pasta dishes (including a number of veggie options).

Garabonciás Pizzeria PIZZERIA €
(360 050; Jurisics tér 7; mains from 980Ft, coffee 350-500Ft; noon-10pm Mon-Sat, 5-10pm Sun) The location, squarely on Fő tér, couldn't be better for people-watching. The pizzas are not for the faint-hearted: come hungry or be prepared to share.

Information

Tourinform (563 120; www.naturpark.hu; Rajnis József út 7; 9am-5pm Mon-Fri, to 1pm Sat mid-Mar–Oct, shorter hours rest of year) Deals out brochures on the town and its surrounds.

Town Website (www.koszeg.hu) Provides a great deal of online information in a variety of languages.

Getting There & Away

Bus departures are frequent to Sopron (1120Ft, 1¼ to 1½ hours, 59km, six daily) and Szombathely (465Ft, 37 minutes, 22km, hourly). Kőszeg is at the end of a railway spur from Szombathely (370Ft, 35 minutes, 18km, hourly).

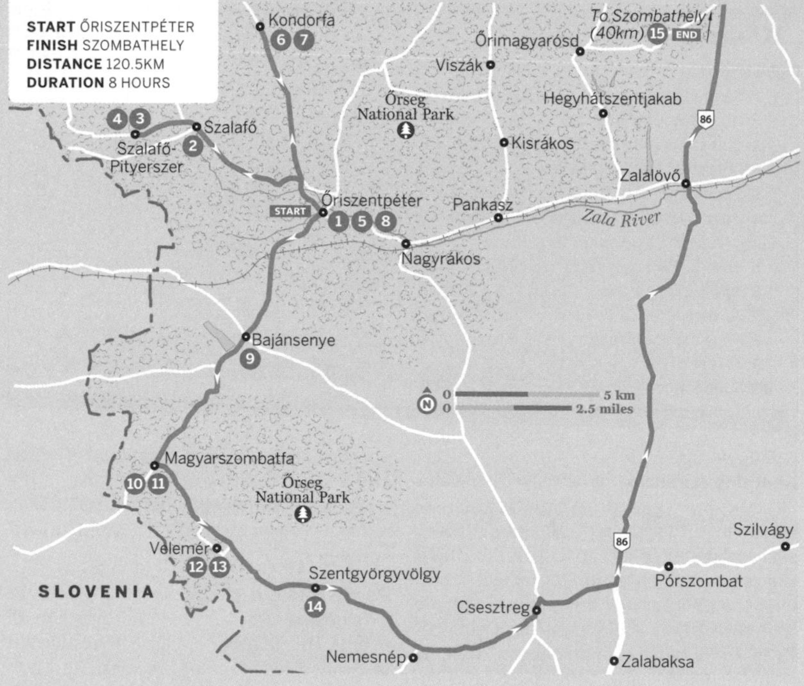

Driving Tour
Őrseg National Park

If you lack the leisure to explore the national park on foot or by bike, a day's driving tour should help you take in the highlights.

Begin your tour at 1 **Őriszentpéter**, the 'capital' of Őrség National Park – an attractive village of thatched wooden dwellings scattered over several hills. Follow the road northwest for 2km towards Szalafő and stop at the remarkably well-preserved 2 **Romanesque church** featuring a wonderful carved portal and an 18th-century altarpiece painted by a student of Franz Anton Maulbertsch. Continue 5km west to 3 **Szalafő-Pityerszer**; the 4 **Open-Air Ethnographical Museum** here is an excellent place to view traditional Őrség architecture: built around a central courtyard, the U-shaped houses are very cute and have large overhangs, which allowed neighbours to chat when it rained. Head back to 5 **Őriszentpéter** and then north for 7.5km to tiny 6 **Kondorfa**. In a restored traditional house you'll find 7 **Vadkörte** – a folksy, kitsch restaurant specialising in Hungarian cuisine that features wild meats, mushrooms, berries and asparagus, depending on the season. After lunch, drive back to 8 **Őriszentpéter** and carry on south for 8km along the E65 to 9 **Bajánsenye**, a village famous for its delicious, locally sourced fish. Another 10km south brings you to 10 **Magyarszombatfa** – an area that has for centuries been known for its pottery, and where the craft is still very much alive. If you don't catch the local potters in action, the 1760 11 **potter's house (Fazekasház)** is an excellent museum featuring some splendid unglazed containers and cooking vessels. Head 7km southeast of Magyarszombatfa; in the forest on the edge of the village of 12 **Velemér** there is a beautiful 13th-century 13 **church** featuring frescos by Austrian painter Johannes Aquilla, designed to be illuminated by the sun at certain times of year. Another 4km along, the Calvinist church at the village of 14 **Szentgyörgyvölgy** has an absolutely splendid ceiling. Head east for 15km to join highway 86 and carry on north for around 60km until you reach your final destination of 15 **Szombathely**.

Őrség National Park

Unspoilt nature and pure rural essence are the biggest drawcards of Őrség, Hungary's westernmost region, where it converges with Austria and Slovenia in forest and farmland. Much of the region forms the boundaries of the 440-sq-km Őrség National Park, founded in 2002 and recently designated a European Destination of Excellence in recognition of the area's commitment to environmental and cultural sustainability. Besides a rich birdlife, the park's villages maintain a strong folk tradition, with local pottery enterprises going back some generations.

The park's **information centre** (☎548 034; http://onp.nemzetipark.gov.hu; Siskaszer 26/a; ⏲8am-4.30pm Mon-Fri, 10am-7pm Sat-Sun mid-Jun–Aug, shorter hours rest of year) is housed in the same building as Tourinform in Őriszentpéter at the turn-off to Szalafő. The park itself is a green belt of dense woods, peaceful meadows, rolling hills and slow streams, which makes it a grand place for hiking, cycling and horse riding. Tourinform can provide information on all of these activities, as well as places to stay in the villages. There are marked hiking trails that link many of Őrség's villages, including Őriszentpéter, Szalafő, Velemér and Pankasz. Cartographia's 1:60,000-scale map *Őrség és a Göcsej* is a good reference for hikers.

An excellent place to stay is **Vadkörte** (☎429 031; www.vadkorte.hu; Alvég 7; s/d/tr/q 6600/12,000/15,000/16,800Ft, apt from 10,500Ft), an adorable country inn in the heart of the park at tiny Kondorfa, with five spacious, pleasant rooms, two fully equipped apartments next door and an excellent restaurant serving hearty seasonal cuisine with a strong emphasis on local ingredients. Guests can rent bicycles (1500Ft per day) and use either the Finnish (5000Ft per day) or infrared sauna (1000Ft per person) after a good day's hiking or biking.

ℹ Getting There and Away

It's best to have your own transport to explore the region, as buses are infrequent. Őriszentpéter can be reached by bus from Körmend (745Ft, one hour, 37km, up to 10 daily) and Kőszeg (1680Ft, two hours, 87km, one daily); there are also buses between Őriszentpéter, Szalafő (250Ft, six to nine minutes, 5.6km, one to two daily) and Kondorfa (250Ft, 11 to 15 minutes, 7.5km, two to four daily).

Lake Balaton & Southern Transdanubia

Includes »

Best Places to Eat

- » Oliva (p172)
- » Mandula (p187)
- » Az Elefánthoz (p183)
- » Rege Café (p163)

Best Places to Stay

- » Bacchus (p153)
- » Kővirag (p157)
- » Mala Garden (p174)
- » Bonvino Hotel (p158)

Why Go?

Extending roughly 80km like a skinny, lopsided paprika, at first glance Lake Balaton seems to simply be a happy, sunny expanse of opaque tourmaline-coloured water to play in. But step beyond the beaches of Europe's biggest and shallowest body of water and you'll encounter the vine-filled forested hills, a national park and a wild peninsula jutting out 4km, nearly cutting the lake in half. Oh, and did we mention Hungary's most famous porcelain producer and a hilltop fairytale fortress? Then there's Southern Transdanubia, where whitewashed farmhouses with thatched roofs dominate a countryside that hasn't changed in centuries. Anchoring its centre is one of Hungary's most alluring cities, Pécs, where a Mediterranean feel permeates streets filled with relics of Hungary's Ottoman past and a headspinning number of exceptional museums. Beyond, a clutch of medieval castles enchant and vineyard cellars beckon you to wine-taste your heart out.

When to Go

Pécs

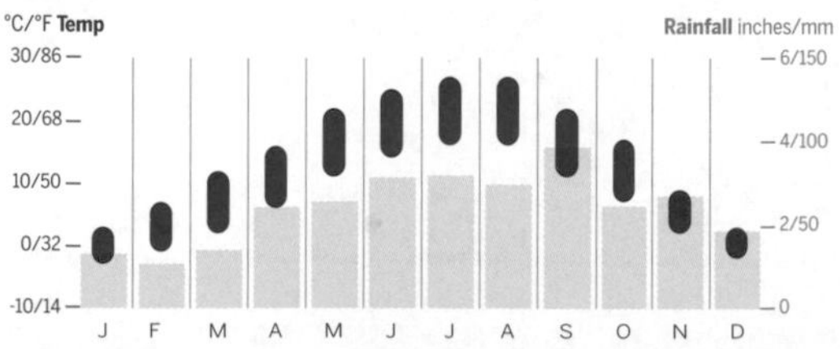

Apr-May Resorts open and Southern Transdanubia bursts with spring flowers

Jul-Aug Hot and humid but guaranteed sunny days and balmy nights

Sep-Oct Fewer crowds and mild temps; this may be the best time to visit

LAKE BALATON REGION

History

The area around Lake Balaton was settled as early as the Iron Age and in the 2nd century AD the Romans, who called the lake Pelso, built a fort at Valcum (now Fenékpuszta), south of Keszthely. Throughout the Great Migrations, Lake Balaton was a reliable source of water, fish, reeds for thatch and ice in winter. The early Magyars found the lake a natural defence line, and many churches, monasteries and villages were built in the vicinity. In the 16th century the lake served as the divide between the Turks, who occupied the southern shore, and the Habsburgs to the northwest. Before the Ottomans were pushed back they had already crossed the lake and razed many of the towns and border castles in the northern hills. Croats, Germans and Slovaks resettled the area in the 18th century, and the subsequent building booms gave towns such as Sümeg, Veszprém and Keszthely their baroque appearance.

Balatonfüred and Hévíz developed early as resorts for the wealthy, but it wasn't until the late 19th century that landowners, their vines destroyed by phylloxera lice, began building summer homes to rent out to the burgeoning middle classes. The arrival of the southern railway in 1861 and the northern line in 1909 increased the tourist influx, and by the 1920s resorts on both shores welcomed some 50,000 holidaymakers each summer. Just before the outbreak of WWII that number had increased fourfold. After the war, the communist government expropriated private villas and built new holiday homes for trade unions. Many of these have been turned into hotels in recent years, greatly increasing the accommodation options.

Activities

The main pursuits for visitors to Lake Balaton - apart from swimming, of course - are boating, fishing and cycling. Motor boats running on fuel are banned entirely, so 'boating' here means sailing, rowing and windsurfing. Fishing is good - the indigenous *fogas* (pikeperch) and the young version, *süllő*, being the prized catch - and edible *harcsa* (catfish) and *ponty* (carp) are in abundance. Area licences are required to fish on the lake - ask at the various Tourinform offices on the lake for places to purchase them.

Lake cruises offered by Balaton Shipping Co (p147) are a fun pastime over the warmest months (June, July and August). Cruises usually last one hour (adult/child 1500/650Ft) and leave from nearly all towns on the lake, including Keszthely, Badacsony, Tihany, Balatonfüred and Siófok. Themed cruises for kids are also offered, along with sunset tours and grill parties.

The 210km designated bike path around the lake is prime for cycling. Most towns on the lake's shores have at least one bike-rental agent operating over the summer months. If you plan to tool around on two wheels, pick up a copy of the free cycling maps available from each town's Tourinform office. In addition to the round-the-lake path, various other shorter cycle routes exist in the Balaton area.

Getting There & Away

Trains to Lake Balaton usually leave from Déli or Kelenföld train stations in Budapest, and buses from Népliget bus station. If you're travelling north or south from the lake to towns in Western or Southern Transdanubia, buses are usually preferable to trains – departure times are more frequent and they serve more destinations.

Getting Around

Rail and bus service on both the northern and southern sides of the lake is fairly frequent. But a better way to see the lake up close is on a ferry run by the **Balaton Shipping Co** (Balatoni Hajózási Rt; 84-310 050; www.balatonihajozas.hu; Krúdy sétány 2, Siófok). Ferries operate on the Siófok–Balatonfüred–Tihany–Balatonföldvár route, and from Fonyód to the Badacsony, up to four times daily from April to May and September to October, with many more frequent sailings from June to August. From late May to early September, ferries ply the lake from Balatonkenese to Keszthely and Révfülöp to Balatonboglár. There is also a regular car ferry between Tihanyi-rév on the northern shore and Szántódi-rév on the southern shore (from early March to late November). There are no passenger services from November to March.

Adults pay 1100Ft for distances of 1km to 10km, 1460Ft for 11km to 20km and 1660Ft for 21km to 70km. Children pay half-price, and return fares are marginally less than double the one-way fare. Bicycle transport costs 1000/1460Ft one way/return.

Car ferries charge 540/475/250/800/1550Ft per adult/child/bicycle/motorcycle/car.

Lake Balaton & Southern Transdanubia Highlights

1. Wondering how tiny Sümeg contains both a striking **hilltop fortress** (p159) and impressive frescoes in its **Church of the Ascension** (p159)
2. Taking a dip in the healing waters of Europe's largest **thermal lake** (p155)
3. Wandering the wild peninsula and poking around in the **Abbey Church** (p161) at Tihany
4. Sailing, swimming and cycling in the **Lake Balaton region** (p147)
5. Embracing nature in the **Kál Basin** (p157), a region of unspoilt beauty in the heart of a national park
6. Marvelling at the greenish- and goldish-hued ceramics at **Zsolnay Porcelain Museum** (p179) in Pécs
7. Sampling big, bold reds in the cellars in and around **Villány** (p186)
8. Exploring one of Hungary's best **skanzens** (p191); open-air museums of folk architecture in the delightfully rural village of Szenna

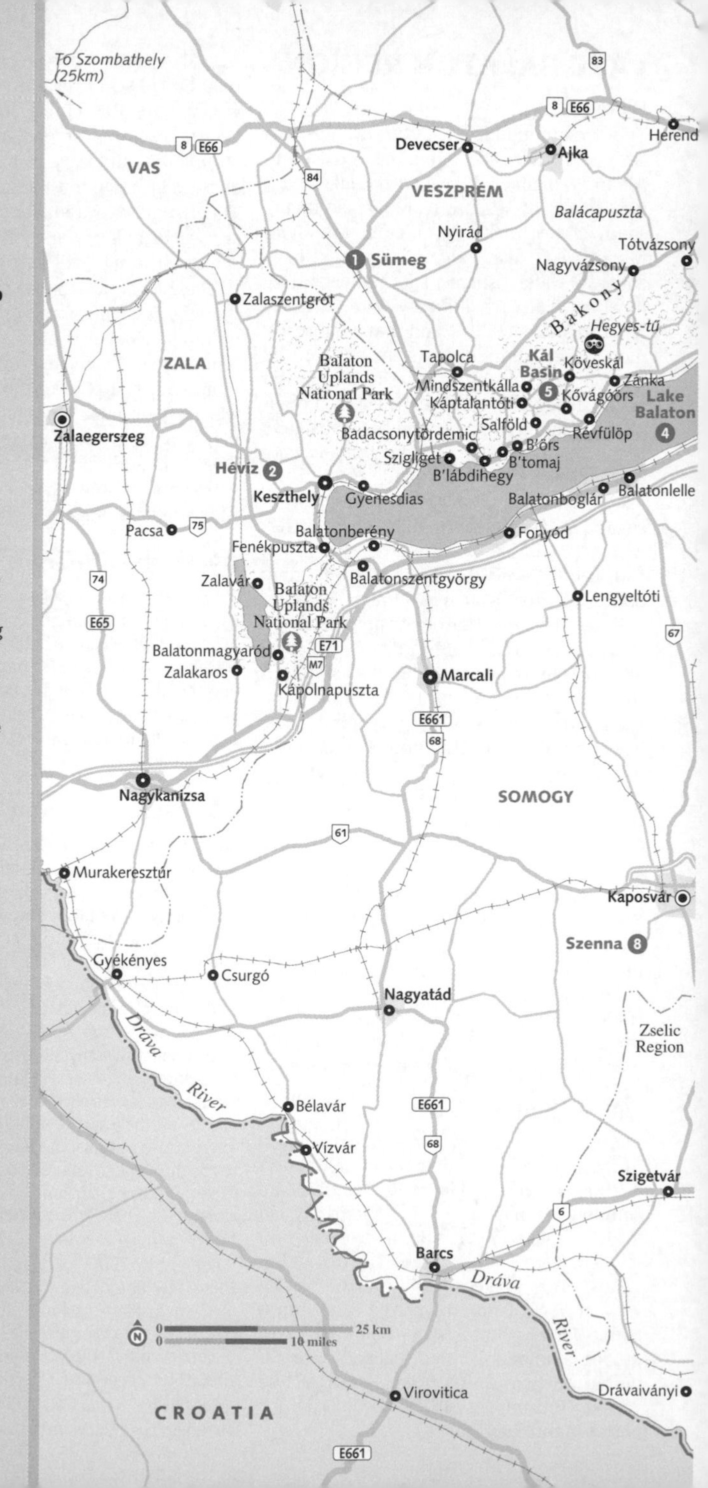

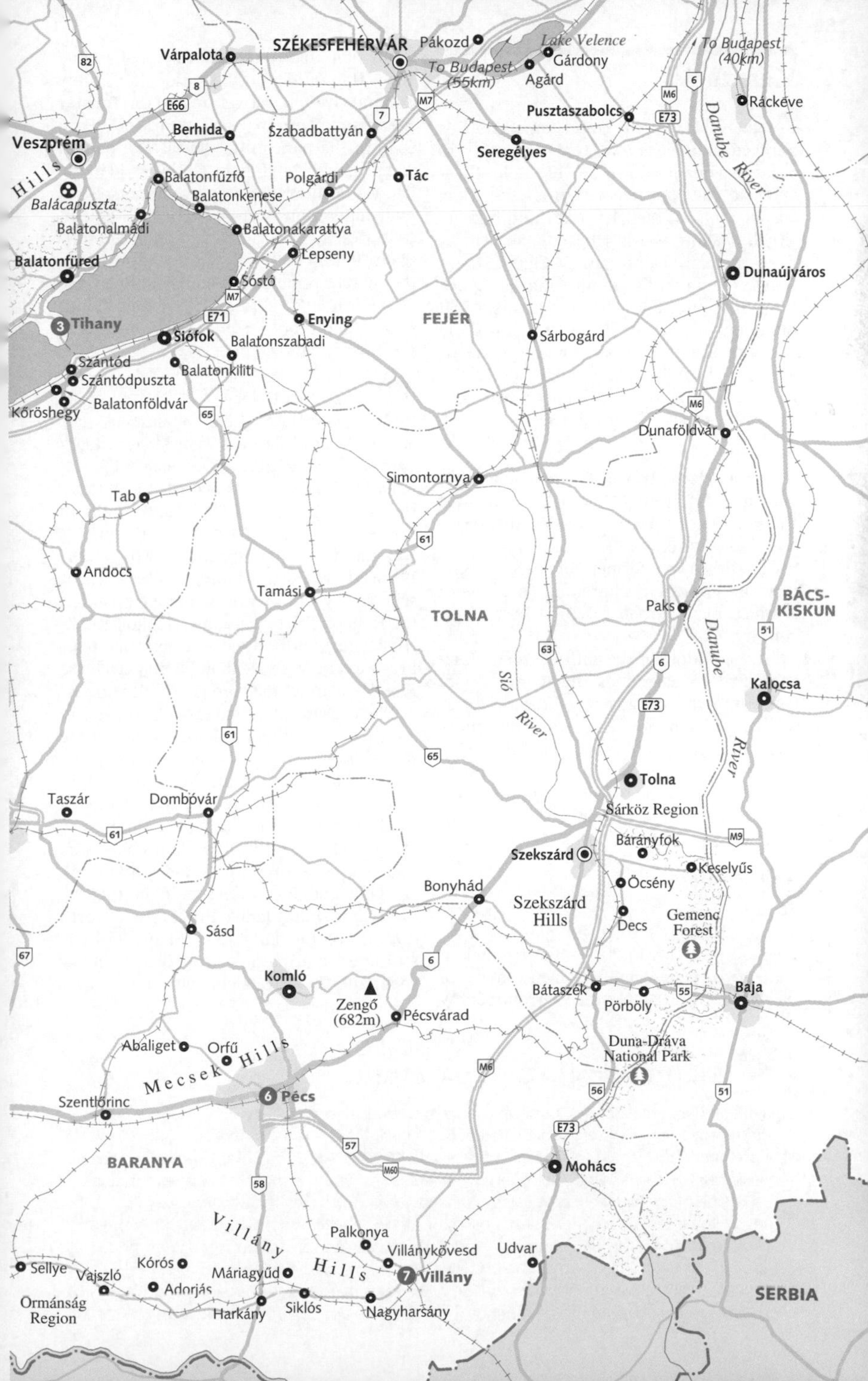
SZÉKESFEHÉRVÁR
Pákozd
Lake Velence
Gárdony
Agárd
To Budapest (55km)
To Budapest (40km)
Várpalota
Veszprém
Hills
Balácapuszta
Berhida
Szabadbattyán
Ráckeve
Pusztaszabolcs
Seregélyes
Tác
Polgárdi
Balatonfűzfő
Balatonkenese
Balatonalmádi
Balatonakarattya
Lepseny
Balatonfüred
Sóstó
Dunaújváros
Danube River
3 Tihany
Enying
FEJÉR
Siófok
Balatonszabadi
Sárbogárd
Szántód
Szántódpuszta
Balatonkiliti
Kőröshegy
Balatonföldvár
Dunaföldvár
Simontornya
Tab
Andocs
Tamási
TOLNA
BÁCS-KISKUN
Paks
Danube
Sió River
Kalocsa
River
Tolna
Taszár
Dombóvár
Sárköz Region
Bárányfok
Szekszárd
Keselyűs
Öcsény
Bonyhád
Szekszárd Hills
Decs
Gemenc Forest
Sásd
Komló
Zengő (682m)
Bátaszék
Pörböly
Baja
Pécsvárad
Abaliget
Orfű
Duna-Dráva National Park
Mecsek Hills
6 Pécs
Szentlőrinc
BARANYA
Mohács
Villány Hills
Palkonya
Villánykövesd
Udvar
Sellye
Kórós
Máriagyűd
7 Villány
Vajszló
Adorjás
SERBIA
Ormánság Region
Harkány
Siklós
Nagyharsány
82
8
E66
M7
7
6
M6
E73
E71
65
61
63
67
55
56
51
M9
57
M60
58

Keszthely

☎83 / POP 20,900

Keszthely, a city of grand town houses perched at the very western end of Lake Balaton, is hands-down one of the loveliest spots to stay, far removed from the tourist hot spots on the lake. You can dip in its small, shallow beaches by day, absorb its lively yet relaxed ambience by night, and get a dose of culture by popping into its handful of museums and admiring its historical buildings. Whatever you do, don't miss the Festetics Palace, a lavish baroque home fit for royalty. Unlike other towns along the lake, Keszthely is a university town and therefore stays awake in winter.

History

The Romans built a fort at Valcum (now Fenékpuszta), around 5km to the south, and their road north to the colonies at Sopron and Szombathely is today's Kossuth Lajos utca. The town's former fortified monastery and Franciscan church on Fő tér were strong enough to repel the Turks in the 16th century.

In the middle of the 18th century, Keszthely and its surrounds (including Hévíz) came into the possession of the Festetics family, who were progressives and reformers very much in the tradition of the Széchenyis. In fact, Count György Festetics (1755–1819), who founded Europe's first agricultural college, the Georgikon, here in 1797, was an uncle of István Széchenyi.

Sights

Fő tér SQUARE, PLAZA

Fő tér, Kezthely's colourful main square, received a facelift in 2012 – the result is a traffic-free, pedestrian-friendly expanse of newly laid white cobblestone surrounded by lovely buildings, including the late-baroque Town Hall on the northern side, the Trinity Column (1770) in the centre and the **former Franciscan church** (Ferences templom; 9am-6pm) in the park to the south. The church was originally built in the Gothic style in the late 14th century for Franciscan monks, but many alterations were made in subsequent centuries, including the addition of the steeple in 1898. The Gothic rose window above the porch remains, though, as does the Gothic ribbing on the nave's ceiling. Count György and other Festetics family members are buried in the crypt below.

TOP CHOICE **Festetics Palace** PALACE

(Festetics Kastély; ☎312 190; www.helikonkastely.hu; Kastély utca 1; Palace & Coach Museum adult/concession 2300/1150Ft; 9am-9pm Jul & Aug, 10am-4pm May, Jun & Sep, reduced hours & closed Mon Oct-Apr) The Festetics Palace, built in 1745 and extended 150 years later, contains 100 rooms in two sprawling wings. The 19th-century northern wing houses a music school, city library and conference centre; the Helikon Palace Museum (Helikon Kastélymúzeum) and the palace's greatest treasure, the renowned Helikon Library (Helikon Könyvtár) are in the baroque south wing.

The museum's rooms (about a dozen in all, each in a different colour scheme) are full of portraits, bric-a-brac and furniture, much of it brought from England by Mary Hamilton, a duchess who married one of the Festetics men in the 1860s. The library is known for its 100,000-volume collection, but just as impressive is the golden oak shelving and furniture carved in 1801 by local craftsman János Kerbl. Also worth noting are the Louis XIV Salon with its stunning marquetry, the rococo music room and the private chapel (1804).

HIGH SEASON IN LAKE BALATON

High season in Lake Balaton is July and August; crowds descend and prices skyrocket. If you're keen to enjoy the water activities but don't want the crowds, try to visit in June or September – the water is still warm (versus a bathtub-like 28°C to 29°C degrees in the heat of summer) yet everything is still open and it feels summery – *without* the intense humidity.

Outside of the high season it's easy to show up without a reservation and wing it, though you'll probably need to settle on midrange or above options. If you arrive in the Lake Balaton area without a hotel booked and you are keen to find budget accommodation, your best bet is to keep an eye out for signs saying *'szoba kiadó'* or *'Zimmer frei'* (Hungarian and German, respectively, for 'room for rent'). In many cases you have the option of renting a room in a private home or an entire apartment in an old villa.

Behind the palace in a separate building is the **Coach Museum** (Hintómúzeum; adult/concession 1000/500Ft; ⏲9am-9pm Jul & Aug, 10am-4pm May, Jun & Sep, reduced hours & closed Mon Oct-Apr), which is filled with coaches and sleighs fit for royalty. Note that the ticket for the palace *always* includes entry to the Coach Museum, but it is possible to visit the Coach Museum only.

Georgikon Farm Museum MUSEUM
(Georgikon Majormúzeum; ☎311 563; Bercsényi Miklós utca 67; adult/child 500/250Ft; ⏲10am-5pm Tue-Sat, to 6pm Sun May-Sep, 10am-6pm Tue-Fri Apr & Oct) Housed in several early-19th-century buildings of what was the Georgikon's experimental farm, the Georgikon Farm Museum is the perfect museum for lovers of early industrial farming tools and farming techniques, with exhibits on the history of viniculture in the Balaton region and traditional farm trades such as those performed by wagon builders, wheelwrights and coopers. Highlights include 19th-century blacksmith tools and an enormous antique steam plough.

Balaton Museum MUSEUM
(☎312 351; www.balatonimuzeum.hu; Múzeum utca 2; adult/child/family 700/350/1600Ft; ⏲10am-6pm Tue-Sun May-Oct, 9am-5pm Tue-Sat Nov-Apr) The Balaton Museum was purpose-built in 1928 and its permanent exhibits focus on the life and history of Lake Balaton. The aquarium of Balaton showcases underwater flora and fauna plus a handful of the lake's fishes (including goldfish, northern pike and several types of bream) and several interconnected rooms detail lake life and culture. Highlights include the exhibit on how bathing culture has evolved over the years (don't miss the 19th-century bathing suits on display) and dioramas on lake fishing, and a room devoted to János Halápy's expressive paintings of life on Lake Balaton – he is known for capturing the vibrant light and colours of the region.

Trophy & Model Railway Museum MUSEUM
(☎312 190; Pál utca; 1 museum adult/student 1000/500Ft, both museums 1800/900Ft; ⏲9am-5pm Jun, 9am-6pm Jul & Aug, 10am-3pm Mon 10am-5pm Tue-Sun Sep-May) This former military attic actually houses two separate museums. If you only have time for one, don't miss the grin-inducing Model Railway Museum on the top floor, which exhibits one of the world's largest mountain railway layouts. Trains whiz round a 40m-long railway network straight out of a picture book: one section contains the historic Vienna to Trieste train line and an awe-inducing section of Austrian mountains complete with mountain tunnels; another goes through Nuremburg and a snow-covered rendition of the Black Forest; and further along you watch train cars make stops at Lake Balaton towns like Keszthely and Badacsony, including amazingly detailed versions of their train stations. It's guaranteed to wow kids and adults alike.

On the two lower floors is the Trophy Museum – although we're not sure we enjoy looking at dead animals, it's impossible not to admit that this collection of hunting trophies from the 1920s and '30s contains spectacular stuffed leopards, cheetahs, lions, a polar bear and even a Siberian tiger, among other animals.

Erotic Panoptikum MUSEUM
(☎318 855; www.szexpanoptikum.hu; Kossuth Lajos utca 10; admission 600Ft; ⏲9am-7pm) Full disclosure: this is an X-rated wax museum. Kind of tacky – yes. Fascinating – absolutely. The tiny subterranean space brings to 'life' lust and sex scenes from illustrated books about Renaissance erotic fiction by the likes of Voltaire, Rousseau and others. Think wax figures of women in bodices

KESZTHELY'S JEWISH HERITAGE

Before WWII Keszthely's Jewish community numbered 1000; at the end of the war it had dropped to 170. Today at most 40 Jews live in the town and attend services at the 18th-century baroque **synagogue** (Kossuth Lajos utca 20; ⏲Bible Garden 5pm to 6pm Fri), located in a quiet courtyard off the main pedestrian drag, Kossuth Lajos utca (enter it through the arched passageway just south of Fejér György utca). It's not possible to visit the interior outside of service times, but if you are in town on Friday late afternoon you can wander the peaceful Bible Garden at the rear. Further evidence of the town's Jewish community can be found at the largely forgotten **Jewish cemetery** (Goldmark karoly utca 33; ⏲10am-4pm, closed Sat), north of the palace.

Keszthely

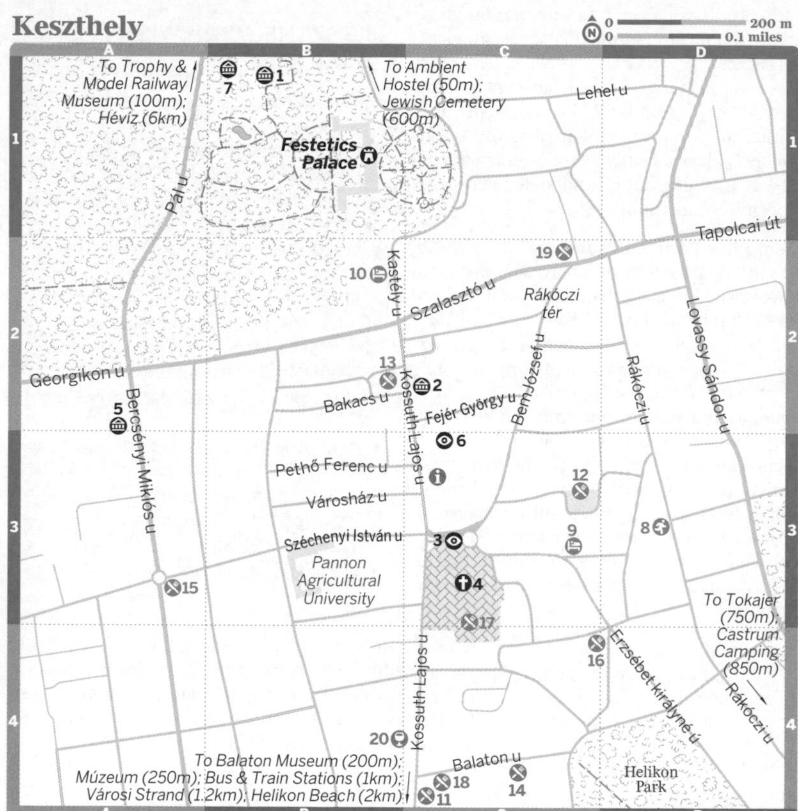

with their hooped skirts hiked up over their knees having kinky intercourse, women on women performing cunnilingus, and acrobatic orgies with extraordinarily real-looking private parts on vivid display. It's a bit like seeing an up-close freeze-frame of a porn film with actors dressed up in medieval garb. Beyond the, er, action scenes, check out the sketches and paintings of erotica gracing the walls or the elaborate terracotta penis sculpture.

Activities

Keszthely's best beaches decent for swimming or sunbathing are **City Beach** (Városi Strand; adult/child 890/630Ft, 3 days 1800/1300Ft; ⏲8am-6pm mid-May–mid-Sept), which is good for kids and close to the ferry pier, and reedy **Helikon Beach** (Helikon Strand; adult/child 500/350Ft, 3 days 1050/840Ft; ⏲8am-6pm mid-May–mid-Sept) further south. They have a unique view of both the north and south shores of the lake. There's windsurfing and kitesurfing rental at City Beach in summer.

The Balaton Shipping Co (p147) runs lake cruises from late March to late October; in high season there are up to four daily departures.

The 210km Balaton cycle path passes through Keszthely, and a 4km path connects the town with Hévíz (home to Europe's largest thermal lake; p155). Rent bicycles from **GreenZone** (☎315 463; Rákóczi utca 15; 3hr/1 day 1000/2200Ft; ⏲9am-6pm Mon-Fri, 10am-3pm Sat).

Festivals & Events

The biggest annual cultural event in Keszthely is the annual week-long **Balaton Festival** (⏲mid-May), featuring free outdoor classical, rock and pop-music concerts

Keszthely

around town and streets filled with jugglers, comedians, mimes and other street performers. Every summer brings the lovely two-day **Wine Festival** (Festetics Palace; 2000Ft; late August), where local winemakers, restaurants and food purveyors sell their wares and bands perform anything from rock to pop to jazz concerts. The admission cost gains you entry to the venue and two glasses of wine.

Sleeping

Tourinform can help find private rooms (from roughly 3500Ft per person per night), otherwise strike out on your own. Móra Ferenc utca always has a number of signs advertising for rooms and apartments.

Pension Sissy PENSION €

(www.villasissy.hu; Erzsébet királyné utca 70; r with/without bathroom per person 6000/3500Ft, 3-12yr half-price;) Sweet, quiet little pension in an old villa steps across from leafy Helikon Park. Simple rooms vary considerably – some with wood floors and stained-glass French doors, others with dull (but new) carpet, but all feature small refrigerators.

Ambient Hostel HOSTEL €

(06 30 460 3536; http://keszthely-szallas.fw.hu; Sopron utca 10; dm/d from 3600/7900Ft;) Only a short walk north of the palace ground is this new hostel. It has basic, cheap dorm rooms, each of which comes with its own en suite bathroom. Ambient also has a colourful, modern roadside cafe and is a hub for the under-30 crowd.

Múzeum PENSION €€

(313 182; Múzeum utca 3; s/d 9000/12,000Ft;) Rooms in this cute yellow cottage are well aired and very clean, and the whole place has a homey feel. It's an easy walk to the bus and train stations. This is one of the best-value pensions in town, so book early.

Párizsi Udvar INN €€

(311 202; www.parizsi.huninfo.hu; Kastély utca 5; d/tr/apt 10,500/13,400/16,500Ft;) There's no closer accommodation to Festetics Palace than Párizsi Udvar. Rooms are a little too big to be cosy, but they're well kept and face onto a sunny inner courtyard (a corner of which is taken over by a daytime restaurant and beer garden).

Tokajer GUESTHOUSE €€

(Tokaji Panzió Keszthely; 319 875; www.pensiontokajer.hu; Apát utca 21; s/d/apt from 9200/15,000/18,000Ft;) Spread over four buildings in a quiet area of town, Tokajer has slightly dated rooms, but they're spacious and some have balconies. Added extras include two pools, free use of bicycles and the fitness room, and a mini wellness centre.

TOP CHOICE **Bacchus** HOTEL €€€

(510 450; www.bacchushotel.hu; Erzsébet királyné utca 18; s 13,500Ft, d 16,900-25,000Ft, apt 27,000Ft;) Bacchus' central position and immaculate rooms make it a popular choice with travellers and rightly

so – rooms are simple but extra clean and inviting with solid wood furnishings. Equally pleasing is its atmospheric cellar, which includes a lovely restaurant that features wine tastings.

Eating & Drinking

Food Market MARKET
(Piac tér; ⌚7am-2pm Mon-Sat) Keszthely's lively food market combines the best and worst of Hungary's markets, packed with overflowing fruit and vegetable stands, stalls selling overwhelming amounts of home-made honey, jam and home-made paprika paste alongside tacky T-shirts with Harleys, and housewares that look like they'd last less than a month.

Pizzeria Donatello PIZZERIA €
(☎315 989; Balaton utca 1; pizza 850-1200Ft) A student favorite that still manages to attract families and diners wanting a quick bite – it's always bustling, and pizzas are standard but extra crispy with fresh vegetables and home-made sauce.

TOP CHOICE **Margareta** HUNGARIAN €
(www.margaretaetterem.hu; Bercsényi utca 60; mains 1400-3200Ft; ⌚11am-10pm) Ask any local where they like to eat and one answer dominates: Margareta. It's no beauty, but the wraparound porch and hidden backyard terrace heave with chatter and laughter any night of the week in the warm months, and the small interior packs them in the rest of the year. Food sticks to basic but hearty Hungarian staples but be warned – portions are huge.

Lakoma HUNGARIAN €€
(☎313 129; Balaton utca 9; mains 1600-3200Ft; ⌚11am-10pm) With a good vegetarian and fish selection (for Hungarian-restaurant standards), grill/roast specialities and a back garden that transforms itself into a convivial dining area in the summer months, it's hard to go wrong with Lakoma.

Vegetárius VEGETARIAN €
(☎311 023; Rákóczi tér 3; mains 460-1200Ft; ⌚11am-4pm Mon-Fri) It may have changed its name, but this small vegetarian restaurant down the hill from the palace has buckets of good energy and healthy pickings during the midweek lunch-hour rush.

Park HUNGARIAN €
(☎311 654; Vörösmarty utca 1/a; mains 1500-3300Ft) The orange decor might be too much for sensitive folk and the service can be a little haphazard, but Park does some damn fine Hungarian cuisine. If you're a party of two, you can't go wrong with the grilled platter, and if at the end you can fit in a Drunken Monk, the house dessert, you're doing better than us.

TOP CHOICE **Bacchus** HUNGARIAN €€
(☎510 450; www.bacchushotel.hu; Erzsébet királyné utca 18; mains 1300-3000Ft; ⌚11am-11pm) Oenophiles and foodies should head straight to this restaurant and wine mecca, which serves simple but lovingly prepared Hungarian fare including local faves like fish from Lake Balaton (the catfish with paprika curded cheese pasta is divine), and the knowledgeable staff will guide you to a lovely glass of local tipple. The restaurant also runs friendly wine tastings (six to eight wines 2500Ft per person, 10 to 12 wines 3500Ft) including cheese and fruit in the vaulted cellar. The ivy-covered outdoor terrace is a cool reprieve from the heat, or pop into the subterranean restaurant – the chunky furniture is made from old wine barrels and presses.

Pelso Café CAFE €
(Fő tér; coffee & cake from 300Ft; ⌚10am-10pm; 📶) This modern two-level cafe boasts a fantastic terrace overlooking the southern end of the main square. It does decent cake and has a selection of teas from around the world plus the usual coffee concoctions. But we like it best as a prime spot for an alfresco sundowner – the wine and beer list is small, but the vantage point is lovely.

Korzó CAFE €
(☎311 785; Kossuth Lajos utca 7; cakes 360Ft) Korzó is one of the few cafes worthy of your attention on pedestrian Kossuth Lajos utca. It's a simple place with street seating, but the cakes are divine and the music thankfully not too intrusive.

Kolibri BAR
(Kossuth Lajos utca 81) Kolibri is a cocktail bar that attracts relaxed over-30ish types – it's an excellent choice if you are keen to veer away from the ubiquitous beer and wine selections that dominate the Lake Balaton region.

Béke WINE BAR
(☎318 219; Kossuth Lajos utca 50) This bar-restaurant hybrid is a colourful, lively spot with a large inner courtyard and live music on weekends.

☆ Entertainment

Festetics Palace CLASSICAL MUSIC
(Festetics Kastély; ☎312 190; www.helikonkastely.hu; Kastély utca 1; ⏰8pm Thu) Operetta concerts are held every Thursday throughout the year in the music hall of the palace.

ℹ Information

Tourinform (☎314 144; keszthely@tourinform.hu; Kossuth Lajos utca 28; ⏰9am-8pm Mon-Fri, to 6pm Sat mid-Jun–mid-Sep, 9am-5pm Mon-Fri, to 12.30pm Sat mid-Sep–mid-Jun) An excellent source of information on Keszthely and the entire Balaton area.

ℹ Getting There & Away

Air

At press time **Héviz Balaton Airport** (formerly FlyBalaton Airport; ☎554 060; www.hevizairport.com; Sármellék), 15km southwest of Keszthely, only served Dusseldorf, Frankfurt, Hamburg and Berlin between April and November, though there was talk of additional flights being added from other countries in the coming years. Check the website for updates.

Bus

Keszthely is well served by buses. Some, including those to Hévíz, Nagykanizsa and Sümeg, can be boarded at the bus stops in front of the Franciscan church on Fő tér. Catch buses to the lake's northern shore (Badacsony, Nagyvázsony and Tapolca) along Tapolcai út.

DESTINATION	PRICE	TIME	KM	FREQUENCY
Badacsony	560Ft	35min	27	7-8 daily
Budapest	3410Ft	2½-4hr	190	7-8 daily
Hévíz	250Ft	15min	8	half-hourly
Pécs	2830Ft	3½hr	152	up to 5 daily
Sümeg	650Ft	50min	31	hourly
Tapolca	560Ft	35-60min	28	hourly
Veszprém	1680Ft	1¾hr	77	hourly

Train

Keszthely has train links to the following destinations. Most trains to/from Budapest go to Budapest Déli station, but occasionally go to Budapest Keleti.

DESTINATION	PRICE	TIME	KM	FREQUENCY
Badacsony (change at Tapolca)	745Ft	1hr	39	8 daily
Budapest	3410Ft	3½-4hr	190	6 daily
Szombathely	2570Ft	2hr	126	2 daily
Tapolca	465Ft	30min	25	hourly

ℹ Getting Around

Buses run from the train and bus stations to the Franciscan church on Fő tér, but unless there's one waiting on your arrival it's just as easy to walk. You can also make a booking for a **taxi** (☎333 666).

Around Keszthely

HÉVÍZ

A short hop west of Keszthely lies Hévíz, the most famous of Hungary's spa towns, and rightly so, for it is home to **Gyógy-tó** (Hevíz Thermal Lake; ☎501 700; www.spaheviz.hu; 3hr/5hr/whole day 2500/2800/3800Ft; ⏰8am-7pm Jun-Aug, 9am-6pm May & Sep, 9am-5pm Apr & Oct, 9am-4pm Mar & Nov-Feb), Europe's largest thermal lake. In fact, some argue Hévíz is the slowest town in the country, partly because the average visitor age is well over 60, but mostly because it's impossible to move quickly after experiencing the lake's therapeutic waters. But no matter your age, a dip into this waterlily-filled lake is essential for anyone visiting the Lake Balaton region.

It's an astonishing sight: a surface of 4.4 hectares in the Park Wood, covered for most of the year in pink and white lotuses. The source is a spring spouting from a crater some 40m below ground that disgorges up to 80 million litres of warm water a day, renewing itself every 48 hours or so. The surface temperature averages 33°C and never drops below 22°C in winter, allowing bathing throughout the year, even when there's ice on the fir trees of Park Wood. Do as the locals do and rent a rubber ring and just float. This is a place where you're urged to reach a dreamy meditative state while floating on the water.

A covered bridge leads to the thermal lake's fin-de-siècle central pavilion, which contains a small buffet, sun chairs, showers, changing rooms and steps down into the lake. Catwalks and piers fan out from the central pavilion to sun decks and a second pavilion where massage treatments are offered. You can swim protected beneath the pavilions and piers or swim out into the lake and rest on wooden planks secured to the lake's bottom. There are some piers along the shore for sunbathing as well, and the on-site indoor spa offers every kind of thermal remedy, massage and scrub imaginable.

The best way to reach Hévíz is by bike via the 4km bicycle path connecting Keszthely to Hévíz, ending at the southern entrance to the thermal lake (the path is well marked; ask for the local bike map at Tourinform). Alternatively, hop on one of the buses travelling west from Keszthely (250Ft, 15 to 20 minutes, 8km) almost every half-hour. Buses also service Badacsony (745Ft, 45 to 55 minutes, 35km, six daily) and Balatonfüred (1490Ft, 1½ to two hours, 75km, six daily). The bus station is on Deák tér, a few steps from the northern entrance to the lake.

KIS-BALATON

Around 20km southwest of Keszthely is Kis-Balaton (Little Balaton), a small lake far removed from the hustle and bustle of its bigger cousin. The lake and the marshes that spread eastwards from it are primarily a haven for bird life (over 250 species of birds have been identified) and a wetland paradise of flora and fauna; both fall under the protection of the **Balaton Uplands National Park** (www.bfnp.hu). The best place to start exploring is at the **Kis-Balaton House** (☎87-710 002; ⏰9am-noon & 1-6pm Tue-Sun Mar-Nov), in the village of Zalavár near the northern end of the lake. Staff are friendly and offer a wealth of information about the area.

Tiny **Kányavári Island** (parking per hr/day 300/800Ft), near the lake's eastern edge and accessible via a wooden footbridge, is one of the better spots to view avian life; there are bird-watching towers and picnic tables scattered its length and breadth. At the southern end of Kis-Balaton is a **Buffalo Reserve** (☎87-555 291; adult/child/student 659/300/500Ft; ⏰9am-6pm), which is home to some 200 water buffalo; the best time to visit is late afternoon, when the buffalo gather near the reserve headquarters. The reserve is 3km south of Balatonmagyaród.

Despite there being hourly buses from Keszthely to Zalavár (370Ft, 30 to 45 minutes, 18km) and two to Balatonmagyaród from Monday to Saturday (560Ft, 30 to 45 minutes, 26km), you're better off exploring the region under your own steam.

Badacsony & Environs

☎87 / POP 2230

Badacsony is a conglomeration of four towns: Badacsonylábdihegy, Badacsonyörs, Badacsonytördemic and Badacsonytomaj. When Hungarians say Badacsony, they usually mean the little resort at the Badacsony train station, near the ferry pier southwest of Badacsonytomaj. The entire shore between Szigliget and Tihany is dotted with lovely lakeside villages and the vineyard-filled hills jutting up from them, sprinkled with little wine-press houses and 'folk baroque' cottages. The area also has a laid-back feel and development has been slow to pick up here, making it just dandy for a couple of days of relaxation.

The primary draw is swimming and boating in and on the lake and hitting the hills for some hiking, but on rainy days the local museums are worth a gander. Lake cruises, run by the Balaton Shipping Co (p147), leave from Badacsony's pier two to three times daily in high season.

Sights & Activities

József Egry Museum MUSEUM

(☎431 044; Egry sétány 12; adult/child 600/300Ft; ⏰10am-8pm daily Jul-Aug, to 4pm Tue-Sun May-Jun & Sep-Oct) The József Egry Museum is devoted to the Balaton region's leading painter (1883–1951) and Hungary's equivalent to Kokoschka, an Austrian artist known for his experssionist art, especially landscapes and portraits. Many of his works powerfully capture the essence of village and fishing life on the lake through the use of strong, dark colours.

Róza Szegedi House MUSEUM

(☎430 906; Szegedi Róza utca; adult/child 500/250Ft; ⏰10am-6pm Tue-Sun May-Sep) The dramatic slopes and vineyards above the town centre are sprinkled with little wine-press houses and 'folk baroque' cottages. One of these is the Róza Szegedi House, which belonged to the actress wife of the poet Sándor Kisfaludy from Sümeg. Established in 1790, it contains a literature museum.

Walking & Hiking HIKING

The best place to start a hike is at Kisfaludy House restaurant (p158), where a large map of the marked trails is posted by the car park. Several paths across the area lead to lookouts – at 437m, Kisfaludy Lookout (Kisfaludy kilátó) is the highest – and to neighbouring hills like Gulács-hegy (393m) and Szentgyörgy-hegy (415m) to the north. The landscape includes abandoned quarries and basalt towers that resemble organ pipes; of these, Stone Gate (Kőkapu) is the most dramatic. Several of the trails take you past

Rose Rock (Rózsakő). A plaque explains an unusual tradition: 'If a lad and a lass sit here together with their backs to the lake, they will be married in a year.' Good luck – or regrets (as the case may be).

Swimming BEACH
(adult/child 700/350Ft; ⏱May-Sep) The postage stamp-sized beach in Badacsony is reedy but lovely for sunbathing; alternatively head a few kilometres northeast to Badacsonytomaj or Badacsonyörs for additional beaches.

Sleeping

Tourinform has a list of private rooms for the entire Badacsony area; expect to pay anything from 3000Ft per person. It generally costs more for stays of less than three nights. If you want to strike out on your own, there are plenty of places with signs advertising rooms for rent along Római út and Park utca and among the vineyards.

THE KÁL BASIN

Only a few kilometres north of the lake in the heart of the Balaton Uplands National Park (p156) is a tiny pocket of rural paradise where time stands still. Of all the spots close to Lake Balaton, there is no better place to escape the hubbub of the lake and relax.

For such a small place (it covers around 120 sq km), Kál Basin (Káli-medence) offers more variety than entire regions. Protected by forested hills and rocky basalt outcrops, it has a mild climate that has attracted settlers for centuries. Their endeavours can be seen in the form of crumbling ruins, forgotten monasteries and disused water mills. Vineyards cling to gently undulating hills, and much of the land is either farmed or home to horse studs. Of its handful of small villages, **Salföld** is the most interesting architecturally; its streets are lined with beautifully restored cottages with whitewashed walls and shingled roofs.

Geographically, the basin is unusual. Sandstone is commonplace here, and fields of boulders can be seen in the so-called **Seas of Stones** near the villages of Salföld, Kővágóörs and Szentbékkálla – look for the **swinging rock** at Szentbékkálla. **Hegyestű** (Pointed Needle), at the eastern border of the basin, is a dramatic basalt formation, featuring 20m-high rock columns.

Preservation of Hungary's rural past is important to the locals. Many farmers only farm or grow organic produce native to the country, such as at **Kecskefarm** (☎87-707 601), 4km west of Kékkút village on the road to Tapolca; pick up Mangalica sausage and freshly made goat's cheese here. At the **Salföld Ranch** (Salföld Major; ☎87-702 857; Salföld; shows adult/child 500/300Ft, horse rides incl shows adult/child 3000/2000Ft; ⏱9am-7pm May-Aug, to 5pm Mar-Apr & Sep-Nov) you can see cowboys ride 'five-in-hand', head out on horse treks (which includes local schnapps and bread on one of your stops), and take a peek at Mangalica pigs and Racka sheep.

Few hotels and pensions are located in the basin, but two special places in **Köveskál** beckon if you're keen to explore the area in detail and embrace a rugged rural retreat worlds away from the lakeside resorts. Surrounded by vineyards is **Kali Art Inn** (☎30 922 8715; www.kaliartinn.hu; Fő utca 8; d 30,000-37,000Ft, tr/q 39,000/40,000Ft, apt from 42,000Ft; P❄📶🏊), an antique-filled former officers' mess decorated with warmth and rustic touches. It caters to both artists (there's an on-site studio and the owners can provide easels and brushes) and active types – free bikes are on hand and staff can arrange local horseback rides. Or opt for **Kővirág** (☎06 20 568 4724; www.kovirag.hu; Fő út 9/a; per person apt 6900Ft), in the back alleys of the village: its handful of apartments are housed in lovingly restored 19th-century cottages, which are filled with folk-art furniture you normally see in museums. Each has a lounge, clay oven and small patio, and prices include use of bikes. Its restaurant is next door, in another of the basin's distinct stone cottages; it serves exceptional regional and seasonal cuisine made using local produce, and you can sample wines from the surrounding vineyards.

The basin is best approached from Tapolca or Révfülöp and can be tackled as a day trip from either – as long as you have your own transport. Buses are infrequent but the basin is small enough to explore by bicycle. Pick up a bike, along with information on the basin, from Hullám Hostel (p158).

Note that much of Badacsony's accommodation opens weekends only from November to April – some close entirely over the winter period.

TOP CHOICE **Hullám Hostel** HOSTEL €
(☎463 089; www.balatonhostel.hu; Füredi út 6, Révfülöp; dm/s/d per person from 3500/4900/4900Ft; ⊙late Mar-Sep; @) With a decidedly relaxed air, young staff happy to share a drink and a tale, and bright colours splashed across its basic rooms, Hullám appeals to those looking for a fun yet relaxed time. The newly renovated house at the rear, with three attic rooms, private terrace and separate bathroom, is perfect for families, and the secluded garden is inviting for all. Staff organise a film festival in mid-July, regular barbecues and parties, and can provide information on self-guided bicycle tours of the Kál Basin and lake. Facilities include bicycles for hire (four hours/one day 1500/2500Ft), laundry (1500Ft per load), internet access (250Ft per hour) and kitchen. It's located 9km east of Badacsony in the township of Révfülöp.

Neptun GUESTHOUSE €€
(☎431 293; www.borbaratok.hu; Római út 156; s/d 8500/12,000Ft) This very central town house has basic rooms, some of which have views of the lake. In summer its large garden turns into a restaurant where breakfast is served (1300Ft).

TOP CHOICE **Bonvino Hotel** BOUTIQUE HOTEL €€€
(www.hotelbonvino.hu; Park utca 22; d/apt from 44,000/64,000Ft; P❄@🛜≋) One of the snazziest boutique hotels on Lake Balaton, this spiffy newcomer is all modern and plush with stylish features of a design hotel. Choose from rooms with the 'rustic' look (Hungarian motifs on pillows and walls and chunky wood headboards paired with simple modern pieces), or just 'modern' (same but minus Hungarian touches – think minimalist heaven). With its full-service spa it's a great choice year-round and staff can arrange wine-cellar visits tailored to what you want. The elegant on-site restaurant serves predictable international fare but we're bigger fans of the wine bar (oodles of local options on the menu and knowledgable staff to guide you through it).

Eating & Drinking

Many of the best restaurants sit among the vineyards up in the hills rising up from the lakeside towns. But if you can't make it up the hill and are looking for a range of fish dishes to choose from, head to **Halászkert** (☎431 054; Park utca 5; mains 1200-2800Ft); it may be crowded and touristy at times, but the food is top rate. For quick fare, food stalls with picnic tables dispensing sausage, fish soup, *lángos* (deep-fried dough) and gyros (meat skewers) line the pedestrian walkway between the train station and Park utca, and are intermingled with **wine stalls** (per glass 100Ft, per litre 500-700Ft) serving cheap plonk.

Borbarátok INTERNATIONAL €€
(☎471 597; Római út 78; mains 1700-2600Ft) A lively bar and restaurant where the food is served on wooden plates (adds to the flavour perhaps?). It's a good place to try a glass of Badacsony's premier white wines, Kéknyelű (Blue Stalk) or Szürkebarát (Pinot Gris).

Szent Orbán HUNGARIAN €€
(☎431 382; Szegedi Róza utca 22; mains 1700-3300Ft) A combination of restaurant and wine tavern in the vineyards above Badacsony, Szent Orbán is a fine destination for anyone looking to sample above-par local produce alongside regional cuisine. The views from its vine-laced terrace are extensive, and it's not such a long stumble back down to the lake afterwards.

TOP CHOICE **Kisfaludy House** EUROPEAN €€
(☎431 016; Szegedi Róza utca 87; mains 1500-3000Ft, 3/5 wine flights 1500/2100Ft; ⊙to midnight Apr–mid-Oct) Perched high on the hill overlooking the vineyards and the lake is Kisfaludy House, a charming stone cottage built in 1798 that was once a press house of the Kisfaludy family. Views are impressive and food reflects the usual regional specialties from the lake, such as pikeperch in breadcrumbs, grilled goose liver and cold fruit soup, plus a good selection of Central European staples like Wienerschnitzel and Cordon Bleu. It also offers excellent wine-tasting menus – the flights of local wines are served with cheese nibbles.

Information

Tourinform (☎431 046; Park utca 6; ⊙9am-7pm daily mid-Jun–mid-Sep, 10am-3pm Mon-Fri mid-Sep–mid-Jun) Informed staff with details on the region.

Getting There & Away

Up to eight buses connect Badacsony with Keszthely (560Ft, 35 minutes, 27km) daily; seven or eight travel to Balatonfüred (840Ft, 50 minutes, 44km) and six to Hévíz (650Ft, 45 minutes, 35km). At least three daily go to Tapolca (370Ft, 30 minutes, 16km), Veszprém (1300Ft, 1½ hours, 62km) and Budapest (3130Ft, three hours, 170km).

Badacsony is on the train line linking all the towns on Lake Balaton's northern shore with Budapest (3130Ft, 3½ to four hours, 170km, five or six daily). Révfülöp (310Ft, 17 minutes, 13km, 10 daily) and Tapolca (310Ft, 20 minutes, 14km, hourly) are easily reached by train; to get to Keszthely (745Ft, 55 to 90 minutes, 39km) you must change at Tapolca.

Sümeg

87 / POP 6350

Sümeg may be small in size but it's big on two major attractions: a rocky, basalt hill topped by a proud castle holding court over the town and the surrounding countryside; and a church containing the best baroque frescoes in the country.

Like a page straight out of a fairy-tale storybook, the imposing **Sümeg Castle** (87-352 737; adult/child 1500/1200Ft, jeep one way/return 500/900Ft; 9am-7pm May–mid-Oct, to 4pm mid-Oct–Apr) sits on a 270m-high cone of limestone (a rare substance in this region of basalt) and towers above Sümeg. It fell into ruin after the Austrians abandoned it early in the 18th century, but was restored in the 1960s. Today it is the largest and best preserved castle in all of Transdanubia and boasts sweeping views east to the Bakony Hills and south to the Keszthely Hills. There's a small Castle Museum (Vármúzeum) of weapons, armour and castle furnishings in the 13th-century Old Tower (Öregtorony); pony rides and archery in the castle courtyard; a snack bar; and a restaurant. Medieval tournaments and feasts within the castle walls are organised throughout the year. You can still see bits of the old town walls below the castle at the northern end of Kossuth Lajos utca (Nos 13 to 33). A 16th-century tower is now the living room of the house at No 31.

Reach the castle by climbing Vak Bottyán utca, which is lined with lovely baroque *kúriak* (mansions), from Szent István tér and then following Városoldal utca past the castle stables, which now house a riding school. The castle is also accessible via jeep from the parking lot at the end of Városoldal utca.

Sümeg Castle may dominate the town, but for many people it is not Sümeg's most important sight. For them that distinction is reserved for the **Church of the Ascension** (church office 352 003; Szent Imre tér; admission free; 9am-5pm Mon-Fri, 11am-noon & 4-6pm Sat & Sun May-Sep, 9am-noon & 1-5pm Mon-Fri, services only Sat & Sun Mar, Apr, Oct & Nov). Architecturally, the building (1756) is unexceptional. But step inside and marvel at what has been called the 'Sistine Chapel of the rococo'.

That's perhaps an overstatement, but it's true that Franz Anton Maulbertsch's frescoes (1757–58) are the most beautiful baroque examples in Hungary and by far the prolific painter's best work. Despite now needing a good clean, the frescoes, with subjects taken from the Old and New Testaments, are still brilliant expressions of light and shadow. Pay special attention to the crucifixion scene in Golgotha on the northern wall in the nave; the Adoration of the Three Kings, with its caricature of a Moor opposite Golgotha; the Gate of Hell, across the aisle under the organ loft on the western side under the porch; and the altarpiece of Christ ascending airily to the clouds. Maulbertsch managed to include himself in a couple of his works, most clearly among the shepherds in the first fresco on the southern wall (he's the one holding the round cheeses and hamming it up for the audience). The commissioner of the frescoes, Márton Padányi Bíró, bishop of Veszprém, is shown on the western wall near the organ. Drop a coin in the machine to illuminate the frescoes and to view them at their best.

Getting There & Away

Buses depart for Sümeg hourly each day from Hévíz (560Ft, 35 to 55 minutes, 27km) and Keszthely (650Ft, 50 minutes, 31km); departures to Veszprém (1300Ft, two hours, 68km) are also frequent. Sümeg is also on the train line that links to Keszthely (840Ft, 50 minutes, 45km).

Tihany

87 / POP 1370

The place with the greatest historical significance on Lake Balaton is Tihany, a peninsula jutting 5km into the lake. It's helpful to think of it in two parts: Tihany village, perched on an 80m-high plateau

Tihany

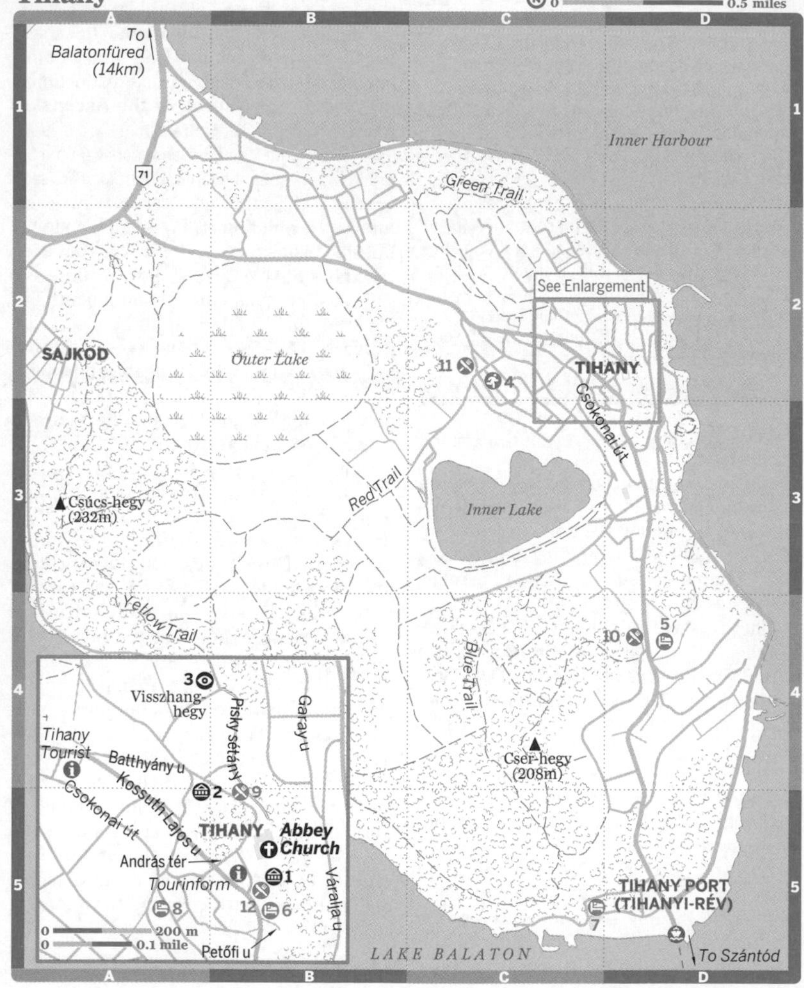

along the peninsula's eastern coast, of the same name, is home to the celebrated Abbey Church and in the height of summer the church attracts so many people it's hard to find space to breathe. Visit the church but then escape the madness by wandering around the tiny town, which is filled with lovely thatched-roof houses.

Juxtaposing this claustrophobic vibe is the peninsula itself – a nature reserve of hills and marshy meadows that has an isolated, almost wild feel to it. Two inland basins on the peninsula are fed by rain and ground water. The Inner Lake (Belső-tó) is almost in the centre of the peninsula and visible from the village, while the Outer Lake (Külső-tó), to the northwest, has almost completely dried up and is now a tangle of reeds. Both basins attract considerable bird life.

Tihany is a popular recreational area with beaches on its eastern and western coasts and a big resort complex on its southern tip. The waters of the so-called Tihany Well, off the southern end of the peninsula, are the deepest – and coldest – in the lake, reaching an unprecedented 12m in some parts.

Tihany

History

There was a Roman settlement in the area, but Tihany first appeared on the map in 1055, when King Andrew I (r 1046–60), a son of King Stephen's great nemesis, Vászoly, founded a Benedictine monastery here. The Deed of Foundation of the Abbey Church of Tihany, now in the archives of the Pannonhalma Abbey, is one of the earliest known documents bearing any Hungarian words – some 50 place names within a mostly Latin text. It's a linguistic treasure in a country where, until the 19th century, the vernacular in its written form was spurned – particularly in schools – in favour of the more 'cultured' Latin and German.

In 1267 a fortress was built around the church and was able to keep the Turks at bay when they arrived 300 years later. But the castle was demolished by Habsburg forces in 1702 and all you'll see today are ruins.

Sights

Open-air Folk Museum MUSEUM

(Szabadtéri Néprajzi Múzeum; Pisky sétány 10; adult/concession 400/300Ft; ⏲10am-6pm May-Sep) This cluster of folk houses with thick thatch roofs have been turned into a small outdoor museum.

TOP CHOICE **Abbey Church** CHURCH

(Bencés Apátság templom; http://tihany.osb.hu; András tér 1; adult/concession incl museum 1000/500Ft; ⏲9am-6pm May-Sep, 10am-5pm Apr & Oct, 10am-3pm Nov-Mar) This twin-spired and ochre-coloured church is the dominating feature in the small village of Tihany. Built in 1754 on the site of King Andrew's church, this impressive house of God contains fantastic altars, pulpits and screens carved between 1753 and 1779 by an Austrian lay brother named Sebastian Stuhlhof, all baroque-rococo masterpieces in their own right.

Upon entering the main nave, turn your back to the sumptuous main altar and the abbot's throne and look right to the side altar dedicated to Mary. The large angel kneeling on the right supposedly represents Stuhlhof's fiancée, a fisherman's daughter who died in her youth. On the Altar of the Sacred Heart across the aisle, a pelican (Christ) nurtures its young (the faithful) with its own blood. The figures atop the pulpit beside it are four doctors of the Roman Catholic church: Sts Ambrose, Gregory, Jerome and Augustine. The next two altars on the right- and left-hand sides are dedicated to Benedict and his twin sister, Scholastica; the last pair, a baptismal font and the Lourdes Altar, date from 1896 and 1900 respectively.

Stuhlhof also carved the magnificent choir rail above the porch and the organ with all the cherubs. The frescoes on the ceilings by Bertalan Székely, Lajos Deák-Ébner and Károly Lotz were painted in 1889, when the church was restored.

The remains of King Andrew I lie in a limestone sarcophagus in the atmospheric Romanesque crypt. The spiral swordlike cross on the cover is similar to ones used by 11th-century Hungarian kings.

Benedictine Abbey Museum MUSEUM

(Bencés Apátsági Múzeum; admission incl with Abbey Church entry fee; ⏲9am-6pm May-Sep, 10am-5pm Apr & Oct, 10am-3pm Nov-Mar) This museum, next door to the Abbey Church in the former Benedictine monastery, is entered from the church crypt. It contains exhibits on Lake Balaton, liturgical vestments, religious artefacts, a handful of manuscripts and a history of King Andrew.

WORTH A TRIP

TAPOLCA

Despite being only 14km northwest of Badacsony, **Tapolca** is far removed from the touristy atmosphere of the resorts lining the Balaton and is a fun spot to bring the kids, who can run riot around the two small lakes at the centre of the town, or head underground to explore the town's underground lake cave.

Tapolca's **Mill Lake** (Malom-tó), just south of Fő tér, is reached through the gateway at No 8 or by walking south along Arany János utca. A small footbridge divides it in two: to the north is the Big Lake (Nagy-tó), which is about the size of a large pond, and to the south is the Little Lake (Kis-tó). Created in the 18th century to power a water mill, the lake has been artificially fed since the nearby bauxite mine lowered the level of the water. But it remains a picturesque area, with pastel-coloured houses reflected in the water of the Big Lake, and a church and museum near the Little Lake. In the centre are the slowly turning blades of the mill house, which is now a hotel.

Lake Cave (Tavasbarlang; ☎412 579; Kisfaludy utca 3; adult/child/student 1200/1000/750Ft; ⏲9am-7pm Jul & Aug, 10am-5pm mid-Mar–Jun, reduced hours Sep–mid-Mar) is a superb jaunt underground for kids and adults alike. At only 250m long, it's technically a rather tiny cave, but over two-thirds of it is a series of underground waterways (the water returned to the caves since mining ended in 1990). You explore it using self-propelled boats – as you make your way through the labyrinth you wind through wee tunnels where you can touch the top (head-ducking required!); other tight spots require a bit of creativity (personally, we abandoned the oar and propelled ourselves along by pushing away from the cave walls with our own hands). The whole circuit takes about 15 to 20 minutes, depending on how fast or slow the boat ahead of you goes.

Tapolca is an easy day bus trip from Keszthely (560Ft, 35 to 60 minutes, 28km, hourly), Balatonfüred (1120Ft, 1½ to two hours, 55km, two to three daily) and Sümeg (520Ft, 25 to 50 minutes, 18km, hourly). It is also the main terminus for the train line linking most of the towns along Lake Balaton's northern shore. The bus station is located on Hősök tere, 1km southwest of the Lake Cave, and the train station is on Dózsa György út, 1.3km southwest of the cave.

Visszhang-hegy HILL

(Echo Hill; Pisky sétány) You'll find Visszhang-hegy at the end of Pisky sétány. At one time, up to 15 syllables of anything shouted in the direction of the Abbey Church would bounce back but, alas, because of building in the area (and perhaps climatic changes) you'll be lucky to get three nowadays. From Visszhang-hegy you can descend Garay utca and Váralja utca to the Inner Harbour and a small beach, or continue on to the hiking trails that pass this way.

Activities

Hiking HIKING

Hiking is one of Tihany's main attractions; there's a good map outlining the trails in the center of the village. Following the Green Trail northeast of the village centre for an hour will bring you to the Russian Well (Oroszkút) and the ruins of the Old Castle (Óvár) at 219m, where Russian Orthodox monks, brought to Tihany by Andrew I, hollowed out cells in the soft basalt walls.

The 232m-high Csúcs-hegy (Csúcs Hill), with panoramic views of Lake Balaton, is about two hours west of the church via the Red Trail. From here you can join up with the Yellow Trail originating in Tihanyi-rév, which will lead you north to the ruins of the 13th-century Apáti Church (Ápáti templom) and to Rte 71. From the church, it's possible to follow the Yellow Trail south till it crosses the Blue Trail near Aranyház, a series of geyser cones formed by warm-water springs and resembling (somewhat) a 'Golden Horse'. From here, you can take the Blue Trail north to the Inner Lake and on to the town centre.

Sail & Surf WATER SPORTS

(☎06 30 227 8927; www.wind99.com; Rév utca 3, Club Tihany; windsurf rental/rental & lessons per 3hr 5000/10,000Ft, boat rental/sailing lessons per 3hr from 8000/14,000Ft) A sailing and windsurfing centre offering private lessons in both activities, along with boat and windsurf rental.

Tihany Lovasudvar HORSE RIDING
(☎06 30 275 3293; Kiserdőtelepi utca 10; 3hr ride 5000Ft) Horses are available for hire at the Tihany Lovasudvar, just north of the Inner Lake.

Sleeping

Accommodation in Tihany is limited and expensive; if you are watching your budget visit it as a day trip by bus from Balatonfüred or Badacsony. Note that most of the hotels listed here are closed between mid-October or November and March or April.

For private rooms (from 9000Ft per double), consult Tihany Tourist or Tourinform. Many houses along Kossuth Lajos utca and on the little streets north of the Abbey Church have *Zimmer frei* (Room for Rent) signs.

Centrum Vendégház GUESTHOUSE €€
(☎06 30 997 8271; www.centrumvendeghaz.hu; Petöfi utca 13; d 10,000-12,000Ft, tr/apt 13,000/18,000Ft; ❄) This family-run guesthouse offers simple but tastefully decorated rooms with polished wood floors in thatched houses a short hop from the main sights.

Kántás Panzió GUESTHOUSE €€
(☎448 072; www.kantas-panzio-tihany.hu; Csokonai út 49; r 13,000Ft; ❄📶) Kántás is a fine example of Tihany's cheaper accommodation; it's small and personal, with pleasant attic rooms (some with balcony) above a restaurant. Views are across the Inner Lake.

Club Tihany HOTEL €€€
(☎538 564; www.clubtihany.hu; Rév utca 3; s 16,900-25,000Ft, d 28,500-39,000Ft, bungalows 14,000-34,000Ft; P❄📶🏊) Close to the car-ferry pier, this massive 13-hectare resort has over 300 hotel rooms and over 150 bungalows, along with every sporting, munching and quaffing possibility imaginable. Its bungalows are simple affairs, while the rooms are more luxurious and have lake views from their balconies.

Adler BOUTIQUE HOTEL €€€
(☎538 000; www.adler-tihany.hu; Felsőkopaszhegyi utca 1/a; r 14,700-16,900Ft, apt 29,700-32,400Ft; ❄📶🏊) Large, whitewashed rooms with balconies; good for families and has a Jacuzzi, sauna and restaurant.

Eating

Like the hotels, most restaurants are closed between mid-October or November and March or April.

Cheap food stalls greet passengers to-ing and fro-ing across the lake at Tihany Port.

Rege Café CAFE €
(Kossuth Lajos utca 22; cakes from 350Ft; ⏰10am-6pm) A prime spot for a photo op! From its high vantage point near the Benedictine Abbey Museum, this modern cafe has an unsurpassed panoramic view of the Balaton. On a sunny day, there is no better place to enjoy coffee, cake and the sparkling lake.

Balatoni Ház INTERNATIONAL €
(☎448 608; Pisky sétány; mains 1500-3500Ft) With fabulous views of the lake from its enormous terrace, this thatched-cottage restaurant attracts the attention of many passers-by. Its welcoming staff and Hungarian menu, featuring touches of Italian cuisine, manage to convince them to stay put.

TOP CHOICE **Ferenc Pince** HUNGARIAN €€
(☎448 575; Cserhegy 9; mains from 2500Ft; ⏰noon-11pm, closed Tue) Ferenc is both a wine- and food-lover's dream; not only does its chef cook up a Hungarian storm in the kitchen, but some of Tihany's best wine is served by the very people who produce the stuff. During the day, its open terrace offers expansive views of the lake, while at night the hypnotic twinkling lights of the southern shore are in full view from the cosy thatched-roof house. Ferenc Pince is just under 2km south of the Abbey Church.

Miska Pince HUNGARIAN €€
(☎06 30 929 7350; Kiserdőtelepi utca; mains 2200-2580Ft) Miska Pince is a cute thatch-roof cottage down near the banks of the Inner Lake. It serves big portions of Hungarian cuisine, and its secluded, sunny terrace is just the place to escape the madding crowds up near the church.

Information

Tihany Tourist (☎448 481; www.tihanytourist.hu; Kossuth Lajos utca 11; ⏰9am-5pm May-Sep, 10am-4pm Apr & Oct) Organises accommodation and local tours.

Tourinform (☎448 804; tihany@tourinform.hu; Kossuth Lajos utca 20; ⏰9am-7pm Mon-Fri, 10am-5pm Sat & Sun mid-Jun–mid-Sep, shorter hours rest of year)

Getting There & Around

Buses cover the 14km from Balatonfüred's bus and train station to and from Tihany 13 to 15 times daily (310Ft, 30 minutes). The bus stops at both ferry landings before climbing to Tihany village.

The Inner Harbour (Belső kikötő), where ferries to/from Balatonfüred and Siófok dock, is below the village. Tihany Port (Tihanyi-rév), to the southwest at the tip of the peninsula, is Tihany's recreational area. From here, car ferries run to Szántódi-rév and passenger ferries to Balatonföldvár. The Balaton passenger ferries (p147) from Siófok, Balatonfüred and elsewhere stop at Tihany from early April to early October. Catch them at the Inner Harbour ferry pier or at Tihanyi-rév. From early March to late November the car ferry takes 10 minutes to cross the narrow stretch of water between Tihanyi-rév and Szántódi-rév, and departs every 40 minutes to an hour.

If you arrive by boat and you aren't keen to huff it up the hill to the 80m-high village, a **tourist train** (adult/child 400/200Ft; ⏲ever half-hour May-Sep) runs between the ferry terminal and the Abbey Church (p161).

Balatonfüred

☎87 / POP 13,580

Balatonfüred is not only the oldest resort on the Balaton's northern shore, it's also the most fashionable. In former days the wealthy and famous built large villas on its tree-lined streets, and their architectural legacy can still be seen today. It's an excellent place to base yourself on Lake Balaton, with endless lodging and dining options, and it boasts a superb tree-lined promenade along the shore where everyone goes for their pre- or post-dinner stroll. The town also has the most stylish marina on the lake and is known for the thermal waters of its world-famous heart hospital.

History

The thermal water here, rich in carbonic acid, has been used as a cure for stomach ailments for centuries, but its other curative properties were only discovered by scientific analysis in the late 18th century. Balatonfüred was immediately declared a spa with its own chief physician in residence.

Balatonfüred's golden age was in the 19th century, especially the first half, when political and cultural leaders of the Reform Era (roughly 1825–48) gathered here in the summer; it was also the site chosen by István Széchenyi to launch the lake's first steamship, *Kisfaludy,* in 1846.

By 1900 Balatonfüred was a popular place for increasingly wealthy middle-class families to escape Budapest's heat. Wives would base themselves here all summer along with their children while husbands would board the 'bull trains' in Budapest at the weekend. It is a sign of the times that even Balatonfüred has begun to modernise itself in the last couple of years.

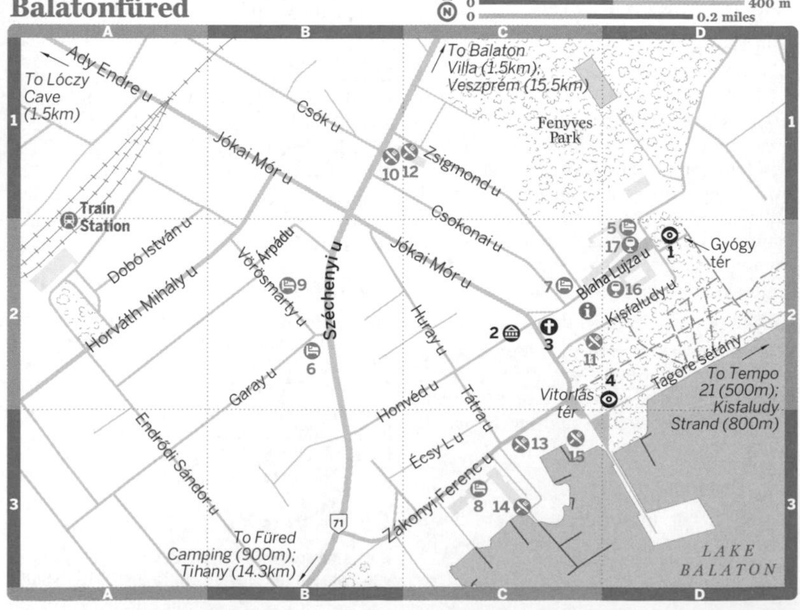

Sights

Jókai Memorial Museum MUSEUM
(Jókai emlékmúzeum; ☎343 426; Honvéd utca 1; adult/concession/family 900/450/2200Ft; ⏲10am-6pm May-Sep, reduced hours rest of year) The Jókai Memorial Museum is housed in the summer villa of the prolific writer Mór Jókai, just north of Vitorlás tér. In his study here, Jókai churned out many of his 200 novels under the stern gaze of his wife, the actress Róza Laborfalvi. The museum is filled with family memorabilia and period furniture. All the signage is in Hungarian but ask for the laminated English guide at the entrance.

FREE **Round Church** CHURCH
(Kerek templom; ☎343 029; Blaha Lujza utca 1; admission free; ⏲services only) Inspired by the Pantheon in Rome, the tiny neoclassical Round Church was completed in 1846. The *Crucifixion* (1891) by János Vaszary sits above the altar on the western wall and is the only notable thing inside.

Gyógy tér SQUARE
(Cure Sq; Gyógy tér) This leafy square is home to the State Hospital of Cardiology, which put Balatonfüred on the map; although Balatonfüred is a major spa, the mineral baths are reserved for patients of the hospital. In the centre you'll encounter the Kossuth Pump House (1853), a natural spring that dispenses slightly sulphuric, but drinkable, sparkling thermal water. If you can ignore the water's pale-yellow hue join the locals lining up to fill their water bottles (after all, how often do you get to access free sparkling water!). On the northern side of the square is the Balaton Pantheon, with memorial plaques from those who took the cure at the hospital.

Tagore Sétány OUTDOORS
(Lake Promenade) The entire town seems to stroll the leafy lake-hugging promenade all day; it gets especially crowded in the early evenings. But if you tear your eyes away from the lake you'll discover the promenade hides a number of statues, including a bust of Nobel Prize–winning poet Rabindranath Tagore in front of a lime tree that he planted in 1926 to mark his recovery from illness after treatment here. Diagonally opposite and closer to the lake is a disturbing memorial of a hand stretching out of the water in memory of those who drowned in the lake when the *Pajtás* boat sank in 1954. Additionally, two very proud statues – one a fisherman, the other a boatman – stand guard over the harbour entrance.

Activities

Balatonfüred has three public beaches, of which **Kisfaludy Strand** (Aranyhíd sétány; adult/concession 900/540Ft; ⏲8am-6pm mid-May–mid-Sep) to the east of Tagore sétány is the best.

Popular lake cruises by the Balaton Shipping Co (p147) leave Balatonfüred up to five times daily between late May and mid-September.

The 210km Balaton cycle path runs through Balatonfüred, and cycling around exploring the town along the water is a fine way to spend the day (but note that as soon as you head away from the lake it's all uphill). Rent bicycles from **Tempo 21** (☎480 671; Deák Ferenc utca 56; per hr/day 450/1700Ft; ⏲9am-6pm mid-May–mid-Sep) at the eastern end of the promenade.

Balatonfüred

Sights
1 Gyógy tér D2
2 Jókai Memorial Museum C2
3 Round Church C2
4 Tagore Sétány D2

Sleeping
5 Anna Grand Hotel D2
6 Aqua Haz B2
7 Hotel Blaha Lujza C2
8 Hotel Silver Resort C3
9 Korona B2

Eating
10 Arany Csillag Pizzéria B1
11 Balaton C2
12 Cafe Bergman C1
13 Food Stalls C3
14 La Riva C3
15 Stefánia Vitorlás C3

Drinking
Karolina .... (see 14)
16 Kredenc Borbisztró D2
17 Vivamus Borharapó D2

For a break from the beach scene, walk or cycle to **Lóczy Cave** (Lóczy-barlang; Öreghegyi utca; adult/child 500/400Ft; ⏲10am-6pm Tue-Sun Apr–mid-Sep), north of the old town centre. Around 40m of cave is accessible to the public, and the highlight inside is the thick layers of limestone.

Sleeping

Tourinform (p167) can help find private rooms (from roughly 4000Ft per person per night).

Füred Camping CAMPGROUND €
(☎580 241; fured@balatontourist.hu; Széchenyi utca 24; campsite per adult/child/tent 1600/1200/5500Ft, bungalows/caravans from 17,000/23,000Ft ; ⏲mid-Apr–early Oct; @) This is one of the the largest camping grounds on the lake and can accommodate 3500 people. In addition to places to pitch your tent you can rent bungalows (they sleep up to four people). The property has direct access to the lake.

Korona PENSION €
(☎343 278; www.koronapanzio.hu; Vörösmarty utca 4; s/d/tr/apt 7500/9500/12,000Ft; P) The homey decor borders on kitsch but rooms are big, bright and offer some of the best value in town if you're not keen to camp.

Balaton Villa HOTEL €€
(☎788 290; www.balatonvilla.hu; Deák Ferenc utca 38; s/d 6400/13,000Ft;) The large, bright upstairs rooms of this pastel-yellow villa uphill from the lake are available for rent. Each has its own balcony overlooking a sunny garden and grape vines, and guests can make use of a well-equipped kitchen and grill area.

Hotel Blaha Lujza HOTEL €€
(☎581 219; www.hotelblaha.hu; Blaha Lujza utca 4; s 11,000Ft, d 16,000-18,000Ft;) This small hotel's rooms are on the boring side, but the lovingly restored villa they're housed in more than makes up for it, as does the prime location two blocks from the water. It was the summer home of the much-loved Hungarian actress-singer of the same name from 1893 to 1916.

Aqua Haz PENSION €€
(☎342 813; www.aquahaz.hu; Garay utca 2; s 9500Ft, d 11,200-13,500Ft; P) Dependable, family-run place conveniently located between the lake and the train/bus station. They go out of their way to make you feel right at home, most rooms feature bright balconies, and free bikes are available for tooling around town.

Hotel Silver Resort RESORT €€€
(☎583 001; www.silverresort.hu; Zákonyi Ferenc utca 4; r/ste from 20,000/33,000Ft;) Overlooking the lake, the four-star Silver Resort sports small, modern rooms bedecked in calming shades of brown. The more expensive variety have balconies, and suites are great for families. The wellness centre, which is free for guests, has a fitness centre, whirlpool and Finnish sauna.

TOP CHOICE **Anna Grand Hotel** HOTEL €€€
(☎342 044; www.annagrandhotel.eu; Gyógy tér 1; s/d from 25,000/35,000Ft; @) Formerly the Anna Grand was a sanatorium, but these days it is the town's best luxury hotel. Choose from rooms with either period antiques or modern furnishings, and views of the hotel's peaceful inner courtyard or tree-shaded Gyógy tér. Activities are plentiful for a hotel of this size, and include a wellness centre, bowling alley and climbing wall. The hotel is also home to a huge wine shop and a lovely, low-key wine bar called Vivamus Borharapó (p166); enter from the corner of Blaha Lujza utca and Gyógy tér.

Eating & Drinking

For cheap eats, a plethora of **food stalls** (Tagore sétany) run along the lake both north and south of the promenade. Oodles of restaurant-bars spots line the waterfront – the majority are excellent for a beer or a glass of local wine with a little people-watching mixed in, but the food tends to be rather samey with Hungarian staples, though the fish will generally be fresh from the lake.

Vivamus Borharapó (Anna Grand Hotel Wine Bar; ☎580 200; Gyógy tér 1; cheese and meat plates 1800-2800Ft, wine flights with snacks 1000-3500Ft; ⏲11am-10pm) is part of the top-end Anna Grand hotel and serves an excellent selection of local wines and small plates in a rustic wood-panelled cellar.

Arany Csillag Pizzéria PIZZERIA €
(☎482 116; Zsigmond utca 1; mains 1200-2800Ft) A convivial pizzeria away from the flashy waterfront, Arany Csillag is a local favourite that attracts a mix of people from every age group. Its small shaded terrace fills up quickly in summer, so either come early (6pm ish) or reserve in advance.

Karolina CAFE

(Zákonyi Ferenc sétány 4) Hands-down the most popular place in town to grab a drink or a bite, Karolina is a sophisticated cafe-bar that does an excellent job of serving fresh coffee, aromatic teas and quality local wines. The interior, with its Art Nouveau wall hangings and subtle lighting, has a certain decadent – yet inviting – air about it, while the terrace area with sofas couldn't be more laid-back.

Cafe Bergman DESSERTS €

(☎341 087; Zsigmond utca 3; ⏰10am-7.30pm) Ignore the ice-cream stands down by the lake and head uphill to this elegant cafe for scoops of the best ice cream in town (including local favorite poppy-seed ice cream). Located on a quiet street, this is a relaxing escape from the crowds and has a lovely tree-shaded exterior terrace. In addition, it offers a handsome selection of cakes and sandwiches.

Balaton HUNGARIAN €€

(Kisfaludy utca 5; mains 1800-3000Ft) This cool, leafy oasis amid all the hubbub is set back from the lake in the shaded park area. It serves generous portions and, like so many restaurants in town, has an extensive fish selection.

Stefánia Vitorlás HUNGARIAN €€

(Tagore sétány 1; mains 2000-3800Ft) This enormous wooden villa sits right on the lake's edge at the foot of the town's pier. It's a prime spot to watch the yachts sail in and out of the harbour from the terrace while munching on Hungarian cuisine and sipping local wine.

La Riva ITALIAN €€€

(☎06 20 391 4039; http://larivaristorante.hu; Zákonyi Ferenc sétány 4; mains 2000-4500Ft) Taking pride of place on the modern marina's waterfront is La Riva, a restaurant that combines imaginative cooking and the prospect of a relaxed table over the water. Pasta and pizza are the mainstays of the menu, but don't overlook the daily blackboard specials.

TOP CHOICE **Kredenc Borbisztró** WINE BAR

(☎518 99-60; Blaha Lujza utca 7) This family-run combination wine bar and bistro is a peaceful retreat only steps away from the lakefront. The menu is stacked with oodles of local wines and the owner, Mr Dobai, is often on hand to thoughtfully recommend the best tipple according to your tastes. The wine bar doubles as a retail shop and sells everything they serve, plus an extensive selection of regional wines. The small but lovely food menu (cheese plates, salads, antipasti) also makes this an excellent choice for a light meal.

Festivals & Events

Anna Ball BALL

(www.annabal.hu; Anna Grand Hotel; tickets from 25,000Ft) The annual Anna Ball on 26 July is a prime event on the Hungarian calendar. Even if you don't attend the ball it's worth joining the crowds gathering to watch the guests decked out in in their finest threads file into the venue, and on the following day the ball queen parades around town in an elaborate horse and carriage. Concerts accompany the days around the ball too, so keep your eyes peeled if you visit in late July.

Information

Tourinform (☎580 480; balatonfured@tourinform.hu; Blaha Lujza utca 5; ⏰9am 7pm Mon-Fri, to 6pm Sat, to 1pm Sun Jul & Aug, 9am-5pm Mon-Fri, to 1pm Sat Jun & Sep, 9am-4pm Mon-Fri Oct-May) Well-stocked tourist office run by helpful staff.

Getting There & Away

Boat

From April to June and September to October, at least four daily Balaton Shipping Co (p147) ferries link Balatonfüred with Siófok and Tihany. Up to seven daily ferries serve these ports from July to August.

Bus

Bus connections from Balatonfüred include the following destinations.

DESTINATION	PRICE	TIME	KM	FREQUENCY
Budapest	2520Ft	2-3hr	136	5-8 daily
Győr	1860Ft	2½hr	100	6 daily
Keszthely	1300Ft	1-1½hr	67	7 daily
Herend (change in Veszprém)	745Ft	55-65min	37	7-10 daily
Tihany	310Ft	30min	14	at least 13 daily
Veszprém	370Ft	40min	20	half-hourly

Train

Trains travel from Balatonfüred to Badacsony (745Ft, one hour, 38km, 12 daily), Budapest

(2520Ft, 2½ hours, 132km, five to seven daily) and Tapolca (1120Ft, 1¼ hours, 52km, 12 daily).

Getting Around

Balatonfüred is small enough to get around on foot, but you can reach Vitorlás tér and the lake from the train and bus stations on buses 1, 1/a and 2; bus 1 continues on to Füred Camping (p166).

You can also book a local **taxi** (☎444 444).

Veszprém

☎88 / POP 64,340

Spreading over five hills between the northern and southern ranges of the Bakony Hills, Veszprém offers a huge dollop of culture paired with one of the most dramatic locations in the Lake Balaton region. The walled castle district, atop a plateau, is one of the oldest castles in Hungary and is a living museum of baroque art and architecture. It's a delight to stroll along the windy Castle Hill district's single street, admiring the embarrassment of fine churches. The town also boasts one of the liveliest food markets in the region and hosts a fantastic music festival each August. As the townspeople say, 'Either the wind is blowing or the bells are ringing in Veszprém'. Add a collection of excellent hotels and restaurants, and this is a superb place to base yourself for a few days.

History

The Romans settled 8km to the southwest at Balácapuszta, where important archaeological finds have been made. Prince Géza, King Stephen's father, founded a bishopric in Veszprém late in the 10th century, and the city grew as a religious, administrative and educational centre (the university was established in the 13th century). It also became a favourite residence of Hungary's queens.

The castle at Veszprém was blown up by the Habsburgs in 1702, and lost most of its medieval buildings during the Rákóczi war of independence (1703–11) shortly thereafter. But this cleared the way for Veszprém's golden age, when the city's bishops and rich landlords built most of what you see today. The church's iron grip on Veszprém prevented it from developing commercially, however, and it was bypassed by the main railway line in the 19th century.

> **CASTLE HILL COMBINATION TICKET**
>
> If you plan to visit Castle Hill's top four sights – Bishop's Palace, Gizella Chapel, Queen Gizella Museum and the Chapel of St George – buy the **combined ticket** (adult/child 2100/1200Ft), which includes entry to all four.

Sights

Make sure to check out the Art Nouveau masterpiece housing the Petőfi Theatre (p172) – even if you don't catch a concert here (which you should try to do!) the exterior is *almost* as magnificent as the interior.

TOP CHOICE **Castle Hill** HISTORIC SITE

(Vár-hegy) Any tour of Castle Hill, Veszeprém's elevated walled castle district, should begin at at the foot of hill at Óváros tér, the medieval market place. Of the many fine 18th-century buildings in the square, the most interesting is the late-baroque **Pósa House** (Óváros tér 3), built in 1793 and now a bank, and fans of the fin-de-siècle style will appreciate the pale yellow facade and Art Nouveau flourishes of the **Chinese House** (Óváros tér 22).

As you begin to ascend Castle Hill and its sole street, Vár utca, you'll pass through Heroes' Gate (Hősök kapuja), an entrance built in 1936 from the stones of a 15th-century castle gate.

Firewatch Tower

To your left is the 48m-high **firewatch tower** (tűztorony; ☎425 204; Vár utca 9; adult/child/family 400/300/800Ft; ⏲10am-6pm Mar-Apr, to 6pm May-Oct) which, like the one in Sopron, is an architectural hybrid of Gothic, baroque and neoclassical styles. You can climb to the top for excellent views of the rocky hill and the Bakony Hills.

Piarist Church

Squeezed between two town houses further up Vár utca is the extremely rich **Piarist church** (Piarista templom; ☎426 088; Vár utca 12; admission free; ⏲10am-5pm Tue-Sun May–mid-Oct), which was built in 1836 in neoclassical style.

Bishop's Palace

Only a couple of doors along from the Piarist church is the U-shaped **Bishop's Palace** (Püspöki palota; ☎426 088; Vár utca 16; adult/child 1200/800Ft; ⏲10am-5pm Tue-Sun May–mid-Oct), designed by Jakab Fellner of Tata in the mid-18th century. It is thoroughly baroque inside and out, and stands on the site where the

WORTH A TRIP

THE WORKER-OWNED HEREND PORCELAIN FACTORY

The **Herend Porcelain Factory** (☎523 190; www.herend.com; Kossuth Lajos utca 140; adult/child/family factory & museum 1900/700/3800Ft; ⊙9am-5.30pm) has been producing Hungary's finest handpainted chinaware for over 180 years. Initially it specialised in copying and replacing the nobles' broken chinaware settings imported from Asia. To avoid bankruptcy in the 1870s, the factory began mass production; tastes ran from kitschy pastoral and hunting scenes to the ever-popular animal sculptures with the distinctive scale-like triangle patterns. In 1992, 75% of the factory was purchased by its 1500 workers and became one of the first companies in Hungary privatised through an employee stock-ownership plan. The state owns the other quarter.

You can witness how ugly clumps of clay become delicate porcelain in 40-minute mini factory guided tours (in English, every 20 minutes from 9.30am). The museum displays the most prized pieces of the rich Herend collection, including some pretty kooky 19th-century interpretations of Japanese art and Chinese faces, plus its own patterns; many, like the 'Rothschild bird' and 'petites roses', were inspired by Meissen and Sèvres designs from Germany and France. There's also a short film tracing the porcelain's history.

Herend is 13km west of Veszprém. Buses from Veszprém leave at least every 30 minutes (425Ft, 20 minutes, 21km); other destinations include Sümeg (1000Ft, 1½ hours, 52km, eight daily) and Balatonfüred (800Ft, one hour, 37km, two daily). Six trains run through Herend daily from Veszprém (350Ft, 12 minutes, 14km).

queen's residence stood in the Middle Ages. The Palace faces Szentháromság tér, named for the Trinity Column (1751) in the centre.

Gizella Chapel

Next to the Bishop's Palace is the early Gothic **Gizella Chapel** (Gizella-kápolna; ☎426 088; Vár utca 18; adult/child 800/400Ft; ⊙10am-5pm Tue-Sun May–mid-Oct), named after the wife of King Stephen, who was crowned near here early in the 11th century. The chapel was discovered when the Bishop's Palace was being built in the mid-18th century. Inside the chapel are valuable Byzantine-influenced 13th-century frescoes of the apostles. The **Queen Gizella Museum** (☎426 088; Vár utca 35; adult/child 800/500Ft; ⊙10am-5pm May–mid-Oct) of religious art is slightly north of the chapel.

Cathedral of St Michael

Parts of this dark and austere **cathedral** (Székesegyház; ☎328 038; Vár utca 18-20; admission free; ⊙10am-5pm May–mid-Oct) date from the beginning of the 11th century, but it has been rebuilt many times since then – the early Gothic crypt is original, though. Vibrant stained-glass windows back the church's modest altar, and little of the nave's high walls are left bare of intricate designs. Beside the cathedral, the octagonal foundation of the 13th-century **Chapel of St George** (Szent György kápolna; ☎426 088; Vár utca; adult/child 800/400Ft; ⊙10am-5pm Tue-Sun May-Oct) sits under an ugly concrete dome.

World's End

From the rampart known as World's End, at the end of Vár utca, you can gaze north to craggy Benedek-hegy (Benedict Hill) and the Séd Stream, and west to the concrete viaduct (now St Stephen's Valley Bridge) over the Betekints Valley. In Margit tér, below the bridge, are the ruins of the medieval Dominican Convent of St Catherine, and to the west is what little remains of the 11th-century Veszprém Valley (Betekints Valley) Convent, whose erstwhile cloistered residents are said to have stitched Gizella's crimson silk coronation robe in 1031. The King Stephen and Queen Gizella statues at World's End were erected in 1938 to mark the 900th anniversary of King Stephen's death.

Galleries

Vár utca is home to a number of art galleries specialising in 20th-century contemporary pieces from Hungary and abroad; they include the **Váss Galéria** (☎561 310; www.vasscollection.hu; Vár utca 7; adult/concession 600/400Ft; ⊙10am-6pm daily mid-Apr–mid-Oct, to 5pm Tue-Sun mid-Oct–mid-Apr) and the **Csikász Galéria** (☎425 204; Vár utca 17; adult/child 350/250Ft; ⊙10am-6pm May-Oct, to 5pm Mon-Sat Nov-Apr).

Dubniczay Palace, a lovely 18th-century baroque structure, is home to two museums. The **Carl László Collection** (☎560 507; www.carllaszlocollection.hu; Vár utca 29; adult/student 800/400Ft; ⊙10am-6pm Tue-Sun)

Veszprém

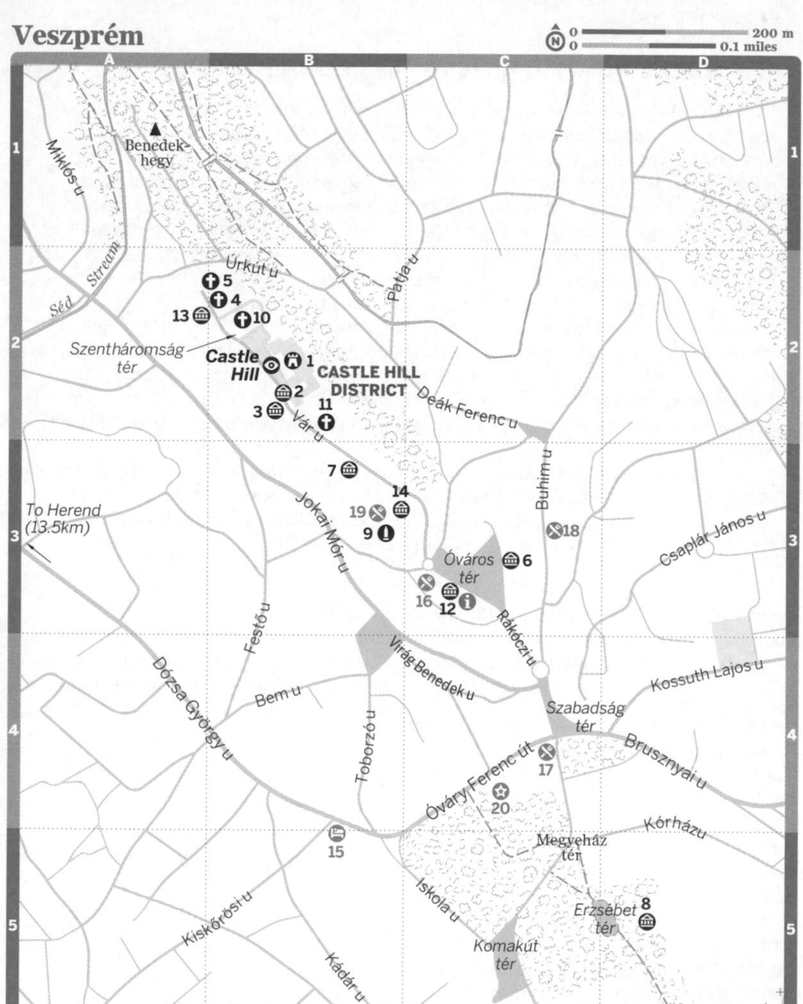

is a brilliant display of modern art acquired by the Pécs-born László, who survived several concentration camps including Auschwitz and eventually landed in Switzerland, where he became a prolific art collector, artist and psychoanalyst. The museum represents a small but significant portion of his collection, with lithographs and pop-art pieces highlighting the avant-garde inclination in Hungary and beyond in the 1920s, the artistic achievements between WWI and WWII and artists hitting the global and local scene in the past 50 years. The **Brick Collection** (admission 350Ft) is a nod to the fact that the region used to be a major brick-producer home to eight brick factories – all have closed down now, but the displays of multicoloured bricks stamped with elaborate coats of arms, royal motifs and religious symbols are oddly captivating for their tremendous detail and the precision of their imprints.

Dezső Laczkó Museum & Bakony Ethnographical House MUSEUM
(☎Bakony 564 330, museum 564 310; Erzsébet sétány 1; adult/child 500/300Ft; ⏰10am-6pm Tue-Sun mid-May–mid-Oct, reduced hours rest of

Veszprém

Top Sights
Castle Hill ... B2

Sights
1 Bishop's Palace ... B2
2 Brick Collection ... B2
3 Carl László Collection ... B2
4 Cathedral of St Michael ... B2
5 Chapel of St George ... B2
6 Chinese House ... C3
7 Csikász Galéria ... B3
8 Dezső Laczkó Museum & Bakony Ethnographical House ... D5
9 Firewatch Tower ... B3
10 Gizella Chapel ... B2
11 Piarist Church ... B2
12 Pósa House ... C3
13 Queen Gizella Museum ... A2
14 Váss Galéria ... B3

Sleeping
Oliva ... (see 18)
15 Péter Pál ... B5

Eating
16 Café Piazza ... C3
17 Mackó Snack ... C4
18 Oliva ... C3
19 Várkert ... B3

Entertainment
20 Petőfi Theatre ... C4

year) The Dezső Laczkó Museum is south of Megyeház tér. It has archaeological exhibits (the emphasis is on the Roman settlement at Balácapuszta), a large collection of Hungarian, German and Slovak folk costumes, and superb wooden carvings, including objects made by the famed outlaws of the Bakony Hills in the 18th and 19th centuries.

Next door to the museum is Bakony House, a copy of an 18th-century thatched peasant dwelling in the village of Öcs, southwest of Veszprém. It has the usual three rooms found in Hungarian peasant homes, and the complete *kamra* (workshop) of a flask-maker has been set up. Its roof suffered fire damage in May 2008, so what you see today is very new.

Festivals & Events

FREE **Veszprém Festival** MUSIC
(www.veszpremfest.hu; headline performers 6000-25,000Ft) The Veszprém Festival in mid-July is one of the premier festivals in the region and attracts big names in jazz and classical music (past internationally recognised performers include the Buena Vista Social Club and George Benson), and there are plenty of free musical performances in between. Stages are set up across town, and everywhere you turn you'll find music, food and drink stalls and general merriment. Note: accomodation books out at least four to six months in advance, so either plan ahead or stay elsewhere and pop in for the event.

Sleeping

Két Lotti PENSION €
(☎566 520; www.ketlotti.hu; József Attila utca 21; s/d/tr 7500/9000/11,000Ft;) A peaceful and relaxing stay is almost always guaranteed at Két Lotti, a boutique villa-pension west of the centre. Rooms are spacious and tastefully decorated in calming hues, and there's a large, manicured garden to enjoy. Additionally, guests can use the sauna and arrange massages on-site.

Péter Pál PENSION €€
(☎328 091; www.peterpal.hu; Dózsa György utca 3; s/d 7900/10,200Ft;) Péter Pál is a lovely little pension bordering on boutique class. It has a fine choice of simple yet stylish rooms, a lovely garden, above-average restaurant, and very friendly and helpful staff.

TOP CHOICE **Oliva** HOTEL €€€
(☎403 875; www.oliva.hu; Buhim utca 14-16; s/d/tr from 13,900/16,000/25,000Ft; P @) This exquisite hotel is located in a beautifully restored town house just below Castle Hill. Rooms are modern, spacious and furnished with pseudo-antiques, and its restaurant is first rate. It recently added a spa area where you can book treatments from massage to reiki or just relax in the Jacuzzi and Finnish sauna

Eating & Drinking

For quick or cheap eats, hit the large **covered market** (Piac tér) or join students and workers at **Mackó Snack** (Szabadság tér; burgers & pizza from 500Ft; ⏱8am-5pm Mon-Fri), which offers mainly pizzas, sandwiches and a salad bar.

Café Piazza CAFE €
(☎444 445; Óváros tér 4; mains from 1600Ft; ⏲8.30am-10pm) With seating on pretty Óváros tér and plentiful lunchtime specials with a focus on salads and sandwiches, Café Piazza attracts workers and tourists by the droves. Excellent for a coffee, a small bite or something stronger.

TOP CHOICE **Oliva** HUNGARIAN €€
(☎403 875; Buhim utca 14-16; mains 2200-4000Ft) Subdued lighting and vaulted ceilings help make Oliva an intimate setting for a romantic evening. The menu changes with the seasons, but regularly features Hungarian specialities cooked with care. A substantial wine selection supplements the menu, and in summer the restaurant's huge outdoor patio often features live bands.

Várkert INTERNATIONAL €€€
(☎560 468; Vár utca 17; mains 1800-4500Ft) Bubbling with energy, Várkert is one of the most popular venues in Veszprém's dining scene. Its menu features unusual dishes, such as wild game ragout and rabbit stew, alongside imaginative Hungarian specialities. There's live music most evenings, and its sunny inner courtyard is an attraction in its own right over summer.

☆ Entertainment

Petőfi Theatre THEATRE
(☎424 235; www.petofiszinhaz.hu; Óváry Ferenc út 2) The Petőfi Theatre is one of Veszprem's highlights not only for its performances, but for its visual wow effect. Designed by István Medgyaszay in 1908, this pink, grey and burgundy building is a gem of Hungarian Art Nouveau architecture. It's also important structurally, as the theatre was the first building in the country to be made entirely of reinforced concrete. The huge round stained-glass window entitled *The Magic of Folk Art* by Sándor Nagy depicts the connection between Hungarians and their fertile land. Plays are only in Hungarian but check the website for concerts (mainly classical).

ARRIVING IN VESZPRÉM

The bus station (on Piac tér) is smack next to the food market, a few minutes' walk northeast from Kossuth Lajos utca, a pedestrian street of shops and banks. If you turn north at the end of Kossuth Lajos utca at Szabadság tér, and walk along Rákóczi utca, you'll soon reach the entrance to Castle Hill (Vár-hegy) at Óváros tér.

The train station is 4km north of the bus station at the end of Jutasi út.

Information

Tourinform (☎404 548; www.veszpreminfo.hu; Óváros tér 2; ⏲9am-6pm Mon-Fri, 10am-4pm Sat & Sun May, Jun & Sep, 9am-7pm Mon-Fri, 10am-8pm Sat & Sun Jul & Aug, 9am-5pm Mon-Fri Oct-Apr) Extremely helpful information office with plenty of brochures on Veszprém and its surrounds.

Getting There & Away

Bus

Connections with Veszprém are excellent.

DESTINATION	PRICE	TIME	KM	FREQUENCY
Balatonfüred	370Ft	40min	20	half-hourly
Budapest	2200Ft	2¼hr	112	hourly
Győr	1680Ft	2hr	86	9 daily
Herend	465Ft	20min	21	half-hourly
Keszthely	1490Ft	1¾hr	77	hourly
Pápa	930Ft	1¼hr	50	hourly
Siófok	840Ft	1¼hr	48	7 daily
Sümeg	1300Ft	2hr	68	up to 18 daily
Tapolca	930Ft	1-1½hr	49	hourly

Train

For destinations along the northern and southern shores of Lake Balaton, a change at Székesfehérvár is required. Direct connections include Budapest (2200Ft, two hours, 112km, six daily), Győr (1490Ft, two to three hours, 79km, three daily), Pannonhalma (1120Ft, 1¾ hours, 58km, four daily) and Szombathely (2570Ft, two hours, 124km, 12 daily).

Getting Around

Buses 1, 2 and 4 run from the train and bus stations to Szabadság tér. You can also book a local **taxi** (☎444 444).

Siófok

☎84 / POP 24,345

Siófok is officially known as 'Hungary's summer capital' but unofficially it's called

KID-FRIENDLY FUN

Beyond the beaches there's not a whole lot in the way of cultural or historical importance in a place where hedonism rules the roost, but kids like to watch the **canal locks** system at work. (Cool historial fact: the locks were partly built by the Romans in AD 292 and used extensively by the Turks in the 16th and 17th centuries.) The best view is from Krúdy sétány, the walkway near the ferry pier, or Baross Bridge to the south. From there you're likely to wander about the tower on the western tip of the canal entrance – this is the **weather observatory** (Vitorlás utca) of the National Meteorological Service.

'Hungary's Ibiza'; though tourist numbers have been dwindling, come July and August this is still the party town of Lake Balaton – come here for massive drinkfests with lots of people under 30, not for local culture. Outside the summer months Siófok returns to relative normality, and is largely indistinguishable from the other resorts on the southern shore.

Sights & Activities

Imre Kálmán Museum MUSEUM
(☎311 287; Kálmán Imre sétány 5; adult/child 320/160Ft; ⏲9am-5pm Tue-Sun Apr-Oct, 10am-4pm Tue-Sun Nov-Mar) North of the weather observatory, on narrow Hock János köz, you'll reach the Imre Kálmán Museum. It is devoted to the life and works of the composer of popular operettas, Imre Kálmán, who was born in Siófok in 1882.

Evangelist Church CHURCH
(Evangélikus templom; www.siofok-lutheran.eu; ⏲services 10am Sun) East of Szabadság tér in Oulu Park, Hungary's maverick architect Imre Makovecz strikes with his winged and 'masked' Evangelist church, which bears a strong resemblance to an Indonesian *garuda* (mythical bird).

Nagy Strand BEACH
(Big Beach; adult/concession 1000/500Ft; ⏲8am-7pm) Nagy Strand is centre stage on Petőfi sétány; free concerts are often held here on summer evenings. There are many more managed swimming areas along the lakeshore, which cost around the same as Nagy Strand.

Galerius SWIMMING
(☎506 580; www.galerius-furdo.hu; Szent László utca 183; pools adult/concession 2900/2500Ft, sauna & pools 3600/3200Ft; ⏲9am-9pm) On a rainy day head here for the plethora of indoor thermal pools, saunas and massages. It's 4km west of downtown Siófok.

Yamaha Kölcsönző CYCLING
(☎06 20 945 1279; Vitorlás utca; 1hr/day 450/2500 Ft; ⏲10am-6pm mid-May–mid-Oct) On the canal's western bank you'll find Yamaha Kölcsönző, where you can hire bicycles.

Sleeping & Eating

Siófok is one of the few places on the lake where you will have trouble finding accommodation in July and August. Also, many small establishments only open during this time. Prices quoted here are for July and August – expect reductions of 50% to 75% outside of the summer months.

Tourinform can help find you a private room (€20 to €35 per person) and an apartment for slightly more. Singles are rare and those staying only one or two nights are generally unwelcome; if you want to do it alone, check for *Zimmer frei* signs along Erkel Ferenc utca and Damjanich utca on the Silver Coast, and Petőfi sétány and Beszédes József sétány on the Gold Coast.

There are over two-dozen campsites on Balaton's southern shore, and Siófok has nine, most with bungalows sleeping up to four people. They are open from May to September; the highest rates apply during most of July and August.

For quick eats, attack one of a bunch of **food stalls** (Petőfi sétány) by the Nagy Strand.

Siófok Város College HOSTEL €
(☎312 244; www.siofokvaroskollegiuma.sulinet.hu; Petőfi sétány 1; dm 2800Ft) Situated close to the action in central Siófok, it's hard to beat this college accommodation for price and location. Rooms are basic, and with all that partying going on at the nearby beach don't expect to get much sleep. There are a handful of rooms available year-round.

Hotel Yacht Club BOUTIQUE HOTEL €€
(☎311 161; www.hotel-yachtclub.hu; Vitorlás utca 14; s/d from €55/115; ❄@🛜≋) Overlooking the harbour is this excellent little hotel,

with cosy rooms, some of which sport balconies overlooking the lake. Its inviting wellness centre has whirlpools, saunas and a private sunbathing terrace. Bicycles can be rented.

TOP CHOICE **Mala Garden** BOUTIQUE HOTEL €€€
(☎506 687; www.malagarden.hu; Petőfí sétány 15/a; r 22,500-38,000Ft; ❄@🛜) Most of Siófok's accommodation options pale in comparison to this gorgeous boutique hotel. It's all very reminiscent of Bali, with Indonesian art lining the walls, a small, manicured flower garden at the rear of the hotel, and a quality restaurant serving Asian cuisine downstairs. Rooms are immaculate and bedecked in pleasing shades of orange, brown and red, and there are enough pillows for a group pillow fight. All in all, Mala Garden does a wonderful job of creating an elegant setting – a rarity in this town.

Roxy INTERNATIONAL €
(Szabadság tér; mains 1300-3000Ft) This pseudo-rustic restaurant-pub on busy Szabadság tér attracts diners with its wide range of international cuisine and surprisingly imaginative Hungarian mains. Don't arrive too late in the evening or you'll be hard pressed to find a table.

TOP CHOICE **Mala Garden Restaurant** INTERNATIONAL, ASIAN €€€
(☎506 687; Petőfi sétány 15/a; mains 1600-4200Ft) This is Siófok's only true top-class international eatery. Carrying on the theme of the hotel in which it's located, the restaurant has a menu featuring plenty of Asian influences, including delectable Thai noodles, spicy Thai vegetable soups and a satisfying *tikka masala* (hard to find in provincial Hungary). But the global cuisine doesn't stop there – Uruguay steaks, sea bass, goose liver and home-made pastas are just some of the myriad choices. Pick a wicker chair or comfy couch indoors, or a terrace table near the lake, and enjoy.

Drinking & Entertainment

Siófok is the region's club central and the turnover rate of bars and clubs is high, but our picks manage to attract punters year after year. In the summer months your best bet is to hit the cluster of the town's bars on Nagy Strand; in July and August free music concerts (from hard rock to pop) are also held on Nagy Strand two to three times per week – ask Tourinform (p174) for details and schedules.

Palace CLUB
(www.palace.hu; Deák Ferenc utca 2) Hugely popular club on the Silver Coast, with Hungarian DJs on Friday and their international counterparts on Saturday. Accessible by free bus from outside Tourinform between 9pm and 5am daily from mid-May to mid-September.

Renegade BAR
(Petőfi sétány 9) Wild pub near the beach where tabletop dancing and live music are the norm.

Information

Tourinform (☎310 117; tourinform@siofokportal.hu; Fő utca 174-176; ⌚8am-7pm Mon-Fri, 10am-7pm Sat & Sun mid-Jun–mid-Sep, 8am-4pm Mon-Fri, 9am-noon Sat mid-Sep–mid-Jun) Based in the old *víztorony* (water tower); very knowledgeable about Siófok.

Getting There & Away

Boat

From April to June and September to October ferries run by Balaton Shipping Co (p147) between Siófok and Balatonfüred; some stop at Tihany enroute. Up to eight ferries follow the same route in July and August.

Bus

Buses serve a lot of destinations from Siófok, but compared with train connections, they're not very frequent.

DESTINATION	PRICE	TIME	KM	FREQUENCY
Budapest	2200Ft	1½-2½hr	108	5 daily
Hévíz	1680Ft	1¾-2hr	86	up to 3 daily
Kaposvár	1680Ft	2hr	85	10 Mon-Sat
Keszthely	1490Ft	1¾hr	78	up to 3 daily
Pécs	2520Ft	3hr	133	3-6 daily
Szekszárd	1860Ft	2¼hr	97	8 daily
Veszprém	930Ft	1¼hr	48	7 daily

Train

Budapest (2200Ft, two hours, 115km, eight daily) and Kaposvár (1860Ft, 3½, hours, 100km, four daily) can be reached by train from Siófok.

Getting Around

Leaving from the bus station, just outside the train station, buses 1 and 2 run south and north along the coast, respectively. There are also **taxis** (☎317 713) around town.

SOUTHERN TRANSDANUBIA

History

Southern Transdanubia was settled by the Celts and then the Romans, who built towns at Alisca (Szekszárd) and Sophianae (Pécs) and introduced grape-growing. The north-south trade route passed through here, and many of the settlements prospered during the Middle Ages.

The region was a focal point of the Turkish occupation; indeed the battle that led to the Ottoman domination of Hungary was fought at Mohács in 1526 and Pécs was an important political and cultural centre under the Turks.

Late in the 17th century the abandoned towns of Southern Transdanubia were resettled by Swabian Germans and Southern Slavs, and after WWII ethnic Hungarians came from Slovakia and Bukovina in Romania as did Saxon Germans. They left a mark that can still be seen and felt today in local architecture and food, and in certain traditions.

Getting There & Away

Trains and buses to Southern Transdanubia generally go to Pécs, the capital and transport hub of Southern Transdanubia. Trains usually leave from Déli or Kelenföld train stations in Budapest, and buses from Népliget bus station.

Getting Around

Pécs is the transport hub for both bus and railway service around Southern Transdanubia, but bus service is far more extensive.

Pécs

72 / POP 157,720

Blessed with a mild climate, an illustrious past and a number of fine museums and monuments, Pécs is one of the most pleasant and interesting cities to visit in Hungary. With a handful of universities, the nearby Mecsek Hills and a lively nightlife, many travellers put it second only to Budapest on their Hungary 'must-see' list.

Lying equidistant from the Danube to the east and the Dráva to the south on a plain sheltered from the northern winds by the Mecsek Hills, Pécs enjoys a microclimate that lengthens the summer and is ideal for viticulture and fruit production, especially almonds. A fine time to visit is during a warm *indián nyár* (Indian summer), when the light seems to take on a special quality.

TRAIN TOURS

An easy way to see the city's highlights is from the **Pécs Little Train** (Pécsi Kisvonat; 06 70 454 5610; www.pecsikisvonat.hu; adult/child 1350/700Ft; 10am-5pm), which departs from the northeast corner of Széchenyi tér.

History

The Romans may have settled here for the region's fertile soil and abundant water, but it's more likely that they were sold by the protection offered by the Mecsek Hills. They called their settlement Sophianae, and it quickly grew into the commercial and administrative centre of Lower Pannonia. The Romans brought Christianity with them, and reminders of that can be seen in the early clover-shaped chapels unearthed here.

Pécs' importance grew in the Middle Ages, when it was known as Quinque Ecclesiae after the five churches dotting the town; it is still called just that – Fünfkirchen – in German. King Stephen founded a bishopric here in 1009, the town was a major stop along the trade route to Byzantium and Hungary's first university opened here in 1367. The 15th-century bishop Janus Pannonius, who wrote some of Europe's most celebrated Renaissance poetry in Latin, made Pécs his home.

The city walls – a large portion of which still stand – were in such poor condition in the 16th century that the Turks took the city with virtually no resistance in 1543. The occupiers moved the local populace out and turned Pécs into their own administrative and cultural centre. When the Turks were expelled almost 150 years later, Pécs was virtually abandoned, but still standing were monumental souvenirs that now count as the most important Turkish structures in the country.

The resumption of wine production by German and Bohemian immigrants and the discovery of coal in the 18th century spurred Pécs' development. The manufacture of luxury goods (gloves, Zsolnay porcelain, Angster organs, Pannonvin sparkling wine) would come later.

Pécs

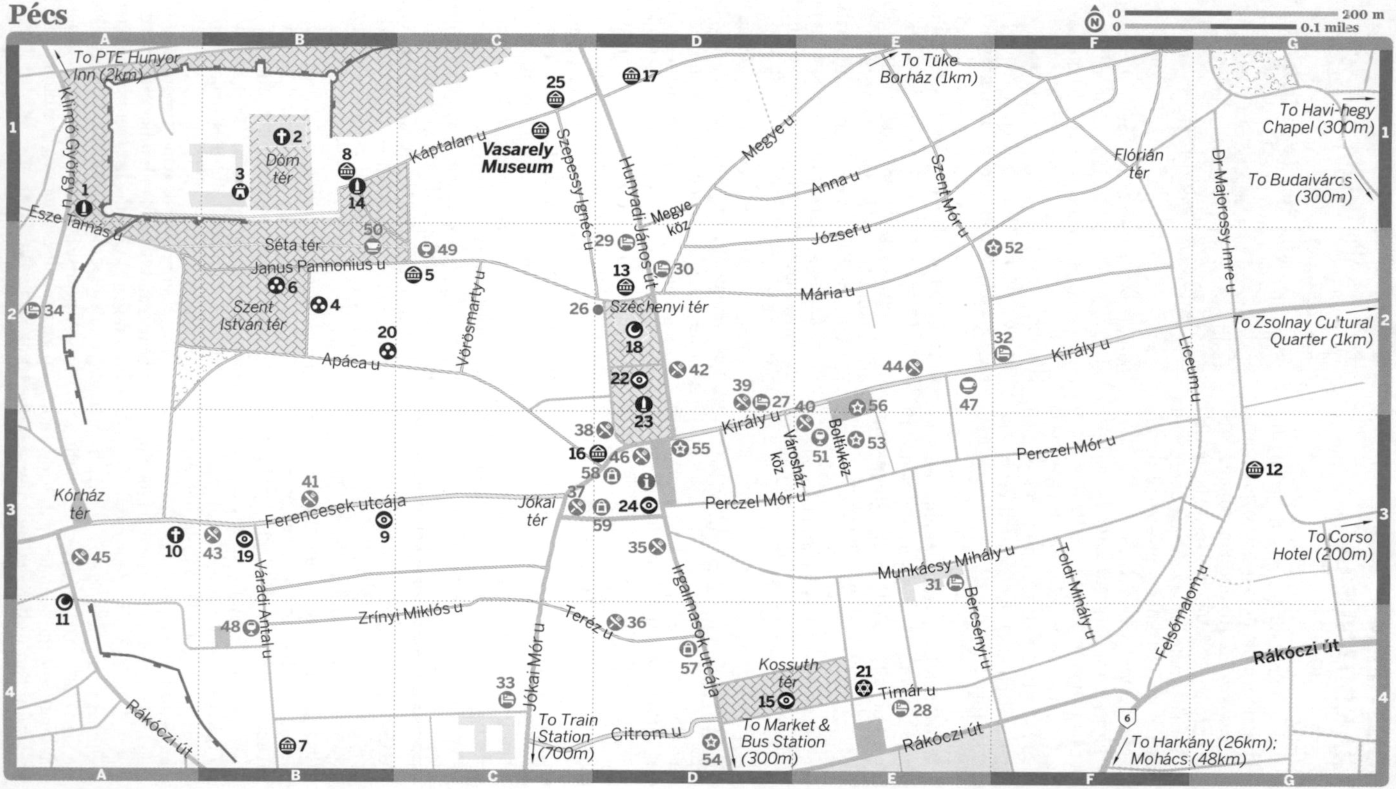

0 200 m
0 0.1 miles

To PTE Hunyor Inn (2km)
Klimó György u
Esze Tamás u
Dóm tér
Vasarely Museum
Káptalan u
Szepessy Ignéc u
Hunyadi János út
Megye u
Megye köz
Anna u
József u
Mária u
Szent Mór u
To Tüke Borház (1km)
Flórián tér
Dr Majorossy Imre u
To Havi-hegy Chapel (300m)
To Budaivárcs (300m)
Séta tér
Janus Pannonius u
Szent István tér
Széchenyi tér
Vörösmarty u
Apáca u
Király u
Liceum u
To Zsolnay Cultural Quarter (1km)
Városház köz
Boltívköz
Perczel Mór u
Kórház tér
Ferencesek utcája
Jókai tér
Váradi Antal u
Zrínyi Miklós u
Teréz u
Irgalmasok utcája
Munkácsy Mihály u
Toldi Mihály u
Bercsényi u
Felsőmalom u
Rákóczi út
To Corso Hotel (200m)
Jókai Mór u
Kossuth tér
Timár u
To Train Station (700m)
Citrom u
To Market & Bus Station (300m)
To Harkány (26km); Mohács (48km)

Pécs

Top Sights
Vasarely Museum C1

Sights
1 Barbican A1
2 Basilica of St Peter B1
3 Bishop's Palace B1
4 Cella Septichora Visitors Centre B2
5 Csontváry Museum C2
6 Early Christian Tomb Chapel B2
7 Ethnographic Museum B4
8 Ferenc Martyn Museum B1
9 Ferencesek utcája B3
10 Franciscan Church A3
11 Hassan Jakovali Mosque A4
12 Historical Museum G3
13 Janus Pannonius Archaeology Museum D2
14 Jug Mausoleum B1
15 Kossuth tér D4
16 Marzipan Museum D3
17 Modern Hungarian Gallery D1
18 Mosque Church D2
19 Pasha Memi Baths B3
20 Roman Tomb Sites B2
21 Synagogue E4
22 Széchenyi tér D2
23 Trinity Column D2
24 Zsolnay Fountain D3
25 Zsolnay Porcelain Museum C1

Activities, Courses & Tours
26 Pécs Little Train D2

Sleeping
27 Aranyhajó Fogadó D2
28 Diána Hotel E4
29 Hotel Arkadia D2
30 Hotel Főnix D2
31 Lenau House E3
32 Nap Hostel F2
33 Pollack Mihály Kollégium C4
34 Szinbád Panzió A2

Eating
35 Áfium D3
36 Aranykacsa D4
37 Az Elefánthoz C3
Cellárium ..... (see 30)
38 Coffein Café D3
39 Dóm D2
40 Enoteca & Bistro Corso E3
41 Giuseppe B3
42 Mecsek D2
43 Minaret B3
44 Oázis E2
45 Otthon Étkezde A3
46 Virág D3

Drinking
47 Cooltour Café E2
48 Csinos Presszó B4
49 Káptalani Borozó C2
50 Kioszk B2
51 Korhely Pub E3

Entertainment
52 Bóbita Puppet Theatre E2
53 Chamber Theatre E3
54 Club 5 Music Pub D4
55 Pécs Cultural Centre D3
56 Pécs National Theatre E2

Shopping
57 Blázek D4
58 Corvina Art Bookshop D3
59 Zsolnay D3

Sights

TOP CHOICE Mosque Church MOSQUE

(Mecset templom; Széchenyi tér; adult/concession 750/500Ft; ⌚10am-4pm mid-Apr–mid-Oct, to noon mid-Oct–mid-Apr, shorter hours Sun) The former Pasha Gazi Kassim Mosque is now the Inner Town Parish Church (Belvárosi plébánia templom), but it's more commonly referred to as the Mosque Church. It is the largest building still standing in Hungary from the time of the Turkish occupation, and the symbol of the city.

Turks built the square mosque with its green copper dome in the mid-16th century with the stones of the ruined Gothic Church of St Bertalan. The Catholics moved back in the early 18th century, and the northern semicircular part was added in the 20th century. The Islamic elements on the south side are easy to spot: windows with distinctive Turkish ogee arches; a *mihrab* (prayer niche) carved into the southeast wall; faded verses from the Koran to the southwest; and lovely geometric frescoes on the corners. The mosque's minaret was pulled down in 1753 and replaced with a bell tower; bells are rung at noon and 7pm.

Széchenyi tér SQUARE

(⏲noon-6pm Tue-Sun Apr-Oct, 10am-4pm Tue-Sun Nov-Mar) Surrounded by largely baroque buildings, Pécs' sprawling main square is the hub of the city – on summer days everyone gathers here to relax, unwind with a scoop of ice cream and people-watch. The square is anchored by the **Trinity Column** (Széchenyi tér) in the centre and, further down at the southern end, the porcelain **Zsolnay Fountain** (cnr Munkácsy Mihály & Irgalmasok utca) boasts the lustrous eosin glaze and four bull's heads; the fountain was donated to the city by the Zsolnay factory in 1892. The eosin creates an iridescent, metallic sheen that most people either love or hate.

The **Janus Pannonius Archaeology Museum** (Janus Pannonius Régészeti múzeum; ☎312 719; www.kepzo.jpm.hu; Széchenyi tér 12; ⏲10am-3pm Tue-Sat) is also located here but was closed for renovations at the time of research; the expected opening date was late 2013 but check the website for details.

Marzipan Museum MUSEUM

(☎225 453; www.szabomarcipan.hu; Apáca utca 1; adult/child 350/200Ft; ⏲10am-6pm) This combination museum and marzipan shop features intricate marzipan sculptures with colourful re-creations of the Mosque Church, embroidered Hungarian lace and more.

Kossuth tér SQUARE

This square southeast of Széchenyi tér has two important buildings: the Eclectic town hall (1891) to the north and synagogue to the east. The **synagogue** (Zsinagóga; Kossuth tér; adult/concession 600/400Ft; ⏲10am-noon & 12.45-5pm May-Oct, closed Sat) was built in the Romantic style in 1869, and a seven-page fact sheet, available in 11 languages, explains the history of the building and the city's Jewish population. Some 2700 of the city's Jews were deported to Nazi death camps in May 1944; only 150 Jews now live here. The pews hewn from Slavonian oak and the Angster organ are particularly fine.

HUNGARY'S GREATEST PAINTER: TIVADAR KOSZTKA CSONTVÁRY

The small but perfectly formed **Csontváry Museum** (☎310 544; Janus Pannonius utca 11; adult/child 1500/750Ft; ⏲10am-6pm, closed Mon) exhibits the major works of master 19th-century painter Tivadar Kosztka Csontváry, a unique symbolist artist whose tragic life is often compared with that of his great contemporary Vincent Van Gogh. He is considered one of Hungary's greatest painters. Born in Kisszeben, now Sabinov in northeastern Slovakia, Csontváry trained and worked as a pharmacist until, at the age of 27, he heard voices telling him that he would go on to become the 'world's greatest *plein air* painter, greater than Rafael'. He allowed himself 20 years to prepare for this seemingly unachievable task by studying painting and travelling (and dispensing drugs on the side to pay the bills). Though he did some charcoal portraits and painted landscapes in the last decade of the 19th century, Csontváry produced his major works in just half a dozen years starting in 1903. His efforts met with praise at his first exhibition in 1907 in Paris, but critics panned his work at a showing in Budapest the following year. This lack of understanding and recognition by his peers pushed what was already an unstable, obsessive personality into insanity, and he died penniless and alone in Budapest. Many of Csontváry's massive (up to 30 sq metres) canvases are masterpieces. Though he belonged to no specific school of art per se, elements of post-Impressionism and expressionism can be seen in such works as *East Station at Night* (1902), *Storm on the Great Hortobágy* (1903) and his most famous work, *Solitary Cedar* (1907). But arguably his best and most profound work is *Baalbeck* (1906), an artistic search for a larger identity through religious and historical themes. And while contemplating it at the museum devoted to his work in Pécs, spare a thought for one Gedeon Gerlóczy, the young architect who recognised Csontváry's genius and bought much of his œuvre at auction from his family, who were trying to flog it for the high-quality canvases the artist had used.

Entry to the museum also gives you access to the **Ferenc Martyn Museum** (Káptalan utca 6; ⏲10am-4pm Tue-Sun), which displays works by the eponymous painter and sculptor who died in Pécs in 1986.

Basilica of St Peter CHURCH

(Szent Péter bazilika; Dóm tér; adult/concession 900/600Ft; ⏲9am-5pm Mon-Sat, 1-5pm Sun) The foundations of the four-towered basilica dedicated to St Peter date from the 11th century and the side chapels are from the 1300s. But most of what you see today of the neo-Romanesque structure is the result of renovations carried out in 1881.

The most interesting parts of the basilica's very ornate interior are the elevated central altar and four chapels under the towers and the crypt, the oldest part of the structure. The Chapel of Mary on the northwest side and the Chapel of the Sacred Heart to the northeast contain works by 19th-century painters Bertalan Székely and Károly Lotz. The Mór Chapel to the southeast has more works by Székely as well as magnificent pews. The Corpus Christi Chapel on the southwest side (enter from the outside) boasts a 16th-century red marble tabernacle, one of the best examples of Renaissance stonework in the country.

Bishop's Palace PALACE

(Püspöki palota; ☎513 030; Szent István tér 23; adult/child 1900/1000Ft; ⏲tours 2pm, 3pm & 4pm Thu late Jun–mid-Sep) The Bishop's Palace, dating to 1770, keeps very limited hours, but have a look at the curious statue of Franz Liszt (Imre Varga; 1983) peering over from the palace balcony.

Early Christian Tomb Chapel RUIN

(Ókeresztény sírkápolna; Szent István tér 12; adult/concession 500/300Ft; ⏲10am-6pm Tue-Sun) The early Christian tomb chapel dates from about AD 350 and has frescoes of Adam and Eve and Daniel in the lion's den. Two **Roman tomb** (Apáca utca 8 & 14; adult/child/family 450/250/850Ft; ⏲10am-5pm Tue-Sun) sites containing 110 graves from the same era are a little further south.

Cella Septichora Visitors Centre RUINS

(Cella Septichora látogatóközpont; www.pecsorokseg.hu; Janus Pannonius utca; adult/concession 1200/600Ft; ⏲10am-6pm Tue-Sun) This early Christian burial site illuminates a series of early Christian tombs that have been on Unesco's World Heritage list since 2000. The highlight is the so-called **Jug Mausoleum** (Korsós sírkamra; adult/child 300/150Ft; ⏲10am-6pm Tue-Sun), a 4th-century Roman tomb; its name comes from a painting of a large drinking vessel with vines.

PÉCS MUSEUM PASS

If you plan to visit more than two or three museums in Pécs purchase the Museum Pass (adult/student 3000/1500Ft), which gives you entry to the Csontváry Museum (p178), Zsolnay Porcelain Museum (p179), Vasarely Museum (p179), Ethnographic Museum (p180), Modern Hungarian Gallery (p179), Archaeology Museum (p178) and the Historical Museum (p180). The pass is valid for one day and can be purchased at any of the participating museums.

Zsolnay Porcelain Museum MUSEUM

(Zsolnay Porcélan Múzeum; Káptalan utca 2; adult/concession 1200/600Ft; ⏲10am-5pm Tue-Sun) The Zsolnay Porcelain Museum traces the history of the porcelain factory established in Pécs in 1853. At the forefront of European art and design for more than half a century, many of its majolica tiles were used to decorate buildings throughout the country and contributed to establishing a new pan-Hungarian style of architecture. Zsolnay's darkest period came when the postwar communist government turned it into a plant for making ceramic electrical insulators. It's producing art (well, knick-knacks, really) again, but contemporary Zsolnay can't hold a candle to the *chinoiserie* pieces from the late 19th century and the later Art Nouveau and Art Deco designs done in the lustrous eosin glaze. The museum was once the home of the Zsolnay family and contains many original furnishings and personal effects.

TOP CHOICE **Vasarely Museum** MUSEUM

(☎514 040; Káptalan utca 3; adult/child 1200/600Ft; ⏲10am-5pm, closed Sun) Completely revamped in 2010, the Vasarely Museum exhibits the work of the father of Op Art, Victor Vasarely. Pieces are exhibited with clever illuminations that intensify the 3D experience, though there have been arguments about whether or not this visual distortion represents what Vasarely had in mind. But overall the well-curated selection is evocative, tactile and just plain fun.

Modern Hungarian Gallery MUSEUM

(Modern Magyar Képtár; www.pecsimuzeumok.hu; Papnövelde u 5; adult/concession 700/350Ft; ⏲noon-6pm Apr-Oct, to 4pm Nov-Mar, closed Mon) The Modern Hungarian Art Gallery exhibits the art of Hungary from 1850 till today; pay special attention to the works of Simon Hollósy, József Rippl-Rónai and Ödön Márffy. More abstract and constructionist artists include András Mengyár, Tamás Hencze, Béla Uitz and Gábor Dienes.

Barbican FORT
(Barbakán; Esze Tamás utca 2; garden 7am-8pm May-Sep, 9am-5pm Oct-Apr) Fronted by a lovely garden, the circular barbican, the only stone bastion to survive in Pécs, dates from the late 15th century and was restored in the 1970s.

Hassan Jakovali Mosque MOSQUE
(Hassan Jakovali mecset; adult/concession 600/300Ft; 9.30am-6pm Wed-Sun late Mar-Oct) Though wedged between two modern buildings, this 16th-century mosque is more intact than its larger cousin, the Mosque Church (p177), and comes complete with a minaret. There's a small museum of Ottoman history inside.

Ethnographic Museum MUSEUM
(Néprajzi Múzeum; 315 629; Rákóczi út 15; adult/child 500/250Ft; 10am-2pm) The Ethnography Museum showcases ethnic Hungarian, German and South Slav folk art in the region.

Ferencesek utcája STREET
One of Pécs' most enjoyable pedestrian streets, Ferencesek utcája, runs east from Kórház tér to Széchenyi tér and boasts the magnificent baroque **Franciscan Church** (Ferences templom; Ferencesek utca 37) dating from 1760 as well as another relic of the Turkish period: the ruins of the 16th-century **Pasha Memi Baths** (Memi pasa fürdője; Ferencesek utcája 33-35).

Historical Museum MUSEUM
(Várostörténeti múzeum; 310 165; Felsőmalom utca 9; adult/child 350/180Ft; 10am-2pm Tue-Sat) This museum traces Pécs' history across two floors of a former tannery with period costumes and clothing, photos and exhibits walking you through the Turkish occupation and explaining how coal mining in the area boosted the development of local factories, including Zsolnay Porcelain.

All Saints' Church CHURCH
(Mindenszentek temploma; 512 400; Tettye utca 14) The suburb of Budaiváros to the northeast of Pécs' town centre is where most Hungarians settled after the Turks banned them from living within the city walls. The centre of this community was the All Saints' Church. Originally built in the 12th century, it was reconstructed in Gothic style 200 years later.

All Saints was the only Christian church allowed in Pécs during the occupation and was shared by three sects – who fought bitterly for every square centimetre. Apparently it was the Muslim Turks who had to keep the peace among the Christians.

Zsolnay Cultural Quarter CULTURAL BUILDING
(www.zskn.hu) The biggest project to evolve out of the 2010 Capital of Culture has been the Zsolnay Cultural Quarter, a development that sprawls across 4.5 hectares on the grounds of the original Zsolnay Family Factory. Divided into four quarters (craftsman, family and children's, creative and university) the area was still evolving at the time of writing, but it's a lovely place to stroll with plenty of green spaces and cafes dotted around. Highlights include the actual functioning **factory** (Zsolnay utca 37, Zsolnay Cultural Quarter; adult/child 500/300Ft; 3-6pm Mon-Sat, 10am-6pm Sun), which now takes up just a section of the grounds, where you can watch the actual pieces being created by hand, and the **Bóbita Puppet Theatre** (Bóbit Bábszínház; 210 301; www.bobita.hu; Felsővámház utca 50, Zsolnay Cultural Quarter; grand hall performances 900Ft, cabin shows 700Ft, puppet museum 400Ft), which moved from its previous location in town to the quarter in late 2011.

Festivals & Events

Among the big annual events in this party town are the late-March **Pécs Spring Festival** (www.pecsitavaszifesztival.hu), a month-long 'everything-but-the-kitchen-sink' event; the late-July **International Culture Week** (www.icwip.hu) which focuses on theatrical performances; the late-September **Pécs Days Heritage Festival** (www.oroksegfesztival.hu), a 10-day festival of dance and music with a couple of wine-related events; and the late-September **European Wine Song Festival** (www.winesongfestival.hu), Europe's only festival exclusively for male choruses.

Sleeping

In July and August more than a dozen of the city's colleges open up their doors to travellers, and prices average 4000Ft to 6000Ft for a dorm bed; Tourinform (p184) has the complete list. The most central is **Pollack Mihály Kollégium** (315 846; Jókai utca 8; dm from 2400Ft), with rooms of between two and five beds.

LOCAL KNOWLEDGE

ANDRÁS GÜTH – TOUR GUIDE

András Güth has been a tour guide in Pécs for over five years. He lets us in on some of his insider tips and explains why he never tires of exploring his adopted city.

What do you love most about living and working here? The fact that you get a laid-back atmosphere that's buzzy but never rushed, paired with an amazing collection of art – yet unlike Budapest, it still feels a bit undiscovered.

Indeed, with all these museums it can feel a bit overwhelming! Are there any iconic pieces of art that you absolutely must see? Vasarely's *Zebras* [in the Vasarely Museum] wows everyone and draws you in with its 3D-like geometric patterns. Also Csontváry's *Solitary Cedar* [in the Csontváry Museum] – it's slightly haunting and almost personifies the artist and his lonely state of mind, I think.

The main square, Széchenyi tér, is a focal point of the city. Any tips on maximising the experience here? I always tell people to hit it around dusk, when the Mosque Church is all lit up. In the warmer months everyone hangs out there and it's a prime spot for people-watching.

Indeed, everyone seems to gather there, and it is so photogenic. Where's the best spot for photo? If you stand just south of the Zsolnay Fountain (with the church right behind you) you can get a fantastic shot of the mosque and the hills in the background with the greenish-goldish iridescent hue of the fountain's bull heads in the foreground. And the modern, floor-level fountains just north of Zsolnay Fountain. It's an amazing juxtaposition of colours.

Speaking of hills, I heard there are some prime spots for drinks with a view. What's your favourite? Definitely Tüke Borház (p183). It's a wine bar nestled in the hills with a huge terrace and plenty of wine barrels used for decoration. It always feels authentic and local. They have a nice selection of local wine which you can sip while taking in a lovely view of Pécs.

While we are on the subject of drinking, where do you send people when they ask about ruin bars in Pécs? There is a new-ish place that I love, Csinos Presszó (p183). It's always lively and as it is a bit tucked away from the main arteries in the centre, you get the sense that you have stumbled upon something slightly hidden.

People love taking home small souvenirs – when people ask you for recommendations, what do you suggest? If you want to spend a small amount on something easy to transport, head to the market (p182) and pick up some local honey. Alternatively, if you are willing to splurge and carry something breakable, pick up a piece of Zsolnay Porcelain – there are a handful of antique shops just east of the main square lining Ferencesek utcája between Jókai tér and Váradi Antál utca that carry excellent selections. Or pick one up at the Zsolnay Porcelain Museum (p179).

Szinbád Panzió PENSION €
(www.szinbadpanzio.hu; Klimó György utca 9; s/d from 10,500/13,500Ft; P❄@) Cosy, standard pension with excellent service and well-maintained rooms. An excellent choice if you want budget prices but don't want the hostel vibe.

Hotel Főnix HOTEL €
(☎311 682; www.fonixhotel.hu; Hunyadi János út 2; s/d from 8200/14,000Ft; ❄@🛜) Főnix appears to be a hotel too large for the land it's built on and some of the 16 rooms and suites are not even big enough to swing, well, a phoenix in. Try to bag a room with a balcony; the Mosque Church is just within reach.

Nap Hostel HOSTEL €
(☎950 684; www.naphostel.com; Király utca 23-25; dm/d from 2800/12,350Ft; @🛜) The best budget choice in Pécs, this place has three dorm rooms with between six and eight beds and a double with washbasin on the 1st floor of a former bank (1885). One of the six-bed dorm rooms has a corner balcony and there's something of a garden at

the rear. There's a large communal kitchen and the on-site **Nappali Bár** (⏲10am-2am) is one of the hippest gathering spots in town for a coffee, breakfast or drinks. Enter the hostel Szent Mór utca through the bar's main entrance.

Aranyhajó Fogadó HOTEL €€
(☎210 685; www.aranyhajo.hu; Király utca 3; s 9500-11,000Ft, d 12,500-15,000Ft, tr 16,000-18000Ft; ❄@📶) Aranyhajó Fogadó claims to be Hungary's oldest hotel, and judging by the lovely, listed medieval building it's situated in, we're ready to believe it. The rooms are traditionally furnished; not exactly antiques, not exactly modern. The standard rooms are quite basic, but clean and very neat with white linen contrasting with the sharp, dark-brown lines of the wooden bed and table. It feels a bit like a grandmother's home that could use a slight revamp, but is excellent value in the center of town.

Lenau House GUESTHOUSE €€
(☎332 515; lenau@t-online.hu; Munkácsy Mihály utca 8; s/d/tr 10,000/14,000/16,000Ft; @) The cultural centre of the German minority in Baranya (Branau in German) County offers accommodation on its top floor. The welcome here is hardly the warmest, but the five rooms are large and spotless with private bathroom, and the location can't be faulted.

Diána Hotel PENSION €€
(☎328 594; www.hoteldiana.hu; Tímár utca 4/a; s 9500-12,000Ft, d 14,000-16,000Ft, tr/q 19,000/22,000Ft; P❄@📶🐾) This very central pension offers spotless rooms, comfortable kick-off-your-shoes decor and a warm welcome. It's a great choice overlooking the synagogue and staff are extra friendly. If you reserve online and pay in cash they'll usually knock 500Ft to 1000Ft off the nightly rate.

Corso Hotel HOTEL €€€
(☎421 900; www.corsohotel.hu; Koller utca 8; s/d/ste from 19,500/23,200/32,000Ft; P❄@📶) One of the newest additions to the top-end hotel scene in Pécs, this is a prime choice if you want the amenities of a business class hotel within a short (10-minute) walk of the town centre. Rooms are inviting with plush carpets and velvet curtains, and all suites have their own outdoor terrace and some also feature private saunas. There's also an on-site restaurant serving solid international and Hungarian fare.

TOP CHOICE **Hotel Arkadia** BOUTIQUE HOTEL €€€
(☎512 550; www.hotelarkadiapecs.hu; Hunyadi János útca 1; s/d/tr 17,000/25,000/28,500Ft; P❄@📶🐾) This minimalist bastion is a welcome addition to the centre of town. Spread across two structures connected by a glass corridor, common areas with polished steel, exposed brick and plenty of Corbusier furniture cement, this is a firm student of Bauhaus. Rooms follow the same vein with lots of straight lines and solid colours, but thick throws, plush carpets and ample doses of natural light lend a cosy vibe to what could otherwise be austere spaces.

Eating

There's an ongoing debate in Pécs over which *cukrászda* (cake shop) serves the better cakes: **Mecsek** (☎315 444; Széchenyi tér 16; cakes from 600Ft; ⏲9am-9pm), next to the former Nádor hotel, or the **Virág** (☎313 793; Irgalmasok utca; cakes from 550Ft; ⏲8am-10pm). Try them both and come to your own conclusions. Pécs' excellent fruit and vegetable **market** (Zólyom utca; sandwiches & sausages 700-1000Ft; ⏲10am-6pm, closed Mon) is next to the bus station; food stalls lining the interior sell gut-busting sandwiches and sausages. Coffein (p184) and Korhely Pub (p184) are also excellent choices for budget meals. The **Árkád Shopping Centre** (Bajcsy-Zsilinszky utca 11; ⏲7am-9pm Mon-Thu & Sat, to 10pm Fri, 8am-7pm Sun) has a huge grocery store, **Interspar** (basement, Árkád shopping centre; ⏲7am-9pm Mon-Thu & Sat, to 10pm Fri, 8am-7pm Sun), with plenty of sandwiches and salads to take away and the food court on the ground floor is home to a local fast-food joint called **Lecsó** (set meals 700-1200Ft), which serves the eponymous sauce of peppers, tomatoes and onions on just about everything.

Giuseppe ICE CREAM €
(Ferencesek utcája 28; ice cream per scoop 160Ft; ⏲11am-8pm Mon-Fri, from 2pm Sat & Sun) This place has been serving its very own Italian-style *lapátos fagyalt* (scooped ice cream) since 1992.

Otthon Étkezde HUNGARIAN €
(☎212 323; Rákóczi utca 1; set menu 750Ft; ⏲11am-3pm Mon-Fri) Ultra-cheap lunch spot at the start of pedestrian Ferencesek utcája, with rib-sticking Hungarian favourites.

Oázis MIDDLE EASTERN €
(Király utca 17; kebabs & dishes 550-1450Ft; ⏲10am-11pm Mon-Thu, to 4am Fri & Sat) A cheap

little kebab house serving a mix of Turkish and Middle Eastern dishes, this is a great central spot for a meal on the run.

Áfium BALKAN €
(☎511 434; Irgalmasok utca 2; mains 1500-2200Ft; ⏰11am-1am) With Croatia and Serbia so close, it's a wonder that more restaurants don't offer cuisine from south of the border. No matter – this restaurant will fill the needs (and stomachs) of most diners searching for such tastes. Don't miss the 'hatted' (actually a swollen bread crust) bean soup with trotters. Set lunch, which changes daily, is 520Ft during the week.

Minaret HUNGARIAN €€
(☎311 338; Ferencesek utcája 35; mains 2200-3900Ft; ⏰noon-4pm Sun & Mon, to 9pm Tue-Thu, to 11pm Fri & Sat; ☑) Boasting one of the loveliest gardens in the city, this eatery in the shadow of the Pasha Memi Baths serves predictable but tasty Hungarian favourites plus plenty of vegetarian options.

Aranykacsa INTERNATIONAL €€
(☎518 860; Teréz utca 4; mains 2220-4340Ft; ⏰11.30am-10pm Tue-Thu, to midnight Fri & Sat, to 3pm Sun) This stunning wine restaurant takes pride in its silver service and venue; the Zsolnay Room is not to be missed. The menu offers at least eight duck dishes – its name means 'Golden Duck' – including such memorables as duck liver with green apple and duck ragout with honey and vegetables.

Cellárium HUNGARIAN €€
(☎314 453; Hunyadi János út 2; mains 2300-3800Ft) This subterranean eatery with vaulted stone ceilings offers excellent value for money in the city centre, and weekends bring a variety of live music – often a small folk band or just a guy playing guitar.

Az Elefánthoz ITALIAN €€
(☎216 055; www.elefantos.hu; Jókai tér 6; mains 2600-4500Ft, pizza 1400-2600Ft) With its enormous terrace and quality Italian cuisine, 'At the Elephant' is a sure bet for first-rate food in the city centre. Pizzas emerging from its wood-burning stove are the best in town and the atmosphere always manges to be elegant but unpretentious.

Dóm INTERNATIONAL €€€
(☎210 088; Király utca 3; mains 3200-5200Ft) This restaurant with wonderful *fin-de-siècle* paintings and stained-glass windows is just behind the Palatinus. It has a full range of mains, but its speciality is steak – from pepper to Chateaubriand.

TOP CHOICE **Enoteca & Bistro Corso** INTERNATIONAL €€€
(☎525 198; www.enotecapecs.hu; Király utca 14; mains 3200-5500Ft) One of Hungary's top restaurants and arguably the most prestigious meal in town. Dining is on two levels, with the top featuring refined Hungarian cooking with Italian and French influences. The ground floor is slightly less expensive, but equally good. The alfresco terrace is also a popular spot for snacks and drinks in the warmer months.

Drinking

Dozens of pubs and bars line Király utca, so if you're undecided about where to go take a stroll here and you should have no problem finding one that suits.

Tüke Borház WINE BAR
(☎06 20 317 8178; Böckh János utca 39/2; ⏰4-10pm Mon-Thu, from 3pm Fri, from noon Sat, noon-7pm Sun) This wine bar tucked away in a stone house in the hills above Pécs offers a fantastic selection of local wines served by gracious and knowledgeable staff. The vast terrace has panoramic views across the city and if you're feeling peckish meat plates and small snacks are always on hand.

Kioszk CAFE
(Sétatér 1; ⏰10am-10pm May-Oct) Open only in the warmer months, this outdoor cafe is a quiet piece of heaven with shaded tables placed amid a jungle-like patch of greenery.

TOP CHOICE **Csinos Presszó** PUB
(☎06 30 988 2665; Váradi Antal utca 8; ⏰noon-midnight, to 4pm Sun) One of the newest ruin pubs in town, Csinos has quickly become a local favourite. Between the alfresco garden with mismatched furniture painted in bright pastels, the Christmas lights strung from the trees and the vast interior with low lights it's easy to see why it packs in relaxed patrons every weekend. A small food menu with wraps and snacks accompanies an inventive drinks menu (a number of the cordials are house-made) and in afternoons it's also a prime spot to grab a coffee and press pause.

Cooltour Café CAFE
(☎310 440; http://cooltourcafe.hu; Király utca 26; ⏰noon-2am) One of the most popular places

MOVING ON?

For tips, recommendations and reviews, head to shop.lonelyplanet.com to purchase a downloadable PDF of the Croatia chapter from Lonely Planet's *Eastern Europe* guide.

in town, Cooltour embodies so many, er, cool things it's hard to choose what we love best. It's a ruin pub, yet it's open all day, making it fine for both coffee and snacks or cocktails and mellow chit-chat. It's right on the main drag in town but its rear garden feels like a secret spot. Outside or inside, the eclectic mishmash of flea-market furniture and whimsical colours exudes a bohemian charm. It also features occasional live music in the evenings.

Coffein Café CAFE €
(Széchenyi tér 9; ⌚8am-midnight Mon-Thu, to 2am Fri & Sat, 10am-10pm Sun; 📶) For the best views across Széchenyi tér to the Mosque Church and Király utca, find a perch at this cool cafe done up in the warmest of colours. It's a divine choice for good-value budget meals like salads and sandwiches.

Korhely Pub TAVERNA
(☎535 916; Boltív köz 2) This outrageously popular *csapszék* (tavern) with the in-your-face name of 'Drunkard' has peanuts on the table, shells on the floor, a half-dozen beers on tap and a retro sorta-socialist/kinda–Latin American decor. It works. It also serves budget-friendly Hungarian stalwarts.

Káptalani Borozó WINE BAR
(Janus Pannonius utca 8-10; ⌚10am-2am Mon-Sat, to midnight Sun) This funny little 'wine bar' opposite the Csontváry Museum has outdoor seating on a tiny terrace next to another early Christian site and serves white Cirfandli, a speciality of the Mecsek Hills, in spades. There's a story behind all those padlocks on the outside gate.

☆ Entertainment

Music & Theatre

Pécs is always a city of culture – not just in 2010 and because Europe said so. The list of theatres and concert venues is enormous for a city of its size, and most times of the year you can find something going on. For information visit the **Pécs Cultural Centre** (☎336 622; www.pecsikult.hu; Szécheny ter 1; ⌚8am-4pm Mon, 9am-5pm Tue-Fri) or pick up a copy of the biweekly freebie *Pécsi Est.*

Pécs National Theatre THEATRE
(Pécsi nemzeti színház; ☎512 660; www.pnsz.hu; Színház tér 1; tickets 1300-2600Ft) Pécs is renowned for its opera company and the Sophianae Ballet, both of which perform at this theatre. Advance tickets can be purchased from the theatre's **box office** (☎211 965; ⌚10am-5pm Mon-Fri, 1hr before performances Sat & Sun). The **Chamber Theatre** (Kamaraszínház; ☎512 660; Perczel Mór utca) next door stages smaller, more experimental productions.

Nightclubs

Pécs is a big university town; it goes without saying that the nightlife is good, but don't expect everything to be heaving in summer, which is the low season in these parts.

Club 5 Music Pub CLUB
(☎06 20 535 5090, 212 621; Irgalmasok utca 24; ⌚7pm-2am Tue-Thu, to 4am Fri & Sat) This basement bar transforms itself into a small (and very central) club on weekends.

Cyrano Club CLUB
(Czindery utca 6; men 800-1200Ft, women free; ⌚8pm-5am Fri & Sat) A big club, popular with a big-haired, big-nailed crowd that's been around for ages. It attracts mainly 20-something trendoids who boogie to the house and techno or sip cocktails and look pretty in the outdoor garden.

Shopping

Pécs has been known for its leatherwork since Turkish times, and you can pick up a few bargains in several shops around the city, including **Blázek** (☎332 460; Teréz utca 1), which deals mainly in handbags and wallets. **Corvina Art Bookshop** (☎310 427; Széchenyi tér 7-8) stocks English-language books and guides, and **Zsolnay** (☎310 220; Jókai tér 2) has a porcelain outlet south of Széchenyi tér. About 3km southwest of the inner town, a weekend **Flea Market** (Vásár tér) attracts people from the countryside, especially on the first Sunday of each month.

ℹ Information

Tourinform (☎213 315; baranya-m@tourinform.hu; Széchenyi tér 9; ⌚9am-5pm Mon-Fri, 10am-3pm Sat & Sun Jun-Aug, closed Sun May, Sep & Oct, closed Sat & Sun Nov-Apr) Knowledgeable staff, copious information on Pécs and Baranya County.

Getting There & Away

Bus

DESTINATION	PRICE	TIME	KM	FREQUENCY
Abaliget (Mecsek Hills)	650Ft	1hr	32km	at least 4-5 daily, more in summer
Budapest	3010Ft	4½hr	215	5 daily
Győr	3440Ft	4½hr	256	2 daily
Harkány	1120Ft	1½-2hr	52km	10-12 daily
Kaposvár	1860Ft	1½hr	91km	9-10 daily
Kecskemét	3010Ft	4¼hr	200	2 daily
Mohács	930Ft	1¼hr	48km	10-12 daily
Orfű (Mecsek Hills)	370Ft	40min	18km	at least 6-8 daily, more in summer
Siklós	1120Ft	45min	55km	10-12 daily
Siófok	2040Ft	3hr	133	3-6 daily
Szeged	3010Ft	4½hr	207	8 daily
Szekszárd	1680Ft	1½hr	88km	9-10 daily
Szigetvár	650Ft	50min	35km	13-15 daily
Veszprém	2780Ft	4¼hr	183	2-3 daily
Villány	900Ft	1½hr	52	1-2 daily

Train

Up to nine direct trains daily connect Pécs with Budapest (3950Ft to 4455Ft, three to four hours, 228km) and Villány (745Ft, 45 minutes, 36km); one daily train goes direct to Kaposvár (1860Ft, 1½ hours, 95km); most other destinations in Southern Transdanubia are best reached by bus.

Getting Around

To get to the PTE Hunyor Inn, take bus 32 from the train station or from opposite the Mosque Church. Buses 34 and 35 run direct to the Fenyves Panoráma Hotel from the train station, with bus 35 continuing on to the TV tower. Buses 3 and 50 from the train station are good for the flea market.

You can also order a local **taxi** (☎333 333/777 777).

Around Pécs

MECSEK HILLS

A string of hills and valleys dotted with villages and the odd lake to the north of Pécs, the Mecsek form both the city's green lungs and playground. There's good hiking here, too, but a copy of Cartographia's 1:40,000 map *A Mecsek,* available at Corvina Art Bookshop (p184), will be invaluable as the trails are not very well marked.

To get a mere taste of the Mecsek Hills, walk northeast from the centre of Pécs to Tettye and the **Garden of Ruins** (Romkert; Tettye), what's left of a bishop's summer residence built early in the 16th century and later used by Turkish dervishes as a lodge or monastery. To the northwest, up Fenyves sor, a winding road leads to Misina Peak (535m) and a **TV tower** (☎336 900; adult/student/child 650/550/450Ft; ⏲9am-10pm daily May-Sep, Mon-Thu Oct-Apr), an impressive 194m-tall structure with a viewing platform.

Further afield, **Orfű** is the most accessible of the Mecsek Hills resorts and the one with the most recreational facilities. It's a series of settlements on four artificial lakes, including the largest, Lake Pécs (Pécsi-tó), where you can swim, row, canoe and fish; seek information from Tourinform (p184). There's a riding school at the **Tekeresi Lovaspanzió** (Tekeres Horse Pension; ☎06 30 227 1401, 498 032; www.tekeresilovaspanzio.hu; Petőfi utca 3; riding per hr 3200Ft, instructor per 10-12 people 7000Ft) on the lake's northern shore. From Széchenyi tér on the lake's southeastern shore you can walk south along tiny Lake Orfű to the **Mill Museum** (Malommúzeum; ☎06 20 466 5506; www.orfuivizimalom.hu; per person/family 550/1800Ft; ⏲10am-5pm Tue-Sun May-Sep), which encompasses pump houses still in use and a horse-driven dry mill.

Abaliget (www.abaliget.hu), about 3km north of Orfű and accessible by bus or on foot via a trail up and over the hill, is quieter and more relaxed (though not quite as attractive as Orfű). But it's worth a jaunt to explore **Abaliget Cave** (Abaligeti-barlang; ☎06 30 377 3387, 498 766; www.abaligetibarlang.hu; adult/student & child 1000/800Ft, combined ticket with Bat Museum 1250/1000Ft; ⏲9am-6pm mid-Mar–mid-Oct, 10am-3pm mid-Oct–mid-Mar), which, at 1.3km, is the longest stalactite cave open to the public in Southern Transdanubia; 460m of it can be visited on a 50-minute tour but dress warmly as the temperature is 10°C to 12°C and the humidity a very damp 97%. Next door, the **Bat Museum** (Denevérmúzeum; ☎06 30 377 3426, 498 684; adult/student & child 450/350Ft; ⏲9am-6pm mid-Mar–mid-Oct, 10am-3pm mid-Oct–mid-Mar) looks at the order Chiroptera both at home and abroad.

The Mecsek Hills are well connected by bus to Pécs; see the bus timetable for details (p185).

Villány

72 / POP 2450

Some 13km northeast of Siklós and dominated by cone-shaped Mt Szársomlyó (422m) to the west, Villány is a village of vineyards, vines and grapes. It was the site in 1687 of what has become known as the 'second battle of Mohács', a ferocious confrontation in which the Turks got their comeuppance and were driven southward by the Hungarians and slaughtered in the Dráva marshes. Serbs and Swabians moved in after the occupation and viticulture resumed. Today Villány is one of Hungary's principal producers of wine. And from the looks of the buildings in the village centre, it's surviving very nicely on plonk, thank you very much.

The best time to visit is during the September harvest, when the town is a hive of activity. Human chains pass buckets of almost black grapes from trucks to big machines that chew off the vines, reduce the fruit to a soggy mass and pump the must – the unfermented grape juice – into enormous casks.

Sights & Activities

FREE **Wine Museum** MUSEUM

(Bormúzeum; 492 130; Bem József utca 8; 9am-5pm Tue-Sun) The Wine Museum, housed in a 200-year-old tithe cellar, has a collection of 19th-century wine-producing equipment, such as barrels and hand corkers. Downstairs in the cellars, Villány's celebrated wines age in enormous casks, and vintage bottles dating from 1895 to 1971 are kept in safes. There's a small shop at the entrance selling Villány and Siklós wines.

Wine Cellars WINERY

(Baross Gábor utca south of the Wine Museum, Batthyány utca 15; tastes 400-1200Ft; 10am-6pm) You can sample wines in many of the family cellars that line Baross Gábor utca – some of the best to try are **Pólya** (No 58), **Szende** (No 87), **Fritsch** (Baross Gábor utca 97) and **Blum** (No 103); **Bock** (Batthyány itca 15) is around the corner from Blum. Consistent opening hours make this is a lovely way to sample wines of the area.

Villánykövesd Cellars WINERY

(Petőfi út; tastes 400-1200Ft) Wine cellars cut directly into the loess soil at Villánykövesd, about 3.5km northwest of Villány along the road to Pécs. Cellars line the main road and the narrow lane (Pincesor) above it; most of those open to the public are along the latter. On Petőfi út, try Pinnyó at No 35 or the deep Polgár cellar at No 51. On Pincesor, Blum is at No 4-5, while Schwarzwalter is at No 16. In between, at No 13-15, is the cellar of master vintner Imre Tiffán. The cellars keep odd hours, so it's a hit-or-miss proposition.

Sleeping

Kővári GUESTHOUSE €

(492 117; Rákóczi utca 25; per person 4000Ft; P) This small pension is more like Grandma's big, rambling house in the countryside, with oil heating stoves and old, mismatched furniture, where guests are assured of a warm, hearty welcome. Everything is spotlessly clean and there's a huge garden out the back.

Cabernet HOTEL €€

(493 200; www.hotelcabernet.hu; Petőfi utca 29; s 12,000-15,000Ft, d 15,000-18,000Ft, tr 19,500-24,000Ft; P@) This appropriately named hotel in Villánykövesd is worth considering if you really want to plonk (sorry) yourself in the heart of the wine area. It has basic rooms (some with balconies), a restaurant and offers wine tastings. There are discounts of 5% to 10% for stays of two nights or longer.

TOP CHOICE **Crocus Gere Bor Hotel** RESORT €€€

(492 195; www.gere.hu; Diófás tér 4-12; s/d/ste from 22,000/29,000/35,000Ft; P) If you're keen to indulge yourself silly, you shouldn't miss the chance to stay at this self-proclaimed wine and wellness centre run by Gere Attila, one of the region's foremost winemakers. Rooms are all ample and luxurious – some feature exposed brick and views over the vines, others exude warm tones but have more of a business-hotel vibe. There's a peaceful garden to laze around in and the full-service spa offers standard treatments with a nod to the region (think wine-infused scrubs and potions to make your skin happy and healthy). A slew of ever-changing packages mixing wine tastings, special wine-pairing dinners, winery visits and spa treatments (see the website) make this one of the best ways to experience the area. It also holds one of the best restaurants in town, the Mandula.

Eating

Oportó HUNGARIAN €

(☎492 582; Baross Gábor utca 33; starters 900-1150Ft, mains 1200-2400Ft; ⏰10am-10pm) Villány's most central restaurant, Oportó is huge, has an inviting, vine-covered terrace and a great selection of local wines.

Júlia HUNGARIAN €€

(☎702 610; Baross Gábor utca 73/b; mains 1690-2900Ft; ⏰noon-10pm Thu-Sun) This intimate little restaurant serves excellent veal *pörkölt* (stew) and has wine tastings.

TOP CHOICE **Mandula** INTERNATIONAL €€€

(☎490 952; www.gere.hu; Diófás tér 4-12; mains 6000-9000Ft, 6-course menu with matching wines 14,900Ft) Oenophile and foodie alert: this is *the* place to book an extravagant belt-challenging wine extravaganza. Like the Crocus Gere Bor Hotel it is located in, Mandula is run by Gere Attila, one of the area's most prominent and well-respected winemakes. The fine-dining restaurant serves high-end international and Swabian (southern German) fare with inventive twists on Hungarian basics in an elegant but unpretentious wood-panelled space along with some of the best wine in these parts, of course. A la carte options are divine, but for a dose of it all go for the seasonal six-course, two-hour degustation menus. Reserve early to avoid disappointment.

Information

Villány-Siklós Wine Route Association (☎492 181; www.borut.hu; Deák Ferenc utca 22; ⏰8am-4pm Mon-Fri) Friendly wine tourism office that produces the handy *Villány Siklós Wine Route* booklet, covering places to buy and sample local wines in the region, and organises tours. It's 250m north of the town hall and bus stop.

Getting There & Around

There are one or two buses daily to Pécs (1120Ft, 1½ hours, 52km), and seven or eight to Siklós (310Ft, 20 minutes, 14km) and Harkány (370Ft, 30 to 40 minutes, 18km). Villánykövesd (250Ft, 10 minutes, 3.5km) can be reached between four and eight times daily on weekdays but only twice daily on Saturday. Trains run east to Mohács (465Ft, 25 minutes, 24km, up to seven daily) and north to Pécs (745Ft, 45 minutes, 36km, up to nine daily).

You can also make a booking for a **taxi** (☎06 30 335 5495).

Siklós

☎72 / POP 9,730

Until recently, the medieval fortress at Siklós, Hungary's southernmost town, was the longest continuously inhabited castle in the country. But Siklós hardly needs superlatives to delight. Protected from the north, east and west by the Villány Hills, it has been making wine (mostly white) since the Romans settled here. Siklós is also close to Villány, famed for its big red wines, and a hop, skip and a jump to the spa centre at Harkány. But come here for the castle, period, and save the wine tasting for Villány (p186) and the cellars at Villánykövesd.

Sights

TOP CHOICE **Siklós Castle** CASTLE

(Vár körút; ☎579 501; adult/student/child 1500/750/700Ft; ⏰9am-6pm Apr-Oct, 10am-4pm Nov-Mar, closed Mon) Though the original foundations of the castle date back to 1249, what you see when you look up from the town is an 18th-century baroque palace, girdled by 15th-century walls and bastions. Reach it either from Kossuth tér via Batthyány Kázmér utca, or up Váralja utca from the bus station on Szent István tér.

The entrance is at the red-brick barbican, topped with loopholes and a circular lookout. It leads to the Castle Museum (Vármúzeum) in the south wing. To the right as you enter the main door is an unusual exhibit devoted to the manufacture and changing styles of gloves, fans and umbrellas since the Middle Ages. The exhibit's emphasis is very much on the Hamerli and Hunor factories at Pécs, which produced some of Europe's finest kid gloves in the 19th century. The woman's mourning outfit from the 1870s, complete with black feather fan, is stylishly sombre. The cellar contains Gothic and Renaissance stone fragments from the castle. Most of the 1st floor is given over to the history of the castle; don't miss the wonderful Sigismund Hall (Zsigmond terem), with its Renaissance fireplace and enclosed balcony with star vaulting and fresco fragments. There's a gallery of modern art on the 2nd floor.

To the right of the museum entrance, two doors lead to the dark and spooky cells – a real dungeon if ever there was one. The walls here are several metres thick, and up to five grilles on the window slits

WORTH A TRIP

HARKANY'S THERMAL BATHS

It's a wonder that no statue stands in honour of János Pogány in Harkany, a spa town 6km west of Siklós. He was the well-digger from nearby Máriagyűd who cured himself of swollen joints in 1823 by soaking in a hot spring he had discovered here. Wealthy landowners recognised the potential almost immediately and the following year bathing huts were erected near the 62°C spring, which has the richest sulphuric content in Hungary. Today, aside from Pécs, no town in Baranya County brings in as much money as Harkány.

Of course, all that means crowds (now topping over a million visitors per year) and stalls selling *lángos* (deep-fried dough topped with cheese and sour cream) in spades and an all-pervasive stench of rotten eggs. But locals and visitors flock to Harkány to socialise; it's not as brash or tacky like some other spa towns, but a chance to soak your muscles among a friendly crowd.

The main entrance to Harkány's **thermals baths** (Gyógyfürdő; ☎72-480 251; www.harkanyfurdo.hu; Kossuth utca 7; adult/student day ticket 2900/2200Ft, week ticket 17,400/13,200Ft; ⏲9am-6pm) and **outside pools** (adult/student 1320/1000Ft; ⏲9am-6pm, to 10pm Jul & Aug), which are meant to cure just about every ailment under the sun (but especially locomotive disorders, gynaecological problems and psoriasis), is on Bajcsy-Zsilinszky utca. The services here range from mud cures and water-jet massages to an enticing 'winous foam bath', but it's just as enjoyable to swim in the 38°C outdoor pool, especially in cool weather.

Four streets (Bartók Béla utca to the north, Ady Endre utca to the south, Kossuth Lajos utca, with several restaurants, to the west and Bajcsy-Zsilinszky utca, with most of the hotels and the bus station, to the east) surround the thermal complex, which essentially domintaes Gyógyfürdő, a 13.5-hectare green square filled with the pools plus fountains, grassy 'beaches' and walkways.

Once- or twice-hourly buses to Harkany depart from Pécs (1120Ft, 1½ hours, 52km) and Siklós (250Ft, 10 minutes, 6km).

discouraged would-be escapees. Woodcuts on the walls of the upper dungeon explain how the various torture devices on display were used – there's a great emphasis on impaling – but even scarier is the bold Russian graffiti dating back to the 1970s, when all was right with the Soviet world. After this the Gothic Chapel of St John of Capistrano (Kapisztrán Szent János kápolna) is a vision of heaven itself, with its brilliant arched windows behind the altar, web vaulting on the ceiling and 15th-century frescoed niches.

On the northern side of the courtyard is a hunting exhibit featuring lots of heads and antlers on walls. Stairs lead to the castle terrace, with fine views of the Villány Hills and the towers to the north and east. Also be sure to check out the small statue of Dorottya Kanizsai that stands on the moat; she was the heroic noblewoman who presided over the burial of the dead at the battle at Mohács.

Franciscan Church CHURCH
(Vajda János 2, south of Siklós castle; ⏲10am-6pm) The 15th-century Gothic Franciscan church, rebuilt after the Turks were driven out, contains lovely 13th-century frescoes on the interior walls including religious imagery and the coat of arms of the Garai family (who had control over this area in the late 12th and early 13th century). Opening times can be unpredictable.

Malkocs Bej Mosque MOSQUE
(Malkocs bej dzsámija; ☎579 279; Vörösmarty utca 14; adult/child 350/250Ft; ⏲10am-noon & 1.30-6pm Tue-Sun May-Sep) Beyond the town hall is the restored 16th-century Malkocs Bej Mosque housing Turkish-era elements (carpets, ornate housewares) and temporary exhibits.

Sleeping & Eating

Accommodation and food options here are extremely thin on the ground, but **Tourinform** (☎579 090; siklos@tourinform.hu; Vajda János tér 8; ⏲9am-5pm Mon-Fri year-round, plus 10am-7pm Sat & Sun Jun-Aug) has a small list of private rooms (per person from 3000Ft).

Hotel Agora HOTEL €€
(☎352 513; www.agorasiklos.hu; Kossuth tér 5; s 9000-10,000Ft, d 14,000-17,000Ft; P❄@📶🐾) Smack in the center of Siklós, the Hotel Agora recently changed owners and has been given a facelift – no, rooms are not overly interesting but new carpets and beds plus excellent service and a top location make this the only viable hotel option in town. There's also a sauna, Jacuzzi and fitness room.

Agora Hotel Restaurant HUNGARIAN €€
(☎352 513; www.agorasiklos.hu; Kossuth tér 5; mains 1350-2250Ft; ⏰11am-10pm) The only real restaurant in town serves solid Hungarian staples and is one of just a few places to eat in the town centre – in warmer months opt for the secluded backyard courtyard or people-watch out the front: tables stretch into the main square and it's an excellent, shaded spot to unwind.

Mennyei Rétes CAFE €
(Mária utca 10; strudel from 210Ft; ⏰8am-6pm Mon-Fri, to 1pm Sat) Delightful Mennyei Rétes (note folk motifs decorating the walls) on Siklós' short pedestrian street specialises in *rétes* (strudel).

WORTH A TRIP

ZRÍNYI'S BIG SALLY & SZIGETVÁR'S CASTLE

For more than a month at Szigetvár in late 1566, Captain Miklós Zrínyi and the 2500 Hungarian and Croatian soldiers under his command held out against Turkish forces numbering up to 80,000. The leader of the Turks was Sultan Suleiman I, who was making his seventh attempt to march on Vienna and was determined to take what he derisively called 'this molehill' of Szigetvár. On 7 September, when the defenders' water and food supplies were exhausted – and Habsburg Emperor Maximilian II had refused reinforcements from Győr – Zrínyi could see no other solution but a suicidal sally. As the moated castle went up in flames, the opponents fought hand to hand, and most of the remaining 200 soldiers on the Hungarian side, including Zrínyi himself, were killed. An estimated one-quarter of the Turkish forces died in the siege; Suleiman died of a heart attack and his corpse was propped up on a chair during the fighting to inspire his troops and avoid a power struggle until his son could take command.

More than any other heroes in Hungarian history, Zrínyi and his men are remembered for their self-sacrifice in the cause of the nation and for saving Vienna – and thereby Europe – from Turkish domination. *Peril at Sziget*, a 17th-century epic poem by Zrínyi's great-grandson and namesake (himself a brilliant general), immortalises the siege and is still widely read in Hungary.

Tucked away in Szigetvár, a quiet town 40km town south of Kaposvár and 35km west of Pécs, are the remains of what is now called **Zrínyi Castle** (☎311 442; Vár utca; adult/child 800/500Ft; ⏰9am-5pm Tue-Sun May-Sep, to 3pm Apr & Oct). But the hero who so valiantly fought to save it more than 400 years ago probably wouldn't recognise his four-cornered castle today. The Turks strengthened the bastions and added buildings, and the Hungarians rebuilt much of the castle again in the 18th century. Today there are only a few elements of its architectural beginnings left, but its remaining shell is an enjoyable wander: walls from up to 6m thick are linked by four bastions; the square Baroque Tower crowns the southern wall; the 16th-century Sultan Suleiman Mosque (Szulejmán pasa dzsámija), with its truncated minaret, scream photo-op; and, attached to it, a summer mansion built by Count Andrássy in 1930 now houses the Castle Museum (Vár Múzeum).

Naturally, the museum's exhibits focus on the siege and its key players: Zrínyi's praises are sung throughout and there's a detailed account of how Suleiman built a bridge over the Dráva River in 16 days to attack Szigetvár. The mock-ups of the battle, especially the Turkish encampment (complete with carpets), are quite effective. The mosque, completed in the year of the siege, contains an art gallery of little interest, but the arches, prayer niches and Arabic inscriptions on the walls are worth a look. At the entrance to the castle is a statue of the impish-looking Sebestyén Tinódi, the beloved 16th-century poet and wandering minstrel who was born in Szigetvár.

Szigetvár has excellent bus connections to Pécs (650Ft, 45 minutes, 35km, eight to 10 daily) and Kaposvár (745Ft, 1¼ hours, 40km, two to seven daily) and is on the train line from Pécs (650Ft, 45 to 50 minutes, 34km).

Egerszegi CAFE €
(☎351 226; Felszabadulás utca 22-24; cakes from 200Ft; ⊙9am-9pm) Situated on a quiet leafy pedestrian street, Egerszegi is a stylish cake shop and cafe with a wonderful selection of sweet things.

Borozó WINE BAR €
(☎06 20 566 9131; Felszabadulás utca 7; small plates 800-1200Ft, mains 1600-2100Ft; ⊙2-8pm Tue-Sun) Borozó (wine bar in Hungarian) is a retro-style wine bar-cum-bistro that has it all: enjoy local tipples served by knowledgeable staff who go out of their way to guide you through the wine list, nibble on small plates (sausage, cheese, olives) or feast on hearty Hungarian dishes. Note the early closing hours.

Getting There & Away

Generally you won't wait more than 30 minutes for buses to Pécs (1120Ft, 45 minutes, 55km) or Harkány (250Ft, 10 minutes, 5km); hourly buses leave for Villány (310Ft, 20 minutes, 14km). For Mohács (1120Ft, 1½ hours, 55km), count on between three and seven buses daily.

Kaposvár

☎82 / POP 67,980

Situated in the Zselic foothills along the valley of the Kapos River, Kaposvár is, at its core, an attractive city. But don't come to 'Kapos Castle' looking for a fortress like the one at Siklós or Szigetvár; the Turks and then the Habsburgs dispatched that long ago. Instead, visit Kaposvár for its art (the city is associated with four great painters: the post-Impressionists József Rippl-Rónai and János Vaszary, as well as Aurél Bernáth and Ferenc Martyn) and the Gergely Csiky Theatre, among the best in provincial Hungary.

In among the pretty, pastel-coloured buildings lining Fő utca is the former county hall (1820) at No 10, which now houses the **Somogy County Museum** (Rippl-Rónai Museum; ☎314 114; www.smmi.hu; adult/child 450/250Ft; ⊙10am-4pm, closed Mon), where you'll find two sections: the county museum houses a large ethnographical collection and a gallery of contemporary art on the ground floor. There is a grand collection of paintings on the 1st floor, which includes works by Vaszary, Bernáth and Béla Kádár.

The folk collection is noteworthy for its wood and horn carvings (at which the swineherds of Somogy County excelled); examples of famous *kékfestő* (indigo-dyed cotton fabrics); an exhibition on the county's infamous outlaws (including the paprika-tempered 'Horseshoe Steve'); and costumes of the Croatian minority, who dressed and decorated their houses in white fabric during mourning periods as the Chinese do. The top floor, otherwise known as the Rippl-Rónai Museum, is full of paintings by Ödön Rippl-Rónai, the brother of Kaposvár's most celebrated – and arguably Hungary's best – painter, József Rippl-Rónai (1861–1927).

József Rippl-Rónai was born at Fő utca 19, above the lovely **Golden Lion Pharmacy** (Aranyoroszlán Patika; Fő utca 19; ⊙7.30am-6pm Mon-Fri), built in 1774. Most of his work is exhibited in the **Rippl-Rónai Memorial Museum** (Rippl-Rónai Emlékmúzeum; ☎422 144; Róma-hegy 88; adult/child 500/250Ft; ⊙10am-6pm, closed Mon), a graceful 19th-century villa about 3km southeast of the city centre.

Built in 1911, the cream- and lemon-coloured Secessionist **Gergely Csiky Theatre** (☎528 450; Rákóczi tér 2), with its hundreds of arched windows, is worth admiring from the outside even if you are not attending a performance.

Check out Kaposvár's **City of Painters Festival** (Festők Városa Hangulatfesztivál), which plays and preys on the town's nickname with dozens of graphic art exhibitions, held in early June, or the mid-October **Kapos Autumn Days** (Kaposi Őszi Napok), a convivial barrel of fun that celebrates the local Zselic grape vintage with – you guessed it – lots of stalls selling wine (surrounded by lots and lots of smiles). It's a great way to taste regional wines shoulder-to-shoulder with the locals and sip to your heart's content. The **Tourinform** (☎512 921; www.tourinformkaposvar.hu; Fő utca 8; ⊙9am-6pm Mon-Fri, to 5pm Sat, to 2pm Sun mid-Jun–Aug, reduced hours rest of the year) website has more information.

The town is an easy day trip by bus from Pécs (1300Ft, 1½ hours, 65km).

Szekszárd

☎74 / POP 35,200

The wine-producing city of Szekszárd lies south of the Sió River, which links Lake Balaton with the Danube, among seven of

THE OPEN-AIR ETHNOGRAPHICAL COLLECTION

The smallest but one of the best *skanzens* (open-air museums of folk architecture) in the country is housed in the **Open-Air Ethnographical Collection** (Szabadtéri néprajzi gyűtemény; ☎484 223; Rákóczi utca 2, Szenna; adult/student & child 700/350Ft; ⏰10am-6pm, closed Mon). What makes it unique is that its centrepiece, the large 18th-century Calvinist church (1815), with its 'crowned' pulpit, coffered and painted ceiling, loft and pews, still functions as a house of worship for villagers.

Half a dozen *porták* (farmhouses with outbuildings) from central Somogy County and the Zselic region surround the 'folk baroque' church – as they would in a real village – and the caretaker will point out the most interesting details: the 'smoke' kitchens with stable doors; the woven-wall construction of the stables and barns; lumps of sugar suspended from the ceiling to soothe irritable children (bread soaked in the Hungarian fruit brandy *pálinka* was given to the particularly pesky); a coop atop the pigsty to keep the chickens warm in winter; and ingenious wooden locks 'so secure that even God couldn't get in'.

The museum is located in Szenna, a 9km bus ride southwest of Kaposvár (250Ft, 20 minutes, up to a dozen daily).

the Szekszárd Hills. It is the centre of the Sárköz folk region, but more than anything else Szekszárd is the gateway to Southern Transdanubia. In fact, you can actually see the region start in the town's main square (Garay tér), where the Great Plain, having crossed the Danube, rises slowly, transforming into the Szekszárd Hills.

Mild winters and warm, dry summers combined with favourable soil help Szekszárd produce some of the best red wines in Hungary. The premier grape here is the Kadarka, a late-ripening and vulnerable varietal that is produced in limited quantities.

History

Szekszárd was a Celtic and later a Roman settlement called Alisca. The sixth Hungarian king, Béla I, conferred royal status on the town and founded a Benedictine abbey here in 1061. The Turkish occupation left Szekszárd deserted, but the area was repopulated late in the 17th century by immigrant Swabians from Germany, and the economy was revitalised in the next century by wheat cultivation and viticulture.

Sights

County Hall HISTORIC BUILDING
(vármegyeháza; ☎419 667; Béla tér 1; adult/student & child 450/250Ft; ⏰9am-5pm, closed Mon) The neoclassical county hall, designed by Mihály Pollack in 1828, sits on the site of Béla's abbey and an earlier Christian chapel; you can see the excavated foundations in the central courtyard. Upstairs is the Franz Liszt Memorial Room and across the hallway is the Eszter Mattioni Gallery, where works in striking mosaics invoke peasant themes with a twist.

Inner City Catholic Church CHURCH
(Belvárosi templom; Béla ter 9) The yellow baroque church (1805) on the main square is the largest single-nave church in Hungary.

Augusz House HISTORIC BUILDING
(Széchenyi utca 36-40) Admire the eye-catching neo-Gothic Augusz House (Liszt stayed and performed here several times in the late 19th century when it was the Black Elephant Inn; today it houses a music school).

Deutsche Bühne Ungarn THEATRE
(Német Színház Magyarország; ☎316 533; www.dbu.hu; Garay tér 4) This 1913 German theatre stages performances *auf Deutsch* but it's worth strolling past to simply look at its delightful Romantic-style elements.

Mihály Babits Memorial House MUSEUM
(Babits Mihály emlékház; ☎312 154; Babits Mihály utca 13; adult/student & child 500/300Ft; ⏰9am-5pm, closed Mon) One of Hungary's most celebrated poets, Mihály Babits (1883–1941) wrote avant-garde, deeply philosophical verse that may be obscure (even in Hungarian), but this house where he was born is a good place to see how a middle-class family lived in 19th-century provincial Hungary.

Calvary Hill HISTORIC SITE
For a great view over Szekszárd and its surrounds, follow Munkácsy Mihály utca and then Kálvária utca from the Tourinform

(p193) office southwest until you reach Calvary Hill (Kálvária-hegy; 205m). Its name recalls the crucifixion scene and the chapel was erected here in the 18th century by grief-stricken parents who lost their child (still remembered in a famous poem by Mihály Babits). The Danube and the Great Plain are visible to the east, the Sárköz region beyond the hills to the south and the Szekszárd Hills to the west. On a clear day you can see Hungary's sole nuclear power station at Paks, 30km to the north.

Today the hill is dominated by a modern sculpture, done by István Kiss for the city's 925th anniversary. It looked fine and unassuming when unveiled in 1986 – just a stylised bunch of grapes representing Szekszárd's lovely wine, sheaves for its wheat and a large bell for Béla's 11th-century abbey. But on closer inspection, the inscriptions on the grape leaves revealed not just the names of Hungarian heroes and literary greats but those of local communist officials.

Mór Wosinszky County Museum MUSEUM
(☎316 222; Szent István tér 26; adult/student & child 500/300Ft; ⏰10am-5pm, closed Mon) This museum, purpose-built in 1895, contains objects left behind by some of the various peoples who passed through the Danube Basin ahead of the Magyars. Don't miss the fine Celtic and Avar jewellery and the large folk collection of Serbian, Swabian and Sárköz artefacts. Three period rooms – that of a well-to-do Sárköz farming family and their coveted spotted-poplar furniture, another from the estate of the aristocratic Apponyi family of Lengyel, and a poor gooseherd's hut – illustrate very clearly the different economic brackets that existed side by side in the region a century ago. Also interesting are the exhibits related to the silk factory that was started in Szekszárd in the 19th century with Italian help and employed so many of the region's young women.

House of Arts MUSEUM, CONCERT VENUE
(Művészetek Háza; ☎511 247; Szent István tér 28; ⏰10am-6pm, closed Mon) The Moorish flourishes of the House of Arts reveals its former life as a synagogue, but these days it's a gallery and concert hall. Four of its original iron pillars have been placed outside and enclosed in an arch, suggesting the tablets of the Ten Commandments.

Festivals & Events

Among the events staged annually in Szekszárd is the one-day late-June **Wine and Strings Festival** (County Hall), a lucious sip-and-listen event with free guitar concerts all afternoon (and plenty of local wine on offer), and the late-September **Harvest Festival** (www.szekszardiszuretinapok.hu), where much wine quaffing is accompanied by folk music and plenty of stalls selling local embroidery, handicrafts and snacks.

Sleeping

Korona Hotel PENSION €€
(☎529 160; hotelkorona.mindenkilapja.hu/; Fáy András utca 2; s/d/tr 12,000/17,000/23,000Ft; P ❄) Typical of many family-owned places to rest your head, this basic pension offers simple but spotless rooms above a Hungarian restaurant with plenty of local wine gracing the menu (of course). Bonus points are the 24-hour reception and extremely helpful staff who will arrange excursions and offer stacks of local tips.

Hotel Zodiaco HOTEL €€
(☎511 150; www.hotelzodiaco.hu/; Szent László utca 19; s/d/tr 13,000/18,000/24,000Ft; ❄@📶) No prizes for guessing that this hotel sports an astrological theme – each room is named after a Zodiac sign. It's by far the best midrange place in town and the owners have made an effort to make the rooms more cheerful than your usual basic midrange Hungarian hotel with thick duvets and plenty of bright blue colours. The large, 2nd-floor rooms 'parade' themselves around the inner courtyard of a bizarre modern block.

Eating & Drinking

Főispán HUNGARIAN €€
(☎06 30 746 2824, 312 139; Béla tér 1; mains 1400-2650Ft; ⏰11am-11pm Mon-Thu, 11.30am-midnight Fri & Sat, 11.30am-9pm Sun) Housed in a renovated wine cellar, Főispán is an atmospheric option, with a small but interesting collection of assorted wine-making implements.

TOP CHOICE **Arany Kulacs** INTERNATIONAL €€€
(☎413 369; Nefelejcs köz 3; mains 1900-4800Ft; ⏰noon-midnight) For fine dining and even finer wine, head for the 'Golden Flask', probably the best restaurant in Szekszárd. Once there, choose the outside terrace with

partial views of the town, or the cellar-like surroundings inside.

TOP CHOICE **Garay Pince** WINE BAR
(412 828; Garay tér 19; 9am-5pm Mon-Fri, 9am-2pm Sat) Sample the local vintages and munch on small plates.

Information

Tourinform (315 198; szekszard@tourinform.hu; Béla tér 7; 9am-5pm, closed Sun) Information on the town and Tolna County.

Getting There & Away

Bus

There are up to a dozen daily departures to Budapest (2830Ft, three hours, 154km) and Pécs (1680Ft, 1½ hours, 88km). At least five daily buses leave for Baja (840Ft, one hour, 41km) and Mohács (930Ft, one hour, 49km).

Train

Two direct trains leave Budapest's Déli train station daily for Szekszárd (2350Ft, three hours, 149km). To travel east (to Baja), west (to Kaposvár) or south (to Pécs) you must change trains at Bátaszék, 20km to the south.

Around Szekszárd

SÁRKÖZ REGION

The folkloric region of Sárköz, the centre of folk weaving in Hungary, consists of five towns southeast of Szekszárd between Rte 56 and the Danube, including **Öcsény** (population 2380) and **Decs** (population 4100), with its high-walled cottages, late Gothic Calvinist church and folk houses.

WORTH A TRIP

GEMENC FOREST

The Gemenc, an 18,000-hectare flood forest of poplars, willows, oxbow lakes and dikes 8km east of Szekszárd, is part of Duna-Drava National Park. Until engineers removed some 60 curves in the Danube in the mid-19th century, the Gemenc would flood to such a degree that the women of the Sárköz region would come to the market in Szekszárd by boat.

Today the backwaters, lakes and ponds beyond the earthen dams, which were built by wealthy landowners to protect their farms, offer sanctuary to black storks, white-tailed eagles, herons, kingfishers and woodpeckers, as well as game animals like red deer and boar. Hunting is restricted to certain areas; for information contact the Budapest-based **Hungarian National Hunting Protection Association** (OMVV; 06 30 239 4659, 1-355 6180; www.vadaszati vedegylet.hu; II Medve utca 34-40)

The main entrance is at the **Gemenc Excursion Centre** (74-312 552; Gemenci Kiránduló Központ; carriage rides adult/child from 1300/800Ft; 9am-5pm) in Bárányfok, about halfway down Keselyűsi út between Szekszárd and the forest. It offers activities such as horse carriage rides and can supply you with a map of walking and cycling trails through the forest. (Keselyűsi út was once the longest stretch of covered highway in the Austro-Hungarian Empire, and in the late 19th century mulberry trees were planted along it to feed the worms at the silk factory in Szekszárd.)

A **narrow-gauge forest train** (one way adult 1100-2200Ft, child 750-1750Ft; late Apr-late Sep), that once carried wood out of the Gemenc Forest, is a fun – but difficult – way to go. The train runs several routes and timetables change frequently: from Bárányfok to Pörböly, some 30km to the south, via Keselyűs. Two other trains go only as far as the Gemenc Dunapart 11km south, where you'll need to change trains for Pörböly.

At the time of writing departures were as follows, but it's a good idea to double-check the times by phone with Tourinform (p193) in Szekszárd before you set out. From Pörböly, a train leaves at 8.35am to Bárányfok. Two other trains leave at 9.30am, 11.25am and 1.35pm, but they go only as far as the Gemenc Dunapart, where you can make connections to Bárányfok. The abridged trip in itself is worthwhile and the best of the bunch, weaving and looping around the Danube's remaining bends.

Buses run between Szekszárd and Bárányfok (310Ft, 23 minutes, 12km, five or six daily), Pörböly (560Ft, 25 to 45 minutes, 28km, eight to 10 daily) and Keselyűs (310Ft, 23 minutes, 13km, four to six daily). The same local buses bound for Keselyűs will drop you off near the Gemenc Excursion Centre in Bárányfok.

The Sárköz became a very rich area after flooding was brought under control in the mid-19th century. In a bid to protect their wealth and land, most families had only one child. Judging from the displays at the **Regional & Artisan House** (Tájház és Kézművesház; ☎06 30 360 2127, 74-495 414; Kossuth utca 34-36; adult/child 200/100Ft; ⏰9am-noon & 1-5pm Tue-Sat), located in a peasant house in Decs, these families spent a lot of their money on lavish interior decoration and some of the most ornate (and Balkan-looking) embroidered folk clothing in Hungary. Don't miss the ingenious porcelain 'stove with eyes' (concave circles) to radiate more heat. The house was built in 1836 from earth and woven twigs, so that when the floods came only the mud had to be replaced.

Elsewhere in the Sárköz, be on the lookout for local pottery decorated with birds, the distinctive black-and-red striped woven fabric so common that it was once used as mosquito netting in this bug-infested region, and the unique *írókázás fazékok* (inscribed pots), usually made as wedding gifts.

Up to 10 buses daily head from Szekszárd for Őcsény (250Ft, 12 minutes, 8km), while departures to Decs (310Ft, 20 minutes, 12km, three to eight daily) are less frequent. Őcsény (250Ft, seven minutes, 4km) and Decs (250Ft, 15 minutes, 8km) are also on the train line from Szekszárd to Bátaszék.

Mohács

☎69 / POP 18,880

Mohács is a sleepy little port on the Danube that wakes up only during the annual **Busójárás festival** (⏰late February or March, procession Sunday before Ash Wednesday), a pre-Lenten free-for-all carnival celebration where men adorned with freakish, horned wooden masks (busós) parade through town to scare off winter and welcome spring. But history buffs won't want to give this place a miss: it's a must-do for its significant role in Hungarian history.

The defeat of the ragtag Hungarian army by the Turks at Mohács on 29 August 1526 was a watershed in the nation's history, and with it came partition and foreign domination that would last almost five centuries. It is not hyperbole to say that the effects of the battle at Mohács can still be felt in Hungary even now. You'll get the full scoop 6km southwest of town at the **Mohács Historical Memorial Site** (Mohácsi Történelmi Emlékhely; ☎06 20 918 2779, 382 130; 1km off route 56; adult/child 1500/1200Ft; ⏰9am-6pm late Mar-early Nov) at Sátorhely (literally 'encampment'). Originally opened in 1976 to mark the 450th anniversary of the Mohács battle, it's a fitting memorial to the dead over a common grave that was only discovered in the early 1970s. The visitor centre allows you to gain insight into the line of battle through clever images of the battle projected on the walls, a section with archaelogical remains and three educational films geared to different age groups (adults, kids and small children roughly under seven). Outside, scores of carved wooden markers in the shape of bows, arrows, lances and crosses lean this way and that and represent the defeated Hungarians. Those topped with turbans, crescents and scimitars and standing bolt upright are the Turks. The subterranean entrance leads to a circular courtyard with 10 panels with (somewhat one-sided) explanations in English. 'Here began the ruination of a once strong Hungary' proclaims one.

Beyond the memorial, the actual town boasts two lovely museums: the **Dorottya Kanizsai Museum** (☎311 536; Városház utca 1; adult/child 300/150Ft; ⏰10am-3pm Tue-Sat Apr-Oct) has a large collection of costumes worn by the Sokác, Slovenes, Serbs, Croats, Bosnians and Swabians who repopulated this devastated area in the 17th century. The distinctive grey-black pottery of Mohács also figures. More interesting is the surprisingly well-balanced exhibit devoted to the 1526 battle, with both sides getting the chance to tell their side of the story. And if you can't make the festival just before Lent, **Busóház** (☎06 20 331 3671, 302 677; Kossuth Lajos utca 54; adult/child 300/200Ft; ⏰9am-5pm Mon-Fri, to noon Sat) is the place to come: it tells the story of the Busójárás festival, from its origins as a South Slav spring rite to a fancy-dress mummery directed at the erstwhile enemy, the Turks. The horrifying devil's and ram's-head masks are on frightening display.

Last but not least, Mohács is an excellent place to start exploring the Mohács-Bóly White Wine Route. Ask for the leaflet at the local **Tourinform** (☎505 515; mohacs@tourinform.hu; Széchenyi tér 1; ⏰7.30am-5pm

Mon-Fri, 8am-5pm Sat & Sun mid-Jun–mid-Sep, 8am-4pm Mon-Fri, 8am-4.30 Mon-Fri mid-Sep–mid-Jun), located in the Moorish Town Hall in the center of town; it pinpoints about a dozen villages in the area where you can sample the local drop.

Bus services from Mohács aren't as frequent as other towns, but to Pécs (1120Ft, 1¼ hours, 48km) and Baja (745Ft, 1¼ hours, 39km) they leave almost hourly. Other destinations include Villány (840Ft, one hour, 42km, three to six daily), Siklós (1120Ft, 1½ hours, 55km, three to seven daily), Harkány (1300Ft, 1½ hours, 66km, five to eight daily) and Szekszárd (930Ft, one hour, 49km, five to seven daily).

The Great Plain & Northeast Hungary

Includes »

Why Go?

Like the Outback for Australians or the Wild West for Americans, the Nagyalföld (Great Plain) holds a romantic appeal for Hungarians. Many of these notions come as much from the collective imagination as they do from history, but there's no arguing the spellbinding potential of big-sky country, especially around Hortobágy and Kiskunság National Parks. The Great Plain is home to cities of graceful architecture and history. Szeged is a centre of art and culture, Kecskemét full of Art Nouveau gems and Debrecen is the 'Calvinist Rome'.

By contrast, if you want to experience village life – steeped in folk culture, replete with dirt roads, horse-drawn carts and tiny wooden churches – Northeast Hungary is the place to go. The best way to explore is to hire a car, motorbike or bicycle and head out from the capital, Nyíregyháza, a spa town with all the creature comforts.

Best Places to Eat

» Ikon (p205)
» Hortobágyi Csárda (p208)
» Cézár (p215)
» Százéves Cukrászda (p227)
» Igrice Csárda (p231)

Best Places to Stay

» Centrum Panzió (p204)
» Fábián Panzió (p214)
» Elizabeth Hotel (p227)
» Dóm Hotel (p223)
» Hotel Hódi (p233)

When to Go

Szolnok

°C/°F Temp | Rainfall inches/mm
30/86, 20/68, 10/50, 0/32, -10/14 | 6/150, 4/100, 2/50, 0
J F M A M J J A S O N D

Apr–May Wet, maybe, but spring is glorious, with grasslands coming to life and everything in flower

Jul–Aug Warm on the *puszta* (plain) but this is the time for outdoor pursuits and Debrecen's festivals

Sep–Oct Excellent bird-watching in the Hortobágy while the Northeast dons its autumnal colours

THE GREAT PLAIN

The Great Plain – also known as the *puszta* ('deserted' or 'abandoned') – covers some 45,000 sq km, encompassing half the nation's territory but only about a third of the population. The Central Plain, the smallest of the Great Plain's three divisions, stretches east-ward from Budapest to the Tisza River. The biggest attraction here is Lake Tisza, Hungary's second-largest lake and a water-lover's paradise.

The Hortobágy region of the Eastern Plain is where the myth of the lonely *pásztor* (shepherd) in billowy trousers, the wayside *csárdák* (inns) and Gypsy violinists was born – kept alive in literature and fine art. The horse and herding show at the national park re-creates this pastoral tradition.

The Southern Plain, spanning the lower regions of the Danube and Tisza Rivers, holds the lion's share of the Great Plain's more intriguing towns and cities, including Kecskemét and Szeged. Bugac, in Kiskunság National Park, is one of the best places in Hungary to learn about life on the plain.

History

Five hundred years ago the Great Plains was not a steppe but forest land at the constant mercy of the flooding Tisza and Danube Rivers. The Turks chopped down most of the trees, destroying the protective cover and releasing the topsoil to the winds; villagers fled north or to the market towns and *khas* (settlements under the sultan's jurisdiction). The region had become the *puszta* and home to shepherds, fisher folk, runaway serfs and outlaws. You'll find few fortifications outside Gyula on the Great Plain; the Turks required they be destroyed as part of the agreement of retreat. In the 19th century regulation of the rivers dried up the marshes and allowed for methodical irrigation, paving the way for intensive agriculture, particularly on the Southern Plain, but flooding still occurs.

Tiszafüred

☎59 / POP 10,800

This may not be the 'Lake Balaton of the Great Plain', as tourist brochures put it, but Lake Tisza (Tisza-tó) on the Central Plain offers outdoors enthusiasts a quiet, laid-back alternative. Few visitors came to town before the 1980s, when they dammed the Tisza River and opened more than 127 sq km of lakes to holiday-makers. Tiszafüred, on the northeastern edge, is recreation central. Bungalows, camping grounds and eateries line the shore; the small town core has little more than a few restaurants.

Sights

Pál Kiss Museum MUSEUM

(☎352 106; www.museum.hu/tiszafured/kisspal; Tariczky sétány 6; adult/child 300/150Ft; ⏲9am-noon & 1-5pm Tue-Sat) Housed in a beautiful old manor (1840) and surrounded by parkland southeast of the Tourinform office, this fine old museum has a collection focusing on the everyday lives of Tisza fisherfolk and the work of local craftspeople, especially potters.

Potters' Houses HISTORIC BUILDING

The area south of the main square (Piac tér) is a patchwork of traditional thatched cottages. One of them houses the **Gáspár Nyúzó House** (Nyúzó Gáspár Fazekas Tájház; ☎352 106; http://www.museum.hu/museum/index_hu.php?ID=460; Malom utca 12; adult/child 300/150Ft; ⏲1-5pm Tue-Sat May-Sep), a former potter's residence with antique potting wheels, drying racks, furniture and plates in pale primary colours and patterns of stars, and birds and flowers unique to the region. In the same district ceramic artist **Zsóka Török Nagyné** (☎06 70 521 4460, 353 538; http://www.tiszafured.hu/info.php?id=55; Szőlősi út 27; ⏲8am-5pm Mon-Fri) has her studio; call ahead before setting out.

Activities

Swimming and sunbathing on the narrow lake's sandy strip are popular activities; the beach is ringed by food stalls, drinks stands and a changing pavilion. If the lake is too cold for you, Tiszafüred's **Thermal Bath** (Tiszafüredi Gyógyfürdő; ☎352 911; www.termalfurdo.net/furdo/tiszafuredi-strand-es-gyogyfurdo-tiszafured; Fürdő utca 2; adult/child 1100/800Ft; ⏲10am-6pm Sun-Fri, noon-8pm Fri & Sun) has four open-air and covered pools, as well as a sauna and a wide range of spa services.

To the west of the beach is a series of boat-rental stands (open 10am to 8pm June to August), where you can get outfitted with a canoe or kayak (per hour 600Ft), paddle boat (per hour 1000Ft) or 5HP motor boat (per hour 4000Ft).

In addition to boat rental both **Albatrosz Kikötő** (☎06 30 234 5108; www.albatroszkikoto.com; Tiszapart) and **Horgászcentrum**

The Great Plain & Northeast Hungary Highlights

1. Go birding in the **Hortobágy** (p206) and sample its namesake meat-filled pancake in a century-old inn
2. Enjoy the Art Nouveau architecture and pretty pedestrian squares of **Kecskemét** (p211)
3. Take to the Tisza in a boat and see **Szeged** (p218) from an entirely new perspective
4. Feel the earth move under your feet as a Hungarian cowboy rides by 'five-in-hand' at the horse show in **Bugac** (p216)
5. Decide how real the Hortobágy portrayed in the work of Mihály Munkácsy is at the Déri Museum in **Debrecen** (p202)
6. Soak in the thermal baths beneath the only castle on the plain at **Gyula** (p226) and enjoy treats at its celebrated Százéves cake shop
7. Visit the evocative town of **Nyírbátor** (p232), steeped in Transylvanian history
8. Try to crack the code on the boat-shaped grave markers at the cemetery in **Szatmárcseke** (p235)
9. Marvel at the patterns of the painted wooden ceiling in the 'peasant's cathedral' at **Tákos** (p235)
10. Immerse yourself in the thoroughly modern Aquarius Adventure Baths before dinner at the lakes in **Nyíregyháza** (p228)

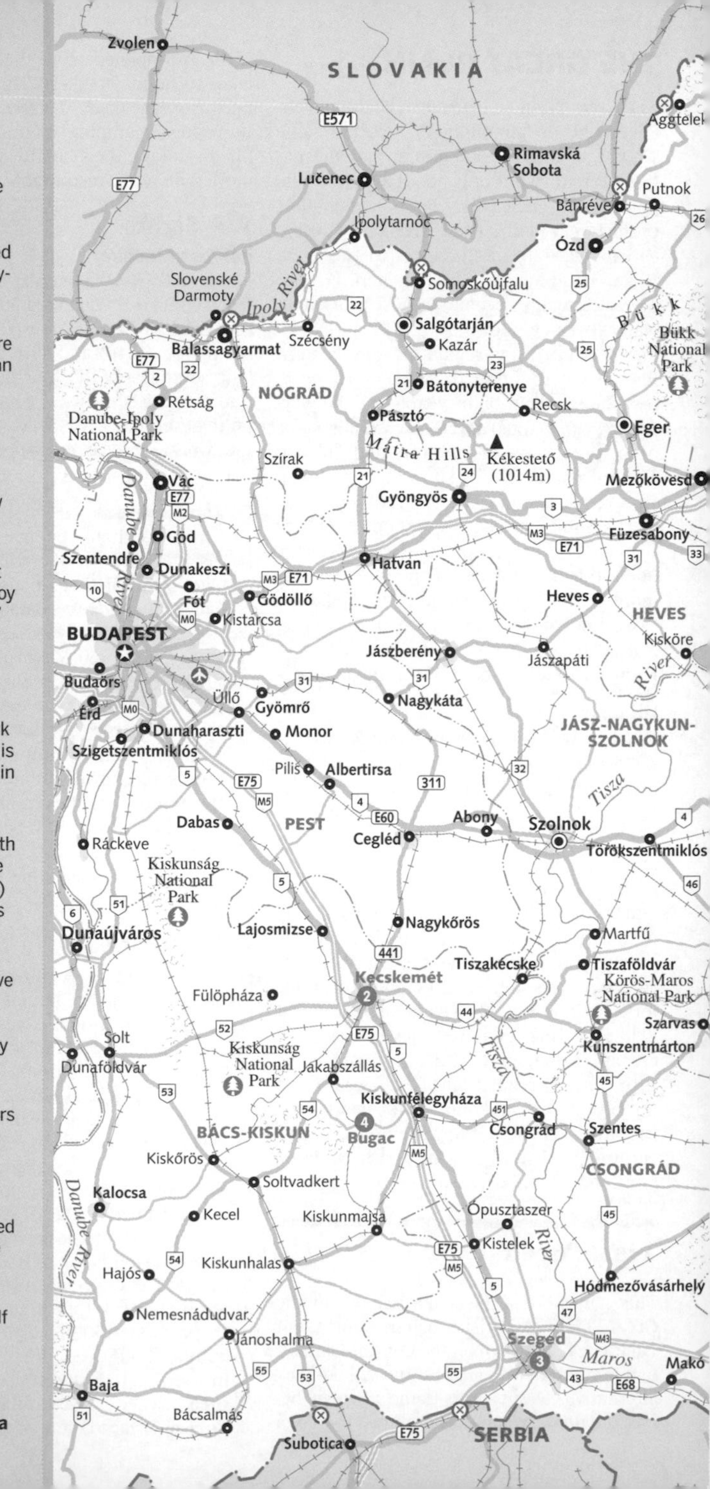

SLOVAKIA
UKRAINE
ROMANIA
Aggtelek National Park
BORSOD-ABAÚJ-ZEMPLÉN
Zemplén Hills
Slovenské Nové Mesto
Sátoraljaújhely
Sárospatak
Encs
Edelény
Kazincbarcika
Sajószentpéter
Szerencs
Miskolc
Chop
Záhony
Dámoc
Lónya
Mándok
Mukačeve
Karcsa
Cigánd
Dombrád
Tiszacsermely
Kisvárda
Tiszatelek
SZABOLCS-SZATMÁR-BEREG
Tákos
Berehove
Gávavencsellő
Tokaj
Rakamaz
Ibrány
Kemecse
Demecser
Vásárosnamény
Kisar
Tiszabecs
Szatmárcseke
Kótaj
Székely
Fehérgyarmat
Tiszalök
Vaja
Nyíregyháza
Tiszavasvári
Mátészalka
Jánkmajtis
Garbolc
Csengersima
Nyékládháza
Tiszaújváros
Nagykálló
Máriapócs
Ököritófülpös
Polgár
Hajdúnánás
Nyírbátor
Csenger
Újfehértó
Mérk
Hajdúdorog
Balkány
Bátorliget
Nyírmihálydi
Hajdúhadház
Carei
Hajdúböszörmény
Nyíradony
Poroszló
Tiszafüred
Balmazújváros
Hajdúsámson
Tiszaörvény
Hortobágy
Debrecen
Lake Tisza
Hortobágy National Park
Abádszalok
Nádudvar
Hajdúszoboszló
Berekfürdő
Kunhegyes
HAJDÚ-BIHAR
Săcueni
Karcag
Püspökladány
Berettyóújfalu
Kisújszállás
Körös-Maros National Park
Borş
Túrkeve
Oradea
Dévaványa
Szeghalom
Mezötúr
Körös River
Gyomaendrőd
Vésztő
Körös-Maros National Park
Mezőberény
BÉKÉS
Salonta
Békés
Sarkad
Kötegyán
Békéscsaba
Gyula
Orosháza
Körös-Maros National Park
Chişineu-Criş
Körös-Maros National Park
Mezőhegyes
Battonya
Nagylak
Arad
0 50 km
0 25 miles

WORTH A TRIP

AROUND LAKE TISZA

Lake Tisza has almost 80km of shoreline, and small towns and resorts are connected by bike paths, trails and country roads. The marinas and waterfront hotel-restaurant at **Tiszaörvény**, just 2km north, are really an adjunct of Tiszafüred. Wide-open water near **Abádszalok** (www.szalok.hu), at the south end of the lake, makes this an ideal place for jet-skiing and wake boarding. On the west side, in **Poroszló** (http://poroszlo.hu/), bird-watchers shouldn't miss the 1500m of boardwalk, **Lake Tisza Water Trail** (Tisza-tavi Vízi Sétány; www.vizisetany.hu; admission free; ⏲10am-8pm daily Jul-Aug, Sat & Sun Sep-Jun) and the all-new (and quite amazing) **Lake Tisza Ecocentre** (☎36-553 033; Kossuth Lajos utca 41, Poroszló; adult/child from 1890/1590Ft; ⏲9am-6pm), a multifunctional visitor centre that focuses on the marine life of the lake and the wildlife of the Tisza Valley. All the shoreline settlements have camping, canoe rental and food options available.

Kikötő (☎06 30 965 9824; www.horgaszcentrum.hu; Tiszapart) offer guided fishing and nature trips from around 8000Ft. The **Ady Fishing Shop** (Ady Horgász Bolt; ☎511 393; Ady Endre utca 35; ⏲7am-6pm Mon-Fri, 7am-3pm Sat, 8am-noon Sun) south of the lake has tackle and permits.

Rent a bicycle (per hour/day 300/1200Ft) from **Horgász Camping** (☎351 220; Kasthély út; ⏲8am-10pm). The towns along the east side of the lake are all cycling friendly and connected by a bike path following the lake shore. You could circuit the lake by continuing north along the waterfront trail to Poroszló and crossing back via Rte 33 (38km).

Lake Tisza Bird Reserve BIRD-WATCHING
(Tisza-tavi Madárrezervátum; www.tisza-to.hu) The expanse west and north of the water connected to Tiszafüred's shoreline is protected as part of the Lake Tisza Bird Reserve, a 2500-hectare division of Hortobágy National Park. More than 200 birds breed in the area; following one of the outlined water routes by kayak or canoe is a great way to see them. Ask for a route map when you rent a boat, as certain areas are off-limits, especially during breeding season (February to May). To go into the park by motor boat, you'll need a guide costing from 3000Ft and available from boat-rental companies. **Szabics Kikötő** (☎06 70 363 7109, 353 250; www.szabicskikoto.hu; Tiszafüred-Örvény) offers daily scheduled bird-watching excursions on its *Kingfisher* boat from 10am to 3pm, from 2900Ft per person.

Sleeping

Horgász Camping CAMPGROUND €
(☎06 30 943 4768, 351 220; www.hotels.hu/horgcamp; Kasthély út; campsites per person/tent/caravan 800/600/800Ft, d/q 5900/8600Ft, bungalows with bathroom/without 9900/6400Ft; ⏲Apr-Oct; @ wi-fi) This 600-site camp ground, a stone's throw from the beach, has plenty of amenities: bike and kayak rental, volleyball court, full restaurant and internet access. Some of the bungalows are well worn. Cabins for two people with private bathroom and full kitchen cost 9900Ft.

Albatrosz Kikötő CAMPGROUND €€
(☎06 30 234 5108; www.albatroszkikoto.hu; Bán Zsigmond út 67; campsites 1500Ft, bungalows without bathroom 10,000Ft; @ wi-fi) At a long-established marina, Albatrosz offers the the closest camping option to the water as well as on-site boat rental and tour arrangements. The tributary location is quiet and shady, too. Showers cost 100Ft extra.

Nádas Panzió RESORT €€
(☎511 401; www.nadaspanzio.hu; Kismuhi utca 2; s/d/apt 10,000/12,000/22,000Ft; air-con @ wi-fi pool) Nádas has a Jacuzzi, swimming pool, sauna, tennis court and even a kids' playground. Staff rent bikes and boats and can arrange nature tours of waterways in the area. The rough-hewn beams and wooden doors make the dozen rooms feel rustic. Apartments come with full kitchens.

Tisza Balneum RESORT €€€
(☎886 200; www.balneum.hu; Húszöles út 27; r 19,000-25,000Ft; air-con wi-fi pool) Flat-screen TVs hang on the walls of the minimalist guestrooms, where wicker, wood and natural linens provide a perfect complement to the lake view off the balcony. A private thermal spring supplies the water for one outdoor and two indoor pools; a private harbour offers boat rentals and trips. There are 52 rooms in the main building and 18 self-contained apartments in the garden outbuilding.

Eating & Drinking

König PIZZERIA €
(☎350 512; Fő utca 15; mains 850-1450Ft; ⏲11am-10pm Sun-Thu, to 11pm Fri & Sat) A welcoming little place in the centre of the village with unsurprising but substantial pizzas and pasta dishes.

Nemzeti Étterem HUNGARIAN €
(☎352 349; Fő út 8; mains 1000-1500Ft; ⏲11am-3pm) The bright yellow restaurant in the village with a red-tile roof hides a rather plain-Jane interior. It's a lunch option only and excellent value with a two-course menu for 700Ft.

Zöld Béke HUNGARIAN €
(Green Frog; Bán Zsigmond út 63; mains 1500-2600Ft) Grilled fish and meat dishes are the speciality at this small, open-air eatery next to Albatrosz Kikötő. It does pizza, too.

Molnár Vendéglõ HUNGARIAN €€
(☎352 705; Húszöles út 31/b; mains 1850-2600Ft) This restaurant near the Nádas Panzió has a decent freshwater fish selection, as well as a handful of game and vegetarian dishes. Its breezy terrace (protected from mosquitoes by netting) is a welcome respite in summer.

Korona Cukrászda CAFE
(☎350 458; Örvényi út 41; cakes 220-480Ft; ⏲9am-8pm) Coffee, cakes, pastries and ice creams... A cool treat from Korona provides a lovely respite from the summer heat.

Information

OTP Bank (Piac út 3) Opposite the market in the village.
Post Office (Fő út 14)
Tourinform (☎511 123; www.tiszafured.hu; Fürdő út 29; ⏲9am-5pm Apr-Oct) On the main road near the thermal bath.

Getting There & Away

From the bus and train stations, opposite one another on Vasút utca, walk 10 or 15 minutes west and then southwest to Tourinform, the beach and the camp grounds. The town centre is another kilometre south.

Direct buses connect Tiszafüred with Budapest (3410Ft, 3½ hours, 190km, four daily) and Eger (1120Ft, 1¼ hours, 55km, 10 daily).

Tiszafüred is on a spur train line that passes through the Hortobágy region on the way to Debrecen (1490Ft, 1½ hours, 73km, nine daily); from Füzesabony (560Ft, 30 minutes, 30km, 10 daily) you can connect to other points on the Budapest–Nyíregyháza rail line.

Debrecen

☎52 / POP 208,000

Debrecen is Hungary's second-largest city, and its name has been synonymous with wealth and conservatism since the 16th century. Flanked by the golden Great Church and the historic Aranybika Hotel, Debrecen's central square sets the rather subdued tone for this city. During summer frequent street festivals fill the pedestrian core with revellers, and old-town bars and nightclubs create a lively scene for night crawlers on weekends year-round. The array of museums and thermal baths in this 'Capital of the Eastern Plain' will keep you busy for a day or two, but then you'll want to day trip out to the *puszta* to explore natural wonders, see a cowboy show, soak in the country's largest spa and shop for pottery.

History

The area around Debrecen has been settled since the earliest times. When the Magyars arrived late in the 9th century, they found a colony of Slovaks here who called the region Dobre Zliem for its 'good soil'. Debrecen's wealth, based on salt, the fur trade and cattle raising, grew steadily through the Middle Ages and increased during the Turkish occupation; the city kept all sides happy by paying tribute to the Ottomans, the Habsburgs and the Transylvanian princes at the same time.

By the mid-16th century much of the population had converted to Protestantism and churches were being erected with gusto, earning the city the nickname 'Calvinist Rome'. Debrecen played a pivotal role in the 1848–49 War of Independence, and it experienced a major building boom in the late 19th and early 20th centuries.

Sights

Great Church CHURCH
(Nagytemplom; ☎412 694; http://nagytemplom.hu; Paic tér 4-6; adult/concession 350/250Ft; ⏲9am-6pm Mon-Fri, 9am-2pm Sat, 10am-4pm Sun Apr-Oct, 10am-1pm daily Nov-Mar) Built in 1822, the iconic Great Church accommodates 3000 people and is Hungary's largest Protestant house of worship. The nave is rather austere apart from the magnificent organ; climb the 210 steps to the top of the west clock tower for grand views over the city. It was in the Great Church that Lajos Kossuth read the Declaration of Independence from Austria on 14 April 1849.

Debrecen

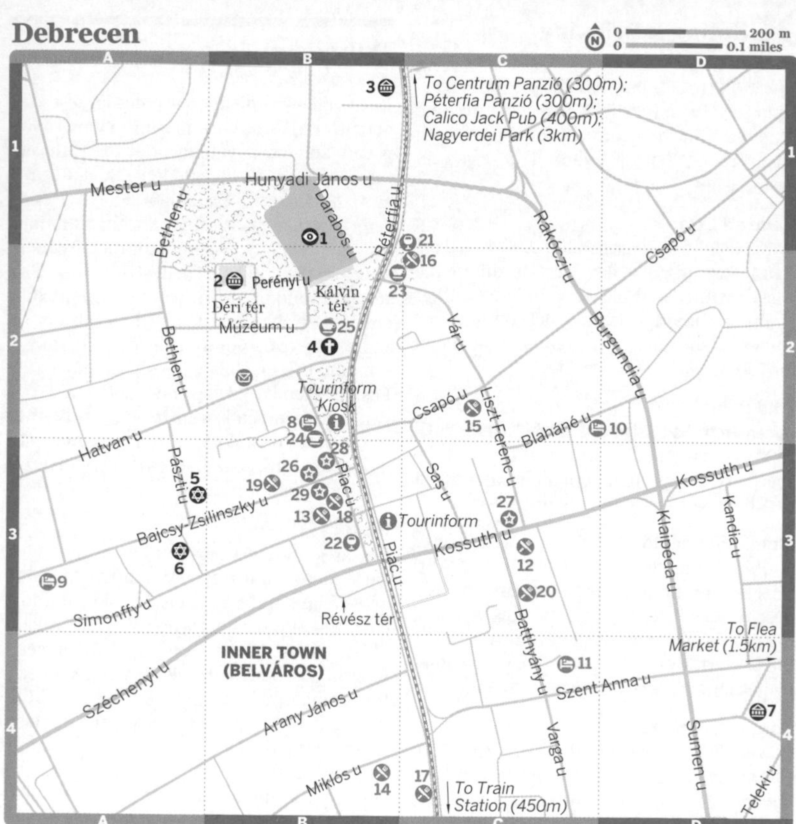

Calvinist College LIBRARY

(Református Kollégium; ☎414 744; www.reformatuskollegium.ttre.hu; Kálvin tér 16; adult/concession 800/400Ft ; ⏰10am-4pm Mon-Fri, 10am-1pm Sat) North of the church stands the Calvinist College, built in 1816 on the site of a theological college dating back to the Middle Ages. Downstairs there are exhibits on religious art and sacred objects (including a 17th-century chalice made from a coconut) and on the regimented school's history. Upstairs is the relatively bland 560,000-volume library and the bright, white oratory, where the breakaway National Assembly met in 1849 and Hungary's postwar provisional government was declared towards the end of WWII in 1944.

Déri Museum MUSEUM

(☎322 207; www.derimuz.hu; Déri tér 1; adult/child 500/300Ft; ⏰10am-6pm Apr-Oct, 10am-4pm Nov-Mar, closed Mon) Folklore exhibits at the Déri Museum, a short walk west of the Calvinist College, offer excellent insights into life on the plain and the bourgeois citizens of Debrecen up to the 19th century. Mihály Munkácsy's mythical interpretations of the Hortobágy and his *Christ's Passion* trilogy usually take pride of place in a separate art gallery but it was under renovation at research time. The museum's entrance is flanked by four superb bronzes by sculptor Ferenc Medgyessy, a local boy who merits his own **Medgyessy Museum** (Medgyessy Ferenc Emlékmúzeum; ☎413 572; http://www.derimuz.hu/medgyessy/medgyessy_nyito.html; Péterfia utca 28; adult/child 500/250Ft; ⏰10am-4pm, closed Mon) in an old burgher house a short distance to the northeast.

Synagogues JEWISH

Debrecen had a Jewish population of 12,000 people up to the end of WWII. The **Status Quo Conservative Synagogue** (☎415 861; Kápolnási utca), just south of Bajcsy-Zsilinszky

Debrecen

Sights
1 Calvinist College ... B1
2 Déri Museum ... B2
3 Ferenc Medgyessy Memorial Museum ... B1
4 Great Church ... B2
5 Orthodox Synagogue ... A3
6 Status Que Conservative Synagogue ... A3
7 Tímárház ... D4

Sleeping
8 Aranybika ... B2
9 Belvárosi Panzió ... A3
10 György Maróthi College ... C2
11 Stop Panzió ... C4

Eating
12 Csokonai Söröző ... C3
13 Eve's Cofe & Lounge ... B3
14 Flaska Vendéglő ... B4
15 Fruit and Vegetable Market ... C2
16 Gilbert Pizzeria ... C2
17 Grocery Shop ... C4
18 Ikon ... B3
19 Klári Salátabár ... B3
20 Trattoria Trinacria ... C3

Drinking
21 B4 Gösser ... C1
22 Bohém Belgian Beer Café ... B3
23 Gara Cukrászda ... B2
24 Magda Szabó Bookshop & Cafe ... B2
25 Romkert ... B2

Entertainment
26 Cool Music & Dance Club ... B3
27 Csokonai Theatre ... C3
28 Home: The Club ... B3
29 Skorpió Bar ... B3

utca, dates from 1909. The facade of the older 1893 **Orthodox synagogue** (Pászti utca 6) has had a lick of paint but its interior is still waiting for a much-needed renovation.

Tímárház GALLERY
(Tanner House; ☎321 260; www.debrecenimuvkozpont.hu/; Nagy Gál István utca 6; adult/child 300/150Ft; ⊙10am-6pm Tue-Fri, to 2pm Sat) East of the city centre, the Tímárház is a folk-craft centre and workshop, where embroiderers, basket weavers and carvers (but no tanners) do their stuff in rotation.

Flea Market MARKET
(Vágóhíd utca; ⊙7am-1pm Wed-Sun) The colourful flea market attracts a motley group of hawkers selling everything from socks to live animals. It's served by buses 15 and 30 from the train station.

Activities

You can wander along leafy trails and rent a **paddle boat** (per hr 1000Ft; ⊙9am-8pm Jun-Aug) in Nagyerdei Park, about 3km north of the city centre. But the main attraction here is **Aquaticum Debrecen** (☎514 174; www.aquaticum.hu; Nagyerdei Park; adult/concession 2350/1900Ft; ⊙11am-9pm Mon-Thu, 10am-9pm Fri-Sun), a huge complex of 'Mediterranean Pleasure Baths' with all manner of slides, waterfalls and grottos – both indoors and out. Choose from a full menu of massages (3800Ft for 25 minutes) and other treatments. Go to the 2nd storey in the old building to the left to get to the **Thermal Baths** (Termálfürdő; ☎514 174; www.aquaticum.hu/; adult/child from 1330/1050Ft; ⊙7am-9pm), older pools filled with nonfiltered, purely mineral (read: muddy-coloured) waters, unlike the Aquaticum's pristine blue Mediterranean variety.

Festivals & Events

Annual events include the pre-Lenten **Masquerade Carnival** in February, the **Spring Festival** of performing arts in March and **Jazz Days** in September. The granddaddy of Debrecen's festivals, though, is the **Flower Carnival** (www.iranydebrecen.hu/info/flower-carnival) held in mid-August, which includes a flowery float parade.

Sleeping

Loads more dormitory accommodation is available in July and August; ask Tourinform for details.

György Maróthi College HOSTEL €
(Maróthi György Kollégium; ☎502 780; www.marothikollegium.hu/; Blaháné utca 15; s/d 4130/6490Ft, without bathroom 2655/4550Ft; @) Just off the main pedestrian lanes, this central dormitory has fairly basic rooms, and bathroom facilities are shared. There's a kitchen on each floor and a basketball court for guests' use.

TOP CHOICE **Centrum Panzió** GUESTHOUSE €
(☎442 843; www.panziocentrum.hu; Péterfia utca 37/a; s/d 6500/8500Ft; ❄@📶) A bit north of the centre but every bit worth the extra half kilometre, the Centrum looks a little like your grandmother's house – if she collected Victorian bric-a-brac. Flowery odds and ends line the bright reception and public areas; some of the 25 large rooms (eg room 15) are out the back, facing a long garden that seems to go on forever. All have both minifridge and microwave. Bike rental is available.

Stop Panzió GUESTHOUSE €
(☎420 302; www.stop.at.tf; Batthányi utca 18; s/d/tr 6900/8900/11,900Ft; 📶) The dozen renovated rooms here fill up because they're the right price for the right location – in a courtyard off a cafe-filled pedestrian street. The brightly tiled, plant-filled lobby and the staff are welcoming, as is the well-stocked in-house bar.

Belvárosi Panzió GUESTHOUSE €€
(Downtown Guesthouse; ☎322 644; www.belvarosipanzio.hu; Bajcsy-Zsilinszky utca 60; s/d 7800/10,600Ft; @📶) Bright, clean and modern, the 24-room 'Downtown' is less homey and more hotel-y than some others. Some 2nd-floor rooms have a balcony looking onto a quiet street.

Péterfia Panzió GUESTHOUSE €€
(☎418 246; www.peterfiapanzio.hu; Péterfia utca 37/b; s/d 8200/9400Ft; ❄📶) Natural-wood furniture fills this guesthouse's 19 comfy rooms, and the staff make you welcome by inviting you to relax in the very long back garden, which also has rooms facing it.

Aranybika HOTEL €€€
(☎508 600; www.hotelaranybika.com; Piac utca 11-15; s €46-88, d €56-106; ❄📶🏊) This landmark Art Nouveau hotel has been *the* place to stay in Debrecen since 1915 but – alas – standards have fallen. Many of the 205 rooms retain their drab carpets and plain, proletarian furnishings of a different era. Superior rooms have a bit more space than standard, though, as well as antique reproduction furniture. Room 333 is in a medieval-looking turret should you be looking for a little romance. The upgraded wellness centre is a bonus.

Szív Panzió GUESTHOUSE €
(Heart Guesthouse; ☎322 200; www.szivpanzio.hu; Szív utca 11; s/d/apt 6000/8200/13,400Ft; ❄📶) Staying at a guesthouse on a tree-lined street not far from the train station helps make day trips a breeze, but the 'Heart' is a bit away from the action. Warm colours enliven the 16 simple rooms with low-slung beds and well-stocked minibars; most face a quiet courtyard.

Aquaticum Wellness Hotel RESORT €€€
(☎514 100; www.aquaticum.hu; Nagyerdei Park 1; s/d €105/140; ❄@📶🏊) Kids' programs, babysitting, bike rental, spa services, swimming pools and loads of other amenities make the 96-room Aquaticum attractive to both adults and children. And you don't have to leave the premises to get from your room to the spas and pools (entry included in the rates).

Eating

There's a **grocery shop** (Piac utca 75; ⏰24hr) within walking distance of the train station, and the small covered **fruit and vegetable market** (Csapó utca; ⏰5am-3pm Mon-Sat, 5-11am Sun) is right in the city centre.

Eve's Cofe & Lounge CAFE €
(☎322 222; http://hovamenjek.hu/debrecen/eves-cofe-lounge; Simonffy utca 1/b; sandwiches 800-1000Ft; ⏰8am-midnight Mon-Thu, 8am-1am Fri & Sat, 9am-10pm Sun) Pleasantly upscale cafe (that's what we think 'cofe' means) serves breakfasts as well as very good sandwiches and salads throughout the day along a pedestrianised street that is tailormade for people-watching.

Gilbert Pizzeria PIZZERIA €
(☎537 373; www.gilbert.hu; Kálvin tér 5; pizzas & pasta 950-1250Ft; ⏰24hr; 🅥) Some of the best pizza in town awaits in an interior courtyard just off the main square. A substantial number of the 50 choices are vegetarian and, best of all, it's open round the clock.

Klári Salátabár VEGETARIAN €
(☎412 203; Bajcsy-Zsilinszky utca 3; per 100g 140-350Ft; ⏰10am-midnight Mon-Thu, 10am-4am Fri & Sat) Broccoli egg rolls, fried mushrooms, peas and white rice – the dishes at this self-service shopfront may not all be super healthy, but they are for the most part vegetarian.

Trattoria Trinacria ITALIAN €€
(☎416 988; http://dvklub.wix.com/trinacria; Batthyány utca 4; mains 1500-3500Ft) Charming Italian terrace eatery on a pedestrian

side-street serves well-prepared pasta dishes, including homemade ravioli, as well as very good wood-fired pizzas.

Csokonai Söröző HUNGARIAN €€
(☎410 802; http://www.csokonaisorozo.hu/eng; Kossuth utca 21; mains 1850-3490Ft) Medieval decor, sharp service and excellent Hungarian specialities all help to create one of Debrecen's most recommended eating experiences. This cellar pub-restaurant also serves pasta and (go figure) Mexican dishes like *fajitas* (1450Ft to 2150Ft).

Flaska Vendéglő HUNGARIAN €€
(☎06 30 998 7602, 414 582; http://flaska.hu; Miklós utca 4; mains 1350-3100Ft) You can't miss the giant terracotta-red flask jutting out from the wall – a landmark in these parts – and you shouldn't skip the food either. Poultry and pork top the Hungarian menu; try the authenic *Hortobágyi palacsinta* (meat-filled pancakes with paprika sauce) or the Debreceni stuffed cabbage.

TOP CHOICE **Ikon** INTERNATIONAL €€€
(☎06 30 555 7766; www.ikonrestaurant.hu; Piac utca 23; mains 2900-6900Ft) The best restaurant in Debrecen, if not all of Hungary, Ikon commands a prominent position on the main square, but despite the postmodern decor and classily clad wait staff, it's discreet and very upscale. Enjoy such inventive dishes as risotto of roasted and marinated peppers, goat's cheese and rosemary (1900Ft), grilled fois gras on *pain d'épices* (spice bread) with pear (2500Ft), and rabbit poached in white wine with carrots (4200Ft). We shall return!

Drinking

B4 Gösser BAR
(☎06 70 943 7752; http://b4gosser.hu; Kálvin tér 4; ⊙10am-2am Sun-Thu, to 4am Fri & Sat) Tucked away in a courtyard just far enough east of the Great Church so as not to disturb the faithful, this pub-club-jazz bar is party central at the weekend.

Calico Jack Pub PUB
(☎455 999; http://www.calicojackpub.hu; Bem tér 15; ⊙8am-2am Mon-Fri, 10am-2am Sat, 10am-midnight Sun) A classic setting for *sör* (beer) drinking just north of the centre, with an interior done up like an 1882 sailing vessel (look for our mate Jack climbing the mast). Extensive beer selection and large outside terrace.

Bohém Belgian Beer Café BEER HALL
(☎536 373; www.belgianbeercafe.hu; Piac utca 29; ⊙10am-midnight Mon-Thu, to 2am Fri & Sat) Why locals drink Belgian beer when neighbouring countries makes such great brew is anyone's guess. But there's no denying the popularity of this streetside cafe with its beer-hall atmosphere.

Romkert CAFE
(Ruin Garden; ☎249 203; www.romkertdebrecen.hu; ⊙noon-8pm mon-Sat) Directly behind the Great Church, this glassed-in cafe and exhibition hall with ancients bits and bobs excavated from the area and rotating exhibitions is a welcome addition to Debrecen's arts and cafe world.

Gara Cukrászda CAFE
(☎530 460; www.garacukraszda.hu; Kálvin tér 6; sweets 250-500Ft; ⊙9am-7pm) Debrecen's preeminent cafe and cake shop for almost two decades, Gara has some of the best cakes and ice cream (made with real fruit and loads of it) outside Budapest.

Magda Szabó Bookshop & Cafe CAFE
(Szabó Magda Könyvesbolt és Kávézó; ☎532 309; Piac tér 11-15; ⊙9am-7pm) Cafe-bookshop named after the late doyenne of Hungarian letters, with novels, maps and coffee.

Entertainment

The eastern end of Bajcsy-Zsilinszky utca is home to a half-dozen clubs that change name and beat with the speed of summer lightning. Pick up a copy of the biweekly entertainment freebie *Debreceni Est* (www.est.hu) for listings.

Cool Music & Dance Club CLUB
(Bajcsy-Zsilinszky utca 1-3; admission 500-800Ft; ⊙11pm-5am Mon, Fri & Sat) DJs spin house and techno tunes here most weekends; Fridays (and sometimes Mondays) see frequent theme parties.

Skorpió Bar BAR
(Bajcsy-Zsilinszky utca 4; ⊙10am-2am Sun-Thu, 10am-4am Fri & Sat) This subterranean music bar has a big open-air terrace out the back in summer. It's a good place to relax over an evening beer.

Home: The Club CLUB
(☎06 30 408 7621; www.homeclub.hu; Piac utca 11; ⊙4pm-4am Fri & Sat) House parties, techno, electro-funk – you never know what kind of music you'll get at Debrecen's craziest (read trashiest) club.

Bed Beach Club CLUB
(☎06 30 408 7621; www.facebook.com/bedbeachdebrecen; Nagyerdei Park 6) Hard-rockin' club overlooking the lake in Nagyerdei Park.

Csokonai Theatre THEATRE
(☎455 075; www.csokonaiszinhaz.hu; Kossuth utca 10) Three-tier gilt balconies, ornate ceiling frescoes and elaborate chandeliers: the Csokonai is everything a 19th-century theatre should be. Musicals and operas are staged here, too.

Information

Debrecen website (www.debrecen.hu) Lots of helpful info.

Ibusz (☎415 555; www.ibusz.hu; Révész tér 2; ⊙9am-5pm Mon-Fri) Travel agency; rents private apartments.

Main Post Office (Hatvan utca 5-9)

OTP Bank (Piac utca 45) Has ATM.

Tourinform (☎412 250; www.iranydebrecen.hu; Piac utca 20; ⊙9am-5pm year-round plus 9am-1pm Sat Jun-Sep) The unbelievably helpful Tourinform office in the town hall has more information than you can carry about the whole region. There's a **Tourinform kiosk** (Kossuth tér; ⊙10am-8pm Thu-Sun Jun-Sep) in Kossuth tér in summer.

Getting There & Away

Bus

Buses are quickest if you're going direct to the following destinations.

DESTINATION	PRICE	TIME	KM	FREQUENCY
Gyula	2520Ft	3hr	130	5 daily
Eger	2520Ft	2½hr	133	6 daily
Nádudvar	840Ft	1hr	41	5 daily
Miskolc	1860Ft	2hr	99	16 daily
Szeged	3950Ft	4½hr	230	3 daily

Train

DESTINATION	PRICE	TIME	KM	FREQUENCY
Budapest	3950Ft	3¼hr	221	Hourly
Hajdúszoboszló	370Ft	15min	20	Half-hourly
Hortobágy	840Ft	45min	42	Half-hourly
Nyíregyháza	930Ft	45min	49	Every 20 minutes
Tokaj	2250Ft	1¼hr	81	7 daily

Trains leave from Debrecen for Satu Marie (3½ hours, 106km) in Romania at 9.12am and 3.12pm. You have to transfer in Záhony to get to Csap (Čop; 120km) in Ukraine, where the train lines are of a different gauge. The night train from Budapest to Moscow stops here at 9.35pm.

Getting Around

Tram 1 – the only line in town at present – is ideal both for transport and sightseeing. From the train station, it runs north along Piac utca to Kálvin tér and then carries on to Nagyerdei Park, where it loops around for the same trip southward. Tickets are 290Ft from newsagents and 370Ft from the driver. Most other city transport can be caught at the southern end of Petőfi tér. Trolleybuses 2 and 3 link the train and bus stations.

Hortobágy

☎52 / POP 1500

This village, some 40km west of Debrecen, is the centre of the Hortobágy region, and was once celebrated for its sturdy cowboys, inns and Gypsy bands. You can see the staged re-creation of all this, complete with traditionally costumed *csikósok* (cowboys), at a *puszta* horse show. But you'll want to explore more of the 810-sq-km Hortobágy National Park and wildlife preserve – home to hundreds of birds, as well as plant species that are usually found only by the sea. Unesco promoted the park to World Heritage status in 1999.

Sights & Activities

Máta Stud Farm HORSE SHOW
(Mátai Ménes; ☎589 369; http://www.hortobagy.eu/en/matai-menes/idegenforgalom/; Hortobágy-Máta; adult/child 2700/1500Ft; ⊙10am, noon, 2pm & 4pm Apr-Oct) Staged it may be, but the *puszta* show at the 300-year-old Máta Stud Farm, 3km north of the village, *is* Hungarian. During the 1½-hour program you (and about 50 others) ride in a horse-drawn wagon train across the prairie, making stops to peer into the pens of *racka* sheep, see great grey cattle grazing, witness a semi-wild herd of horses herded past and watch Hungarian *csikósok* perform tricks. A *csikós* riding full gallop five-in-hand – standing balanced on the back of the two rear horses, with three more reined in front – is something to see. To get to the stud on foot, cross the train tracks from the station and find the path through the brush (to the right). This well-worn track through the fields, over the river and past the Hortobágy Club Hotel cuts the walk to 1.5km, down from 3km if you follow the road.

Hortobágy National Park PARK
(www.hnp.hu) With its varied terrain and water sources, the patchwork Hortobágy National Park has some of the best bird-watching in Europe. Indeed, some 340 species (of the continent's estimated 400) have been spotted here in the past 20 years, including many types of grebe, heron, shrike, egret, spoonbill, stork, kite, warbler, eagle and kestrel. The great bustard, one of the world's largest birds, standing 1m high and weighing in at 20kg, has its own reserve, with limited access to two-legged mammals. Some 160 species nest here.

Stop first at the Hortobágy National Park Visitor Centre (p208) to get an overview of the flora and fauna of the region, both from the helpful staff and the excellent exhibition. On-site there's also a traditional **Craftsmen's Yard** (Kézmûvesudvar; Petőfi tér 9; per craft 70Ft; ⏲9am-5pm Tue-Fri, 10am-5pm Sat & Sun May-Oct), where you can watch artists work in leather, clay, straw, wood and iron in 10 different workshops.

Park passes, also available from the visitor centre, allow entry to three restricted 'demonstration areas' within driving distance (each area 600Ft, all three 1000Ft). One of the most interesting areas is the **Hortobágy Great Fishponds** (Hortobágy Nagyhalastó; off Hwy 33; ⏲10am-5pm daily mid-Jun–Aug, 10am-6.30pm Sat & Sun Apr–mid-Jun & Sep-Oct) 7km west, where you can walk along interpretive trails and climb a watchtower to see the amazing amount of aquatic birdlife that inhabits this 20-hectare swathe. From April to October a **narrow-gauge train** (kisvonat; one way adult/child 800/500Ft, return 1200/700Ft; ⏲10am, noon, 2pm & 4pm daily Jul & Aug, Sat & Sun Apr-Jun & Sep-Oct) runs back and forth across pond bridges four times at the weekend (daily in July and August). A bike path connects the ponds with Hortobágy village. Rent bikes from the Hortobágy Club Hotel (p208) or Ökotúra Vendégház (p208).

Ask the visitor centre about the occasional local weekend bird-watching tours, too. October is a great month to visit; between 60,000 and 100,000 common cranes stop over on the Hortobágy plain during their annual migration.

Nine-Hole Bridge BRIDGE
(Kilenclyukú-híd) The Nine-Hole Bridge, built in 1833 and spanning the marshy Hortobágy River, is the longest – and certainly the most sketched, painted and photographed – stone bridge in the country. Just in front stands the still-operating Hortobágyi Csárda, one of the original eating houses (1781) used by salt traders on their way from the Tisza River to Debrecen. As you'll discover at the small **Hortobágy Inn Museum** (Hortobágyi Csárda Múzeum; ☎589 321; http://www.hortobagy.eu/en/idegenforgalom/hortobagyi-csarda; Petőfi tér 1; adult/child 200/100Ft; ⏲9am-6pm Jul & Aug, shorter hours Mar-Jun & Sep-Nov) inside, the inns provided itinerant Roma fiddlers with employment. Gypsy music and *csárdak* (inns) have been synonymous ever since.

Animal Parks ZOO
There are two open-air zoos in the national park south of Hortobágy village. The **Puszta Animal Park** (Pusztai Állatpark; ☎701 037; http://www.hortobagy.eu/en/idegenforgalom/pusztai-allatpark; off Hwy 33; adult/child 600/400Ft; ⏲9.30am-6pm Apr-Sep, to 5pm Mar & Oct), 2km south of the Nine-Hole Bridge, with its weird and wonderful animals, is a fun place for kids of all ages. Here's you'll see the rare breeds of the *puszta* up close: the heavy-set long-horned grey cattle, the curly haired *mangalica* pig and the *racka* sheep, whose corkscrew-like horns are particularly devilish. About 5km further south at Malomháza is the **Hortobágy Wild Animal Park** (Hortobágyi Vadaspark; ☎589 321; http://www.hnp.hu/index_en.php; Hortobágy-Malomháza; adult/child 1500/700Ft; ⏲10am-7pm Jul & Aug, shorter hours Apr-Jun, Sep & Oct), which hosts animals that lived on the *puszta* before it was farmed: wolves, jackals, wild horses, vultures, pelicans etc. Visitors are transported by 'safari bus', which departs hourly from the Herder Museum.

Bird Park Centre WILDLIFE RESERVE
(Madárpark Központ; ☎369 181; www.madarapark.hu; Petőfi tér 6; adult/child 800/600Ft; ⏲9am-6pm) Get up close with ailing feathered friends as they convalesce at the Bird Park Centre. Walk through the 'hospital' section of this sanctuary (including an operating room), among ambling storks in the park and into an aviary with hawks. Fidgety kestrels stay behind one-way glass. Kids can learn about conservation from simple displays before they head off to the playground.

Herder Museum MUSEUM
(Pásztormúzeum; ☎589 000; Petőfi tér 1; adult/child 600/400Ft; ⏲9am-6pm Jul & Aug, shorter hours

Mar-Jun & Sep-Nov) Housed in an 18th-century carriage house across from the *csárda* (inn), this museum illustrates life on the plains for shepherds, swineherds and cowboys in the 19th century.

FREE **Round Theatre** MUSEUM
(Körszín; ☎369 025; Petőfi tér; adult/child 200/100Ft; ⊙9am-6pm Jul & Aug, shorter hours Mar-Jun & Sep-Nov) Next door to the Herder Museum, the Round Theatre has a small exhibit on traditional crafts and a gift shop.

Hortobágy Club Hotel HORSE RIDING
(☎369 020; www.hortobagyhotel.hu; Hortobágy-Máta) About 2km north of the village, the Hortobágy Club Hotel is an activity centre where beginners can take horse-riding lessons and experienced riders can gallop into the sunset across the *puszta* (per hour from 3600Ft); two-hour carriage rides (per person 2700Ft) are available, too. Rent a bike here for 500/2000Ft per hour/day.

Festivals & Events

The area is busiest the first weekend in July, when Máta hosts the **International Equestrian Day**; on Pentecost in late May and June, when the **National Herdsmen Competition & Shepherd's Meeting** is held; and on 19 and 20 August during the **Hortobágy Bridge Fair**.

Sleeping & Eating

Ökotúra Vendégház GUESTHOUSE €
(☎369 075; www.okoturavendeghaz.hu; Borsós utca 13; campsite per person/tent/caravan 1000/1000/3000Ft, s/d/tr 5000/8000/10,500Ft) The best thing to happen to the accommodation scene in Hortobágy in recent years is the opening of this guesthouse and campground 2km east of the village just off Rte 33. The 20 rooms are large, bright and spotlessly clean with wood-laminate floors; they look onto a large open green space that accommodates campers in the warmer months. There's a kitchen here for their use, too. Rent bikes for 300/1500Ft per hour/day.

Hortobágy Inn GUESTHOUSE €
(Hortobágyi Fogadó; ☎06 30 286 6793; Kossuth utca 1; s/d 3500/7000Ft) This small inn is begging for an update. But it is the most central place to stay, the 10 basic rooms come with balconies, and there's a bar and restaurant on-site (mains 1000Ft to 1800Ft).

Hortobágy Club Hotel RESORT €€€
(☎369 020; www.hortobagyhotel.hu; Hortobágy-Máta; s/d/apt €67/83/134; @☜≋) This hotel's low-lying buildings were constructed in traditional style to blend with the environment, and it works. Use of thermal pools, saunas and tennis courts is included, though horse-riding and bike and canoe rental cost extra. The 54 rooms are spacious; apartments for four are equipped with kitchens, though the in-house restaurant (mains 1890Ft to 2490Ft) is the best in town.

TOP CHOICE **Hortobágyi Csárda** HUNGARIAN €€
(☎589 010; http://www.hortobagy.eu/en/idegenforgalom/hortobagyi-csarda; Petőfi tér 1; mains 1490-2290Ft; ⊙8am-10pm Apr-Sep, to 8pm Oct-Mar) This is Hungary's most celebrated roadside inn, built at the end of the 18th century. Sit back and admire the Hortobágy kitsch taking up every square centimetre of wall space; Gypsy violinists often play as you tuck into your *bográcś gulyas* (goulash served in a small kettle) or game dishes. You can even try the meat of the famous grey cattle and the wooly mangalica pig, whose relatives you may have met at the Puszta Animal Park. Don't miss the famous *Hortobágyi palacsinta* as an appetiser.

Information

Hortobágy National Park Visitor Centre (Hortobágyi Nemzeti Park; ☎589 321; www.hnp.hu; Petőfi tér 9; ⊙8am-6pm Mon-Fri, 10am-6pm Sat & Sun Jun-Sep, shorter hours Mar-May & Oct)

Post Office (Kossuth utca 2)

Takarékszövetkezet (Petőfi tér) In the shopping complex, with an ATM.

Tourinform (☎589 000; hortobagy@tourinform.hu; Petőfi tér 9) Shares the same space and hours as the visitor centre.

Getting There & Away

Buses stop on both sides of the main road (Rte 33) just opposite the vistor centre; the train station is to the northeast at the end of Kossuth utca.

Six buses stop daily at Hortobágy village on runs between Debrecen (745Ft, 40 minutes, 38km) and Eger (1680Ft, two hours, 90km). A couple of buses connect daily with Hajdúszoboszló (1300Ft, 1¼ hours, 58km).

Hortobágy is on the main train line linking Debrecen (840Ft, 45 minutes, 42km), Tiszafüred (650Ft, 40 minutes, 31km) and Füzesabony (1300Ft, 1¼ hours, 61km), served by up to a dozen trains daily. Connect to Eger from Füzesabony.

Hajdúszoboszló

52 / POP 23,300

Thousands of visitors flock to Hajdúszoboszló, the country's largest thermal bathing centre and water park. The small town is well spread out; from the train station or even central Hősök tere you'd never suspect the hubbub to the north. Hotels after guesthouses after apartment rentals line the streets surrounding the 40-hectare holiday spa complex.

Sights & Activities

István Bocskai Museum MUSEUM
(362 165; http://www.derimuz.hu/bocskai/bocskai_nyito.html; Bocskai utca 12; adult/child 600/300Ft; 10am-6pm Apr-Oct, to 4pm Nov-Mar, closed Mon) The Bocskai Museum is a temple to the memory of Prince István Bocskai and his *hajdúk* (Heyduck) helpers. Among the saddles, pistols and swords hangs Bocskai's banner – the standard of the Heyduck cavalry, picturing the prince doing battle with a leopard (which mysteriously changes into a lion in later versions). There's a good collection on local history and folk art. Next door is the **International Modern Museum** (Nemzetkőzi Modern Múzeum; Bocskai utca 14), with works by local painters and graphic artists.

FREE **Calvinist Church** CHURCH
(Kálvin tér 9; admission free) In the centre of town on Kálvin tér is this Calvinist church built in 1711. Behind it is a 20m-long stretch of wall and a small tower – all that remains of a 15th-century Gothic fortress destroyed by the Turks in 1660. Ask at the **City Cultural Centre** (558 800; Szilfákalja út 2) about the church's organ and choral concerts.

Hungarospa Thermal Baths SPA
(558 558; www.hungarospa.hu; Szent István Park 1-3) Hungarospa Thermal Baths is a huge complex spread over 30 hectares and comprising more than a dozen pools – including the 'Mediterranean Shore' pool, Europe's largest – set in a gigantic park, with food and souvenir stands, full restaurants and lakeside rowing-boat rental (per hour 1000Ft). Forty different spa services are also available. The nine slides, outdoor pools and beaches at the **Aquapark** (adult/child day pass 2800/1400Ft; 10am-6pm Jun-Aug), towards the back of the complex, are now complemented by the thermal pools (name the temperature) of the snazzy new **Aqua Palace** (adult/child day pass from 3200/2200FT; 10am-8pm Mon-Thu, to 9pm Fri-Sun) close to the main entrance. All of the thermal and enjoyment pools here are undercover, making this a year-round attraction. There's also the original **Thermal Spa & Beach** (Termálfürdő és Strand; adult/child 1800/1300Ft; indoor baths 7am-7pm year-round, outdoor pools 8am-7pm May-Sep) and a small island in the lake reserved for naturists. Outside the baths' open-air entrance stands the striking Forest of Bells Monument honouring Hungary's war dead.

Sleeping

Less than a three-night stay in midsummer will almost certainly incur a surcharge.

Thermal Camping CAMPGROUND €
(558 552; thermalcamping@hungarospa.hu; Böszörményi út 35/a; campsites per person/tent/caravan 2200/1100/2000Ft; @) Owned by Hungarospa Thermal Baths, this campground is at the northern end of the holiday complex; rates quoted here include admission to the baths. It's a flat, basic site with some cover and a minimart, adjacent to farmers' fields.

HEY WHAT?

The names of Hungarian towns often reflect the heritage of original settlers, such as the Kun (Cuman) people of Turkic decent in Kiskunság. The Hajdúság region was settled in the 15th century predominantly by the *hajdúk* (Heyducks or Haiduks in English), a community of drovers and brigands turned mercenary soldiers and renowned for their skill in battle. When the Heyducks helped István Bocskai (1557–1606), prince of Transylvania, rout the Habsburg forces at Álmosd, southeast of Debrecen, in 1604, they were raised to the rank of nobility and some 10,000 were granted land – as much to keep the ferocious brigands in check as to reward them. Thus the more than a dozen town names starting with Hajdú in Hajdú-Bihar county.

WORTH A TRIP

NÁDUDVAR

Though you can buy its famous black pottery elsewhere, **Nádudvar** (www.nadudvar.hu), a village of 8800 people 18km west of Hajdúszoboszló, is likely to be where it originated. The characteristic black colour comes from minerals in the area's clay soil and designs are made by etching into the clay with pebbles. The Fazekas, the appropriately named 'Potter' family, has carried on the pottery tradition for centuries and they have several businesses on the main street, Fő út. See the youngest generation's work at the studio of **István Fazekas** (☎06 20 423 1850, 54-480 562; www.fazekasiostvan.hu; Fő út 64; ⏲8am-6pm Mon-Fri); there's a much larger showroom almost opposite at Fő út 77. **Ferenc Fazekas** (☎06 30 481 3441, 54-480 569; www.nadudvarifazekas.hu; Fő út 152; ⏲8am-6pm Mon-Fri) is often on hand to give a demonstration, and his wares are for sale in his workshop further up the road. The little **Fazekas Ház Museum** (☎54-480 425; Fő út 159; admission 450Ft; ⏲8am-6pm Mon-Fri) almost next door contains 18th-century pottery and an old foot-operated potter's wheel.

According to professional potter István Fazekas, the methods and materials used in Nádudvar pottery make it unique. 'Our clay has an extremely high content of red ferric oxides, which during the firing process yield high-quality black iron oxides', he says. 'The firing takes place in wood-burning furnaces where the resulting smoke further contributes to the colouring process. In fact, this is one of the oldest firing techniques in the trade. It works today as it did some thousands of years before.'

At least five daily buses daily (more on weekdays) run to and from Hájduszoboszló (370Ft, 30 minutes, 19km) and Debrecen (465Ft, 30 minutes, 24km).

Arany Oroszlán GUESTHOUSE €€
(☎06 30 591 1888, 610 790; www.aranyoroszlanpanzio.hu; Bessenyei utca 14; s/d 9000/11,000Ft; @📶) Nine simple and very yellow guestrooms with little more than a low-lying bed and chair are what you'll find at this innlike guesthouse. The quiet location at the end of a cul-de-sac is a plus.

Bungalló Panzió GUESTHOUSE €€
(☎270 607; www.hajduszoboszlo-panzio.hu; Mátyás király sétány 16; s/d 7000/12,000Ft, 4-person bungalow 12,000Ft; ❄@📶) This bungalow complex has that old-fashioned, family feel, with barbecues and ball courts. Each of the 31 rooms has a kitchenette, while two-storey bungalows have three bedrooms but only a refrigerator. There's a reasonable restaurant (mains 1290Ft to 1980Ft) with set lunch for just 950Ft.

Hotel Aurum LUXURY HOTEL €€€
(☎271 431; www.hotelaurum.hu; Mátyás király sétány 3; s/d 25,000/34,000Ft; ❄@📶🏊) Set back from the road, you approach this rather luxurious 55-room hotel through elegant terraces along a lamppost-lit lane. The neoclassical exterior hides clean-lined rooms, each with kitchen and wi-fi. A bit over the top – but it works.

Eating

There are also plenty of sausage, *lángos* (deep-fried dough) and ice-cream stalls in the spa park as well as along Mátyás király sétány and Szilfákalja út.

Szilfa SELF-SERVICE €
(József Attila utca 2; mains 360-1250Ft; ⏲11.30am-4pm) Survey the counter filled with sausages and sandwiches, then pick and buy. Primarily a takeaway, this simple eatery also has a covered terrace for escaping the summer heat. Good *rétes* (strudel).

Kemencés Csárda HUNGARIAN €€
(☎362 221; www.kemencescsarda.com; Darug zug 1/a; mains 1700-3300Ft) With its pseudo-rustic trappings and folksily clad waiters, this themed restaurant on the corner of Szilfákalja út (the main street) is cashing in on *puszta* tourism big time, but it is near the baths and the food is substantial (if not great).

Nelson INTERNATIONAL €€€
(☎270 226; www.nelsonpub.hu; Hősök tere 4; mains 1850-3590Ft) Like a captain's luxurious cabin on a 19th-century ship, the interior of this hotel-restaurant is very Horatio – all dark wood and brass. Upscale offerings include chicken fillet with goose liver and apricot purée, but there are simpler, vegetarian dishes, too. There's a great *cukrászda* (cake shop) atached.

Information

Main Post Office (Kálvin tér 1)

OTP Bank (Szilfákalja út 10) Next to the Coop supermarket; has an ATM.

Tourinform (☎558 929; www.hajduszoboszlo.hu; Szent István Park 1-3; ⏰9am-9pm daily Jun-Sep, 9am-5pm Mon-Sat Oct-May) At the spa's main entrance.

Getting There & Away

The bus station on Fürdő utca is just south of Mátyás király sétány. From Hajdúszoboszló at least five buses a day depart for Nádudvar (370Ft, 30 minutes, 19km) and Miskolc (2520Ft, 2½ hours, 120km). Up to 20 a day head for Debrecen (370Ft, 30 minutes, 19km).

The train station on Déli sor is a long 3km walk south via Rákóczi utca; take bus 1 or 1/a to the bus station.Trains headed from Debrecen (370Ft, 15 minutes, 20km) to Budapest (3690Ft, three hours, 201km) stop here half-hourly.

Kecskemét

☎76 / POP 113,300

Lying halfway between the Danube and the Tisza Rivers in the heart of the Southern Plain, Kecskemét is a city ringed with vineyards and orchards that don't seem to stop at the limits of this 'garden city'. Indeed, Kecskemét's agricultural wealth was used wisely – it was able to redeem all its debts in 1832 – and today it boasts some of the finest architecture of a small city in the country. Along with colourful Art Nouveau and Secessionist architecture, its fine museums and the region's excellent *barackpálinka* (apricot brandy) attract. And Kiskunság National Park, the *puszta* of the Southern Plain, is right at the back door. Day-trip opportunities include hiking in the sandy, juniper-covered hills, a horse show at Bugac or a visit to one of the region's many horse farms.

Sights

Kecskemét is a city of multiple squares that run into one another without definition. Walking northeast into Szabadság tér, for example, you'll pass the 17th-century Calvinist church and adjoining Calvinist New College (Református Újkollégium) from 1912, a later version of the Hungarian Romantic style that looks like a Transylvanian castle and is now a music school.

FREE Great Church CHURCH

(Nagytemplom; ☎487 501; Kossuth tér 2; ⏰9am-noon year-round plus 3-6pm May-Sep, closed Mon) The late-baroque Great Church, dedicated in 1806, dominates Kossuth tér, the southeasternmost of the main squares. Large tablets on the front honour (from left to right) a mounted regiment of Hussars that served in WWI; citizens who died in the 1848–49 War of Independence; and the Kecskemét victims of WWII. The 73m-tall tower offering views of the city's sun-bleached rooftops was closed at research time.

Franciscan Church of St Nicholas CHURCH

(Szent Miklós Ferences Templom; ☎497 025; Lestár tér) On the eastern side of Kossuth tér is the Franciscan Church of St Nicholas, dating in part from the late 14th century. It was shared by squabbling Catholics and Protestants during the Turkish occupation in the 16th century.

Zoltán Kodály Institute of Music Education MUSEUM

(Kodály Zoltán Zenepedagógiai Intézet; ☎481 518; www.kodaly-inst.hu; Kéttemplom koz 1; adult/child 150/100Ft; ⏰10am-6pm) The world-renowned music institute, established in 1975, occupies the baroque monastery behind the Franciscan church. There's a small exhibit inside devoted to the life and work of the eponymous founder-composer.

FREE City Hall ARCHITECTURE

(☎513 513 ext 2263; Kossuth tér 1; admission free; ⏰by arangement) The sandy-pink Town Hall, where you'll find the Tourinform office, is a lovely late-19th-century building designed by Ödön Lechner. With a mixture of Art Nouveau/Secessionist and folkloric elements, Lechner produced a uniquely Hungarian style. The exterior tilework is from the renowned Zsolnay porcelain factory in Pécs, and the carillon chimes out works by Ferenc Erkel, Kodály, Mozart, Handel and Beethoven several times during the day. The floral ceilings and frescoes of Hungarian heroes in the Ceremonial Hall (Díszterem) were painted by Bertalan Székely. Other beautiful examples of this architectural style are the restored **Otthon Cinema** (Széchenyi tér 4), on the corner of pedestrian Görögtemplom utca, and the Ornamental Palace (p211).

Ornamental Palace ARCHITECTURE

(Cifrapalota; Rákóczi út 1) The masterful Art Nouveau-style Ornamental Palace, which

Kecskemét

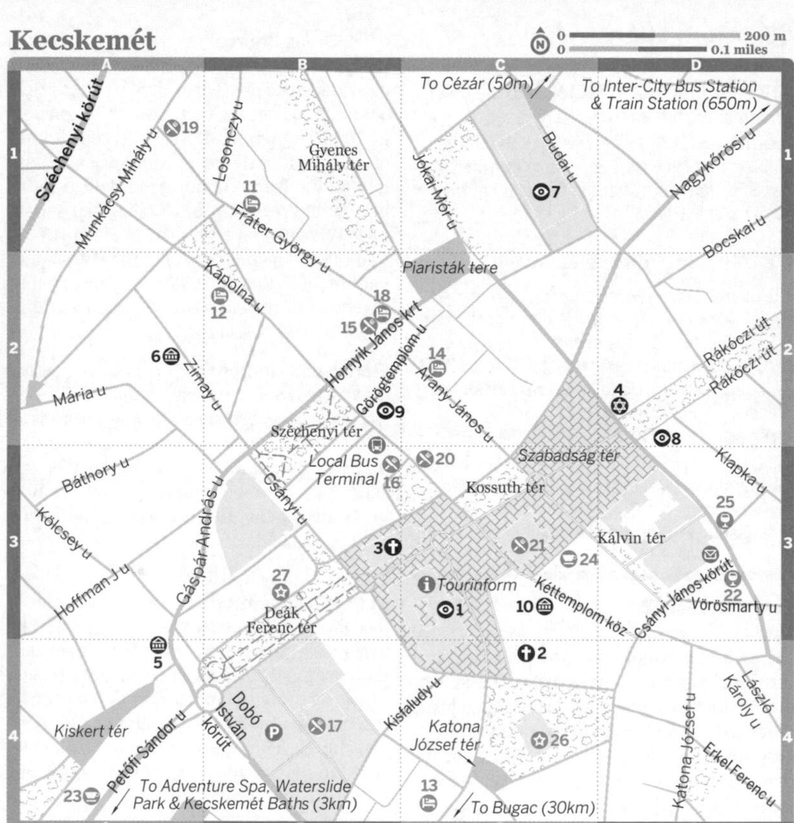

dates from 1902, has multicoloured majolica tiles decorating its 'waving' walls. The palace contains the **Kecskemét Gallery** (Kecskeméti Képtár; ☎480 776; www.museum.hu/kecskemet/keptar; adult/concession 500/270Ft; ⏰10am-5pm Tue-Sun). Its collection of 20th-century Hungarian art is large and important, but visit mainly to view the aptly named Decorative Hall (Díszterem) and its amazing stucco peacock, bizarre Secessionist windows and more colourful tiles.

House of Science & Technology JEWISH
(Tudomány és Technika Háza; ☎487 611; www.mtesz.hu; Rákóczi út 2; adult/child 300/150Ft; ⏰8am-4pm Mon-Fri) A Moorish-looking structure dating from 1871, this was once a synagogue and is now used for conferences and temporary exhibitions, including plaster copies of 15 statues by Michelangelo. There's a cafe here open till 9.30pm daily if you just want to catch a glimpse of the interior.

Hungarian Museum of Naive Artists MUSEUM
(Magyar Naiv Művészek Múzeuma; ☎324 767; www.museum.hu/kecskemet/naivmuzeum; Gáspár András utca 11; adult/child 450/250Ft; ⏰10am-5pm mid-Mar–Oct, closed Mon) Arguably the city's most interesting museum and one of the few of its kind in Europe, the Hungarian Museum of Naive Artists is in Stork House (1730) just off Petőfi Sándor utca. There are lots of folksy themes here, but the warmth and craft of Rozália Albert Juhászné's work, the druglike visions of Dezső Mokry-Mészáros, and the bright and comical paintings of András Süli should hold your attention. Something extra special is the work of István Kada – a Hungarian Grandma Moses – and János Balázs, whose glass paintings are somehow Magritte-like.

Toy Museum & Workshop MUSEUM
(Szórakaténusz Játékmúzeum; ☎481 469; www.szorakatenusz.hu; Gáspár András utca 11; adult/

Kecskemét

Sights

1 City Hall C3
2 Franciscan Church of St Nicholas C4
3 Great Church B3
4 House of Science & Technology D2
5 Hungarian Museum of Naive Artists A4
Kecskemét Gallery ..... (see 8)
6 Leskowsky Musical Instrument Collection A2
7 Market C1
8 Ornamental Palace D2
9 Otthon Cinema B2
Toy Museum & Workshop ..... (see 5)
10 Zoltán Kodály Institute of Music Education C3

Sleeping

11 Barokk Antik Panzió B1
12 Fábián Panzió B2
13 Hotel Három Gúnár C4
14 Pálma C2
15 Teachers' College B2

Eating

16 Aranyhomok Gyorsétterem B3
17 Géniusz B4
18 Italia Pizzeria B2
19 Kisbugaci Csárda A1
20 Lordok C3
21 Rozmaring C3

Drinking

22 Black Cat Pub D3
23 Jakó Cukrászda A4
24 Vincent C3
25 Wanted Söröző D3

Entertainment

26 József Katona Theatre C4
27 Kecskemét Cultural Centre B3

child 450/250Ft; ⏲10am-5pm Tue-Sun) Next door to the Hungarian Museum of Naive Artists, this museum has a large collection of rather spooky 19th- and early-20th-century dolls. Also in the rows of glass cases are wooden trains and board games. The museum organises events and classes for kids.

Hungarian Folk Craft Museum MUSEUM
(Népi Iparművészeti Múzeum; ☎327 203; www.nepiiparmuveszet.hu; Serfőző utca 19/a; adult/concession 500/250Ft; ⏲10am-5pm Tue-Sat Mar-Oct, to 4pm Nov-Feb) A dozen rooms of a 200-year-old farm complex are crammed with embroidery, weaving, woodcarving, furniture, agricultural tools and textiles at the Hungarian Folk Craft Museum, the granddaddy of all Kecskemét museums. Styles from across the entire region are represented and a few local handicrafts are for sale at the reception. It's located about 2km southwest of Kossuth tér.

Leskowsky Musical Instrument Collection MUSEUM
(Leskowsky Hangszergyűjtemény; ☎486 616; www.hangszergyujtemeny.hu; Zimay László utca 6/a; adult/child 1000/750Ft; ⏲by arrangement) This private collection traces the development of music-making over the centuries and has an assemblage of some 150 musical instruments from five continents. Visits must be arranged in advance.

Market MARKET
(Jókai Mór utca; ⏲6am-noon Tue-Sun) One of the liveliest on the Great Plain, Kecskemét's market north of the centre is worth a trip but get there as early as you can.

Activities

Adventure Spa & Waterslide Park SWIMMING
(Élményfürdő és Csúszdapark; ☎417 407; www.csuszdapark.hu; Csabay Géza körút 2; adult/child 1500/1150Ft; ⏲9am-8pm mid-May–Aug) Kecskeméts main summer attraction is this huge waterpark 3km southwest of the centre, which is loaded with fun things for the kids (five slides, huge pools, ball courts, grassy park) but is also equipped with three spas to soothe any aches and pains among older folk.

Kecskemét Baths SPA
(Kecskeméti Fürdő; ☎500 320; www.kecskemetifurdo.hu; Csabay Géza körút 5; adult/child 3600/2800Ft; ⏲6am-9pm) A year-round, rather extravagant complex with thermal baths, swimming pools, full spa facilities and every wellness treatment known to man, woman or child.

Festivals & Events

Kecskemét is a festive town indeed, with spring (March), summer (June through August) and winter (mid-December) cultural festivals that bring classical concerts to town. Mid to late August is especially celebratory: a weekend **International Air Show** kicks things off every other year, followed by the **Hirős Week Festival**, with folk and popular concerts, run concurrently with the **Wine Festival**, at which vintners from all across Hungary set up tasting booths on the squares.

Sleeping

Tourinform has a list of summer college accommodation.

TOP CHOICE Fábián Panzió GUESTHOUSE €€
(☎477 677; www.panziofabian.hu; Kápolna utca 14; s 9800-10,800Ft, d 11,000-12,800Ft; ❄@📶) We love, love, love this 10-room guesthouse on a quiet street that looks onto an inner courtyard garden. Four of the rooms are upstairs in the terraced main building; they're smaller and a bit cheaper than the six at nose level with the flowers and trees in the garden. The world-travelling family that owns the place seem to know exactly what their guests want: fridges and tea- and coffee-making facilities are room standards; there are local restaurant menus and tourist brochures to peruse; and bikes are available for rent. If the fabulous and very friendly service doesn't keep you coming back, the home-made scones and jam at breakfast will.

Hotel Három Gúnár HOTEL €€€
(☎483 611; www.hotelharomgunar.hu; Batthyány utca 1-7; s €54-73, d €60-79; ❄@📶) Four multihued town houses cobbled together to form a charming hotel on a quiet street in the late 1980s have now been renovated to within an inch of their lives and joined by a somewhat garish modern building with wellness facilities and a big conference centre. Guestrooms in the orginal hotel are small but have character. If size does matter, choose one of the 25 larger (but rather soulless) ones in the new building. There's a large restaurant on-site.

Pálma HOTEL €€
(☎321 045; www.hotelpalma.hu; Arany János utca 3; s 6100-8500Ft, d 8900-10,900Ft; ❄📶) As central in Kecskemét as you could possibly want to be, the Pálma has 40 simple guestrooms in two modern buildings. The more expensive ones are on the 1st floor and have TV, fridge and air-conditioning. Cheaper rooms are upstairs and have sloping ceilings, but are quiet and bright. Free self-service laundry facilities available.

Barokk Antik Panzió GUESTHOUSE €€
(☎260 3215; www.barokkantik-panzio.hu; Fráter György utca 17; s/d incl breakfast 8500/11,500Ft; 📶) A sombre painting or two does lend a bit of an old-world feel, but we wouldn't say the five rooms here have actual antiques; at least not baroque ones. Thankfully, the rooms are bright and spotlessly clean, and have minibars and very modern bathrooms.

Teachers' College HOSTEL €
(Tanítóképzö Főiskola; ☎486 977; www.kefo.hu; Piaristák tere 4; s/d 3500/7000Ft; ⊙mid-Jun–Aug; @) The most central and friendly of Kecskemét's summer college accommodation, this dormitory has basic rooms with twin beds and (mostly) en suite bathrooms.

Eating

Aranyhomok Gyorsétterem FAST FOOD €
(☎06 20 479 9199; Kossuth tér 3; mains 450-950Ft; ⊙7am-midnight Sun-Thu, to 2am Fri & Sat) Locals love the quick and tasty self-service cafeteria on the ground floor of the city's ugliest hotel.

Lordok SELF-SERVICE €
(☎06 70 866 0223; Kossuth tér 6-7; mains 500-900Ft; ⊙7am-midnight) This popular self-service canteen and adjoining trendier cafe-bar does triple duty as a cheap and tasty lunch option, a place for a mid-afternoon caffeine break and a comfortable spot for an after-dinner beer or cocktail.

Italia Pizzeria PIZZERIA €
(☎327 328; www.italiapizzeria.hu; Hornyik János körút 4; pizza 1090-1250Ft) Italia is a little short on atmosphere, but it does a roaring trade with students from the nearby teachers' college. A full menu also includes pasta dishes (950Ft to 1150FT) and meat mains (1490Ft to 1650Ft). Set lunch is just 990Ft.

Kisbugaci Csárda HUNGARIAN €€
(☎322 722; www.kisbugaci.hu/; Munkácsy Mihály utca 10; mains 1600-3800Ft; ⊙11am-11pm Mon-Sat, noon-4pm Sun) This place trades on folksy charm, with its wooden benches, plates on the wall and Gypsy music. But the food, which comes in huge meaty portions, holds its own. Try the *Erdélyi flekken* (Transylvanian barbecue) or the *betyár pörkölt* (thief's stew).

TOP CHOICE **Cézár** ITALIAN €€

(☎328 849; www.clubcaruso.hu; Kaszap utca 4; mains 2200-4200Ft) As authentic a *ristorante italiano* as you'll find in the Hungarian provinces, Cézár serves dishes made with ingredients almost entirely sourced in Italy. The minestrone and tomato and mozzarella salad are out of this world. The choice of pizza (980Ft to 1400Ft) and pasta dishes (1800Ft to 2700Ft) is huge but don't be frightened off by the gargantuan sizes of the main course as it does half-portions. The Caruso house wine is, in fact, Hungarian from Kiskunhalas and quite drinkable.

Rozmaring HUNGARIAN €€€

(☎509 175; www.rozmaringbisztro.hu; Szabadság tér 2; mains 1800-4300Ft; ✎) Artistic presentations come standard at this silver-service restaurant, whether you order the traditional stuffed cabbage or the mixed sautéed chicken with eggplant. This is modern Hungarian done right. Streetside tables on the pedestrian square have the best seats in town for people-watching.

Géniusz INTERNATIONAL €€€

(☎497 668; www.geniuszetterem.hu; Kisfaludy utca 5; mains 2200-4500Ft; ✎) This is business-lunch territory but not for nothing as the rather inventive menu changes seasonally, and options might include stuffed trout with almonds or Thai chicken. What it calls 'light dishes' (1750Ft to 2250Ft) are largely vegetarian.

Drinking

Wanted Söröző PUB

(☎415 923; Csányi János körút 4; ⏲8am-midnight Mon-Thu, 10am-2am Fri & Sat, 10am-midnight Sun) This Western-themed pub just down from the Ornamental Palace is where Kecskemét's young bloods congregate.

Black Cat Pub PUB

(☎06 70 299 4040; Csányi János körút 6; ⏲11am-midnight Sun-Thu, to 2am Fri & Sat) Diagonally opposite the Wanted Söröző, the Black Cat – more a bar than a pub – offers an alternative night on the town.

Vincent CAFE

(☎06 30 570 0518; Szabadság tér 6; ⏲8am-10pm Mon-Fri, 9am-midnight Sat, to 10pm Sun) We've always tended to avoid the eating and drinking outlets on Szabadság tér like the plague but we make an exception for Vincent. It serves excellent coffee and is a decent place for such a central (read touristy) location.

Jakó Cukrászda CAFE

(Petőfi Sándor utca 7; cakes 130-350Ft; ⏲9am-8pm) This is where locals go in season for cake and ice cream when they are trying to avoid tourist-rammed Szabadság tér.

Entertainment

Kecskemét is a city of music and theatre; cultural festivals are on nearly year-round. Check out the free weekly *Kecskeméti Est* (www.est.hu) for listings.

Kecskemét Cultural Centre PERFORMING ARTS

(Kecskeméti Kulturális Központ; ☎503 890; Deák Ferenc tér 1) The cultural centre sponsors some events and is a good source of information.

József Katona Theatre THEATRE

(Katona József Színház; ☎501 170; www.kecskemetikatona.hu; Katona József tér 5) This attractive 19th-century theatre named after the eponymous local boy who brought new life to Hungarian theatre stages dramatic works, as well as operettas and concerts.

Information

Ibusz (☎486 955; www.ibusz.hu; Korona utca 2, Malom Centre) In central shopping plaza; for apartment rental.

Main Post Office (Kálvin tér 10)

OTP Bank (Korona utca 2, Malom Centre) Foreign exchange and ATM; in central shopping centre.

Tourinform (☎481 065; www.kecskemet.hu; Kossuth tér 1; ⏲8am-5pm Mon-Fri, 9am-1pm Sat & Sun Jun-Aug, 8am-6pm Mon-Fri Sep-May) In the northeastern corner of City Hall; rents bikes and can advise on excursions to Kiskunság National Park.

Getting There & Away

The intercity bus and main train stations are opposite one another near József Katona Park, a 10-minute walk northeast along Nagykőrösi utca from Szabadság tér.

Bus

DESTINATION	PRICE	TIME	KM	FREQUENCY
Baja	2200Ft	2½hr	110	4 daily
Budapest	1680Ft	1½hr	84	hourly
Debrecen	3950Ft	4hr	235	1 daily
Eger	3410Ft	4hr	186	3 daily
Gyula	2830Ft	3¼hr	144	2 daily
Pécs	3690Ft	4½hr	200	2 daily
Szeged	1860Ft	2hr	89	hourly

Train

Kecskemét is on the train line linking Nyugati train station in Budapest (2200Ft, 1¾ hours, 106km) with Szeged (1680Ft, 1½ hours, 85km) at least hourly. To get to other towns north and east, you must change at Cegléd (650Ft, 30 minutes, 33km).

Getting Around

Buses 1 and 15 link the intercity bus and train stations with the local bus terminal behind Aranyhomok Gyorsétterem. For the water parks/spas, buses 5 and 22 are good. Rent bicycles at Tourinform (p215) for 1000/3000Ft per hour/day.

Kiskunság National Park

76

Kiskunság National Park (Kiskunsági Nemzeti Park; www.knp.hu) consists of nine 'islands' of land totalling more than 76,000 hectares. Much of the park's alkaline ponds, dunes and grassy 'deserts' are off-limits to casual visitors. Ask about birding and other tours at the park's main office in Kecskemét – the so-called **House of Nature** (Természet Háza; 482 611; www.knp.hu; Liszt Ferenc utca 19; 9am-4pm Tue-Fri, 10am-2pm Sat Apr-Oct, 9am-4pm Mon-Fri Nov-Mar) – or check its useful website.

The easiest place to get up close with this environmentally fragile area and see the famous horse herds go through their paces is at **Bugac** (www.bugac.hu) – population 2850 – on a sandy steppe 30km southwest of Kecskemét. Board a **horse-driven carriage** (adult/child incl cowboy show 3500/2500Ft; 11.30am May-Oct), walk or drive the 1.5km along the sandy track to the **Herder Museum** (Pásztormúzeum; 575 112; www.museum.hu/bugac/pasztormuzeum; admission free; 10am-5pm May-Oct), a circular structure designed to look like a horse-driven dry mill. It's filled with stuffed fauna and shepherds' implements – carved wooden pipes, embroidered fur coats and a tobacco pouch made from a gnarled old ram's scrotum.

The highlight of a trip here is the chance to see the *puszta* **cowboy show** (csikósbemutató; www.bugacpuszta.hu; admission 1400Ft; 12.15pm May-Oct). In addition to making noble Nonius steeds perform tricks that most dogs would be disinclined to do, the *csikósok* crack their whips, race one another bareback and ride 'five-in-hand'. This is a breathtaking performance in which one *csikós* gallops five horses around the field at full tilt while standing on the backs of the rear two.

There are several nature and educational hiking trails in the vicinitiy with explanatory sign-posting in English where you can get out and see this amazing ecosystem of dunes, bluffs and swamps. The circular 2km Juniper Trail (Boróka Sáv), behind the stables, is an interpretive track that leads you to the edge of the juniper forest and sandy hills (a restricted area). You can take an offshoot trail to a nearby tower for a better look before heading back.

The food is surprisingly good at the entirely kitschy **Karikás Csárda** (575 112; www.bugacpuszta.hu/en/?pid=310; Nagybugac 135; mains 1600-3800Ft; 10am-10pm May-Sep, to 8pm Apr & Oct), next to the park entrance. The *gulyás* (beef goulash soup; 900Ft) is hearty and the accompanying folk-music ensemble will get your foot tapping on the large and shady terrace.

Getting to the show without your own vehicle is difficult. There's a morning bus from Kecskemét to Bugac (745Ft, one hour, 37km) but it won't get you there in time for the 12.15pm show. (Buses before that leave at an ungodly 5.25am weekdays and 6.30am at the weekend.) An alternative but complicated way to go is to take the hourly train to Kiskunfélegyháza (465Ft, 16 minutes, 25km) at 9.11am and then the hourly bus to Bugac (370Ft, 30 minutes, 18km).

Kalocsa

78 / POP 17,200

Kalocsa is as celebrated for its paprika and folk art as for its long and rich history. Together with Esztergom, Kalocsa was one of the two bishopric seats founded by King Stephen in 1009 from the country's 10 dioceses. The brilliantly flowered folk art originating here – embroidery, painting and pottery – is recognised all over the country.

Sights

Almost everything of interest in Kalocsa is on or near the main drag, Szent István király út, beginning at Szentháromság tér, where the Trinity Column (1786) is corroding into sand.

Kalocsa Cathedral CHURCH

(Kalocsai Főszékesegyház; Astrik tér) Kalocsa Cathedral (1754) was completed by András Mayerhoffer and is a baroque masterpiece, with a dazzling pink-and-gold interior full

HUNGARY'S RED GOLD

Along with Szeged, Kalocsa is the largest producer of paprika, the *piros arany* ('red gold') so important to Hungarian cuisine. It is used to season *halaszlé* (fish soup), *gulyás* (beef goulash soup), *pörkölt* (stew) and *paprikas* (dishes in a creamy piquant sauce), and Hungarians consume about a half-kilo of the spice per person per year. You can learn all about its development (first mentioned in documents in the 16th century), production and beneficial qualities (it's higher in vitamin C than citrus fruits) at not one, but two museums in Kalocsa: the central **Paprika Museum** (☎461 819; www.puszta.com/eng/programs/cikk/paprika_muzeum_kalocsa; Szentháromság tér 2-3; adult/child 800/500Ft; ⏲10am-5pm May-Oct) and the larger **Kalocsa Paprika House** (Kalocsai Paprika Ház; ☎462 998; www.paprikart.hu; Kossuth Lajos utca 15; adult/child 600/300Ft; ⏲10am-4pm mid-May–Oct). Perhaps the best way to learn all about *Capsicum annum* is to come during **Kalocsa Paprika Festival** in mid-September where you can sample both the *édes* (sweet) and *csipős* or *erös* (hot or strong) versions of the spice in a range of dishes.

of stucco, reliefs and tracery. Some believe that the sepulchre in the crypt is that of the first archbishop of Kalocsa, Asztrik, who brought King Stephen the gift of a crown from Pope Sylvester II, thereby legitimising the Christian convert's control over Hungary. A statue of the Asztrik on Szent István király út recalls this event. Franz Liszt was the first to play the cathedral's magnificent 3560-pipe organ.

Archbishop's Palace HISTORIC BUILDING
(Érseki palota; Szentháromság tér 1) The Great Hall and the chapel of the Archbishop's Palace built in 1766 contain magnificent frescoes by Franz Anton Maulbertsch, but you won't get to see these unless a concert is being held. More than 100,000 volumes, including 13th-century codices and a Bible belonging to Martin Luther that is annotated in the reformer's hand, make the **Archbishop's Library** (Érseki könyvtár; ☎465 280; http://konyvtar.asztrik.hu/; adult/child 800/500Ft; ⏲9am-5pm Apr-Oct, tours noon & 2pm, closed Mon) here one of the most impressive in Hungary.

Cathedral Treasury MUSEUM
(Főszékesegyházi kincstár; ☎462 641; Hunyadi János utca 2; adult/child 800/500Ft; ⏲9am-5pm May-Oct, closed Mon) The Cathedral Treasury, just east of the cathedral across Kossuth Lajos utca, is a trove of gold and bejewelled objects, vestments and church plate. The large bust of St Stephen was cast for the Millenary Exhibition in 1896 and contains 48kg of silver and 2kg of gold. Among other valuable objects is a 16th-century reliquary of St Anne and a gold and crystal baroque monstrance.

Károly Viski Museum MUSEUM
(☎462 351; www.museum.hu/museum/index_hu.php?ID=117; Szent István király út 25; adult/child 500/250Ft; ⏲9am-5pm Wed-Sun mid-May–mid-Sep, Tue-Sat mid-Mar–mid-May & mid-Sep–Oct) This museum is very rich in folk art, and highlights the life and ways of the Swabian (Sváb), Slovak (Tót), Serbian (Rác) as well as the Magyar peoples of the area. It's surprising to see how colourful interiors of peasant houses became as wealth increased; walls, furniture, doors – virtually nothing was left undecorated by the famous 'painting women' of Kalocsa. The museum also has a large collection of coins dating back to Roman times, as well as minerals.

House of Folk Arts MUSEUM
(Népmüvészeti tájház; ☎461 560; www.museum.hu/kalocsa/nepmuveszeti; Tompa Mihály utca 5-7; adult/child 400/200Ft; ⏲10am-5pm mid-Apr–mid-Oct, closed Mon) You'll see lavish examples of wall and furniture painting at this museum in a former peasant's cottage. There's a good selection of Kalocsa embroidery in the adjoining gift shop.

Kalocsa Painted Porcelain Factory CRAFT
(Kalocsai porcelánfestő manufaktúra; ☎462 017; www.porcelanfesto.hu; Malatin tér 5; adult/child 500/400Ft; ⏲8am-5pm Mon-Fri, 10am-2pm Sat) Tour this factory to see the making of the modern version of Kalocsa painted plates before you buy. Some find the bright tulips, daisies and paprikas rather garish – we rather like them.

Nicolas Schöffer Collection MUSEUM
(Nicolas Schöffer gyűjtemény; ☎462 256; http://nicolasschoffer.blogspot.co.uk; Szent István király

út 76; adult/child 500/250Ft; ⌚10am-5pm, closed Mon) An exhibition of the futuristic work of the Paris-based modern artist Nicolas Schöffer (1912–76), who was born in Kalocsa and is celebrated for his kinetic sculptures, can be seen at this small but enlightening museum. Near the bus station, Schöffer's Chronos 8 kinetic light tower (1982) is a Meccano-set creation of steel beams and spinning reflecting mirrors that two decades ago was supposed to portend the art of the future.

Festivals & Events

Embroidered folk costumes are best seen at the **Danube International Multicultural Festival**, held in mid-June. The **Kalocsa Paprika Festival**, held over two days in mid-September, celebrates the harvest of the town's 'red gold' with cauldrons of paprika-infused foods, handicrafts for sale and entertainment.

Sleeping

Club Hotel Kalocsa HOTEL €€
(☎562 804; www.clubhotelkalocsa.hu; Szent István király út 64; d 7600-10,000Ft, tr 11,400Ft; ❄📶) Seven rooms above a popular pub and pizzeria with a dubious name do not a luxury hotel make. While the cheaper ground-floor rooms are forgettable in the extreme, the ones above have balconies and air-conditioning. The place is very central to the bus station.

Hotel Kalocsa HOTEL €€€
(☎469 000; www.hotelkalocsa.hu; Szentháromság tér 4; s 13,500-15,500Ft, d 20,000-22,000Ft; ❄📶🏊) Carved mouldings on the furniture and tapestry drapes feel entirely appropriate in this 1780 building that used to house church offices, but the 31 guestrooms in two buildings are beginning to look a bit threadbare. Your stay includes entry to the on-site thermal pool, Jacuzzi and sauna. There's a fine restaurant and cafe here, too.

Eating & Drinking

Karona HUNGARIAN €
(☎463 102; www.koronaetterem.hu; Szent István király út 6; mains 1000-2800Ft; ⌚11am-4pm Sun & Mon, to 10pm Tue-Sat) Descend the brick stairs to the cellar for excellent fish soup or a pork chop stuffed with onions, garlic and paprika. In the warmer months, though, plump for a seat in the lovely garden or on the terrace overlooking Szent István király ú.

Club 502 S&M PIZZERIA €
(☎462 295; www.club502.hu; Szent István király út 64; pizza 990-1440Ft) This may be a garrison town, but the bar scene is pretty dire. The intriguingly named Club No 502 S&M is a boisterous option for those looking to have a pizza and (perhaps) more than their fair share of beer and other entertainment.

Barokk Kavéház CAFE
(☎06 30 896 2558; Szent István király út 2-4; cakes 280-400Ft; ⌚8am-8pm Mon-Fri, 9am-9pm Sat & Sun) This cafe opposite the cathedral attracts many locals with its location and relaxed atmosphere.

Dublin Irish Pub PUB
(Szent István király út 87; ⌚24hr) It's a long way to Tipperary – and Dublin for that matter – from eastern Hungary but this rough-and-ready pub will keep you entertained all through the night.

Shopping

You can buy embroidered aprons, handkerchiefs and tablecloths at the House of Folk Arts (p217), Károly Viski Museum (p217) and the small **Kalocsa Folk Art Shop** (Népművészeti Bolt Kalocsa; Szentháromság tér 3; ⌚10am-4pm Mon-Sat, to noon Sun) across from the cathedral.

Information

Kalocsa website (www.kalocsa.hu) Useful multilingual official website.

OTP Bank (Szent István király út 43-45) With ATM.

Post Office (Szent István király út 44)

Getting There & Away

The bus station lies at the southern end of tree-lined Szent István király út. Buses connect Kalocsa with Budapest (2520Ft, 2¼ hours, 122km, eight daily), Kecskemét (1680Ft, two hours, 86km, two daily) and Szeged (2200Ft, three hours, 117km, four daily).

Szeged

☎62 / POP 170,300

It's hard to name the single thing that makes Szeged such an appealing city. Is it the the shady, garden-like main square with all the park benches or the the abundant street-side cafe seating in a pedestrian area that seems to stretch on forever? Maybe it's the interesting architecture of the old-town palaces. Then again, it could be the year-round cultural performances and lively university-town vibe. Szeged – a corruption of the Hungarian word *sziget* (island) – sits astride the Tisza River, with a thermal bath complex and park opposite the old town. Famed local edibles include Pick salami and its own local paprika that marries so well with spicy *Szegedi halaszlé*. From here it's a hop, skip and a jump to the national historic park in Ópusztaszer or the lovely town of Hódmezővásárhely.

History

Remnants of the Körös culture suggest that these goddess-worshipping people lived in the Szeged area 4000 or 5000 years ago, and one of the earliest Magyar settlements in Hungary was at Ópusztaszer to the north. By the 13th century the city was an important trading centre, helped by the royal monopoly it held on the salt shipped in via the Maros River from Transylvania. Under the Turks, Szeged was given some protection as the sultan's estates lay in the area, and it continued to prosper in the 18th and 19th centuries as a royal free town.

The watery fingers of the Tisza almost choked Szeged off the map in 1879, when the river burst its banks, leaving fewer than 300 houses, out of an estimated 6300, standing. At least 600 people died and 60,000 were left homeless. The town bounced back and rebuilt in great haste. As a result, Szeged has an architectural uniformity unknown in most other Hungarian cities, and the leafy, broad avenues that ring the city in an almost perfect circle were named after the European cities that helped bring Szeged back to life. Szeged is an important university centre; students marched here in 1956 even before their classmates in Budapest.

Sights

Dóm Tér SQUARE

(Cathedral Square) 'Cathedral Square' contains Szeged's most important buildings and monuments and is the centre of events during the annual summer festival. The **National Pantheon** (Nemzeti Emlékcsarnok; admission free; ⏲24hr) – statues and reliefs of 80 notables running along an arcade around three sides of the square – is a crash course in Hungarian art, literature, culture and history. Even the Scotsman Adam Clark, who supervised the building of Budapest's Chain Bridge, wins a place of honour, but you'll look high and low for a woman.

The Romanesque **St Demetrius Tower** (Dömötö-torony; Dóm tér), the city's oldest structure, is all that remains of a church erected here in the 12th century. Adjacent stands the twin-towered **Votive Church** (Fogadalmi templom; ☎420 157; www.dom.szeged.hu; Dóm tér; admission free; ⏲6.30am-7pm Mon-Sat, from 7.30am Sun), a disproportionate brown brick monstrosity that was pledged after the 1879 flood but built from 1913 to 1930. About the only things worth seeing inside are the organ, with more than 11,500 pipes; the dome covered with frescoes; and the choir. The **Serbian Orthodox church** (Görögkeleti Szerb ortodox templom; ☎424 246; Dóm tér; adult/child 400/300Ft; ⏲8am-5pm), at the northeastern end of the square, was built in 1778. Take a peek inside at the fantastic iconostasis: a central gold 'tree', with 70 icons hanging from its 'branches'. Back on Dóm tér, duck into the **Diocesan Museum & Treasury** (Egyházmegyei Múzeum és Kincstár; ☎420 932; www.museum.hu/szeged/egyhazmegyei; Dom tér 5; adult/concession 100/50Ft; ⏲10am-6pm Apr-Oct, closed Mon) and wade through the collection of monstrances, chalices and other liturgical objects.

Ferenc Móra Museum MUSEUM

(☎549 040; www.mfm.u-szeged.hu; Roosevelt tér 1-3; adult/concession 900/600Ft; ⏲10am-6pm Tue, Wed & Fri-Sun, to 8pm Thu) The erstwhile Palace of Education built in 1896 now houses this excellent museum containing a colourful collection of folk art from Csongrád County as well as traditional trades. After the 1879 flood claimed many of the walls of Szeged's riverfront castle built around 1240, the city demolished the rest. Behind the Ferenc Móra Museum you can see ongoing excavations of the foundation; for a closer look at the ancient subterranean walls, visit the nearby **Castle Museum & Lapidarium** (Varmuzéum és kötár; ☎549 040; Stefánia sétány 15; adult/child 300/200Ft; ⏲10am-5pm, closed Mon), a small gallery with some archaeological finds.

New Synagogue JEWISH

(Új Zsinagóga; ☎423 849; www.zsinagoga.szeged.hu; Jósika utca 10; adult/concession 400/200Ft; ⏲10am-noon & 1-5pm Apr-Sep, 10am-2pm Oct-Mar, closed Sat) For many people, Szeged's most compelling sight is the Hungarian Art Nouveau New Synagogue, which was designed by Lipót Baumhorn in 1903. It is the most beautiful Jewish house of worship in Hungary and is still in use, though the comunity has dwindled from 8000 before WWII to about

Szeged

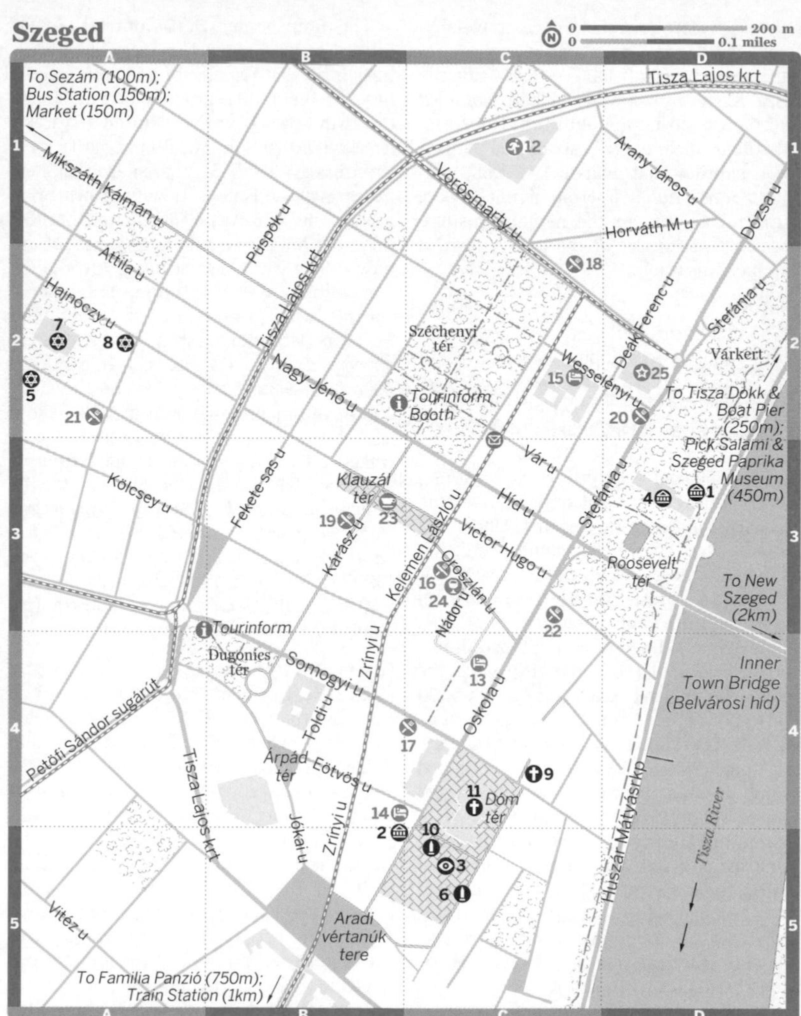

50 people. If the grace and enormous size of the exterior don't impress you, the blue-and-gold interior will. The cupola, decorated with stars and flowers (representing infinity and faith), appears to float skyward, and the tabernacle of carved acacia wood and metal fittings is a masterpiece. The stained glass is the work of Miksa Róth. There are a few other buildings of interest in this area, the former Jewish quarter, including a **former Jewish community centre** (Zsidó Hitközség; Gutenberg utca 20) built in 1902, which once served as an old-age home, and the neoclassical **Old Synagogue** (Ózsinagóga; Hajnóczy utca 12), built in 1843. It now houses theatre workshops.

Pick Salami & Szeged Paprika Museum MUSEUM
(Pick szalámi és Szegedi paprika múzeum; ☎06 20 989 8000; www.pickmuzeum.hu; Felső Tisza-part 10; adult/child incl salami tasting & paprika sample 980/740Ft; ⏱3-6pm, closed Mon) Between the two bridges spanning the Tisza is this museum with two floors of exhibits showing the methods of salami production and the cultivating, processing and packaging of Szeged's 'red gold'. It's a lot more interesting than

Szeged

Sights
1 Castle Museum & Lapidarium D3
2 Diocesan Museum & Treasury B5
3 Dóm Tér C5
4 Ferenc Móra Museum D3
5 Former Jewish Community Centre A2
6 National Pantheon C5
7 New Synagogue A2
8 Old Synagogue A2
9 Serbian Orthodox Church C4
10 St Demetrius Tower C5
11 Votive Church C4

Activities, Courses & Tours
12 Anna Baths C1

Sleeping
13 Dóm Hotel C4
14 István Apáthy College B4
15 Tisza Hotel C2

Eating
16 Bistorant C3
17 Boci Tejivó C4
18 Classic Cafe C2
19 Graffito Pizzeria B3
20 Port Royal Étterem D2
21 Taj Mahal A2
22 Vendéglő A Régi Hídhoz C3

Drinking
23 A Cappella B3
24 John Bull Pub C3

Entertainment
25 Szeged National Theatre D2

you might think and you even get samples. There's a pub-restaurant (set lunch 950Ft) in the factory building and a delicatessen-cum-butcher around the corner.

Activities

The lovely cream-coloured **Anna Baths** (☎553 330; www.szegedsport.hu; Tisza Lajos körút 24; adult/child 1650/1350Ft; ⏰6am-8pm) were built in 1896 to imitate the tilework and soaring dome of a Turkish bath. Rich architectural detail surrounds all the modern aromatherapy saunas and bubbly pools you'd expect.

Across the Tisza in what is called New Szeged (Újszeged), there is a small public beach on the bank south of the bridge. But the main attraction nowadays is **Napfényfürdő Aquapolis** (☎566 488; www.napfenyfurdoaquapolis.com; Torontál tér 1; ⏰6am-9pm, outdoor pools 8am-8pm May-Sep), a positively enormous spa and waterpark with all manner of pools inside and out, basins with thermal water, saunas and steam rooms and treatment centres. Flanking the complex is New Szeged Park (Újszegedi Liget), a great place for walking and biking.

See Szeged from a different vantage point altogether by taking a **boat cruise** (Hajókirándulás; ☎06 20 230 8817, 402 302; www.hajokirandulas.hu; adult/child 1200/900Ft; ⏰1pm & 3pm May-Sep, 11am, 1pm, 3pm & 5pm Sat & Sun mid-Mar–Oct), which departs from the Mahart pier at the eastern end of Tisza Lajos körút between two and four times a day. The excursion lasts an hour and takes you northward to where the Maros flows into the Tisza and then southward past the old town.

Festivals & Events

The **Szeged Open-Air Festival** (☎541 205; www.szegediszabadteri.hu) unfolds on Dóm tér in July and August. The outdoor theatre in front of the Votive Church seats some 6000 people. Main events include an opera, an operetta, a play, folk dancing, classical music, ballet and a rock opera. Other events include the 10-day **Wine Festival** in the second half of May and the pretty (and fragrant) three-day **Rose Festival** in late June.

Sleeping

Tourinform has a full list of summer college accommodation.

István Apáthy College HOSTEL €
(Apáthy István Kollégium; ☎545 896; www.apathy.szote.u-szeged.hu; Apáthy utca 4; dm/s/d 4100/5500/6500Ft; @📶) Strong feelings about the Apáthy? This supremely central option offers pretty bare-bones dormitory accommodation. More than 200 rooms are available in July and August, but only a handful throughout the rest of the year. There are communal kitchens and a laundry room on each floor.

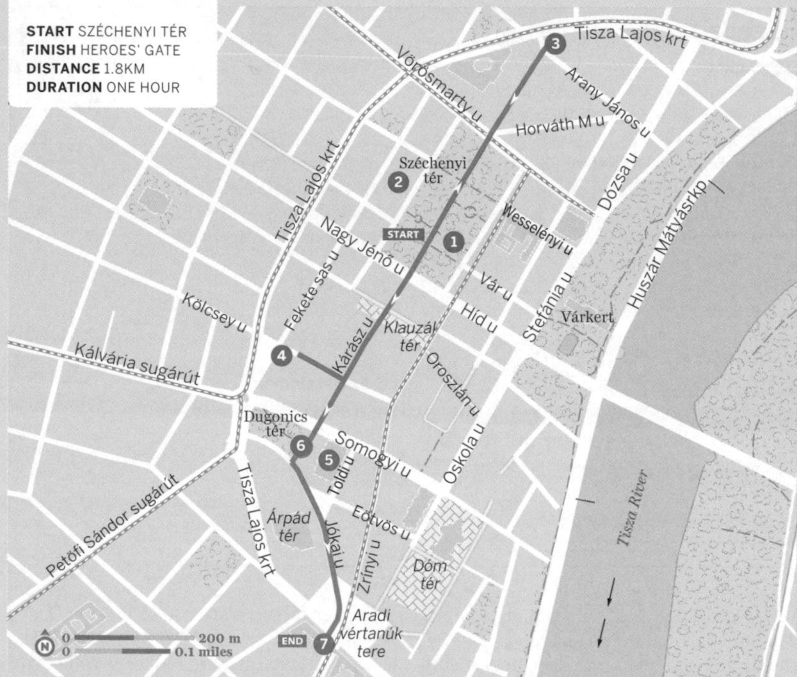

Walking Tour
Szeged

Begin your walking tour of Szeged in Széchenyi tér, a square so large it's almost a park.

On the southeast side under the plane and linden trees, the 1 **Pál Vásarhelyi monument** immortalises the man who designed the regulation of the Tisza River. Marble plaques on the plinth indicate the high-water levels of floods in 1970 and 2006. On the west side of the square is the neobaroque 2 **town hall**, with its bizarre, top-heavy tower and colourful tiled roof. Take a quick detour north of the square to the 3 **Gróf Palace**, a Secessionist office building completed in 1913.

Pedestrian Kárász utca leads south through redesigned Klauzál tér. Turn west on Kölcsey utca and walk for about 100m to the 4 **Reök Palace**, a mind-blowing green-and-lilac Art Nouveau structure built in 1907 that looks like an aquarium decoration. It now serves as an exhibition space and cafe.

Further south, Kárász utca meets Dugonics tér, site of the 5 **Attila József Science University** (abbreviated JATE in Hungarian), named after its most famous alumnus. József (1905–37), a much-loved poet, was actually expelled from here in 1924 for writing controversial verse during the ultraconservative rule of Admiral Miklós Horthy. A 6 **music fountain** in the square plays at irregular intervals throughout the day.

From the southeast corner of Dugonics tér, walk along Jókai utca into Aradi vértanúk tere. 7 **Heroes' Gate** to the south was erected in 1936 in honour of Horthy's White Guards, who were responsible for 'cleansing' the nation of 'reds' after the ill-fated Republic of Councils in 1919. The brutish sculptures will send a chill down your spine.

New Szeged Bath & Camping CAMPGROUND €
(Újszegedi partfürdő és kemping; ☎430 843; www.szegedcamping.hu; Középkikötő sor 1-3; campsites per person/tent 990/390Ft, s/d/tr from 3000/5400/6900Ft, bungalows 8000-11,500Ft; ⏲May-Sep;) The large grassy camping ground with sites for 700 happy campers, volleyball courts and a beach on the Tisza River looks a bit like a public park. Bungalows on stilts, containing both rooms and apartments (with kitchens), are also available.

Familia Panzió GUESTHOUSE €€
(☎441 122; www.familiapanzio.hu; Szentháromság utca 71; s/d/tr from 7000/9500/14,000Ft;) Families and international travellers often book up this family-run guesthouse with contemporary, if nondescript, furnishings in a great old-town building close to the train station. The reception may be dim, but the two dozen rooms have high ceilings and loads of light from tall windows. Air-conditioning costs an extra 1200Ft.

Illés Panzió GUESTHOUSE €€
(☎315 640; www.illespanzio-vadaszetterem.hu; Maros utca 37; d 13,000Ft;) The cheery facade of this former mansion northeast of the centre stands in stark contrast to its 14 rooms' dark-wood veneers and woven rugs. The courtyard garden with pool is quite pleasant, though. Walk 10 minutes to the city centre, or rent a bike (per day 1000Ft). There's a cellar restaurant here too.

Tisza Hotel HISTORIC HOTEL €€€
(☎478 278; www.tiszahotel.hu; Széchenyi tér 3; s/d classic 15,700/17,900Ft, superior 17,800/20,800Ft;) Szeged's fine old-world hotel drips with crystal chandeliers and gilt mirrors, but many of its 49 rooms don't match up to the public elegance. All in all, it's a lovely (if somewhat frayed) place with large, bright and airy rooms. Go for the superior ones if you can afford to.

Dóm Hotel BOUTIQUE HOTEL €€€
(☎423 750; www.domhotel.hu; Bajza utca 6; s/d/apt 26,500/30,500/47,000Ft; @) A welcome addition to Szeged top-end accomodation scene is this very smart and extremely central 16-room hotel. There's a small wellness centre with Jacuzzi, sauna and massage, a very popular inhouse restaurant and a 21st-centry underground carpark accessed by lift. But the main draw here is the extremely helpful multilingual staff for whom no request is too much.

Hotel Forrás HOTEL €€€
(☎566 466; www.hotelforras.hunguesthotels.hu; Szent-Györgyi Albert utca 16-24; s/d €101/142; @) This enormous hotel on the doorstep of the Napfényfürdő Aquapolis spa (entry included in the room price) in New Szeged underwent a massive renovation in 2010 and has come up trumps. The 196 rooms are large and most have balconies; the preference for orange, chocolate and tan is rather masculine, but somehow works. As bowlers from way back, we love the four fully equipped lanes just begging for a strike. Bike rental is available.

Eating

Boci Tejivó FAST FOOD €
(☎423 154; www.bocitejivo.hu; Zrínyi utca 2; mains 260-500Ft; ⏲24hr) This is a very modern take on an old-fashion idea – the 'milk bar' so popular during socialist times. Order from among the dozens of meatless dishes – cheese and mushroom omelettes, noodles with walnuts or poppyseed and anything with the ever-popular *túró* (curds), especially *túrógombóc* (curd dumplings; 590Ft).

Sezám SELF-SERVICE €
(London körút 17; mains 280-590Ft; ⏲11am-9pm Mon-Fri, to 7pm Sat) Eatery with cafeteria-style food offers good value just opposite the bus station.

Graffito Pizzeria PIZZERIA €
(☎423 830; www.graffitopizzeria.hu; Kárász utca 5; 1250-2950Ft) Ask any local where the best palace for pizza and pasta is and they'll send you to this lively spot on Szeged's main pedestrian drag. It does more serious mains as well as Mexican *quesadillas*, but when in Rome, take Roman advice.

Kiskőrössy Halászcsárda FISH €€
(☎555 886; www.kiskorossyhalaszcsarda.hu; Felső Tisza-part 336; mains 1100-3300Ft) Housed in a traditional fisherman's cottage with terrace on the banks of the Tisza a few kilometres east of the centre, this excellent fish restaurant is an atmospheric place to dine. Have one of the many fish soups on offer, a whole roasted pike with garlic or fillet of carp, and watch the boats go by. To reach it take trolleybus 9 to Etelka sor then walk 300m east along Felső Tisza part.

Vendéglő A Régi Hídhoz HUNGARIAN €€
(At the Old Bridge; ☎420 910; www.regihid.hu; Oskola utca 4; mains 1400-2400Ft) For an authentic meal that won't break the bank, head for

WORTH A TRIP

ÓPUSZTASZER & HÓDMEZŐVÁSÁRHELY

Two easy day trips from Szeged, which can be combined if you're travelling under your own steam, are to Ópusztaszer, 28km to the north, and Hódmezővásárhely, 31km to the northeast.

Visit Ópusztaszer (population 2300) to see **Ópusztaszer National Historical Heritage Park** (Ópusztaszeri nemzeti történeti emlékpark; ☎275 133; www.opusztaszer.hu; adult/child day pass 3200/2400Ft; ⊙10am-6pm daily Apr-early Nov, 10am-4pm Tue-Sun early Nov-Mar), which commemorates the 9th-century *honfoglalás* (conquest) of the Carpathian Basin by the Magyars. The enormous 360° panorama painting in the Rotunda entitled *The Arrival of the Hungarians* completed by Árpád Feszty for the Millenary Exhibition in Budapest in 1896 is worth the trip as is the **open-air museum** (skanzen; ⊙10am-6pm daily Apr-early Nov, 10am-4pm Tue-Sun early Nov-Mar).

Hódmezővásárhely (population 47,000; its long, funny name simply means 'Beaver Meadow Marketplace'), is the quintessential well-groomed Hungarian town and well worth the trip for its sights. It was once an artist colony; view a vast collection of local pottery at the renovated **János Tornyai Museum** (☎242 2234; www.tornyaimuzeum.hu; Dr Rapcsák András utca 16-18; adult/child 600/300Ft; ⊙10am-5pm, closed Mon) or visit the **Downtown Pottery House** (Belvárosi Fazekasház; ☎233 666; fazekashaz@vnet.hu; Lánc utca 3; adult/child 1000/500Ft; ⊙10am-6pm Mon-Fri, to 2pm Sat) to watch a master at work. Other attractions include the world-class **Remembrance Point** (Emlékpont; ☎530 940; www.emlekpont.hu; Andrássy utca 34; adult/child 800/400Ft; ⊙10am-5pm, closed Mon), a multimedia exhibition space that recalls the communist era, and the restored **synagogue** (☎241 968; Szent István tér 2; ⊙9am-1pm, closed Sat) with its small **Holocaust Exhibition** (Magyar Tragédia 1944; Szent István tér 2; donations welcome; ⊙9am-1pm, closed Sat). The **Fekete Sas** (☎249 326; Kossuth tér 5; mains 1500-3000Ft; ⊙9am-10pm Sun, from 8am Mon-Thu, 8am-midnight Fri & Sat) overlooking central Kossuth tér is a great place to recharge the batteries.

Buses from Szeged go to Ópusztaszer and Hódmezővásárhely every half-hour and each costs 560Ft. If driving, when leaving Hódmezővásárhely head northeast for 9km for Mindszent where a tiny **car ferry** (☎06 30 635 7339; per person/bicycle/car 50/100/500Ft; ⊙6.30am-6.30pm) will take you across the Tisza. Ópusztaszer is about 8km to the west.

'At the Old Bridge', a traditional Hungarian restaurant with all the favourites and a great terrace just a block in from the river. Mains are mostly meaty – in fact, very meaty.

Taj Mahal INDIAN €€
(☎452 131; www.tajmahalszeged.hu; Gutenberg utca 12; mains 1540-2290Ft; 🅥) This pleasantly authentic Indian-Pakistani restaurant is just metres from the New Synagogue. If you get a hankering for a curry or a spot of tandoor, this is the place to come. There are up to 10 vegetarian dishes (1250Ft to 1490Ft) on offer too.

Classic Cafe SERBIAN €€
(☎422 065; www.classiccafe.hu; Széchenyi tér 5; mains 2050-2350Ft) This welcoming Serbian place with its lovely inner courtyard garden (fine for a quiet drink too) serves up grills like *csevap* (spicy meatballs of beef or pork) and *plyeszkavica* (meat patties).

Port Royal Étterem INTERNATIONAL €€
(☎547 988; www.portroyal.hu/; Stefánia 4; mains 1690-2990Ft; ⊙11am-midnight Mon-Thu, to 2am Fri & Sat, to 11pm Sun) The leafy terrace of this interesting place dating to 1892 and facing quiet Vaszy Viktor tér is enough reason to make this restaurant your destination on a warm summer evening. Add people-watching to that as the nattily dressed come and go from the National Theatre next door, and the fact that in any season the modern kitchen turns out tasty traditional dishes, international faves and veggie options, and you have a winner. Set lunch is a mere 680Ft.

Bistorant INTERNATIONAL €€€
(☎555 566; www.bistorant.hu; Oroszlán utca 8; mains 1790-4450Ft) Many consider this stylish eatery and wine bar to be Szeged's finest restaurant. The ever-changing menu includes everything from *sous vide* dishes to pasta (1600Ft to 1950Ft) and grills (2300Ft to 3600Ft). Three-course set lunches are 1500Ft

and 1950Ft. Choose to sit inside, on the lively front terrace or in the back courtyard.

Drinking

John Bull Pub PUB

(☎484 217; www.johnbullpubszeged.hu; Oroszlán utca 6; ⏲11am-1am) This place does a grand 'English pub' imitation, with mock Turkish carpets, proper pints and bar stools, and there's a full menu (mains 1380Ft to 4870Ft). Its garden courtyard, which backs into a former synagogue, is a welcome respite.

A Cappella CAFE

(☎559 966; Kárász utca 6; cakes 385-625Ft; ⏲7am-9pm) This giant sidewalk cafe overlooking Klauzál tér has a generous choice of cakes, ice creams and frothy coffee concoctions.

Entertainment

Your best sources of entertainment information in this culturally active city are Tourinform and the free biweekly entertainment guide *Szegedi Est* (www.est.hu).

Jazz Kocsma LIVE MUSIC

(☎06 70 250 9279; jazzkocsma.blog.hu; Kálmány Lajos 14; ⏲5pm-midnight Mon-Thu, to 2am Fri & Sat) The kind of small, smoky music club that no self-respecting university town would be without. Gets pretty crowded during the academic year for live music on Friday and Saturday nights. Things slow down in summer, but it's still worth searching out for a drink.

Tisza Dokk CLUB

(www.tiszadokk.hu; Arany János utca 1; ⏲10am-1am Sun-Thu, to 5am Fri & Sat) This bar-cum-dance club sitting on a dock on the Tisza attracts Seged's beautiful people with its streamlined decor and lighting, sophisticated music and excellent cocktails.

Sing Sing CLUB

(☎420 314; www.sing.hu; Mars tér, C pavilion; ⏲11pm-5am Wed, Fri & Sat) Long-established warehouse club near the bus station has rave parties and theme nights.

Szeged National Theatre THEATRE

(Szegedi Nemzeti Színház; ☎479 279; www.szinhaz.szeged.hu; Deák Ferenc utca 12-14) This theatre, where operas, ballet and classical concerts are staged, has been the centre of cultural life in Szeged since 1886.

Information

Main Post Office (Széchenyi tér 1)

OTP Bank (Klauzál tér 4) With ATM.

Tourinform (☎488 690; http://tip.szegedvaros.hu; Dugonics tér 2; ⏲9am-5pm Mon-Fri, to 1pm Sat) This exceptionally helpful main office is tucked away in a quiet courtyard near the university. There is a seasonal **Tourinform booth** (Széchenyi tér; ⏲8am-8pm Mon-Fri, 9am-6pm Sat & Sun mid-Jun–mid-Sep) in Széchenyi tér.

Getting There & Away

The main train station is south of the city centre on Indóház tér. The bus station, to the west of the centre, is on Mars tér, within easy walking distance via pedestrian Mikszáth Kálmán utca.

Bus

DESTINATION	PRICE	DURATION	KM	FREQUENCY
Debrecen	3950Ft	4½hr	230	2-3 daily
Gyula	2830Ft	3½hr	150	6 daily
Hódmezővásárhely	560Ft	30min	26	hourly
Mohács	2830Ft	3¼hr	155	4 daily
Ópusztaszer	560Ft	30min	28	12 daily
Pécs	3410Ft	4hr	195	8 daily

Buses also head for Nagylak (1120Ft, 1½ hours, 54km) on the Romanian border where you can catch buses to Arad and points beyond. Buses run to Novi Sad (2400Ft, 3½ hours) in Serbia at 2.30pm and 3.40pm daily, and to Subotica (1200Ft, 1½ hours) two to four times daily.

Train

Szeged is on several rail lines, including a main one to Budapest's Nyugati train station. You have to change at Békéscsaba for Gyula. Southbound trains leave Szeged for Subotica (1500Ft, two hours, 48km) in Serbia twice daily.

DESTINATION	PRICE	DURATION	KM	FREQUENCY
Békéscsaba	1860Ft	2hr	97	half-hourly
Budapest	2420Ft	2½hr	191	hourly
Hódmezővásárhely	650Ft	35min	31	half-hourly
Kecskemét	2100Ft	1hr	85	hourly

Getting Around

Trams 1 and 2 from the train station will take you north to Széchenyi tér. From the bus station catch bus 2 for New Szeged. Rent bikes at Tourinform (p225) for 1000/3000Ft per hour/day.

Gyula

☎66 / POP 32,000

A town of spas with the last remaining medieval brick castle on the Great Plain, Gyula is a wonderful place to rest before crossing the border into Romania just 4km to the east. This place was made for a holiday, but don't think Hungarians don't know it – even the many private rooms fill up on summer weekends. Thankfully there are numerous museums to keep you busy on a rainy day.

Sights

Gyula Castle CASTLE
(Gyulai Vár; ☎464 117; www.gyulaimuzeumok.hu; Várfürdő utca 1; adult/child 1500/700Ft; ⊙9am-5pm, closed Mon) Gyula Castle, overlooking a picturesque moat, was originally built in the mid-15th century but has been expanded and renovated many times over the centuries. Two dozen rooms are done up as medieval living quarters; in the vaulted former chapel there's a small museum tracing the history of the castle and city. Much attention is paid to the Ottoman Turks and the weapons used to finally fend them off. Like any self-respecting castle, there's a wall 2m to 3m thick to wander along, a tower to climb and a dungeon to explore.

György Kohán Museum MUSEUM
(☎06 70 310 6722; www.gyulaimuzeumok.hu; Béke sugárút 35; adult/child 600/300Ft; ⊙9am-1pm, closed Mon) The György Kohán Museum, in a quiet little park, is Gyula's most important art museum, with more than 3000 paintings and graphics bequeathed to the city by the artist upon his death at age 56 in 1966. The large canvases of horses and women in dark blues and greens, and the relentless summer sun of the Great Plain, are quite striking and worth a look.

Ladics House MUSEUM
(Ladics ház; ☎06 70 310 6722; www.gyulaimuzeumok.hu; Jókai Mór utca 4; adult/child 600/350Ft; ⊙9am-1pm, closed Mon) A fascinating – and, for Hungary, unusual – museum is Ladics House, the perfectly preserved and beautifully furnished late baroque residence (1801) of Dr György Ladics and his prosperous bourgeois family. It offers an excellent look into what life was like in a Hungarian market town in the mid-19th century.

Ferenc Erkel Memorial House MUSEUM
(Erkel Ferenc emlékház; ☎06 70 340 1570; http://erkelemlekhaz.hu; Apor Vilmos tér 7; adult/child 1000/600Ft; ⊙9am-5pm, closed Mon) The birthplace of Ferenc Erkel (1810–93), the man who composed operas and the music for the Hungarian national anthem, contains memorabilia about his life and work. A striking new extension has doubled the exhibition space here.

Virgin Mary Museum MUSEUM
(Szűz Mária Kegy és Emléktárgyak Gyűjteménye; ☎362 169; www.turizmus.bekesmegye.hu; Apor tér 11; donations welcome; ⊙9am-noon & 12.30-3pm Mar-Oct, closed Mon) For contemporary icons at their kitschiest, no place compares with this museum. With more than 3000 'devotional objects' from as far away as Papua New Guinea, you've never seen the Virgin in so many guises.

Churches CHURCH
There are a couple of churches in the town centre worth a quick look. The Romanian Orthodox **St Nicholas Cathedral** (☎361 281; www.episcopiagyula.eu; Szent Miklós Park), built in the Zopf style in 1824 but only consecrated 170 years later, has a beautiful iconostasis containing almost three dozen painted images. The baroque **Inner City Church** (Belvárosi templom; Harruckern tér 1; ⊙8am-6pm) from 1777 has interesting contemporary ceiling frescoes highlighting events in Hungarian and world history – including an astronaut in space!

Activities

Rent kayaks, canoes and row boats on the canal at **Kikötő Vizitura** (☎06 30 670 0934; Varosház utca 11; ⊙10am-6pm May-Oct) for 1000/1500/6000Ft per half-hour/hour/day. Bikes go for 2000Ft a day at a bike shop called **Lipi Bici** (Lipi Bici Kerékpár; ☎278 6657; Diófa utca 2; ⊙9am-5pm Mon-Fri, 9am-noon Sat) near the Castle Baths entrance.

Castle Baths SPA
(Várfürdő; ☎561 350; www.varfurdo.hu; Várkert utca 2; adult/child 2300/1900Ft; ⊙8am-6pm year-round, outdoor pools 8am-7pm May-Oct) Beneath the fortified castle walls, the 30-hectare Castle Garden is a grand, flower-filled setting for the Castle Baths, boasting 18 indoor and outdoor pools and a thoroughly modern wellness complex of the highest standards. Some of the 'curative' pools have small geysers to help massage tired muscles. Treatments cost 1050Ft to 2100Ft.

Festivals & Events

Gyula has festivals year-round – medieval games in July, a New Year's street dance, a Renaissance fair in February – but the not-to-miss event of the year is the **Gyula Castle Theatre Festival** (Gyulai Várszínház; ☎463 148;

www.gyulaivarszinhaz.hu), with performances in the castle courtyard from July to mid-August. The first two weeks are devoted to Shakespeare, but operettas, operas, concerts – even puppet shows – are performed during the rest of the festival. There's also a big three-day **All-Hungarian Folkdance Festival** around 20 August.

MOVING ON?

For tips, recommendations and reviews, head to shop.lonelyplanet.com to purchase downloadable PDFs of the Romania, Serbia and Ukraine chapters from Lonely Planet's *Eastern Europe* guide.

Sleeping

Márk Camping CAMPGROUND €
(☎06 30 428 8600; www.markcamping.hu; Vár utca 5; campsites 4000Ft; @) This friendly and very pretty (think flower gardens) campground is the size of a postage stamp with 50 sites but in full view of Gyula Castle.

Thermál Camping CAMPGROUND €
(☎650 111; http://gyulatermalkemping.hu/; Szélső utca 16; campsites per person/tent/caravan 1200/1000/1200Ft, s/d 6000/8000Ft, cabin from 10,000Ft;) About 700m east of the town centre, this large campground has 400 sites spread over three shady hectares. There are barbecue areas and a shared kitchen and dining room with a fantastic traditional stove. The renovated motel rooms and holiday cabins sleep up to five people.

Lux Panzió GUESTHOUSE €€
(☎06 20 974 4655; www.luxpanzio.hu; Kossuth Lajos tér 2; d/tr 8000/9000Ft;) Located on the floor above the Sörpince Vendéglő, this is a small guesthouse with spotlessly clean and very bright contemporary-style accomodation. All five rooms have kitchenettes and three have balconies overlooking the 'new look' Kossuth Lajor tér, Gyula's pride and joy.

Aqua Hotel HOTEL €€
(☎463 146; www.aqua-hotel.hu; Part utca 7/c; s/d 7300/11,900Ft; @) The outside is not much to look at, but the 38 renovated rooms at the Aqua are up to international-chain standards (minibar, nondescript but nice veneer furniture). And you can't beat being just acoss the canal from the main entrance to the Castle Baths.

TOP CHOICE **Elizabeth Hotel** HISTORIC HOTEL €€€
(☎560 240; www.elizabeth-hotel.hu; Vár utca 1; s/d €66/96; @) Ever wondered what it would be like to live in a neoclassical mansion opposite a castle? See for yourself when you stay at the Almásy manor house (1905) that is now the 49-room Elizabeth Hotel. Brocade bedclothes and draperies recall rich tapestries, and Italian marble covers every bit of the bathroom. Look out your full-length window onto the castle; room 205 is a top choice. Though you are within diving distance of the Castle Baths, the hotel's own wellness centre, with saunas, steam rooms, swimming pools and even salt and aromatherapy rooms, will keep you close to home

Eating

TOP CHOICE **Százéves Cukrászda** PATISSERIE €
(Century Cakeshop; ☎362 045; Erkel tér 1; cakes 280-350Ft; 10am-7pm Sun-Thu, to 8pm Fri & Sat) One of the most beautiful *cukrászdák* (cake shops or patisseries) in Hungary, the 'Century' is a visual and culinary delight. Established around 1840, the Regency-blue interior is filled with Biedermeier furniture and mirrors in gilt frames. If that's not enough, it moonlights as a museum, with mockups of antique kitchens and cake-making paraphernalia.

Passzió Udvar TURKISH €
(Hobby Courtyard; ☎06 30 392 2265; Kossuth Lajos utca 36; mains 480-950Ft; 4-10pm Sun-Thu, to 11pm Fri & Sat) Engorged with *gulyás*? Try Turkish – or a close facsimile – at the 'Hobby Courtyard', where the owner's pastime seems to be grilling shish kebabs and *köfte* and making eggplant dip. Lovely garden seating.

Gelateria Maestro Toscano ICE CREAM €
(☎06 70 206 5480; Kossuth Lajos utca 18; ice cream 175Ft; 9am-7pm) The best ice cream and Italian ices in town are available at this stunning *gelateria* opposite Tourinform.

Bols Café CAFE €
(☎06 30 978 7407; Kossuth Lajos utca 1/b; mains 1800-3200Ft) Salads, gyros and pizzas (920Ft to 1580Ft) are on the menu at this cheap and cheerful cafe-restaurant. Many come just to drink on the terrace overlooking the town hall. Set lunch is a snip at 750Ft.

Halászcsárda FISH €€
(☎466 303; www.hotelhalaszcsarda.hu; Part utca 3; mains 1500-2900Ft) When fish is what you crave, this is where you go. Some 10 varieties of fish soup, including the local *Körösi halászlé* (1200Ft), as well as trout, carp and catfish are served in a leafy, canalside garden or inside the rustic inn.

Sörpince Vendéglő HUNGARIAN €€
(Beer Cellar Guesthouse; ☎362 382; Kossuth Lajos tér 2; mains 1600-3300Ft) The name just means 'beer cellar' and to be sure there's plenty of *sör* to go around. But locals also swear by the traditional Hungarian dishes served here, and there's a terrace in addition to the cellar seating overlooking lovely Kossuth Lajor tér.

Drinking

Mergés Kobold Pub PUB
(Angry Leprechaun Pub; ☎06 20 230 5660; www.angry-leprechaun.hu; Béke sugárút 8; ⌚8am-3am Mon-Thu, 10am-3am Fri & Sat, 10am-11pm Sun) Any place with a name like the 'Angry Leprechaun' gets our undivided attention (and our custom) but especially as chilled a spot as this, with its great music and wide choice of whiskies.

Rondella Terasz BAR
(☎463 544; Várkert; ⌚8am-2am) This late-closing bar occupies a squat 16th-century tower near the castle, with a delightful terrace in summer. Live music at the weekend.

Information

Erste Bank (Városház utca 16) With ATM.

Post Office (Eszperantó tér)

Tourinform (☎561 681; www.turizmus.bekesmegye.hu; Kossuth Lajos utca 7; ⌚8am-6pm Mon-Fri & 10am-6pm Sat & Sun Jun-Aug, 8am-6pm Mon-Fri Sep-May) East of the castle.

Getting There & Away

Gyula's bus station on Vásárhelyi Pál utca is just south of central Kossuth Lajos tér. The train station is at the northern end of Béke sugárút, which leads into the same square.

Gyula is connected by bus with Debrecen (2520Ft, three hours, 130km, four daily), Kecskemét (2830Ft, 3¼ hours, 144km, two daily) and Hódmezővásárhely (1680Ft, 2½ hours, 87km).

Some 15 trains daily run west on line 128, the spur between Gyula and Békéscsaba (310Ft, 20 minutes, 15km), where you can transfer to Budapest (4260Ft, 2½ hours, 196km, 10 daily) or Szeged (1860Ft, two hours, 97km, 12 daily).

NORTHEAST HUNGARY

On a map, Hungary's northeastern corner may appear to be a continuation of the Great Plain. But it is so different physically, culturally and historically from both of those regions that most consider it separate. Essentially it encompasses just one county (Szabolcs-Szatmár-Bereg) and is divided into three regions: the Nyírség (Birch) containing the major towns and therefore the majority of museums and city-bound attractions; Bereg, where some women still eke out a living embroidering pillowcases in age-old patterns and men work the land; and Rétkõz, squeezed up against Ukraine and of little interest to travellers.

Getting There & Around

The best way to see the small region is under your own steam, be it car, motorbike or bicycle. From Nyíregyháza, connected to the rest of Hungary by rail, there is a really slow train to towns like Nyírbátor and Vásárosnamény. Bus services in Bereg exist but are not very good.

Nyíregyháza

☎42 / POP 118,000

You have to look at Nyíregyháza from the inside out. Stand in the old town centre and notice the checkerboard of well-tended squares and gardens and then survey the forests, pavilions and reedy lakeshore at the park in Sóstófürdő, 5km to the north. The problem is, what rings these pleasant views is the ugly high-rises and industrial architecture of a commercial and administrative centre. Still, give Nyíregyháza a chance; the town's spas and low-key lifestyle make up for the ugliness and this is the springboard for visiting other towns and villages in the Northeast.

Sights

Central Buildings ARCHITECTURE
It is worth taking the time to check out the architecture in the centre of town, including the eclectic-style **County Hall** (Megyeháza; Hősök tere) dating from 1892; the blue-and-white **Art Nouveau building** (Országzászló tér), which houses a bank and offices; and the restored **Korona Hotel** (Dózsa György utca 1-3). Bizarre in the extreme is the **Mihály Váci Cultural Centre** (☎411 822; Szabadság tér 9; ⌚9am-5pm Mon-Fri), built in 1981 and

Nyíregyháza

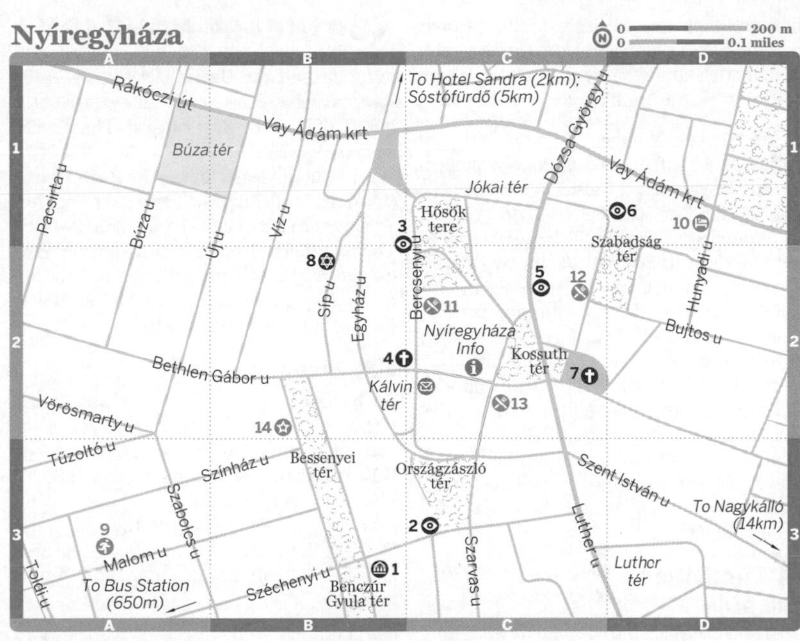

Nyíregyháza

Sights

1 András Jósa Museum B3
2 Art Nouveau Building C3
3 County Hall B1
4 Greek Catholic Church B2
5 Korona Hotel C2
6 Mihály Váci Cultural Centre D1
7 Roman Catholic Cathedral C2
8 Synagogue B2

Activities, Courses & Tours

9 Julia Baths A3

Sleeping

10 Európa Hotel D1
Korona Hotel .... (see 5)

Eating

11 Belvárosi Főzi C2
12 Da Paolo C2
13 La Bodega Bistro C2

Drinking

John Bull Pub .... (see 5)
Omnia Kávéház .... (see 2)

Entertainment

14 Zsigmond Móricz Theatre B2

inspired, we are told, by 'the principles of Japanese metabolism'.

Houses of Worship CHURCH, SYNAGOGUE

There are many houses of worship in the inner city. Dominating Kossuth tér, the red-brick neo-Romanesque **Roman Catholic cathedral** (☎409 691; Kossuth tér 4; admission free; ⏲6am-6.15pm) dating from 1904 has arabesque painted pastel-coloured tiles inside. Near Kálvin tér the **Greek Catholic church** (☎500 006; Bethlen Gábor utca 7; admission free; ⏲8am-4pm), built in 1895, contains a rich liturgical collection of vestments and church plate. The **synagogue** (☎06 20 243 9714; Mártírok tere 6; admission free; ⏲8am-2pm Mon-Thu) still functions as a house of worship and has a small collection of Jewish artefacts.

András Jósa Museum MUSEUM

(☎315 722; www.josamuzeum.hu; Benczúr Gyula tér 21; adult/child 800/400Ft; ⏲9am-5pm Apr-Oct, 8am-4pm Nov-Mar, closed Mon) This huge museum built in 1918 has exhibits devoted to antiquities as far back as the Iron Age, the region's rich ethnography and Nyíregyháza's history since the Middle Ages.

Sóstó Museum Village MUSEUM
(Sóstói Múzeumfalu; ☎500 552; www.muzeumfalu.hu; Tölgyes utca 1, Sóstófürdő; adult/child 700/350Ft; ⏲9am-5pm Apr-Oct) Nyíregyháza's most interesting sight is the *skanzen* (open-air museum) in Sóstófürdő. Its two dozen reconstructed structures – three-room cottages, school, wells, fire station, general store, church and even a cemetery (with Jewish headstones) – offer an easy introduction to the traditional architecture and way of life in the Northeast. All the nationalities that make up this ethnically diverse region are represented, including the Tirpák, ethnic Slovaks who lived in isolated 'bush farms' (*bokor tanyák*) and the often overlooked Roma.

Activities

Julia Baths SPA
(Julia Fürdő; ☎tel, info 315 800; http://www.sostort.hu/julia-furdo; Malom utca 19; adult/child around 1400/1300Ft; ⏲10am-8pm Mon-Fri, 9am-8pm Sat & Sun) A central option is this modernised indoor thermal spa with three pools. Unlike the modern facilities at Sóstófürdő Spas, here you get see how spa culture in Hungary used to be – both warm and chilled.

Sóstófürdő Spas SPA
In the park called 'Salt Lake Thermal Baths' north of town you have your choice of three or four (depending on how you count) spas. The **Aquarius Adventure Baths** (Aquarius Élményfürdő; ☎726 140; www.aquariusfurdo.hu; Sóstói út; adult/child 2200/1700Ft; ⏲9am-8pm Jun-Aug) is the newest and shiniest indoor-outdoor complex. Thermal World, with hot-water pools, Jacuzzis etc is for adults; kids love the Adventure World waterpark with squirting castle and kamikaze slide. Add another 1000Ft (for both adults and children) for Sauna World.

Admission to the Aquarius complex also allows entry to the **Park Baths** (Parkfürdő; ☎475 736; www.parkfurdo.hu; Berenát utca 1-3; adult/child 800/600Ft; ⏲9am-8pm, open-air baths 9am-7pm May-Sep), which is the original spa. A renovation in 2011 doubled the number of indoor and outdoor pools to 10; the 50m athletic swimming pool also got spruced up.

A portion of the southern half of the Salt Lake itself has been cordoned off for swimming at the **Lake Baths** (Tófürdő; ☎479 701; www.sostort.hu; Blaha Lujza sétány; adult/child 1400/1200Ft; ⏲9am-8pm Jun-Aug). There's also a grassy 'beach' .

Last but not least, there's the **Bath House** (Fürdőház; ☎411 191; www.furdohaz.hu; Sóstói út, Víztorony; adult/child 1900/1200Ft; ⏲10am-9pm). The two thermal pools and associated cold plunge pool and whirlpool are mainly frequented by guests of the attached Fürdőház Panzió, but you bathe here too.

Sleeping

Sóstó Kemping CAMPGROUND €
(☎500 692; www.hotelsosto.hu; Sóstói út 76, Sóstófürdő; campsites per person/tent/caravan 1100/800/2000Ft, 4-person bungalow 11,800Ft; ⏲May-Sep; @) A large green space allows for plenty of room to play on the ball courts at Sóstó Kemping. It's in a forested area and has a restaurant, sauna and tennis court.

Hotel Sandra HOSTEL €
(☎505 400; www.hotelsandra.hu; Sóstói út 31/b; s/d without bathroom 7000/8000Ft; ⏲Jul & Aug; @) This overachieving college dorm has 210 renovated rooms with bright red chairs, plus a self-service cafeteria, coffee bar and even a dance club. It's 2km north of the centre near the stadium and en route to Sóstófürdő. Take bus 8 and get off at the Etelköz stop.

Blaha Panzió GUESTHOUSE €€
(☎403 342; www.blahapanzio.hu; Blaha Lujza sétány 7, Sóstófürdő; s/d incl breakfast 8000/10,800Ft;) Relaxing under the 100-year-old oaks by the swimming pond, you'd never know you're actually only a few hundred metres away from the holiday-spa central that is Sóstófürdő. The yellow half-timber building looks a lot like a sprawling house; with only a dozen rooms, it feels cosy. And that's how it is with the friendly owners who make excellent booked-ahead meals for their guests.

Európa Hotel HOTEL €€
(☎508 670; www.europahotel.hu; Hunyadi utca 2; s/d 9000/11,000Ft; @) Stay at this so-so 58-room hotel only if eveything else is booked up. It has a very handy location near the centre and bus lines but it's on a major crossroads and feels removed from the action.

It's colourful on the outside, but rooms look to be furnished with hand-me-downs.

Korona Hotel HISTORIC HOTEL €€
(☎409 300; www.korona.cs.hu; Dózsa György utca 1-3; s/d 12,800/13,900Ft; ❄@📶) Like a big blue wedding cake with frilly white icing, the Korona Hotel has decorated Nyíregyháza's main square since 1895. At these prices, the three dozen ho-hum rooms could use an update, but you do have easy access to the John Bull Pub, Da Paolo Italian restaurant and all of downtown at your doorstep. Small wellness centre too. Staff are very welcoming and helpful.

Eating

Belvárosi Főzi HUNGARIAN €
(☎06 20 421 8818; Bercsény utca 4; mains 270-470Ft; ⏰10am-4pm Mon-Fri) For a cheap and filling lunch you couldn't do better than this place specialising in *főzelék,* the traditional 'twice-cooked' way of preparing vegetables. Set lunches are 580Ft and 750Ft.

Da Paolo ITALIAN €
(☎06 70 200 9192; Szabadság tér 1; mains 950-1950Ft; ⏰noon-10pm Mon-Thu, to 10.30pm Fri & Sat) For simple, quick and authentic pasta and pizza (the owner is Italian) this is your best bet. It's in the same building as the Korona Hotel.

TOP CHOICE **Igrice Csárda** HUNGARIAN €€
(☎06 20 583 4319, 444 200; www.igricecsarda.hu; Blaha Lujza sétány 4-6, Sóstófürdő; mains 1080-3590Ft) As the sun sets and you look out over the reeds to the lake beyond, you might think you've found the best terrace in town. Just avoid the place when cold weather forces you inside, unless you like synthesised Hungarian music. Try the Szeged-style turkey breast with locally made plum jam (1690Ft) or the grilled plate for two (3990Ft), which actually serves three.

424 Irish Pub INTERNATIONAL €€
(☎424 000; www.424etterem.hu; Blaha Lujza sétány 1, Sóstófürdő; mains 1490-2790Ft) The only thing Irish about this place is the Guinness sign hanging out the front and the frantic session music on the website. But this cute pavilion pub-restaurant has views of the lake and serves decent international favourites too.

La Bodega Bistro INTERNATIONAL €€
(Zrínyi utca1-2; mains 1850-3200Ft; 🖉) A light-touch Mediterranean eatery with steaks and a half-dozen vegetarian dishes on offer as well, this is one of the more upbeat restaurants in central Nyíregyháza. Sit outside on the terrace, inside on the ground floor or upstairs looking out onto Kossuth tér.

Drinking & Entertainment

Your best source of entertainment information is the free biweekly entertainment guide *Nyíregyházi Est* (www.est.hu).

John Bull Pub PUB
(☎409 300; www.korona-hotel.hu; Dózsa György utca 1) This convivial place at the Korona Hotel serves full meals but most people come here to drink pints of English ale and listen to live music at the weekend.

Omnia Kávéház CAFE
(Széchenyi utca 1; ⏰8am-10pm Mon-Thu, to 11pm Fri & Sat, 10am-10pm Sun) Fantastic old-style coffee house in a lovely Art Nouveau building; great cakes.

Zsigmond Móricz Theatre THEATRE
(☎311 333; www.moriczszinhaz.hu; Bessenyei tér 13) Though most performances here are plays in Hungarian, you will find the occasional dance or operetta.

Information

Ibusz (☎311 817; www.ibusz.hu; Országzászló tér 6; ⏰8am-6pm Mon-Fri, to 1pm Sat) Brokers private rooms and flats.

Main Post Office (Bethlen Gábor utca 4)

Nyíregyháza Info (☎310 735; www.nyiregyhaza-info.hu; Kossuth tér 1; ⏰9am-5pm Mon-Fri) This county-run tourist office with bankers' hours is the only game in town in Nyíregyháza.

OTP Bank (Kossuth tér 2) Has an ATM.

Sóstófürdő Tourinform (☎411 193; sostofurdo@tourinform.hu; Víztorony, Sóstófürdő; ⏰9am-5pm Mon-Fri, to 1pm Sat & Sun mid-Jun–mid-Sep) A seasonal office at the landmark water tower in Sóstófürdő.

Getting There & Away

The main train station, on Állomás tér, is about 1.5km southwest of the centre at the end of Arany János utca. The bus station is on Petőfi tér, just north of the train station, at the western end of Széchenyi utca.

Bus

Heading west to Eger (2520Ft, 2½ hours, 132km, two daily), buses are most convenient. Regionally, buses are very frequent to Nagykálló (370Ft, 35 minutes, 16km) and up to seven a day go to Máriapócs (650Ft, one hour, 31km). At least three buses (with many more on weekdays) connect daily with Nyírbátor (745Ft, one hour, 38km).

Train

The Tisza Express train to Kyiv (22 hours, 1235km) stops here every day at just after 10pm. To get to the Ukrainian border town of Csop (Čop), 14km from Uzhgorod, you have to change in Záhony (1300Ft, one hour, 66km, hourly).

Direct destinations include the following:

DESTINATION	PRICE	TIME	KM	FREQUENCY
Budapest (Keleti station)	4430Ft	4hr	270	8 daily
Budapest (Nyugati station)	4430Ft	3½hr	270	hourly
Debrecen	930Ft	30min	49	hourly
Kisvárda	840Ft	45min	43	hourly
Máriapócs	560Ft	1hr	30	4 daily
Nyírbátor	745Ft	1½hr	38	5 daily
Tokaj	650Ft	30min	32	half-hourly
Vásárosnamény	1120Ft	1¾hr	59	6 daily

Getting Around

Take bus 7 or 8 from the train or bus station to reach the centre of the old town (Egyház or Kossuth Lajos utca stops); bus 8 carries on to Sóstófürdő.

Nyírbátor

☎42 / POP 12,200

Anyone with a passion for medieval or Transylvanian history should put Nyírbátor on their itinerary. Several of the town's Gothic buildings were originally constructed in the latter part of the 15th century by István Báthory, the ruthless Transylvanian prince whose family is synonymous with this town and its sights.

Sights

Calvinist Church CHURCH

(Református templom; ☎281 749; www.nyirbator.hu/a_keso_gotikus_reformatus_templom; Báthory István utca; admission 200Ft; ⌚9am-noon & 1-4pm Tue-Sat, 1-4pm Sun) The interior of the Calvinist church, on a small hill just north of Báthory István utca, is refreshingly plain and its long lancet windows, which flood the nave with light, accentuate the church's masterpiece – the ribbed vaulted ceiling. István Báthory's remains lie in a marble tomb at the back of the church; the family's coat of arms embellished with wyverns (dragon-like creatures) is on top of the tomb. The 17th-century wooden bell tower, standing apart from the church (as was once required of Calvinists in this Catholic country), has a Gothic roof with four little turrets.

Báthory Castle CASTLE

(Báthory Várkastély; ☎510 216; www.nyirbator.hu/bathori_varkastely; Szentvér utca; adult/child 800/400Ft; ⌚10am-6pm, closed Mon) The starkly white, 15th-century Báthory Castle is a small fortified palace with a striking 2nd-storey loggia. The building is mostly used as a conference centre, but a couple of rooms are outfitted in Renaissance style. Also here is the Báthory Panoptikum, with 45 wax figures tracing the history of Nyírbátor and the Báthory family.

Minorite Church CHURCH

(Minorita templom; ☎281 770; www.nyirbator.hu/a_minorita_templom_es_kolostor; Károlyi Mihály utca 19; ⌚9-11am & 4-5pm, closed Sun) The Minorite Church was originally late Gothic but was ravaged by the Turks in 1587 and rebuilt in the baroque style 130 years later. Five spectacular altars carved in Presov (now eastern Slovakia) in the mid-18th century fill the nave and chancel. The most interesting is the first on the left, the Krucsay Altar of the Passion (1737).

István Báthory Museum MUSEUM

(☎281 760; www.nyirbim.hu; Károlyi Mihály utca 15; adult/child 300/150Ft; ⌚10am-6pm Tue-Sun Apr-

BLOODY FAMILY

István Báthory (1430–93) ruled as prince-ruler *(voivod)* of Transylvania between 1479–93. He palled around in battle with Vlad the Impaler (aka Dracula) and was deposed as prince in 1493 for extreme cruelty. You may have heard of his grand-grandniece, Erzsébet Báthory, who was accused of killing peasant girls and bathing in their blood for beauty. Blood lust ran in the Báthory family, it would seem.

WORTH A TRIP

NAGYKÁLLÓ

Observant Jews or anyone who might answer to a Higher Authority will want to make a pilgrimage to the town of Nagykálló (population 10,000), 14km southeast of Nyíregyháza, to pay their respects at the **tomb of Isaac Taub** (06 30 224 7349; Nagybalkányi út; 9am-4pm Mon-Thu, 9am-2pm Fri & Sun), especially on the anniversary of his death on 7 Adar in the Hebrew calendar (February/March). Known as the 'Wonder Rabbi of Kálló' (a *tzaddik*, or righteous man, in Yiddish), Isaac Taub was an 18th-century philosopher who advocated a humanistic approach to Judaic study and prayer. Be aware that unless you call ahead, the cemetery gates, less than 1km due south of central Szabadság tér, will be locked.

Óbester Étterem (264 496; Korányi Ferenc utca 1; mains 1100-1600Ft), serving Hungarian staples, is a central option for a full meal; its outside tables on Szabadság tér are popular on summer evenings. **Üvegtigris Kávézó** (Kossuth Lajos utca 2; 7am-9pm), a short distance north of the square, is mostly for coffee and drinks but sells ice cream too.

Four daily trains link Nagykálló with Nyíregyháza (310Ft, 20 minutes, 14km) and with Nyírbátor (465Ft, 50 minutes, 24km).

Sep, 8am-4pm Mon-Fri Sep-May) Housed in the 18th-century monastery next to the Minorite church, this museum showcase the trades of the town's heyday – barrel-making, leatherworking, hat-making and pottery. It has some medieval pieces connected with the Báthory family.

Festivals & Events

In early July, actors, musicians and puppets perform during the **Week of the Winged Dragon International Street Theatre Festival.** In mid-August, the **Nyírbátor Music Days** hosts concerts in the town's churches.

Sleeping

Bástya Wellness Hotel HOTEL €€
(281 657; www.bastyawellnesshotel.eu; Hunyadi utca 8-10; s/d/tr 6800/9200/11,800Ft;) Stone walls on the exterior and in the grotto-like pool seem to hint at a medieval theme at this hotel, with sauna and Jacuzzi too. The 26 rooms are comfortable but a bit over-decorated in a kind of tacky eclectic style. It offers remarkabaly good value though.

TOP CHOICE **Hotel Hódi** BOUTIQUE HOTEL €€
(281 012; www.hotelhodi.com; Báthory István utca 11; s/d 11,900/12,900Ft;) Set in a small leafy courtyard east of Szabadság tér, this charming hotel has 15 rooms that exude an old-world atmosphere, with high ceilings and antique furniture. You can't get much more secluded than the heated indoor swimming pool and sauna, which are tucked away at the back of the hotel.

Eating & Drinking

Csekő Kávéház & Pizzéria CAFE €
(281 289; www.csekokavehaz.hu; Bajcsy-Zsilinszky utca 62; cakes 150-300Ft, mains 750-1750Ft; 9am-8pm) Once inside the door, go right and ogle the cream filled cakes in the cafe case or go left and sit down in a light-filled eatery. Unexpected options include main-dish salads like the 'Hawaiian' with chicken and pineapple, and the savoury crêpes stuffed with fillings like seafood in a sour-cream sauce. Come for lunch or early dinner.

Kakukk HUNGARIAN €€
(281 050; kakukketterem.hu; Szabadság tér 21; mains 1490-3690Ft) This old-style eatery on the main square, which has recently got a new lease of life, has a lunchtime set menu for just under 1000Ft that packs 'em in at midday. Other Hungarian specialities are served as well.

Port Side Pub PUB
(06 30 938 9677; www.portsidepub.hu; Radnóti Miklós út 5; noon-midnight Sun-Thu, to 2am Fri & Sat) Ahoy matey, come aboard this fun bar that impersonates a pirate ship and sees them bopping in the aisles at weekends.

Information

Main Post Office (Szabadság tér 3)

Nyírbátor website (www.nyirbator.hu) Official town website.

OTP Bank (Zrínyi utca 1) Opposite central Szabadság tér; has an ATM.

Getting There & Away

The train and bus stations are on Ady Endre utca, which is about 1km north of Szabadság tér via Kossuth Lajos utca.

Three buses a day connect to Nyíregyháza (745Ft, one hour, 38km) via Nagykálló (745Ft, 30 minutes, 37km); many go to both places directly during the week. One daily bus goes into Máriapócs (310Ft, 20 minutes, 14km) proper; the others stop at the train station.

Eight daily trains from Nyíregyháza (745Ft, one hour, 38km) call at Nagykálló (465Ft, 50 minutes, 24km) and Máriapócs (250Ft, 20 minutes, 8km) first. Trains also arrive direct from Debrecen (1120Ft, 1½ hours, 58km, 10 daily).

Bereg Region

Folksy blue and red painted flowers enliven the walls of a church in Csaroda, a kerchief-clad grandmother sits by the fence in Tákos selling her needlework, and row after row of boat-shaped wooden grave markers stand sentinel in Szatmárcseke. The pleasures of Northeastern Hungary are simple and rural ones. Regular flooding of the Tisza and Szamos Rivers cut Bereg off from the rest of Hungary, and isolation discouraged development and preserved folkways.

Bring your sense of adventure; the simple life is not always so simple. Each small village has only one sight, and the guy who keeps the church key may not be home. It might be best to base yourself in the region's only sizeable town, Vásárosnamény. And remember that having your own transport is key, as a negligible number of buses connect the villages.

VÁSÁROSNAMÉNY

☎45 / POP 8700

Vásárosnamény was once an important trading post on the Salt Road, which ran from the forests of Transylvania, via the Tisza River and across the Great Plain to Debrecen. Today it's a nondescript little town, but it does offer the closest city services for Bereg villages.

The **OTP Bank** (Szabadság tér 28-31) and its ATM are on the same square as **Tourinform** (☎570 206; vasarosnameny@tourinform.hu; Szabadság tér 9; ⏰8am-4.30pm Mon-Fri), where the friendly staff will help you plan your rural excursions. There's a seasonal **Tourinform kiosk** (☎570 206; vasarosnameny@tourinform.hu; Atlantika Waterpark; ⏰11am-7pm mid-Jun–Aug) at the Atlantika Waterpark.

The **Bereg Museum** (☎470 638; www.beregi-muzeum.hu; Szabadság tér 26; adult/child 400/200Ft; ⏰8.30am-4.30pm Tue-Fri, 8am-4pm Sat & Sun Apr-Oct, 8am-4pm Mon-Fri Nov-Mar), inside Tomcsány Manor, contains an excellent collection of Bereg cross-stitch, pottery, iron stoves and painted Easter eggs. A whole room is dedicated to how local textiles are woven. You can buy examples of cross-stitch and food products like jam made from the famous local plums in the main Tourinform office. Ask staff for the *Plum Route* map or check out www.szilvaut.hu.

The five indoor and outdoor pools at **Szilva Thermal Baths** (☎470 180; www.szilvafurdo.hu; Beregszászi út 1/b; adult/child 1300/1100Ft; ⏰10am-9pm Mon-Fri, 9am-1am Sat, 9am-8pm Sun) are close to the town centre. Some 2km east across the Rte 41 bridge in Gergelyiugornya, near the free Tisza-part (Tisza bank) beach, is the more ambitious **Atlantika Waterpark** (Atlantika vízividámpark; ☎570 112; www.atlantika.hu; Gulácsi út 56; adult/child 3000/2500Ft; ⏰9am-6.30pm Jun-Aug) with a plethora of slides and rides.

Sleeping & Eating

Turistaszálló HOSTEL €
(Tourist Hostel; ☎06 30 65 0012; www.turistaszallo-vasarosnameny.hu; Szabadság tér 26; per person 2400Ft; @) Very basic accommodation available in this very cheap and very central hostel in an old townhouse. It has nine rooms with between four and 12 beds.

Diófa Kemping CAMPGROUND €
(☎712 298; www.diofakemping.hu; Gulácsi út 71; campsite per person/tent/caravan 1000/1000/1500Ft, bungalow 7000Ft; @ 🏊) Not only does this small campground have an indoor pool and fitness room, it's right across the street from the Atlantika Waterpark. Pitch your tent in the field, or bunk in an above-average bungalow. There's a restaurant (mains 1000Ft to 1800Ft) too.

Winkler Ház Panzió-Étterem GUESTHOUSE €€
(☎470 945; www.winkler.hu; Rákóczi utca 5; s/d 8000/10,000Ft; ❄) This cute little guesthouse is the most comfortable place to stay in Vásárosnamény. Handwoven neutral textiles are the highlight of its 15 pleasantly plain guestrooms; each has a minibar. The restaurant is tops in town and especially popular at lunch (mains 1500Ft to 2000Ft). Check out the poignant black-and-white photographs of locals on the walls by Rádi Bálint.

Getting There & Away

Eight daily trains connect with Nyíregyháza (1200Ft, 1¾ hours, 59km). Up to six weekday-only buses linking Vásárosnamény with Tákos (250Ft, 15 minutes, 8km) continue on to Csaroda (310Ft, 20 minutes, 13km). Up to nine weekday buses serve Tarpa (465Ft, 40 minutes, 20km). To get to Szatmárcseke, you have to change in Fehérgyarmat (840Ft, 1¼ hours, 40km, nine daily), but runs are few and far between.

TÁKOS

☎45 / POP 360

A village must for anyone interested in folk art, Tákos is 8km northeast of Vásárosnamény on Rte 41. The 18th-century wattle-and-daub **Calvinist church** (Református templom; ☎06 20 254 7131, 701 718; www.takos.hu; Bajcsy-Zsilinszky utca 25; admission 300Ft; ⏲7am-7pm) has a spectacularly painted coffered ceiling of blue and red flowers, a beaten-earth floor and an ornately carved 'folk baroque' pulpit sitting on a large millstone. Outside the church, which villagers call the 'Barefoot Notre Dame of Hungary', stands a perfectly preserved bell tower (1767). The keeper of the keys lives at Bajcsy-Zsilinszky utca 29.

The **provincial house** (Tájház; ☎701 606; www.takos.hu; ⏲7am-7pm), opposite the church, sells works by local craftspeople and local plum jam.

CSARODA

☎45 / POP 580

A lovely **Romanesque church** (☎06 20 444 7624, 484 905; Kossuth utca 2; adult/child 250/200Ft; ⏲10am-6pm Mon-Fri Mar-Oct) from the 13th century stands in this village some 3km east of Tákos. It is a wonderful hybrid, with both Western- and Eastern-style frescoes (some from the 14th century), as well as some fairly crude folk murals dated 1647. Nearby are two wooden bell towers of a more recent vintage.

You can find repose in these peaceful rural surrounds at the three-room **Székely Vendégház** (☎06 20 261 9497, 484 830; József Attila utca 48; s/d 3000/6000Ft). The long, yard-oriented traditional peasant house-turned-lodging – with thick whitewashed walls, dark wood and red geraniums – has more than a little rustic appeal. Home-cooked meals (from 1000Ft) are available. More central (and commercial) is **Julianna Vendégház** (☎06 30 643 2512; www.juliannavendeghaz.honlapom.com/; Kossuth Lajos utca 15; s/d 3000/6000Ft) opposite the church.

TARPA

☎45 / POP 2100

A bit more of a town than the other Bereg villages, with actual shops, Tarpa lies 16km southeast of Csaroda. It's known for its plum products, but one of Hungary's last examples of a working, horse-driven, 19th-century **dry mill** (szárazmalom; ☎06 20 358 2938; Árpád utca 36; adult/child 300/150Ft; ⏲by appointment) can also be seen here. Nearby is a decorated **Calvinist church** (Kossuth utca 13; admission free; ⏲8am-noon Mon-Fri). Shop for home-made *szilva lekvár* (plum jam) and 20 types of *pálinka* at **Bereg Kincsei** (☎06 20 986 2937, 488 488; www.tarpanatura.hu; Kölcsey utca 10; ⏲10am-4pm), which also sells cross-stitch and other folk crafts.

Near the church the **Kuruc Panzió-Étterem** (☎488 121; tarpakurucpanzio@freemail.hu; Kossuth út 25; d/tr 6000/8000Ft) has a dozen comfortable rooms with between two and four beds and a restaurant serving hearty Hungarian dishes (mains 1000Ft to 2200Ft).

On a bend in the river, **Tivadar** (www.tivadar.hu), 5km south of Tarpa, is a quiet little beachfront settlement with alternative lodging, a campsite and an eatery or two.

SZATMÁRCSEKE

☎44 / POP 1400

This village is the site of a famous **cemetery** (temető; Táncsics utca) with intriguing prow-shaped grave markers. To get here from Tarpa, cross at the Tivadar, turn east and carry on another 7km northeast. The 600 carved wooden markers that resemble up-ended boats are unique in Hungary; the notches and grooves represent a complicated language detailing marital status, social position and so on. No one knows how the tradition (which is still carried on today) started, but scholars generally agree it's not Finno-Ugric (ancestral Hungarian). One of the few stone markers in the cemetery is that of native son Ferenc Kölcsey (1790–1838), who wrote the lyrics to *Himnusz*, the Hungarian national anthem. The **Szatmár Fogadó** (☎06 20 468 7882; www.szatmarifogadok.hu; Petőfi út 7; dm/s/d 1500/2000/4000Ft) on the main road and at the turning to the cemetery has six rooms and hearty meals from 800Ft.

Northern Uplands

Includes »

Best Places to Eat

- » Kékes Étterem (p242)
- » Imola Udvarház Borétterem (p251)
- » Mátyás Restaurant (p260)
- » Toldi Fogadó (p263)

Best Places to Stay

- » Hotel Senator Ház (p250)
- » La Contessa Kastély Hotel (p255)
- » Hotel Palota (p260)
- » Kastélyhotel Sasvár (p245)
- » Gróf Degenfeld Castle Hotel (p261)
- » Palóc Holiday Houses (p240)

Why Go?

Forested hiking trails, superb wine regions, traditional folk culture and hilltop castle ruins beckon you to the Northern Uplands. OK, the highest peak here – Kékestető in the Mátra Hills – is only just over 1000m. But in a country as flat as a *palacsinta* (pancake), these foothills of the Carpathians soar above most of Hungary. After exploring Bükk National Park on foot or caving in Lillafüred, why not sample the spectacular red wines of Eger or the honey-sweet whites of Tokaj? The five ranges that make up the Northern Uplands – Cserhát, Mátra, Bükk, Aggtelek and Zemplén – are not just about nature. This is a land where the Palóc and Mátyo people hold strong in traditional villages such as Hollókő and Mezőkövesd. As reminders of far too many battles won and lost, ageing castles and evocative ruins punctuate the landscape. Outdoor recreation, culture, history – it's time to head for the hills!

When to Go

Eger

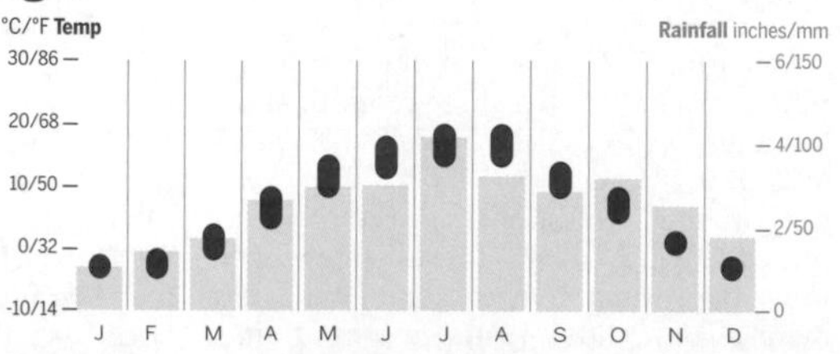

Mar & Apr Easter in Hollókő or Mezőkövesd, when everyone dons their traditional finery for Mass

Jul & Aug Crowded it may be but this is the time for medieval tournaments at castles such as Boldogkő

Dec–Mar Snow (usually) falls and Hungary's only ski centre at Kékestető comes to life

HOLLÓKŐ

☎32 / POP 360

The Cserhát Hills may not be graced with soaring peaks (none of them is higher than 650m), but they are cloaked in a rich folk-culture tapestry belonging to the Palóc people. Hollókő (Raven Rock), a two-street village nestled in a tranquil valley, is the epicentre. What sets Hollókő apart is its restored 13th-century castle and the architecture of the so-called Old Village (Ófalu), where some 65 houses and outbuildings have been on Unesco's World Heritage list of cultural sites since 1987. The village has burned to the ground many times since the 13th century (most recently in 1909), but the residents have always rebuilt their houses exactly to plan in traditional wattle and daub.

Sights

The Old Village's folk architecture is the main attraction. Stroll down one cobblestone street and up the other, past whitewashed houses with carved wooden porches and tiled roofs. Few people live in the Old Village any more, preferring the more modern accommodation of the New Village, which you'll pass on the way here.

Hollókő Castle CASTLE

(Hollókői Vár; ☎06 30 968 1739; adult/child 700/350Ft; ⏲10am-5.30pm Apr-Oct) At 365m on Stalk Hill (Szár-hegy), Hollókő Castle commands a striking view of the surrounding hills. The fortress was built at the end of the 13th century and strengthened 200 years later. Captured by the Turks, it was not liberated until 1683 by the Polish king Jan Sobieski (r 1674–96). It was partially destroyed after the war of independence early in the 18th century but the shell is fairly intact. Climb to the top of the pentagonal keep to look out across fields and forested hills without a trace of human occupation. Exhibits inside focus on weaponry and heraldry. There's also a small wax museum.

Hollókő Church CHURCH

(Kossuth utca) The focus of the village's spiritual and social life, this adorable wooden church is on the corner where Petőfi utca, the Old Village's 'other' street, branches off from Kossuth utca. Built as a granary in the 16th century and sanctified in 1889, it is a fairly austere affair both inside and out.

Village Museum MUSEUM

(Falumúzeum; ☎379 255; Kossuth utca 82; adult/child 250/100Ft; ⏲10am-6pm Apr-Oct) The award-winning Village Museum contains the usual three rooms of a Hungarian peasant house, with local folk pottery, painted furniture and embroidered pillows. In the backyard there's an interesting carved wine press dating from 1872.

Postal Museum MUSEUM

(Postamúzeum; ☎379 288; Kossuth utca 80; adult/child 750/375Ft; ⏲10am-6pm Apr-Oct) The Postal Museum is a branch of the one in **Budapest** (Postamúzeum; Map p68; ☎1-269 6838; www.postamuzeum.hu; VI Andrássy út 3; adult/child/family 500/250/1000Ft; ⏲10am-6pm Tue-Sun; M1 Bajcsy-Zsilinszky út). If you must skip one, choose this overpriced museum.

Country House MUSEUM

(Tájház; ☎379 157; Kossuth utca 99-100; adult/child 250/130Ft; ⏲10am-5pm daily Apr-Oct, Sat & Sun Nov-Mar) A nature exhibition at the Country House deals with the flora, fauna and human inhabitants of the Eastern Cserhát Landscape Protection Reserve, part of which surrounds the village.

Doll Museum MUSEUM

(Babamúzeum; ☎379 088; Kossuth utca 96; adult/child 250/150Ft; ⏲10am-5pm Apr-Oct) This museum exhibits more than 200 porcelain dolls in traditional costumes from all across Hungary.

Legend House MUSEUM

(Legendák Háza; ☎06 30 597 8952; Kossuth utca 62; adult/child 400/200Ft; ⏲10am-5pm Apr-Oct) Rather hokey mini-museum tells the story of Hollókő Castle and its legends through costumed figures in three rooms.

Activities

There are some gentle **walks** into the hills and valleys of the 140-hectare landscape protection reserve to the west and south of the castle. *Cserhát,* the 1:60,000 map (No 8; 1215Ft) from Cartographia, will help you plan your route.

Kézművesporta COURSE

(☎06 20 569 7525; www.kezmuvesporta.hu; Kossuth utca 53; per craft 300-1400Ft; ⏲10am-4pm Wed-Fri, to 5pm Sat & Sun) You can learn to weave straw baskets, dip candles and sew cloth dolls the old-fashioned way at Kézművesporta.

Northern Uplands Highlights

1. Savour **Eger** (p246), the unequalled jewel of the Northern Uplands celebrated for its legendary wine, baroque architecture and easy-going temperament

2. Ride the narrow-gauge **railway** (p258) through the forest from Miskolc to the lakeside resort town of Lillafüred

3. Scale the heights of **Boldogkő Castle** (p265), perched high on a craggy cliff, transporting yourself back to the Middle Ages

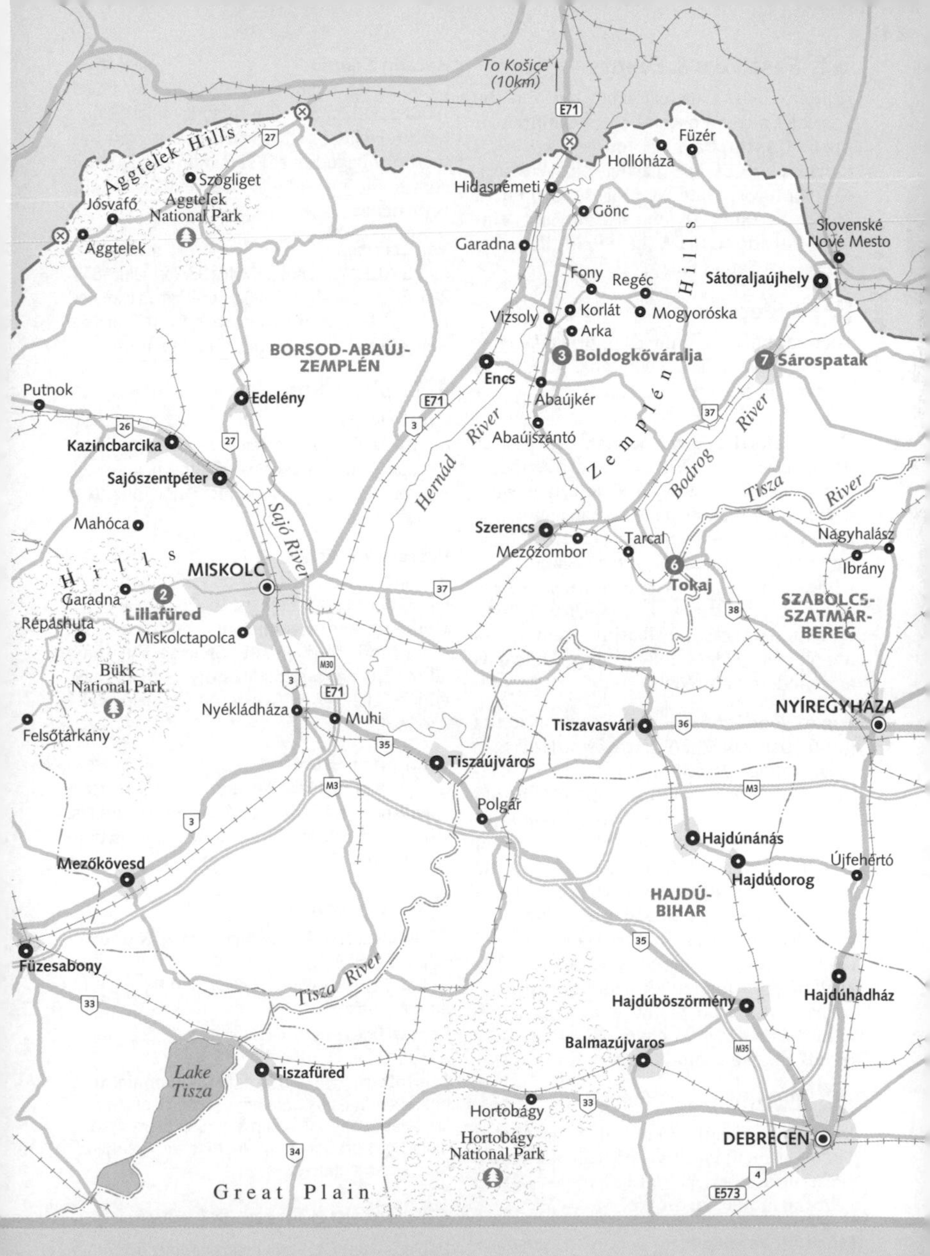

4 Hike through the lush green forests of the **Bükk Hills** (p246) after visiting the magnificent white **Lipizzaner stallions** (p255) at home in Szilvásvárad

5 Spend the night and listen to the silence in **Hollókő** (p237), a tiny village where folk art and tradition live on

6 Taste the famous 'wine of kings and the king of wines' in situ at **Tokaj** (p261)

7 Marvel at the trompe l'oeil ceiling of the Great Library in the **Calvinist College** (p266) at Sárospatak

Festivals & Events

Hollókő marks its calendar red for the annual **Easter Festival** in late March or April, **Castle Days**, a touristy medieval tournament at the castle, on Whitsunday/Pentecost (late May or June) and St Stephen's Day (20 August), and the **Vintage Parade** to mark the end of the grape harvest in September.

Sleeping

There are quite a number of private rooms in the New Village, charging 3000Ft to 4000Ft per person.

TOP CHOICE **Palóc Holiday Houses** HOMESTAY €€
(Palóc üdülőházak; ☎579 010; www.holloko.hu/en/accomodation; s/d 6750/13,500Ft) Nine wonderfully traditional houses that could easily double as folk museums are available for rent throughout the village. Some of the whitewashed cottages with dark beams have antiques and curios – hand-carved beds, hanging lanterns, washbasins – and others are plainer. All have fully equipped kitchens and modern bathrooms.

Tugári Vendégház GUESTHOUSE €€
(☎06 20 379 6132, 379 156; www.holloko-tugarivendeghaz.hu; Rákóczi út 13; r 7500-9500Ft) Though in the New Village, this 75-year-old cottage with four attractive rooms is charmingly traditional. You can tell the cheerful owners Ádám and Tünde worked in the London hospitality industry before coming home to start this guesthouse – they provide electric kettles in every room and will deliver a king's breakfast basket discreetly to your door for 1200Ft. Note that private baths may be down the hall. One apartment has its own kitchen; the other three rooms share a common one.

Eating

Places close early here, so plan ahead. There's a small grocery store called **Piroska** (József Attila utca; ⏲7.30am-3.30pm Mon-Sat) up near the municipal car park.

Muskátli Vendéglő HUNGARIAN €€
(☎379 262; Kossuth utca 61; mains 1850-2250Ft; ⏲11am-7pm Wed-Fri, to 5pm Sat & Sun) The traditional dishes at this traditional cottage restaurant are the best in the village. The flower-bedecked courtyard out the back is a positive delight in the warmer months but is often booked out by groups.

Katalin Csárda HUNGARIAN €
(☎06 30 499 0558; Kossuth utca 69; mains 1390-1900Ft; ⏲11am-6pm Sun-Fri, to 8pm Sat) Come here for classic Hungarian fare served in a quaint village house. The staff are extra accommodating and will change dishes to suit your needs.

Vár Étterem HUNGARIAN €€
(☎06 30 29 4528; Kossuth utca 93-95; mains 1850-2250Ft; ⏲11am-6pm Tue-Sun, to 10pm in summer) A third restaurant to choose from, but one that offers later opening time in summer.

Shopping

Craft House HANDICRAFTS
(Mívesház; ☎380 016; Petőfi utca 4; ⏲11am-5pm Tue-Sun) This artisans' workshop is an excellent place to admire and buy Palóc folk dress and costumes.

Pottery Workshop HANDICRAFTS
(Fazekas műhely; ☎06 70 456 7116; Kossuth utca 65; ⏲10am-6pm) This is the only place in Hollókő where ceramic pots and plaques are made and fired on-site. Sharing the same address is **Fakanálás Műhely** (⏲10am-6pm), which sells carved wooden items (especially spoons).

Grandma's Store FOOD
(Nagymama Kamrája; Kossuth utca 86; ⏲noon-6pm Mon, from 10am Tue-Sun) Jams, jellies, wines and spices fill the shelves in this pantry of a shop.

Information

ATM (cnr József Attila & Sport utca) Next to Piroska grocery store.

Hollókő Website (www.holloko.hu) Bilingual official website.

Post Office (Kossuth Lajos utca 72; ⏲8am-2.30pm Mon-Fri)

Tourinform (☎579 011; holloko@tourinform.hu; Kossuth Lajos utca 68; ⏲8am-6pm Mon-Fri, 10am-2pm Sat & Sun May-Sep, 8am-4pm daily Oct-Apr) Very helpful office with useful map and brochures.

Getting There & Away

One bus a day (3.15pm) heads directly from Budapest (1860Ft, 2¼ hours, 91km) to Hollókő; it returns at 5am weekdays, and 4pm Saturday and Sunday. Otherwise you have to change in Szécsény (370Ft, 30 minutes, 18km, at least three daily). To reach Balassagyarmat (745Ft, one hour, 36km) you must also change there. The bus stops on Kossuth utca at Dósza György utca; from there the Old Village is downhill.

WORTH A TRIP

BALASSAGYARMAT & THE PALÓC PEOPLE

The Palóc people are a distinct Hungarian group living in the fertile hills and valleys of the Cserhát Hills. Ethnologists are still debating whether they were a separate people who later mixed with the Magyars, or a Hungarian ethnic group that, through isolation and Slovakian influence, developed its own unique ways. What's certain is that the Palóc continue to speak a distinct dialect of Hungarian. Hollókő, with its uniformly traditional cottages, is undoubtedly Palóc central. Villages like **Rimóc** (www.rimoc.hu) and **Kazar** (www.kazar.hu) may have more mixed architecture, but they preserve their traditions with small ethnographic exhibits and elaborate celebrations on feast days. The **Palóc Road** (Palóc út; www.palocut.hu) will take you to places associated with these people in Hungary and Slovakia.

If you'd like to know a whole lot more, head for the town of **Ballasagyamat** and its purpose-built **Palóc Museum** (☎300 168; www.palocmuzeum.hu; Palóc liget 1; adult/child 700/350Ft; ⊙10am-6pm Tue-Sun). The standing exhibit 'From Cradle to Grave' on the 1st floor takes you through the important stages in the life of the Palóc people, and includes pottery, superb carvings and mock-ups of a birth scene, a classroom and a wedding. There are also ex-voto objects used for the all-important *búcsúk* (church patronal festivals). But the Palóc women's needlework – from the distinctive floral embroidery in blues and reds to the almost-microscopic white-on-white stitching – leaves everything else in the dust. An **open-air museum** (adult/child 400/200Ft; ⊙10am-4pm Tue-Sat May-mid-Nov), including an 18th-century Palóc-style house, stable and church, stands in the garden behind the main museum. For refreshment try the popular **Orchidea Cukrászda** (☎311 450; Bajcsy-Zsilinszky utca 12; ice cream 150Ft; ⊙9am-7pm Mon-Fri, from 8am Sat & Sun), just opposite the museum.

Eight daily buses go to Szécsény (370Ft, 20 minutes, 18km) from here, where you can change for Hollókő (370Ft, 30 minutes, 18km). At least 10 daily buses link Budapest (1680Ft, 1½ hours, 82km) with Balassagyarmat.

GYÖNGYÖS

☎37 / POP 33,650

The Mátra Hills, which include Hungary's tallest 'peaks', are the most accessible of the ranges. Gyöngyös, a colourful, small city at the base of the Mátras, is the gateway. With its important museum, ancient churches and rich medieval library, it's easy to let the delights of the hills wait a while. Or you may simply want to hang out on the shaded main square and sample a glass or two of the region's fine wines. Gyöngyös is the centre of the Mátraalja wine-growing region, noted especially for Hárslevelű (Linden Leaf), a green-tinted white wine that is both spicy and slightly sweet.

Sights

Mátra Museum MUSEUM
(☎505 530; www.matramuzeum.hu; Kossuth Lajos utca 40; adult/child 1100/550Ft; ⊙10am-5pm Tue-Sun) It's hard to believe the fine old Orczy manor house that now holds the lion's share of the Mátra Museum began as a family hunting lodge in the 1760s. Here you'll find exhibits dealing with the history of Gyöngyös in the 18th and 19th centuries, area ethnography and a room dedicated to the 1800 local Jewish Holocaust victims, as well as minerals and fossils (including a mini mammoth). In the new **Natural History Pavilion** (Természettudományi Pavilon; adult/child 1100/550Ft) there are copious amounts on animal and plant life as well as a palm house and aquarium. The displays at this award-winning museum are all very well done, with English summaries. A combined ticket costs adult/child 1550/750Ft. City lore has it that the wrought-iron railings enclosing the elaborate flower gardens were made from gun barrels taken during the *kuruc* uprising.

St Bartholomew's Church CHURCH
(Szent Bertalan utca 1; ⊙during services only) St Bartholomew's Church, at the northeastern end of Fő tér, was built in the 14th century and is the largest Gothic church in Hungary. You'd hardly know it though, with the baroque restoration (including an unusual upper-storey gallery inside) that was carried out 400 years later. Look for the twin Gothic-arch windows on each side, which are original.

House of the Holy Crown MUSEUM
(Szent Korona-ház; Szent Bertalan utca 3) The presbytery of St Bartholomew's Church, under renovation at the time of research, served as a safe house for the Crown of St Stephen three times from 1806 to 1809 during the Napoleonic Wars. Today it contains the city's **Ecclesiastical Treasury** (Egyházi Kincstár; ☎311 143; adult/child 600/300Ft; ⏲10am-noon & 2-5pm Tue-Sun), a rich collection of liturgical objects and church plate.

FREE **Hungarian Franciscan Memorial Library** LIBRARY
(Magyar Ferencesek Műemlék Könyvtára; ☎311 971; Barátok tere 2; adult/child 250/160Ft; ⏲10am-noon Mon-Fri, 10am-1pm Sat) The former Franciscan Monastery (built 1730) contains the only historical archive in Hungary to have survived the Turkish occupation intact. Among its 14,000 volumes are some of the rarest books written in Hungarian.

Synagogues JEWISH
(Zsinagogák) Gyöngyös was home to a relatively large Jewish community from the 15th century to WWII, and two splendid synagogues bear witness to this fact. The older of the two, the neoclassical **Memorial Synagogue** (Műemlék zsinagóga; Eszperantó utca), built in 1820, faces Gyöngyös Stream and now houses the city's TV studios. The Moorish-Secessionist **New Synagogue** (Új zsinagóga; Kőrösi Csoma Sándor utca), on the corner with Gárdonyi Géza utca, was designed by Lipót Baumhorn in 1930, two decades after he completed his masterpiece in Szeged (p219). It is currently being used as a warehouse.

Activities

Narrow-Gauge Train TRAIN TOUR
(☎320 025; Dobó István utca 1) Easily the most enjoyable way to enter the Mátra Hills is by the narrow-gauge forest train that departs from Előre station on Dobó István utca just east of the Mátra Museum. From April to late August, up to five daily trains make the 20-minute run (adult/child one way 490/290Ft, return 895/540Ft) to Mátrafüred, 7km to the northeast. On the way back, you can get off at Farkasmály-Borpincék, where there's a row of wine cellars, and then jump onto any bus coming down Rte 24 to return the 4km to Gyöngyös.

A second train chugs along the 11km (40 minutes) line to Lajosháza up to five times a day from early April to late October. The slow ride (adult/child one way 590/350Ft, return 995/590Ft) gives you a good feel for what's on offer further into the hills. Check out www.matrahegy.hu for more suggestions.

Festivals & Events

Gyöngyös parties hard at the twice-annual **Wine Festival** in mid-May and again in mid-September and kicks up its heels at the **Folk Dance Festival** in August.

Sleeping

Hotel Opál HOTEL €€
(☎505 400; www.opalhotel.hu; Könyves Kálmán tér 12; s/d 10,000/15,000Ft; ❄@📶) Housed in a former college, this 35-room hotel has recently undergone a total revamp and is now the pride of Gyöngyös – despite its boxy, slightly clinical-looking exterior. Staff are friendly, rooms are up to date and added extras, such as a fitness room, sauna and cafe-bar, add to Opál's overall good value.

Vincellér Panzió GUESTHOUSE €€
(☎311 691; www.vincellerpanzio.hu; Erzsébet királyné út 22; d/apt 10,000/16,000Ft; ❄📶) Its proximity to the hills attracts travellers to this 15-room guesthouse on the way to Mátrafüred. The outside is old, but colourful duvets complement warm wood veneers inside. The restaurant is very popular with local people, especially at weekends.

Károly Róbert Diákhotel HOSTEL €
(☎518 100; www.krhotel.hu; Bene út 69; s/d 5000/7000Ft; @📶) This 'student hotel' (read hostel), with 175 comfortable, spotlessly clean and modern rooms with bathroom in two buildings 2km north of the centre, welcomes guests year-round.

Eating

TOP CHOICE **Kékes Étterem** MODERN HUNGARIAN €€
(☎311 915; www.kekesetterem.hu; Fő tér 7; mains 1850-4800Ft) With a full list of regional specialities, Kékes is simply tops in town and exceptionally inventive for a provincial Hungarian restaurant. Try a glass of local Hárslevelű with your chicken breasts braised in honey mustard, or pork cutlet in a wild forest mushroom sauce.

Giardinetto d'Italia ITALIAN €€
(☎300 709; www.giardinetto.hu; Rózsa utca 8; mains 2900-4300Ft) How can you beat a real-deal Italian restaurant in provincial Hungary that has *Blues Brothers* statues kicking back at the entrance just south of the main square? The garden at Giardinetto is good for both drinks

BUS

The bus station is on Koháry út, a 10-minute walk southeast of Fő tér and just south of the Mátra Museum. You won't wait more than an hour for buses to/from Budapest (1490Ft, 1¾ hours, 79km) or Eger (1120Ft, one hour, 52km). Several daily buses traverse the hills from Gyöngyös to Eger (1300Ft, 1¾ hours, 61km) via Parád. Other destinations in the Mátra Hills include the following:

DESTINATION	PRICE	TIME	KM	FREQUENCY
Kékestető	370Ft	45min	18	9 daily
Mátrafüred	250Ft	10min	6	half-hourly
Mátraháza	310Ft	15min	15	half-hourly
Parád	560Ft	1¼hr	30	9 daily
Recsk	650Ft	1¼hr	35	9 daily

and food, which includes pizza (1250Ft to 2250Ft) and pasta dishes (1370Ft to 2580Ft).

Karma 2 INTERNATIONAL
(☎301 701; Páter Kiss Szaléz utca 22; mains 1050-1950Ft) This restaurant, on the 1st floor of a modern shopping arcade, offers a mixed bag of international favourites - Caribbean jerk chicken, anyone? - and pizza, and its set lunches (750Ft to 1000Ft) are particularly good value. It's a club on Saturday night.

☆ Entertainment

Mátra Cultural Centre PERFORMING ARTS
(Mátra Művelődési Központ; ☎312 282; www.gyongyok.com; Barátok tere 3) Done up in 'Finnish functionalist style', with huge (52 sq metres!) and very colourful stained-glass windows, this 1978-vintage building is where Gyöngyös entertains itself.

Information

OTP Bank (Fő tér 1) On the main square.

Post Office (Páter Kiss Szaléz utca 9-11)

Tourinform (☎311 155; gyongyos@tourinform.hu; Fő tér 10; ⏲9am-5pm Mon-Fri, to 2pm Sat & Sun May-Sep, 8am-4pm Mon-Fri Oct-Apr) Opposite the town hall on the main square.

Getting There & Away

Train

Gyöngyös is on a dead-end spur, 13km from the Vámosgyörk stop (310Ft, 15 minutes), where you can switch to the Budapest–Miskolc trunk line. Hourly trains connect Vámosgyörk with Budapest (1680Ft, 1½ hours, 87km). You'd have to change a second time, in Füszabony, to get to Eger (1120Ft, one hour, 5km) by train. Gyöngyös train station is on Vasút utca, near the eastern end of Kossuth Lajos utca.

GYÖNGYÖS TO EGER

Rte 24 wends its way through the Mátra Hills north of Gyöngyös to Parádsasvár and then cuts eastward onto Eger (60km); if you're travelling under your own steam, it's one of the prettiest drives in the country. The section to Mátraháza is popular with bikers, who constantly attack the road and its hairpin corners with wanton abandon on weekends. There's a shrine to the (many) victims at Kékestető, Hungary's highest point. The most idyllic approach is via the narrow-gauge train (p242) to Mátrafüred. From Gyöngyös, buses to (and between) Mátrafüred, Mátraháza and Kékestető are frequent. The further east you go, the more sporadic the services become. For general information on the Mátra Hills, see www.matrahegy.hu.

Mátrafüred

☎37 / POP 980

Hungarians come to this village, 6km north of Gyöngyös, to breathe the forest air and walk in nature at 340m. The many easy trails in the area are the main draw. Arm yourself with a copy of the 1:40,000 *Mátra* map (No 14; 1215Ft) from Cartographia.

Sights & Activities

Palóc Doll Museum MUSEUM
(Palócbaba Múzeum; ☎320 137; Pálosvörösmarti út 2; adult/child 400/300Ft; ⏲9.30am-5pm Apr-Nov, 10am-4pm Dec-Mar) South of the narrow-gauge train stop, this cute little museum is well worth a visit. Rita Juhász Lovásné is not only an artist with her sculpted cloth dolls, she's an ethnographer too – replicating

each of the region's three-dozen Palóc village costumes for different stages of life. Some crafts on sale.

Walking & Hiking HIKING

Off Akadémia utca, the red trail leads less than 1km north up to the small ruins of Bene Castle (Benevár). From the west side of the village, off Hegyalja utca, you can follow the yellow triangle trail past Közmáry watchtower and Dobogó Hill, up to the next watchtower and bus stop at Sástó (2.5km, 300m elevation change).

Sleeping & Eating

Back streets west of Rte 24 have the bulk of signs advertising private rooms (per person 3000Ft to 4000Ft), while holiday hotels surround the park. Food stands congregate at the intersection of the main route and Béke utca.

Hotel Anna HOTEL €€€

(☎320 317; www.anna-hotel.hu; Üdülősor utca 55; s/d 15,000/19,000Ft; @🛜🏊) The warm colours – lemon and peach predominate – of the 18 comfortable rooms detract from the relatively small size. Still, there's a full wellness centre (fitness, sauna, whirlpool) and the park-like surrounds are restful. There's a fancy restaurant here, too.

Gyöngyvirág HOTEL €€

(☎520 001; www.gyongyvirag.hu; Béke utca 8; s/d/apt 9000/10,100/15,000Ft; 🛜) A fully equipped playground and minigolf make this otherwise institutional-looking hotel kid-central. Parents on a budget will love the self-catering apartment, and the attached Hungarian eatery (mains 1200Ft to 1800Ft) is quite reasonable.

Fekete Rigó HUNGARIAN €€

(Blackbird; ☎320 052; www.feketerigo.hu; Avar utca 2; mains 1200-2500Ft) The 'Blackbird' is an easy-going choice for dining, with a lovely beer garden nestled among the pines. The fruit and ham-stuffed pork (yes, meat-stuffed meat – a common Hungarian predilection) is actually quite good.

Sástó

☎37

About 3km northwest of Mátrafüred, Sástó is little more than a reedy lake and an ever-extending recreation and camping complex. Rowing boats and a 54m-high lookout tower are just the beginning. At the **Oxygen Adrenalin Park** (☎316 480; www.adrenalin-park.hu; Sástó-Kőbánya; admission 550-4400Ft; ⌚9am-7pm Sun-Thu, to 8pm Sat & Sun May-Aug, 10am-6pm Sun-Thu, to 7pm Fri & Sat mid-Mar–Apr & Sep–mid-Nov, 10am-4pm Fri-Sun mid-Nov-mid-Mar) you can ride a chain-assisted, roller-coaster-like bobsled, climb a rope course, ride a four-wheeler, do a mini bungee jump, go to a petting zoo, swoop down a zip line or scale a rock wall. Activities cost between 550Ft and 4400Ft apiece.

With all that adrenaline, you can well imagine that **Mátra Camping** (☎374 025; www.matrakemping.hu; Sástó-Kőbány; campsites per person/tent 1200/1000Ft, motel r 7500Ft, bungalows with/without bathroom 10,500/6500Ft; ⌚Apr-Oct) is far from quiet. Tents are pitched willy-nilly in a field, and snack stands clutter the clearing's edge. 'Comfortable' wood bungalows come with bathroom and TV; the others have shared facilities; both sleep three. Motel rooms have twin beds but are small.

The plain-Jane guest quarters at the **Panorama Panzió** (☎574 026; www.adrenalin-park.hu/panzio; Sástó-Kõbány; s/d 7500/9600Ft) are much nicer – trimly made beds and crisply painted walls. Music plays on the terrace on summer evenings, when the restaurant (mains 1650Ft to 2250Ft) is open daily (October through April, it opens only on weekends).

Mátraháza

☎37 / POP 290

Holidaymakers have been coming to Mátraháza since the first hotel was built in the 1920s. On a slight incline, 715m above sea level, the village is about 5km north of Sástó. It has an Alpine feel to it and is smaller and more secluded than Mátrafüred.

Follow the **yellow trail** (triangle then square) 4.5km west through the hills to Lajosháza and the terminus of a narrow-gauge train, or the **red trail** south through Kalló Valley (Kalló-völgy) past the Bene Castle ruins to Mátrafüred (4.5km). The real test is the 3.4km **red and blue cross trail** that leads through a gentle valley before climbing steeply the last 1km to Kékestető.

If you feel like splashing out, **Residence Hotel Ózon** (☎506 000; www.hotelozon.hu; r 15,000-29,000Ft; ❄@🛜🏊) is a four-star spa hotel with 79 rooms halfway between Sástó and Mátraháza. With 1000 sq metres of pools inside and out, a full wellness centre and spectacular views of Kékestető, this is the place to pamper yourself. In the centre of

Mátraháza, the **Tölgy Kisvendéglő** (☎322 7711; mains 1650-3150Ft; ⏰11am-8pm Thu-Sun), with its large covered deck, is just the place to enjoy a carb-loaded meal of dumplings and cheese before heading up the nearby trail to Kékestető.

Kékestető

☎37 / POP 80

Every Hungarian knows that Kékestető, 4km west of Mátraháza, is the highest point in the country; that it's only 1014m doesn't seem to affect the enthusiasm. You do have quite a view on clear days, and it only gets better if you take the elevator up the 178m-tall **TV tower** (☎367 086; adult/child 480/350Ft; ⏰9am-6pm May-Aug, to 5pm Apr, Sep & Oct, to 4pm Nov-Mar).

Things liven up when snow falls (roughly late December until March) and the **Kékestető Ski Centre** (☎567 007; www.kekesteto.hu; half/full day lift ticket adult 4500/3500Ft, child 3500/2500Ft; ⏰9am-4.30pm Sun-Thu, to 8pm Fri, to 9pm Sat) opens up. Three tow-lifts serve nine runs, including two advanced ones, and skis are for rent (from 3500Ft per day). **Skimobile rides** (per 2hr 9900Ft; ⏰11am-2pm) are offered nearby.

If you follow the blue and red cross trail through the forest, crossing over the road, you'll reach Mátraháza in 3.4km (you can also take a shortcut, 2km, down the ski hill). The even more scenic 7km green trail leads past waterfalls and valleys to Mátrafüred.

The seven uncomplicated log-cabin lodge rooms at **Kékesi Vendégház** (☎06 30 623 1759, 567 007; info@matracentrum.hu; s/d 5000/9000Ft; ⏰10am-8pm Wed-Sun), opposite the ski lift from Mátraháza, are your best bet for sleeping; the nearby **Kányai Uram Fogodója** (☎367 064; Üdülötelep 1; d 7600Ft) has cheaper but much more basic accommodation. There's a restaurant at the Kékesi Vendégház (mains 1650Ft to 2400Ft). Nearby **Tető Étterem** (mains 650-1250Ft; ⏰10am-6pm) offers self-service cafeteria options.

Parádsasvár

☎36 / POP 420

Parádsasvár, 12km north of Mátraháza, is where the country's most odoriferous *gyógyvíz* (medicinal drinking water) is bottled. Stop for a glass at the public fountain, if you can stand the stench of this sulphuric brew.

Nearly 3 hectares of parkland surround the 57-room **Kastélyhotel Sasvár** (☎444 444; www.khs.hu; Kossuth Lajos utca 1; r 22,800-38,000, ste 45,900-64,900Ft; ❄@📶🏊), a 'destination' place to stay. Miklós Ybl, the same man responsible for the Hungarian State Opera House in Budapest, constructed the Renaissance-style hunting manor and its outbuildings in 1882. Rooms range from the romantic (swagged canopies and dusty rose silk) to the utilitarian. A stay includes spa admission, tennis, bowling and billiards. A grand meal is to be had at the silver-service restaurant (mains 2600Ft to 4200Ft).

Parád & Parádfürdő

☎36 / POP 1950

Five kilometres further east, Parád and Parádfürdő run into one another and effectively make up one long village. The **Coach Museum** (Kocsimúzeum; ☎364 083; Kossuth Lajos utca 217; adult/child 500/300Ft; ⏰10am-5pm Apr-Sep, to 4pm Tue-Sun Oct-Mar), housed in the red marble Ornamental Stables (Cifra Istálló) of Count Károlyi, is an excellent small museum. Silk brocade richly decorates the 19th-century diplomatic and state coaches; the bridles contain as much as 5kg of silver (for the record, the word 'coach' comes from Kocs, a small village in Transdanubia, where these lighter horse-drawn vehicles were first used in place of the more cumbersome wagons). The stables can arrange **horse riding** (per hr from 3000Ft) as well.

The lovely **Erzsébet Park Hotel** (Queen Elizabeth Park Hotel; ☎444 044; www.erzsebetparkhotel.hu; Kossuth Lajos utca 372; r 21,500-32,000Ft; @📶🏊) is more hotel than palace, but it was also designed by the very busy Miklós Ybl in 1893. Tasteful furnishings in its 99 rooms reflect today's pared-down interpretations of imperial classics. Bathe in the thermal waters of the Elizabeth's own medicinal pools, or do laps in the Olympic-size swimming pool outdoors before retiring to the cafe or the formal restaurant.

Recsk

☎36 / POP 2700

From Parádfürdő the road continues for 2km to Recsk, a place that lives in infamy as the site of Hungary's most brutal forced-labour camp during the communist regime. Set up by Mátyás Rákóczi in 1950, it was closed down by the reformer Imre Nagy three years later. As a memorial to those who slaved and died here, the **Recsk Forced-Labour Death Camp** (Recski Kényszermunka Haláltábor; ☎06 20 935 9043; www.recsk.hu; adult/child 500/250Ft; ⏰9am-5pm May-Sep, 9am-3pm Sat & Sun Oct-Apr) has been partially reconstructed near the quarry, about 5km south of the village.

EGER

☎36 / POP 56,500

Blessed with beautifully preserved baroque architecture, Eger is a jewellery box of a town with loads to see and do. Explore the bloody history of Turkish occupation and defeat at the hilltop castle, climb an original Ottoman minaret, listen to an organ performance at the colossal basilica, or relax in a renovated Turkish bath. Then spend time traipsing from cellar to cellar in the Valley of Beautiful Women, tasting the celebrated Eger Bull's Blood (Egri Bikavér) and other local wines from the cask. Flanked by the Northern Uplands' most inviting range, the Bükk Hills, hiking and horse-riding excursions are never far away.

History

It was at Eger in 1552 that the Hungarians fended off the Turks for the first time during the 170 years of occupation. The Turks came back in 1596 and this time captured the city, turning it into a provincial capital and erecting several mosques and other buildings, until they were driven out at the end of the 17th century. Eger played a central role in Ferenc Rákóczi II's attempt to overthrow the Habsburgs early in the 18th century, and it was then that a large part of the castle was razed by the Austrians. Having enjoyed the status of an episcopate since the time of King Stephen in the 11th century, Eger flourished in the 18th and 19th centuries, when the city acquired most of its wonderful baroque architecture.

Sights

Eger Castle FORTRESS

(Egri Vár; www.egrivar.hu; Vár köz 1; castle grounds adult/child 800/400Ft, incl museum 1400/700Ft; ⏰exhibits 9am-5pm Tue-Sun Mar-Oct, 10am-4pm Tue-Sun Nov-Feb, castle grounds 8am-8pm May-Aug, to 7pm Apr & Sep, to 6pm Mar & Oct, to 5pm Nov-Feb) The best view of the city can be had by climbing up cobblestone Vár köz from Dózsa György tér to Eger Castle, erected in the 13th century after the Mongol invasion. Much of the castle is a modern reconstruction, but you can still see the foundations of 12th-century **St John's Cathedral** on the eastern side of the complex. Models and drawings in the István Dobó Museum, housed in the former Bishop's Palace (1470), painlessly explain the history of the castle. On the ground floor, a statue of Dobó takes pride of place in the **Heroes' Hall**. The 19th-century building on the northwestern side of the courtyard houses the **Eger Art Gallery**, with works by Canaletto and Ceruti. The

BÜKK HILLS

Much of the Bükk range forms 43,250-sq-km **Bükk National Park** (☎in Eger 36-411 581; www.bnpi.hu). The range takes its name from the beech (*bükk*) trees growing here. Karst formations, upland plateaus, thick pine forests and abundant wildlife attract hikers and cyclists to hillside villages such as Szilvásvárad, famous for its Lipizzaner horses. Southern slopes support wine production, including the famous Bull's Blood red. Sample it in the baroque treasure of a town, Eger, one of the country's true treasures. To the east, the valleys around industrial Miskolc have been scarred by ore mining. But you needn't linger there when you can visit verdant resorts like Lillafüred.

Nearly in the dead-centre of Bükk National Park, **Répáshuta** (www.repashuta.hu) makes an excellent base for exploring nearby caves and, further afield, the Bükk Plateau. The long and windy hillside village has a handful of guesthouses and private rooms, a game restaurant, a folk-craft exhibition and a grocery store. Just 24km from Lillafüred, buses connect to Miskolc (650Ft, 1¼ hours, 31km) between two (daily) to eight (weekdays) times a day. The hilly drive from Eger through Répáshuta to Miskolc is extremely enjoyable, but the bus only makes the journey once weekly, on Sunday at 8.30am.

Cartographia (www.cartographia.hu) puts out a 1:40,000 *Bükk* map (No 29; 1215Ft) and a useful atlas-guide (2690Ft).

terrace of the renovated 1549 **Dobó Bastion** (Dobó Bástya; adult/concession 500/250Ft), which collapsed in 1976, offers stunning views of the town; it now hosts changing exhibits. Beneath the castle are **casemates** hewn from solid rock, which you may tour with a Hungarian-speaking guide included in the price (English-language guide 800Ft extra). Other attractions, including the **Panoptikum** (Waxworks; waxworks adult/concession 500/350Ft) and **3D film** (admission 400-600Ft) cost extra. Alternatively, you can just wander the castle grounds, which are also open Monday, when most exhibits are closed.

Kossuth Lajos Utca STREET

Kossuth Lajos utca is a fine, tree-lined street with dozens of architectural gems. The first of interest is the former **Orthodox synagogue** (Kossuth Lajos utca 17), built in 1893 and now the **Zsinagóga Galéria** (Synagogue Gallery; ☎785 027; Kossuth Lajos utca 17; adult/concession 500/300Ft; ⏲10am-6pm Tue-Sun) with rotating exhibitions. The former **neoclassical synagogue** (Dr Hibay Károly utca 7), dating from 1845, is around the corner and is a modern-art gallery. You'll pass several outstanding baroque and Eclectic buildings along the way, including the **county hall** (Megyeháza; Kossuth Lajos utca 9), with a wrought-iron grid above the main door of (from left) Faith, Charity and Hope by Henrik Fazola, a Rhinelander who settled in Eger in the mid-18th century. Walk down the passageway and you'll see two more of his magnificent works: baroque wrought-iron gates decorated on both sides. The one on the right shows the seal of Heves County at the top and has a comical figure on its handle. The more graceful gate on the left is decorated with flowers and grapes. The wrought-iron balcony and window grilles of the rococo **Provost's Palace** (Kispréposti palota; Kossuth Lajos utca 4) were also done by Fazola.

Eger Basilica CHURCH

(Egri Bazilika; Pyrker János tér 1; 7.30am-6pm Mon-Sat, from 1pm Sun) A highlight of the town's amazing architecture is the basilica. This neoclassical monolith was designed in 1836 by József Hild, the same architect who later worked on the cathedral at Esztergom. A good time to see the place is when the ornate altars and a soaring dome create interesting acoustics for the half-hour **organ concert** (admission 800Ft; ⏲11.30am Mon-Sat, 12.45pm Sun mid-May–mid-Oct).

City Under the City HISTORIC SITE

(Pyrker János tér, Város a Város Alat; adult/concession 950/500Ft; ⏲9am-7pm Apr-Sep, 10am-5pm Oct-Mar) To the right of the main steps to the basilica is the entrance to the former archbishop's cellars. A history-oriented tour leads you through the caverns and takes 45 minutes.

Lyceum HISTORIC BUILDING

(Líceum; ☎325 211; www.mheger.hu; Eszterházy tér 1; library adult/student 800/550Ft; ⏲9.30am-3.30pm Tue-Sun Apr–mid-Oct, 9.30am-1pm Sat & Sun mid-Oct–mid-Dec, 9.30am-1.30pm Tue-Sun Feb & Mar) Directly opposite the basilica is the recently renovated Zopf-style Lyceum (1765). The 60,000-volume library on the 1st floor of the south wing contains hundreds of priceless manuscripts and codices. The trompe l'oeil ceiling fresco (1778) depicts the Counter-Reformation's Council of Trent (1545–63), with a lightning bolt setting heretical manuscripts ablaze. The **Astronomy Museum** (Csillagászati Múzeum; ☎520 400; www.varazstorony.ektf.hu; Eszterházy tér 1, 6th fl, Lyceum; adult/student 1000/800Ft) on the 6th floor of the east wing contains 18th-century astronomical equipment, an observatory and a planetarium with regularly scheduled shows. Climb three more floors up the so-called Magic Tower (Varász Torony) to the observation deck to try out the camera obscura, the 'eye of Eger', designed in 1776 to entertain townspeople.

Archbishop's Palace HISTORIC BUILDING

(Érseki Palota; Széchenyi István utca 5) Northeast of the basilica is the Archbishop's Palace and its **Ecclesiastical Collection** (Egyházi Gyűjtemény; ☎517 751; http://egyk.uw.hu; adult/child 600/300Ft; ⏲10am-3.30pm Tue-Fri, 10am-2pm Sat Apr-Oct, 10-11.30am Tue-Fri Nov-Mar), with priceless vestments, church plate and liturgical objects. Entry is under the sign reading 'Szent István Rádió'.

György Kepes International Art Centre GALLERY

(Kepes György Nemzetközi Művészeti Központ; ☎420 044; Széchenyi utca 16; adult/child 1200/600Ft; ⏲10am-6pm Tue-Sun) Eger's newest gallery exhibits the work of Hungarian-born American artist and designer György Kepes, who is celebrated for – among other things – his light installations.

Eger

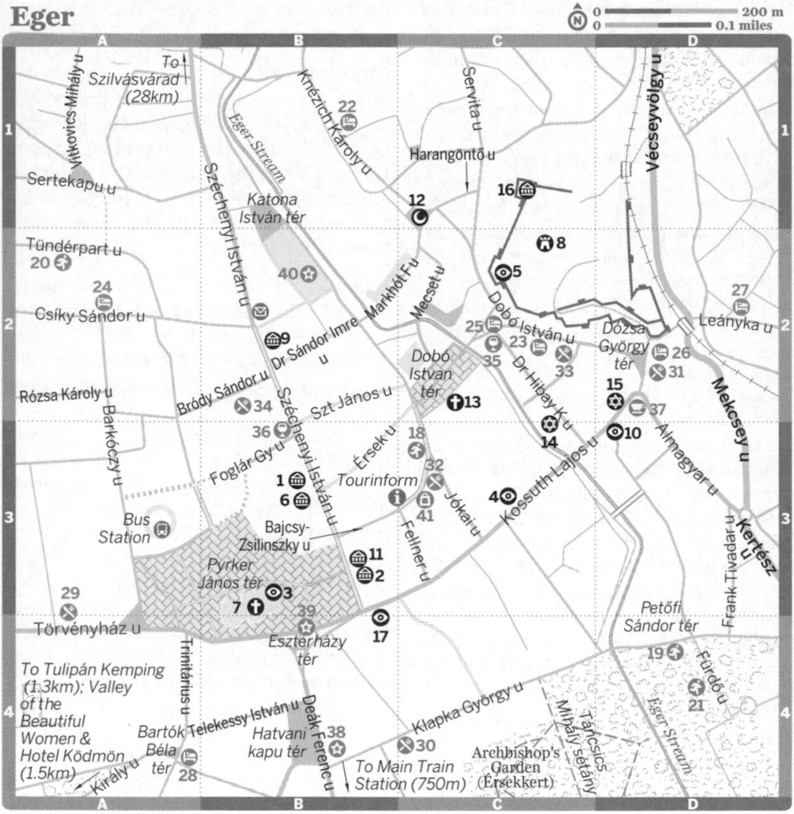

Minorite Church of St Anthony of Padua CHURCH

(Páduai Szent Antal Minorita Templom; Dobó István tér 6; ⏲9am-5pm Tue-Sun) On the southern side of Eger's main square stands the Minorite church, built in 1771 by Bohemian architect Kilian Ignaz Dientzenhofer and one of the most glorious baroque buildings in Hungary. The altarpiece of the Virgin Mary and St Anthony of Padua is by Johann Kracker, the Bohemian painter who also did the fire-and-brimstone ceiling fresco in the Lyceum library.

Minaret ISLAMIC

(☎06 70 202 4353; Knézich Károly utca; admission 200Ft; ⏲10am-6pm Apr-Oct) This 40m-tall minaret, topped incongruously with a cross, is the only reminder of the Ottoman occupation of Eger. Nonclaustrophobes will brave the 97 narrow spiral steps to the top for the awesome view.

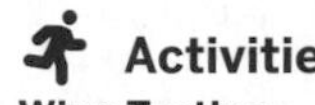

Activities

Wine Tasting

You can taste Eger's famous wines at many places around town, including at restaurants at the base of the castle and in the **István Cellar** (☎313 670; www.koronahotel.hu; Hotel Korona, Tündérpart 5; wine tasting 2200-5500Ft; ⏲noon-10pm Tue-Sat). But why bother drinking in town when you can do the same in the cellars of the evocatively named Valley of the Beautiful Women (Szépasszony-völgy)? Here, more than two dozen *pincék* (cellars) have been carved into the horseshoe-shaped rock. For an average of 100Ft you can have a one-decilitre taste of a range of reds, such as Bull's Blood, and whites, such as Olaszrizling and Hárslevelű. The choice of wine cellars can be a bit daunting, so walk around and have a look yourself (hint: we like numbers 40, 43 and 46 on the west side of the green). It's not to be missed.

Eger

Sights

1 Archbishop's Palace ... B3
2 Astronomy Museum ... B3
3 City Under the City ... B3
4 County Hall ... C3
5 Dobó Bastion ... C2
6 Ecclesiastical Collection ... B3
7 Eger Basilica ... B3
8 Eger Castle ... C2
9 György Kepes International Art Centre ... B2
10 Kossuth Lajos Utca ... D3
11 Lyceum ... B3
12 Minaret ... C1
13 Minorite Church of St Anthony of Padua ... C2
14 Neoclassical Synagogue ... C3
15 Orthodox Synagogue ... D2
16 Panoptikum ... C1
17 Provost's Palace ... B4

Activities, Courses & Tours

18 Eger Bike ... C3
19 Eger Thermal Baths ... D4
20 István Cellar ... A2
21 Turkish Bath ... D4

Sleeping

22 Agria Retur Panzió ... B1
23 Dobó Vendégház ... C2
24 Hotel Romantik ... A2
25 Hotel Senator Ház ... C2
26 Imola Apartman Hotel ... D2
27 Imola Hostel ... D2
28 Szent Kristóf Panzió ... A4

Eating

29 Agria Park ... A3
30 Fehérszarvas Vadásztanya ... C4
31 Imola Udvarház Borétterem ... D2
32 König Pizza ... C3
33 Palacsintavár ... C2
Senator Ház Étterem ... (see 25)
34 Szántófer Vendéglő ... B2

Drinking

35 Bikavér Borház ... C2
36 La Isla ... B3
37 Marján Cukrászda ... D2

Entertainment

38 Géza Gárdonyi Theatre ... B4
39 Gödör Kult Klub ... B4
40 Hippolit ... B2

Shopping

41 Magvető Könyvesbolt ... C3

The valley is a little over 1km southwest across Rte 25, off Király utca. Catch the **City Eye Bus Tour** (☎06 20 457 7871; Dobó István tér; 700Ft; ⌚8am-6.30pm Apr-Oct) from the west side of Dobó István tér. A taxi costs about 1000Ft.

Other Activities

Eger Thermal Baths SPA
(Egri Térmalfürdő; ☎510 558; www.egertermal.hu; Petőfi tér 2; adult/child 1700/1500Ft, swimming pool only 900Ft; ⌚6am-8pm Apr-Sep, 9am-6.30pm Oct-Mar) After strolling in the Archbishop's Garden (Érsékkert), once the private reserve of papal princes, you can further unwind in the Eger Thermal Baths. Admission gains you access to a variety of pools, including bubbling massage pools and a castle-themed kids' pool, and other recreational and spa features spread over 5 hectares.

Turkish Bath SPA
(Török Fürdő; ☎510 552; www.egertermal.hu; Fürdő utca 3-4; 2½hr session adult/child 1900/1500Ft; ⌚4.30-9pm Mon & Tue, 3-9pm Wed-Fri, 9am-9pm Sat & Sun) After a hard day's drinking in the Valley of the Beautiful Women, nothing beats a soak and steam at this historic spa, which has a bath dating to 1617 at its centre. A multimillion-forint addition opened in 2009 has five pools, saunas, steam room and a hammam (Turkish bath). Various kinds of massage and treatments are also available. Recommended.

Eger Bike BICYCLE RENTAL
(☎06 30 233 5814; www.egerbike.hu; Bajcsy-Zsilinszky utca 17-19; 6hr/full day/week 2000/3000/10,000Ft; ⌚9am-8pm Mar-Nov) In a courtyard off Bajcsy-Zsilinszky utca

Festivals & Events

Annual events include the **Spring Festival** in late March/April, the **Border Fortress Merrymaking Festival and Games** at the castle at the end of July, **Baroque Weeks** in late July/August, the **Agria International Folkdance Meeting** in August and the **Grape Harvet Festival** in mid-September.

THE SIEGE OF EGER

The story of the Turkish attempt to take Eger Castle is the stuff of legend. Under the command of István Dobó, a mixed bag of 2000 soldiers held out against more than 100,000 Turks for a month in 1552. As every Hungarian kid in short trousers can tell you, the women of Eger played a crucial role in the battle, pouring boiling oil and pitch on the invaders from the ramparts.

Eger's wine apparently also played a significant role. It's said that Dobó sustained his troops with a ruby-red local wine. When they fought on with increased vigour – and stained beards – rumours began to circulate among the Turks that the defenders were drinking the blood of bulls. The invaders departed – for the time being – and the name Bikavér (Bull's Blood) was born.

View the mock-up of the siege in miniature in the castle museum or read Géza Gárdonyi's *Eclipse of the Crescent Moon* (1901), which describes the siege in thrilling detail.

Sleeping

TOP CHOICE **Hotel Senator Ház** BOUTIQUE HOTEL €€€
(Senator House; ☎411 711; www.senatorhaz.hu; Dobó István tér 11; s/d €50/70; ❄) Eleven warm and cosy rooms with traditional white furnishings fill the upper floors of this delightful 18th-century inn on Eger's main square. The ground floor is shared between a quality restaurant and a reception area stuffed with antiques and curios. If you'd like more space, stay at its nearby sister property called **Pátria Panzió** (Szúnyo köz 3; s/d €50/70, apt for 2/3 €90/110; ❄@📶), with three rooms and two huge apartments.

Hotel Romantik HOTEL €€€
(☎310 456; www.romantikhotel.hu; Csíky Sándor utca 26; s/d €40/65; ❄@📶) This cosy 15-room hotel, with a pretty back garden and delightful breakfast room, is an easy walk from the city centre, but far enough away to escape any noise in the summer months. Room 20 has its own balcony facing the garden. The friendly owner rents bicycles for 30000Ft a day.

Agria Retur Panzió GUESTHOUSE €
(☎416 650; http://agria.returvendeghaz.hu; Kné-zich Károly utca 18; s/d 3800/6400Ft; @📶) You couldn't find sweeter hosts than the daughter and mother who own this guesthouse near the minaret. Walking up three flights of stairs, you enter a cheery communal kitchen/eating area central to four rooms. Out the back is a huge garden with tables and barbecue at your disposal.

Dobó Vendégház HOTEL €€
(☎421 407; www.vendeghaz.hu; Dobó István utca 19; s/d 9000/13,500Ft; 📶) Tucked away along one of the old town's pedestrian streets, just below the castle, this lovely little hotel is a boon for sightseers. The seven rooms are spic and span and some have little balconies. Check out the museum-quality Zsolnay porcelain collection in the breakfast room.

Imola Apartman Hotel APARTMENT €€€
(☎516 180; www.imolaudvarhaz.hu; Dósza György tér 4; s/d 19,000/23,000Ft; ❄📶) With six sleek and stylish apartments under the very nose of the castle, this is where you want to stay if you are looking for a central location and the freedom to prepare your own meals. Kitchens come fully equipped.

Imola Hostel HOSTEL €
(Leányka úti Kollégium; ☎520 430; www.imolanet.hu/imolahostel; Leányka út 2; s/d 3700/7400Ft; @) This former college dormitory has been modernised and comfortable beds and large desks now fill quite smart twin rooms. Each floor shares a kitchen and a computer with internet.

Szent Kristóf Panzió GUESTHOUSE €
(☎06 20 436 7877; http://www.stkristofpanzioeger.hu; Arany János utca 1; d 6500-8500Ft, tr 8500-10,500Ft; 📶) This guesthouse, just south of the basilica and on the way to the Valley of the Beautiful Women, has eight rather small but comfortable rooms. Ceilings slope but that's the price you pay for staying in an old building. We like the round turreted room on the corner.

Hotel Ködmön RESORT €€€
(☎515 803; www.szepasszonyvolgy.eu; Szépasszonyvölgy utca 1; r €98-120; ❄@📶🏊) If you like the idea of staying out in the Valley of the Beautiful Women, choose this relatively new, modern-design resort hotel with 20 rooms. Awaken to a view of the vineyards

and then take advantage of its fully equipped wellness centre. There's a popular *csárda* (Hungarian-style inns) on-site.

Tulipán Kemping CAMPGROUND €
(☎311 542; www.tulipancamping.com; Szépasszonyvölgy utca 71; campsites per person/tent/caravan 800/900/1600Ft, bungalows d/q 5000/6000Ft) Many of the caravan and tent sites at Tulipán Kemping are in an open, shadeless field. But you're surrounded by vineyards and just stumbling distance from the wine cellars of the Valley of the Beautiful Women. The bungalow is just a cabin, with no bath or kitchen.

Eating

Lining the entry path to the Valley of the Beautiful Women are 10 food-stand-like eateries, with waiters who come to your covered picnic table with menus at which to point (mains 850Ft to 1400Ft). There are also several *csárdák* among the wine cellars to choose from.

TOP CHOICE **Imola Udvarház Borétterem** HUNGARIAN €€
(☎516 180; www.imolaudvarhaz.hu; Dósza György tér 4; mains 1930-3970Ft) This very stylish eatery at the foot of the castle, with its inventive menu and excellent wine card, has been named among the top dozen restaurants in Hungary and who are we to disagree? We'll come back in particular for the four-course tasting menu (4570Ft), which changes every two months.

Szántófer Vendéglő HUNGARIAN €€
(Plough; ☎517 298; www.szantofer.hu; Bródy Sándor utca 3; mains 1700-2400Ft) Choose the 'Plough' for hearty, home-style Hungarian fare. Farming equipment and cooking utensils hang like prize kills on the walls, and a covered courtyard out the back is perfect for escaping the summer heat. Two-course weekday lunches are a snip at 850Ft.

Senator Ház Étterem INTERNATIONAL €€
(☎320 466; www.senatorhaz.hu; Dobó István tér 11; mains 1500-3500Ft) Seats in the antique-filled dining room of this charming hotel are coveted, but the outdoor ones are the hot seat of Eger's main square. Try the cream of garlic soup served with Camembert (650Ft), the smoked local trout (1700Ft) with pineapple and walnut oil salad, and the *borjúpaprikás* (veal stew; 2000Ft).

Palacsintavár CREPERIE €
(Pancake Castle; ☎413 986; www.palacsintavar.hu; Dobó István utca 9, enter from Fazola Henrik utca; mains 1490-1820Ft) Pop art and a fascinating collection of antique cigarettes still in their packets line the walls, and groovy music fills the rest of the space in this eclectic eatery. Savoury *palacsinták* – pancakes, for a better word – are served with an abundance of fresh vegetables and range in flavour from Asian to Italian. There's a large choice of sweet ones too, but be prepared to wait; service is below standard.

Fehérszarvas Vadásztanya HUNGARIAN €€€
(White Deer Hunters' Farm; ☎411 129; www.feherszarvasetterem.hu; Klapka György utca 8; mains 2200-4800Ft) With its game specialities and cellar setting, the White Deer Hunters' Farm is really a place to enjoy in season – autumn and winter. Cold fruit soups and goose liver pâté are particular specialities, but try those in the warmer months.

König Pizza PIZZERIA €
(Bajcsy-Zsilinszky utca 4; pizza 690-1250Ft) Very simple hole-in-the-wall place serving innumerable varieties of pizza, with a fair number of vegetarian options.

Agria Park INTERNATIONAL €
(www.agriapark.hu; Törvényház utca 4; mains 500-1000Ft; ⏰8am-10pm Mon-Sat, to 9pm Sun) Chinese, Hungarian and Greek self-service restaurants are among your choices on the top floor of the Agria Park shopping centre west of the basilica.

Drinking

Bikavér Borház WINE BAR
(☎413 262; Dobó István tér 10; ⏰9am-10pm) Try one or two of the region's best wines at this central wine bar. The waiters can guide you with the right selection and supply a plate of cheese or grapes to help you cleanse your palate.

La Isla COCKTAIL BAR
(☎06 30 405 0817; www.laislabarandgrill.hu; Foglár György utca 2; ⏰10am-midnight Sun-Thu, to 2am Fri & Sat) As much a Latin cocktail bar as a cafe, this is a fine place to kick back after a hard day's sightseeing.

Marján Cukrászda CAFE
(☎312 784; Kossuth Lajos utca 28; cakes 180-480Ft; ⏰9am-10pm Jun-Sep, 9am-7pm Oct-May) Linger over coffee and sweets on the big terrace south of Dozsa György tér and directly below the castle.

Entertainment

Eger has a year full of cultural programs listed in the free monthly magazine *Belváros,* available at Tourinform. For cultural programs, especially music concerts, check out the listings in the free Egri Est (www.est.hu) biweeky magazine.

Géza Gárdonyi Theatre THEATRE
(Gárdonyi Géza Színház; ☎510 700; www.gardonyiszinhaz.hu; Hatvani kapu tér 4) Dance, opera and drama are staged at the town's theatre, due south of the basilica.

Hippolit CLUB
(☎412 452; www.hippolit.hu; Katona István tér 2; ⊙10pm-5am Wed, Fri & Sat) Eger's classic club, where the dance floor doesn't heave but buckles until the wee hours, is downstairs from the circular Elefanto restaurant near the city market.

Gödör Kult Klub CLUB
(Pyrker János tér 3; ⊙10pm-6am Wed, Fri & Sat) This bizarre, cave-like DJ dance club beneath the cathedral steps parties hard on weekends. Seriously underground.

Shopping

Magvető Könyvesbolt BOOKS
(☎517 757; www.lira.hu/hu/bolthalozat/eger1; Bajcsy-Zsilinszky utca 4; ⊙9am-6pm Mon-Fri, to 1pm Sat) Small bookstore with a selection of English titles and maps.

Information

Eger Website (www.eger.hu) Multilingual official site.

OTP Bank (Széchenyi István utca 2) With ATM.

Post Office (Széchenyi István utca 22)

Tourinform (☎517 715; http://mheger.hu; Bajcsy-Zsilinszky utca 9; ⊙9am-6pm Mon-Fri, to 1pm Sat & Sun mid-Jun–mid-Sep, 9am-5pm Mon-Fri, to 1pm Sat mid-Sep–mid-Jun) Covers both the town and surrounding areas.

Getting There & Away

Train

The main train station is on Vasút utca, south of the Archbishop's Garden. To reach the city centre, walk north on Deák Ferenc utca and then head along pedestrian Széchenyi István utca, Eger's main drag. The Egervár train station, which serves Szilvásvárad and other points north, is on Vécseyvölgy utca, about a five-minute walk north of Eger Castle.

Up to seven direct trains a day connect to/from Budapest's Keleti train station (2830Ft, two hours, 120km). Otherwise, Eger is on a minor train line linking Putnok and Füzesabony, so you have to change at the latter for Miskolc (1490Ft, 1½ hours, 74km) or Debrecen (2200Ft, 2¾ hours, 120km).

AROUND EGER

Mezőkövesd

☎49 / POP 16,600

Around 18km southeast of Eger, Mezőkövesd is not much of a town, but it is the centre of the Matyó, a Magyar people famous for their fine embroidery, wood painting and folk dress. Here you have the opportunity to see some of the most distinctive folk art in Hungary.

Sights & Activities

Matyó Museum MUSEUM
(☎311 824; www.hermuz.hu/hom/index.php/hu/muzeumaink/muzmezokovesd/muzmatyo; Szent László tér 8; adult/child 600/300Ft; ⊙9am-3pm Tue-Sat) Your first port of call in the capital city of Matyóland is this museum, with rich

BUS

DESTINATION	PRICE	TIME	KM	FREQUENCY
Debrecen	2520Ft	2½hr	131	7 daily
Gyöngyös	1120Ft	1hr	52	hourly
Kecskemét	3130Ft	4½hr	166	3 daily
Miskolc	1300Ft	1½hr	68	8 daily
Szeged	3950Ft	5¾hr	237	2 daily
Szilvásvárad	560Ft	45min	29	hourly

The only bus that goes through the Bükk Hills via Felsőtárkány to Miskolc leaves on Sunday at 8.30am.

ROZI VÁCZI: MATYÓ MAVEN

Rozi Váczi spent the first five years and every subsequent summer of her childhood in Tard, a one-horse Matyó town 12km northwest of Mezőkövesd, blind to the colourful embroidery around her. But then she went back, had a closer look-see and with her sister, Borbála, founded Matyó Design (p84), a fashion company that has pulled this traditional craft into the 21st century by using it to brighten up everyday clothes.

OK, so the eureka moment... When was that exactly? I came to Tard to convalesce after a difficult pregnancy and had one of the village *nénék* (aunties) embroider a shirt as a birthday gift. I thought, 'Oh my God, this is what I should be doing next! Why not start a business?'

'Traditional' and 'conservative' usually go hand in hand. Can you, in fact, teach old dogs new tricks? We usually stick to the usual Matyó colours, but if someone wants blue roses, that's fine with us. Of course, the women minded. 'But, Rozi,' they'd say, 'it can't be like this. A rose has to be red, a leaf green.' It took a year to win them over. But look at it from their point of view. If you were 82 and had been looking at Matyó roses ever since you were two, you wouldn't be able to see them any colour but red.

Are you telling Tard 'thanks for the memories'? Our big dream is for the whole village to live from Matyó Design. There are 1100 people here, there's almost no work, and old people do everything – gardening, cooking, cracking walnuts, making honey and, of course, embroidering from 5am to 10pm daily. Why not have them earn something for their labour?

But isn't that labour pool going to dry up pretty soon? The seamstresses are getting older and the knowledge is under threat. We need to focus our attention on setting up an apprentice scheme. The challenge is getting the younger generation interested in this sort of work.

Is Matyó embroidery the next big thing? What has become trendy nowadays in this world of mass production is to have something others do not. And the whole craft is self-perpetuating as no two items are ever the same.

So we defer to your expertise... How do you tell the difference between kézimunka (needlework, literally 'hand work') and machine-made stuff? Turn it over and you'll see imperfections; a handmade item is never perfect. Also the thread is a little thicker in needlework. One may not be visually superior to the other but intellectually there's a huge difference. Machine work takes five minutes, handmade five hours.

So where do we go from here? When we started up Matyó Design I assumed Kalocsa Design and Palóc Design would follow. But I soon realised that the whole point of this business is that we are here in Tard and have this connection. We understand Matyó and what we make we sell from our hearts. We know where these things come from.

displays explaining the regional differences and historical development of Matyó needlework – from white-on-white stitching and patterns of blue-and-red roses, to the metallic fringe that was banned in the early 1920s because the high cost was ruining families.

Hadas District HISTORIC SITE

(Hadas Városrész) From Hősök tere, a short distance southwest of Szent László tér, enter any of the small streets running southward to dicover Hadas district, a completely different world of thatched and whitewashed cottages. Interesting lanes to stroll along are Patkó köz, Kökény köz and Mogyoró köz, but the centre of activity is Kisjankó Bori utca, the street named after Hungary's own 'Grandma Moses', who lived and stitched her famous rose patterns here for almost 80 years. The family's 200-year-old cottage is now the **Bori Kisjankó Memorial House** (Kisjankó Bori Emlékház; ☎312 759; www.mezokovesd.tajhaz.hu; Kisjankó Bori utca 22; adult/child 200/100Ft; ⊙10am-6pm daily Jul & Aug, 10am-4pmTue-Sun Apr-Jun, Sep & Oct, 10am-2pm Tue-Sat Nov & Dec, 10am-2pm Fri-Sun Jan-Mar), filled with needlework and brightly painted furniture. 'Aunt Bori' and her apprentices eschewed symmetry and improvised on tradition, stitching intensely bright flowers flowing across dark backgrounds. She is credited with creating 100 rose embroidery patterns.

You can see occasional embroidery demonstrations and dance performances at the **House of Folk Art & Dance** (☎411 686; www.matyofolk.hu; Kisjankó Bori utca 5-7). Check out traditional Matyó wood-painting techniques at **Szabolcs Kovács Furniture Folk Artist** (☎500 288; Kis Jankó Bori utca 10). Several other artists have their studios on this street – making intricately decorated honey cakes at No 6, embroidering (No 8), throwing pots (No 38) – or on Mogyoró köz (eg toys at No 4), where you can also buy the crafts. Studios are generally open the same hours as Aunt Bori's house.

The best time to visit is during a festival, such as Easter, when you can see some townsfolk in full traditional regalia. Check the Mezőkövesd website (p254) for program schedules.

Sleeping & Eating

Rozmaringos Vendégház GUESTHOUSE €
(☎06 30 935 0827; www.hidaskapus.hu/rozmaringos.htm; Kisjankó Bori út 42; d 6000Ft) An older home in the historic district with thatched roof, the four rooms here have antiques and a dark-wood decor. There are shared bathrooms and a kitchen.

Tulipános Vendégház GUESTHOUSE €
(☎06 30 228 7119, 411 686; www.tulipan.ini.hu; Mogyoró köz 1; d 6000Ft) Sleep in the heart of Matyóland opposite the Bori Kisjankó Memorial House. This self-catering cottage has three fairly modern double rooms that share a kitchen and garden.

Hungária HUNGARIAN €€
(☎416 800; Alkotmány út 2; mains 1400-3150Ft) The Hungária's interior may be a bit stiff, but the chicken cordon bleu and other fried meat dishes are solid. There's a huge dessert menu, too. It's across from Tourinform.

Pizza Néró PIZZERIA €
(☎415 676; Eötvös utca 9; mains 850-1100Ft; ⏰10am-11pm Sun-Thu, to 1am Fri & Sat) Simple pizzas and pastas are available till late on the northern edge of the Hadas District.

Information

Mezőkövesd Website (www.mezokovesd.hu)

OTP Bank (Mátyás király út 149) At the western edge of town, near the bus station.

Post Office (Alkomány utca 1)

Tourinform (☎500 285; meokovesd@tourinform.hu; Szent László tér 23; ⏰9am-5pm Mon-Fri, to 2pm Sat Jul & Aug, 10am-4pm Mon-Fri Sep-Jun) Very helpful information office.

Getting There & Around

The bus station is on Rákóczi utca. Walk south for 50m and then east along Mátyás király út for 500m to Szent László tér and Tourinform. From the train station, head north on Széchenyi István utca and then east on Mátyás király út.

Buses run to/from Eger (465Ft, 30 minutes, 21km) and Miskolc (930Ft, one hour, 46km) every hour as do trains to/from Miskolc (840Ft, 40 minutes, 44km).

Szilvásvárad

☎36 / POP 1675

Home to graceful white Lipizzaner horses, carriage races, a narrow-gauge train and

THE MAGNIFICENT WHITE STALLIONS

The celebrated white Lipizzaner (Lipicai in Hungarian) horses are well known for their graceful, ballet-like dressage movements at the Spanish Riding School in Vienna. In Szilvásvárad they are bred as carriage horses. As a result they are bigger and stronger than the Austrian breed and those raised for riding and show at Lipica in Slovenia.

Breeding, as they say, is paramount. Six families with 16 ancestors (including Spanish, Arabian and Berber breeds) can be traced back to the early 18th century, and their pedigrees read like those of medieval royalty. When you walk around the stables at the stud farm (p255) you'll see charts on each horse stall with complicated figures, dates and names like Maestoso, Neapolitano and Pluto. It's all to do with the horse's lineage.

A fully mature Lipizzaner measures about 15 hands (around 153cm), weighs between 500kg and 600kg and lives an average of 25 to 30 years. Lipizzaners are not born white, but grey or even chestnut brown. The celebrated 'imperial white' coat does not come about until they are between five and 10 years of age, when their hair loses its pigment. Think of it as part of the maturing process. Their skin remains grey, however, so when they are ridden hard enough to sweat, they become mottled.

forest trails, Szilvásvárad makes an excellent day's excursion from Eger, 28km to the south. But hikers and horse lovers especially may want to extend their stay in this peaceful, green village in the hills.

Sights & Activities

Horse Museum MUSEUM
(Lovasmúzeum; ☎564 400; Park utca 8; adult/child 500/400FT; ⏲9am-noon & 1-5pm Fri-Tue) You can learn a whole lot more about the intelligent Lipizzaner horses by visiting the whiffy Horse Museum about 1km northeast of town. Exhibits focus on bloodlines, but the real sight is the breeding mares who live in this five-star stable built in 1860. The stallions at the **Lipizzaner Stud Farm** (Lipicai Ménes; ☎564 400; www.menesgazdasag.hu; Fenyves utca 4; adult/child 500/400Ft; ⏲9am-noon & 1-4.30pm Wed-Mon) to the southwest can also be visited; there's a **Coach Museum** (Kocsimúzeum; ☎564 400; Fenyves utca 4) attached. Arrange ahead for horse rides up into the protected areas of the Bükk Plateau (3000Ft per hour) or for coach rides (from 7000Ft per hour). Horse parades, coach races and special events, such as the **Lipizzaner Horse Festival** in mid-July, take place in the open and closed **racecourses** in the centre.

Orbán House Museum MUSEUM
(Orbán-ház Múzeum; ☎816 233; Miskolci utca 58; adult/child 300/200Ft; ⏲9am-5pm Tue-Sun mid-Apr–Oct) Displays in this 17th-century farmhouse are devoted to ethnography – especially that of the Palóc people – and the history of the area that now forms Bükk National Park.

Narrow-Gauge Train TRAIN TOUR
(Erdei Kisvonat; ☎355 197; www.szalajka-volgy.hu; Szalajka-völgy 6; one way adult/child 800/460Ft; ⏲Apr-Oct) A little open-air narrow-gauge forest train chugs its way for 4km into the Szalajka Valley between four and 10 times a day from April to October.

From the terminus at Szalajka-Fátyolvízesés you can walk for 1km to **Istállóskő Cave**, where Stone Age pottery shards were discovered in 1911, or climb 959m **Mt Istállóskő**, the highest peak in the Bükk Hills. To return to Szilvásvárad, either board the train for the return trip or walk back 1¼ hours along shady paths and past trout-filled ponds. Towards the end of the path, there's the small **Aladár Zilahy Forestry Museum** (Zilahy Aladár Erdészeti Múzeum; ☎355 112; adult/child 400/200Ft; ⏲9am-4.30pm) and a turn-off where you can veer for a 2.1km hike to the **Millennium Lookout Tower** (Milleniumi Kilátó; adult/child 350/210Ft; ⏲10am-5pm Mon-Fri, 10am-7pm Sat & Sun May-Oct) with great views across the valley.

At the mouth of the Szalajka Valley, and south of the narrow-gauge train station, there's a line of paid amusements, including a trampoline jump, **pony rides** (per ride 400Ft; ⏲11am-5pm Mon-Fri, from 1pm Sat & Sun May-Oct), an exhibition on the endangered imperial eagle and the somewhat hokey **Archeopark** (☎06 20 491 6531; www.archeopark.hu; Szalajka-völgy; adult/child 450/350Ft) about prehistoric local life. The **mountain bike rental shop** (☎06 30 335 2695; www.kerekparkolcsonzo.hu; per hr/day 1000/2500Ft; ⏲9am-6pm) also sells gear and maps.

Sleeping

TOP CHOICE **La Contessa Kastély Hotel** HISTORIC HOTEL €€€
(☎564 065; www.lacontessa.hu; Park utca 6; r 46,900-52,900Ft;) At long last what was once the Szilvás hotel, housed in the 19th-century Palavicini mansion, has returned to the land of the living as the rather prissily named Contessa following extensive reconstruction. No worries, for she's a beaut, with 80 rooms in the manor house and extension linked by corridors with vaulted ceilings. There's a huge wellness centre with everything, a lovely covered pool and parkland surrounds the property.

Jókai Vendégház GUESTHOUSE €
(☎816 604; www.jokaivendeghaz.hu; Jókai út 5/1; s 5000-600Ft, d 8000-10,000Ft; @) Each of the dozen brightly hued rooms has light wood furnishings and minibars; some rooms have balconies and views, including room 111. The friendly owners will arrange bicycle rental and horse riding. There's a spa and sauna on-site.

Szalajka Liget Hotel RESORT €€€
(☎564 300; www.szalajkaliget.hu; Park utca 25/a; r/house 20,000/38,000Ft; @) Rooms are super-comfortable but oatmeal bland at this full-blown resort with huge outdoor pool and playground, indoor whirlpools and sauna, spa services and treatments, and bike rental. The free-standing holiday houses (with kitchen) sleep four to six. It's east of the centre.

Hegyi Camping CAMPGROUND €
(☎355 207; www.hegyicamping.com; Egri út 36/a; campsites tent & 2 people 3500Ft, 2-/3-/4-bed

bungalows 6600/7500/9000Ft; ⌚May-Oct) A small, shady campground close to walks. White-and-wood bungalows are a bit dated but the on-site restaurant is good and reasonably priced (mains 1150Ft to 1400Ft).

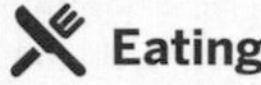

Eating

Numerous food stands and eateries line the entrance to Szalajka Valley, opposite the narrow-gauge train station. Most of them serve *pistrang* (trout; per 100g 60Ft), the area's speciality, in some form or another.

Lovas Étterem HUNGARIAN €€
(☎564 057; www.lovasetterem.hu; Szalajka-völgy; mains 1550-3650Ft) The dining-room walls here serve as an informal gallery of coach racing and Lipizzaner glory. As the main restaurant in town, Lovas hosts loads of events – from dances and horse riding to sleigh rides with hot drinks in winter.

Csobogó Étterem HUNGARIAN €€
(☎06 70 326 2759; www.csobogoetterem.hu; Szalajka-völgy; mains 1750-2750Ft) Next to a stream-powered waterwheel under the trees at the start of the Szalajka Valley is a truly lovely place to dine. In summer you can watch your grilled dishes being fired nearby on the open outdoor pit.

Táltos Vigadó HUNGARIAN €
(☎355 752; www.taltosvigado.hu; Fenyves út 2; mains 990-1590Ft) Hearty Hungarian faves top the menu at this rustic neighbourhood inn northwest of the town centre. Sit outside if you don't relish trophy animals staring down at you.

Information

Coop Mini (Egri út 8) This central grocery store has an ATM.

Information Kiosk (www.szilvasvarad.hu; Szalajka-völgy; ⌚10am-6pm Tue-Sun Jun-Oct) At other times of the year, check with Tourinform in Eger.

Post Office (Egri út 12)

Getting There & Away

Buses, which stop along Egri út, connect with Eger (560Ft, 45 minutes, 30km) at least hourly. There are two daily buses to Budapest (2830Ft, three hours, 157km) via Eger and Gyöngyös.

There are four trains a day to/from Eger (630Ft, one hour, 34km). Get off at the Szilvásvárad-Szalajkavölgy stop and walk northeast for about 10 minutes to the centre; the main station is 3km north.

Miskolc

☎46 / POP 168,000

Miskolc, Hungary's fourth-largest city after Budapest, Debrecen and Szeged, is not so attractive in its own right, but its position at the foot of the Bükk Hills makes it a convenient springboard for trips to the thermal cave baths of nearby Miskolctapolca, the castle ruins in the western suburb of Diósgyőr and a forest train ride to the picturesque hillside village of Lillafüred, from where you can hike into Bükk National Park. The town is sizeable enough to have a number of churches and museums, a few bars and even its own tramline.

Sights

Széchenyi István út is lined with some fairly interesting old buildings, especially those around the so-called **Dark Gate** (Sötétkapu), an 18th-century vaulted passageway.

Hungarian Orthodox Church CHURCH
(Deák Ferenc tér 7) The tourist board likes to vaunt Miskolc as the 'city of churches', and it isn't wrong. The Hungarian Orthodox Church, a splendid late-baroque structure, has a Greek Orthodox iconostasis (1793) that is 16m high with 64 icons. A guide will escort you to the impressive **Orthodox Ecclesiastical Museum** (Ortodox Egyházi Múzeum; ☎tel, info 415 441; Deák tér 7; adult/child 300/150Ft; ⌚10am-6pm Tue-Sun May-Sep, 10am-4pm Tue-Sat Oct-Apr) near the main gate. Look out for the Black Madonna of Kazan, presented to the church by Catherine the Great, and the jewel-encrusted Mt Athos Cross, brought to Miskolc by Greek settlers in the 18th century.

Other Houses of Worship CHURCH
Southeast of the Hungarian Orthodox Church stands the large **Orthodox Synagogue** (☎505 043; Kazinczy Ferenc utca 7), designed in 1861 by Ludwig Förster, architect of the Great Synagogue in Budapest. The Calvinist **Plank Church** (Deszkatemplom; ☎413 590; Petőfi tér) is a 1938 replica of a 17th-century Transylvanian-style wooden church. It has been completely rebuilt and renovated after being badly damaged by fire in 1997. Below Avas Hill is the large Gothic 1410 **Avas Calvinist Church** (Avasi Református Templom; Papszer 14, Avas-hegy), with a painted wooden interior. The bell tower, which chimes musically on the hour, dates from the mid-16th century. From here you can stroll up leafy

Miskolc

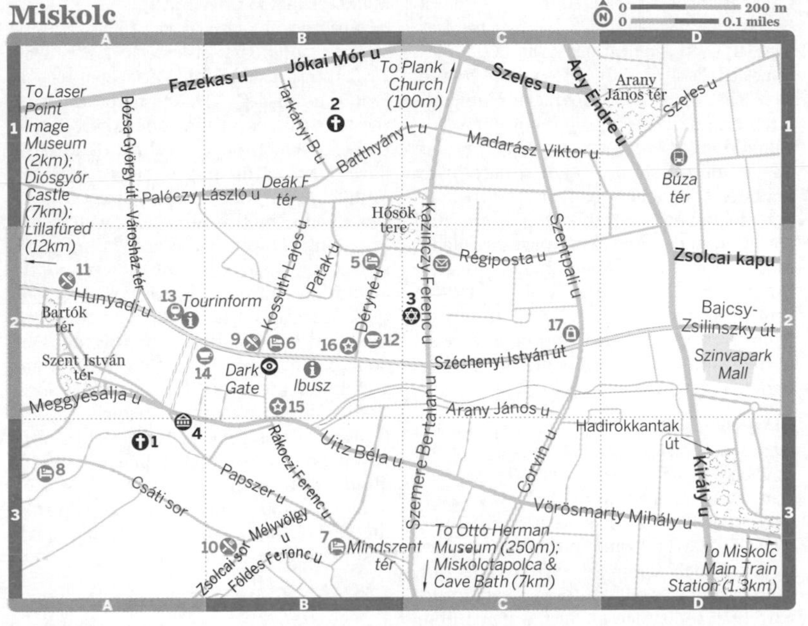

NORTHERN UPLANDS MISKOLC

Miskolc

Sights

1 Avas Calvinist Church A3
2 Hungarian Orthodox Church B1
3 Orthodox Synagogue C2
4 Ottó Herman Museum Exhibition Gallery A3

Sleeping

5 Dolce Vita Panzió B2
6 Hotel Pannónia Miskolc B2
7 Székelykert B3
8 Völgyzugoly Vendégház A3

Eating

9 Impresszó Club-Restaurant B2
10 Palacsinta Ház B3
11 Via Piano A2

Drinking

12 Cafe Dali B2
13 Green Gecko Bar A2
14 Sarokház A2

Entertainment

15 House of Arts B2
16 Miskolc National Theatre B2

Shopping

17 Géniusz C2

Avas Hill along narrow lanes and past some of the more than 800 wine cellars cut into the limestone. The best approach is via Mélyvölgy utca, off Papszer utca, or Földes Ferenc utca, off Mindszent tér.

Ottó Herman Museum MUSEUM
(☎560 170; www.hermuz.hu; Görgey Artúr utca 28; adult/child 600/300Ft; ⏲8am-4pm Tue-Sun) The Ottó Herman Museum has two branches. This, the main branch, southeast of the city centre, has one of the country's richest regional collections of Hungarian paintings dating from the 18th to 20th centuruies. Also here is a large assembly of Neolithic finds (many from the Bükk region) and a good ethnographical collection. Visit the **Ottó Herman Museum Exhibition Gallery** (Herman Ottó Múzeum Kiállítóhelye; ☎346 875; Parszer 1; adult/child 600/30Ft; ⏲8am-4pm Tue-Sun), south of Tourinform, for a permanent exhibition on photography as well as rotating exhibitions.

Laser Point Image Museum MUSEUM
(Lézerpont Látánytár; ☎428 111; www.nepviseleteink.hu; Győri kapu 57; admission 800-1900Ft, combined ticket 3500Ft; ⏰9am-6pm Mon-Fri, 9am-2pm Sat) One of provincial Hungary's largest and most unusual museums has something for everyone – from Carpathian Basin folk costumes and disappearing crafts to odds and ends from the socialist era, including motorbikes, posters and consumer goods. Add to that old office machines and and optical equipment, Russian bronze icons from the 18th and 19th centuries, and a vast mineral collection from Transylvania. The museum is west of the centre. Take bus 1 bound for Majális Park and get off at Aba utca.

Diósgyőr Castle CASTLE
(☎533 355; www.diosgyorivar.hu; Vár utca 24; adult/child 900/60Ft; ⏰9am-6pm May-Oct, 9am-5pm Nov-Apr) Four-towered Diósgyőr Castle, almost an icon of Miskolc, is in a suburb 7km to the west. Begun in the 13th century, it was heavily damaged early in the 18th century and was only restored – very insensitively in some places – in the 1950s. Tour the castle's history displays, wax museum, medieval weapon collection and ramparts. The castle hosts numerous summer events, including plays staged in the castle courtyard and **Medieval Castle Days** in mid-August. Take tram 1 to the Diósgyőr stop. Then head east on Nagy Lajos Király útja and south on Vár utca.

Activities

Lillafüred Narrow-Gauge Train TRAIN TOUR
(Lillafüredi Állami Erdei Vasút; LÁEV; ☎530 593; www.laev.hu; adult/child 650/550Ft) One of the most enjoyable forest train trips in Hungary connects Miskolc with the resort town of Lillafüred and should be experienced even if you're not interested in the destination! From April to late October the little narrow-gauge train leaves from Dorottya út in western Miskolc, accessible via tram 1 (stop: LÁEV), on weekdays at 9am, 11.30am, 2pm and 4.30pm; on weekends there are additional departures at 10.15 am, 12.45pm and 3.15pm. During the rest of the year, trains leave at 11.30am and 2pm at weekends only, with extras scheduled during school holidays. After the 8km, 30-minute ride to Lillafüred, the train carries on 6km (one hour) further to Garadna, another Bükk National Park hiking destination.

Miskolctapolca Cave Bath SPA
(Miskolctapolcai Barlangfürdő; ☎560 030; www.barlangfurdo.hu; Pazár István sétány 1; adult 1950-2350Ft, child 1350-1750Ft; ⏰9am-8pm Jun-Aug, 9am-6pm Sep-May) The curative waters of the thermal spa in the suburb of Miskolctapolca, 7km from the centre of Miskolc, have been attracting bathers since the Middle Ages. Today's Cave Bath, with its earth walls, 'mildly radioactive waters' and thrashing shower at the end, is unique in the country. Go with the flow from the atrium pool through a series of cave pools that, because of the skylights, at times feel like you're in a not-too-hot volcano. Outdoor pools have a few jetted bubbles and a climbing apparatus for the kids. Choose from a full complement of medical, spa and fitness services. Special events – like night bathing or musical theme nights – are held often. Miskolctapolca is part of Miskolc public transport: buses 2 and 20 run from the Miskolc bus station on Búzá tér, northeast of the centre.

Festivals & Events

The city has a calendar full of cultural events, including the **Miskolc Winter Festival** in late February; **Miskolc City Days** in mid-May; the **Miskolc International Opera Festival** at the end of June; and the **Jameson Cinefest International Film Festival** in the second half of September.

Sleeping

Völgyzugoly Vendégház GUESTHOUSE €
(☎353 676; www.volgyzugolyvendeghaz.hu; Toronyalja utca 61; s 6000-7000Ft, d/apt 8000/10,000Ft; 📶) Bold hues and avant-garde decor, including poetry books displayed on the walls, pep up this charming litle guesthouse with six rooms. One room – a single – has a bathroom on the corridor. The owner is a JRR Tolkien fan, which you may gather from some of the artwork.

Dolce Vita Panzió GUESTHOUSE €€
(☎505 045; www.freund.hu; Déryné utca 7; s/d 11,000/13,000Ft; ❄@📶) A central location and a good cafe are the main selling points at this small guesthouse. Lace doilies and fake flowers in the rooms are a bit old-fashioned, but the owners have spiffed up the restaurant (mains 1850Ft to 3500Ft) with colourful broken-tile mosaics. Beef stroganoff, Mexican bean chilli and pizza are on the mixed international menu.

Székelykert INN €€
(☎411 222; www.szallasinfo.hu/szekelykert; Földes Ferenc utca 4; s/d/tr 9500/12,500/14,500Ft; @) The seven rooms in this old Transylvanian-style inn at the base of Avas Hill may not be large enough to swing much of a cat, but the basic twin-beds-and-TV-table set-up is surrounded by cheery golden-coloured walls. The restaurant below does a decent lunch for 70Ft.

Hotel Pannónia Miskolc HOTEL €€€
(☎504 980; www.hotelpannonia-miskolc.hu; Kossuth Lajos utca 2; s/d 16,900/18,900Ft; ❄ ☎) The Pannónia is Miskolc's most central option and targets itself largely at a business clientele. Its 34 rooms (there are seven apartments in a separate building) are renovated, though not particularly stylish, but we love the original sweeping staircase. Room 213, looking to the pedestrian street, is well situated.

Eating

Palacsinta Ház CREPERIE €
(☎06 70 374 3671; www.papacsintahaz.com; Mélyvölgy út 12; mains 1680-2380Ft; ⏰noon-10pm) This pancake house and wine cellar at the start of Avas Hill has savoury *palacinták* in main-course sizes as well as sweet pancakes (1390Ft to 1480Ft) for afters. It's huge and very popular.

Impresszó Club-Restaurant INTERNATIONAL €€
(☎509 669; www.impresszo.hu; Széchenyi István út 3-9; mains 1690-2290Ft; ⏰7.30am-midnight Mon-Fri, 9.30am-2am Sat, 10am-midnight Sun) A generous choice of vegetarian dishes, such as an aubergine moussaka, and light meals are the strengths of this stylish restaurant-cafe-cum-gallery that turns into a club at the weekend. Excellent breakfasts (600Ft to 800Ft) and set lunches (1400Ft), too.

Via Piano INTERNATIONAL €€
(☎320 486; Hunyadi utca 4; mains 1850-3500Ft) Miskolc's classiest eatery has a subdued, somewhat stark feel to it, enlivened by the music theme. International favourites with a leaning towards Mediterranean and an excellent wine list.

Drinking

Green Gecko Bar BAR
(☎780 743; Városház tér 3; ⏰8pm-2am) Branch of a popular upscale bar in Miskolctapolca that attracts hip young things clamouring for some of the more than 50 shots and mixed drinks on the menu. There are snacks and light meals (390Ft to 1200Ft), too.

Cafe Dali CAFE
(Déryné utca 10; ⏰10am-midnight Mon-Thu, 10am-2am Fri & Sat, 11am-10pm Sun) With big sofas, a funky decor and chilled tunes, Dali is perfect for lolling around sipping cocktails.

Sarokház CAFE
(☎789 919; Széchenyi István út 2; cakes 180-350Ft; ⏰7.30am-midnight Mon-Fri, 10am-midnight Sat, 10am-8pm Sun) The 'Corner' coffee house has an old-world theme and some pretty tasty pastries to go along with the assortment of java and juice. Just opposite the Erzsébet tér fountain.

Entertainment

For listings, see the free biweekly *Miskolci Est* (www.miskolciest.hu) or *Miskolci Műsor* (www.miskolctour.hu).

House of Arts PERFORMING ARTS
(Művészetek Háza; ☎507 573; www.muveszetekhazamiskolc.hu; Rákóczi utca 5) Cutting-edge multicultural complex with concert hall, theatre, cinema, gallery and cafe.

Miskolc National Theatre THEATRE
(☎516 700; www.mnsz.eu; Széchenyi István út 23; ⏰box office 10am-6pm Mon-Fri) Built in 1857 this expanded theatre is where the beloved 19th-century actress Róza Széppataki Déryné once walked the floorboards. It stages plays and operas.

Shopping

Géniusz BOOKS
(☎412 932; Széchenyi István út 107; ⏰9am-5.30pm Mon-Fri, 9am-1pm Sat) Bookstore with travel guides on Hungary and novels in English.

Information

Ibusz (☎508 210; www.ibusz.hu; Széchenyi István út 14; ⏰9am-5pm Mon-Fri, 9am-1pm Sat) Can broker private rooms and apartments.

Main Post Office (Kazinczy Ferenc út 16)

OTP Bank (Széchenyi István út 15) Next to the Dark Gate.

Tourinform (☎350 425; www.miskolctour.hu; Városház tér 13; ⏰8.30am-4.30pm Mon-Fri, 8.30am-1.30pm Sat Jun-Sep, 8.30am-4.30 Mon-Fri Oct-May) Extremely helpful office has bundles of information on Miskolc and its surrounds.

Getting There & Away

Heading to Eger (1300Ft, 1½ hours, 68km, eight daily), it's best to go by bus. Buses depart for Debrecen (1860Ft, 2¼ hours, 100km) at least every hour.

Miskolc's state-of-the-art train station lies to the southeast on Kandó Kálmán tér, a 15-minute tram ride from the city centre. The city is served by hourly trains between Budapest (4260Ft, 2¾ hours, 182km), Nyíregyháza (1680Ft, 1½ hours, 88km) and Tokaj (1120Ft, one hour, 56km). Seven trains a day connect to Debrecen (1860Ft, 1½ hours, 100km). About 12 trains leave Miskolc each day for Sárospatak (1490Ft, 1¼ hours, 74km) via Szerencs. Two trains a day (at 8.34am and 8.34pm) depart Miskolc for Košice in Slovakia (1½ hours).

Getting Around

Tram 1 (300Ft) begins at the train station (Tiszai pályaudvar) and travels through the centre of the city (Városház tér is near Tourinform) and past the narrow-gauge train (LÁEV) and Diósgyőr before reaching the terminus at Felső-Majláth. You can transfer from there to bus 5 to Lillafüred. Tram 2 also tracks from the train station through the centre, but it ends up in the industrial quarter of Diósgyőr-Vasgyár.

AROUND MISKOLC

Lillafüred

☎46 / POP 475

The mountain feel of Lillafüred, a tiny resort at the junction of two valleys formed by the Garadna and Szinva Streams, stands in stark contrast to the urban sprawl of Miskolc only 12km to the east. Take the narrow-gauge train up to feel the change unfold. Other than a couple of caves and a palatial hotel and gardens, there are no real sights. It's just a nice spot to enjoy some fresh air, and a good springboard for walks and hikes. The village is in the eastern expanses of Bükk National Park. The Tourinform (p259) office in Miskolc can provide all the information you need.

Activities

Reach Lillafüred via the stunningly picturesque **narrow-gauge train** (☎530 593; www.laev.hu; adult/child 650/550Ft) from Miskolc. If you don't have the time and/or inclination to do the round-trip, take the bus up and the little train back.

Below the Palota hotel, stone steps and terraces lead down to the 20m **waterfall** *(vízesés)* and to **Anna Cave** (☎334 130; www.bnpi.hu; adult/child 1000/600Ft, minimum 10 people; ⏲10am-4pm Apr–Oct), sometimes called Petőfi Cave. On a 25-minute tour of the labyrinth of tunnels, you'll come across fossilised leaves, branches and even entire trees. Tours depart more or less on the hour.

István Cave (☎334 130; www.bnpi.hu; adult/child 1000/600Ft, minimum 10 people; ⏲9am-6pm Apr-Sep, 9am-3pm Oct-Mar) is about 500m up the mountain road leading to Eger, past the souvenir and food stands. Hour-long tours (on the hour) take in stalagmites, stalactites, sinkholes and large chambers.

Jade-coloured **Foundry Lake** (Hámori-tó) was named after the proto-blast furnace set up here by a German named Frigyes Fazola in the early 19th century to exploit the area's iron ore. The reconstructed **Fazola Furnace** (Fazola-kohó) at Újmassa, 3km from Lillafüred and accessible on the narow-gauge train to Garadna, recalls this development. **Row boats** (⏲10am-6pm May-Sep) cost 600Ft per person per half-hour, while paddle boats cost 1000Ft. The Hotel Palota rents out bicycles for 3000Ft per day, but only to guests when it's busy.

A lovely walk leads along the red/green trail from the east side of the car park, south of István Cave, to **Fehérkő Overlook** (3km, 1¼ hours). When the green triangle veers off, follow it up a steep incline and narrow trail for panoramic views of Szinva Valley. Longer hikes can be undertaken from the terminus of the narrow-gauge train at Garadna, but accommodation is sparse in those parts. Be sure to have a copy of Cartographia's 1:40,000 *Bükk* map (No 29; 1215Ft) and carry extra water.

Sleeping & Eating

Sidle up to any of the several food stalls serving *lángos* (deep-fried dough with toppings) and sausage near the narrow-gauge train station, or climb uphill towards István Cave for even more food-stand options.

TOP CHOICE **Hotel Palota** HISTORIC HOTEL €€€
(Palace Hotel; ☎331 411; www.hotelpalota.hunguesthotels.hu; Erzsébet sétány 1; s/d 23,000/31,000Ft; @📶🏊) Dominating Lillafüred with its regal air, fancy turrets and formal gardens, the 'Palace' hotel is a piece of old-world luxury. Look out from many of its 133 traditional rooms onto views of the lake or forest. Stained-glass windows brighten the silver-service **Mátyás** (mains 2300-4200Ft) restaurant, where waiters look like they're dressed to serve a medieval banquet. There's also a wine cellar and

terrace restaurant on-site. Services include bike rental, saunas, billiards, a fitness centre and swimming pool.

Tókert HOTEL €€
(Lake Garden; ☎531 203; www.hoteltokert.hu; Erzsébet sétány 3; s/d 12,500/16,500Ft; @) In the shadow of the Palota, this 15-room hotel housed in the former Weidlich Villa (1899) offers more affordable accommodation with expansive views of the lake from the balconies of two of the rooms and the fabulous terrace restaurant (mains 1990Ft to 2690Ft). Both game and fish dishes are pretty good, especially the trout farmed just up the road.

Lillafüred Camping CAMPGROUND €
(☎333 146; http://kovatt.lillacamp.hu/camping.htm; Erzsébet sétány 39; campsites per adult/child/tent/caravan 1000/600/700/1000Ft; May-Sep) This small, shady campground is tent and caravan only. There's a shared fridge and laundry station in addition to bathrooms.

Getting There & Away

From Miskolc you can reach Lillafüred by the narrow-gauge train, or from the end station of tram 1 at Felsõ-Majláth, where you transfer to bus 5. In addition, between two to six long-distance buses stop in Lillafüred en route between Miskolc (310Ft, 30 minutes, 15km) and Répáshuta (650Ft, 1¼ hours, 31km).

Tokaj

☎47 / POP 4900

The world-renowned sweet wines of Tokaj (pronounced *toke*-eye) have been produced here since the 15th century. Today Tokaj is a picturesque little town of old buildings, nesting storks and wine cellars, offering plenty of opportunities to sample its famous tipple. And lying at the confluence of the Bodrog and Tisza Rivers, there are ample options for recreation.

Sights

Tokaj Museum MUSEUM
(Tokaji Múzeum; ☎352 636; www.tokaj.hu/tokaj/culture/museum/index; Bethlen Gábor utca 7; adult/concession 600/300Ft; 10am-4pm Tue-Sun) The Tokay Museum, in an 18th-century mansion built by Greek wine traders, leaves nothing unsaid about the history of Tokaj and the production of its wines. There's also a superb collection of Christian liturgical art, including icons, medieval crucifixes and triptychs, Judaica from the former Great Synagogue, and temporary exhibits by local artists.

Great Synagogue JEWISH
(Nagy Zsinagóga; ☎552 000; Serház utca 55) The 19th-century Eclectic Great Synagogue, which was used as a German barracks during WWII, is once again gleaming after a total reconstruction. It is now used as a conference and cultural centre. There's a large **Orthodox Jewish cemetery** in Bodrogkeresztúr, 6km northwest of Tokaj.

Activities

WINE TASTING

Private cellars *(pincék)* and restaurants for wine tastings are scattered throughout town. Start with 100mL glasses; you may swallow more than you think! If you're

A LONG & WINEY ROAD

The 7000-hectare Tokaj-Hegyalja wine-producing region, a microclimate along the southern and eastern edges of the Zemplén Hills, which were declared a Unesco World Heritage site in 2002, is just right for creating Tokaj wine. The 'wine of kings' that most people know is a golden sweet dessert nectar, but the area also produces some wonderful, apple-scented dry whites, notably Furmint. In addition to Tokaj, there are 27 villages in the Tokaj-Hegyalja region with cellars to sample the local wine. Pick up a wine map at Tourinform in Tokaj, or check out **Tokaj Wine Road** (www.tokaji-borut.hu) to help plan your itinerary. Picture-pretty **Tarcal** (www.tarcal.hu), 6km west and the self-proclaimed 'gateway to Tokaj', is a good place to start – particularly since you can stay in the restored **Gróf Degenfeld Castle Hotel** (☎580 400; www.hotelgrofdegenfeld.hu; Terézia kert 9, Tarcal; s/d €108/118; @) with vineyards and parklands as backdrop. The owners rank among the top vintners in the region so there's plenty of excellent wine on hand, but you can also rent a bicycle there and toodle off to visit another of the dozen-or-so local cellars and restaurants. Tarcal is easily accessed by train from Tokaj (250Ft, 10 minues, 8km, hourly).

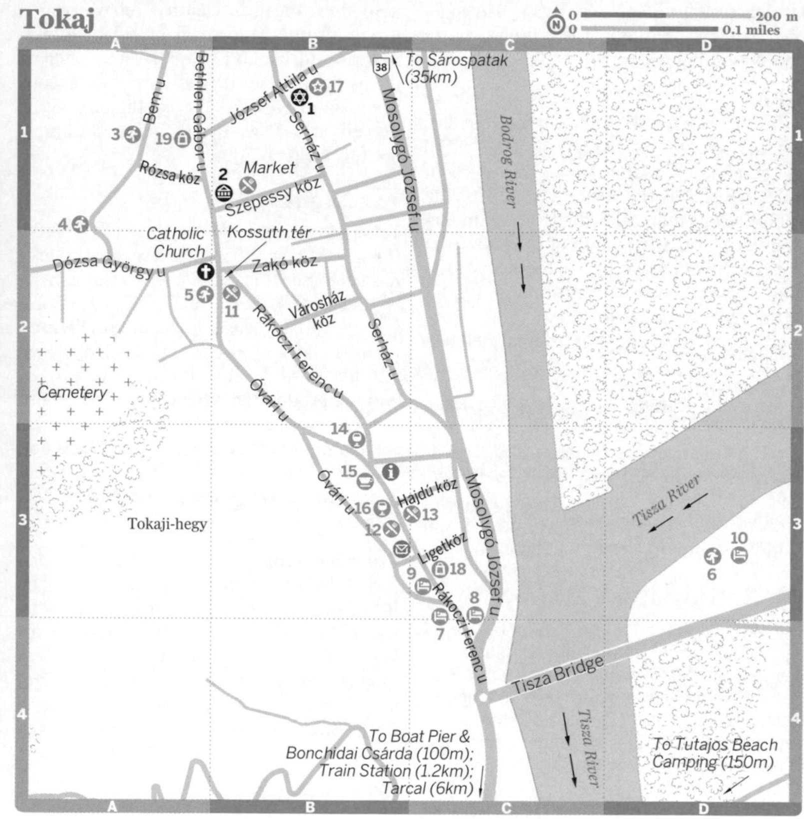

serious, the correct order is to move from dry to sweet: Furmint, dry Szamorodni, sweet Szamorodni and then the Aszú wines. The last, dessert-like wines have a rating of four to six *puttony* (a measure of how much of the sweet essence of noble rot grapes has been used). A basic flight of six Tokaj wines costs 2600Ft to 3200Ft; an all-Aszú tasting can run between 4200Ft and 6000Ft.

The granddaddy of tasting places is the 600-year-old **Rákóczi Cellar** (Rákóczi Pince; ☎352 408; www.rakoczipince.hu; Kossuth tér 15; ⏲11am-6pm), where bottles of wine mature in long corridors (one measures 28m by 10m). **Erzsébet Cellar** (☎06 20 802 0137; www.erzsebetpince.hu; Bem utca 16; ⏲10am-6pm, by appointment) is a smaller, family-run affair that usually needs to be booked ahead. The most friendly of all is **Hímesudvar** (☎352 416; www.himesudvar.hu; Bem utca 2; ⏲10am-6pm), with an atmospheric 16th-century cellar and shop northwest of the town centre. Smaller cellars line Hegyalja utca, off Bajcsy-Zsilinszky utca, at the base of the vine-covered hill above the train station.

OTHER ACTIVITIES

There's a grassy riverfront beach for swimming at **Tutajos Beach Camping** (☎06 30 239 6300; adult/child 500/300Ft; ⏲9am-7pm Jun-Aug), across the Tisza River Bridge from town.

You can rent canoes, kayaks and bicycles from **Vízisport Turistaház** (☎552 187; www.tokaj-info.hu; Horgász utca 3; canoe & kayak per hr/day 450/1700Ft, bicycle 300/1200Ft; ⏲8am-8pm); enquire inside the restaurant.

From May through October, hour-long **sightseeing boat tours** (☎06 20 971 6564; www.tokaj-info.hu; Hajókikötő; adult/child 1200/900Ft; ⏲11am & 3pm, plus 11am & 5pm Sat & Sun Jun-Aug) ply the Tisza and Bodrog waters. Board at the pier next to the Bonchidai Csárda.

Tokaj

Sights
1 Great Synagogue B1
2 Tokaj Museum B1

Activities, Courses & Tours
3 Erzsébet Cellar A1
4 Hímesudvar A1
5 Rákóczi Cellar A2
6 Vízisport Turistaház D3

Sleeping
7 Huli-Bodrog Panzió C3
8 Tokaj Hotel C3
9 Vaskó Panzió C3
10 Vízisport Turisztaház D3

Eating
11 Bacchus B2
12 Fakapu B3
13 Toldi Fogadó C3

Drinking
14 Cafe Műhely Borbr B3
15 Óváros Kavéház B3
16 Veresszekér B3

Entertainment
17 Ede Paulay Theatre B1

Shopping
18 Borostyán Wine Shop C3
19 Furmint Vinotéka A1

Festivals & Events

The **Tokaj Wine Festival**, held in late May, attracts oenophiles from far and wide, as do the **Tokaj VIntage Days** during harvest season, on the first weekend of October. In mid-July the **Hegyalja Festival** rocks Tokaj out with bands from across Europe.

Sleeping

Private rooms on offer along Hegyalja utca are convenient to the train station and surrounded by vineyards. Bring lots of mosquito repellent if you're camping.

Huli-Bodrog Panzió GUESTHOUSE €
(☎06 20 465 5903; www.hulipanzio.hu; Rákóczi út 16; s 4000-5000Ft, d 8000Ft; ❄📶) A sunny yellow covers both the walls and the flowered duvet covers in down-to-earth rooms spread across the 1st floor of a popular counter-service restaurant (mains 1100Ft to 1600Ft). The 19 rooms aren't huge and decor is basic, but what do you need besides a sturdy wooden bed and table? Oh, there are small fridges and the possibility of air-con (1500Ft). A welcoming place.

Vaskó Panzió GUESTHOUSE €
(☎352 107; http://vaskopanzio.hu; Rákóczi út 12; r 8000Ft; ❄📶) The very central Vaskó has 11 tidy rooms with window sills bedecked with flower pots. It's above a private wine cellar and the proprietor can organise tastings.

Tokaj Hotel HOTEL €
(☎352 344; www.tokajhotel.hu; Rákóczi út 5; s 5000-9200Ft, d 5900-9900Ft) A recent renovation could not change the overall appearance of this 1960s time-warp place located close to where the two rivers meet, but it's comfortable enough. A full 30 of the 42 rooms have balconies, some overloking the Tisza. The cheaper rooms are on the 4th floor, have sloping ceilings and showers only. The pretty terrace restaurant (mains 1090Ft to 1690Ft) specilalises in game (as you might have guessed from all the trophies on the walls).

Vízisport Turisztaház HOSTEL €
(☎06 20 971 6564, 552 187; www.tokaj-info.hu; Horgász utca 3; campsites/dm 1000/2000Ft; @) Three- and four-bed rooms share a bathroom at this bare-bones hostel (beds only, no kitchen or common room). It rents bikes, canoes and kayaks, and organises canoe trips. There's a restaurant on-site offering full board (1800Ft).

Tutajos Beach Camping CAMPGROUND €
(☎06 20 221 2112, 06 20 969 1088; Honfoglalás utca 24; campsites/bungalows per person 300/2000Ft; ⊙Apr-Oct) Shady tent sites and basic bungalows are adjacent to a beach with boat rental. Showers cost 100Ft for three minutes.

Eating

Toldi Fogadó HUNGARIAN €€
(☎353 403; www.toldifogado.hu; Hajdú köz 2; mains 1650-2590Ft; 🖉) A lovely restaurant offering quasi-fine dining down a small *köz* (lane) off the main drag, Toldi excels at fish dishes (try the catfish) but also has some excellent duck dishes (duck leg with *lecsó*, a kind of ratatouille) and a generous selection of vegetarian mains.

Fakapu HUNGARIAN €
(Wooden Gate; ☎06 20 972 6307; Rákóczi út 27; mains 1200-1850Ft) Enter the 'Wooden Gate' through its impressive, well, wooden gate and find a cute wine restaurant that offers simple Hungarian soups, stews and plates of smoked meats to accompany wine tastings in a a romantic, candlelit atmosphere.

Bonchidai Csárda SEAFOOD €€
(☎352 632; www.etterem.hu/519; Bajcsy-Zsilinszky utca 21; mains 1500-3800Ft) Nine types of *halászlé* (fish soup) are just the beginning of the offerings made from the water's bounty. Sit on the large terrace overlooking the recreational boat pier on the Tisza River (with your back to the car park) or inside the rustic fish house.

Bacchus HUNGARIAN €
(☎352 054; www.borostyanbacchus.hu; Kossuth tér 17; mains 1000-1800Ft; ⏰9am-8pm) Head for this simple little eatery on the main square under two leafy lindens for lunch or early dinner. It serves the usual Hungarian staples as well as pizza.

Drinking

Cafe Műhely Borbr WINE BAR
(☎06 20 454 1188; Rákóczi út 40; ⏰10am-10pm Mon-Thu, 10am-3am Fri-Sun) Very stylish wine bar that's just the place to sate your thirst, should you want to try Tokaj's vintages in a relaxed atmosphere.

Veresszekér PUB
(Red Cart; ☎06 20 488 9993; Rákóczi út 30-32; ⏰5pm-4am) Should your palate tire of wine, turn your taste buds hopsward at this congenial pub in a little courtyard.

Óváros Kávéház CAFE
(☎552 124; Rákóczi út 38; ⏰9am-10pm) Enjoy a full selection of hot beverages to warm you on chilly mornings. The coffee house has a pleasant, cherrywood interior, but not much outdoor seating.

Entertainment

Ede Paulay Theatre THEATRE
(Paulay Ede Színház; ☎352 003; http://szinhaz.tokaj.hu; Serház utca 55) From folk dance to full drama, something's always on at Tokaj's fantastic theatre behind the synagogue.

Shopping

Wine, wine and more wine – from a 10L plastic jug of new Furmint to a bottle of six-*puttony* Aszú – is available in shops and cellars throughout Tokaj. **Furmint Vinotéka** (☎353 340; www.furmintvinoteka.hu; Bethlen Gábor utca 14; ⏰10am-4pm) is perhaps the most helpful, with some information in English. You can also head to the shop at the Rákóczi Cellar (p262) or the **Borostyán wine shop** (Borostyán Bor Üzlet; ☎352 054; www.borostyanbacchus.hu; Rákóczi út 11; ⏰10am-9pm Mon-Fri, to 10pm Sat & Sun).

Information

OTP Bank (Rákóczi Ferenc út 35) With ATM.

Post Office (Rákóczi Ferenc út 24)

Tourinform (☎950 603; www.tokaj-turizmus.hu; Serház utca 1; ⏰9am-5pm Mon-Sat, 10am-3pm Sun Jun-Aug, 9am-4pm Mon-Fri Sep-May) Just off Rákóczi út. Has a handy booklet of wine cellars in the area and organises weekend 'wine bus' tours (from 5170Ft per person) with visits to two or three wineries, depending on the day. Bikes for rent for 1200/2400Ft per half-/full day.

Getting There & Away

Bus travel in the Zemplén Hills requires frequent changes and careful timing; few buses run daily, though you can reach Debrecen (1680Ft, two hours, 86km) via Nyíregyháza (650Ft, 40 minutes, 33km) twice a day and Sárospatak (650Ft, one hour, 32km) two to three times daily. Buses arrive and depart from Serház utca 38, east of Kossuth tér.

Tokaj's train station is 1.2km south of the town; walk north for 15 minutes along Baross Gábor utca and Bajcsy-Zsilinszky utca to Rákóczi Ferenc út. Up to 16 trains a day head west through Miskolc (1120Ft, one hour, 56km) to Budapest Keleti (3950Ft, 2¾ hours, 238km), and east through Nyíregyháza (650Ft, 30 minutes, 32km) to Debrecen (2250Ft, 1¾ hours, 81km). If you want to travel north to Sárospatak (840Ft, 1½ hours, 44km), change at Mezőzombor or Szerencs.

Getting Around

Cycling is an excellent way to get around Tokaj, and the Hegyalja region in general – especially if you're wine tasting. Most lodgings can arrange rental in this bike-friendly town, or rent from Vízisport Turisztaház (p263) or Tourinform (p264).

Boldogkőváralja

The picturesque Hernád Valley, which basically runs from Szerencs to Hidasnémeti, near the Slovakian border, is dotted with quaint wine-producing towns, perfect for sampling the region's fine vintages. Boldogkőváralja (population 1150), 39km north of Tokaj, would be just another of these charming places if it weren't for its impressive castle ruins, seamlessly grafted to a rocky outcrop

WORTH A TRIP

ACTIVE IN THE ZEMPLÉN HILLS

The northern Zemplén Hills, on the border with Slovakia, is full of hiking opportunities and romantic castles and castle ruins like those at **Boldogkőváralja** and **Sárospatak**. The long-distance Eurovelo 11 cycling route skirts the hills, entering from Slovakia near **Göncs** and continuing east to **Sátoraljaújhely** before beginning to follow the Tisza River's path south at **Tokaj**. For more on the region, check out www.zemplen.hu. Make sure to invest in Cartographia's 1:40,000 *Zempléni-hegység* (No 23; 1215Ft) map. For further information, head to shop.lonelyplanet.com to purchase a downloadable PDF of the Slovakia chapter from Lonely Planet's *Eastern Europe* guide.

above the valley. Heading north on the train, sit on the right-hand side to see the dramatic fortress as it comes into view.

Atop a basalt mountain, **Boldogkő Castle** (adult/child 650/350Ft; ⌚10am-6pm Apr-Oct), literally 'Happy Rock' Castle, is exactly what most people imagine a castle to be: impossibly perched on solid rock, strong walls and turrets commanding 360-degree views of the southern Zemplén Hills, the Hernád Valley and nearby vineyards. Originally built in the 13th century, the castle was strengthened 200 years later, but gradually fell into ruin in the 17th century. A series of rooms has been reconstructed to contain small exhibits on minerals in the area, medieval armour and weapons, and mock-ups of key battles in Hungarian history with lead soldiers. There's also a dungeon with requisite torture exhibit. But most satisfying is just walking through the uneven courtyard up onto the ramparts and looking out over the surrounding countryside in the late afternoon from the awesome triangular-shaped keep. It's easy to see how the swashbuckling lyric poet Bálint Balassi (1554–94) produced some of his finest work here.

Boldogkőváralja doesn't hold much reason to linger, but **Bodóvár Wellness Panzió** (☎306 613; www.bodovar.hu; Kossuth Lajos utca 61; s/d 9000/14,000Ft; 📶🏊), at the bottom of the road to the castle, has a heated pool and hot tub great for soaking after a hike. Some of the 14 mostly basic rooms have views of the castle. At the restaurant (mains 1200Ft to 2500Ft), hearty Hungarian dishes like pork steak with green beans, bacon and sour cream can be paired with a local Tokaj wine.

Boldogkőváralja is not the easiest place to get to without a vehicle. By train, you have to change (no wait) at Abaújszántó (250Ft, 10 minutes, 7km, six daily) to get to Szerencs (465Ft, 30 minutes, 21km, 10 daily), where you can connect to Tokaj and Debrecen to the east and Miskolc and Budapest to the west.

Sárospatak

☎47 / POP 13,000

An attractive town on the Bodrog River, Sárospatak means 'Muddy Stream' (OK, so it's not a *big* river). Sárospatak became a free, royal wine-producing town in the early 15th century and has never looked back. Here, beneath the Zemplén Hills, 35km northeast of Tokaj, you'll find the finest example of a Renaissance fort extant in Hungary. The town is also known for its centuries-old college and its long history.

Sights & Activities

Rákóczi Castle CASTLE

(Rákóczi-vár; ☎311 083; www.rakoczimuzeum.hu; Szent Erzsébet utca 19; grounds free, permanent exhibits adult/child 840/420Ft, with temporary exhibiits 1640/820Ft; ⌚10am-6pm Tue-Sun) The Rákóczi Castle should be your first stop in Sárospatak. The oldest part of the castle, the five-storey **Red Tower** (Vörös-torony), dates from the late 15th century – inside you'll find period rooms in excellent condition. Note that this can only be visited by guided tour.

The Renaissance-style **Palace Wing** (Palotaszárny), connected to the Red Tower by a 17th-century loggia called the **Lorántffy Gallery**, was built in the 16th century and later enlarged by its most famous owners, the Rákóczi family of Transylvania. Today, along with some 19th-century additions, it contains the **Rákóczi Exhibition**, devoted to the 1703–11 uprising and the castle's later occupants. Bedrooms and dining halls overflow with furniture, tapestries, porcelain and glass. Of special interest is the small five-windowed bay room on the 1st floor near the **Knights' Hall**, with its stucco rose in the middle of a vaulted ceiling. It was here that nobles put their names sub rosa (literally 'under the rose' in Latin) to the *kuruc* uprising against the Habsburg emperor in

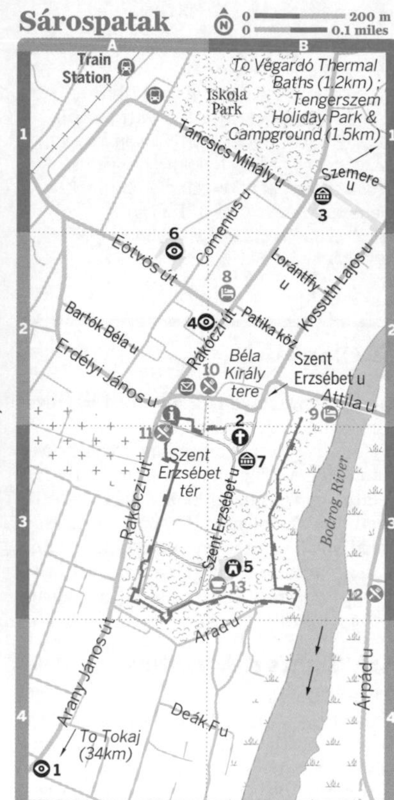

Sárospatak

Sights

1 Árpád Vezér College A4
2 Basilica Minor B3
3 Calvinist College & Great Library B1
4 Hild Udvar Shopping Mall A2
5 Rákóczi Castle B3
6 Sárospatak Cultural House A2
7 St Elizabeth House B3

Sleeping

8 Rákóczi Panzió B2
9 Retel Vitéz Vendégház B2

Eating

10 András Ötödik (V András) B2
11 Ristorante Collegno A3
12 Vár Vendéglő B3

Drinking

13 Vár Caffe Bar B3

1670. The expression, which means 'in secret', is thought to have originated here.

Basilica Minor CHURCH
(Basilika Minor; ☎311 183; www.cometohungary.com/basilica-minor-sarospatak.html; Szent Erzsébet utca 7; ⊙10am-4pm Tue-Sat, noon-4pm Sun) Just north of the castle, the Basilica Minor is one of Hungary's largest Gothic hall churches (those within castle walls), and has flip-flopped from serving Catholics to Protestants and back many times since the 14th century. The enormous baroque altar was moved here from the Carmelite church in Buda Castle late in the 18th century; the 200-year-old organ from Kassa (now Košice in Slovakia) is still used for concerts. The statue (1985) by Imre Varga outside the church depicts the Sárospatak-born and much revered St Elizabeth, a 13th-century queen of Hungary and her husband Louis IV. Her relics are within the church.

St Elizabeth House MUSEUM
(Szent Erzsébet Ház; ☎314 107; www.szenterzsebet.hu; Szent Erzsébet utca 7; adult/child 500/300Ft; ⊙10am-6pm Mon-Sat Apr-Oct, 10am-4pm Nov-Mar) Opposite the Basilica Minor and housed in what was once a boys' elementary school dating from the 16th century, St Elizabeth House contains a small but well-formed art collection as well as an assemblage of liturgical objects and vestments dating from the 18th and 19th centuries.

Calvinist College & Great Library MUSEUM, LIBRARY
(Református Kollégium és Nagykönyvtár; ☎06 20 419 0914; www.patakarchiv.hu; Rákóczi út 1; adult/child 600/400Ft; ⊙9am-5pm Mon-Sat, to 1pm Sun Apr-Oct, 9am-5pm Mon-Thu, 9am-2pm Fri Nov-Mar) The history of the celebrated Calvinist College is told in words and displays at the **School History Exhibition** (Iskolatörténeti Kiállítás) in an 18th-century physics classroom. The list of the school alumni reads like a who's who of Hungarian literary and political history, and includes the patriot Lajos Kossuth, the poet Mihály Csokonai Vitéz and the novelist Géza Gárdonyi. The main reason for visiting the college, though, is to see its 25,000-volume **Great Library** (Nagy Könyvtár) in the main building, a long oval-shaped room with a gallery and a trompe l'oeil ceiling simulating the inside of a cupola. Guided tours leave on the hour.

Sárospatak Cultural House ARCHITECTURE
(Sárospataki Művelődés Háza; ☎311 811; Eötvös utca 6) Sárospatak counts a number of buildings designed by the 'organic' architect

Imre Makovecz, including this anthropomorphic cultural house, the **Hild Udvar shopping mall** (Béla Király tere) and the cathedral-like **Árpád Vezér College** (Arany János utca 3-7).

Végardó Thermal Baths SPA
(Végardó Fürdő; ☎655 317; www.vegardofurdo.hu; Határ út 2; adult/child 1500/1200Ft May–mid-Sep, 900/650Ft mid-Sep–Apr; ⏲8am-7pm) These hugely popular baths and pools, recently renovated with the assistance of the architect Imre Makovecz from the look of things, are 2km northeast of the city centre.

Festivals & Events

At Pentecost in May or June, **St Elizabeth Days** is a popular weekend festival celebrating the saint in the castle quarter. Sárospatak hosts some of the events of the **Zemplén Festival** in mid-August.

Sleeping

Retel Vitéz Vendégház GUESTHOUSE €
(☎315 428; www.retelvitez.extra.hu; Attila út 2; s/d 6000/8000Ft) About as central as you'll find in Sárospatak, at the very foot of the bridge crossing over the Bodrog River, this little guesthouse with 10 comfortable and eminently affordable rooms can at times feel like it's right in the water. If you want to get closer still, ask the owners to take you out on their little excursion boat for a one-hour twirl (adult/child 1000/800Ft).

Rákóczi Panzió GUESTHOUSE €€
(☎312 111; www.hotels.hu/rakoczipanzio; Rákóczi utca 30; s/d 7000/13,000Ft; ❄@) Sauna, solarium, coffee bar and restaurant: Rákóczi has the most services of any hostelry in the area. Staff will help you rent bicycles (per hour/day 300/1200Ft) and can arrange castle tours and water sports. The 17 rooms are of a good size; avoid the ones facing busy Rákóczi utca.

Tengerszem Holiday Park & Campground CAMPGROUND €€
(Tengerszem Üdülőpark és Camping; ☎312 744; www.tengerszem-camping.hu; Herceg Ferenc utca 2; campsites per person/tent/caravan 1500/1500/1800Ft, bungalows 6850-10,900Ft; @📶🏊) Basic bungalows sleep two to five with shared facilities near the thermal baths. Superior apartments (17,900Ft) really are just that: cosy whitewashed buildings with kitchenettes and cable TV around a large swimming pool.

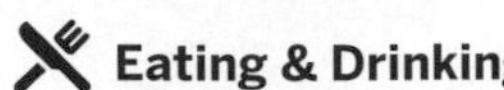

Eating & Drinking

Vár Vendéglő HUNGARIAN €€
(☎311 370; www.varvendeglo.hu; Árpád utca 35; mains 1400-3300Ft) The best restaurant in Sárospatak has quite the view of the castle from across the Bodrog River. Try a speciality, such as *harcsapaprikás túrós* (catfish in a sour cream and paprika sauce; 2400Ft), and enjoy it with an excellent local wine on the covered terrace out the back.

Ristorante Collegno ITALIAN €
(☎314 494; Szent Erzsébet utca 10; mains 830-1890Ft) Really good wood-fired pizzas, homemade bread and hearty pastas come out of this rustic Italian kitchen – eventually. The college students who always pack the cellar and terrace seating don't seem to mind the wait.

András Ötödik (V András) HUNGARIAN €€
(Andrew the Fifth; ☎312 415; Béla Király tere 3; mains 1600-3100Ft) With its inner courtyard, quick service and healthy range of Hungarian cuisine, 'Andrew the Fifth' is quite popular. The modern art on the walls is local.

Vár Caffe Bar CAFE
(Szent Erzsébet utca 26/a; dishes 650-1300Ft; ⏲10am-2am Mon-Thu, to 4am Fri & Sat, to midnight Sun) Drinks – hot and cold and of variable strengths – in the castle garden. Snacks and light meals available all day.

Information

Main Post Office (Rákóczi út 45)

OTP Bank (Eötvös utca 3)

Tourinform (☎513 150; www.sarospatak.hu; Szent Erzsébet utca 3; ⏲8am-4pm Mon-Sat, 8am-1pm Sun mid-Jun–Aug, 8am-4pm Tue-Sat Sep–mid-Jun) Loads of info on the area, with attached cafe.

Getting There & Away

The bus and train stations sit cheek by jowl at the end of Táncsics Mihály utca, northwest of the city centre. Much of the Zemplén region is not easily accessible by bus without multiple transfers; only two or three buses a day travel between Sárospatak and Tokaj (650Ft, one hour, 32km). Two daily buses also travel to Debrecen (2200Ft, 2¾ hours, 118km) and Nyíregyháza (1300Ft, 1½ hours, 65km). Direct trains connect Sárospatak with Miskolc (1490Ft, 1¼ hours, 74km, eight daily). If you are coming from Debrecen, Nyíregyháza or Tokaj, change trains at Mezőzombor (650Ft, one hour, 31km, hourly).

Understand Hungary

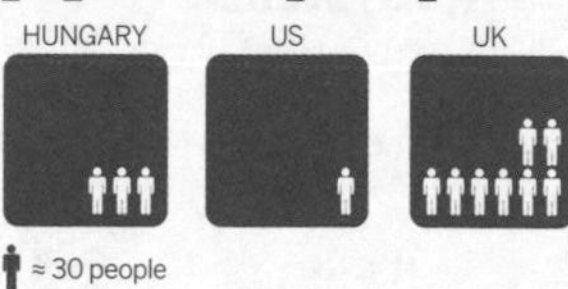

Hungary Today

Change of Guard

In 2010 Viktor Orbán once again became prime minister after his Fidesz-MPP party won a decisive victory in the parliamentary elections. Viktátor (as he's known in certain circles) moved quickly to make his mark. He has changed the constitution: Hungary is no longer 'the republic of', and an extended preamble called the National Creed dispenses with the period from March 1944 (the Nazi occupation of Hungary) to May 1990 (the first free election since 1945) simply by declaring it legally nonexistent. Orbán has weakened the national press with a controversial media law and was read the riot act for that in public by MEP Daniel Cohn-Bendit – known as 'Danny the Red' for his revolutionary activities in Paris in 1968 – as Hungary took control of the EU presidency in 2011. To add to his misery, the right-wing Jobbik (which is a kind of pun on the word 'right') garnered over 16% of the vote in the national elections and its uniformed militia wing, Magyar Gárda (Hungarian Guard), resumed bullying and intimidating Roma people in villages of the northeast. And those rumours about Orbán's Roma ancestry just won't go away.

» Population: 9.96 million

» Area: 93,028 sq km

» GDP: US$195.6 billion

» GDP per capita: US$19,600 (ranked 63 in world)

» GDP growth: -0.5%

» Inflation: 4%

» Unemployment: 11%

Economic Woes

It seems the bad news just won't go away... Hungary was badly affected in the last recession, and with the world's financial markets in what looks like a trampoline trip to hell at press time, the economy, already on its knees, was in danger of meltdown. It's a position Hungarians call *a béka segge alatt* ('under the arse of the frog'). Think about it – you can't get much lower than that. Growth is in the negative numbers (in fact, at -0.5%, the lowest among the the 10 Central and Eastern European countries that joined the EU in 2004), inflation is at 4% and unemployment

Who-Knew Hungarians

» **Laszlo Biro** (Bíró László) Ballpoint pen inventor

» **Brassaï** (Halász Gyula) French photographer

» **Robert Capa** (Friedmann Endre Ernő) US photojournalist

» **Tony Curtis** (Bernard Schwartz) US actor

» **Harry Houdini** (Weisz Erich) American escape artist

» **Estée Lauder** (Josephine Esther Mentzer) US cosmetics baroness

» **Bela Lugosi** (Blaskó Béla) American 'Dracula' actor

» **Ernő Rubik** Puzzle cube inventor

Top Films

» **Moszkva tér** (2001) End-of-communism comedy with kids

» **Children of Glory** (Szabadság, Szerelem; 2006) About the 'blood in the water' water-polo match in 1956

» **Zimmer Feri** (1998) Jokes about German tourists on the Balaton

belief systems

(% of population)

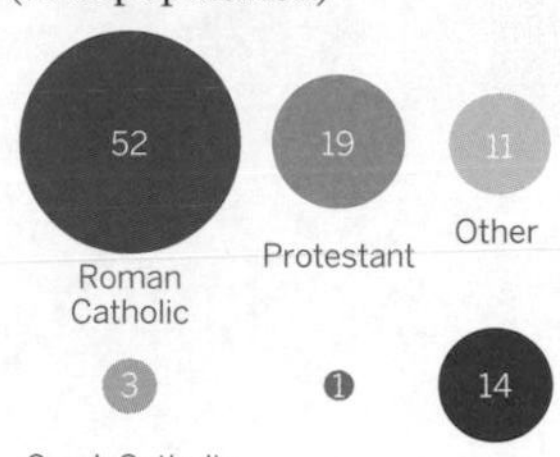

if Hungary were 100 people

68 would live in towns and cities
32 would live in rural areas

has reached an unconscionable 11%. And everyone, but everyone, still holds a mortgage in Swiss francs, which now cost a wheelbarrow full of weak forint to repay. Not good.

Now the Good News

But always look on the bright side of life… Through all this mess Hungarians have gone about their business as only Hungarians can – with a large dash of reality mixed with dollops of pride in their homeland. Slowly the focus is turning from quantity to quality: boutique hotels are popping up everywhere, not just in Budapest; world-class restaurants can be found as easily in Debrecen and Pécs as they can in the capital; and superior thermal retreats are replacing dated eyesores well past their use-by date. Despite the rising tide of commercialism, Hungary's roots remain firmly entwined with its folk traditions, as a trip to any part of the country will testify to. Thankfully Hungary has held on to the one factor that makes it special – being Hungarian. That means different things to different people but the good thing is Magyarország likes to be different. It's been that way for centuries. It's not going to change tomorrow.

Hungary can no longer claim the dubious distinction of having the world's highest suicide rate, but it still ranks at No 6, surpassed only by Lithuania, South Korea, Guyana, Kazakhstan and Belarus. An average 22 people (against Lithuania's 32) per 100,000 population take their lives each year.

Top Books

» **Prague** (Arthur Phillips, 2002) Mixed-up young American does Budapest

» **Twelve Days: The Story of the 1956 Hungarian Revolution** (Victor Sebestyen, 2007) Day-by-day account of the Uprising

Top Albums

» **Live at the Liszt Academy**

» **Romano Trip: Gypsy Grooves from Eastern Europe** Romano Drom mixes Roma folk with world music

» **Lechajem Rebbe** Traditional Jewish music

Etiquette

» **Greeting** Shake hands with everyone, even if it hurts

» **Requesting** Say *legyen szíves* (be so kind as…) to attract attention, *bocsánat* (sorry) to apologise

» **Celebrating** Bring/give flowers or a good bottle of wine

History

Hungary's impact on Europe's history has been far greater than its present size and population would suggest. Hungarians – who call themselves the Magyar – speak a language and form a culture unlike any other in the region, which has been both a source of pride and an obstacle for more than 1100 years. Indeed, Hungarian nationalism has been the cause (and the result) of an often paranoid fear of being gobbled up by neighbouring countries – particularly the 'sea of Slavs' that surrounds much of the country. Yet, despite endless occupations and wars, the Hungarians have been able to retain their own identity without shutting themselves off from the world. It is to the credit of the nation's heroes, its patriots and the everyday people who just get on with their lives that Hungary doesn't just exist but thrives.

The updated Corvinus Library of Hungarian History (www.hungarianhistory.com) is a font of all knowledge and an excellent first step on the subject; the links to related topics – from language to painting – are endless.

Early Inhabitants

The Carpathian Basin, in which Hungary lies, has been populated for at least half a million years. Bone fragments found at Vértesszőlős, about 5km southeast of Tata, in the 1960s are believed to be that old. Stone Age pottery shards and bone-tipped arrowheads have been found at Istállóskő Cave near Szilvásvárad.

Indo-European tribes from the Balkans stormed the Carpathian Basin in horse-drawn carts in about 2000 BC, bringing with them copper tools and weapons. After the introduction of the more durable metal bronze, horses were domesticated, forts were built and a military elite was developed.

Over the next millennium, invaders from the west (Illyrians, Thracians) and east (Scythians) brought iron, but it was not in common use until the Celts arrived at the start of the 4th century BC. They introduced glass and crafted some of the fine gold jewellery that can still be seen in museums (eg the Mór Wosinszky County Museum in Szekszárd).

TIMELINE

AD 106

Roman Aquincum in today's Óbuda becomes the administrative seat of the province of Pannonia Inferior and a fully fledged colony less than a century later.

Late 430s

Aquincum offers little protection to the civilian population when the Huns burn the colony to the ground, forcing the Romans and other settlers to flee.

896–98

Nomadic Magyar tribes set up camp in the Carpathian Basin, with five of the seven original tribes settling in the area that is now Budapest.

The Roman Conquest

The Romans conquered the area west and south of the Danube River in about 35 BC; two dozen years later they were in the Danube Bend. By AD 10 they had established the province of Pannonia, which would later be divided into Upper (Superior) and Lower (Inferior) Pannonia. The Romans introduced writing, viticulture and stone architecture, and established garrison towns and other settlements, the remains of which can still be seen in Óbuda (Aquincum in Roman times), Szombathely (Savaria), Pécs (Sophianae) and Sopron (Scarbantia).

Although Hungarians are in no way related to the Huns, Attila remains a very common given name for males in Hungary today.

The Great Migrations

The first of the so-called Great Migrations of nomadic peoples from Asia reached the eastern outposts of the Roman Empire early in the 3rd century AD. Within two centuries, however, they were forced to pull out of Pannonia by the Huns, whose short-lived empire had been established by Attila.

Other Germanic tribes occupied the region for the next century and a half until the Avars, a powerful Turkic people, gained control of the Carpathian Basin in the late 6th century. They in turn were subdued by the Frankish king Charlemagne in 796 and converted to Christianity. By that time the Carpathian Basin was virtually unpopulated, except for groups of Turkic and Germanic tribes on the plains and Slavs in the northern hills.

The Magyars

The origin of the Magyars is a complex issue, not helped by the similarity (in English) of the words 'Hun' and 'Hungary', which are *not* related. One thing is certain: Magyars are part of the Finno-Ugric group of peoples who inhabited the forests somewhere between the middle Volga River and the Ural Mountains in western Siberia and began migrating as early as 4000 BC.

By about 2000 BC population growth had forced the Finnish-Estonian branch of the group to move westward, ultimately reaching the Baltic Sea. The Ugrians migrated from the southeastern slopes of the Urals into the valleys, and switched from fishing, hunting and gathering to primitive farming and raising livestock, especially horses. The Magyars' equestrian skills proved useful half a millennium later when climatic changes brought drought, forcing them to move north to the steppes.

If you'd like to learn more about the nomadic Magyars, their history, civilisation and/or art, go to http://ancientmagyarworld.tripod.com, which also offers a number of useful and interesting links.

On the plains, the Ugrians turned to nomadic herding. After 500 BC, by which time the use of iron had become widespread among the tribes, some of the groups moved westward to the area of Bashkiria in central Asia. Here they lived among Persians and Bulgars and began

955

Hungarian raids outside the Carpathian Basin as far as Germany, Italy and Spain are stopped for good by German king Otto I at the Battle of Augsburg.

1000

Stephen (István in Hungarian) is crowned 'Christian King' of Hungary at Esztergom on Christmas Day; he is canonised as St Stephen later in the century (1083).

1222

King Andrew II signs the Golden Bull, according the nobility increased rights and powers; it is renewed nine years later.

1241–42

Mongols sweep across Hungary, reducing the national population by up to a half and killing some 100,000 people in Pest and Óbuda alone.

referring to themselves as Magyars (from the Finno-Ugric words *mon*, 'to speak', and *er*, 'man').

After several centuries another group split away and moved south to the Don River under the control of the Turkic Khazars. Here they lived among different groups under a tribal alliance called *onogur* (or '10 peoples'), thought to be the derivation of the word 'Hungary'. The Magyars' last migration before the so-called conquest *(honfoglalás)* of the Carpathian Basin brought them to what modern Hungarians call the Etelköz, the region between the Dnieper and lower Danube Rivers above the Black Sea.

The Will to Survive: A History of Hungary (Bryan Cartledge, 2011), written by a former British diplomat, is the best all-round general history of Hungary.

The Conquest of the Carpathian Basin

In about 895 and under attack, seven tribes under the leadership of Árpád, the chief military commander *(gyula)*, struck out for the Carpathian Basin. They crossed the Verecke Pass in today's Ukraine three years later.

Known for their ability to ride and shoot, the Magyars began plundering and pillaging on their own, taking slaves and amassing booty. Their raids took them as far as Spain, northern Germany and southern Italy, but in 955 they were stopped in their tracks by German king Otto I at the battle of Augsburg.

This and subsequent defeats forced them to form an alliance with the Holy Roman Empire. In 973 Prince Géza, the great-grandson of Árpád, asked Emperor Otto II to send Catholic missionaries to Hungary. Géza was baptised in his capital, Esztergom, as was his son Vajk, who took the Christian name Stephen (István). When Géza died Stephen ruled as prince but on Christmas Day in the year 1000 he was crowned 'Christian King' Stephen I.

Eclipse of the Crescent Moon (Géza Gárdonyi, 1901) is a *Boy's Own*–style page-turner that tells the story of the siege of Eger by the Turks in 1552 and an orphaned peasant boy who grows up to become one of the greatest (fictional) heroes in Hungarian history.

King Stephen I

Stephen set about consolidating royal authority by expropriating the land of the independent-minded clan chieftains and establishing a system of counties *(megyék)* protected by fortified castles *(várak)*. Stephen shrewdly transferred much land to loyal (mostly German) knights. He also sought the support of the church and established 10 episcopates, two of which – Kalocsa and Esztergom – were made archbishoprics. When Stephen died in 1038, Hungary was a nascent Christian nation, increasingly westward-looking and multiethnic.

The House of Árpád

The next two and a half centuries – the extent of the Árpád Dynasty – were marked by dynastic intrigues and relentless struggles between rival pretenders to the throne, which weakened the young nation's defences against its powerful neighbours. In the mid-13th century the Mongols

1458–90

Medieval Hungary enjoys a golden age under the enlightened reign of King Matthias Corvinus and Queen Beatrix, daughter of the king of Naples.

1514

A peasant uprising is crushed, with 70,000 people executed, including leader György Dózsa, who dies on a red-hot iron throne wearing a scalding crown.

1526

Hungary is soundly defeated by the Ottomans at the Battle of Mohács and young King Louis is killed; the ensuing Turkish occupation lasts more than a century and a half.

1541

Buda Castle falls to the Ottomans; Hungary is partitioned and shared by three separate groups: the Turks, the Habsburgs and the Transylvanian princes.

BIRDS DO IT

The ancient Magyars believed in magic and celestial intervention, and the *táltos* (shaman) enjoyed an elevated position in their society. Certain animals – for example, bears, stags and wolves – were totemic, and it was taboo to mention them directly by name. No other ancient totemic animal is better known to modern Hungarians than the *turul*, a hawklike bird that had supposedly impregnated Emese, the grandmother of Árpád. That legend can be viewed as an attempt to foster a sense of common origin and group identity, as an effort to bestow a sacred origin on the House of Árpád and its rule, or just as a good story.

swept through Hungary, burning it virtually to the ground and killing an estimated one-third to one-half of its two million people. The Árpád line died out at the start of the next century with the death in 1301 of Andrew III, who left no heir.

Medieval Hungary

The struggle for the Hungarian throne after the fall of the House of Árpád involved several European dynasties, with the crown first going to Charles Robert (Károly Róbert) of the French House of Anjou in 1307.

In the following century an alliance between Hungary and Poland gave the latter (with the pope's blessing) the Hungarian crown. When Vladislav I (Úlászló), son of the Polish Jagiellonian king, was killed fighting the Turks at Varna in 1444, János Hunyadi, a Transylvanian general, was made regent. His decisive victory over the Turks at Belgrade (Hungarian: Nándorfehérvár) in 1456 had checked the Ottoman advance into Hungary for 70 years and assured the coronation of his son Matthias (Mátyás), the greatest ruler of medieval Hungary.

Through his military exploits Matthias (r 1458–90), nicknamed 'the Raven' (Corvinus) from his coat of arms, made Hungary one of Central Europe's leading powers. Under his rule the nation enjoyed its first golden age. His second wife, the Neapolitan princess Beatrix, brought artisans up from Italy and extended the royal palace at Visegrád.

But while Matthias busied himself with centralising power for the crown and being a good king, he ignored the growing Turkish threat. Under his successor, Vladislav II (Úlászló; r 1490–1516), what had begun as a crusade in 1514 turned into a peasant uprising against landlords under György Dózsa.

The revolt was brutally repressed by Transylvanian leader John Szapolyai (Zápolyai János); some 70,000 peasants, including Dózsa, were tortured and executed. The retrograde Tripartitum Law that followed

Habsburg Emperor Joseph II was called the 'hatted king' because he was never actually crowned within the borders of Hungary.

In what must be one of the oddest footnotes in Hungarian history, Napoleon Bonaparte entered Hungarian territory and spent the night of 31 August 1809 in Győr, which was near a battle site.

1686

Austrian and Hungarian forces backed by the Polish army liberate Buda from the Turks; peace is signed with the Ottomans at Karlowitz (now in Serbia) 13 years later.

1703–11

Ferenc Rákóczi II fights and loses a war of independence against the Habsburgs; he is given asylum in Thrace by the Turkish sultan Ahmet III.

NEALE CLARK / GETTY IMAGES ©

» Statue of Ferenc Rákóczi II outside Hungarian Parliament

THE CROWN OF ST STEPHEN

That Asztrik, the first abbot of the Benedictine monastery at Pannonhalma, presented a crown to Stephen as a gift from Pope Sylvester II around AD 1000 is the stuff of legend. In actual fact, the two-part crown, with its characteristic bent cross, pendants hanging on either side and enamelled plaques of the Apostles, dates from the 12th century. It is the very symbol of the Hungarian nation. After WWII American forces in Europe transferred the crown to Fort Knox in Kentucky for safe-keeping; it was returned in 1978, to the nation's great relief. Because legal judgements in Hungary had always been handed down 'in the name of St Stephen's Crown', it was considered a living symbol and had thus been 'kidnapped'.

codified the rights and privileges of the barons and nobles and reduced the peasants to perpetual serfdom.

John Lukacs' classic *Budapest 1900: A Historical Portrait of a City and Its Culture* is an illustrated social history presenting the Hungarian capital at the height of its *fin-de-siècle* glory.

The Battle of Mohács

The defeat of the ragtag Hungarian army by the Ottoman Turks at Mohács in 1526 is a watershed in Hungarian history. On the battlefield south of the small town in Southern Transdanubia, a relatively prosperous and independent medieval Hungary died, sending the nation into a tailspin of partition, foreign domination and despair that would last for centuries.

It would be unfair to put all the blame on the weak and indecisive teenage King Louis II (Lajos). Bickering among the nobility and the brutal response to the peasant uprising had severely diminished Hungary's military power, and there was virtually nothing left in the royal coffers. By 1526 Ottoman sultan Suleiman the Magnificent (r 1520–66) had occupied much of the Balkans and was poised to march on Buda.

Unwilling to wait for reinforcements from Transylvania under his rival John Szapolyai, Louis rushed south with a motley army of just over 25,000 and was soundly thrashed in less than two hours. Among the 18,000 dead was the king himself, who drowned while trying to retreat across a stream.

Paul Lendvai's lively *The Hungarians: A Thousand Years of Victory in Defeat* takes a look at why Hungarians have contributed so disproportionately, relative to their numbers, to modern sciences and arts.

Turkish Occupation

After the Turks returned and occupied Buda Castle in 1541, Hungary was divided in three. The central section, including Buda, went to the Turks, while parts of Transdanubia and what is now Slovakia were governed by the Austrian House of Habsburg and assisted by the Hungarian nobility based at Bratislava (Hungarian: Pozsony). The principality of Transylvania prospered as a vassal state of the Ottoman Empire. This arrangement would remain in place for more than a century and a half.

1795

Seven pro-republican Jacobites, including the group's leader Ignác Martonovics, are beheaded at Vérmező (Blood Meadow) in Buda for plotting against the Habsburg throne.

1848–49

Poet Sándor Petőfi dies fighting during the War of Independence; and Lajos Batthyány and 13 of his generals are executed for their roles; leader Lajos Kossuth goes into exile.

1867

The Act of Compromise creates the Dual Monarchy of Austria (the empire), based in Vienna, and Hungary (the kingdom), with its seat at Budapest.

1896

Millennium of the Magyar 'conquest' of the Carpathian Basin is marked by a major exhibition in City Park that attracts four million people over six months.

Ottoman power began to wane in the 17th century, especially after the Turkish attempt to take Vienna was soundly defeated. Buda was liberated from the Turks in 1686 after a 77-day siege, and an imperial army under Eugene of Savoy wiped out the last Turkish army in Hungary at the Battle of Zenta (now Senta in Serbia) 11 years later.

Miklós Jancsó's 1967 film *Csend és Kiáltás* (Silence and Cry; 1967) is a political thriller about a 'red' who takes refuge among politically suspicious peasants after the overthrow of Béla Kun's Republic of Councils in 1919.

The Habsburgs

The expulsion of the Turks did not result in independence, and the policies of the Catholic Habsburgs' Counter-Reformation and heavy taxation further alienated the nobility. In 1703 the Transylvanian prince Ferenc Rákóczi II assembled an army of *kuruc* forces against the Austrians at Tiszahát in northeastern Hungary. The rebels 'dethroned' the Habsburgs as the rulers of Hungary in 1706 but were defeated five years later.

Hungary was now a mere province of the Habsburg Empire. Under Maria Theresa (r 1740–80) and her son, Joseph II (r 1780–90), Hungary took great steps forward economically and culturally. But Joseph's attempts to modernise society by dissolving the all-powerful (and corrupt) monastic orders, abolishing serfdom and replacing 'neutral' Latin with German as the official language of state administration were opposed by the Hungarian nobility, and he rescinded many orders on his deathbed.

Liberalism and social reform found their greatest supporters among certain members of the aristocracy including Count György Festetics (1755–1819), who founded Europe's first agricultural college at Keszthely, and Count István Széchenyi (1791–1860), a true Renaissance man, who advocated the abolition of serfdom and returned much of his own land to the peasantry. But the radicals, dominated by the dynamic lawyer and journalist Lajos Kossuth (1802–94), demanded more immediate action.

The 1848–49 War of Independence

A perplexed US President Franklin D Roosevelt asked an aide in the early days of WWII: 'Hungary is a kingdom without a king, run by a regent who's an admiral without a navy?'

The Habsburg Empire began to weaken as Hungarian nationalism strengthened early in the 19th century and certain reforms were introduced, including a law allowing serfs alternative means of discharging their feudal service obligations and increased Hungarian representation in the Council of State in Vienna.

The reforms were too limited and too late. On 15 March 1848 a group calling itself the Youth of March, led by the poet Sándor Petőfi, took to the streets of Pest with hastily printed copies of the Twelve Points to press for more radical reforms and even revolution. Habsburg patience began to wear thin.

In September 1848 Habsburg forces launched an attack. The Hungarians hastily formed a national defence commission and moved the

1918

Austria-Hungary loses WWI in November and the political system collapses; Hungary declares itself a republic under the leadership of Count Mihály Károlyi.

1919

Béla Kun's Republic of Councils, the world's second communist government after the Soviet Union's, lasts for five months until Kun is driven into exile by the Romanian army.

1920

Treaty of Trianon carves up much of central Europe, reducing historical Hungary by almost two-thirds and enlarging the ethnic Hungarian populations in Romania, Yugoslavia and Czechoslovakia.

1939

Nazi Germany invades Poland; Britain and France declare war on Germany two days later but Hungary remains neutral for two years when it joins the Axis led by Germany and Italy.

government seat to Debrecen, where Kossuth was elected governor-president. In April 1849 the parliament declared Hungary's full independence and 'dethroned' the Habsburgs again.

The new Habsburg emperor, Franz Joseph (r 1848–1916), quickly took action. He sought the assistance of Tsar Nicholas I, who obliged with 200,000 troops. Weak and vastly outnumbered, the rebel troops were defeated by August 1849. Martial law was declared and a series of brutal reprisals ensued. Kossuth went into exile. Habsburg troops then went around the country systematically blowing up castles and fortifications lest they be used by resurgent rebels.

German director Rolf Schübel's romantic drama *Ein Lied von Liebe und Tod* (Gloomy Sunday, 1999) is set in a Budapest restaurant just before the Nazi invasion and revolves around the song 'Gloomy Sunday', which was so morose it had people committing suicide in Budapest.

The Dual Monarchy

Hungary was again merged into the Habsburg Empire as a conquered province. But disastrous military defeats for the Habsburgs, by the French and then the Prussians in 1859 and 1866, pushed Franz Joseph to the negotiating table with liberal Hungarians under the leadership of reformer Ferenc Deák.

The result was the Act of Compromise of 1867, which created the Dual Monarchy of Austria (the empire) and Hungary (the kingdom) – a federated state with two parliaments and two capitals: Vienna and Budapest. This 'Age of Dualism' would carry on until 1918 sparked an economic, cultural and intellectual renaissance in Hungary, culminating with the six-month exhibition in 1896 celebrating the millennium of the Magyar arrival in the Carpathian Basin.

But all was not well in the kingdom. The working class had virtually no rights and the situation in the countryside remained almost medieval. Despite an 1868 law protecting their rights, minorities under Hungarian control – Czechs, Slovaks, Croatians and Romanians – were under increased pressure to 'Magyarise'. Many viewed their new rulers as oppressors.

The website of the National Szécheny Library's 1956 Institute and Oral History Archive (www.rev.hu) will walk you through the build-up, outbreak and aftermath of Hungary's greatest modern tragedy through photographs, essays and timelines.

WWI & the Republic of Councils

On 28 July 1914, a month to the day after the assassination of Archduke Franz Ferdinand, heir to the Habsburg throne, by a Bosnian Serb in Sarajevo, Austria-Hungary declared war on Serbia and entered WWI allied with the German Empire. The result was disastrous, with widespread destruction and hundreds of thousands killed on the Russian and Italian fronts. After the armistice in 1918 the fate of the Dual Monarchy – and Hungary as a multinational kingdom – was sealed with the Treaty of Trianon.

A republic under the leadership of Count Mihály Károlyi was established but the fledgling republic would not last long. Rampant inflation, mass unemployment, the occupation of Hungary by the Allies and dismemberment of 'Greater Hungary' and the success of the Bolshevik

1944

Germany invades and occupies Hungary; most Hungarian Jews, who had largely been able to avoid persecution under strongman Miklós Horthy, are deported to Nazi concentration camps.

1945

Budapest is liberated by the Soviet army in April, a month before full victory in Europe, with three-quarters of its buildings and all of its bridges in ruins.

STUART BLACK / GETTY IMAGES ©

» Soviet army memorial, Budapest (p52)

Revolution in Russia all combined to radicalise much of the Budapest working class.

In March 1919 a group of Hungarian communists under a former Transylvanian journalist called Béla Kun seized power. The so-called Republic of Councils (Tanácsköztársaság) set out to nationalise industry and private property, but Kun's failure to regain the 'lost territories' brought mass opposition to the regime and the government unleashed a reign of 'red terror' around the country. In August Romanian troops occupied the capital, and Kun fled to Vienna.

Szabadság, Szerelem (Children of Glory, 2006) by Krisztina Goda is the simplified (but effective) history of the 1956 Uprising, as seen through the eyes of a player on the Olympic water polo team and his girlfriend, who is one of the student leaders.

The Horthy Years & WWII

In March 1920 parliament chose a kingdom as the form of state and – lacking a king – elected as its regent Admiral Miklós Horthy. He embarked on a 'white terror' – every bit as brutal as the red one of Béla Kun – that attacked social democrats, communists and Jews for their roles in supporting the Republic of Councils. Though the country had the remnants of a parliamentary system, Horthy was all-powerful, and very few reforms were enacted.

Everyone agreed was that the return of the 'lost' territories was essential for Hungary's development. Hungary obviously could not count on the victorious Allies to help recoup its land; instead, it sought help from the fascist governments of Germany and Italy.

Hungary's move to the right intensified throughout the 1930s, though it remained silent when WWII broke out in September 1939. Horthy hoped an alliance would not mean actually having to enter the war, but Hungary joined the German- and Italian-led Axis, declaring war on the Soviet Union in June 1941. The war was as disastrous for Hungary as WWI had been, and Horthy began secret discussions with the Allies.

A Good Comrade: János Kádár, Communism & Hungary by Roger Gough, arguably the definitive biography of a communist official, does much to explain the tour de force that transformed Kádár from traitor and most hated man in the land to respected reformer.

When Hitler caught wind of this in March 1944 he dispatched the German army. Ferenc Szálasi, the deranged leader of the pro-Nazi Arrow Cross Party, was installed as prime minister and Horthy was deported to Germany.

The Arrow Cross Party arrested thousands of liberal politicians and labour leaders. The puppet government introduced anti-Jewish legislation similar to that in Germany, and Jews, who lived in fear but were still alive under Horthy, were rounded up into ghettos. From May to July of 1944, less than a year before the war ended, some 450,000 men, women and children – 60% of Hungarian Jewry – were deported to Auschwitz and other labour camps, where they starved to death, succumbed to disease or were brutally murdered.

Hungary now became an international battleground for the first time since the Turkish occupation, and bombs began falling on Budapest. Fierce fighting continued in the countryside, especially near Debrecen

1949
The Communists, now in complete control, announce the formation of the 'People's Republic of Hungary'; Stalinist show trials of 'Titoists' and other 'enemies of the people' begin.

1956
Budapest is in flames after riots in October; Hungary briefly withdraws from the Warsaw Pact and proclaims its neutrality but the status quo is restored and János Kàdár installed as leader.

1958
Imre Nagy and others are executed by the communist regime for their role in the uprising and buried in unmarked graves in Budapest's New Municipal Cemetery.

1963
Amnesty is extended to those involved in the 1956 Uprising by the communist government after a UN resolution condemning the suppression of the rebellion is struck from the agenda.

and Székesfehérvár, but by Christmas Day 1944 the Soviet army had encircled Budapest. By the time Germany had surrendered in April 1945, many of Budapest's homes, historical buildings and churches had been destroyed. The vindictive retreating Germans blew up Buda Castle and knocked out every bridge spanning the Danube.

The last Soviet troops left Hungary in June 1991 to great fanfare, and an annual festival still marks the date, but what few people know is that the Russians actually left two weeks ahead of schedule.

The People's Republic of Hungary

When free parliamentary elections were held in November 1945, the Independent Smallholders' Party received 57% of the vote. But Soviet political officers, backed by the occupying army, forced three other parties – the Communists, Social Democrats and National Peasants – into a coalition. Two years later in a disputed election held under a complicated new electoral law, the communists declared their candidate, the oafish Mátyás Rákosi, victorious. The following year the Social Democrats merged with the communists to form the Hungarian Workers' Party.

Rákosi, a big fan of Stalin, began a process of nationalisation and unfeasibly rapid industrialisation at the expense of agriculture. Peasants were forced into collective farms and all produce had to be delivered to state warehouses. A network of spies and informers exposed 'class enemies' (such as Cardinal József Mindszenty) to the secret police, the ÁVO (ÁVH after 1949). Up to a quarter of the adult population faced police or judicial proceedings. Stalinist show trials became the norm and in August 1949 the nation was proclaimed the 'People's Republic of Hungary'.

After Krushchev's denunciation of Stalin in 1956, Rákosi's tenure was up and the terror began to abate. Executed apparatchiks were rehabilitated, and people like former Minister of Agriculture Imre Nagy, who had been expelled from the party for suggesting reforms, were readmitted. By October of that year murmured calls for a real reform of the system – 'socialism with a human face' – were being heard.

NO, NO, NEVER!

In June 1920, the victorious Allies drew up a postwar settlement under the Treaty of Trianon at Versailles, near Paris, that enlarged some countries, truncated others and created several 'successor states'. As one of the defeated enemy nations and with large numbers of ethnic minorities demanding independence, Hungary stood to lose more than most. It was reduced to 40% of its historical size and, while it was now a largely uniform, homogeneous state, millions of ethnic Hungarians in Romania, Yugoslavia and Czechoslovakia were now the minority.

'Trianon' became the most hated word in Hungary and '*Nem, Nem, Soha!*' (No, No, Never!) was the rallying cry during the interwar years. Many of the problems the *diktátum* created remained in place for decades, and it has coloured Hungary's relations with its neighbours for almost a century.

1968

Plans for a liberalised economy are introduced in an attempt to overcome the inefficiencies of central planning but are rejected as too extreme by conservatives.

1978

The Crown of St Stephen is returned to Hungary from the USA, where it had been held at Fort Knox in Kentucky for safekeeping since the end of WWII.

1988

János Kádár is forced to retire in May after more than three decades in power; he dies and is buried in Budapest's Kerepesi Cemetery the following year.

1989

The electrified fence separating Hungary and Austria is removed in July; communist power is relinquished; the Republic of Hungary is declared in October.

The 1956 Uprising

The nation's greatest tragedy – an event that rocked communism, shook the world and pitted Hungarian against Hungarian – began on 23 October, when some 50,000 university students assembled at Bem tér in Buda, shouting anti-Soviet slogans and demanding that Imre Nagy be named prime minister. That night a crowd pulled down the colossal statue of Stalin near Heroes Sq, and shots were fired by ÁVH agents on another group gathering outside Hungarian Radio. Hungary was in revolution.

The following day Nagy formed a government, while János Kádár was named president of the Central Committee of the Hungarian Workers' Party. Over the next few days the government offered amnesty to all those involved in the violence, promised to abolish the ÁVH and announced that Hungary would leave the Warsaw Pact and declare its neutrality.

At this, Soviet tanks and troops crossed into Hungary and within 72 hours began attacking Budapest and other urban centres. Kádár had slipped away from Budapest to join the Russian invaders; he was now installed as leader.

Fierce street fighting continued for several days – encouraged by Radio Free Europe broadcasts and disingenuous promises of support from the West, which was embroiled in the Suez Canal crisis at the time. When the fighting was over, 25,000 people were dead. Then the reprisals began. About 20,000 people were arrested and 2000 – including Nagy and his associates – were executed. Another 250,000 refugees fled to Austria.

Alan Parker's 1996 film *Evita* was filmed in Budapest. The Buenos Aires cathedral on screen is St Stephen's Basilica, the grand, tree-lined boulevard is Andrássy út and the swarthy horse guards belong to the Hungarian mounted cavalry.

Hungary under Kádár

After the revolt, the ruling party was reorganised as the Hungarian Socialist Workers' Party, and Kádár began a program to liberalise the social and economic structure based on compromise. He introduced market socialism and encouraged greater consumerism. By the mid-1970s Hungary was light years ahead of any other Soviet-bloc country in its standard of living, freedom of movement and opportunities to criticise the government. The 'Hungarian model' attracted much Western investment.

But the Kádár system of 'goulash socialism' was incapable of dealing with such 'unsocialist' problems in the 1980s as unemployment, soaring inflation and the largest per-capita foreign debt in the region. Kádár and the 'old guard' refused to hear talk about party reforms. In June 1987 Károly Grósz took over as premier and Kádár retired.

The Magyars were so skilled (and brutal) as archers on horseback that a common Christian prayer during the early Middle Ages was 'Save us, O Lord, from the arrows of the Hungarians.'

Renewal & Change

Throughout the summer and autumn of 1988, new political parties were formed and old ones resurrected. In January 1989 Hungary, seeing the handwriting on the wall as Mikhail Gorbachev launched his reforms in

1990

The centrist MDF wins the first free elections in 43 years in April; Árpád Göncz is chosen as the republic's first president in August.

1991

The last Soviet troops leave Hungarian soil in June, two weeks ahead of schedule; parliament passes the first act dealing with the return of property seized under communist rule since 1949.

1994

Socialists win a decisive victory in the general election and form a government under Gyula Horn for the first time since the changes of 1989.

1995

Árpád Göncz of the SZDSZ, arguably the most popular politician in Hungary, is elected for a second (and, by law, final) five-year term as president of the republic.

the Soviet Union, announced that the events of 1956 had been a 'popular insurrection' and not a 'counter-revolution'. In June some 250,000 people attended the reburial of Imre Nagy and other victims of 1956 in Budapest.

The next month Hungary began to demolish the electrified wire fence separating it from Austria. The move released a wave of East Germans holidaying in Hungary into the West and the opening attracted thousands more. The collapse of the communist regimes around the region had become unstoppable.

If you are in search of reminders of the 1956 Uprising in Budapest, look around you – in many buildings in Pest the bullet holes and shrapnel scorings on the exterior walls still cry out in silent fury.

The Republic of Hungary Reborn

The communists agreed to give up their monopoly on power, paving the way for free elections in March 1990. On 23 October 1989, the 33rd anniversary of the 1956 Uprising, the nation once again became the Republic of Hungary.

The 1990 vote was won by the centrist Hungarian Democratic Forum (MDF), which advocated a gradual transition to full capitalism. The social-democratic Alliance of Free Democrats (SZDSZ), which had called for much faster change, came second and the former communists (now socialists) trailed far behind. Hungary had changed political systems with scarcely a murmur.

János Kádár's most quoted line was 'Whoever is not against us is for us' – a reversal of the Stalinist adage that 'Those not for us are against us'.

In coalition with two smaller parties – the Independent Smallholders and the Christian Democrats (KDNP) – the MDF provided Hungary with sound government during its painful transition to a free-market economy. Those years saw Hungary's neighbours to the north (Czechoslovakia) and south (Yugoslavia) split along ethnic lines, and Prime Minister József Antall did little to improve Hungary's relations with Slovakia, Romania and Yugoslavia by claiming to be the 'emotional and spiritual' prime minister of the large Magyar minorities in those countries. He died in December 1993 after a long fight with cancer and was replaced by interior minister Péter Boross.

In the May 1994 elections the Socialist Party, led by Gyula Horn, surprisingly won an absolute majority in parliament. Árpád Göncz of the SZDSZ was elected for a second five-year term as president in 1995.

Many Hungarians refer to the four decades from 1949 to the change of regime in 1989 as *az átkos 40 év* (the accursed 40 years).

The Road to Europe

After its dire showing in the 1994 elections, the Federation of Young Democrats (Fidesz), which until 1993 had limited membership to those aged under 35 in order to emphasise a past untainted by communism and privilege, moved to the right and added the extension 'MPP' (Hungarian Civic Party) to its name to attract the support of the burgeoning middle class. In the 1998 elections, during which it campaigned for integration with Europe, Fidesz-MPP won by forming a coalition with the

1999
Hungary becomes a fully fledged member of NATO, along with the Czech Republic and Poland; NATO aircraft heading for Kosovo begins using Hungarian air bases.

2004
Hungary is admitted to the EU along with nine other new member-nations, including neighbouring states Slovakia and Slovenia, with Romania following three years later.

2006
Socialist Ferenc Gyurcsány is re-elected as prime minister; Budapest is rocked by rioting during the 50th anniversary celebrations of the 1956 Uprising.

2008
Government loses key referendum on health-care reform; SZDSZ quits coalition, leaving the socialists to form a minority government; Hungary is particularly hard hit by the world economic crisis.

MDF and the conservative Independent Smallholders. The party's youthful leader, Viktor Orbán, was named prime minister.

The electorate grew increasingly hostile to Fidesz-MPP's strongly nationalistic rhetoric and unseated the government in April 2002, returning the MSZP, allied with the SZDSZ, to power under Prime Minister Péter Medgyessy, a free-market advocate who had served as finance minister in the Horn government. In August 2004, amid revelations that he had once served as a counterintelligence officer, Medgyessy resigned and Sports Minister Ferenc Gyurcsány of the MSZP was named premier.

In 2007 János Kádár's grave in Budapest's Kerepesi Cemetery was broken into and his skull and assorted bones were removed. The only clue was a note that read: 'Murderers and traitors may not rest in holy ground 1956–2006'. The remains were not recovered.

At Home at Last

Hungary became a fully fledged member of NATO in 1999 and, with nine so-called accession countries, was admitted into the EU in May 2004.

Reappointed prime minister in April 2006 after the electorate gave his coalition 55% of the vote, Gyurcsány began a series of austerity measures to tackle Hungary's budget deficit, which had reached a staggering 10% of the GDP. But in September, just as these unpopular steps were put into place, an audiotape recorded shortly after the election at a closed-door meeting of the prime minister's cabinet had Gyurcsány confessing that the party had 'lied morning, noon and night' about the state of the economy since coming to power and now had to make amends. Gyurcsány refused to resign, and public outrage led to a series of demonstrations near the Parliament building in Budapest, culminating in widespread rioting that marred the 50th anniversary of the 1956 Uprising.

The Minister of Culture in Béla Kun's short-lived Republic of Councils was one Béla Lugosi, who fled to Vienna in 1919 and eventually made his way to Hollywood, where he achieved fame as the lead in several Dracula films.

Since then sometimes violent demonstrations have become a not-infrequent feature on the streets of Budapest and other large cities, especially during national holidays. The radical right-wing nationalist party Jobbik Magyarországért Mozgalom (Movement for a Better Hungary), and its uniformed militia arm, the Magyar Gárda (Hungarian Guard), have been at the centre of many of these demonstrations and riots.

Gyurcsány led a feeble minority government until general elections in 2010 when Fidesz-MPP won a majority of 52% in the first round of voting and joined forces with the Christian Democratic People's Party (KDNP) to rule with a two-thirds majority in parliament

Hungary's most recent appearance on the world stage came in 2011 when it assumed presidency of the EU Council. A new constitution went into effect at the start of 2012.

2010

Fidesz-MPP wins a 52% majority in general elections; Viktor Orbán resumes the premiership and governs with a two-thirds majority of 263 of 386 seats.

2011

In its most high-profile role on the European stage to date Hungary assumes presidency of the EU council; a new Constitution of Hungary is ratified.

» Parliament (p46), Budapest

The Arts

Hungarian art has been both stunted and spurred on by pivotal events in the nation's history. King Stephen's conversion to Catholicism brought Romanesque and Gothic art and architecture, while the Turkish occupation nipped most of Hungary's Renaissance in the bud. The Habsburgs opened the doors wide to baroque influences. The arts thrived under the Dual Monarchy, through Trianon and even under fascism. The early days of communism brought the aesthetics of wheat sheaves and muscle-bound steelworkers to a less-than-impressed populace, but much money was spent on music and 'correct art' such as classical theatre. Under current economic conditions funding for the arts is being slashed.

Architecture

You won't find as much Romanesque and Gothic architecture in Hungary as you will in, say, Slovakia or the Czech Republic – the Mongols, Turks and Habsburgs destroyed most of it here – but the Benedictine Abbey Church (p137) at Ják is a fine example of Romanesque architecture, and there are important Gothic churches in Nyírbátor and Sopron.

The yellow ochre that became the standard colour for all Habsburg administrative buildings and many churches in the late 18th century, and that is ubiquitous throughout Hungary, is now called 'Maria Theresa yellow'.

Baroque architecture abounds in Hungary; you can see examples in virtually every town in the land. For something on a grand scale, visit the Esterházy Palace (p130) at Fertőd or the Minorite church (p248) in Eger.

Distinctly Hungarian architecture didn't come into its own until the mid-19th century, when Mihály Pollack, József Hild and Miklós Ybl were changing the face of Budapest or racing around the country building mansions and cathedrals like Esztergom Basilica (p108). The Romantic Eclectic style of Ödön Lechner – see the Museum of Applied Arts (p50) in Budapest, and Hungarian Secessionist or Art Nouveau style in Szeged at **Reök Palace** (Reök Palota; ☎541 205; www.reok.hu; Tisza Lajos körút 56) – brought unique architecture to Hungary at the end of the 19th century and the start of the 20th. Art Nouveau fans will find in cities such as Budapest, Szeged and Kecskemét some of the best examples of the style in Europe.

Post-WWII architecture in Hungary is almost completely forgettable. One exception is the work of Imre Makovecz, who developed his own 'organic' style using unusual materials like tree trunks and turf. His work is everywhere, but among the best (or strangest) examples are the Sárospatak Cultural House (p266) and the Evangelist church (p173) in Siófok. Equally controversial is the work of Mária Siklós (Budapest's National Theatre; p84).

Painting & Sculpture

For Gothic art, have a look at the 15th-century altarpieces done by various masters at the Christian Museum (p108) in Esztergom. The Bakócz Chapel in Esztergom Basilica and the Royal Palace (p105) at Visegrád contain exceptional examples of Renaissance sculpture and masonry.

The finest baroque painters in Hungary were the 18th-century artists Franz Anton Maulbertsch, who did the frescoes in the Church of the Ascension (p159) at Sümeg, and István Dorffmeister, whose work can be seen in the sublime murals in the Bishop's Palace (p135) in Szombathely. The ornately carved altars in the Minorite church (p232) at Nyírbátor and the Abbey Church (p161) in Tihany are masterpieces of baroque carving.

The saccharine Romantic Nationalist school of heroic paintings, best exemplified by Bertalan Székely (1835–1910) and Gyula Benczúr (1844–1920), gave way to the realism of Mihály Munkácsy (1844–1900), the 'painter of the *puszta*'. The greatest painters from this period were Tivadar Kosztka Csontváry (1853–1919; p178), who has been compared with Van Gogh, and József Rippl-Rónai (1861–1927), the key exponent of Secessionist painting in Hungary. There are museums dedicated to their work in Pécs and Kaposvár, respectively.

Hungary's favourite artists of the 20th century include Victor Vasarely (1908–97), the so-called father of Op Art, and the sculptor Amerigo Tot (1909–84). There are museums dedicated to the former in both Pécs and Budapest.

The **Studio of Young Artists Association** (FKSE; http://studio.c3.hu), a branch of the National Association of Hungarian Artists, is a showcase for contemporary Hungarian art by people under the age of 35.

Folk Art

From the beginning of the 18th century, as segments of the Hungarian peasantry became more prosperous, ordinary people tried to make their world more beautiful by painting and decorating ordinary objects and clothing. As a result Hungary has one of the richest folk traditions in Europe and, quite apart from its music, this is where the country has come to the fore in art.

Three groups of people stand out for their embroidery, the acme of Hungarian folk art: the Palóc of the Northern Uplands, especially around the village of Hollókő; the Matyó from Mezőkövesd; and the women of Kalocsa. Also impressive are the waterproof woollen coats called *szűr*, once worn by herders on the Great Plain, which were masterfully embroidered by men using thick, 'furry' yarn.

Folk pottery is world-class here and no Hungarian kitchen is complete without a couple of pairs of matched plates or shallow bowls hanging on the walls. The centre of this industry is in the Great Plain towns of Hódmezővásárhely and Tiszafüred. There are jugs, pitchers, plates, bowls and cups, but the rarest and most attractive are the *írókázás fazékok* (inscribed pots), usually celebrating a wedding day, or produced in the form of animals or people, such as the *Miskai kancsó* (Miska jugs), not unlike English Toby jugs, from the Tisza River region. Nádudvar near Hajdúszoboszló on the Great Plain specialises in striking black pottery.

Most people made and decorated their own furniture in the old days, especially cupboards for the *tiszta szoba* (parlour) and *tulipán ládák* (trousseau chests with tulips painted on them).

One art form that ventures into the realm of fine art is ceiling and wall folk painting. Among the best examples of the former can be found in churches, especially in the Northeast (see Tákos). The women of Kalocsa also specialise in colourful wall painting, some of it very overdone.

Music

One person stands head and shoulders above the rest: Franz (or, in Hungarian, Ferenc) Liszt (1811–86). He established the Academy of Music (p54) in Budapest and liked to describe himself as 'part Gypsy'. Some

Though a commercial site, www.folk-art-hungary.com is an excellent introduction and primer to embroidery and other textile folk art by artisans in Hollókő, Kalocsa and Mezőkövesd.

Franz Liszt was born in the Hungarian village of Doborján (now Raiding in Austria) to a Hungarian father and an Austrian mother, but never learned to speak Hungarian fluently.

of his works, notably his 20 *Hungarian Rhapsodies,* do in fact echo the traditional music of the Roma people.

Ferenc Erkel (1810–93) is the father of Hungarian opera, and two of his works – the nationalistic *Bánk Bán,* based on József Katona's play of that name, and *László Hunyadi* – are standards at the Hungarian State Opera House (p49).

Imre Kálmán (1882–1953) was Hungary's most celebrated composer of operettas. *The Gypsy Princess* and *Countess Marica* are two of his most popular works and standard fare at the Budapest Operetta (p83).

The former US president Theodore Roosevelt (1858–1919) enjoyed *St Peter's Umbrella* by Kálmán Mikszáth so much that he insisted on visiting the ageing novelist during a European tour in 1910.

Béla Bartók (1881–1945) and Zoltán Kodály (1882–1967) made the first systematic study of Hungarian folk music, travelling together and recording throughout the Magyar linguistic region in 1906. Both incorporated some of their findings in their music – Bartók in *Bluebeard's Castle,* for example, and Kodály in the *Peacock Variations.*

Pop music is as popular here as anywhere – indeed, Hungary has one of Europe's biggest pop spectacles, the annual **Sziget Music Festival** (www.sziget.hu). It boasts more than 1000 performances over a week and attracts an audience of up to 400,000 people.

Folk Music

When discussing folk music, it's important to distinguish between 'Gypsy' music and Hungarian folk music. Gypsy music is schmaltzy and based on tunes called *verbunkos* played during the Rákóczi independence wars. At least two fiddles, a bass and a cymbalom (a curious stringed instrument played with sticks) are de rigueur. You can hear this music at almost any fancy hotel restaurant in the country or get hold of a recording by Sándor Déki Lakatos and his band.

Hungarian folk musicians play violins, zithers, hurdy-gurdies, bagpipes and lutes on a five-tone diatonic scale. Watch out for Muzsikás, Marta Sebestyén, Ghymes (a Hungarian folk band from Slovakia), and the Hungarian group Vujicsics that mixes elements of South Slav music. Another folk musician with eclectic tastes is the Paris-trained Beáta Pálya, who combines such sounds as traditional Bulgarian and Indian music with Hungarian folk.

Roma – as opposed to Gypsy – music is different altogether, and traditionally sung a cappella. Some modern Roma music groups – Kalyi Jag (Black Fire) from northeastern Hungary, Romano Drom (Gypsy Road) and Romani Rota (Gypsy Wheels) – have added guitars, percussion and even electronics to create a whole new sound. Gyula Babos' Project Romani has used elements of avant-garde jazz.

TÁNCHÁZ

For a complete and up-to-date listing of the times, dates and places of *táncház* meetings and performances in Budapest and elsewhere in Hungary, check out www.tanchaz.hu.

Dance

Táncház (literally 'dance house') is an excellent way to hear Hungarian folk music and to learn traditional dance, and they're good fun and relatively easy to find, especially in Budapest. You'll rarely – if ever – encounter such traditional dances as the *karikázó* (circle dance) and *csárdás* outside the capital these days.

Hungary also has ballet companies based in Budapest, Pécs and Szeged (contemporary), but the best by far is the Győr Ballet.

Literature

Sándor Petőfi (1823–49) is Hungary's most celebrated and widely read poet, and a line from his work *National Song* became the rallying cry for the 1848–49 War of Independence. A deeply philosophical play called *The Tragedy of Man* by Imre Madách (1823–64), published a decade after Hungary's defeat in the War of Independence, is still considered the country's greatest classical drama.

Hungary's defeat in 1849 led many writers to look to Romanticism for comfort and inspiration: winners, heroes and knights in shining armour became popular subjects. Petőfi's comrade-in-arms, János Arany (1817–82) wrote epic poetry (including the *Toldi Trilogy*) and ballads. Another friend of Petőfi, the prolific novelist and playwright Mór Jókai (1825–1904), gave expression to heroism and honesty in such accessible works as *The Man with the Golden Touch* and *Black Diamonds*. Another perennial favourite, Kálmán Mikszáth (1847–1910), wrote satirical tales such as *The Good Palóc People* and *St Peter's Umbrella,* in which he poked fun at the gentry in decline.

Zsigmond Móricz (1879–1942) was a very different type of writer. His works, in the tradition of Émile Zola, examined the harsh reality of peasant life in Hungary in the late 19th century. His contemporary Mihály Babits (1883–1941), poet and editor of the influential literary magazine *Nyugat* (West), made the rejuvenation of Hungarian literature his lifelong work.

Two 20th-century poets are unsurpassed in Hungarian letters. Endre Ady (1877–1919), sometimes described as a successor to Petőfi, was a reformer who ruthlessly attacked Hungarians' growing complacency and materialism, provoking a storm of protest from right-wing nationalists. The work of socialist poet Attila József (1905–37) expressed the alienation felt by individuals in the modern age; his poem *By the Danube* is brilliant even in translation. József ran afoul of both the underground communist movement and the Horthy regime. Tragically, he threw himself under a train near Lake Balaton at the age of 32. A perennial favourite is the late Sándor Márai (1900–89), whose crisp style has encouraged worldwide interest in Hungarian literature.

The difficulty and subtlety of the Magyar tongue has always excluded outsiders from Hungarian literature in the original, prompting the poet Gyula Illyés (1902–83) to write: 'The Hungarian language is at one and the same time our softest cradle and our most solid coffin.'

Among Hungary's most important contemporary writers are Imre Kertész (1929–), György Konrád (1933–), Péter Nádas (1942–) and Péter Esterházy (1950–). Konrád's *A Feast in the Garden* (1985) is an almost autobiographical account of a Jewish community in a small eastern Hungarian town. *A Book of Memoirs* (1986) by Nádas traces the decline of communism in a style reminiscent of Thomas Mann. In *The End of a Family Story* (1977), Nádas uses a child narrator as a filter for the adult experience of 1950s communist Hungary. Esterházy's partly autobiographical *Celestial Harmonies* (2000) paints a favourable portrait of the protagonist's father. His later *Revised Edition* (2002) is based on documents revealing his father to have been a government informer during the communist regime.

Novelist and Auschwitz survivor Kertész won the Nobel Prize for Literature in 2002, the first time a Hungarian had gained that distinction. Among his novels available in English are *Fatelessness* (1975), *Detective Story* (1977), *Fiasco* (1988), *Kaddish for an Unborn Child* (1990) and *Liquidation* (2003). Hungary's foremost female contemporary writer, the widely read Magda Szabó, died in 2007 at age 90. Her works include *Katalin Street* (1969), *Abigail* (1970) and *The Door* (1975), a compelling story of a woman writer and the symbiotic relationship she has with her peasant housekeeper.

Hungarian Literature Online (www.hlo.hu) leaves no page unturned in the world of Hungarian books, addressing everyone from writers and editors to translators and publishers, with a useful list of links as well.

Making a big spalsh in literarty circles both at home and abroad these days is László Krasznahorka, whose demanding postmodernist novels (*Satantango*, 1985; *The Melancholy of Resistance*, 1988) are called 'forbidding' in Hungary.

Cinema

For classic Hungarian films look out for works by Oscar-winning István Szabó *(Sweet Emma, Dear Böbe, The Taste of Sunshine),* Miklós Jancsó *(Outlaws)* and Péter Bacsó *(The Witness, Live Show)*. Other favourites are *Simon Mágus,* the surrealistic tale of two magicians and a young woman in Paris, from Ildikó Enyedi, and her *Tender Interface,* about the brain drain from Hungary after WWII.

In Anthony Minghella's film *The English Patient* (1996), when László Almásy (Ralph Fiennes) plays a Hungarian folk song on the phonograph for Katharine Clifton (Kristin Scott Thomas), the voice you hear is that of Marta Sebestyén singing '*Szerelem, Szerelem*' (Love, Love).

Péter Timár's *Csinibaba* is a satirical look at life – and film production quality – during communism. *Zimmer Feri,* set on Lake Balaton, pits a young practical-joker against a bunch of loud German tourists; the typo in the title is deliberate. Timár's *6:3* takes viewers back to that glorious moment when Hungary defeated England in football. Gábor Herendi's *Something America* is the comic tale of a film-making team trying to profit from an expatriate Hungarian who pretends to be a rich producer.

Of more recent vintage is Hungarian-American director Nimród Antal's *Kontroll,* a high-speed romantic thriller set almost entirely in the Budapest metro in which assorted outcasts, lovers and dreamers commune. Kornél Mundruczó's award-winning *Delta* is the brooding tale of a man's return to his home in Romania's Danube Delta and his complex relationship with his half-sister.

Two films that use pivotal events in Hungarian history as backdrops are *Children of Glory* by Krisztina Goda, which recounts the 1956 Uprising through the eyes of a player on the Olympic water polo team, and Ferenc Török's *Moszkva Tér,* the comic tale of high-school boys in 1989 oblivious to the important events taking place around them.

The Hungarian People

The vast majority of Hungary's 10 million people are Magyars, an Asiatic people of obscure origins who do not speak an Indo-European language and who found their way to the Carpathian Basin after a rather long and circuitous route in the late 9th century. Their only cousins in Europe are the far-flung Finns and the Estonians.

A Polite Formality

Hungarians are not uninhibited people like the gregarious Romanians or the sentimental Slavs. Forget about the impassioned, devil-may-care, Gypsy-fiddling stereotype – it doesn't exist here. Hungarians are a reserved and somewhat formal people. They are almost always extremely polite in social interactions, and the language can be very courtly. But while all this civility certainly oils the wheels that turn a sometimes difficult society, it can be used to keep 'outsiders' (both foreigners and other Hungarians) at a distance.

Penchant for the Blues

Himnusz, the national anthem, describes Hungary as a country 'long torn by ill fate' and the overall mood here is one of *honfibú*, literally 'patriotic sorrow' but really a penchant for the blues. This mood certainly predates communism. To illustrate what she saw as the 'dark streak in the Hungarian temperament', the late US foreign correspondent Flora Lewis recounted a story in *Europe: A Tapestry of Nations* that was the talk of the early 1930s. 'It was said', she wrote, 'that a song called "Gloomy Sunday" so deeply moved otherwise normal people [in Budapest] that whenever it was played, they would rush to commit suicide by jumping off a Danube bridge.' The song has been covered in English by many artists, including Billie Holiday, Sinéad O'Connor, Marianne Faithfull and Björk. It is a real bummer.

When the Italian-American Nobel Prize–winning physicist Enrico Fermi (1901–54) was asked whether extraterrestrial beings existed, he replied: 'Of course they do...[and] they are already here among us. They are called Hungarians.' He had worked with Hungarian scientists on the so-called Manhattan Project, which led to the development of the atomic bomb.

Scientific Minds

Hungary is a highly cultured and educated society, with a literacy rate of over 99% among those 15 years and older. The nation's contributions to specialised education and the sciences have been far greater than its present size and population would suggest. A unique method of music education, devised by the composer Zoltán Kodály (1882–1967), is widespread and Budapest's Pető Institute, founded by András Pető (1893–1967) in 1945, has a very high success rate in teaching children with cerebral palsy to walk. Albert Szent-Györgyi (1893–1986) won the Nobel Prize in 1937 for his discovery of vitamin C.

Lifestyle

If Kovács János and his wife, Kovácsné Szabó Erzsébet, invite you home for a meal, be flattered. By and large, Hungarians meet their friends outside the home at cafes and restaurants. If you do go along, bring a bunch of flowers or a bottle of good local wine.

You can talk about anything under the sun chez Kovács – from religion and politics to whether their language really is more difficult than Japanese and Arabic – but money is a touchy subject. Traditionally, the discussion of wealth – or even wearing flashy bling and clothing – was considered gauche. Though it's almost impossible to calculate (with the 'black economy' being so widespread and significant), the average monthly salary at the time of writing was just under €900 – but after taxes and social security deductions, only half of that went home.

Like more than two-thirds of all Hungarians, the Kovácses live in a town but retain a connection with the countryside with a hut in a wine-growing region. Friends have a more coveted *nyaralóház* (summer cottage) by the lake. During *szüret* (grape harvest), they head for the hills and probably attend a *disznótor,* which involves the slaughtering of a pig followed by a party.

There's not much gay or lesbian life in the countryside unless you take it with you; both communities keep a very low profile outside Budapest. Since 2009 Hungary has allowed registered partnerships *(bejegyzett élettársi kapcsolat)*, which offer almost all the benefits of marriage, except adoption, to same-sex couples. However, same-sex marriage is prohibited by the Hungarian constitution, which was rewritten in 2011 by the current government.

Life expectancy in Hungary is very low by European standards: just over 71 years for men and almost 79 for women. Kovács Jánosné can expect to outlive Kovács János by almost eight years (but that might have something to do with the amount of alcohol János puts away).

Drinking is an important part of social life in a country that has produced wine and fruit brandies for thousands of years. Consumption is high at an annual average of 16.3L of pure alcohol per person; only citizens of Moldova and the Czech republic drink more. Alcoholism in Hungary is not as visible to the outsider as it is in, say, Russia, but it's here nonetheless; official figures suggest that 10% of the population are fully fledged alcoholics. And it must be said that even social drinking is not always a happy affair and can often end (willingly) in tears. Indeed, Hungarians have an expression for this bizarre arrangement: *sírva vigadni*, or 'to take one's pleasure sadly'.

The latest edition of *Culture Shock! Hungary: A Guide to Customs & Etiquette* by Zsuzsanna Ardó goes beyond the usual anecdotal information and observations offered in this kind of book and is virtually an anthropological and sociological study of the Magyar race.

Multiculturalism

Just over 92% of the population is ethnically Magyar. Non-Magyar minorities include Germans (2.6%), Serbs and other South Slavs (2%), Slovaks (0.8%) and Romanians (0.7%). The number of Roma is officially put at 1.9% of the population (or just under 200,000 people), but some people believe the figure is twice as high, and members of the Roma community itself put the number at 800,000.

For the most part, ethnic minorities in Hungary aren't discriminated against and their rights are inscribed in the constitution. Yet this has not stopped the occasional attack on nonwhite foreigners, a rise in anti-Semitism and the widespread discrimination against Roma.

The Roma

The origins of the Gypsies (Hungarian: *cigány*), who call themselves the Roma (singular Rom) and speak Romani, a language closely related to several still spoken in northern India, remain a mystery. It is generally

WHERE THE FIRST COME LAST

In a practice unknown outside Asia, Hungarians reverse their names in all usages, and their 'last' name (or surname) always comes first. For example, John Smith is never János Kovács but Kovács János, while Elizabeth Taylor is Szabó Erzsébet.

Most titles also follow the structure: Mr John Smith is Kovács János úr. Many women follow the practice of taking their husband's full name. If Elizabeth was married to John, she might be Kovács Jánosné (Mrs John Smith) or, increasingly popular among professional women, Kovácsné Szabó Erzsébet.

accepted, however, that they began migrating to Persia from India sometime in the 10th century and had reached the Balkans by the 14th century. They have been in Hungary for at least 500 years, and they officially number around 190,000, although that figure could much be higher.

Though traditionally a travelling people, in modern times the Roma have by and large settled down in Hungary and worked as smiths and tinkers, livestock and horse traders, and as musicians. As a group, however, they are chronically underemployed and have been the hardest hit by economic recession (statistically, Roma families are twice the size of *gadje*, or 'non-Roma' ones.)

Unsettled people are often persecuted in one form or another by those who stay put, and Hungarian Roma are no exception. They are widely despised and remain the scapegoats for everything that goes wrong in certain parts of the country, from the rise in petty theft and prostitution to the loss of jobs. Though their rights are inscribed in the constitution, along with those of other other ethnic minorities, their housing ranks among the worst in the nation, police are regularly accused of harassing them and, more than any other group, they fear the revival of right-wing nationalism. In recent years members of the thuggish Magyar Gárda (Hungarian Guard), the uniformed militia wing of the right-wing Jobbik party with 46 seats in Parliament, have resumed bullying and intimidating Roma people in villages of the northeast.

You will probably be shocked at what even educated, cosmopolitan Hungarians say about Roma and their way of life. Learn the truth from Budapest-based Romedia Foundation (www.romediafoundation.org), whose remit is to use media as a tool to bring about social change.

Religion

Hungarians tend to have a much more pragmatic approach to religion than most of their neighbours; it has even been suggested that this generally sceptical view of matters of faith has led to Hungary's high rate of success in science and mathematics. Except in villages and on the most important holy days (Easter, the Assumption of Mary and Christmas), churches are never full. The Jewish community in Budapest, on the other hand, has seen a great revitalisation in recent years, mostly due to an influx of Chasidic Jews from the USA and Israel.

Of those Hungarians declaring religious affiliation in the most recent census, just under 52% said they were Roman Catholic, 16% Reformed (Calvinist) Protestant and 3% Evangelical (Lutheran) Protestant. There are also small Greek Catholic and Orthodox (2.7%) and other Christian (1%) congregations. Hungary's Jews (not all practising) number around 80,000, down from a pre-WWII population of 10 times that amount.

For a list of people who you may or may not have known were Magyar get hold of *Eminent Hungarians* by Ray Keenoy.

The Wines of Hungary

Wine has been made in Hungary since at least the time of the Romans. It is very much a part of Hungarian culture, but only in recent years has it moved on from the local tipple you drank at Sunday lunch with the rels or the overwrought and overpriced thimble of rarefied red sipped in a Budapest wine bar, to the all-singin', all-dancin', all embracin' obsession that it is now. It is no exaggeration to say that wine is just about the sexiest thing you'll find in Hungary today.

Choosing Wine

The Wineportal (www.wineportal.hu) website is an excellent source for basic and background information on Hungarian wine. It also lists accommodation options in the various wine regions and wine restaurants around the country.

Wine is sold by the glass or bottle everywhere – at food stalls, wine bars, restaurants, supermarkets and 24-hour grocery stores – and usually at reasonable prices. Old-fashioned wine bars ladle out plonk by the *deci* (decilitre, or 0.1L), but if you're into more serious wine, you should visit one of Budapest's excellent wine bars such as DiVino Borbár (p78) or Dobló (p79), a wine restaurant like Klassz (p74), or speciality wine shops (the Bortársaság, p86, chain is among the best).

When choosing a Hungarian wine, look for the words *minőségi bor* (quality wine) or *különleges minőségi bor* (premium quality wine), Hungary's version of the French quality regulation *appellation d'origine contrôlée*. On a wine label the first word indicates the region, the second the grape variety (eg Villányi Kékfrankos) or the type or brand of wine (eg Tokaji Aszú, Szekszárdi Bikavér). Other important words that you'll see include: *édes* (sweet), *fehér* (white), *félédes* (semisweet), *félszáraz* (semi-dry or medium), *pezsgő* (sparkling), *száraz* (dry) and *vörös* (red).

Very roughly, anything costing more than 2000Ft in the shops is a serious bottle of Hungarian wine. Pay more than 3000Ft and you'll be getting something very fine indeed.

Wine Regions

Hungary is divided into seven wine-growing and -producing regions. In the west are Észak Dunántúl (Northern Transdanubia), Balaton, Sopron and Pannonia (Southern Transdanubia). In the east are Eger, Tokaj and Duna ('Danube') encompassing parts of the Great Plain. Subdivisions range in size from tiny Somló in Transdanubia, to the vast vineyards of the Kunság on the Southern Plain, with its sandy soil nurturing more than a third of all of the vines grown in the country.

It's all a matter of taste but the most distinctive (and big) Hungarian red wines come from Villány in Southern Transdanubia and Eger in the Northern Uplands. The reds from Szekszárd, also in Southern Transdanubia, are softer and more subtle. The best dry whites are produced around Lake Balaton's northern shore and in Somló, though the latest craze is for bone-dry, slightly tart Furmint from Tokaj, which also produces the world-renowned sweet wine. If you're looking for sparkling wine *(pezsgő)* go for Hungaria Extra Dry, which retails for just under 2000Ft.

What's New

Hungary is moving away from technology-driven wine production to *terroir*-based cultivation and vineyard-specific bottling. Let's face it – anyone with the money and know-how can produce a decent Cabernet or Chardonnay. What people are looking for now is wine that speaks of the region and the soil – the *terroir*. There's even talk of introducing village denomination. Until recently these phenomena occurred only in Tokaj and Villány; they're now becoming the norm in places like Badacsony on the northern shore of Lake Balaton. Most vintners now produce their own premium *cuvée* (blend) – often named after themselves, such as Gere's eponymous Attila. And some winemakers have adopted biodynamic cultivation methods, including Pendits in Tokaj and Franz Weninger in Sopron.

Tokaj

The volcanic soil, sunny climate and protective mountain barrier of the Tokaj-Hegyalja (Tokaj Uplands) region in northern Hungary make it ideal for growing grapes and making wine. Tokaj wines were exported to Poland and Russia in the Middle Ages and reached the peak of their popularity in Europe in the 17th and 18th centuries.

Tokaj dessert wines are rated according to the number – from three to six – of *puttony* (butts, or baskets for picking) of sweet Aszú grapes added to the base wines. These are grapes infected with 'noble rot', the *Botrytis cinera* mould that almost turns them into raisins on the vine.

For Tokaji Aszú, one name to look out for is István Szepsy; he concentrates on both the upscale six-puttony type and the Esszencia – so sweet and low in alcohol it's hardly even wine. His Szepsy Cuvée, aged in stainless steel barrels for a year or two (against the usual five for Tokaji Aszú), is a complex, elegant blend comparable to Sauternes. That said, Zoltán Demeter's version is almost pushing Szepsy aside in terms of quality. Other names to watch out for are Hétszőlő, Gróf Degenfeld, Pendits and, for Furmint, Oremus and Béres.

Tokaj also produces less-sweet wines, including dry Szamorodni (an excellent aperitif) and sweet Szamorodni, which is not unlike an Italian *vin santo;* for the latter try Disznókő's version. Of the four grape varieties

WINE OF KINGS

Louis XIV famously called Tokaj 'the wine of kings and the king of wines', while Voltaire wrote that 'this wine could be only given by the boundlessly good God'!

PÉTER LENGYEL'S TOP FIVE

We know what we like but we're no experts. So we turned to 'he-who-knows-all' – Budapest-based wine translator and maven Péter Lengyel – for his favourite five wines.

» **Laposa Badacsonyi Olaszrizling** (Balaton) Among the best dry white wines for everyday drinking; a straw-blonde Welschriesling high in acid that has a tart aftertaste and is reminiscent of burnt almonds.

» **Szepsy Tokaji Furmint** (Tokaj) With a flavour recalling apples, dry Furmint has the potential to become the best white wine in Hungary; Szepsy's version could pass for a top-notch white Burgundy.

» **Ráspi Soproni Kékfrankos** (Sopron) This is an increasingly popular red wine known as Blaufränkisch in neighbouring Austria; full flavour belies pale colour.

» **Gere Villányi Syrah** (Pannonia) Hungary's 'newly discovered' variety of grape is making quite a splash; this one is full-bodied, rustic, simple.

» **Szepsy Tokaji Aszú** (Tokaj) With six *puttonyos*, Hungary's sweetest 'noble rot' wine from the acknowledged leader of Tokaj vintners.

grown here, Furmint and Hárslevelű (Linden Leaf) are the driest. Some Hungarian wine experts believe Tokaj's future is in dry white wine, with sweet wines just the icing on the cake. They say that dry Furmint, with a flavour recalling apples, has the potential to become the best white wine in the country.

Vintage has always played a more important role in Tokaj than elsewhere in Hungary. Though it is said that there is only one truly excellent year each decade, the wines produced in 1972, 1988, 1999, 2000, 2003, 2006 and 2009 were all superb.

Eger

Flanked by two of the Northern Uplands' most beautiful ranges of hills and on the same latitude as Burgundy in France, Eger is the home of the celebrated Egri Bikavér (Eger Bull's Blood). By law, Hungarian vintners must spell out the blend of wine on their label; the sole exception is Bikavér, though it is usually a blend of Kékfrankos (Blaufränkisch) mixed with other reds, sometimes Kadarka. Bikavér producers to watch out for are Tibor Gál and István Toth; the latter's Bikavér easily compares with any of the 'big' reds from Villány and is said to have set the standard for Bull's Blood in Hungary. Look out for Kékfrankos and Merlot from János Bolyki.

Eger's signature grape is Pinot Noir; try the versions from Tibor Gál *fils* and Vilmos Thummerer, whose vintages have been on par with the *premiers crus* from Burgundy. The latter's Vili Papa Cuvée, a blend of Cabernet Franc, Cabernet Sauvignon and Merlot, is a monumental wine aged in new wood, with fleshy fruit flavours. You'll also find several decent whites in Eger, including Leányka (Little Girl), Olaszrizling (Italian Riesling) and Hárslevelű from Debrő.

Two excellent tomes on Hungarian wines are the rather, err, sober *The Wines of Hungary* by Alex Liddell and the much flashier and colourful *Hungary: Its Fine Wines & Winemakers* by David Copp. Both books don't just look at wines but at the whole wine-making process.

Villány

Villány, in Hungary's warm south and on the same latitude as Bordeaux in France, is especially noted for red wines: Blauer Portugieser (formerly called Kékoportó here), Cabernet Sauvignon and, in particular, Cabernet Franc and Merlot. The region has also been experimenting in Pinot Noir in recent years. Red wines here are almost always big-bodied, Bordeaux-style and high in tannins.

Among the best vintners in Villány is József Bock, whose Royal Cuvée is a special blend of Cabernet Franc, Pinot Noir and Merlot. Other ones to watch out for are Márton Mayer and Alajos Wunderlich. Wines to try from this region include Attila Gere's elegant and complex Cabernet Sauvignon or his Solus Merlot as well as Ede and Zsolt Tiffán's elegant and complex Blauer Portugieser and Cabernet Franc.

A HEAVENLY MATCH

The pairing of food with wine is as great an obsession in Hungary as it is in France. Everyone agrees that sweets like strudel go very well indeed with a glass of Tokaji Aszú, but what is less appreciated is the wonderful synergy that this wine enjoys with savoury foods like *foie gras* and cheeses such as Roquefort, Stilton and Gorgonzola. A bone-dry Olaszrizling from Badacsony is a superb accompaniment to any fish dish, but especially the *fogas* (pikeperch) indigenous to Lake Balaton, while dry Furmint goes well with river fish like *harcsa* (catfish). Villány Sauvignon Blanc is excellent with creamy and salty goat's cheese.

It would be a shame to 'waste' a big wine like a Vili Papa Cuvée from Eger on Hungarian staple dishes like *pörkölt;* instead try a Kékfrankos or Szekszárd Kadarka. Cream-based dishes stand up well to late-harvest Furmint and pork dishes are nice with new Furmint or any type of red, especially Kékfrankos. Try Hárslevelű with poultry.

VINTAGE ADVANTAGE

Generally speaking, the *évjárat* (vintage) of Hungarian wines has only become important in the past decade or so.

» **2000** Very hot summer raised alcohol levels in whites, impairing acids and lowering quality; excellent for reds in Eger, Szekszárd and Villány.

» **2001** Decent year for whites in general; very good for some top-end reds (eg from Eger and Villány).

» **2002** No great whites, but the reds were firm and have cellared well, depending on the grower.

» **2003** Very hot year, with a long, very even ripening season. Whites suffered from burned acids and preponderant alcohol; reds were full-bodied and big, with almost a Californian flair.

» **2004** Inferior year throughout, with aggressive whites and thin reds.

» **2005** The very wet summer was catastrophic for whites, but the quality of reds beat the previous year.

» **2006** Bad start with a cool summer but the long, very hot autumn proved excellent for whites and certain reds; good late-harvest sweet whites.

» **2007** Much hotter summer created more rounded acidity in whites, especially in Tokaj.

» **2008** Nice quantity of noble rot produced some decent but not outstanding sweet wines.

» **2009** Favourable weather conditions brought excellent reds and good Tokaj.

» **2010** Inferior year with incessant rain produced thin and diluted red and white wines. Avoid.

» **2011** Balanced weather, with a hot summer and sufficient precipitation produced wine drinkable after just one year.

» **2012** Too early to call but the most arid summer in memory produced tiny qualities of grapes in most regions; the potential for excellent quality wine from top growers is great.

Szekszárd

Mild winters and warm, dry summers combined with favourable loess soil help Szekszárd in Southern Transdanubia to produce some of the best affordable red wines in Hungary. They are not like the big-bodied reds of Villány, but softer and less complex, with a distinct spiciness and are easy to drink. In general they are much better value too.

The premier grape here is Kadarka, a late-ripening variety produced in limited quantities. The best Kadarka is made by Ferenc Takler and Pál Mészáros. Kadarka originated in the Balkans – the Bulgarian Gamza grape is a variety of it – and is a traditional ingredient here in making Bikavér, a wine usually associated with Eger. In fact, many wine aficionados in Hungary prefer the Szekszárd's 'Bull's Blood'; try Zoltán Heimann's version.

Ferenc Vesztergombi produces some excellent Szekszárd Merlot and Kékfrankos. Syrah from Takler is making quite a splash in Szekszárd. Tamás Dúzsi is acknowledged to be the finest producer of rosé; sample his Kékfrankos Rosé.

Badacsony

Badacsony is named after the 400m-high basalt massif that rises like a bread loaf from the Tapolca Basin along the northwestern shore of Lake Balaton. Wine has been produced here for centuries and the region's signature Olaszrizling, especially produced by Huba Szeremley and Ambrus

Bakó, is among the best dry white wine for everyday drinking that is available in Hungary. It's a straw-blonde Welschriesling high in acid that is related to the famous Rhine vintages in name only. Drink it young – in fact, the younger, the better. The most reliable Chardonnay is from Ottó Légli on Balaton's southern shore.

The best website for Hungarian wines is www.bortarsasag.hu/en/. It appraises vintners and their vintages and lists prices from the Bortársaság (Budapest Wine Society), Hungary's foremost wine society and wine retail chain.

The area's volcanic soil gives the unique, once-threatened Kéknyelű (Blue Stalk) wine its distinctive mineral taste; it is a complex tipple of very low yield that ages well; Szeremley's version is the only reliably authentic example. Another big-name producer of quality Badacsony white wines (eg Nagykúti Chardonnay, Csopaki Rizling) is Jásdi.

Somló

Somló is a single volcanic dome and the soil (basalt talus and volcanic tuff) helps to produce wine that is mineral-tasting, almost flinty. The region boasts two indigenous grape varieties: Hárslevelű and Juhfark (Sheep's Tail). Firm acids give 'spine' to this wine, and it reaches its peak in five years.

Béla Fekete is foremost among the producers of Somlói Hárslevelű and Juhfark; another excellent producer of the latter is Kreinbacher. Imre Györgykovács' Olaszrizling is a big wine with a taste vaguely reminiscent of burnt almonds. His Hárslevelű is a golden wine, with a tart, mineral finish.

Outdoor Activities

Hungarians love a day out in the country to escape their relatively cramped quarters and the pollution of the towns and cities, and nothing is more sacred than the *kirándulás* (outing), which can be a day of horse riding, cycling, canoeing or just a picnic of *gulyás* (a thick beef soup) cooked in a *bogrács* (cauldron) in the open air by a river or lake.

Thermal Baths

Many spas, such as those at Hajdúszoboszló, Sárvár, Gyula and on Margaret Island in Budapest, are serious affairs and for centuries people have come to 'take the waters' to treat their specific complaints. But most bathers go just to relax (the baths are also an excellent cure for a hangover). The most unusual in the country is the Thermal Lake (p155) in Hévíz, but the Cave Bath (p258) in Miskolctapolca, the outdoor thermal pools at Harkány (p188), the Castle Baths (p226) at Gyula and Budapest's Turkish-style baths such as the Király (p55) and the Rudas (p55) also have their own following.

There are more than 3000 thermal springs registered in Hungary.

The advent of massive waterparks for kids with giant wellness centres attached for adults has broadened the fan base of spas in recent years. The spa complex at Hajdúszoboszló (p209) is king of recreation – the largest in Hungary (40 hectares), with more than a dozen outdoor pools that have themes, slides, wave action, sunbathing decks and the like. Other noteworthy complexes include those at Győr in the west and Nyíregyháza in the east.

The **Hungarian National Tourist Office** (www.gotohungary.com) puts out a booklet called *Hungary: A Garden of Well-Being* and has listings online. Also try the **Spas in Hungary** (www.spasinhungary.com) website.

Horse Riding

There's a Hungarian saying that the Magyars were 'created by God to sit on horseback' – just look at any statue of Árpád. Most stables that we recommend offer follow-the-leader treks up to scenic spots, but the emphasis is usually on lessons. English riding and saddles are the preferred style. Book ahead.

Nonius horses, bred at Máta in the Hortobágy, have been raised in Hungary since the late 17th century.

The nonprofit **Hungarian Equestrian Tourism Association** (Magyar Lovas Turisztikai Szövetség (MLTSZ); Map p68; ☎215 3560; www.equi.hu; I Aranyhal utca 4, Budapest) classifies stables countrywide and has full information on riding facilities and tours. See too the Hungarian National Tourist Office website and its helpful *Hungary on Horseback* brochure. **Equus Tours** (☎325 6349; www.equi.hu/equus/eng; II Őzgida utca 32, Budapest) leads seven-night horseback tours (from €750) in the Hortobágy, Mátra Hill and the Nyírség region of Northeast Hungary. Prices include transfers to/from Budapest.

GETTING INTO HOT WATER

The procedure for getting out of your street clothes and into the water requires some explanation. All baths and pools have cabins or lockers. In many of the baths nowadays you are given an electronic bracelet which directs you to and then opens your locker or cabin. Some of the others still employ the old, more personal method. Find a free locker or cabin yourself (it's vision flight rules here). After getting changed in (or beside) it, seek out an attendant, who will lock it for you and hand you a numbered tag to tie on your costume or 'apron'. Please note: in order to prevent theft should you lose or misplace the tag, the number is not the same as the one on the locker, so commit the locker number to memory. Always bring a swimsuit in case it is a 'mixed' day and your own towel.

Not surprisingly, the two places where you can see horsemen do their tricks – Hortobágy (p207) and Kiskunság National Park (p216) – are also the best places for individual riding. Look, too, for good schools at Orfű, in Southern Transdanubia, and around the Lake Balaton region, including the Kál Basin, Tihany and Siófork. Riding a white Lipizzaner horse through the wooded hills of Szilvásvárad is the stuff of dreams (see p246).

Hungary's indigenous populations of great white egrets (3000 nesting pairs), great bustards (about 1300 birds), red-footed falcons (900 pairs) and white-tailed eagles (180 pairs) are among the most important in Europe. More saker falcons (200 pairs) and eastern imperial eagles (90 pairs) nest here than anywhere else on the continent.

Bird-Watching

Some 360 of Europe's 400-odd bird species have been sighted in Hungary, and a full 250 are resident or regular visitors. Spring and autumn are always great for bird-watching (May and October, especially). Huge white storks nesting atop chimneys in eastern Hungary are a striking sight from May through October.

There are dozens of excellent birding sites in Hungary, but the grassy, saline steppe, large fish ponds and marshes of the Hortobágy and Kiskunság are some of the best. Look for birds of prey, egrets, herons, storks, bee-eaters and rollers. In October up to 100,000 common cranes and geese stop on the plains as they migrate south.

The wooded hills of Bükk National Park (p246) hold woodpeckers and other woodland birds year-round; April to June sees the most activity in the reed beds of the shallow, saline Lake Fertő, and autumn brings white-fronted and bean geese. Freshwater lakes Tisza and Öregtó are prime sites for wading birds and waterfowl.

For a guided outing, go to the expert: Gerard Gorman, author of *The Birds of Hungary* and *Birding in Eastern Europe*. He owns and operates **Probirder** (www.probirder.com), an informational website and guide service out of Budapest. Fixed tours take in the woodland birds of the Bükk Hills, the sites on the Great Plain and typically last a week.

University-based **Sakertour** (☎06 30 995 7765; www.sakertour.com), out of Debrecen, offers bird-watching tours around Hortobágy and in the Zemplén Hills. Hungarian Bird Tours (p315) operates similar woodland and plains tours from a base near Eger. For both companies, three-night tours cost from €350 to €450 and seven-night tours are €770 to €950.

The **Hungarian Ornithological & Nature Conservation Society** (Magyar Madártani és Természetvédelmi Egyesület, MNE); ☎1-275 6247; www.mme.hu) works to protect the nation's feathered friends.

Find out the latest on the rare eastern imperial eagle (*Aquila heliaca*), a globally threatened Eurasian bird species, with a world population of only a few thousand breeding pairs at www.imperialeagle.hu.

Cycling

Hungary counts some 2200km of cycle tracks, with thousands more kilometres of relatively quiet country roads. Three **EuroVelo** (www.eurovelo.org) routes sponsored by the **European Cycling Federation** (www.ecf.com) cross Hungary, including the new so-called Iron Curtain Trail (Route 13). Many cities, including Budapest, Szeged, Kecskemét and Nyíregyháza, have dedicated bike lanes.

The Danube Bend is among the best areas to explore on two wheels. In the Lake Balaton region a 200km track circles the entire lake. You can also cycle 70km around Lake Tisza from Tiszafüred on the Central Plain. Bicycles are banned from motorways as well as national highways 0 to 9, and they must be fitted with lights and reflectors. On certain train lines, bicycles can be transported in special carriages for 235Ft per 50km travelled.

Local tourist offices are good sources of information about suggested routes, and some routes are posted on the Hungarian National Tourist Office website under 'Active Holidays' and 'Cycling'. **Frigoria** (www.frigoriakiado.hu) publishes a very useful 1:250,000-scale atlas and guide called *Cycling around Hungary* (3360Ft), which outlines 100 tours, with places of interest and service centres listed in several languages. It also does guides to Lake Balaton and Tisza, the Danube Bend and Budapest.

Happy Bike (Map p44; ☎06 30 560 1824; www.happybike.hu; XIII Pannónia utca 36, Budapest) organises ambitious week-long cycle tours of Lake Balaton and the Danube Bend, as does **Hooked on Cycling** (☎+44 1501 740 985; www.hookedoncycling.co.uk) from €800 for a week. **Velo-Touring** (p315), a large cycling travel agency, has a great selection of seven-night trips in all regions, from a seniors-friendly Southern Transdanubia wine tour (€835) to a bike ride between spas on the Great Plain (€750). **Ecotours** (☎06 30 645 9318; www.ecotours.hu) has cycle trips through Transdanubia (six days, €450), the Zemplén Hills (five days, €360) and around Balaton (three days, €190).

Travel the EuroVelo cycle Route 6 from the Atlantic Ocean to the Black Sea via Hungary virtually at www.eurovelo6.org.

Canoeing & Kayaking

Many of Hungary's more than 4000km of waterways are navigable by *kajak* (kayak) or *kenu* (canoe) from April to September. The most famous long-haul routes course from Rajka to Mohács (386km) on the Danube and from Tiszabecs to Szeged (570km) on the Tisza River. Rentals are available at tourist centres in places such as Tiszafüred and Tokaj.

There's a full range of lake and river-route maps (1300Ft to 2000Ft) available online from **Vízitúra** (http://vizitura.hu/vizitura-terkep). **Ecotours** (p315) leads week-long Danube River canoe and camping trips for about €500 (tent rental and food extra), as well as shorter Danube Bend and Tisza River trips. Tokaj-based **Kékcápák** (☎47-353 227; www.turak.hu; Malom utca 11, Tokaj) organises four-day trips on the smaller rivers in north and eastern Hungary, with transport to/from Tokaj included.

Hiking

The forests of the Bükk Hills are the best in Hungary for serious trekkers; much of the national park there is off-limits to cars. The Mátra and Zemplén Hills, to the east and west respectively, also offer hiking possibilities. There are also good short hikes in the forests around Visegrád, Esztergom, Badacsony, Kőszeg and Budapest.

Cartographia (p306) publishes two-dozen hiking maps (average scales 1:40,000 and 1:60,000; 1215Ft) of the hills, plains and forests of Hungary. On all hiking maps, paths appear as a red line and with a letter indicating the colour-coding of the trail. Colours are painted on trees or the letter of the colour in Hungarian appears on markers: 'K' for *kék* (blue), 'P' for *piros* (red), 'S' for *sárga* (yellow) and 'Z' for *zöld* (green).

The Danube Cycleway, by John Higginson, maps the 2875km-long riverfront route along the Danube from Donaueschingen near Basel in Germany through Slovakia and Hungary and to the river's mouth in the Black Sea.

Fishing

Hungary's lakes and sluggish rivers are home to pike, perch, carp and other coarse fish. You'll see locals fishing in waterways everywhere, but Lake Balaton and Tiszafüred are particularly popular. You'll need a national fishing licence valid for a year as well as a local one issued for the day, week or year for your area. You can usually buy local ones at tackle shops, anglers' clubs and fishing associations. The **National Federation of Hungarian Anglers** (MOHOSZ; ☎1-248 2590; www.mohosz.hu; XII Korompai utca 17, Budapest) sells national licences.

Survival Guide

Accommodation

Except during the peak summer season (ie July and most of August) in Budapest, most of Lake Balaton, the Danube Bend and the Mátra Hills, you should have no problem finding accommodation to fit your budget in Hungary. Campsites are plentiful, university and college dormitories open their doors to guests during summer and other holiday periods, the number of hostels and decent hotels is on the increase, and family-run pensions and inns are everywhere. Although they are decreasing in number, private rooms are another option in many towns, particularly near tourist centres.

Price Ranges

In this book, the price breakdown is as follows:

» **Budget** (campsites, hostels, pensions and cheap hotels): less than 9000Ft per night (less than 15,000Ft in Budapest)

» **Midrange** (pensions and hotels): 9000Ft to 16,500Ft per night (15,000Ft to 33,500Ft in Budapest)

» **Top end** (luxury hotels): more than 16,500Ft per night (more than 33,500Ft in Budapest)

Prices in this book are full price in high season (except for Budapest, where price ranges cover all seasons) and include private bathrooms, unless otherwise stated. High season tends to be June to August, while prices tend to be highest during the August Formula 1 season in Budapest and over the New Year period countrywide. Exceptions are noted in specific listings.

Tourist tax is often not quoted in the advertised price, so your bill may be higher than expected. Some top-end hotels in Budapest do not include the 27% Value Added Tax (VAT) in their rack rates; make sure you read the fine print. As a general rule, hotels and pensions include breakfast in their rates, but not always; if not included, it can cost between 800Ft and 2500Ft.

Camping

Campsites are the cheapest places to stay. One of the best resources for finding a campsite in a particular part of the country is en.camping.info; another good website is www.camping.hu. Campsites range from small, private sites with few facilities to the large, fully equipped sites that accommodate camper vans and have restaurants on their premises. On average, you'll end up paying around 800Ft per tent, plus another 1000Ft per person on top of that, but it could be significantly more on Lake Balaton in the height of summer.

Most campsites open from April or May to September or October, and some offer simple bungalows *(üdölőházak* or *faházak)* from around 2500Ft to around 18,500Ft; book ahead in summer. A Camping Card International (www.campingcardinternational.com) will sometimes get you a discount of up to 10%. Camping 'wild' is prohibited in Hungary.

Farmhouses

'Village tourism' means an introduction to the rural lifestyle by staying at a farmhouse. Most of the places are truly remote, however, and you'll usually need your own transport. For information contact Tourinform, the **National Federation of Rural & Agrotourism** (FATOSZ; Map p60; ☎1-352 9804; www.fatozs.eu; VII Király utca 93; 🚌73, 76) or the **Centre of**

TOURIST TAX

Most cities and towns levy a local tourist tax on accommodation of around 300Ft to 350Ft per night per adult. Some hotels and pensions advertise their prices exclusive of the tax, so don't be surprised when it comes time to pay that a little extra has been added on. Where possible, we've included the tax in Sleeping prices quoted.

Rural Tourism (Map p52; ☎1-321 2426; www.falutur.hu; VII Dohány utca 86; 🚊4, 6) in Budapest.

Hostels

The youth hostel *(ifjúsági szállók)* scene in Budapest has exploded in the last couple of years, leaving backpackers with a massive array of options. However, in the rest of Hungary quality hostels are a rare breed. The **Hungarian Youth Hostel Association** (MISZSZ; www.miszsz.hu) lists a number of places across the country associated with Hostelling International (HI), but not all HI-associated hostels provide discounts to HI cardholders. Useful websites for online booking include www.hostelworld.com and www.hihostels.hu.

Dormitory beds in a hostel cost between 2000Ft and 3000Ft per person and doubles 4500Ft to 6900Ft in Budapest; the prices drop considerably in the countryside. A HI card sometimes gets you a small discount. Many hostels, particularly the ones in the capital, come with a plethora of services – from laundry and tour bookings to free wi-fi, guest kitchen and more.

Hotels

Hotels, called *szállók* or *szállodák*, run the gamut from luxurious five-star palaces to the run-down old socialist-era hovels that still survive in some towns, and the star rating may not always paint an accurate picture of a hotel's facilities.

As a rule of thumb, two-star hotels usually have rooms with a private bathroom, whereas one-star places offer basic rooms with shared facilities; prices start from around 7000Ft. Three stars and up (from around 13,000Ft), and you're usually looking at TV and telephone as extras; some come with saunas and/or a pool. Four- and five-star hotels (from around 25,000Ft to 30,000Ft) tend to have a gym and spa and most hotels apart from the cheapest tend to have their own restaurant. A buffet breakfast is usually included in the price at the cheaper hotels, whereas at the top-end ones you may end up paying extra. Then there are the 'wellness hotels' which make the most of Hungary's thermal waters and come equipped with spas offering a variety of treatments – from pampering packages to medical treatments aimed at rheumatism, asthma and more.

For the big splurge, or if you're romantically inclined, check out Hungary's network of castle hotels *(kastély szállók)* or mansion hotels *(kúria szállók)*.

> **BOOK YOUR STAY ONLINE**
>
> For more accommodation reviews by Lonely Planet authors, check out http://hotels.lonelyplanet.com. You'll find independent reviews, as well as recommendations on the best places to stay. Best of all, you can book online.

Pensions & Inns

Privately run pensions (*panziók*) and inns (*fogadók*) have been springing up like mushrooms over the past decade. Some are really just little hotels in all but name, charging from an average 9000Ft for an en-suite double. They are usually modern and clean, and often have an attached restaurant, a sauna or even a pool. Others are cosy, family-run B&Bs and offer great value for money, as they tend to have all the facilities of a hotel (TV, wi-fi) in the same price range as well as the personal touch of an owner who really cares about the clientele. A useful website is www.panzio.lap.hu.

Private Rooms

Hungary's 'paying-guest service' *(fizetővendég szolgálat)* or homestay essentially means a simple room in a private house, with facilities shared with the owner/family. It's inexpensive – around 3800Ft to 7000Ft per night (6500Ft to 9000Ft in Budapest) – but the lack of facilities and the advent of *pensions* means that it's not as widespread or popular as it once was. Most Tourinform offices no longer keep a list of private rooms in the region, but it's worth inquiring about if you're short of other options. In resort areas look for houses with signs reading 'szoba kiadó' or 'Zimmer frei', advertising private rooms in Hungarian or German.

University Accommodation

From 1 July to 20 August (or later) and sometimes during the Easter holidays, Hungary's cheapest rooms are available at vacant student dormitories, known as *kollégium* or *diákszálló,* where beds in double, triple and quadruple rooms start as low as 1800Ft per person. There's no need to show a student or hostel card, and facilities are usually basic and shared.

Business Hours

With rare exceptions, opening hours *(nyitvatartás)* are posted on the front door of businesses; *nyitva* means 'open' and *zárva* 'closed'. Our reviews only include business hours if they differ from the standard hours listed here.

» **Banks** 7.45am to 5pm or 6pm Monday, to 4pm or 5pm Tuesday to Thursday, to 4pm Friday

» **Bars** 11am to midnight Sunday to Thursday and to 1am or 2am Friday and Saturday

» **Businesses** 9am or 10am to 6pm Monday to Friday, to 1pm Saturday

PRACTICALITIES

» **Newspapers** Budapest has two English-language newspapers: the *Budapest Times*, with good reviews and opinion pieces, and the biweekly *Budapest Business Journal*. There is also the long-established tabloid *Budapest Sun* (online only), featuring local news, and arts and entertainment reviews.

» **Radio** Magyar Radio has three main stations: MR1-Kossuth (107.8FM; jazz, talkback and news); MR2-Petőfi (94.8FM; popular music); and MR3-Bartók (105.3FM; classical music). Juventus Rádió (103.9FM) is a good mix of local and international pop music; Rádió C (88.8FM) addresses issues concerning the Roma people; and Budapest 92.1FM features the BBC World Service between 4pm and 6pm.

» **TV & Video** Like Australia and most of Europe, Hungary uses PAL, which is incompatible with the North American and Japanese NTCS system.

» **Weights & Measures** Hungary uses the metric system.

» **Clubs** 4pm to 2am Sunday to Thursday and to 4am on Friday and Saturday; some only open on weekends

» **Grocery stores and supermarkets** 6am or 7am to 6pm or 7pm Monday to Friday and 7am to 3pm Saturday; some also 7am to noon Sunday

» **Restaurants** 10am or 11am to 11pm or midnight; breakfast venues open by 8am

» **Shops** 9am or 10am to 6pm Monday to Friday, to 1pm Saturday

Customs Regulations

The usual allowances apply to duty-free goods purchased outside the EU: 200 cigarettes, 50 cigars or 250g of loose tobacco; 2L of wine and 1L of spirits; 50mL of perfume; 250mL of eau de toilette. You must declare the import/export of any currency exceeding the sum of €10,000.

When leaving the country, you are not supposed to take out valuable antiques without a 'museum certificate', which should be available from the place of purchase.

Discount Cards

Hungary Card

Those planning on travelling extensively in the country might consider buying a **Hungary Card** (www.hungarycard.hu; basic/standard/plus 2550/5800/9300Ft), which comes in three denominations. Depending on the denomination, benefits may include free admission to many museums nationwide; a 50% discount on a number of return train fares and some bus and boat travel, as well as other museums and attractions; up to 20% off selected accommodation; and 25% off the price of the Budapest Card. Cards are available at Tourinform offices nationwide.

Regional Cards

A number of regions in Hungary offer regional-specific discount cards. These include, among others, the Budapest Card, Balaton Card and Badacsony Card.

Student & Youth Cards

The **International Student Identity Card** (ISIC; www.isic.org; 1800Ft) gives students many discounts on certain forms of transport, and cheap admission to museums and other sights. If you're aged under 26 (30 in some countries) but not a student, you can apply for ISIC's **International Youth Travel Card** (IYTC; 1300Ft) or the **Euro<26 card** (2200Ft) issued by the **European Youth Card Association** (EYCA; www.euro26.org), both of which offer the same discounts as the student card.

Embassies & Consulates in Hungary

Selected countries with representation in Budapest (where the area code is 1) are listed here. The opening hours indicate when consular or chancellery services are available, but be sure to confirm these times before you set out as they change frequently.

Australia (☎457 9777; www.hungary.embassy.gov.au; 4th fl, XII Királyhágó tér 8-9; ⊙visas 9-11am, general enquiries 8.30am-4.30pm Mon-Fri)

Austria (☎479 7010; www.austrian-embassy.hu; VI Benczúr utca 16; ⊙8-11am Mon-Fri)

Canada (☎392 3360; www.hungary.gc.ca; II Ganz utca 12-14; ⊙8.30-11am & 2-3.30pm Mon-Thu)

Croatia (☎354 1315; vele poslanstvo.budimpesta@mvpei.hr; VI Munkácsy Mihály utca 15; ⊙9am-5pm Mon-Fri)

France (☎374 1100; www.ambafrance-hu.org; VI Lendvay utca 27; ⊙9am-12.30pm Mon-Fri)

Germany (☎488 3567; www.budapest.diplo.de; I Úri utca 64-66; ⊙9am-noon Mon-Fri)

Ireland (☎301 4960; www.embassyofireland.hu; 5th fl, Granit Tower, Bank Center, V Szabadság tér 7; ⊙9.30am-12.30pm & 2.30-4.30pm Mon-Fri)

Netherlands (☎336 6300; www.netherlandsembassy.hu; II Füge utca 5-7; ⌚10am-noon Mon-Fri)

Romania (☎384 0271; http://budapesta.mae.ro; XIV Thököly út 72; ⌚8.30am-12.30pm Mon-Fri; 🚌5, 7, 173)

Serbia (☎322 9838; ambjubp@mail.datanet.hu; VI Dózsa György út 92/a; ⌚10am-1pm Mon-Fri)

Slovakia (☎273 3500; www.mzv.sk/Budapest; XIV Gervay út 44; ⌚9am-noon Mon-Fri)

Slovenia (☎438 5600; http://budimpesta.veleposlanistvo.si; II Csatárka köz 9; ⌚9am-noon Mon-Fri)

South Africa (☎392 0999; budapest.admin@foreign.gov.za; II Gárdonyi Géza út 17; ⌚9am-12.30pm Mon-Fri)

UK (☎266 2888; http://ukinhungary.fco.gov.uk/en; V Harmincad utca 6; ⌚9.30am-12.30pm & 2.30-4.30pm Mon-Fri)

Ukraine (☎422 4122; www.mfa.gov.ua; XIV Stefánia út 77; ⌚9am-noon Mon-Wed)

USA (☎475 4400; www.usembassy.hu; V Szabadság tér 12; ⌚8.30am-4.30pm Mon-Fri)

Electricity

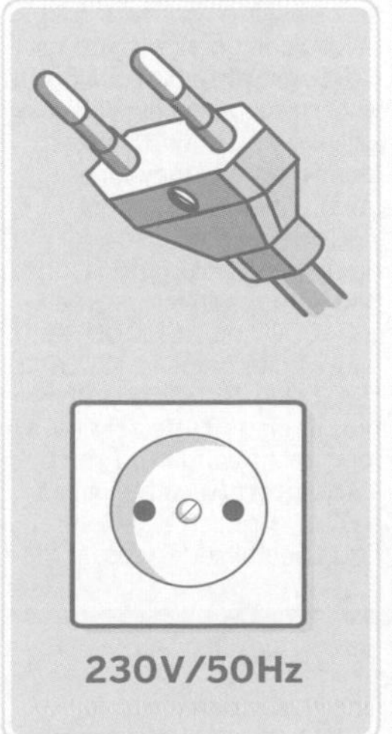

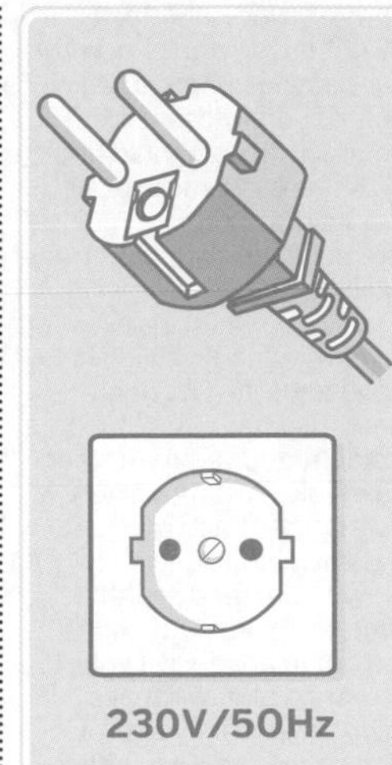

Gay & Lesbian Travellers

There have been a couple of violent far-right demonstrations recently in response to Budapest's Gay Pride parades, and Hungarian society maintains largely conservative views, but attitudes are slowly changing.

There's a good gay nightlife in Budapest (but not elsewhere in Hungary) and Budapest was also the venue for EuroGames 2012 – Europe's largest gay-friendly sporting event.

The **Háttér Gay & Lesbian Association** (☎1-329 2670; www.hatter.hu; ⌚6-11pm) has an advice and help line operating daily. *Company* (www.companymedia.hu) is a monthly magazine featuring info on events, venues and parties (available at gay venues around Budapest), while the **Labrisz Lesbian Association** (☎1-252 3566; www.labrisz.hu) has info on Hungary's lesbian scene.

Health

Recommended Vaccinations

Hungary doesn't require any vaccination of international travellers, but the World Health Organization (WHO) recommends travellers be covered for diphtheria, tetanus, measles, mumps, rubella and polio, regardless of their destination.

Availability & Cost Of Health Care

Medical care in Hungary is generally adequate and good for routine problems but not complicated conditions. Treatment at a *rendelő intézet* (public outpatient clinic) costs little, but doctors working privately will charge much more. Very roughly, a consultation in an *orvosi rendelő* (doctor's surgery) costs from 6000Ft while a home visit is around 10,000Ft to 15,000Ft.

Most large towns and all of Budapest's 23 districts have a *gyógyszertár* or *patika* (rotating 24-hour pharmacy). A sign on the door of any pharmacy will help you locate the closest one.

Emergency dental care is easy and inexpensive to obtain as many Hungarian towns feature an abundance of dentists.

Insect Bites & Stings

Tick-borne encephalitis, a serious infection of the brain, spread by *kullancs* (ticks), which burrow under the skin, has become a common problem in parts of Hungary in recent years. Vaccination is advised for campers and hikers, particularly in Transdanubia and the Northern Uplands between May and September.

Lyme disease is another tick-transmitted infection not unknown in Central and Eastern Europe. The illness usually begins with a spreading rash at the site of the tick bite and is accompanied by fever, headaches, extreme fatigue, aching joints and muscles, and mild neck stiffness. If untreated, these symptoms usually resolve themselves over several weeks, but over subsequent weeks or months disorders of the nervous system, heart and joints might develop. Protect yourself by wearing trousers and long-sleeved shirts when hiking in forests.

Mosquitoes are a real scourge around Hungary's lakes and rivers in summer, so make sure you're armed with a DEET-based insect repellent and wear long-sleeved shirts and long trousers around sundown.

Sexual Health

Emergency contraception is most effective if taken within 24 hours of unprotected sex. The **International Planned Parent Federation** (www.ippf.org) can advise about the availability of contraception in different countries.

The number of registered AIDS cases in Hungary and those who are HIV-positive is relatively low (just over 1100), though Hungarian epidemiologists estimate the actual number of those infected with HIV to be around 3000 or more. That number could multiply substantially as Budapest claims the less-than-distinctive title of 'sex industry capital of Eastern and Central Europe'. An AIDS line to contact in Budapest is the **Anonymous AIDS Association** (☎1-466 9283; www.anonimaids.hu; XI Karolina út 35/b; ⏲5-8pm Mon & Wed, 9am-noon Tue & Fri; 🚌61).

Insurance

A travel insurance policy to cover theft, loss and medical problems is a good idea. There is a wide variety of policies available, so check the small print.

If you're an EU citizen, a European Health Insurance Card (EHIC), available from health centres, covers you for most medical care. It will not cover you for non-emergencies or emergency repatriation. Citizens from other countries should find out if there is a reciprocal arrangement for free medical care between their country and Hungary.

In Hungary, foreigners are entitled to first-aid and ambulance services only when they have suffered an accident and require immediate medical attention; follow-up treatment and medicine must be paid for.

If you do need health insurance while travelling, find out in advance if your insurance plan will make payments directly to providers or reimburse you later for overseas health expenditures. The former option is generally preferable, as it doesn't require you to pay out of pocket in Hungary, but if you have to claim later, make sure you keep all documentation.

If you need to make a claim regarding a loss or theft of possessions, you will need to produce a police report and proof of value of items lost or stolen.

Internet Access

Hungary is a wired country. Many libraries in Hungary have free (or almost free) terminals, and most towns have at least one internet cafe; Budapest has a few such places (between 200Ft and 400Ft per hour), though they're decreasing in number as free wi-fi hotspots become easier to find.

Almost all hostels and hotels offer internet and/or wi-fi, mostly free but sometimes for a small surcharge. Free wi-fi is also available at major airports, and many restaurants and cafes.

Legal Matters

Those violating Hungarian laws, even unknowingly, may be expelled, arrested and/or imprisoned. Penalties for possession, use or trafficking in illegal drugs in Hungary are severe, and convicted offenders can expect long jail sentences and heavy fines.

There is a 100% ban on alcohol when driving and it is taken very seriously. Police conduct routine roadside checks with breathalysers and if you are found to have even 0.005% of alcohol in your blood, you could be fined up to 100,000Ft on the spot; police have been known to fine for less than that, so it's best not to drink at all. In the event of an accident, the drinking party is automatically regarded as guilty.

Maps

Hungary's largest map-making company, **Cartographia** (www.cartographia.hu), publishes a useful 1:450,000-scale sheet map of the country, as well as maps of all the main cities and towns, widely available in kiosks, and its 1:250,000 *Magyarország autó-atlasza* (Road Atlas of Hungary) is indispensable if you plan to do a lot of travelling in the countryside by car. Bookshops in Hungary generally stock a wide variety of maps, or you can go directly to the **Cartographia** (☎1-312 6001; www.cartographia.hu; VI Bajcsy-Zsilinszky út 37; ⏲10am-6pm Mon-Fri; Ⓜ M3 Arany János utca) outlet in Budapest.

Cartographia also produces national, regional and hiking maps (average scales 1:40,000 and 1:60,000), as well as city plans (1:11,000 to 1:20,000). Smaller companies such as **Topográf** (www.topograf.hu) and **Magyar Térképház** (www.terkephaz.hu) also publish excellent city and specialised maps.

Money

The Hungarian currency is the forint (Ft) and today

TIPPING

Hungary is a very tip-conscious society, and virtually everyone routinely tips waiters, hairdressers, hotel porters, tour guides, bar staff and taxi drivers. If you are less than impressed with the service, leave nothing at all.

A 10% to 15% tip is the norm in restaurants, while in bars and taxis it's common to round up the fare. To tip in restaurants, don't leave the money on the table, but tell the waiter how much you're paying in total. If the bill is, say, 2700Ft, you're paying with a 5000Ft note and you think the waiter deserves a gratuity of around 10%, first ask if service is included (some restaurants add it to the bill automatically). If it isn't, say you're paying 3000Ft or that you want 2000Ft back.

there are coins of 5Ft, 10Ft, 20Ft, 50Ft, 100Ft and 200Ft. Notes come in seven denominations: 500Ft, 1000Ft, 2000Ft, 5000Ft, 10,000Ft and 20,000Ft. Prices in shops and restaurants are uniformly quoted in forint, but many hotels and guest houses and even MÁV, the national rail company, give rates for their international routes in euros. In such cases, we have followed suit; you can usually pay in either euros or forint. It's always prudent to carry a little foreign cash, though, preferably euros or US dollars, in case you can't find an ATM nearby.

ATMs

All major banks have ATMs and most ATMs accept cards issued outside Hungary. ATMs are plentiful, particularly in Budapest and larger towns. Be warned that many of the ATMs at branches of Országos Takarékpenztár (OTP), the national savings bank, give out 20,000Ft notes, which can be difficult to break.

Credit Cards & Travelex Cash Passport

Credit cards, especially Visa, MasterCard and American Express, are widely accepted in Hungary, and you'll be able to use them at many restaurants, shops, hotels, car-rental firms, travel agencies and petrol stations. They are not usually accepted at museums, supermarkets, or train and bus stations. Many banks give cash advances on major credit cards but charge both a fee and interest.

A good alternative to credit cards (or travellers cheques) is the **Travelex Cash Passport** (www.travelex.com) – a prepaid travel card that you load up with funds before departure and then withdraw funds in local currency as you go along, throwing it away when you're done.

Moneychangers

For the best rates, change money at banks rather than moneychangers.

Taxes & Refunds

ÁFA, a value-added tax of up to 27% (the highest in Europe), covers the purchase of all new goods in Hungary. It's usually included in the price but not always. Visitors are not exempt, but non-EU residents can claim refunds for total purchases of at least 52,001Ft on one receipt, as long as they take the goods out of the country (and the EU) within 90 days. The ÁFA receipts (available from where you made the purchases) should be stamped by customs at the border, and the claim has to be made within 183 days of exporting the goods. You can then collect your refund (minus commission) from the VAT desk in the departure halls of Terminals 2A and 2B at Ferenc Liszt International Airport in Budapest, and at branches of the Ibusz chain of travel agencies at some nine border crossings.

Travellers Cheques

You can change travellers cheques – American Express, Visa and Thomas Cook MasterCard are the most recognisable brands – at most banks and some post offices. OTP offers among the best rates. As they are becoming increasingly rare, many exchange offices change them at a poor rate. Shops never accept travellers cheques.

Post

The **Hungarian Postal Service** (Magyar Posta; www.posta.hu) has improved in recent years, but at the post offices service can be slow, so buy your *bélyeg* (stamps) at newsagents to beat the crowds.

Prices for postcards or letters sent within Hungary cost 80/105Ft, while postcards or letters within/outside Europe cost 235/270Ft. Look for the window marked with the symbol of an envelope.

To send a parcel, look for the sign 'Csomagfeladás' or 'Csomagfelvétel', but it's best not to send anything of value by regular post. If absolutely necessary, opt for registered post and ask for an *ajánlott levél* form to fill in; you get to keep the stamped form while the package is marked with an ID number.

Hungarian addresses start with the name of the recipient, followed on the next line by the postal code and city or town, and then the street name and number. The postal code consists of four digits. The first one indicates the city, town or region (eg '1' is Budapest, '6' is Szeged), the second and third are the district, and the last is the neighbourhood.

Public Holidays

Hungary celebrates 10 *ünnep* (public holidays) each year.

New Year's Day 1 January

1848 Revolution/ National Day 15 March

Easter Monday March/April

International Labour Day 1 May

Whit Monday May/June

St Stephen's/Constitution Day 20 August

1956 Remembrance Day/ Republic Day 23 October

All Saints' Day 1 November

Christmas holidays 25 & 26 December

Telephone

You can make domestic and international calls from public telephones; they take either coins or phonecards. Phonecards issued by **NeoPhone** (www.neophone.hu) come in values of 1000Ft, 2000Ft and 5000Ft and are available from post offices and newsstands. Other discount phonecards such as **No Limits** (www.nolimits.hu) also offer good rates for international calls. Public phones are rapidly becoming obsolete with the advent of cheap mobile phone calls and Skype.

EMERGENCY NUMBERS

Ambulance ☎104

Crime hotline ☎438 8080

Emergency ☎112

Fire ☎105

International inquiries ☎199

Police ☎107

Local & International Calls

All localities in Hungary have a two-digit telephone area code, except for Budapest, which has just a '1'. Local codes appear under the heading name of each city and town in this book.

To make a local call, pick up the receiver and listen for the continuous dial tone, then dial the phone number (seven digits in Budapest, six elsewhere). For an intercity landline call within Hungary and whenever ringing a mobile telephone, dial 06 and wait for the second, more melodious, tone. Then dial the area code and phone number. Cheaper or toll-free numbers start with 06 40 and 06 80, respectively.

The procedure for making an international call is the same, except that you dial 00, then the country code, the area code and the number. The country code for Hungary is 36.

Mobile Phones

The three main mobile phone providers are: **Telenor** (☎06 20; www.telenor.hu), **T-Mobile** (www.t-mobile.hu) and **Vodafone** (☎06 70; www.vodafone.hu). It is now relatively inexpensive to use a mobile from another EU country in Hungary, as call and SMS rates are now standardised across the board. You can also purchase a rechargeable or prepaid SIM card from any of the three providers, but check first with your service provider, as it may be possible to get an even cheaper rate with your own home network.

Time

Hungary lies in the Central European time zone and is one hour ahead of GMT. Clocks are advanced by one hour on the last Sunday in March and set back on the last Sunday in October.

Hungarians tell the time by making reference to the next hour – not the previous one. Thus 7.30 is *fél nyolc óra* ('half eight'; sometimes written as f8). Also, the 24-hour system is often used in giving the times of movies, concerts and so on. So a film at 7.30pm could appear on a listing as 'f8', 'f20', '½8' or '½20'. A quarter to the hour has a ¾ symbol in front (thus '¾8' means 7.45), while a quarter past is ¼ of the next hour (eg '¼9' means 8.15).

Tourist Information

The Hungarian National Tourist Office has a chain of more than 140 tourist information bureaus called **Tourinform** (☎from abroad 36 1 438 80 80, within Hungary 800 36 000 000; www.tourinform.hu) across the country. They are usually the best places to ask general questions and pick up brochures – and can sometimes provide more comprehensive assistance. Tourist offices in Budapest are run by **Budapest Tourism** (www.budapestinfo.hu).

Travelling with Children

Travelling with children in Hungary poses few problems: the little 'uns receive discounts on public transport and entry to museums and attractions, and the general public attitude to kids is one of acceptance. All car-rental firms in Hungary have children's safety seats for hire and picking up basic supplies is never a problem.

Museums catering specifically to children are few and far between, but many thermal parks across the country have slides, wave pools and designated kiddie pools, and shallow Lake Balaton is perfect for a family holiday.

For general information, Lonely Planet's *Travel with Children* is a good source.

Travellers with Disabilities

Hungary has made great strides in recent years in making public areas and facilities more accessible to the disabled. Wheelchair ramps, toilets fitted for the disabled and inward opening doors, though not as common as they are in Western Europe, do exist, and audible traffic signals for the blind are becoming commonplace in the cities.

For more information, contact the **Hungarian Federation of Disabled Persons' Associations** (MEOSZ; ☎1-250 9013; www.meoszinfo.hu; III San Marco utca 76).

SCAM ALERT!

» In Budapest, gentlemen should beware of being chatted up by so-called *konzumlányok*, attractive 'consume girls' in collusion with rip-off bars and clubs, who will see you relieved of a serious chunk of money.

» Waiters may try to bring you an unordered dish, make a 'mistake' when tallying the bill, or add service to the bill and then expect an additional tip. If you think there's a discrepancy, ask for the menu and check the bill carefully.

» Taxi drivers, particularly in Budapest, are known for overcharging and taking advantage of passengers unfamiliar with local currency – switching large denomination notes for smaller ones and demanding extra payment. Only ever take taxis from reputable companies and make sure you know exactly how much cash you're handing over. Budapest residents don't tent to grab taxis off the street; it's cheaper to call a taxi company. The reputable ones include **Buda** (☎1-233 3333), **City** (☎1-211 1111), **Fő** (☎1-222 2222), **Rádió** (☎1-377 7777) and **Tele** (☎51-355 5555).

» Some travellers in Budapest have complained of men in fake policemen's uniforms who demand to see tourists' passports and money, ostensibly to check for fraudulent notes. They then either run away with the money or switch large denomination notes for small ones.

Visas

Citizens of virtually all European countries, as well as Australia, Canada, Israel, Japan, New Zealand and the USA, do not require visas to visit Hungary for stays of up to 90 days. Check current visa requirements on the website of the **Hungarian Foreign Ministry** (www.mfa.gov.hu).

Visas are issued at Hungarian consulates or embassies, Ferenc Liszt International Airport and the International Ferry Pier in Budapest. They are issued at border crossings only in exceptional circumstances.

Short-stay visas (entry for up to 90 days) and transit visas (five days) both cost €60. Since Hungary is a member of the Schengen Agreement, if you have a visa valid for entry to any of the other Schengen members, it's also valid in Hungary.

Women Travellers

Women should not encounter any particular problems while travelling in Hungary besides some mild local machismo. If you do need assistance and/or information, ring the **Women's Line** (Nővonal; ☎06 80 505 101; ⌚6-10pm, closed Wed).

Transport

GETTING THERE & AWAY

Entering Hungary

Border formalities with Hungary's four EU neighbours – Austria, Romania, Slovenia and Slovakia – are virtually nonexistent. However, Hungary has to implement the strict Schengen border rules, so expect a somewhat closer inspection of your documents when travelling to/from Croatia, Ukraine and Serbia.

Passport

Everyone needs a valid passport, or for many citizens of the EU a national identification card, to enter Hungary.

Air

Airports & Airlines

International flights land at Terminals 2A and 2B of **Ferenc Liszt International Airport** (☎296 7000; www.bud.hu) on the outskirts of Budapest. Budget carriers use Terminal 2B. **Balaton Airport** (SOB; ☎83-554 060; www.flybalaton.com) receives Lufthansa flights from Dusseldorf and Frankfurt, among other German destinations, and is located 15km southwest of Keszthely near Lake Balaton.

Malév Hungarian Airlines, the national carrier, was liquidated due to bankruptcy in 2012.

International Airlines

International airlines that serve Hungary include the following:

Aeroflot (SU; ☎1-318 5955; www.aeroflot.com; hub Moscow)

Air Berlin (AB; ☎06 80 017 110; www.airberlin.com; hub Cologne)

Air France (AF; ☎1-483 8800; www.airfrance.com; hub Paris)

Alitalia (AZ; ☎1-483 2170; www.alitalia.it; hub Rome)

Austrian Airlines (OS; ☎1-296 0660; www.aua.com; hub Vienna)

British Airways (BA; ☎1-777 4747; www.ba.com; hub London)

CSA Czech Airlines (OK; ☎1-318 3045; www.csa.cz; hub Prague)

EasyJet (U2; www.easyjet.com; hub London)

EgyptAir (MS; www.egyptair.com; hub Cairo)

El Al (LY; ☎1-266 2970; www.elal.co.il; hub Tel Aviv)

Finnair (AY; ☎1-296 5486; www.finnair.com; hub Helsinki)

German Wings (4U; ☎1-526 7005; www.germanwings.com; hub Cologne)

LOT Polish Airlines (LO; ☎1-266 4771; www.lot.com; hub Warsaw)

Lufthansa (LH; ☎1-411 9900; www.lufthansa.com; hub Frankfurt)

Ryanair (FR; www.ryanair.com; hub London)

SAS (SK; www.flysas.com; hub Copenhagen)

Tarom Romanian Airlines (RO; www.tarom.ro; hub Bucharest)

Turkish Airlines (TK; ☎1-266 4291; www.thy.com; hub Istanbul)

Wizz Air (W6; ☎06 90 181 181; www.wizzair.com; hub Katowice, Poland)

Tickets

Competition in the European skies has resulted in cheap fares offered by both no-frills airlines and full-service carriers. Discounted web fares are often the best deals for short-haul hops, but as a general rule travel agencies still offer the best options for long-haul flights.

AUSTRALIA & NEW ZEALAND

There are no direct flights from either Australia or New Zealand to Hungary; most fly via London or Frankfurt, with a small minority stopping in at other European capitals.

Consider purchasing a round-the-world ticket or multistop ticket offered by Qantas and British Airways; travel agents will be able to inform you of the most up-to-date prices.

CONTINENTAL EUROPE

There are numerous flights to Budapest from a plethora of European cities, including almost all of the capitals on the continent. Many national airlines duplicate what used to be Malév's coverage, as do the likes of what Hungarians call the *fapados* (wooden-bench) airlines – the super-discount carriers such as Air Berlin, EasyJet, Ryanair and Wizz Air.

MIDDLE EAST

El Al and Wizz Air fly to/from Tel Aviv. Flights from Beirut and Damascus had been suspended at the time of research.

UK & IRELAND

Ryanair connects Budapest with Bristol, Birmingham, Manchester and London Stansted, while EasyJet links the Hungarian capital with London Luton and London Gatwick. Wizz Air also flies between London Luton and Budapest.

USA & CANADA

There are no direct flights to Hungary from the USA or Canada. There are connections via London and several other European capitals.

Land

Hungary is well connected with all seven of its neighbours by road, rail and even ferry, though most transport begins or ends its journey in Budapest.

Timetables for both domestic and international trains and buses use the 24-hour system. Also, Hungarian names are sometimes used for cities and towns in neighbouring countries on bus and train schedules.

Bus

Crossing the continent by bus is cheapest. Most international buses are run by **Eurolines** (www.eurolines.com) and link with its Hungarian associate, **Volánbusz** (☎382 0888; www.volanbusz.hu).

The **Eurolines Pass** (www.eurolines.com/en/eurolines-pass/) allows unlimited travel between 51 European cities, including Budapest. Sample prices for high season include €350/295 over/under 26 years old for 15 days and €460/380 for 30 days.

Car & Motorcycle

Drivers and motorbike riders will need the vehicle's registration papers, liability insurance and an International Driving Permit in addition to their domestic licence.

Train

Hungary is well connected to neighbouring countries, with international services arriving and departing at least once a day.

Magyar Államvasutak (MÁV; ☎06 40 494 949, 1-371 9449; http://elvira.mav-start.hu/), which translates as Hungarian State Railways, links up with the European rail network in all directions. Its trains run as far as London (via Munich and Paris), Stockholm (via Hamburg and Copenhagen), Moscow, Rome and Istanbul (via Belgrade). Almost all international trains bound for Hungary arrive and depart from Budapest's Keleti station; Deli handles trains to Croatia, Slovenia, Bosnia and Herzegovina and Serbia.

The **Thomas Cook European Timetable** (www.europeanrailtimetable.co.uk), updated monthly and available from Thomas Cook outlets, is the train-lover's bible, with a complete listing of train schedules, supplements and reservations information. **The Man in Seat 61** (www.seat61.com) can also help you plan your train journey across Europe.

CLASSES, COSTS & RESERVATIONS

Seat reservations for international destinations usually cost €3 one way. Tickets are normally valid for 60 days from purchase and stopovers are permitted. On long hauls, sleepers are almost always available in both 1st and 2nd class, and couchettes are available in 2nd class. Not all express trains have dining or even buffet cars; make sure you bring along snacks and drinks as vendors can be few and far between. International journeys require seat reservations.

All prices quoted are full-price, one-way, 2nd-class fares; 1st-class seats are around 50% more expensive than 2nd class.

Substantial discounts to a number of European capitals are available on tickets purchased more than three days in advance. Due to limited seating, book early to take advantage of the savings.

TRAIN PASSES

Inter Rail (www.interrailnet.com) Global Pass covers 30 European countries and can be purchased by European nationals or residents of at least six months. Sample costs for 1st/2nd class travel:

CLIMATE CHANGE & TRAVEL

Every form of transport that relies on carbon-based fuel generates CO_2, the main cause of human-induced climate change. Modern travel is dependent on aeroplanes, which might use less fuel per kilometre per person than most cars but travel much greater distances. The altitude at which aircraft emit gases (including CO_2) and particles also contributes to their climate change impact. Many websites offer 'carbon calculators' that allow people to estimate the carbon emissions generated by their journey and, for those who wish to do so, to offset the impact of the greenhouse gases emitted with contributions to portfolios of climate-friendly initiatives throughout the world. Lonely Planet offsets the carbon footprint of all staff and author travel.

TRAIN CONNECTIONS

Eastern Europe

Budapest's Keleti station has services to the following destinations in Romania, Croatia, Slovakia, the Czech Republic, Ukraine and Russia. Note that the Moscow service goes via Kyiv (26 hours) and Lviv (15 hours).

DESTINATION	PRICE	TIME	DEPARTURES
Belgrade via Subotica	€37	8	3 daily
Cluj-Napoca	€35	7	3 daily
Košice via Miskolc	€16	3½	2 daily
Ljubljana (change at Zagreb)	€39	9	daily
Moscow	€154	37¼	daily
Prague via Bratislava	€45	7	up to 5 daily
Sofia (change at Belgrade)	€89	18-31	daily
Timisoara (change in Arad)	€25	4¾	daily
Warsaw	€72	10-12	daily
Zagreb	€42	6¼	1-2 daily

Western Europe

Budapest has connections to the following destinations:

» Berlin (€95, 12 to 13 hours, three daily) via Dresden, Prague and Bratislava

» Frankfurt (€110, 11 to 15 hours, three daily); change in Dresden, Munich or Vienna

» Munich (€95, eight to 10 hours, four daily) via Salzburg (€95, six hours; up to eight daily)

» Venice (€70, 12 to 21 hours, daily); change in Kelenföld or Vienna

» Vienna (€32, three hours, eight daily) via Hegyeshalom and Győr

» Zürich (€94, 12 to 15 hours, two daily); change in Kelenföld

» five days within a 10-day period: €409/267

» 10 days within a 22-day period: €583/381

» 22 continuous days: €656/494

Inter Rail Global Pass for travellers under 26 comes with a substantial discount.

A **Eurail** (www.eurail.com) pass gives you unlimited travel in 21 European countries, including Hungary, but you have to travel intensively to make it worth your while. Passes start from $478 for 15 days for travellers under 26 (2nd class) and from $734 for over 26 (1st class only). Non-European residents may consider a combination ticket allowing you to travel over a fixed period for a set price. These include the Hungary N' Slovenia/Croatia pass, Austria N' Hungary pass and Romania N' Hungary pass, offering five/10 days of travel on those countries' rail networks for around US$214/364 for adults (no discounts for youths); children aged between four and 11 travel for half price.

River

A hydrofoil service on the Danube River between Budapest and Vienna (5½ to 6½ hours) operates daily from late April to early October. Adult one-way/return fares for Vienna are €99/125.

For information and tickets, contact **Mahart PassNave** (Map p68; ☎484 4013; www.mahartpassnave.hu; Landing Stage pier 3, V Belgrád Rakpart; ⊙10am-10pm May-Sep, 11am-8pm Oct-Dec & Apr) in Budapest and **Mahart PassNave Wien** (☎01 72 92 162, 01 72 92 161; Handelskai 265) in Vienna.

GETTING AROUND

Hungary's domestic transport system is efficient, comprehensive and inexpensive. Towns are covered by a system of frequent buses, trams and trolleybuses. The majority of Hungary's towns and cities are easily negotiated on foot. There are no scheduled flights within Hungary; it's small enough to get everywhere by train or bus within the span of a day.

Menetrend (www.menetrendek.hu) has links to all the timetables – bus, train, public transport and boat. EU members over the age of 65 travel for free on all public transport.

Bicycle

Hungary offers endless opportunities for cyclists: challenging slopes in the north, much gentler terrain in Transdanubia, and flat though windy (and hot in summer) cycling on the Great Plain. The cycle-path network is being extended all the time.

Outside the tourist hotspots and summer high season, hiring a bike can be difficult. Your best bets are campgrounds, resort hotels and – very occasionally – bicycle repair shops.

Bicycles are banned from all motorways and national highways with a single digit, and bikes must be equipped with lights and reflectors. Bicycles can be taken on many trains (look for the bicycle symbol on the timetables) at

25% additional cost, and can also be taken on boats, but not on buses.

Boat

From April to late October the Budapest-based **Mahart PassNave** (Map p68; ☎484 4013; www.mahartpassnave.hu; Landing Stage pier 3, V Belgrád Rakpart; ⊙10am-10pm May-Sep, 11am-8pm Oct-Dec & Apr) runs excursion boats on the Danube from Budapest to Szentendre, Vác, Visegrád and Esztergom; and hydrofoils from Budapest to Visegrád, Nagymaros, Esztergom and Komárom between May and September.

From spring to autumn, 24 ports around Lake Balaton are well served by passenger ferries of the **Balaton Shipping Company** (www.balatonihajozas.hu).

Bus

Hungary's **Volánbusz** (☎382 0888; www.volanbusz.hu) network comprehensively covers the whole country. In Southern Transdanubia and many parts of the Great Plain, they are far quicker and more direct than trains, as is the case for short trips around the Danube Bend or Lake Balaton areas.

In most cities and large towns there is at least one direct bus a day to fairly far-flung areas of the country.

Budapest has separate long-distance bus stations *(távolságiautóbusz pályaudvar)* and local stations *(helyiautóbusz pályaudvar)*. Outside the capital the stations are often found side by side or in the same building. Arrive early to confirm the correct departure bay or *kocsiállás* (stand), and check the individual schedule posted at the stop itself; the times shown can be different from those shown on the *tábla* (main board).

Some larger bus stations have left-luggage rooms, but they generally close early (around 6pm). Check your bag at the train station, which is almost always nearby; the left-luggage offices there keep much longer hours.

Tickets are purchased directly from the driver. There are sometimes queues for intercity buses, so arrive around 30 minutes before departure time. Buses are reasonably comfortable and have adequate leg room. On long journeys there are rest stops every two or three hours.

BUS CONNECTIONS

Western Europe

From Népliget station there are buses to many cities across Western Europe. Prices fluctuate depending on day and time of departure.

DESTINATION	PRICE	TIME	DEPARTURES
Amsterdam	21,400Ft	22¼	6 weekly
Athens	24,000Ft	24	up to 3 weekly
Berlin	18,900Ft	4¾	4 weekly
Düsseldorf	20,900Ft	18	4-5 weekly
Frankfurt	16,900Ft	14¼	4 weekly
London via Brussels & Lille	31,900Ft	27¼	4 weekly
Paris	24,400Ft	21¾	Mon, Wed & Fri
Rotterdam via Vienna	21,900Ft	23½	5-6 weekly
Venice	18,400Ft	10¼	Wed, Fri & Sun
Vienna	5900Ft	3	up to 5 daily
Zürich	26,900Ft	14½	Wed & Sat

Eastern Europe

From Budapest's Népliget station there are good bus connections with destinations in Croatia, Romania, the Czech Republic, Poland and Ukraine, among others. Services to Croatia operate between mid-June and mid-September. Prices fluctuate depending on day and time of departure.

Sample destinations and prices include the following.

DESTINATION	PRICE	TIME	DEPARTURES
Bratislava	3400Ft	3	daily
Dubrovnik	9900Ft	14	Fri
Lviv	12,900Ft	11	Mon & Fri
Porec	10,900Ft	11¼	Sat
Prague	6900Ft	7¼	daily
Pula	10,900Ft	9½	Sat
Rijeka	9900Ft	8	Sat
Kraków	3900Ft	7	Wed & Sat
Kyiv	14,900Ft	19½	Mon & Fri
Sofia	12,500Ft	13½	daily
Split	13,900Ft	12¾	Fri
Subotica (Szabadka)	3900Ft	4½	daily

Bus Costs

Bus ticket costs are calculated according to distance:

FARE	DISTANCE
250Ft	up to 10km
370Ft	15-20km
1300Ft	60-70km
2200Ft	100-120km
3690Ft	200-220km
4660Ft	280-300km

Car & Motorcycle

Automobile Associations

In the event of a breakdown, the so-called **Yellow Angels** (Sárga Angyal; ☎nationwide 188; ⏲24hr) of the **Hungarian Automobile Club** (Magyar Autóklub; ☎1-345 1800; www.autoklub.hu; IV Berda József utca 15, Budapest; Ⓜ M3 Újpest Városkapu) are the people to call, as they do basic car repairs free of charge if you belong to an affiliated organisation such as AAA in the USA, or AA in the UK.

For 24-hour information on traffic and public road conditions around Hungary, contact **Útinform** (☎1-336 2400; www.kozut.hu). In the capital, ring **Főinform** (☎1-317 1173; ⏲7am-7pm).

Hire

You must be at least 21 years old and have had your license for a year to rent a car. Drivers under 25 sometimes have to pay a surcharge. All of the big international firms, such as **Avis** (☎318 4240; www.avis.hu; V Arany János utca 26-28; ⏲7am-6pm Mon-Sat, 8am-6pm Sun), **Europcar** (☎505 4400; www.europcar.hu; V Erzsébet tér 7-8; ⏲8am-6pm Mon & Fri, to 4.30pm Tue-Thu, to noon Sat) and **Budget** (☎214 0420; www.budget.hu; Hotel Mercure Buda, VII Krisztina körút 41-43; ⏲8am-8pm Mon-Fri, to 6pm Sat & Sun) have offices in Budapest, and there are scores of local companies throughout the country.

Insurance

Third-party liability insurance is compulsory in Hungary. If your car is registered in the EU, it is assumed you have it. Other motorists must show a Green Card or buy insurance at the border. All accidents should be reported to the **police** (☎107) immediately.

Any claim on insurance policies bought in Hungary can be made to **Allianz Hungária** (☎06 40 421 421; www.allianz.hu) in Budapest. It is one of the largest insurance companies in Hungary and deals with foreigners all the time.

Road Conditions

Roads in Hungary are generally good – in some cases excellent nowadays – and there are several basic types.

There are now nine motorways and seven express roads, preceded by an 'M'. These include the M0 half-ring road around Budapest, the M1 that leads as far as the border with Austria via Győr before turning into A4 and continuing as far as Vienna, and the M7 that leads to Croatia via the southern shore of Lake Balaton, turning into M70 by the Croatian border. They also run along the eastern bank of the Danube Bend (M2), past Vác en route to Slovakia as far as Nyiregyhaza (M3), with the M35 branch reaching as far as Debrecen, and en route to Szeged and Serbia via Kecskemét as far as Kiskunfélegyháza (M5). National highways (dual carriageways) are designated by a single digit without a prefix and fan out mostly from Budapest. Secondary/tertiary roads have two/three digits.

Driving in Hungary – particularly in Budapest – can be quite trying. Overtaking on blind curves, tailgating, making turns from the outside lane, running stop signs and lights, and jumping lanes in roundabouts are everyday occurrences.

Many cities and towns have a confusing system of one-way streets, pedestrian zones and bicycle lanes. Parking is an issue in Budapest. You are required to 'pay and display' when parking your vehicle – parking disks, coupons or stickers are available at newsstands, petrol stations and, increasingly, automated ticket machines. In smaller towns and cities

DECIPHERING BUS TIMETABLES

Posted bus timetables can be horribly confusing for non-Hungarians. Here's a guide to some essential words and symbols:

- *Indulás*: departures
- *Érkezés*: arrivals
- Numbers one to seven in a circle refer to the days of the week, beginning with Monday
- **D** *naponta*: daily except Saturday
- **M** *munkanapokon*: working days
- **O** *szabadnapokon*: Saturday
- **+** *munkaszüneti napokon*: Sunday and holidays
- **I** *iskolai napján:* school days
- *hétköznap:* weekdays
- *szabad és munkaszünetes napokon:* Saturday, Sunday and holidays
- *szabadnap kivételével naponta:* daily except Saturday
- *munkaszünetes nap kivételével naponta:* daily except holidays

ROAD RULES

- You must drive on the right-hand side of the road.
- Speed limits for cars and motorbikes are consistent throughout the country and strictly enforced: 50km/h in built-up areas; 90km/h on secondary and tertiary roads; 110km/h on most highways and dual carriageways; and 130km/h on motorways. Exceeding the limit will earn you an on-the-spot fine of up to 10,000Ft.
- Seat belts are compulsory for the driver and all passengers.
- Using a hand-held mobile phone while driving is prohibited.
- Headlights must be on at all times outside built-up areas. Motorcyclists must illuminate headlights too, but at all times and everywhere. Helmets are compulsory.
- There is a 100% ban on alcohol when you are driving, and this rule is strictly enforced.
- Hungary's motorways may only be accessed with a motorway pass or *matrica* (vignette), to be purchased beforehand from petrol stations and post offices. See www.autopalya.hu for more details; prices start from 2975Ft for a week and 4780Ft for a month.

a warden collects 200Ft or so for each hour you plan to park. In Budapest, parking on the street costs between around 200Ft and 440Ft per hour, depending on the neighbourhood.

Hitching

Hitching is never entirely safe in any country and we don't recommend it. Travellers who decide to hitch are taking a small but potentially serious risk. Hitchhiking is legal everywhere in Hungary except on motorways. Though it isn't as popular as it once was (and can be very difficult), the road to Lake Balaton is always jammed with hitchhikers in the holiday season.

Local Transport

Urban transport is well developed in Hungary, with efficient bus (and, in many cities and towns, trolleybus) services. It usually runs from about 5.30am to 9pm in the provinces and a little longer in the capital.

You'll probably make extensive use of public transport in Budapest, but little (if any) in provincial towns and cities. Most places are manageable on foot, and bus services are not all that frequent. Generally, city buses meet incoming long-distance trains; hop onto anything waiting outside when you arrive and you'll get close to the city centre.

You must purchase transport tickets (around 280Ft to 320Ft) at newsstands or ticket windows beforehand and validate them once aboard. Travelling without a ticket (or 'riding black') is an offence; you'll be put off and fined on the spot.

Boat

Budapest and Lake Balaton have ferry systems.

Bus

Buses are the mainstay of public transport in most villages, towns and cities in Hungary. They are a cheap and efficient way of getting to further-flung places.

Metro

Budapest is the only city in Hungary with a metro.

Taxi

Taxis are plentiful on the streets of most Hungarian cities. Unscrupulous drivers are common, particularly in the capital, so it's best to call a reputable taxi company rather than hail a taxi in the street. If you do hail a taxi, make sure it has the company name on the side and that the meter is switched on. Make sure you know exactly how much cash you're handing over, as switching large denomination notes for small ones and then demanding extra payment is a common scam. Flag fall varies, but a fare between 6am and 10pm is from 250Ft (in Budapest from 300Ft), with the charge per kilometre about the same.

Tram

Hungary's larger cities – Budapest, Szeged, Miskolc and Debrecen – have the added advantage of a tram system. The capital also has a suburban railway known as the HÉV.

Tours

A number of travel agencies offer excursions and special-interest guided tours (horse riding, cycling, bird-watching, Jewish culture etc) to every corner of Hungary. These include the following.

Cityrama (Map p60; ☎1-302 4382; www.cityrama.hu; V Báthory utca 22, Budapest; 🚌15, 115) Sightseeing tours – from Jewish heritage in Budapest to horse shows in Puzsta and Danube Bend Tour.

Ecotours (☎06 30 645 9318; www.ecotours.hu) Specialist in bird-watching, nature and wildlife photography tours.

Hungarian Bird Tours (☎44 7774 574 204; www.hungarianbirdtours.com) Birding tours run by a retired Brit.

Velo-Touring (☎1-319 0571; www.velo-touring.hu; XI Előpatak utca 1, Budapest) Cycling tours all over Hungary.

Vidam Delfin (☎42-443 519; www.vidamdelfin.hu; Szent Miklós tér 7, Nyíregyháza) Canoeing, kayaking and cycling tours.

Vizitura (www.vizitura.hu) 'Water tours' – from canoeing and kayaking trips to thermal water tours.

Train

MÁV (www.elvira.hu) operates clean, punctual and relatively comfortable (if not ultra-modern) train services. Budapest is the hub of all the main railway lines, though many secondary lines link provincial cities and towns. There are three main stations in Budapest, each serving largely (but not exclusively) destinations from the following regions:

Keleti (Eastern Railway) station Northern Uplands and the Northeast

Nyugati (Western Railway) station Great Plain and Danube Bend

Déli (Southern Railway) station Transdanubia and Lake Balaton

All train stations have left-luggage offices, some of which stay open 24 hours. You sometimes have to pay the fee (around 400/600Ft per small/large locker per day) at another office or window nearby, which is usually marked *pénztár* (cashier).

Some trains have a carriage especially for bicycles; on other trains, bicycles must be placed in the first or last cars. You are able to freight a bicycle for 25% of a full 2nd-class fare.

Departures and arrivals are always on a printed timetable: yellow is for *indul* (departures) and white for *érkezik* (arrivals), fast trains are marked in red and local trains in black. The number (or sometimes letter) next to the word *vágány* indicates the platform from which the train departs or arrives.

Classes

» InterCity (IC): the fastest and most comfortable in Hungary; only stops in major towns/cities. Reservation mandatory.

» *Gyorsvonat* and *sebesvonat* ('fast trains', indicated on the timetable by boldface type, a thicker route line and/or an 'S'): stop more frequently. Cheaper than IC trains by around 10%.

» *Személyvonat* (passenger trains or 'snail trains'): stop at every city, town, village and hamlet along the way. Only use for short hops. Most domestic links between smaller towns normally offer 2nd-class services only.

Costs

Train fares are calculated by distance. At the time of writing, MÁV charged the following prices:

FARE	DISTANCE
620Ft	20-30km
1120Ft	50-60km
1300Ft	60-70km
1860Ft	90-100km
2830Ft	140-150km
3950Ft	220-230km

Reservations & Fines

On Hungarian domestic trains, seat reservations are compulsory on intercity express services (indicated by an 'R' in a circle or square on the timetable) or available without needing to book (just a plain 'R').

IC trains normally levy a surcharge that starts from 300Ft (depending on distance), which includes the reservation.

Passengers holding a ticket of insufficient value must pay a fine. If, for example, you're travelling from Budapest to Győr but have only paid for a ticket up to Tatabanya, if you notify the conductor before you reach Tatabanya, you pay the fare between Tatabanya and Győr, plus a fine of 500Ft. If you don't inform the conductor in time, the fine is 2600Ft. If you buy your ticket on the train rather than at the station, there's a 2600Ft fine (unless the station didn't have a ticket office). You can be fined 500Ft plus the price of a seat reservation for travelling on a domestic IC train without having a seat reservation.

Narrow-gauge & 'Nostalgia' Trains

Sixteen *keskenynyomközű vonat* (narrow-gauge trains), 12 run by Állami Erdei Vasutak (ÁEV; State Forest Railways) and the other four by MÁV pass through many wooded and hilly areas of the country. They are usually taken as a return excursion by holiday-makers, but in some cases can be useful for getting from A to B (eg Miskolc to Lillafüred and the Bükk Hills).

An independent branch of MÁV runs vintage *nosztalgiavonat* (steam trains) in summer, generally along the northern shore of Lake Balaton (eg from Keszthely to Tapolca via Badacsonytomaj) and along the Danube Bend from Budapest to Szob or Esztergom. For information, contact **MÁV Nostalgia** (☎1-238 0558; www.mavnosztalgia.hu) at Keleti train station.

Train Passes

The Hungary pass from **Eurail** (www.eurail.com), available to non-European residents only, costs US$92/132 for five/10 days of 1st-class travel in a 15-day period and US$80/101 for youths in 2nd class. Children six to 14 pay half.

The **Inter Rail One Country Pass** (www.interrail.com) offers 1st- and 2nd-class travel for three, four, six or eight days within a month to non-Hungarian European residents from €51. Discounts available for those under 26 (but only for 2nd class).

MÁV (☎1-444 4499; www.mav-start.hu) has a START Klub Card that gives you 50% off all tickets for 2nd-class travel (though not prebooked tickets); it costs 14,900/24,900Ft for those under 26 for six/12 months and 19,900/34,900Ft for those over 26.

Language

WANT MORE?

For in-depth language information and handy phrases, check out Lonely Planet's *Hungarian Phrasebook*. You'll find it at **shop .lonelyplanet.com**, or you can buy Lonely Planet's iPhone phrasebooks at the Apple App Store.

Hungarian is a member of the Finno-Ugric language family; it is related very distantly to Finnish and Estonian. There are approximately 14.5 million speakers of Hungarian.

Hungarian is easy to pronounce, and if you read our coloured pronunciation guides as if they were English, you'll be understood. The stressed syllables are indicated with italics. The symbol ¯ over a vowel (eg ā) means you say it as a long vowel sound. Note that eu is pronounced as in 'her' (without the 'r'), ew as i but with rounded lips, and zh as the 's' in 'measure'. The apostrophe (') indicates a slight y sound. If you see double consonants like bb, dd or tt, draw them out a little longer than you would in English. Polite and informal forms are included where relevant, indicated with the abbreviations 'pol' and 'inf'.

BASICS

Hello.	*Szervusz.* (sg)	*ser*·vus
	Szervusztok. (pl)	*ser*·vus·tawk
Goodbye.	*Viszont-látásra.* (pol)	*vi*·sawnt·laa·taash·ro
	Szia. (inf sg)	*si*·o
	Sziasztok. (inf pl)	*si*·os·tawk
Yes./No.	*Igen./Nem.*	*i*·gen/nem
Please.	*Kérem.* (pol)	*kay*·rem
	Kérlek. (inf)	*kayr*·lek
Thank you.	*Köszönöm.*	*keu*·seu·neum
You're welcome.	*Szívesen.*	*see*·ve·shen
Excuse me.	*Elnézést kérek.*	*el*·nay·zaysht *kay*·rek
Sorry.	*Sajnálom.*	*shoy*·naa·lawm

How are you?	
Hogy van/vagy? (pol/inf)	hawd' von/vod'
Fine. And you?	
Jól. És Ön/te? (pol/inf)	yāwl aysh eun/te
What's your name?	
Mi a neve/neved? (pol/inf)	mi o *ne*·ve/*ne*·ved
My name is ...	
A nevem ...	o *ne*·vem ...
Do you speak English?	
Beszél angolul? (pol)	*be*·sayl *on*·gaw·lul
Beszélsz angolul? (inf)	*be*·sayls *on*·gaw·lul
I don't understand.	
Nem értem.	nem *ayr*·tem

ACCOMMODATION

Where's a ...?	*Hol van egy ...?*	hawl von ed' ...
campsite	*kemping*	*kem*·ping
guesthouse	*panzió*	*pon*·zi·āw
hotel	*szálloda*	*saal*·law·do
youth hostel	*ifjúsági szálló*	*if*·yū·shaa·gi *saal*·lāw

I'd like to book a ... room, please.	*Szeretnék egy ... szobát foglalni.*	*se*·ret·nayk ed' ... *saw*·baat *fawg*·lol·ni
single	*egyágyas*	*ed'*·aa·dyosh
double	*duplaágyas*	*dup*·lo·aa·dyosh
twin	*kétágyas*	*kayt*·aa·dyosh

How much is it per ...?	*Mennyibe kerül egy ...?*	*men'*·nyi·be *ke*·rewl ed' ...
night	*éjszakára*	*ay*·so·kaa·ro
person	*főre*	*fēū*·re

DIRECTIONS

Where's (the market)?
Hol van (a piac)? — hawl von (o *pi*·ots)

What's the address?
Mi a cím? — mi o tseem

How do I get there?
Hogyan jutok oda? — *haw*·dyon *yu*·tawk *aw*·do

How far is it?
Milyen messze van? — *mi*·yen *mes*·se von

Can you show me (on the map)?
Meg tudja mutatni nekem (a térképen)? — meg *tud*·yo *mu*·tot·ni *ne*·kem (o *tayr*·kay·pen)

It's straight ahead.
Egyenesen előttünk van. — *e*·dye·ne·shen *e*·lēūt·tewnk von

Turn ...	*Forduljon ...*	*fawr*·dul·yawn ...
at the corner	*a saroknál*	o *sho*·rawk·naal
at the traffic lights	*a közlekedési lámpánál*	o *keuz*·le·ke·day·shi *laam*·paa·naal
left	*balra*	*bol*·ro
right	*jobbra*	*yawbb*·ro

It's ...	*... van.*	... von
behind ...	*... mögött*	... *meu*·geutt
here	*Itt*	itt
in front of ...	*... előtt*	... *e*·lēūtt
near ...	*... közelében*	... *keu*·ze·lay·ben
next to ...	*... mellett*	... *mel*·lett
on the corner	*A sarkon*	o *shor*·kawn
opposite ...	*...val szemben*	...·vol *sem*·ben
straight ahead	*Egyenesen előttünk*	*e*·dye·ne·shen *e*·lēūt·tewnk
there	*Ott*	ott

EATING & DRINKING

I'd like to reserve a table for ...	*Szeretnék asztalt foglalni ...*	*se*·ret·nayk *os*·tolt *fawg*·lol·ni ...
(eight) o'clock	*(nyolc) órára*	(nyawlts) *āw*·raa·ro
(two) people	*(két) főre*	(kayt) *fēū*·re

The menu, please.
Az étlapot, kérem. — az *ayt*·lo·pawt *kay*·rem

I'd like a local speciality.
Valamilyen helyi specialitást szeretnék. — *vo*·lo·mi·yen *he*·yi *shpe*·tsi·o·li·taasht *se*·ret·nayk

What would you recommend?
Mit ajánlana? — *mit* o·yaan·lo·no

KEY PATTERNS

To get by in Hungarian, mix and match these simple patterns with words of your choice:

Where's (a market)?
Hol van (egy piac)? — hawl von (ej *pi*·ots)

Where can I (buy a padlock)?
Hol tudok (venni egy lakatot)? — hawl *tu*·dawk (*ven*·ni ej *lo*·ko·tawt)

I'm looking for (a hotel).
(Szállodát) keresek. — (*saal*·law·daat) *ke*·re·shek

Do you have (a map)?
Van (térképük)? — von (*tayr*·kay·pewk)

Is there (a toilet)?
Van (vécé)? — von (*vay*·tsay)

I'd like (the menu).
(Az étlapot) szeretném. — (oz *ayt*·lo·pawt) *se*·ret·naym

I'd like to (buy a phonecard).
Szeretnék (telefon kártyát venni). — *se*·ret·nayk (*te*·le·fawn· kaar·tyaat *ven*·ni)

Could you please (write it down)?
(Leírná), kérem. — (*le*·eer·naa) *kay*·rem

Do I have to (pay)?
Kell érte (fizetni)? — kell *ayr*·te (*fi*·zet·ni)

I need (assistance).
(Segítségre) van szükségem. — (*she*·geet·shayg·re) von *sewk*·shay·gem

Do you have vegetarian food?
Vannak önöknél vegetáriánus ételek? — *von*·nok *eu*·neuk·nayl *ve*·ge·taa·ri·aa·nush *ay*·te·lek

I'd like..., please.
Legyen szíves, hozzon egy... — *le*·dyen *see*·vesh *hawz*·zawn ej...

Cheers! (to one person)
Egészségére! (pol) — e·gays·shay·gay·re
Egészségedre! (inf) — e·gays·shay·ged·re

Cheers! (to more than one person)
Egészségükre! (pol) — e·gays·shay·gewk·re
Egészségetekre! (inf) — e·gays·shay·ge·tek·re

That was delicious!
Ez nagyon finom volt! — ez *no*·dyawn *fi*·nawm vawlt

Please bring the bill.
Kérem, hozza a számlát. — *kay*·rem *hawz*·zo o *saam*·laat

Key Words

bar	*bár*	baar
bottle	*üveg*	*ew*·veg
breakfast	*reggeli*	*reg*·ge·li

cafe	*kávézó*	*kaa*·vay·zāw
cold	*hideg*	*hi*·deg
dinner	*vacsora*	*vo*·chaw·ro
fork	*villa*	*vil*·lo
glass	*pohár*	*paw*·haar
hot	*forró*	*fawr*·rāw
knife	*kés*	kaysh
lunch	*ebéd*	*e*·bayd
plate	*tányér*	*taa*·nyayr
restaurant	*étterem*	*ayt*·te·rem
spoon	*kanál*	*ko*·naal
warm	*meleg*	*me*·leg

Meat & Fish

beef	*marhahús*	*mor*·ho·hūsh
chicken	*csirke*	*chir*·ke
fish	*hal*	hol
herring	*hering*	*he*·ring
meat	*hús*	hūsh
pork	*disznóhús*	*dis*·nāw·hūsh
prawn	*garnélarák*	*gor*·nay·lo·raak
tuna	*tonhal*	*tawn*·hol
turkey	*pulyka*	*puy*·ko
veal	*borjúhús*	*bawr*·yū·hūsh

Fruit & Vegetables

apple	*alma*	*ol*·mo
apricot	*sárgabarack*	*shaar*·go·bo·rotsk
banana	*banán*	*bo*·naan
cabbage	*káposzta*	*kaa*·paws·to
carrot	*sárgarépa*	*shaar*·go·ray·po
cauliflower	*karfiol*	*kor*·fi·awl
cherry (sour)	*meggy*	mejj
cherry (sweet)	*cseresznye*	*che*·res·nye
fruit	*gyümölcs*	*dyew*·meulch
grape	*szőlő*	*sēū*·lēū
green bean	*zöldbab*	*zeuld*·bob
mushroom	*gomba*	*gawm*·bo
orange	*narancs*	*no*·ronch
pea	*zöldborsó*	*zeuld*·bawr·shāw
peach	*őszibarack*	*ēū*·si·bo·rotsk
pear	*körte*	*keur*·te
spinach	*spenót*	*shpe*·nāwt
strawberry	*eper*	*e*·per
vegetables	*zöldség*	*zeuld*·shayg

Other

butter	*vaj*	voy
cheese	*sajt*	shoyt
egg	*tojás*	*taw*·yaash
honey	*méz*	mayz
pepper	*bors*	bawrsh
salt	*só*	shāw
sugar	*cukor*	*tsu*·kawr

Drinks

apple juice	*almalé*	*ol*·mo·lay
beer	*sör*	sheur
champagne	*pezsgő*	*pezh*·geu
coffee	*kávé*	*kaa*·vay
draught beer	*csapolt sör*	*cho*·polt sheur
fruit juice	*gyümölcslé*	*dyew*·meulch lay
milk	*tej*	tey
mineral water	*ásvány víz*	*aash*·vaan'·veez
orange juice	*narancslé*	*no*·ronch·lay
red wine	*vörösbor*	*veu*·reush bawr
soft drink	*üdítőital*	*ew*·dee·tēū·i·tal
tea	*tea*	*te*·o
water	*víz*	veez
white wine	*fehér bor*	*fe*·hayr bawr

EMERGENCIES

Help! *Segítség!*	*she*·geet·shayg
Go away! *Menjen el!*	*men*·yen el
Call the police! *Hívja a rendőrséget!*	*heev*·yo o *rend*·ēūr·shay·get
Call a doctor! *Hívjon orvost!*	*heev*·yawn *awr*·vawsht
I'm lost. *Eltévedtem.*	*el*·tay·ved·tem

Signs

Bejárat	Entrance
Kijárat	Exit
Nyitva	Open
Zárva	Closed
Felvilágosítás	Information
Tilos	Prohibited
Toalett/WC	Toilets
Férfiak	Men
Nők	Women

I'm sick.
Rosszul vagyok. raws·sul vo·dyawk

I'm allergic to ...
Allergiás vagyok ... ol·ler·gi·aash vo·dyawk ...

Where are the toilets?
Hol a véce? hawl o vay·tse

SHOPPING & SERVICES

Where's a/an ...?	*Hol van ...?*	hawl von ...
department store	*egy áruház*	ed' aa·ru·haaz
shopping centre	*egy bevásárlóközpont*	ed' be·vaa·shaar·lāw·keuz·pawnt
supermarket	*egy élelmiszeráruház*	ed' ay·lel·mi·ser·aa·ru·haaz

I want to buy ...
Szeretnék venni ... se·ret·nayk ven·ni ...

I'm just looking.
Csak nézegetek. chok nay·ze·ge·tek

Can I look at it?
Megnézhetem? meg·nayz·he·tem

Do you have any others?
Van másmilyen is? von maash·mi·yen ish

How much is this?
Mennyibe kerül ez? men'·yi·be ke·rewl ez

That's too expensive.
Ez túl drága. ez tūl draa·go

Do you have something cheaper?
Van valami olcsóbb? von vo·lo·mi awl·chāwbb

There's a mistake in the bill.
Valami hiba van a számlában. vo·lo·mi hi·bo von o saam·laa·bon

ATM	*bankautomata*	bonk·o·u·taw·mo·to
internet cafe	*Internet kávézó*	in·ter·net kaa·vay·zāw
post office	*postahivatal*	pawsh·to·hi·vo·tol
tourist office	*turistairoda*	tu·rish·to·i·raw·do

Question Words

How?	*Hogyan?*	haw·dyon
How much?	*Mennyi?*	men'·yi
How many?	*Hány?*	haan'
What?	*Mi?*	mi
When?	*Mikor?*	mi·kawr
Where?	*Hol?*	hawl
Who?	*Ki?*	ki
Why?	*Miért?*	mi·ayrt

TIME & DATES

What time is it?
Hány óra? haan' āw·ra

It's (one/10) o'clock.
(Egy/Tíz) óra van. (ed'/teez) āw·ra von

Half past (10).
Fél (tizenegy). fayl (ti·zen·ed')

At what time ...?
Hány órakor ...? haan' āw·ro·kawr ...

At (10).
(Tíz)kor. (teez)·kawr

yesterday	*tegnap*	teg·nop
today	*ma*	mo
tomorrow	*holnap*	hawl·nop

morning	*reggel*	reg·gel
afternoon	*délután*	dayl·u·taan
evening	*este*	esh·te

Monday	*hétfő*	hayt·fēū
Tuesday	*kedd*	kedd
Wednesday	*szerda*	ser·do
Thursday	*csütörtök*	chew·teur·teuk
Friday	*péntek*	payn·tek
Saturday	*szombat*	sawm·bot
Sunday	*vasárnap*	vo·shaar·nop

January	*január*	yo·nu·aar
February	*február*	feb·ru·aar
March	*március*	maar·tsi·ush
April	*április*	aap·ri·lish
May	*május*	maa·yush
June	*június*	yū·ni·ush
July	*július*	yū·li·ush
August	*augusztus*	o·u·gus·tush
September	*szeptember*	sep·tem·ber
October	*október*	awk·tāw·ber
November	*november*	naw·vem·ber
December	*december*	de·tsem·ber

TRANSPORT

Public Transport

Which ... goes (to Budapest)?	*Melyik ... megy (Budapestre)?*	me·yik ... med' (bu·do·pesht·re)
bus	*busz*	bus
train	*vonat*	vaw·not

Numbers

1	*egy*	ed'
2	*kettő*	*ket*·tēū
3	*három*	*haa*·rawm
4	*négy*	nayd'
5	*öt*	eut
6	*hat*	hot
7	*hét*	hayt
8	*nyolc*	nyawlts
9	*kilenc*	*ki*·lents
10	*tíz*	teez
20	*húsz*	hūs
30	*harminc*	*hor*·mints
40	*negyven*	*ned'*·ven
50	*ötven*	*eut*·ven
60	*hatvan*	*hot*·von
70	*hetven*	*het*·ven
80	*nyolcvan*	*nyawlts*·von
90	*kilencven*	*ki*·lents·ven
100	*száz*	saaz
1000	*ezer*	e·zer

Which ... goes (to the Parliament)?	*Melyik ... megy (a Parlamenthez)?*	*me*·yik ... med' (o *por*·lo·ment·hez)
metro line	*metró*	*met*·rāw
tram	*villamos*	*vil*·lo·mawsh
trolleybus	*trolibusz*	*traw*·li·bus

When's the ... (bus)?	*Mikor megy ... (busz)?*	*mi*·kawr med' ... (bus)
first	*az első*	oz *el*·shēū
last	*az utolsó*	oz *u*·tawl·shāw
next	*a következő*	o *keu*·vet·ke·zēū

A ... ticket to (Eger).	*Egy ... jegy (Eger)be.*	ed' ... yej (*e*·ger)·be
one-way	*csak oda*	chok *aw*·do
return	*oda-vissza*	*aw*·do·*vis*·so

What time does it leave?
Mikor indul? *mi*·kawr *in*·dul

What time does it get to (Eger)?
Mikor ér (Egerbe)? *mi*·kawr ayr (*e*·ger·be)

How long does the trip take?
Mennyi ideig tart az út? *men'*·yi *i*·de·ig tort oz ūt

Is it a direct route?
Ez közvetlen járat? ez *keuz*·vet·len *yaa*·rot

Does it stop at (Visegrád)?
Megáll (Visegrád)on? *meg*·aall (*vi*·she·graad)·on

How long will it be delayed?
Mennyit késik? *men'*·yit *kay*·shik

Please tell me when we get to (Eger).
Kérem, szóljon, amikor (Eger)be érünk. *kay*·rem *sāwl*·yawn o·mi·kawr (*e*·ger)·be *ay*·rewnk

Is this taxi available?
Szabad ez a taxi? *so*·bod ez o *tok*·si

Please take me to (this address).
Kérem, vigyen el (erre a címre). *kay*·rem *vi*·dyen el (*er*·re o *tseem*·re)

Please stop here.
Kérem, álljon meg itt. *kay*·rem *aall*·yawn meg itt

Driving & Cycling

I'd like to hire a/an ...	*Szeretnék egy ... bérelni.*	*se*·ret·nayk ed' ... *bay*·rel·ni
4WD	*négykerék-meghajtású autót*	*nayj*·ke·rayk·meg·hoy·taa·shū *o*·u·tāwt
bicycle	*biciklit*	*bi*·tsik·lit
car	*autót*	*o*·u·tāwt
motorbike	*motort*	*maw*·tawrt

LPG	*folyékony autógáz*	*faw*·yay·kawn' *o*·u·tāw·gaaz
premium unleaded	*ólommentes szuper*	*āw*·lawm·men·tesh *su*·per
unleaded	*ólommentes*	*āw*·lawm·men·tesh

Is this the road to (Sopron)?
Ez az út vezet (Sopronba)? ez oz ūt *ve*·zet (*shawp*·rawn·bo)

Where's a petrol station?
Hol van egy benzinkút? hawl von ed' *ben*·zin·kūt

(How long) Can I park here?
(Meddig) Parkolhatok itt? (*med*·dig) *por*·kawl·ho·tawk itt

Do I need a helmet?
Kell bukósisak? kell *bu*·kāw·shi·shok

I need a mechanic.
Szükségem van egy autószerelőre. *sewk*·shay·gem von ed' o·u·tāw·se·re·lēū·re

The car/motorbike has broken down.
Az autó/A motor elromlott. oz *o*·u·tāw/o *maw*·tawr *el*·rawm·lawtt

I have a flat tyre.
Defektem van. *de*·fek·tem von

I've run out of petrol.
Kifogyott a benzinem. *ki*·faw·dyawtt o *ben*·zi·nem

I have a puncture.
Kilukadt a gumim. *ki*·lu·kott o *gu*·mim

GLOSSARY

ÁEV – Állami Erdei Vasutak (State Forest Railways)
ÁFA – value-added tax (VAT)
Avars – a people of the Caucasus who invaded Europe in the 6th century
ÁVO – Rákosi's hated secret police in the early years of communism; later renamed ÁVH

bélyeg – stamp
BKV – Budapest Közlekedési Vállalat (Budapest Transport Company)
bokor tanyák – bush farms
borozó – wine bar; any place serving wine
Bp – commonly used abbreviation for Budapest
búcsú – farewell; also a church patronal festival
büfé – snack bar

centrum – town or city centre
čevapčiči – spicy Balkan meatballs
Compromise of 1867 – agreement that created the dual monarchy of Austria-Hungary
Copf – a transitional architectural style between late baroque and neoclassicism
csárda – a Hungarian-style inn or restaurant
csikós – 'cowboy' from the *puszta*
cukrászda – cake shop or patisserie

Eclectic – an art and architectural style popular in Hungary in the Romantic period, drawing from sources both indigenous and foreign
élelmiszer – grocery shop or convenience store
érkezés – arrivals
eszpresszó – coffee shop, often also selling alcoholic drinks and snacks; strong, black coffee; same as *presszó*
étkezde – canteen that serves simple dishes
étterem – restaurant
fasor – boulevard, avenue
fogas – pikeperch-like fish indigenous to Lake Balaton
forint – Hungary's monetary unit
főkapitányság – main police station
főváros – main city or capital
főzelék – a traditional way of preparing vegetables, where they're fried or boiled and then mixed into a roux with milk
Ft – forint; see also *HUF*

gulyás or **gulyásleves** – a thick beef soup cooked with onions and potatoes and usually eaten as a main course
gyógyfürdő – bath or spa
gyógyszertár – pharmacy
gyógyvíz – medicinal drinking water
gyorsvonat – fast trains
gyűjtemény – collection
gyula – chief military commander of the early Magyar

hajdúk – Hungarian for *Heyducks*
hajóallomás – ferry pier or landing
ház – house
hegy – hill, mountain
hegyalja – hill country
helyiautóbusz pályaudvar – local bus station
HÉV – Helyiérdekű Vasút (suburban commuter train in Budapest)
Heyducks – drovers and outlaws from the *puszta* who fought as mercenaries against the Habsburgs
híd – bridge
honfoglalás – conquest of the Carpathian Basin by the Magyars in the late 9th century
HUF – international currency code for the Hungarian forint
Huns – a Mongol tribe that swept across Europe under Attila in the 5th century AD
Ibusz – Hungarian national network of travel agencies
ifjúsági szálló – youth hostel
indulás – departures

kamra – workshop or shed; one of three rooms in a traditional Hungarian cottage
kastély – manor house or mansion (see *vár*)
kékfestő – cotton fabric dyed a rich indigo blue
kemping – campground
képtár – picture gallery
khas – towns of the Ottoman period under direct rule of the sultan
kincstár – treasury
kirándulás – outing
kocsma – pub or saloon
kolostor – monastery or cloister
könyvesbolt – bookshop
könyvtár – library
konzumlányok – 'consume girls': attractive young women who work in collusion with bars and clubs to rip off unsuspecting male tourists
kórház – hospital
körút – ring road
korzó – embankment or promenade
köz – alley, mews, lane
központ – centre
krt – abbreviation for *körút* (ring road)
kúria – mansion or manor
kuruc – Hungarian mercenaries, partisans or insurrectionists who resisted the expansion of Habsburg rule in Hungary after the withdrawal of the Turks (late 17th/early 18th centuries)

lángos – deep-fried dough with toppings
lekvár – fruit jam
lépcső – stairs, steps
liget – park

Mahart – Hungarian passenger ferry company

Malév – Hungary's national airline

MÁV – Magyar Államvasutak (Hungarian State Railways)

megye – county

menetrend – timetable

mihrab – Muslim prayer niche facing Mecca

MNB – Magyar Nemzeti Bank (National Bank of Hungary)

Moorish Romantic – an art style popular in the decoration of 19th-century Hungarian synagogues

műemlék – memorial, monument

Nagyalföld – the Great Plain (same as the *puszta*)

Nagykörút – 'Big Ring road' in Budapest

népművészeti bolt – folk-art shop

Nonius – Hungarian breed of horse

nosztalgiavonat – vintage steam train

nyitva – open

nyugat – west

önkiszolgáló – self-service

óra – hour, 'o'clock'

orvosi rendelő – doctor's surgery

OTP – Országos Takarékpenztár (National Savings Bank)

Ottoman Empire – the Turkish empire that took over from the Byzantine Empire when it captured Constantinople (Istanbul) in 1453, and expanded into southeastern Europe

pálinka – fruit brandy

palota – palace

pályaudvar – train or railway station

Pannonia – Roman name for the lands south and west of the Danube River

panzió – *pension,* guesthouse

part – embankment

patika – pharmacy

pénztár – cashier

piac – market

pince – wine cellar

plébánia – rectory, parish house

pörkölt – stew

porta – type of farmhouse in Transdanubia

presszó – same as *eszpresszó* (coffee shop; strong, black coffee)

pu – abbreviation for *pályaudvar* (train station)

puszta – literally 'deserted'; other name for the Great Plain (see *Nagyalföld*)

puttony – the number of 'butts' of sweet *aszú* essence added to other base wines in making Tokaj wine

racka – sheep on the Great Plain with distinctive corkscrew horns

rakpart – quay, embankment

sebesvonat – swift trains

Secessionism – art and architectural style similar to Art Nouveau

sétány – walkway, promenade

skanzen – open-air museum displaying village architecture

söröző – beer bar or pub

strand – grassy 'beach' near a river or lake

sugárút – avenue

szálló or **szálloda** – hotel

személyvonat – passenger trains that stop at every city, town, village and hamlet along the way

sziget – island

színház – theatre

szoba kiadó – room for rent

szűr – long embroidered felt cloak or cape traditionally worn by Hungarian shepherds

Tanácsköztársaság – the 1919 Communist 'Republic of Councils' under Béla Kun

táncház – folk music and dance workshop

tanya – homestead or ranch; station

templom – church

tér – town or market square

tere – genitive form of *tér* as in Hősök tere (Square of the Heroes)

tiszta szoba – parlour; one of three rooms in a traditional Hungarian cottage

turul – eagle-like totem of the ancient Magyars and now a national symbol

u – abbreviation for *utca* (street)

udvar – court

ünnep – public holiday

út – road

utca – street

utcája – genitive form of *utca* as in Ferencesek utcája (Street of the Franciscans)

útja – genitive form of *út* as in Mártíroká útja (Street of the Martyrs)

vágány – platform

város – city

városház or **városháza** – town hall

vendéglő – a type of restaurant

vonat – train

zárva – closed

Zimmer frei – German for 'room for rent'

Zopf – German and more commonly used word for *Copf*

ALTERNATIVE PLACE NAMES

On a lot of bus and train timetables, Hungarian-language names are used for cities and towns in neighbouring countries. Many of these are in what once was Hungarian territory, and the names are used by the Hungarian-speaking minorities who live there. You should at least be familiar with the more important ones (eg Pozsony for Bratislava, Kolozsvár for Cluj-Napoca, Bécs for Vienna).

ABBREVIATIONS

(C) Croatian, (E) English, (G) German, (H) Hungarian, (R) Romanian, (S) Serbian, (Slk) Slovak, (Slo) Slovene, (U) Ukrainian

Alba Iulia (R) – Gyula Fehérvár (H), Karlsburg/Weissenburg (G)

Baia Mare (R) – Nagybánya (H)
Balaton (H) – Plattensee (G)
Banská Bystrica (Slk) – Besztercebánya (H)
Belgrade (E) – Beograd (S), Nándorfehérvár (H)
Beregovo (U) – Beregszász (H)
Braşov (R) – Brassó (H), Kronstadt (G)
Bratislava (Slk) – Pozsony (H), Pressburg (G)

Carei (R) – Nagykároly (H)
Cluj-Napoca (R) – Kolozsvár (H), Klausenburg (G)

Danube (E) – Duna (H), Donau (G)
Danube Bend (E) – Dunakanyar (H), Donauknie (G)
Debrecen (H) – Debrezin (G)

Eger (H) – Erlau (G)
Eisenstadt (G) – Kismárton (H)
Esztergom (H) – Gran (G)

Great Plain (E) – Nagyalföld, Alföld, Puszta (H)
Győr (H) – Raab (G)

Hungary (E) – Magyarország (H), Ungarn (G)

Kisalföld (H) – Little Plain (E)
Komárom (H) – Komárno (Slk)
Košice (Slk) – Kassa (H), Kaschau (G)
Kőszeg (H) – Güns (G)

Lendava (Slo) – Lendva (H)
Lučenec (Slk) – Losonc (H)

Mattersburg (G) – Nagymárton (H)
Mukačevo (U) – Munkács (H)
Murska Sobota (Slo) – Muraszombat (H)

Northern Uplands (E) – Északi Felföld (H)

Oradea (R) – Nagyvárad (H), Grosswardein (G)
Osijek (C) – Eszék (H)

Pécs (H) – Fünfkirchen (G)

Rožnava (Slk) – Rozsnyó (H)

Satu Mare (R) – Szatmárnémeti (H)
Senta (S) – Zenta (H)
Sibiu (R) – Nagyszében (H), Hermannstadt (G)
Sic (R) – Szék (H)
Sighişoara (R) – Szegesvár (H), Schässburg (G)
Sopron (H) – Ödenburg (G)
Štúrovo (Slk) – Párkány (H)
Subotica (S) – Szabadka (H)
Szeged (H) – Segedin (G)
Székesfehérvár (H) – Stuhlweissenburg (G)
Szombathely (H) – Steinamanger (G)

Tata (H) – Totis (G)
Timişoara (R) – Temesvár (H)
Tirgu Mureş (R) – Marosvásárhely (H)
Transdanubia (E) – Dunántúl (H)
Transylvania (R) – Erdély (H), Siebenbürgen (G)
Trnava (Slk) – Nagyszombat (H)

Uzhhorod (U) – Ungvár (H)

Vác (H) – Wartzen (G)
Vienna (E) – Wien (G), Bécs (H)
Villány (H) – Wieland (G)
Villánykövesd (H) – Growisch (G)

Wiener Neustadt (G) – Bécsújhely (H)

Behind the Scenes

SEND US YOUR FEEDBACK

We love to hear from travellers – your comments keep us on our toes and help make our books better. Our well-travelled team reads every word on what you loved or loathed about this book. Although we cannot reply individually to postal submissions, we always guarantee that your feedback goes straight to the appropriate authors, in time for the next edition. Each person who sends us information is thanked in the next edition – the most useful submissions are rewarded with a selection of digital PDF chapters.

Visit **lonelyplanet.com/contact** to submit your updates and suggestions or to ask for help. Our award-winning website also features inspirational travel stories, news and discussions.

Note: We may edit, reproduce and incorporate your comments in Lonely Planet products such as guidebooks, websites and digital products, so let us know if you don't want your comments reproduced or your name acknowledged. For a copy of our privacy policy visit lonelyplanet.com/privacy.

OUR READERS

Many thanks to the travellers who used the last edition and wrote to us with helpful hints, useful advice and interesting anecdotes:
Joke Akkerman, Fekete Angelika, Liz Bissett, Martin Hämmerle, Celine Heinbecker, Helene Kaz, Judit Kende, Juha Levo, Sheila Miller, Tanya Neistova, Paco Pastor & Sara Munsterhjelm, Stephanie Pintz, Torben Retboll, Michal Rudziecki, Pascalle Tamis, Bertil Teutelink, Endre Vaitzner, Charlotte Valloe.

AUTHOR THANKS

Steve Fallon

Thanks to Bea Szirti and Ildikó Nagy Moran for their helpful suggestions. Péter Lengyel showed me the correct wine roads to follow again and Gerard Gorman where the birds are. For hospitality on the road I am indebted to Regina Bruckner (Budapest), András Cseh (Eger), Zsuzsi Fábián (Kecskemét), Anita Kolostori (Miskolc), Shandor Madachy (Budapest) and Gabriella Rigó (Hollókő). *Nagyon szépen köszönöm mindenkinek!* As always, I'd like to dedicate my share of this to my partner Michael Rothschild, with love and gratitude.

Anna Kaminski

Many people to thank, not least Dora – for entrusting me with this task, fellow authors Steve and Caroline – for all your help, and everybody else who's aided me along the way. A particular *köszönöm* to Kimo and family for the warm hospitality and advice in Sopron; Krisztián for the drinks; Péter in Szombathely; Gergely in Győr; the indomitable Sándor, as well as Gabor, Petra, Beata, Julia and Mili in Budapest; my interviewees – András Török and Csaba Grózer; and, last but not least, Christina and Simon, my faithful travelling companions.

Caroline Sieg

Thanks to everyone who took the time to share their tips and the countless, friendly conversations at the Tourinform offices across Lake Balaton and Southern Transdanubia. And last but not least, special thanks to András Güth for being my official 'interview dude' and for giving me a sensational night out on the town.

ACKNOWLEDGMENTS

Climate map data adapted from Peel MC, Finlayson BL & McMahon TA (2007) 'Updated World Map of the Köppen-Geiger Climate Classification', *Hydrology and Earth System Sciences*, 11, 163344.

Cover photograph: Parliament building at early dawn, Budapest, George Tsafos/Getty Images.

This Book

This 7th edition of Lonely Planet's *Hungary* guidebook was researched and written by Steve Fallon, Anna Kaminski and Caroline Sieg. Steve wrote the first three editions and was joined by Neal Bedford for the 4th and 5th editions. Neal Bedford, Lisa Dunford and Steve Fallon wrote the 6th edition. This guidebook was commissioned in Lonely Planet's London office, and produced by the following:

Commissioning Editor Dora Whitaker

Coordinating Editor Anne Mason

Coordinating Cartographer Hunor Csutoros

Coordinating Layout Designer Adrian Blackburn

Managing Editor Angela Tinson

Managing Cartographers Anita Bahn, Anthony Phelan, Diana Von Holdt

Managing Layout Designer Jane Hart

Assisting Editors Andrew Bain, Kate James, Kellie Langdon, Ali Lemer, Rosemary Neilson, Kristin Odijk

Assisting Cartographers Mark Griffiths, David Kemp, Chris Tsismetzis

Cover Research Naomi Parker

Internal Image Research Kylie McLaughlin

Language Content Branislava Vladisavljevic

Thanks to Ryan Evans, Larissa Frost, Genesys India, Jouve India, Pászthory László, Korina Miller, Trent Paton, Kirsten Rawlings, Raphael Richards, Gerard Walker

index

000 Map pages
000 Photo pages

E

F

G

H

I

J

000 Map pages
000 Photo pages

000 Map pages
000 Photo pages

NOTES

how to use this book

These symbols will help you find the listings you want:

- Sights
- Beaches
- Activities
- Courses
- Tours
- Festivals & Events
- Sleeping
- Eating
- Drinking
- Entertainment
- Shopping
- Information/ Transport

These symbols give you the vital information for each listing:

- Telephone Numbers
- Opening Hours
- Parking
- Nonsmoking
- Air-Conditioning
- Internet Access
- Wi-Fi Access
- Swimming Pool
- Vegetarian Selection
- English-Language Menu
- Family-Friendly
- Pet-Friendly
- Bus
- Ferry
- Metro
- Subway
- Tram
- Train

Reviews are organised by author preference.

Look out for these icons:

- TOP CHOICE — Our author's recommendation
- FREE — No payment required
- A green or sustainable option

Our authors have nominated these places as demonstrating a strong commitment to sustainability – for example by supporting local communities and producers, operating in an environmentally friendly way, or supporting conservation projects.

Map Legend

Sights
Beach
Buddhist
Castle
Christian
Hindu
Islamic
Jewish
Monument
Museum/Gallery
Ruin
Winery/Vineyard
Zoo
Other Sight

Activities, Courses & Tours
Diving/Snorkelling
Canoeing/Kayaking
Skiing
Surfing
Swimming/Pool
Walking
Windsurfing
Other Activity/ Course/Tour

Sleeping
Sleeping
Camping

Eating
Eating

Drinking
Drinking
Cafe

Entertainment
Entertainment

Shopping
Shopping

Information
Post Office
Tourist Information

Transport
Airport
Border Crossing
Bus
Cable Car/ Funicular
Cycling
Ferry
Monorail
Parking
S-Bahn
Taxi
Train/Railway
Tram
Tube Station
U-Bahn
Underground Train Station
Other Transport

Routes
Tollway
Freeway
Primary
Secondary
Tertiary
Lane
Unsealed Road
Plaza/Mall
Steps
Tunnel
Pedestrian Overpass
Walking Tour
Walking Tour Detour
Path

Boundaries
International
State/Province
Disputed
Regional/Suburb
Marine Park
Cliff
Wall

Population
Capital (National)
Capital (State/Province)
City/Large Town
Town/Village

Geographic
Hut/Shelter
Lighthouse
Lookout
Mountain/Volcano
Oasis
Park
Pass
Picnic Area
Waterfall

Hydrography
River/Creek
Intermittent River
Swamp/Mangrove
Reef
Canal
Water
Dry/Salt/ Intermittent Lake
Glacier

Areas
Beach/Desert
Cemetery (Christian)
Cemetery (Other)
Park/Forest
Sportsground
Sight (Building)
Top Sight (Building)

OUR STORY

A beat-up old car, a few dollars in the pocket and a sense of adventure. In 1972 that's all Tony and Maureen Wheeler needed for the trip of a lifetime – across Europe and Asia overland to Australia. It took several months, and at the end – broke but inspired – they sat at their kitchen table writing and stapling together their first travel guide, *Across Asia on the Cheap*. Within a week they'd sold 1500 copies. Lonely Planet was born.

Today, Lonely Planet has offices in Melbourne, London and Oakland, with more than 600 staff and writers. We share Tony's belief that 'a great guidebook should do three things: inform, educate and amuse'.

OUR WRITERS

Steve Fallon

Coordinating Author, Danube Bend, Northern Uplands, The Great Plain & Northeast Hungary Steve, who has worked on every edition of *Hungary*, first visited Magyarország in the early 1980s by chance – he'd stopped off on his way to Poland (then under martial law) to buy bananas for his friends' children. It was a brief visit but he immediately fell in love with thermal baths, Tokaj wine and *bableves* (bean soup). Not able to survive on the occasional fleeting fix, he moved to Budapest in 1992, where he could enjoy all three in abundance and in Magyarul (Hungarian). Now based in London, Steve returns to Hungary regularly for all these things and more: *pálinka* (fruit brandy), Art Nouveau, the haunting voice of Marta Sebestyén and the best nightlife in Central Europe.

Read more about Steve at:
lonelyplanet.com/members/stevefallon

Anna Kaminski

Budapest, Western Transdanubia Originally from the Soviet Union, Anna finds a lot to appreciate about Hungary, a country she first visited as a dental tourist many years ago and has been drawn back to since, time and again – from the familiar relics of Communism to the world's best poppy-seed strudel. This edition took her from the 'ruin pubs' of Budapest to the splendid churches, castles and remote villages of Western Transdanubia. Anna also wrote the Directory A–Z and Transport chapters.

Caroline Sieg

Lake Balaton & Southern Transdanubia Caroline Sieg is a half-Swiss, half-American freelance writer and editor focusing on travel, food and the outdoors. Born to a Swiss-French mother and a Polish father who emigrated to the US, she has spent most of her life moving back and forth across the Atlantic Ocean. Caroline's relationship with Hungary began when she visited Pécs in 1992 and fell in love with its charms and fantastic mosque. Subsequent trips to the region yielded countless hikes in vineyard-covered hills, dips into Lake Balaton and a profound obsession with greasy, heart-attack-inducing *langos* (deep-fried dough with toppings).

Read more about Caroline at:
lonelyplanet.com/members/carolinesieg

Published by Lonely Planet Publications Pty Ltd
ABN 36 005 607 983
7th edition – July 2013
ISBN 978 1 74179 568 4

10 9 8 7 6 5 4 3 2 1
Printed in China